Teach
Yourself
Database
Programming
with Visual
Basic 4
in 21 Days

Teach Yourself
Database Programming with Visual Basic 4
in 21 Days

Michael Amundsen
Curtis Smith

SAMS
PUBLISHING

201 West 103rd Street
Indianapolis, Indiana 46290

To our families. Their support, patience, and—above all—their love helped
make this book possible.

Copyright © 1996 by Sams Publishing

FIRST EDITION

All rights reserved. No part of this book shall be reproduced, stored in a retrieval system, or transmitted by any means, electronic, mechanical, photocopying, recording, or otherwise, without written permission from the publisher. No patent liability is assumed with respect to the use of the information contained herein. Although every precaution has been taken in the preparation of this book, the publisher and author assume no responsibility for errors or omissions. Neither is any liability assumed for damages resulting from the use of the information contained herein. For information, address Sams Publishing, 201 W. 103rd St., Indianapolis, IN 46290.

International Standard Book Number: 0-672-30832-0

Library of Congress Catalog Card Number: 95-70088

99 98 97 96   4 3 2 1

Interpretation of the printing code: the rightmost double-digit number is the year of the book's printing; the rightmost single-digit, the number of the book's printing. For example, a printing code of 96-1 shows that the first printing of the book occurred in 1996.

Composed in AGaramond and MCPdigital by Macmillan Computer Publishing

Printed in the United States of America

All terms mentioned in this book that are known to be trademarks or service marks have been appropriately capitalized. Sams Publishing cannot attest to the accuracy of this information. Use of a term in this book should not be regarded as affecting the validity of any trademark or service mark.

Publisher	*Richard K. Swadley*
Acquisitions Manager	*Greg Wiegand*
Development Manager	*Dean Miller*
Managing Editor	*Cindy Morrow*
Marketing Manager	*Gregg Bushyeager*

Aquisitions Editor
Bradley L. Jones

Development Editor
Ricardo Birmele

Software Development Specialist
Steve Flatt

Production Editor
Ryan Rader

Copy Editors
Marla L. Reece
Bart Reed

Technical Reviewer
Ricardo Birmele

Editorial Coordinator
Bill Whitmer

Technical Edit Coordinator
Lynette Quinn

Formatter
Frank Sinclair

Editorial Assistants
Sharon Cox
Andi Richter
Rhonda Tinch-Mize

Cover Designer
Tim Amrhein

Book Designer
Alyssa Yesh

Production Team Supervisor
Brad Chinn

Production
Mary Ann Abramson, Carol Bowers, Mona Brown, Charlotte Clapp, Terri Edwards, Michael Henry, Ayanna Lacey, Casey Price, Brian-Kent Proffitt, SA Springer, Susan Van Ness

Indexer
Cheryl Dietsch

Overview

Contents

Acknowledgments

We want to thank all the people at Sams for their assistance. Although many people have worked with us to bring this idea to its final form, we especially want to thank Brad, Marla, and Ryan for their help. Their persistence, insistence, and encouragement got us through the difficult spots and made the not-so-difficult spots even a bit fun. We also want to thank Ricardo Birmele for his unflagging support, even while he was pointing out our shortcomings.

The people mentioned here are just some of those who helped us in putting this book together. Where this book succeeds, it is due in large measure to the dedication and hard work of our friends and colleagues. We thank them all for their efforts and look forward to working with them on future projects.

About the Authors

Michael Amundsen

Michael Amundsen has more than 10 years of database programming experience using dBASE, Clipper, FoxPro, and Visual Basic. He has worked in large corporate IS shops, small accounting offices, and an IS consulting firm. He recently completed his Microsoft Certification in Visual Basic and Windows 3.1 and now holds Microsoft's MCP.

Curtis Smith

Curtis Smith has been working in the computer industry for many years. He has a financial background, which helps to bring a practical real-world flair to *Teach Yourself Database Programming with Visual Basic 4 in 21 Days*. Curtis currently holds both an MBA and a CPA.

Introduction

Welcome to Database Programming in Visual Basic 4

Welcome to *Teach Yourself Database Programming with Visual Basic 4 in 21 Days.* You'll cover a lot of ground in the next 21 lessons—from developing fully functional input screens with less than 10 lines of Visual Basic code, and writing Visual Basic code libraries to handle complex user security and auditing in multiuser applications, to creating online help files for your Visual Basic programs, and much more. Whether you are a power user, a business professional, a database guru, or a Visual Basic programmer, you'll find something in this book to help you improve your Visual Basic and database skills.

Each week you will focus on a different aspect of database programming with Visual Basic. In week one, you learn about issues related to building simple database applications using the extensive collection of data controls available with Visual Basic. In week two, you concentrate on techniques for creating database applications using Visual Basic code. In week three, you study advanced topics such as SQL data definition and manipulation language, and issues for multiuser applications such as locking schemes, database integrity, and application-level security. You'll also learn techniques for creating ODBC-enabled Visual Basic applications.

Database Design Skills

This book will help you develop your database design skills, too. Each week covers at least one topic on database design. Day 2 covers Visual Basic database data types, and Day 3 covers how to use the Visual Basic Data Manager program to create Microsoft JET format databases. Day 8 covers the use of the Visdata program to create and manage databases, and Day 9 teaches you to use SQL SELECT statements to organize existing data into usable data sets. On Days 15 and 16, you'll learn advanced SQL data definition and manipulation techniques, and on Day 17 you'll learn the five rules of data normalization.

Reusable Code Libraries

Throughout the book, we show you how to develop code libraries that you can reuse in all your future Visual Basic programs. These code libraries include routines for input validation, error trapping, report printing, graphing data, creating input forms, user log in/log out, program security features, audit trails, and ODBC API interface. All of these libraries can be added to existing and future Visual Basic programs with very little, if any, modification. After you build these libraries, you'll be able to modify them to fit your specific needs, and even add new libraries of your own.

Who Should Read This Book

This book is designed to help you improve your database programming skills using Visual Basic. You do not have to be a Visual Basic coding guru to use this book. If you are a power user who wants to learn how to put together simple, solid data entry forms using Visual Basic, you'll get a lot from this book. If you have some Visual Basic experience and want to take the next step into serious database programming, you'll find a great deal of valuable information here, too. Finally, if you are a professional programmer, you can take many of the techniques and code libraries described here and apply them to your current projects.

What You Need to Use This Book

All code examples in this book were built using Microsoft Visual Basic 4, Professional Edition. Most of the examples will work using Visual Basic 3, Professional Edition with the Microsoft JET/Access Compatibility Layer installed, but some will not. Version 4 of Visual Basic has several new features not available with version 3. If you are using Visual Basic 3, you can still get a great deal out of this book, but we strongly encourage you to upgrade to Visual Basic 4. There are so many new features in Visual Basic 4 that you'll be glad you upgraded.

If you have Visual Basic 4 Enterprise Edition, you can take advantage of some new features not available in the Professional Edition, but this is not required. It will also help if you have Microsoft Word, which is used in the lesson on building help files.

Visual Basic is available in both 16-bit and 32-bit versions. The 16-bit version of Visual Basic 4 will run under Windows 3.1, Windows for Workgroups, Windows 95, and Windows NT. The 32-bit version of Visual Basic 4 will only run under Windows 95 or Windows NT. We run Visual Basic 4 under Windows 95, but almost all of the examples in this book will run under any version of Windows and Visual Basic 4. In the rare cases in which a feature only exists in the 32-bit version of the software, we let you know ahead of time and show how you can accomplish the same thing in the 16-bit environment.

Quick Course Summary

Here is a brief rundown of what you'll accomplish each week.

Week One: Data Controls and Microsoft JET Databases

In the first week, you will learn about the relational database model, how to use the Visual Basic database objects to access and update existing databases, and how to use the Visual Basic Data Manager program to create and maintain databases. You will also learn how to design and code data entry forms (including use of the Visual Basic bound data controls), and how to create input validation routines at the keystroke, field, and form levels. Lastly, you'll learn how to use the Visual Basic Crystal Reports report writer to design simple reports, and how to use the Crystal Reports control to run those reports from within your Visual Basic programs.

When you complete the work for week one, you will be able to build Microsoft JET databases, create solid data entry forms that include input validation routines, and produce printed reports of your data.

Week Two: Programming with the Microsoft JET Database Engine

Week two will concentrate on topics that are of value to developers in the stand-alone and workgroup environments. We will cover a wide variety of topics including the following:

- [ ] How to use Visdata to build and manage databases.
- [ ] How to use the Structured Query Language (SQL) to extract data from existing databases.
- [ ] What the Microsoft JET engine is, and how you can use Visual Basic code to create and maintain Data Access Objects.
- [ ] How to create data entry forms with Visual Basic code.
- [ ] How to use the Microsoft graph control to create graphs and charts of your data.
- [ ] How to use data-bound list boxes, data-bound combo boxes, and data-bound grids to create advanced data entry forms.
- [ ] How to make applications more solid with error trapping.

When you complete the chapters for week two, you will be able to build advanced database structures using the Visdata program and create complex data entry forms using Visual Basic code, including bound lists and grids, and error handling routines.

Week Three: Advanced Database Programming with SQL and ODBC

In the third and final week, we will cover several very important topics. This week's work focuses on database issues you'll encounter when you develop database applications for multiple users and/or multiple sites. You'll learn advanced SQL language for defining databases (DDL) and manipulating records within existing databases (DML). You'll also learn the five rules of data normalization and how applying those rules can improve the speed, accuracy, and integrity of your databases.

We cover Visual Basic database locking schemes for the database, table, and page levels. We also explain the advantages and limitations of adding cascading updates and deletes to your database relationship definitions. You will learn how to use the Visual Basic keywords BeginTrans, CommitTrans, and Rollback to improve database integrity and processing speed during mass updates.

We show you how to write data entry forms that use the ODBC API calls to link directly with the ODBC interface to access data in registered ODBC data sources. You will also be able to install the ODBC Administrator and create new ODBC data sources for your ODBC-enabled Visual Basic programs.

We review application-level security schemes such as user log in and log out, program-level access rights, and audit trails to keep track of critical application operations.

Finally, you will learn how to design and build online help systems for your Visual Basic applications, including the 10-point checklist for creating quality help systems. You will also learn how to link help files directly to fields on a Visual Basic data form.

When you finish the final week of the course, you will be able to use advanced SQL statements to create and maintain databases. You will also be able to build solid multiuser applications that include database locking schemes, cascades, and transactions; ODBC API interfaces; application security and audit features; and online help files.

What's Not Covered in This Book

Although there is a lot of good stuff in this book, there are some important topics we don't cover in these pages. For example, we don't talk in detail about Visual Basic coding in general. If you are new to Visual Basic, you might want to review the book *Teach Yourself Visual Basic in 21 Days*. This is an excellent introduction to Visual Basic.

Although we discuss issues such as connecting to back-end databases such as SQL Server and Oracle, we do not cover the specifics of these systems. We focus on techniques you'll need for connecting your Visual Basic applications to remote databases, and not on how to operate these remote databases.

We also do not cover any third-party controls or add-ins for Visual Basic 4. That isn't because we don't think they are useful. There are literally hundreds of new and existing third-party products for Visual Basic, and many of them are very good. We have included samples and demo versions of some of those third-party products on the accompanying CD-ROM. However, because we wanted the book to be as accessible as possible to all our readers, we use only those controls or add-in products that are included in the Visual Basic 4 Professional Edition.

What's On the CD

Along with the text, there is a CD-ROM that contains lots of Visual Basic code, sample and demonstration programs, and handy utilities. The following is a brief description of the contents of the CD. Refer to the installation directions on the last page of the book for details on how to install and run these programs.

Chapter Projects and Examples

All examples and exercises mentioned in this book are stored in the TYSDBVB directory of the CD-ROM. You can copy these files directly to your workstation hard disk or enter them from the listings in the book.

Visual Basic Code Libraries

All reusable code libraries mentioned in the text are also included in a separate directory called \LIBS. This directory contains completed, fully documented versions of the code libraries used throughout the text. If you want to save yourself some typing, you can simply add these libraries to your Visual Basic projects. You can also copy these libraries to your workstation hard drive and modify them for your own use.

Recommended Files

Besides what is included on the CD, here are some products that we recommend you pick up on your own to use.

☐ What6 Help Authoring Kit: This is Microsoft Corporation's help authoring kit, which includes all the tools you need to convert Microsoft Word formatted documents into compiled help files for your Visual Basic application. You can obtain this free of charge from the Microsoft site at

http://www.microsoft.com/kb/softlib/mslfiles/what6.exe

☐ Microsoft JET/Access Compatibility Layer for Visual Basic 3.0: If you are using Visual Basic 3.0 Professional with this book, you should install the Microsoft JET/Access Compatibility Layer in order to perform many of the examples in this text. You must have Microsoft Access on your workstation in order to complete the compatibility layer installation. This software can be obtained from the following Microsoft site:

http://www.microsoft.com/kb/softlib/mslfiles/comlyr.exe

Warning: If you are using Visual Basic 4, you do not need to install the Microsoft JET/Access Compatibility Layer. In fact, installing the compatibility layer over Visual Basic 4 could result in disabling your current version of Visual Basic. If you are using Visual Basic 4, *do not* install these files on your workstation.

SQL-VB Interpreter

The \SQLVB directory contains the executables and the source code for the SQL-VB Interpreter program. This program is covered in Appendix A of this book. The SQL-VB program reads ASCII text files containing valid SQL scripts. The SQL-VB Interpreter can be used to create, modify, update, and delete Microsoft JET format databases.

Shareware and Demos

The CD also contains various shareware and demo versions of third-party software. We encourage you to test these software tools and, if you like what you find, support the software authors by purchasing a licensed copy of the programs you find useful.

In addition, the CD contains a complimentary copy of True Grid Pro™ version 2.1c from APEX Software.

This week, you learn the skills you need to create a simple database that contains a master record table, and you design and implement a complete data entry form, including input validation routines. You also design and implement a simple list report that you can call from within your Visual Basic application.

Day 1: If you're new to Visual Basic, you learn basic controls and write a complete Visual Basic database data entry application using no more than three lines of Visual Basic code.

Day 2: You learn the basics of relational database theory including databases, data tables, and fields. You also learn the database data types recognized by Visual Basic and how to use them in your Visual Basic applications.

Day 3: You learn how to use the Data Manager program that ships with Visual Basic 4 to create and maintain databases in Microsoft Access format, as well as other database formats including dBASE, FoxPro, Paradox, and Btrieve.

You also design the CompanyMaster data table, which you use throughout the three-week course.

Day 4: You learn what the Visual Basic database objects are and how to use them to read and write data tables.

Day 5: You learn how to design and build quality data entry forms using Visual Basic bound data controls. You also learn how to design forms that conform to the Windows 95 style specifications.

Day 6: You learn the fundamentals of input validation for data entry forms. You learn how to write keyboard filters, field-level, and form-level validation routines. You also create your first Visual Basic reusable library when you build the LIBVALID.BAS module that contains validation routines you can use in any Visual Basic application.

You also create a complete data entry form for the CompanyMaster data table you created on Day 3.

Day 7: You learn how to use the Crystal Reports report writer that ships with Visual Basic 4 to create and run quality reports from your databases.

You also create a generic Report Print form that prints any report definition created with Crystal Reports. This generic form can be added to any Visual Basic program.

For the last project of the week, you create a list report that prints the customer list from the CompanyMaster data table you created earlier in the week.

Your First
Database Program
in Visual Basic

This chapter is for readers who have never created database applications using Visual Basic. Those who already know how to use the Visual Basic data control and the bound controls to make simple data entry programs might want to skip this chapter and move on to Day 2.

Your project today is to create a completely functional data entry program using Visual Basic. The program you create will be able to access data tables within an existing database; it will also allow users to add, edit, and delete records.

Sound like a lot for one day? Not really. You will be amazed at how quickly you can put together database programs. Much of the drudgery commonly associated with writing data entry programs (screen layout, cursor control, input editing, and so on) is automatically handled using just a few of Visual Basic's input controls. In addition, with Visual Basic's data controls it's easy to add the capability to read and write database tables, too.

So let's get started!

Starting Your New Visual Basic Project

If you already have Visual Basic up and running on your PC, select File | New Project to create a new project. If you haven't started Visual Basic yet, start it now. When you first load Visual Basic, it automatically creates a new project for you. Now you're ready to create the data entry screen.

Adding the Database Control

The first thing you need to do for the database program is open up the database and select the data table you want to access. To do this, double-click on the data control in the Visual Basic toolbox. This will place a data control in the center of the form. When this is done, the form is ready to open a data table. At this point, your screen should look something like the one in Figure 1.1.

Tip: Are you not sure which of those icons in the toolbox is the data control? You can hit F1 while the toolbox window is highlighted to get a help screen describing each of the Visual Basic tools. This screen shows the tool icon and points to additional help, listing the properties, events, and methods available for each of the controls. You can get help on a particular control in the toolbox by clicking on the icon and hitting F1 to activate Visual Basic help.

Tool Tips are also available in Visual Basic 4. Simply rest the mouse pointer on any icon to view a pop-up description of that item. This option can be toggled on and off by selecting Tools | Options, choosing the Environment tab, and then checking the Show Tool Tips checkbox.

Figure 1.1.
The data control as it appears when first added to your form.

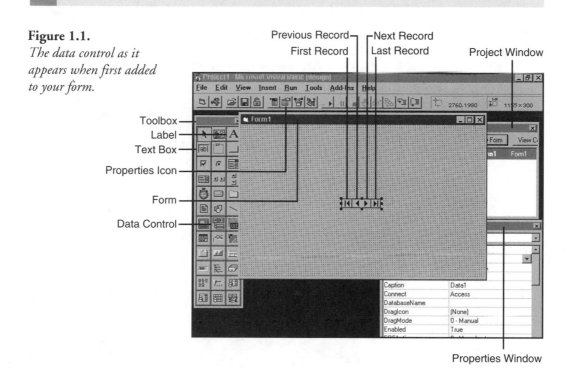

Next you need to set a few of the control's properties to indicate the database and data table you want to access.

Setting the DatabaseName and RecordSource Properties

You must first set the following two properties when linking a data control to a database:

DatabaseName   Selected database

RecordSource   Selected data table in the database

The BIBLIO.MDB database will be used in the exercise that follows. This database can be found in the root directory of Visual Basic 4.

Note: The BIBLIO.MDB database was copied to the Visual Basic 4 directory during installation. If you need a clean copy of this database, you can find it on the accompanying CD-ROM in the \TYSDBVB\CHAP01 subdirectory. This file can also be found on the Visual Basic 4 distribution CD in the VB directory.

Tip: If you do not see the Properties dialog box, press F4 or select View | Properties from the menu, or click the properties icon on the Visual Basic toolbar at the top of the screen.

To set the DatabaseName of the data control, first select the data control by single-clicking on the control. This will force the data control properties to appear in the Visual Basic Properties dialog box. Locate the DatabaseName property (all properties are listed in alphabetical order), and click on the property name. When you do this, three small dots appear to the right of the data entry box. Clicking the three dots brings up Windows standard File | Open dialog box. You should now be able to select the BIBLIO.MDB file from the list of available database files. For the first database program, you will use the Titles data table in the BIBLIO.MDB database. Your screen should look something like the one in Figure 1.2.

Figure 1.2.
*Using the Visual Basic File |
Open dialog box to set the
DatabaseName property.*

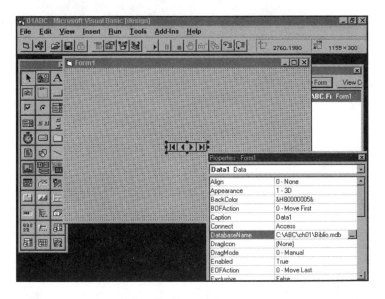

When you have located the BIBLIO.MDB file and selected OK, Visual Basic inserts the complete drive, path, and filename of the database file into the input area, linking the database

and your program together. Always double-check this property to make sure that you correctly selected the desired database.

 **Note:** People often use the words *database* and *data table* interchangeably. Throughout this book, *data table* is used to refer to a single table of data and *database* is used to refer to a collection of related tables. For example, the Titles table and the Publishers table are two *data tables* in the Biblio *database*.

Now that you know what database you will use, you must select the data table within that database that you want to access by setting the RecordSource property of the data control. You can do this by locating the RecordSource property in the Properties window, single-clicking on the property, and then single-clicking on the small down arrow to the right of the property input box. This brings up a list of all the tables in the BIBLIO.MDB database, as shown in Figure 1.3.

Figure 1.3.
Setting the RecordSource property to the Titles table.

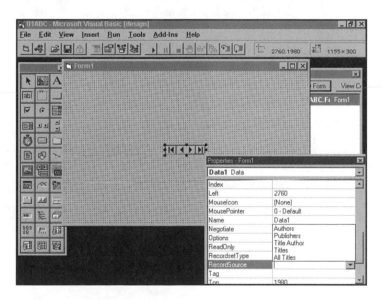

To select the Titles table from this list, simply click on it. Visual Basic automatically inserts the table name into the RecordSource property in the Properties window.

Setting the Caption and Name Properties

You need to set two other data control properties in the project. These two properties are not required, but setting them is a good programming practice because it improves the readability of the programming code. Here are the optional properties:

Caption | Displayed name of the data control
Name | Program name of the data control

Setting the Caption property of the data control sets the text that displays between the record selection arrows on the data control. It is a good habit to set this to a value that makes sense to the user. Setting the Name property of the data control sets the text that will be used by the Visual Basic programmer. This is never seen by the user, but you should set the Name to something similar to the Caption to make it easier to relate the two when working on your program.

For your program, set the Caption property of the data control to Titles and the Name property of the data control to datTitles. Now that you've added the Caption property, use the mouse to stretch the data control so that you can see the complete caption. Your form should look like the one in Figure 1.4.

Note: The name of the data control (datTitles) might seem unusual. It is, however, a logical name if you remove the first three letters, *dat*. This prefix is added to designate this object as a data control. The three character prefix naming convention is Microsoft's suggested nomenclature for Visual Basic 4 and is used throughout this book.

Use the search phrase "Object Naming Conventions" in the Visual Basic 4 Books Online to find a complete listing of the suggested object prefixes.

Figure 1.4.
A data control stretched to show the Caption property.

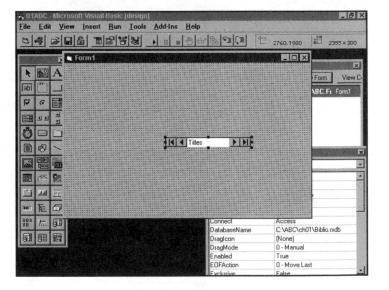

Saving Your Project

1

Now is a good time to save your work up to this point. To save this project, select File | Save Project from the main menu. When prompted for a filename for the form, enter C:\TYSDBVB\CHAP01\DATCNTRL.FRM. You will then be prompted for a filename for the project. Enter C:\TYSDBVB\CHAP01\DATCNTRL.VBP.

It's always a good idea to save your work often.

> **Note:** This, and all other projects that you will complete from this book, can be found on the CD included with this book.

> **Tip:** One way to make sure that you keep an up-to-date copy of your project saved on disk is to set the Save Project Before Run environment variable to Yes. You can do this by selecting Options | Environment from the menu and toggling the Save Project Before Run value to Yes.

Adding the Bound Input Controls

Now that you have successfully linked the form to a database with the data control and selected a data table to access, you are ready to add input controls to the form. Visual Basic 4 supplies you with input controls that can be directly bound (connected) to the data table you want to access. All you need to do is place several input controls on the form and assign them to an existing data control.

> **Note:** Associating a control on a form to a field in a data table is referred to as *binding a control*. When they are assigned to a data source, these controls are called *bound input controls*.

Let's add the first bound input control to the Titles table input form. You place an input control on the form by double-clicking on the text box control in the Visual Basic 4 toolbox. This inserts a text box control directly in the center of the form. When the control is on the form, you can use the mouse to move and resize it in any way you choose. You can copy additional input

controls by double-clicking the text box button in the toolbox as many times as you like. Set the Name property of this control to txtTitle. Add a label to describe this control by double-clicking on the Label control. Set the Name property of the label to lblTitles, and the Caption property to Title. Refer to Figure 1.1 if you have any problems finding a particular Visual Basic control.

Tip: When double-clicking controls onto a form, each instance of the control is loaded in the center of the form. When you add several controls in this manner, each control is loaded in exactly the same place on the form, like a stack of pancakes. It looks as though you still only have one, but they're all there! You can view each of the controls you loaded on your form by using the mouse to drag and drop the topmost control to another portion of the form.

Setting the DataSource and DataField Properties

You must set two text box properties in order for the text box control to interact with the data control. These are the two required properties:

DataSource	Name of the data control
DataField	Name of the field in the table

A relationship is established between a field (the DataField property) in a table (the DataSource property) and a bound control when you set these two properties. When this is done, all data display and data entry in this input control is linked directly to the data table/field you selected.

Setting the DataSource property of the text box control binds the input control to the data control. To set the text box DataSource property, first select the text box control (click on it once), and then click on the DataSource property in the Property window. By clicking on this property's down arrow, you can see a list of all the data controls currently active on this form. You have only added one data control to this form, so you see only one name in the list (see Figure 1.5). Set the DataSource value to Titles by clicking on the word Titles in the drop-down list box.

The second required property for a bound input control is the DataField property. Setting this property binds a specific field in the data table to the input control. Set the DataField property of the current input control by single-clicking on the DataField property in the Property window and then single-clicking the down arrow to the right of the property. You now see a list of all the fields that are defined for the data table that you selected in the DataSource property (see Figure 1.6). Click on the Titles field to set the DataField property for this control.

Figure 1.5.
Setting the DataSource
property of a bound text box.

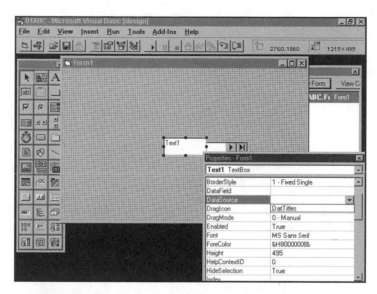

Figure 1.6.
Selecting the DataField
property of the bound text
box control.

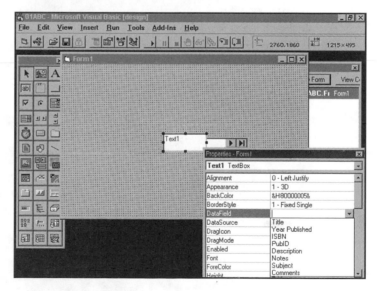

Now that you have the general idea, finish up the data entry form by adding bound input controls for the remaining four fields in the Titles data table. Refer to Table 1.1 for details. While you're at it, add Label controls to the left of the text box controls and set their Caption properties to the values shown in Table 1.2. Size and align the controls on the form, too. Also, size the form by selecting its borders and dragging to a desired shape. Your form will look something like the one in Figure 1.7 when you're done.

Table 1.1. The Input Control DataSource and DataField properties for the Titles form.

Text Box	DataSource	DataField
txtYearPublished	Titles	Year Published
txtAUID	Titles	Au_ID
txtISBN	Titles	ISBN
txtPubID	Titles	Pub_ID
txtDescription	Titles	Description

Table 1.2. The Label Control Caption properties for the Titles form.

Label	Caption
lblTitle	Title
lblYearPublished	Year Published
lblAuthorID	Author ID
lblISBN	ISBN
lblPubID	Pub ID
lblDescription	Description

Figure 1.7.
The completed data entry form for Titles.

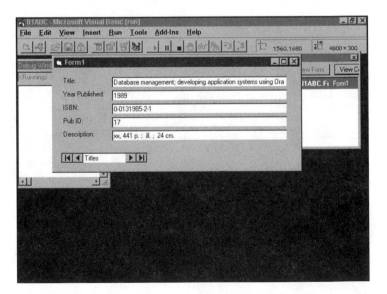

You can now run the program and see the data control in action. Select Run | Start (or press F5) to compile and run your program. You can now walk through the data table by clicking the left and right arrows on the data control at the bottom of the form. The leftmost arrow (the one with the bar on it) moves you to the first record in the data table. The rightmost arrow (which also has a bar) moves you to the last record in the data table. The other two arrows simply move you through the data table one record at a time.

You can make permanent any changes to the data table by moving to a different record in the table. Try this by changing the data in the Title input control, moving the record pointer to the next record, and then moving the pointer back to the record you just edited. You will see that the new value was saved to the data table.

Now let's include the capability to add new records to the data table and to delete existing records from the data table.

Adding the New and Delete Command Buttons

Up to this point, you have not written a single line of Visual Basic code. However, in order to add the capability to add new records and delete existing records, you have to write a grand total of two lines of Visual Basic code: one line for the add record function, and one line for the delete record function.

The first step in the process is to add two command buttons labeled Add and Delete to the form. Refer to Table 1.3 and Figure 1.8 for details on adding the command buttons to your form.

Table 1.3. Command button properties for the Title form.

Name	Caption
cmdAdd	&Add
cmdDelete	&Delete

Note: Adding an ampersand (&) to a Caption of a command button causes the letter immediately following the ampersand to be underlined. The underlined letter (also known as a shortcut key or hot key) serves as a prompt to the user to indicate that it can be pressed in conjunction with the Ctrl key to execute the procedure that the button contains.

Figure 1.8.
The form layout after adding the Add and Delete command buttons.

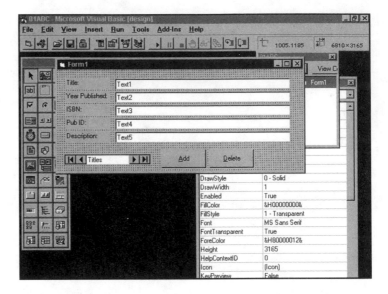

Double-click on the Add button to bring up the Visual Basic code window to add code behind the Add command button. You see the subroutine header and footer already entered for you. All you need to do is add a single line of Visual Basic code between them.

```
Sub cmdNew_Click ()
    datTitles.Recordset.AddNew   ' add a new record to the table
End Sub
```

Note: Visual Basic automatically creates the Sub...End Sub routines for each new procedure you create. When you are performing the exercises in this book, only insert the code between these two lines (in other words, don't repeat the Sub...End Sub statements, or your code will not work properly).

Now open the code window behind the Delete button and add this Visual Basic code:

```
Sub cmdDelete_Click ()
    datTitles.Recordset.Delete   ' delete the current record
End Sub
```

Runtime and Design Time Properties

RecordSet is a *runtime only* property of the data control. This property is a reference to the underlying data table defined in the *design time* RecordSource property. The

RecordSet can refer to an existing table in the database or a virtual table, such as a Visual Basic Dynaset or Snapshot. This is covered in more depth on Day 4, "Visual Basic Database Objects." For now, think of the RecordSet property as a runtime version of the RecordSource property you set when you designed the form.

In the previous two code snippets, you used the Visual Basic methods `AddNew` and `Delete`. You will learn more about these and other Visual Basic methods in the lesson on Day 5, "Creating Data Entry Forms with Bound Controls."

Save the project and run the program again. You can now click the Add button and see a blank set of input controls for data entry. Fill them all with some data (refer to Figure 1.9 for an example of a new record), and then move to another record in the table. The data is automatically saved to the data table. You can also use the Delete button to remove any record from the table. Select the record you just added (it's the last record in the table), and click the Delete button. Now move to the previous record in the table and try to move forward again to view the record you just deleted. You can't. It's not there!

Figure 1.9.
Example data filling in blank fields after clicking the Add button.

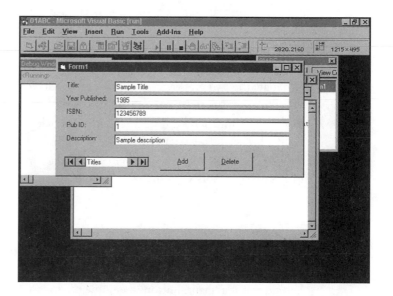

If you didn't enter data into the data entry form that you created in this exercise in quite the same way as Figure 1.9 (for example, you incorrectly entered characters in the Year field, which only accepts numbers), you might have received an error message from Visual Basic 4 saying that you have invalid data in one of the fields. This is supposed to happen! Visual Basic 4 (more precisely, the Microsoft JET Engine) verifies all data entries to ensure that the correct data type is entered in each field. Input validation routines, a means of restricting data entry even further, are covered in depth on Day 6, "Input Validation," and error trapping is reviewed in the lesson on Day 14, "Error Trapping." You can skip over these messages for now.

Summary

In today's lesson you learned the following:

☐ You learned how to use the data control to bind a form to a database and data table by setting the DatabaseName and DataSource properties.

☐ You learned how to use the text box bound input control to bind an input box on the form to a data table and data field by setting the DataSource and DataField properties.

☐ You learned how to combine standard command buttons and the `AddNew` and `Delete` methods to provide Add and Delete record functionality to a data entry form.

Quiz

1. What are the two properties of the data control that must be set when you link a form to an existing database and data table?

2. What property must you set if you want the data control to display the name of the data table in the window between the record pointer arrows?

3. What are the two properties of the text box control that must be set when you bind the input control to the data control on a form?

4. How many lines of code does it take to add a delete record function to a Visual Basic form when using the data control?

5. What environment setting can you use to make sure that Visual Basic will automatically save your work each time you attempt to run a program in design mode?

Exercises

1. Add the caption "The Titles Program" to the data entry form created in this chapter.

2. Place an additional command button labeled Exit on the data entry form. Add code behind this command button to end the program when it is clicked.

3. Modify the Add button to move the cursor to the first input control (Text1) on the data entry form. (Hint: search for SetFocus in the Visual Basic online help.)

Creating Databases

In today's lesson, you will learn a working definition of a *relational database,* as well as the basic elements of a database, including *data table, data record,* and *data field.* You will also learn the importance of establishing and maintaining *data relationships.* These are some of the key elements to developing quality databases for your applications.

You will also learn Visual Basic *database field types,* including their names, storage sizes, and common uses. Along the way, you will create a programming project that explores the limits, possibilities, and common uses of Visual Basic database field types.

Relational Databases

Before looking at the individual components of relational databases, let's first establish a simple definition. For the purposes of this book, a relational database is defined as "a collection of data that indicates relation among data elements"; or, to put it even more directly, a relational database is "a collection of related data."

In order to build a collection of related data, you need three key building blocks. These building blocks are as follows (from smallest to largest):

- Data Fields (somtimes called Data Columns)
- Data Records (also known as Data Rows)
- Data Tables

Let's look at each of these elements in more depth.

Data Fields: Columns

The first building block in a relational database is the *data field.* The data field contains the smallest element of data that you can store in a database, and each field contains only one data element. For example, if you want to store the name of a customer, you must create a data field somewhere in the database and also give that field a name, such as CustomerName. If you want to store the current account balance of a customer, you must create another field, possibly calling it AccountBalance. All the fields you create are stored in a single database (see Figure 2.1).

> **Note:** In formal database theory, a data field is often referred to as a *data column.* Throughout this book, the phrases *data field* and *data column* are used interchangeably.

Although it is possible to store more than one data element in a single field (such as first and last name), it is not good database practice to do so. In fact, storing more than one data element in a field can lead to problems when you or other users try to retrieve or update data.

This concept seems simple in theory, but it's not so easy in practice. The CustomerName field discussed earlier is a good example. Assume that you have a database that contains a list of your customers by name, and you need to sort the list by last name. How would this be done? Can you assume that each CustomerName data field contains a last name? Do some contain only a first name? Possibly some contain both first and last name—but in what order (*last name, first name* or *first name, last name*)? When you look at this situation, you discover that you're actually storing *two* data elements in the CustomerName field (first name and last name). For this reason, many databases contain not just the CustomerName data field, but data fields for LastName and FirstName.

Figure 2.1.
Examples of data fields in a database.

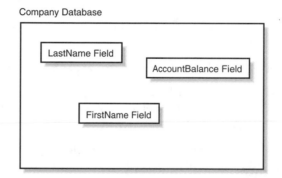

When you begin constructing your database, spend time thinking about the various ways you (and your users) will need to retrieve useful data. The quality and usefulness of your database rests on the integrity of its smallest element—the data field.

Data Records: Rows

Data records are a collection of related data fields. To use the example started earlier, a Customer Record could contain the fields LastName, FirstName, and AccountBalance. All three fields describe a single customer in the database.

> **Note:** Formal database theory refers to a data record as a *data row*. Both *data record* and *data row* are used interchangeably throughout this book.

A single data record contains only one copy of each defined data field. For example, a single data record cannot contain more than one LastName data field. Figure 2.2 shows the Company Database with a Customer Record defined. The Customer Record (row) contains three fields (columns).

Figure 2.2.

An example of a data record in a database.

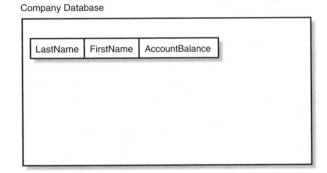

Data Table: Rows and Columns

By combining data fields and data records, you create the most common element of relational databases—the data table. This element contains multiple data records, and each data record contains multiple data fields (see Figure 2.3).

Just as each data record contains related data fields (LastName, FirstName, and AccountBalance), each data table contains related records. Data tables have meaningful names (Customer Table or Invoice Table, for example) in the same way that data fields have meaningful names (LastName, FirstName, AccountBalance, and so on). These names help you and other users to remember the contents of the elements (table elements and field elements).

Figure 2.3.

An example of a data table in a database.

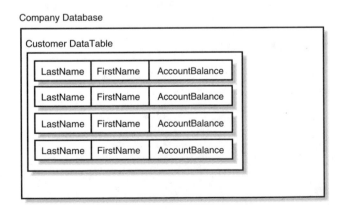

Database Relationships

Just as a data record can contain several related data fields, a database can contain several related tables. Using relationships is a very efficient way to store complex data. For example, a table storing customer names could be related to another table storing the names of items the customer has bought, which could be in turn related to a table storing the names of all the items you have to sell. By establishing meaningful relationships between data tables, you can create flexible data structures that are easy to maintain.

You establish relationships between data tables by using *pointer* or *qualifier fields* in your data table.

You use qualifier fields to point to records in other tables that have additional information. Qualifier fields usually describe what's known as *one-to-one* relationships. A good example of a one-to-one relationship is the relationship between a single customer record and a single record in the shipping address table (see Figure 2.4).

Figure 2.4.
An example of a one-to-one relationship between tables.

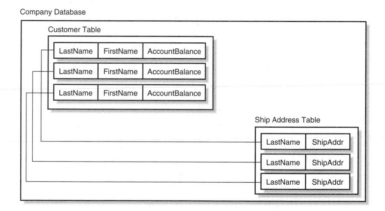

You use pointer fields to point to one or more records in other tables that have related information. Pointer fields usually describe what are known as *one-to-many* relationships. A good example of a one-to-many relationship is the relationship between a single customer master record and several outstanding customer orders (see Figure 2.5).

One-to-One Relationships

One-to-one relationships are used to link records in a master table (such as the Customer Table) to a *single* related record in another table.

Figure 2.5.

An example of a one-to-many relationship between tables.

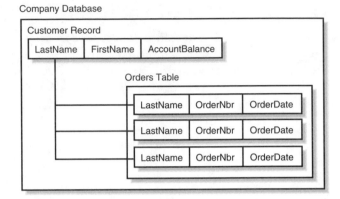

For example, assume you have two types of customers in your Company Database—retail and wholesale. Retail customers get paid commissions on sales, so you will need a Commission field added to the Customers table. Wholesale customers, however, purchase their products at a discount, so you also need to add a Discount field to the Customers table. Now your database users have to remember that, for Retail customers, the Discount field must be left empty, and for Wholesale customers, the Commission field must be left empty. You must remember these rules when adding, editing, and deleting data from the database, and you must remember these rules when creating reports.

This might seem to be a manageable task now, but try adding dozens more data fields to store (along with the exceptions), and you'll have quite a mess on your hands! Instead of establishing all data fields for all customers, what you need is a way to define only the fields you need for each type of customer. You can do this by setting up multiple tables in a single database and then setting up relationships between the tables.

In the example illustrated in Figure 2.6, you have added an additional data field—Type. This data field qualifies, or describes, the type of customer stored in this data record. You can use this type of information to tell you where to look for additional information about the customer. For example, if the Type field is set to Retail, you know you can look for the customer in the Retail Table to find additional information. If the Type field is set to Wholesale, you can find additional information in the Wholesale Table.

By creating the RecordType field, you can establish a one-to-one relationship between records in the Customer Table and the Retail and Wholesale Tables.

Figure 2.6.

Using a qualifier field to establish a one-to-one relationship.

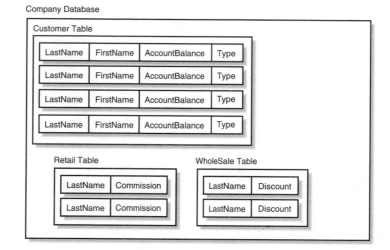

One-to-Many Relationships

One-to-many relationships are used to link records in a master table (such as the Customer Table) to multiple records in another table.

For example, you can keep track of several orders for each customer in your database. If you were not creating a relational database, you would probably add a data field to your customer table called Order. This would contain the last order placed by this customer. But what if you needed to keep track of more than one outstanding order? Would you add two, four, or six more order fields? You can see the problem.

Instead, you can add an additional table (the Orders Table) that can contain as many outstanding orders for a single customer as you need. After you create the Orders Table, you can establish a relationship between the Customer Table and the Orders Table using the LastName field (refer back to Figure 2.4). The LastName field is used as a pointer into the Orders Table to locate all the orders for this customer.

You can use many different ways to establish relationships between tables. This is usually done through a *key field*. Key fields are covered in depth in the next section.

Indexes: Key Fields

Usually, at least one data field in each data table acts as a key field for the table. Key fields in relational databases are used to define and maintain database integrity and to establish relationships between data tables. You create keys in your data table by designating one (or more) fields in your table as either a *primary key* or a *foreign key*. A data table can only have one primary key, but it can have several foreign keys. The primary key is used to control the order in which

the data is displayed. The foreign key is used to relate fields to fields in other (foreign) tables in the database.

Note: Key fields are sometimes referred to as *index fields* or *indexes*. Both key fields and index fields will be used interchangeably throughout the book. It is important to note that in most PC databases (xBase, Paradox, Btreive, and so forth), indexes are used only to speed processing of large files and play only a minor role in maintaining table relationships. The Visual Basic database model (.mdb files) and other true relational database models use key fields to establish database integrity rules as well as to speed database search and retrieval.

As mentioned earlier, a data table can have only one primary key. The primary key is used to define a unique record in the data table. In the Customer table, the LastName field is the primary key field for the data table. This means that no two records in that table can have exactly the same value in the LastName fields (see Figure 2.7). Any attempt to add more than one record with an identical primary key would result in a database error.

Tip: The main role of the primary key is to maintain the internal integrity of a data table. For this reason, no two records in a data table can have the same primary key value. Many companies with large customer bases use social security numbers or area codes and telephone numbers, because they know they are likely to have more than one customer with the same name. In these cases, the SSN or phone number would be the primary key field.

Figure 2.7.
The LastName field is the primary key field of the Customer Table.

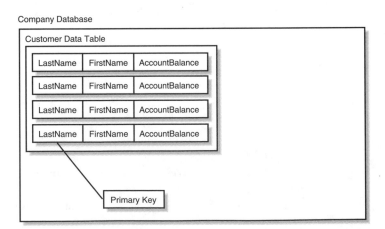

A data table can have more than one foreign key. It can also have no foreign key at all. In the Orders Table, the LastName field would be defined as a foreign key field. This means that it is a nonunique field in this data table that points to a key field in an external (foreign) table. Any attempt to add to the Orders table a record that contains a value in the LastName field, which does not also exist in a LastName field in the Customer Table, would result in a database error. For example, if the Customer table contains three records (Smith, Amundsen, and Jones), and you try to add a record to the Orders Table by filling the LastName field of the Orders Table with Paxton, you would get a database error. By creating foreign key fields in a table, you build data integrity into your database. This is called referential integrity.

Tip: The main role of a foreign key is to define and maintain relationships between data tables in a database. For this reason, foreign key fields are not unique in the data table in which they exist.

Note: Database integrity and foreign keys are covered in depth on Day 17, "Database Normalization," and Day 18, "Multiuser Considerations."

Now that you've worked through the basics of database elements in general, let's look at specific characteristics of Visual Basic data fields.

Visual Basic Database Field Types

Visual Basic stores values in the data table in data fields. Visual Basic recognizes 13 different data field types that you can use to store values. Each data field type has unique qualities that make it especially suitable for storing different types of data. Some are used to store images, the results of checkbox fields, currency amounts, calendar dates, and various sizes of numeric values. Table 2.1 lists the 13 database field types recognized by Visual Basic.

The first column contains the Visual Basic data field type name. This is the name you use when you create data tables using the Visual Basic Data Manager from the Toolbar. You'll learn about using this tool in Day 3, "Using the Data Manager."

The second column shows the number of bytes of storage taken by the various data field types. If the size column is set to "V," the length is variable and is determined by you at design time or by the program at runtime.

The third column in the table shows the equivalent Visual Basic data type for the associated database field type. This column tells you what Visual Basic data type you can use to update the database field.

Table 2.1. Visual Basic data field types.

Data Field Type	Size	VBType	Comments
BINARY	V	(none)	No equivalent VBType
BOOLEAN	1	Boolean	Stores 0 or –1 only
BYTE	1	Integer	Stores 0 to 255 only
COUNTER	8	Long	Auto-incrementing
CURRENCY	8	Currency	Scaled integer
DATETIME	8	Date/Time	Stored as a VBDouble
DOUBLE	8	Double	
INTEGER	2	Integer	
LONG	8	Long	
LONGBINARY	V	(none)	No equivalent VBType
MEMO	V	String	Length varies up to 1.2 gigabytes
SINGLE	4	Single	
TEXT	V	String	Length varies up to 255

Note: It is important to understand the difference between the Visual Basic *data field types* and the Visual Basic *data types.* The data field types are those recognized as valid data types within data tables. The data types are those types recognized by Visual Basic when defining variables within a program. For example, you can store the value 3 in a BYTE field in a data table, but you store that same value in an Integer field in a Visual Basic program variable.

Even though it is true that Visual Basic allows programmers to create database applications that can read and write data in several different data formats, all database formats do not recognize all data field types. For example, xBase data fields do not recognize a CURRENCY data field type. Before developing cross data-engine applications, you'll need to know exactly what data field types will be needed and how they are to be mapped to various data formats. The various data formats are covered in Day 10, "Visual Basic and the Microsoft JET Engine."

A number of things in Table 2.1 deserve additional comment.

☐ LONGBINARY data fields are for storing images and OLE objects. Visual Basic has no corresponding internal data type that maps directly to the LONGBINARY data field types. This information is usually stored as character data in Visual Basic. For example, a bitmap image would be stored in a LONGBINARY data table field, but it would be stored as a string variable in a Visual Basic program.

☐ The BOOLEAN data field type is commonly used to store the results of a bound checkbox input control. It stores only a -1 (True) or 0 (False). For example, if you enter 13 into the input box, Visual Basic will store -1 in the data field. To make matters trickier, Visual Basic will not report an error when a number other than 0 or -1 is entered. You should be careful when using the BOOLEAN data type because any number other than 0 entered into a BOOLEAN data field will be converted into -1.

☐ The BYTE data field type will accept input ranging from –32,768 to 32767 without reporting an error. However, if the input is outside the range of 0 to 255, Visual Basic will store only the right-most byte of the number. For example, if you enter the value 255 (stored as FF in hexadecimal), Visual Basic will store 255 in the data field. If you enter 260 (stored as 0104 in hexadecimal—it takes two bytes!), Visual Basic will store a decimal 4 in the data field because the right-most byte is set to hexidecimal 04.

☐ The COUNTER data field type is a special case. This is an auto-incrementing, read-only data field. Any attempt to write a value to this data field will result in a Visual Basic error. Visual Basic keeps track of the integer value to place in this field; it cannot be altered through the input controls or through explicit programming directives. The COUNTER field is often used as a unique primary key field in sequential processing operations.

☐ MEMO and TEXT data field types both accept any character data as valid input. MEMO data fields are built with a default length of 0 (zero). The physical length of a MEMO field is controlled by the total number of characters of data stored in the field. The length of a TEXT field must be declared when the data field is created. The Data Manager that is shipped with Visual Basic allows the TEXT field to have a length of 1 to 255 bytes.

Building the Visual Basic 4 Field Data Types Project

The following project will illustrate how different Visual Basic data field types store user input. You will also see how Visual Basic responds to input that is out of range for the various data field types.

1. Begin by creating a new Visual Basic project (select File | New Project). Using Table 2.2 and Figure 2.8 as guides, populate the Visual Basic form.

Table 2.2. Controls for the Visual Basic Data Field Types project.

Control	Property	Setting
Form	Caption	Visual Basic Data Field Types
	Name	frmFieldTypes
CommandButton	Caption	&Add
	Name	cmdAdd
CommandButton	Caption	&Delete
	Name	cmdDelete
CommandButton	Caption	E&xit
	Name	cmdExit
DataControl	DatabaseName	DATATYPE.MDB (include correct path)
	RecordSource	FieldTypes
	Name	datFieldTypes

Figure 2.8.
The form for the Visual Basic Data Field Types project.

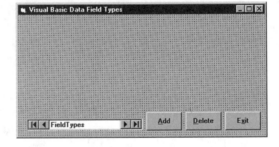

2. Now add the code behind the Add button. Double-click on the Add button to bring up the code window. The following line is all you need to add a new record to the data table.

```
Sub cmdAdd_Click ()
    datFieldTypes.Recordset.AddNew
End Sub
```

3. Next, add the code line behind the Delete button.

```
Sub cmdDelete_Click ()
    datFieldTypes.Recordset.Delete
End Sub
```

4. Finally, add the single Visual Basic keyword End behind the Exit button.

```
Sub cmdExit_Click ()
    End
End Sub
```

Now is a good time to save the project. Save the form as DATATYPE.FRM and the project as DATATYPE.VBP. Run the project just to make sure that you have entered all the code correctly up to this point. If you get error messages from Visual Basic, refer back to Table 2.2 and the preceding code lines to correct the problem.

Testing the BOOLEAN Data Type

Now you can add a text box input control and a label to this form. Set the caption of the label to BOOLEAN:. Set the DataSource property of the text box to datFieldTypes and the DataField property to BOOLEAN. Set the Text property to be blank. Refer to Figure 2.9 for placement and sizing.

Figure 2.9.
Adding the BOOLEAN data type input control.

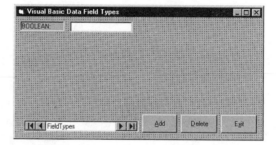

Now run the program. You'll see that the first value in the input box is a 0, the default value for new records. Enter the number 13 in the text box and click on the left-most arrow button on the data control. This will force the data control to save the input field to the data table and update the display. What happened to the 13? It was converted to -1. Any value other than 0, when entered into a BOOLEAN data type field, will be converted to -1.

Testing the BYTE Data Type

Now let's add a label and input control for the BYTE data type field. Instead of picking additional controls from the Toolbox Window and typing in property settings, Visual Basic allows you to copy existing controls. Copying controls saves time, reduces typing errors, and helps to keep the size and shape of the controls on your form consistent.

To copy controls, use the mouse pointer, with the left mouse button depressed, to create a dotted-line box around both the label control and the text box control already on your form (in this case, the label Boolean and its text box). When you release the left mouse button, you'll see that both controls have been marked as selected. Now click on Edit | Copy to copy the selected controls to the Clipboard. Now just use Edit | Paste to copy the controls from the Clipboard back onto your form.

At this point, Visual Basic asks you whether you want to create a Control Array. Say yes, both times. You then see the two controls appear at the top left of the form. Use your mouse to position them on the form (see Figure 2.10).

 Tip: The Textbox and Label controls on this form are part of a control array. Because using control arrays reduces the total number of distinct controls on your forms, using control arrays reduces the amount of Windows resources your program uses. You can copy controls as many times as you like—even across forms and projects!

Figure 2.10.
Copying controls on a form.

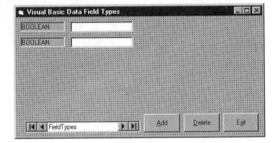

You just created duplicates of the BOOLEAN input control. All you need to do now is change the label caption to BYTE: and the text box DataField property to BYTE, and you have two new controls on your form with minimal typing. Your form should now look like the one in Figure 2.11.

Now save and run the program. This time, enter the value 256 into the Byte input control and hit the left-most arrow button. You'll see that when Visual Basic stored the numeric value into the BYTE data type field, it converted the 256 back to 0. BYTE data type fields can only store from 0 to 255. Try entering a negative number in the Byte text box and see what value gets stored to the data table.

Figure 2.11.
Adding the BYTE data type to your form.

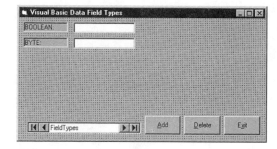

Testing the CURRENCY Data Type

Copy the label and text box control again using the mouse to select the controls for copy, and the Copy and Paste commands from the Edit menu. Change the label caption property to CURRENCY: and the text box DataField property to CURRENCY. Refer to Figure 2.12 for spacing and sizing of the controls.

Figure 2.12.
Adding the CURRENCY data type to the form.

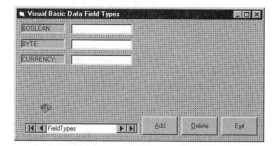

Save and run the program and test the CURRENCY data type text box. Enter the value 1.12345, force Visual Basic to save the value to the data table (press the left-most arrow button), and see what happens. Try entering 1.00001. When storing values to the CURRENCY data type field, Visual Basic will only store four places to the right of the decimal. If the number is larger than four decimal places to the right, Visual Basic will round the value before storing it in the data field. Also, you'll notice that Visual Basic does not add a dollar sign ($) to the display of CURRENCY type data fields.

Testing the DATE Data Type

The Visual Basic DATE data type field is one of the most powerful data types. Visual Basic will perform extensive edit checks on values entered in the DATE data type field. Using DATE data type fields can save a lot of coding when you need to make sure valid dates are entered by users.

Create a new set of label and text box controls by copying the label and text box controls again. Change the label caption property to DATE: and the text box DataField property to DATE. Your form should look like the one in Figure 2.13.

Figure 2.13.
Adding the DATE data type to the form.

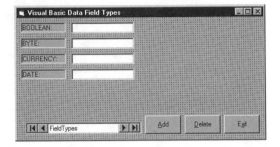

Save and run the program. Try entering 12/32/95. As you can see, Visual Basic gives you an error message whenever you enter an invalid date. Now enter 1/1/0 into the Date text box. Notice that Visual Basic formats the date for you.

How does Visual Basic decide what date format to use? The date format used by Visual Basic comes from the settings in the Windows 95 Control Panel Regional Settings applet. While you have this program running, experiment by calling up the Windows 95 Regional Settings applet. (From the task bar, select Start | Settings | Control Panel, and then select Regional Settings.) Change the date format settings, and return to your Visual Basic program to see the results.

Tip: The Visual Basic DATE data type should always be used to store date values. If you install your program in Europe, where the common date display format is *DD-MM-YY* instead of the common U.S. format of *MM-DD-YY*, your program will work without a problem. If you store dates as strings in the format *MM/DD/ YY* or as numeric values in the format *YYMMDD*, your program will not be able to compute or display dates correctly across international boundaries.

Testing the COUNTER Data Type

You can test one more Visual Basic data type—the COUNTER data type. This data type is automatically set by Visual Basic each time you add a new record to the data table. The COUNTER data type makes an excellent unique primary key field because Visual Basic is able to create and store more than a billion unique values in the COUNTER field without duplication.

Copy another label/text box control set onto the form. Change the label caption property to Counter and the text box DataField property to COUNTER. See Figure 2.14 for positioning and sizing.

Figure 2.14.
Adding the COUNTER data type to the form.

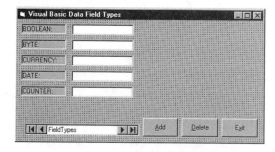

Now save and run the program one more time. Notice that the COUNTER data type already has a value in it, even though you have not entered data into the field. Visual Basic will set the value of COUNTER fields; users do not. Add a new record to the table by pressing the Add button. You'll see a new value in the COUNTER input control. Visual Basic will use the next available number in sequence. Visual Basic is also able to ensure unique numbers in a multiuser setting. If you have three people running the same program adding records to this table, they would all receive unique values in the Counter text box.

Caution: You should never attempt to edit the value in the COUNTER text box! If Visual Basic determines that the counter value has been changed, it displays a Visual Basic error message, and you will be unable to save the record. Even if you reset the value in the COUNTER data field back to its original value, Visual Basic will refuse to save the record.

Additional Visual Basic Data Types

The rest of the Visual Basic data types (INTEGER, SINGLE, DOUBLE, TEXT, MEMO, BINARY, and LONGBINARY) are rather unspectacular when placed on a form. The following are some notes on the various Visual Basic data types that you should keep in mind when you are designing your data tables.

☐ Visual Basic will return an error if you enter more than the maximum number of characters into a TEXT data field. You will get the same error message if you pass the Visual Basic 32K input limit on the MEMO data field.

☐ The BINARY and LONGBINARY data fields are meant to store graphic image data and will allow any alphanumeric data to be entered and saved. The storage of graphic data is covered later in the book (see Day 12).

☐ Check the Visual Basic online help under Visual Basic Data Types for additional information on the high and low ranges for DOUBLE, INTEGER, and SINGLE data fields.

☐ BOOLEAN and BYTE data fields will allow you to enter values beyond their expected range without reporting an error. Notice that Visual Basic will alter the data you entered into these data fields without telling you!

☐ The CURRENCY data field only stores the first four places to the right of the decimal. If you enter values beyond the fourth decimal place, Visual Basic will simply truncate the value to four decimal places and give you no warning.

☐ The DATE data field has some interesting behavior. Visual Basic will not let you store an invalid date or time in the data field; you receive a `Type mismatch` error instead. Also, the display format for the dates and times is determined by the settings you choose in the Windows Control Panel (through the International icon). In fact, when valid data is stored in a DATE data field, you can change the display format (say from 12-hour time display to 24-hour time display), and the next time you view that data record, it will reflect the changes made through the Control Panel.

Summary

Today you learned the following about relational databases:

☐ A relational database is "a collection of related data."

☐ The three key building blocks of relational databases are data fields, data records, and data tables.

☐ The two types of database relationships are one-to-one, which uses qualifier fields, and one-to-many, which uses pointer fields.

☐ There are two types of key (or index) fields: primary key and foreign key.

You also learned the 13 data field types recognized by Visual Basic. You constructed a data entry form that allows you to test the way Visual Basic behaves when attempting to store data entered into the various data field types.

Quiz

1. What are the three main building blocks for relational databases?

2. What is the smallest building block in a relational database?

3. A data record is a collection of related _____.

4. What is the main role of a primary key in a data table?

5. Can a data table have more than one foreign key defined?

6. List all the possible values that can be stored in a BOOLEAN data field.

7. What is the highest value that can be stored in a BYTE data field?

8. What happens when you attempt to edit a COUNTER data field?

9. How many places to the right of the decimal can be stored in a CURRENCY data field?

10. What Windows Control Panel Applet determines the display format of DATE data fields?

Exercises

Answer questions 1, 2, and 3 based on the data in this table:

SSN	Last	First	Age	City	St	Comments
123-45-6789	Smith	Mark	17	Austin	TX	Trans from New York.
456-79-1258	Smith	Ron	21	New York	NY	Born in Wyoming.
987-65-8764	Johnson	Curt	68	Chicago	IL	Plays golf on Wed.

1. How many records are in the previous data table?

2. Which field should you select as the primary key?

3. Identify each data field, its Data Field Type, and its VISUAL BASIC Type.

4. Modify the Visual Basic Data Field Types example from this lesson by creating a checkbox and placing the results in the existing BOOLEAN text box.

Using the Data Manager

Today you will learn how to use the Data Manager that is shipped with Visual Basic 4. This utility program gives you the power to create and maintain basic databases without leaving Visual Basic 4 design mode. You will learn how to use the Data Manager program to do the following:

- ☐ Create a new database
- ☐ Open existing databases
- ☐ Add data tables to a database
- ☐ Link to information contained in other databases
- ☐ Add fields and indexes to a database
- ☐ Set relationships between data tables
- ☐ Enter and find data in data tables
- ☐ Enter and save SQL statements
- ☐ Compact and repair databases
- ☐ Encrypt and decrypt databases

Plus, today is the day you start building your first extended Visual Basic 4 database project—The Company Database Project. You will use the Data Manager to construct the first data table in the database—the CompanyMaster table.

What Is the Visual Basic 4 Data Manager?

The Visual Basic 4 Data Manager is a complete program (written in Visual Basic!) that ships with Visual Basic 4. This program can be used to create new Microsoft Access databases and edit, convert, compact, repair, encrypt, and decrypt existing databases. You can use Data Manager to create or delete data tables and indexes. You can also use the Visual Basic 4 Data Manager to perform simple data entry on data tables.

The Visual Basic 4 Data Manager can create databases in the Microsoft Access database format. It can also be used to attach to and perform field maintenance and data entry on Paradox, dBASE, FoxPro, Btrieve, and ODBC data sources. It can even attach to Excel spreadsheets and DOS text files.

Microsoft Access Database Support

The Visual Basic 4 Data Manager provides nearly complete support for Microsoft Access databases. It allows you to create databases and create and delete tables, indexes, and data fields. You will not, however, be able to delete data fields that are used in indexes.

Advantages and Disadvantages of Using the Data Manager

The Data Manager program has several key features that make it an excellent tool for constructing and maintaining databases for your Visual Basic 4 applications. First, you can launch this program directly from the Visual Basic 4 Add-Ins menu. As long as Visual Basic 4 is up and running in design mode, you can call up the Data Manager and create new databases, open existing databases, or modify data tables and indexes without having to leave Visual Basic 4 or close down your Visual Basic 4 project.

Another advantage of having the Data Manager is that you can use it to do quick data entry into existing data tables. This allows you to quickly create test data for your Visual Basic 4 applications. Do you need to see whether a database lookup routine you wrote really works? You can pop up the Data Manager, add a few records to the appropriate data table, and then return to Visual Basic 4 and run your application.

You can also use the Data Manager to compact out deleted records (in other words, physically remove spaces left by deleted records), and for those occasions when you get the dreaded "corrupted database" error, you can use the Data Manager to repair existing Microsoft Access type databases.

You can even use Data Manager to build and test SQL statements. This is an extremely handy tool to have in order to test the logic of SQL statements as you need to incorporate them into your Visual Basic 4 code. These statements, once tested and working properly, can then be saved by Data Manager.

A major disadvantage of using the Data Manager to create databases for your Visual Basic 4 applications is that it is not a complete database administration tool. Although you can use the Data Manager to construct and maintain data tables and indexes, you cannot print out data structures or index parameters.

Even with this limitation, the Data Manager is a very useful tool. Let's go through a short course on how to use the Data Manager to construct and maintain Microsoft Access-type databases.

Maintaining Databases with Data Manager

First, if you haven't already started the Data Manager, do it now. To start the program from within Visual Basic 4, select Add-Ins | Data Manager.

The first screen shows two menu choices: File and Help. The Help menu lets you bring up an online reference about how to use the Data Manager. All other program options appear underneath the File menu. Let's look at one of the first commands you will use on this menu.

Opening and Closing Existing Microsoft Access Databases

You use the Open command under the File menu to open an existing database. Data Manager allows you to open Microsoft Access databases. When the database is open, you can perform table maintenance functions such as adding new tables, modifying existing tables, and deleting tables.

Now open a Microsoft Access database. Select File | Open Database. Use the Open Database dialog box to locate and select the BIBLIO.MDB database from your Visual Basic 4 directory (see Figure 3.1).

Note: To guard against any accidental changes to the structure of the BIBLIO.MDB database, it is recommended that you copy the pristine BIBLIO.MDB database to a different directory and change its name. A logical choice would be C:\TYSDBVB\CHAP03\DATAMGR.MDB.

Figure 3.1.
Opening a database in Data Manager.

Open Database	? X
Look in: vb4	

bitmaps   samples
clisvr   setup
hc   setupkit
icons   VBOnline
include   winapi
metafile   Biblio.mdb
report

File name: Biblio.mdb   Open
Files of type: Access (*.mdb)   Cancel
☐ Open as read-only

For Users of Visual Basic 3.0

The Visual Basic/Microsoft Access compatibility layer is an upgrade that provides improved database speed and additional SQL language options to Visual Basic 3.0. If you are using Visual Basic 3.0 and have not installed the compatibility layer, you should do so now. Most of the examples in this book will require the added functionality of the Visual Basic/Microsoft Access compatibility layer.

The Visual Basic 4.0 Data Manager can handle all current versions of Microsoft Access database files. If you are using Visual Basic version 3.0 and have installed the Visual Basic/Microsoft Access compatibility layer, you can open version 1.1 and

version 2.0 Microsoft Access databases. If you are using Visual Basic version 3.0 and have not installed the compatibility layer, you can open Microsoft Access version 1.0 and version 1.1 databases only.

After you select the database, Data Manager will load all the tables and display the Tables/QueryDefs and SQL Statement forms. Your screen should look something like the one in Figure 3.2. You can perform all the necessary table maintenance operations from the Tables/QueryDefs form. You can use the SQL Statement form to enter and generate SQL statements. You will perform exercises using both of these forms throughout this chapter.

Figure 3.2.
Viewing the forms of the Data Manager.

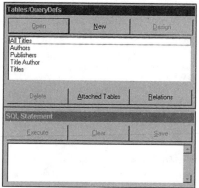

You can close the Microsoft Access database by selecting Close Database from the File menu.

Compacting and Repairing Microsoft Access Databases

The Data Manager has two additional database functions that can only be used on Microsoft Access databases—Compact and Repair. These two functions reduce the amount of disk space used by a database (Compact) and attempt to recover data from damaged databases (Repair).

Occasionally, a database you have been working on becomes corrupted. This usually occurs when there has been a hardware failure during a database update operation. Hardware failures include loss of power to the PC, loss of power to the file server where the database is stored, disk read/write failures due to power fluctuations, component failure—the list is (sadly) endless. If you are unable to open a data table, index, or entire database, and you know you have correct connection information, you might have a corrupted database.

To repair a database using Data Manager, select Repair Database from the File menu. You should now see the Repair Database dialog box (see Figure 3.3). Locate and select a Microsoft Access database to repair (remember that you can only repair Microsoft Access databases with Data Manager). When you click on the OK button, Data Manager will begin the process of repairing any corrupted items in the database. This might result in lost records in a data table or even a lost table or index. It is therefore a good idea to review your data after doing a repair.

In severe cases, Data Manager might report that it cannot repair the database at all. In such cases, your only recourse is to replace the corrupted database with your most recent backup copy.

Figure 3.3.

*Selecting a Microsoft Access
database to repair.*

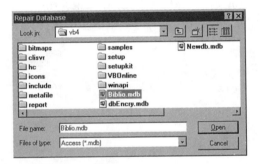

Note: Your database might increase in size after running the Repair Database routine. For this reason, we advise you to run the Compact Database routine after running the Repair Database routine.

As a database is used, records are added and updated, and some are eventually deleted. All this activity in the database tends to increase the overall disk space used to store the database. It is a good practice to run the Compact Database routine to clear out any empty space that can accumulate. This routine also optimizes the storage of the data, based on existing indexes. This optimization not only saves disk space, but it can also improve overall performance of the database.

To compact a database using Data Manager select File | Compact Database. You are asked to locate and select a Microsoft Access database to compact (see Figure 3.4). Remember that you can only compact Microsoft Access databases with Data Manager. After you click the OK button, you will be shown the Compact To Database dialog. You must supply a recipient database to compact to. This is the name of a *new* database (see Figure 3.5). After you enter a new database name, click OK. Data Manager begins copying all valid items (data table and index definitions, actual data and indexes, and system control information) to the new database. When the routine completes successfully, you can erase the old database and rename the new database using the previous name.

Figure 3.4.
Selecting a Microsoft Access database to compact.

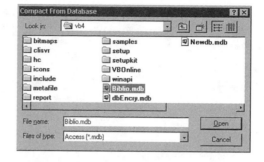

Figure 3.5.
Selecting a recipient database in the Compact To dialog.

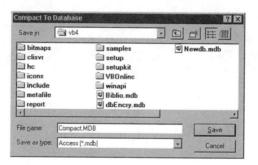

For example, if you want to compact a database named CH03.MDB, you would select CH03.MDB as the database in the Compact From dialog box and COMPACT.MDB as the database filename in the Compact To dialog box. After the compacting is completed, delete CH03.MDB and rename COMPACT.MDB to CH03.MDB.

Encrypting and Decrypting Databases

The Encrypt menu options on the File menu enable you to *scramble* the contents of an existing database. This is a security feature that keeps individuals who do not have a utility that can read Access databases (such as Data Manager) from reading the information stored in them.

To perform an encryption, simply select the File | Encrypt option. You will then be prompted by the Encrypt Database dialog box (see Figure 3.6) to select a database to encrypt.

When you select the on-screen Open button, Data Manager finds the database and prompts you for the name of the new, encrypted database (see Figure 3.7). The New Database filename must be different from the original database name. Also, you cannot have the database open for use when you attempt an encryption.

Figure 3.6.
Selecting a Microsoft Access database to encrypt.

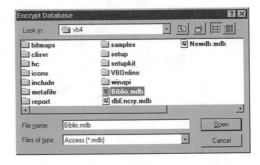

Figure 3.7.
Entering a Microsoft Access database filename to encrypt to.

Data Manager also provides a Decrypt utility to unscramble data that you scrambled with the Encrypt option. This simply reverses the effects of the encryption.

Select Decrypt from the File menu to perform this option. You will be prompted for the name of the database to decrypt (remember, you can't have the database you want to decrypt open at the time of decryption). You will be greeted with a similar dialog box (see Figure 3.8).

Figure 3.8.
Selecting a Microsoft Access database to decrypt.

Click Open to select the highlighted database. Next, a screen will appear to enable you to enter a new database filename (see Figure 3.9). This name cannot be the same as one existing within the same path.

Figure 3.9.
Entering a filename for a decrypted database.

Encryption can provide a useful security feature for your data, but it does have some drawbacks. First, it doesn't provide complete security. A user with appropriate network rights can erase an encrypted file in the same way as an ordinary data file. Secondly, encrypting a database means it can't be read by other applications. One of the main benefits of a database written in Access is that it can be read by numerous programs (Excel, for example). Encrypting can keep users from performing the tasks that they most need in order to perform their work efficiently. Finally, encryption is not selective at the table level and can only be applied at the database level. You will have to encrypt an entire database even if you only want one table of that database encrypted.

Creating New Databases with Data Manager

To create an entirely new Microsoft Access database using Data Manager, select File | New Database. You should now see a New Database dialog box where you can enter a name for the database in the File Name field. For this example, enter MASTER.MDB as the database name (see Figure 3.10).

Figure 3.10.
Entering the name of a new Microsoft Access database.

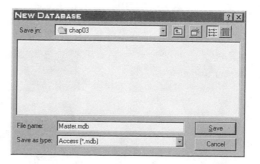

When creating Microsoft Access databases, you should use the .MDB extension. If you leave it off and do not include the period (.) in your filename, Data Manager will add the .MDB to your database name automatically. When you click the Save button, Data Manager creates the Microsoft Access database and presents you with the Tables/Query Defs form (see Figure 3.11). Now you are ready to create and maintain data tables and indexes in your new database. You'll add these in the next section of this chapter.

Figure 3.11.
A new Microsoft Access database ready for table definitions.

Maintaining Tables

After you have opened an existing database or created a new database, you can perform data table maintenance. Data Manager allows you to create new tables, modify existing tables, and delete existing tables. You can add or delete fields and indexes for an existing table. You can even use Data Manager to perform data entry on existing tables.

Using Data Manager to Create a New Table

You must first create a new table before you can add fields and indexes to a database. To do this, you must first open an existing database or create one. In the following example, you will use the MASTER.MDB Microsoft Access database you created in the previous part of this chapter. If you haven't done this already, see the previous section, "Creating New Databases with Data Manager."

To add a new table to this database, click New and enter a table name in the first field of the dialog box that appears. For this example, enter CompanyMaster. (See Figure 3.12.)

Figure 3.12.
Adding a new table to the MASTER.MDB database.

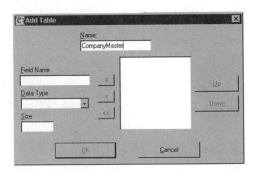

Next, press the Tab key to move to the Field Name field. Enter the first field of this table, EntryNbr. Select the Data Type of LONG INTEGER, and then press the right arrow (>) to move the field into the fields container. Now select OK to create the table with the first field included.

You could have built an entire table in this screen, but for the sake of practice, move on to the Table Edit function to add more fields.

Adding Fields to a Table

The Data Manager Add Table form only allows you to add fields to a table. You need to use the Design function on the Tables/QueryDefs form to add indexes, keys, default values, and validation rules to your data tables.

To go into the Design of the table, first select the table by clicking on its name once with the left mouse button in the Tables/QueryDefs form. Next, click the design button. You should see a screen similar to the one in Figure 3.13.

Figure 3.13.
The Table Editor form.

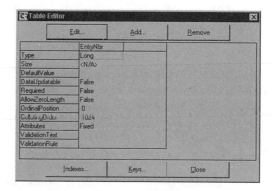

Take a look at the buttons that appear on this form. From here, you can edit an existing field, add fields, remove fields, add indexes, and add keys. The first section covered is Edit.

To edit a field, simply select it by clicking on its field name in the grid that appears, and click Edit. Do this with the EntryNbr field. You should see a form similar to Figure 3.14.

Notice how this form enables you to enter the field type, size, default value, ordinal position, collating order, validation text, and validation rule. Notice also how you can set attributes and confirm whether the data is updatable, required, or can be of zero length.

For this exercise, make the EntryNbr field a counter field. Simply select the Counter checkbox and click OK. You will be notified that this change will delete data that exists. Select Yes to continue because there are currently no data records in the table.

Figure 3.14.
The Field Edit form.

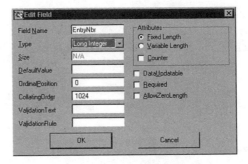

 Tip: Adding a counter field to your Microsoft Access data tables is an excellent way to automatically generate unique record IDs. Each time a new record is added to the table, Visual Basic 4 generates a new counter value and inserts it into the designated field. This works in a multiuser environment, too. Because the underlying data type for a counter field is the Visual Basic 4 type LONG, you can add more than 2 billion records to a single data table before you have to worry about running out of unique values.

Now you need to complete the rest of the CompanyMaster table. This table should contain the basic name and address information for all the customers of the company. Throughout the next three weeks, you will build this Company database and create programs that will access the data you put into this table.

To add a field to a data table, click the Add button on the Design form. Data Manager presents you with the Add Field dialog box. Note that this is the same form you used earlier for editing. Each time you click the OK button on this form, another field is added to the table. You can add as many fields as you like to a data table.

Table 3.1 contains a list of the field names, data types, and lengths for the CompanyMaster data table. Please refer to this listing as you continue with this lesson and construct this table.

Table 3.1. The field list for the CompanyMaster data table.

Number	Field Name	Field Type	Field Length
1.	EntryNbr	Long Integer	
2.	CompanyName	Text	50
3.	LastName	Text	30
4.	FirstName	Text	30

Number	Field Name	Field Type	Field Length
5.	Title	Text	30
6.	Addr1	Text	40
7.	Addr2	Text	40
8.	City	Text	30
9.	StateProv	Text	10
10.	PostalCode	Text	12
11.	Country	Text	20
12.	VoicePhone	Text	20
13.	FAXPhone	Text	20
14.	Extension	Text	10
15.	CustFlag	Boolean	
16.	CompanyLogo	Long Binary	
17.	Notes	Memo	
18.	LastUpdated	Date/Time	

The second field you'll add to the table is the CompanyName field. To do this, click on the Add button of the Design table form. This brings up the Add Field dialog box. First, type CompanyName in the Field Name input box (remember, do not put spaces in field names). Then, click on the down arrow of the Field Type drop-down listbox.

Tip: You can also open a listbox by pressing the F4 key. Field types can also be selected by typing the first letter of the desired type. Repeatedly striking the first letter of a desired type cycles through types that begin with the same first letter.

Select Text as your field type. Then press Tab to move to the size box. Enter the value (50) from Table 3.1. Before you click the OK button for the Add Field dialog, your screen should look like the one in Figure 3.15.

Note: Data can only be entered into the Field Size input box if you have selected the Text data type. The field sizes of all other data types are controlled by the Microsoft JET engine.

Figure 3.15.
Adding the CompanyName field to the CompanyMaster data table.

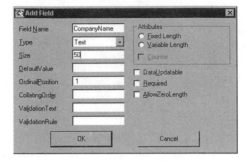

After clicking the OK button on the Add Field dialog box, Data Manager adds the field to the data table and returns to the Design form. You can now see that the CompanyName field has been added to your table (see Figure 3.16).

Figure 3.16.
A view of the Table Design form after adding the CompanyName field.

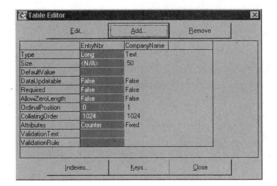

Using the information in Table 3.1, create the remaining data fields for the CompanyMaster table. Be sure to enter the Field Size values for the Text data type fields.

> **Note:** The Visual Basic 4 Data Manager gives you only limited ability to modify existing Microsoft Access data tables. You can add new fields to an existing data table, but you cannot modify or delete existing fields in a table without deleting data in the edited fields.

After you have added all 17 fields to the data table, you are ready to create the indexes.

Indexes

You can speed data processing and establish database integrity by creating indexes for data tables. It is usually a good idea to create at least one index for each data table. This one index should be based on the primary key field of the data table. The primary key field is the one field that will always contain a unique value. Additional indexes can be created to speed data searches or to enforce data integrity across multiple tables. Integrity indexes are covered in Week Two.

Adding Indexes to a Data Table

To add a primary index to a database, you must first open a database and select a data table in design mode.

Now let's add a primary key index to the CompanyMaster data table you created earlier in this chapter. If you have not already done so, create the CompanyMaster data table defined in the previous section. If you already created the data table, start Data Manager and select the MASTER.MDB database. At the Tables/QueryDefs form, select the CompanyMaster data table, and click on the Design button to bring up the Design form. Your screen should look like the one in Figure 3.17.

Figure 3.17.

Adding an index to the CompanyMaster data table.

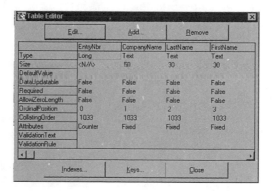

Click on the Indexes button at the bottom of the form. This brings up the Index dialog box. The Index dialog box shows you a listing of all the current indexes for the table on which you are working. From this point, you can either edit, add, or remove an index. Select Add so that you can build the primary key for this table.

The Add Index dialog now appears. The first value you should enter on this form is the Index name. This name will be used in your Visual Basic 4 program when you are selecting the index. Embedded spaces are allowed in the Index name, but don't use them. It is good database practice to have no embedded spaces in data object names. For this example, enter PrimaryKey as the Index name.

Note: Microsoft Access databases allow embedded spaces in field and index names (for example, First Name instead of FirstName). This makes working with Microsoft Access databases very comfortable for novice users. However, most other database systems do not allow embedded spaces in field names or index names. If you build your databases assuming that embedded spaces are allowed, and then convert your database to another system (for example, use an upgrade Wizard to move to Microsoft SQL Server), you will run into problems. It is better to use no embedded spaces in your field and index names.

When you built this table, you added the Counter data type field EntryNbr for use as a unique key field for the data table. This is the field you want to use for the PrimaryKey index. Locate the EntryNbr field in the field list and click on it once to highlight it. Notice that two Add buttons are now enabled. Clicking on either of these buttons will add the highlighted field to the index definition. The ASC stands for Ascending and the DEC stands for Descending. You can use these two buttons to force the index to sort the data from the smallest value to the largest (ascending) or from the largest value to the smallest (descending). You want the PrimaryKey index to run from the smallest EntryNbr to the largest, so click on the Add (ASC) button. Notice that the highlighted field now appears in the list of the Fields in the Index box, followed by (ASC) to denote ascending order.

Before you click the OK button to save the index definition, click the Primary Index checkbox at the top of the form. Clicking this checkbox tells Visual Basic 4 that the values in this field must always be unique. If users attempt to save a record with an index value that duplicates that of another record in the data table, Visual Basic 4 issues an error message. Also, Visual Basic 4 only allows one primary index for each data table. Your index dialog box should look like the one in Figure 3.18.

Figure 3.18.

Defining an index using the Data Manager.

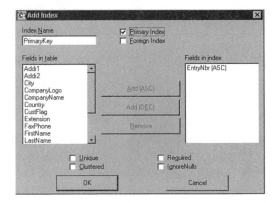

When you have toggled the primary checkbox, click on OK to save the index definition. Data Manager stores the index definition and returns to the Indexes dialog box. You will now see that the PrimaryKey index has been added (see Figure 3.19).

Figure 3.19.
The Indexes form showing the PrimaryKey index.

Select Close from the Indexes dialog to return to the Design grid.

Add two more indexes to this data table. Create an ascending index called Names that contains two fields—LastName and FirstName. Multiple fields can be included in an index by selecting the first field and pressing the Add (ASC) key. Then repeat this process for the second field in the index. Click the Unique checkbox to make this index unique. This prevents two records in the data table from containing the same name. Your Add Index dialog should look like the one in Figure 3.20. Select OK when you are finished.

Figure 3.20.
Creating the Names multifield index.

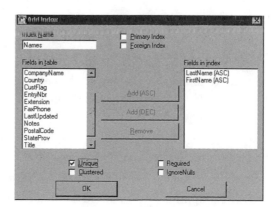

The last index to create will be one built on a descending key. Create a nonunique, descending index called Updates that contains one field—LastUpdated. Be sure to use the Add (DEC) button to add the LastUpdated field to the Fields In Index list. Your Index dialog should look like the one in Figure 3.21. Notice that the field name LastUpdated in the Fields In Index list is followed by (DEC) to denote descending order.

Figure 3.21.

Creating a nonunique, descending key index called Updates.

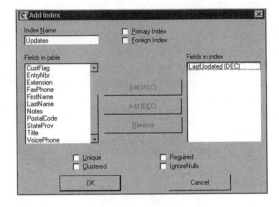

When all three indexes are defined, your Indexes form should look like the form in Figure 3.22.

Figure 3.22.

The completed CompanyMaster data table index definitions.

Deleting Indexes from Data Tables

You can delete an index by clicking on the index name in the Indexes dialog box and clicking the Remove button at the bottom of the form. Before the index is removed, you will see a dialog box asking you to confirm the deletion.

For now, delete the Names index from the CompanyMaster data table. Select the Names index by clicking on the Names line of the Index grid. Click on the Remove button to delete the selected index. Your screen should now look like the one in Figure 3.23.

Click Yes to confirm that you want to delete the index.

Figure 3.23.
Deleting an index from the
CompanyMaster data table.

Editing Indexes of Data Tables

There may be times when an index will need to be edited. For example, you may have forgotten to select the Unique box, or you may want to add another field to the index. Editing an index is very similar to adding an index. Simply select the index you want to edit and press the Edit button. You will then be presented with the same form you used to build the index. Make changes as needed in this form and press OK to save your work.

Deleting an Existing Table

To delete an existing table, select a table from the Tables/QueryDefs window by clicking on it. Then click the Delete button to remove the table from the database. By deleting the table, you also delete all the data stored in that table.

Attaching External Data Sources

One of the beauties of working with Visual Basic 4 and Microsoft Access data tables is the openness that you have with data. Data can be read from MDB databases by off-the-shelf products such as Microsoft Excel and Lotus 123. In addition, MDB databases can incorporate and modify data that exists in other sources. Using data that exists in other data sources is made possible by attaching that data source.

Attaching a data table from another database simply places a pointer in your original database to the external source. You will be able to add and edit data in the attached table just like you would with an ordinary table. This helps you be more productive by eliminating the need to copy or replicate the same data among several applications.

Let's take a look at attaching a table from your MASTER.MDB database. First, start Data Manager and open MASTER.MDB, if you do not currently have it open. Next, select Attached Tables from the Tables/QueryDefs window. You should now see the Attached Tables dialog box (see Figure 3.24).

Figure 3.24.
The Attached Tables dialog box.

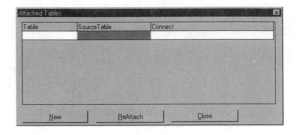

Now, click the New button to display the New Attached Table dialog box (see Figure 3.25).

Figure 3.25.
The Attached Tables definition dialog.

You will now complete this dialog to define the parameters of the attachment. First, enter an Attachment Name. This will serve as the name of the table in your database. Remember that it is good practice to avoid entering spaces in the names of database objects. For this exercise, enter Test.

Now enter the name of the database, including its path, into the Database Name field. You'll want to open the Authors table in the BIBLIO.MDB database that ships with Visual Basic 4, so you can enter C:\PROGRAM FILES\MICROSOFT VISUAL BASIC\BIBLIO.MDB. To play it safe, open the copy of this database (C:\TYSDBVB\CHAP03\DATAMGR.MDB) that you created earlier in this chapter. Please note that you must know the full path and filename of the database you want to attach. Data Manager does not provide an open dialog from which to choose a database.

Select JET Engine MDB as the Connect String. The connect string is the format of the database to which you are attaching. Take a minute to look at the different formats that can be attached.

Finally, open the Table to Attach box. When you click on the down arrow of this box, Data Manager finds the database you entered in the Database Name field and lists its tables. You will receive an error message if you entered an invalid name in the Database Name field. Select Authors as the table to attach.

Compare your form to Figure 3.26. Click Attach to create the attachment and click Close. You should now return to the Attached Tables dialog box, which displays the new table reference.

Figure 3.26.
The completed Attached Tables definition dialog.

Close the Attached Tables dialog to see the Test attachment in the Tables/QueryDefs window. Double-click on it to open it. You have now created an attachment where you can read and write data.

Finish this exercise by closing the Test table and returning to the Tables/QueryDefs window. You no longer have a need for this attachment, so you can delete it. Do this by clicking once on Test and then selecting the Delete button. A confirmation will appear to confirm the deletion. Select OK and the attachment is gone.

Note: Deletion of the attachment does not delete the underlying table, or the data it contains. The deletion simply removes the pointer to the data table.

Establishing Relationships

Relationships are the cornerstone of modern database theory. By setting a relationship between tables, you are actually telling a table to use the information contained within another table and restrict entry to the values that currently exist. This provides benefits by keeping entry consistent. Relationships also make tables more efficient because similar data does not have to be entered into multiple tables. Let's construct relationships to demonstrate what they can do for you.

Open the BIBLIO.MDB database found in your Visual Basic 4 root directory (or your copy in C:\TYSDBVB\CHAP03). Examine the design of the Publishers table by clicking on its name in the Table/QueryDefs window and then pressing Design. Take note of the field names— especially the PubID field.

Now do the same with the Titles table. Note that this table also has a PubID field. You will next build a relationship between these two tables. By doing so, you will be able to restrict entry to the Titles table of only PubIDs that exist in the Publishers table.

Begin this function by selecting the Publishers table and pressing the Relations button. You are then presented with the Relationships form, as shown in Figure 3.27.

Figure 3.27.

The Relationships form.

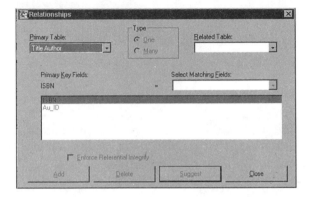

The primary table in this example will be Publishers. Select this table from the Primary combo box. The Related table will be the Titles table. Select this table from the Related Table combo box.

You want to join these two tables with a field that is included in both tables. This is the PubID field. Select this field from the Select Matching Fields combo box if it is not already displayed.

You want to create this as a one-to-many relationship. This means that there can be multiple occurrences of the PubID field of the Publishers table (the one side) to the PubID in the Titles table (the many side). Select the Many option button in the Type group.

Finally, check the Enforce Referential Integrity checkbox at the bottom of the form. This will keep users from deleting records in the Publishers table that are used in the Titles table. Your completed form should match Figure 3.28.

Note: Enforcing referential integrity is the process of telling the database that a record cannot be deleted from a data table if it is used in another data table (in other words, if it is referenced from another table). For example, if you set up a table of customers (the parent), you may want to assign a customer type (child) to each record. This customer type field may be stored in a table that contains numerous fields of information (terms, finance charges, tax status, and so on) that you shouldn't repeat in every customer master. You will want to enforce the integrity of this relationship so that a customer type is not deleted if it is used in a customer master. Failure to do so could lead to having undefined customer types (orphans).

Figure 3.28.
The completed Relationships form.

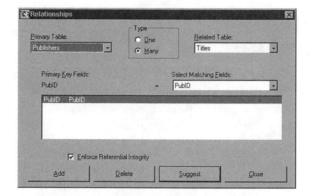

Click on the Add button to create the relationship. Then click Close to return to the main screen. The relationship has been created and is ready for you to test.

To do this, open the Titles table by double-clicking it in the Tables/QueryDefs window and find the PubID that is used in the first record. Close this table and open the Publishers table. Look up the PubID you saw in the first record of the Titles record by pressing the arrow buttons at the bottom of the form. Now press Delete. You should get a message similar to the one in Figure 3.29 that notifies you that this record cannot be deleted because referential integrity rules will be violated.

Figure 3.29.
The error message caused by attempted deletion of a Primary Table record utilized in a related table.

Let's perform one more test on this data. Open the Titles table and select any record. Modify the PubID of the record you selected by entering 4444 in this field. When you select Update, you receive an error message similar to the one displayed in Figure 3.30 stating that referential integrity requires a related record in the Publishers table. Referential integrity is now working to keep your tables consistent.

Figure 3.30.
Enforcement of referential integrity rules.

Working with SQL Statements in Data Manager

In addition to building databases, fields, and indexes, Data Manager provides a function to build and save queries. A query is a program statement that reads a data table and creates a selection of data arranged in a manner most suitable to the task at hand. For example, you might build a query that selects all the customers from a customer table that have invoices greater than 120 days past due. Or, you might build a query to select all students that walk to school rather than ride the bus.

You use Structured Query Language, commonly referred to as SQL (pronounced *S-Q-L*—not *sequel*) to create a query. This book covers SQL in depth on Day 9, "Selecting Data with SQL." For now, let's run a quick exercise to demonstrate the functionality of the Data Manager to manage SQL statements.

If you don't still have it loaded, load BIBLIO.MDB. Now you can test an SQL statement that will produce a listing of all publishers with a publisher ID of less than 12. To do this, enter the following statements in the SQL Statement window, after which, your screen should look like Figure 3.31.

```
SELECT * FROM Publishers WHERE PubID<12
```

Figure 3.31.
Entry of an SQL statement.

This statement will display every field (the * represents all fields) from the Publishers table (FROM Publishers) with an ID of less than 12 (WHERE PubID<12).

Execute this statement by pressing the Execute button. Move through the records that appear. Notice that no records appear with an ID greater than 12.

Data Manager allows you to save a query for future use. To do this, simply select Save from the SQL Statement window. You will then be prompted to enter the name of the Query. For this example, enter ABC. Your screen should look like Figure 3.32. After you select OK, you will be questioned as to whether this is an SQL Passthrough. Answer No.

> **Note:** In the preceding exercise, the Microsoft JET database engine that ships with Visual Basic 4 questioned whether the SQL statement was an SQL Passthrough. When you answered no, the JET engine performed error checking based upon its internal rules on how SQL statements should be composed. If you had answered yes, JET would not have performed any error checking and would have passed the responsibility of error checking on to the next database engine. A passthrough is commonly used in situations where Visual Basic 4 is used as a front-end tool to access databases such as Microsoft SQL Server.

Figure 3.32.
Entering a name for a saved SQL query.

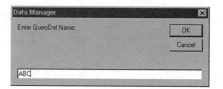

A query based upon the statement you entered is now saved in the same way as a table. Double-click on ABC in the Tables/QueryDefs window and explore the data presented. Next, open the Publishers table to compare your results set. Notice how many more records are in the table than in the query.

This completes the lessons on the construction features of Data Manager. The remainder of today's lesson will focus on using Data Manager to enter data.

Using Data Manager to Perform Data Entry

The Data Manager can be used to enter data into existing data tables. You can do this by opening a database, selecting a data table from the Tables/QueryDefs window, and clicking on the Open button. When you do this, Data Manager will present a data entry form that lists all the fields in the data table along with a set of command buttons for adding, deleting, and locating records. You can also use the data control at the bottom of the form to move forward and backward through the data table. As an example, open the CompanyMaster data table you built earlier in this chapter. You should see a screen similar to the one in Figure 3.33.

To add a record, click on the Add button at the top left of the form. Using Figure 3.34 as a guide, enter information in the first record of the table. Data Manager will save the new record when you click on the Update button.

Figure 3.33.

Initial data entry form for the CompanyMaster data table.

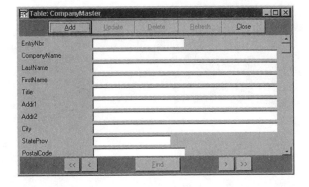

Figure 3.34.

Ready to save a new record to the CompanyMaster table.

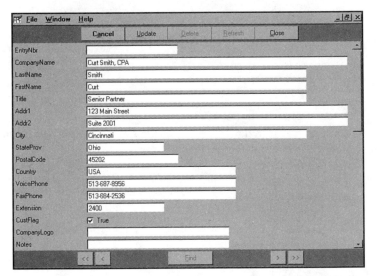

Note: While entering records, you might decide that you don't want to make some fields required entry. If so, you can return to the Design form, select a field, and check its Allow Zero Length checkbox. This will make entry into that field optional.

Caution: Do not enter any data in the EntryNbr field. This is a COUNTER data type field. It will be updated by Visual Basic 4 after you save the record. If you enter any data into the COUNTER data type field, Visual Basic 4 will issue an error message and you will not be able to save the record to the table.

Keep this in mind when designing data entry forms. Set COUNTER fields off by themselves, and don't give users the ability to enter or edit data in a COUNTER field.

Updating an Existing Record

When you update one or more fields in an existing record of a data table, you can save the changed data by clicking on the Update button at the top of the form.

Refreshing an Existing Record

If you have changed one or more fields in a record but then decide you do not want to save the changes, you can use the Refresh button to restore the record to its original state. This is the Data Manager equivalent of an undo feature. Pressing the Refresh button tells Data Manager to forget all the changes you made to the current record and to reset the fields to the values still stored in the data table. The Refresh button restores the entire record; you cannot refresh a single field. After you refresh a record, you cannot change your mind and recall the changes you made. You can't undo your refresh! Also, you will not get a confirmation when you click Refresh.

Finding an Existing Record

When you open a data table that already has records, Data Manager shows you the first record in the data table. You can walk through a data table to locate a record using the arrow buttons on the data control to move forward and backward through the table. This is fine if you have only a few records to review before you find the record you need. However, if the table has several records—possibly hundreds—you need a more effective method for locating a specific record.

That's why the Find button is handy. When you click the Find button, Data Manager pops up an input box that enables you to enter a search string (see Figure 3.35).

Let's give the Find button a try. First, make up and add several additional records to your CompanyMaster table. When you are finished, press the Find button. Select CompanyName from the Fields list and the equal sign (=) from the Operator list, and enter the name of a company record that you entered into your CompanyMaster table into the Value field. Click OK. You should now be at the requested record.

Figure 3.35.
Using Data Manager to
find a record.

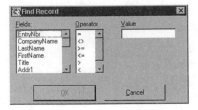

If you enter a valid search string but no record is found that meets your criteria, Data Manager will issue an error message and return you to the same record you were pointing to before the search began.

Deleting an Existing Record

You can use the Delete button on the data entry form to permanently remove a record from the data table. To delete a record, bring up the record you want to delete on the form. You can use the data control to walk through the data table to locate the record, or use the Find button (as described in the preceding section). When you have located the record to delete, simply click on the Delete button and your record will be removed.

You cannot undo a delete operation. If you want to restore a deleted record to the table, you must re-enter the data using the Add button.

Note: When a record is deleted from a Microsoft Access database, it is possible that the physical size of the database will not decrease. This is because a delete operation can leave empty space in the data table where the data record used to reside. You can use the Compact Database option (discussed earlier) to remove the empty space from a database.

Summary

Today you learned how to use the Data Manager that comes with Visual Basic 4 to perform the following database maintenance operations on Microsoft Access databases:

- [ ] Create new databases.
- [ ] Open existing databases.
- [ ] Create, modify, and delete data tables, fields, and indexes.
- [ ] Attach tables residing in other databases.

☐ Enter SQL statements to build and save queries.

☐ Perform data entry on existing tables including adding, updating, finding, and deleting records.

☐ Compact, repair, encrypt, and decrypt databases.

Quiz

1. List the advantages of using the Data Manager to create databases for your Visual Basic 4 applications.

2. List the disadvantages of using the Data Manager.

3. What database types can benefit from the Compact feature of the Data Manager?

4. How many primary keys can you have in an Access data table?

5. Is it possible to delete database indexes in the Data Manager?

6. What does this SQL statement mean?

```
SELECT Names, VoicePhone FROM CompanyMaster
```

Exercise

Create a Microsoft Access database to track mailing addresses. Include fields for social security number, last name, first name, address, city, state, and zip code. Identify and create a primary index. After creating the database, enter records for five individuals.

Visual Basic
Database Objects

In the previous day's lesson, you learned how to use the Data Manager to create databases, data tables, and indexes. Today you will learn about the programmatic data objects of Visual Basic 4. Data objects are used within a Visual Basic program to manipulate databases, as well as the data tables and indexes within the database. The data objects are the representations (in program code) of the physical database, data tables, fields, indexes, and so on. Throughout today's lesson, you will create small Visual Basic programs that illustrate the special features of each of the data objects.

Every Visual Basic program that accesses data tables uses data objects. Even if you are only using the data-aware controls (for example, the data control and bound input controls) and are not writing programming code, you are still using Visual Basic data objects.

These are the three main data objects used in Visual Basic programs:

- ☐ Dynaset object
- ☐ Table object
- ☐ Snapshot object

Any one of these objects can be used to gain access to an existing data table in a database. However, they each have unique properties and behave differently at times. Today you will learn how these three data objects differ and when it is best to use these objects in your programs.

You'll also learn about two additional data objects today:

- ☐ Recordset object
- ☐ Database object

The Database object and the Recordset object are two special Visual Basic data objects. You can use the Database object to get information about the connected database. The Recordset object can be used to get information about the selected data table. These objects are runtime-only objects that exist as subsets of a Visual Basic data control. In this lesson, you will learn about the general properties and behaviors of the Database and Recordset objects of the data control and how you can use them in your programs.

Data Set Oriented Versus Data Record Oriented

Before you learn about Visual Basic data objects, you should first learn some basics of how Visual Basic operates on databases in general. When you understand how Visual Basic looks at databases, you will be better able to create programs that meet your needs.

The database model behind the Microsoft Access database and other SQL-oriented databases is quite different from the database model behind traditional PC databases such as FoxPro, dBASE, and Paradox. Traditional PC databases are *record-oriented* database systems. Stuctured Query Language (SQL) databases are *data set-oriented* systems. Understanding the difference between record-oriented processing and data set-oriented processing is the key to understanding how to optimize database programs in Visual Basic.

In record-oriented systems, you perform database operations one record at a time. The most common programming construct in record-oriented systems is the Loop. The following pseudocode example shows how to increase the price field of an inventory table in a record-oriented database.

```
ReadLoop:
    If EndOf File
        Goto EndLoop
    Else
        Read Record
        Price=Price*1.10
        Write Record
    EndIf
Goto ReadLoop
EndLoop:
End Program
```

Processing in record-oriented systems usually involves creating a routine that reads a single data record, processes it, and returns to read another record until the job is completed. PC databases use indexes to speed the process of locating records in data tables. Indexes also help speed processing by allowing PC databases to access the data in sorted order (by LastName, by AccountBalance, and so on).

In data-oriented systems, such as Microsoft Access, you perform database operations one set at a time, not one record at a time. The most common programming construct in set-oriented systems is the SQL statement. Instead of using program code to loop through single records, SQL databases can perform operations on entire tables from just one SQL statement. The following pseudocode example shows how you would update the price field in the same inventory file in a data set-oriented database.

```
UPDATE Inventory SET Price=Price*1.10
```

The UPDATE SQL command behaves with SQL databases much like keywords behave with your Visual Basic programs. In this case, UPDATE tells the database that it wants to update an entire table (the Inventory table). The SET SQL command changes the value of a data field (in this case, the Price data field). As you can see, in data set-oriented databases, you create a single statement that selects only the records you need to perform a database operation. After you identify the data set, you apply the operation to all records in the set. In data set systems, indexes are used to maintain database integrity more than to speed the location of specific records.

Visual Basic and Data Objects

Visual Basic database objects are data set oriented. Visual Basic programs generally perform better when data operations are done with a data set than when data operations are done on single records. Some Visual Basic objects work well when performing record-oriented operations; most do not. The Visual Basic Table object is very good at performing record-oriented processing. The Visual Basic Dynaset and Snapshot objects do not perform well on record-oriented processes.

A common mistake made by database programmers new to Visual Basic is to create programs that assume a record-oriented database model. These programmers are usually frustrated by Visual Basic's slow performance on large data tables and its slow response time when attempting to locate a specific record. Visual Basic's sluggishness is usually due to improper use of Visual Basic data objects—most often because programmers are opening entire data tables when they only need a small subset of the data in order to perform the required tasks.

Data Set Size Affects Program Performance

Unlike record-oriented systems, the size of the data set you create affects the speed at which Visual Basic programs operate. As a data table grows, your program's processing speed can deteriorate. In heavy transaction-oriented applications, such as accounting systems, a data set can grow quickly and cripple your application's ability to process information. If you are working in a network environment where the machine requesting data and the machine storing the data are separated, sending large data sets over the wire can affect not only your application, but all applications running on the network. For this reason, it is important to keep the size of the data sets as small as possible. This does not mean you have to limit the number of records in your data tables! You can use Visual Basic data objects to select the data you need from the table instead.

For example, you might have a data table that contains thousands of accounting transactions. If you want to modify the payment records in the data table, you can create a data object that contains all of the records (quite a big set), or you can tell Visual Basic to select only the payment records (a smaller set). Or, if you know that you only need to modify payment records that have been added to the system in the last three days, you can create an even smaller data set: The smaller the data set, the faster your program can process the data. Visual Basic data objects give you the power to create data sets that are the proper size for your needs.

The *Dynaset* Data Object

The Visual Basic Dynaset data object is the most frequently used data object in Visual Basic programs. It is used to dynamically gain access to part or all of an existing data table in a database; hence the name Dynaset. When you set the DatabaseName and RecordSource properties of a Visual Basic data control, you are actually creating a Visual Basic Dynaset. You can also create a Dynaset by using the CreateDynaset program statement.

When you create a Visual Basic Dynaset, you do not create a new physical table in the database. A Dynaset exists as a *virtual* data table. This virtual table usually contains a subset of the records in a real data table, but it can contain the complete set. Because creating a Dynaset does not create a new physical table, Dynasets do not add to the size of the database. However, creating Dynasets does take up space in RAM memory on the machine that creates the set (the one that is running the program). Depending on the number of records in the Dynaset, temporary disk space can also be used on the machine requesting the data set.

Strengths of the *Dynaset* Data Object

There are several reasons to use Dynasets when you access data. In general, Dynasets require less memory than other data objects and provide the most update options, including the capability to create additional data objects from existing Dynasets. Dynasets are the default data objects for the Visual Basic data control, and they are the only updatable data object you can use for databases connected through Microsoft's Open Database Connectivity (ODBC) model. The following sections are more detailed listings of the strengths of the Dynaset data object.

Dynasets Are Really Key Sets

Visual Basic Dynasets use relatively little workstation memory, even for large data sets. When you create a Dynaset, Visual Basic selects the records you requested, creates temporary index keys to each of these records, and then sends the complete set of keys to your workstation along with enough records to fill out any bound controls (text boxes and/or grid controls) that appear on your on-screen form. This process is illustrated in the diagram in Figure 4.1.

Note: The actual data request engine used by Visual Basic is called the Microsoft JET, or Joint Engine Technology, data engine. In pure SQL systems all requests for data result in a set of data records. Data requests to the Microsoft JET result in a set of keys that point to the data records. By returning keys instead of data records, the Microsoft JET is able to limit network traffic and speed database performance.

Figure 4.1.

Dynasets contain keys that point to the actual records.

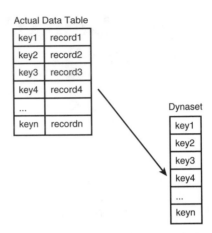

The set of keys is stored in RAM and—if the set is too large to store in RAM—in a temporary file on a local disk drive. As you scroll through the data set, Visual Basic retrieves actual records as needed from the physical table used to create the Dynaset. If you have a single text box on the form, Visual Basic will retrieve the data from the table one record at a time. If you have a grid of data or a loop that collects several records from the table in succession, a small set of the records in the data set will be retrieved by Visual Basic. Visual Basic also caches records at the workstation to reduce requests to the physical data table to speed performance.

If the Dynaset is very large, it is possible to end up with a key set that is so large that it requires more RAM and temporary disk space than the local machine can handle. In that case, you will receive an error message from Visual Basic. For this reason, it is important that you use care in creating your criteria for populating the data set. The smaller the data set, the smaller the key set.

*Dynaset*s Are Dynamic

Even though Dynasets are virtual tables in memory created from physical tables, they are not static copies of the data table. After you create a Dynaset, if anyone else alters the underlying data table by modifying, adding, or deleting records, you will see the changes in your Dynaset as soon as you refresh the Dynaset. Refreshing the Dynaset can be done using the Refresh method. You can also refresh the Dynasets by moving the record pointer using the arrow keys of the data control or using the MoveFirst, MoveNext, MovePrevious, and MoveLast methods. Moving the pointer refreshes only the records you read, not the entire Dynaset.

Although the dynamic aspect of Dynasets is very effective in maintaining up-to-date views of the underlying data table, Dynasets also have some limitations and drawbacks. For example, if another user deletes a record that you currently have in your Dynaset and you attempt to Move to that record, Visual Basic will report an error.

*Dynaset*s Can Be Created from More Than One Table

A Dynaset can be created using more than one table in the database. You can create a single view that contains selected records from several tables, update the view, and therefore update all the underlying tables of the data at one time. This is a very powerful aspect of a Visual Basic Dynaset data object. Using Visual Basic Dynasets, you can create virtual tables that make it easy to create simple data entry screens and display graphs and reports that show specialized selections of data.

Use *Dynaset*s to Create Other *Dynaset*s or *Snapshot*s

Often in Visual Basic programs, you need to create a secondary data set based on user input. The Dynaset data object is the only data object from which you can create another Dynaset.

You can create additional Dynasets by using the Clone method or the CreateDynaset method. When you Clone a Dynaset, you create an exact duplicate of the Dynaset. You can use this duplicate to perform look-ups or to reorder the records for a display. Clone Dynasets take up slightly less room than the original Dynaset.

Let's put together a short code sample that explores Dynasets. You'll do this all in Visual Basic code, too, instead of using the Visual Basic data control.

First start a new Visual Basic project. Double-click on the form to open the code window to the Form_Load event. You will write the entire example in this procedure.

When you open a Dynaset using Visual Basic code instead of using the data control, you must create two Visual Basic objects: a Database object and a Dynaset object. Listing 4.1 shows how you create the objects in Visual Basic code.

Listing 4.1. Creating a Database object and a Dynaset object.

```
Sub Form_Load ()
'
    ' create data object variables
    Dim dat As Database ' create a database object
    Dim dyn1 As Dynasct 'create a dynasct object
```

You must initialize these objects with values before they can access data. This process is similar to setting the properties of the data control. To initialize the values, first you'll create two variables that correspond to the DatabaseName and RecordSource properties of the Visual Basic data control. The code sample in Listing 4.2 shows how it is done.

> **Tip:** The code sample in Listing 4.2 uses the `App.Path` Visual Basic keywords. You can use the `Path` method of the `App` object to determine the drive letter and directory from which the program was launched. In most projects throughout this book, you will find the databases are stored in the same directory as the sample projects. By using the `App.Path` method as part of the database name, you will always point to the correct drive and directory for the required file.

Listing 4.2. Declaring database and data table variables.

```
Private Sub Form_Load()
    '
    ' create data object variables
    Dim dat As Database ' create a database object
    Dim dyn1 As Dynaset 'create a dynaset object
    '
    ' create standard variables
    Dim cDbName As String
    Dim cRecSource As String
    '
    ' initialize variables
    cDbName = App.Path + "\books.mdb"
    cRecSource = "Titles"

End Sub
```

> **Tip:** Notice that you created two string variables and both variable names start with the letter c. This c stands for *character type*. The first letter of the name tells you what type of data is stored in the variable. This is common programming practice. Adhering to a strict naming convention makes it easier to read and maintain your programs.

Before you continue with the chapter, save this form as DBPROJ01.FRM and save the project as DBPROJ01.VBP.

Now that you have created the data objects, created variables to hold database properties, and initialized those variables with the proper values, you are ready to actually open the database and create the `Dynaset`. The code in Listing 4.3 shows how to do this using Visual Basic code.

Listing 4.3. Opening the database and creating the Dynaset.

```
Private Sub Form_Load()
    '
    ' create data object variables
    Dim dat As Database ' create a database object
    Dim dyn1 As Dynaset 'create a dynaset object
    '
    ' create standard variables
    Dim cDbName As String
    Dim cRecSource As String
    '
    ' initialize variables
    cDbName = App.Path + "\books.mdb"
    cRecSource = "Titles"
    '
    ' set values
    Set dat = OpenDatabase(cDbName) ' open the database
    Set dyn1 = dat.CreateDynaset(cRecSource) ' create the dynaset

End Sub
```

There are two added lines in Listing 4.3. The first added line opens the BOOKS.MDB database and sets the Visual Basic database object dat to point to the database. Now you can use the dat data object to represent the open database in all other Visual Basic code in this program. The second line creates a Dynaset that contains the records in the Titles table. The Visual Basic dyn1 object is set to point to this set of records. Notice that the CreateDynaset method is applied to the dat Database object.

The code in Listing 4.3 is all that you need to open an existing Microsoft Access database and create a Dynaset ready for update. However, for this project, you want to see a bit more. Let's add some code that tells you how many records are in the Titles data table.

You need one more variable to hold the record count. You also use the MoveLast Dynaset method to move the record pointer to the last record in the Dynaset. This forces Visual Basic to touch every record in the Dynaset, and therefore gives you an accurate count of the total number of records in the table. You get the count by reading the RecordCount property of the Dynaset. When you have all that, you display a Visual Basic message box that tells you how many records are in the Dynaset. Listing 4.4 contains the code to add.

Listing 4.4. Counting the records in a Dynaset.

```
Sub Form_Load ()
    '
    ' create data object variables
    Dim dat As Database ' create a database object
    Dim dyn1 As Dynaset 'create a dynaset object
```

continues

Listing 4.4. continued

```
        ' create standard variables
        Dim cDbName As String
        Dim cRecSource as String
        Dim nRecs as Integer
        '
        ' initialize variables
        cDbName = "c:\abc\examples\ver11\access\biblio.mdb"
        cRecSource ="Titles"
        '
        ' set values
        Set dat = OpenDatabase(cDbName) ' open the database
        Set dyn1 = dat.CreateDynaset(cRecSource) ' create the dynaset

        dyn1.MoveLast ' move to end of set to force count
        nRecs = dyn1.RecordCount ' get count
        MsgBox cSelect + " :" + Str$(nRecs), 0, "Total Records in Set"
        '
' exit program
    End
End Sub
```

Save the form (DBPROJ01.FRM) and project (DBPROJ01.VBP) again and run the program. You'll see a message box telling you that there are 50 records in the Dynaset.

You can use the CreateDynaset command on an existing Dynaset to create a smaller subset of the data. This is often done when the user is allowed to create a record selection criterion, and then if the data set returned is too large, the user is allowed to further qualify the search by creating additional criteria to apply to the data set.

Let's modify DBPROJ01.VBP to create a smaller Dynaset from the existing Dynaset. You'll need to create a new Dynaset object and a new variable called cFilter that will hold the criteria for selecting records. The code in Listing 4.5 shows how to add the object and variable to the existing DBPROJ01.VBP project.

Listing 4.5. Adding a new Dynaset object and string variable.

```
Private Sub Form_Load()
    '
    ' create data object variables
    Dim dat As Database ' create a database object
    Dim dyn1 As dynaset ' create a dynaset object
    Dim dyn2 As dynaset ' create dynaset object
    '
    ' create standard variables
    Dim cDbName As String
    Dim cRecSource As String
    Dim nRecs As Integer
    Dim cFilter As String
    '
```

```
    ' initialize variables
    cDbName = App.Path + "\books.mdb"
    cRecSource = "Titles"
    cFilter = "[Year Published]>1990"
    '
    ' set values
    Set dat = OpenDatabase(cDbName) ' open the database
    Set dyn1 = dat.CreateDynaset(cRecSource) ' create the dynaset

    dyn1.MoveLast ' move to end of set to force count
    nRecs = dyn1.RecordCount ' get count
    MsgBox cRecSource + " :" + Str$(nRecs), 0, "Total Records in Set"
    '
    ' exit program
    End
    '
End Sub
```

Now that you have the object and the variable, you can add code that will create a new Dynaset. First you set the Filter property of the existing Dynaset using the variable you just created. Then you create the new Dynaset from the old one. See the last two lines of the code in Listing 4.6.

Listing 4.6. Using the Filter property to create a Dynaset.

```
Private Sub Form_Load()
    '
    ' create data object variables
    Dim dat As Database ' create a database object
    Dim dyn1 As dynaset ' create a dynaset object
    Dim dyn2 As dynaset ' create dynaset object
    '
    ' create standard variables
    Dim cDbName As String
    Dim cRecSource As String
    Dim nRecs As Integer
    Dim cFilter As String
    '
    ' initialize variables
    cDbName = App.Path + "\books.mdb"
    cRecSource = "Titles"
    cFilter = "[Year Published]>1990"
    '
    ' set values
    Set dat = OpenDatabase(cDbName) ' open the database
    Set dyn1 = dat.CreateDynaset(cRecSource) ' create the dynaset
    '
    dyn1.MoveLast ' move to end of set to force count
    nRecs = dyn1.RecordCount ' get count
    MsgBox cRecSource + " :" + Str$(nRecs), 0, "Total Records in Set"
    '
    ' create subset of dynaset and count records
    dyn1.Filter = cFilter
```

continues

Listing 4.6. continued

```
        Set dyn2 = dyn1.CreateDynaset()
        '
        ' exit program
        End
        '
End Sub
```

Now that you've created the new Dynaset from the old one, you can get a count of the selected records. You can add the same code you used earlier: Move to the end of the Dynaset, get the RecordCount, and show it in a message box. Listing 4.7 shows the completed program.

Listing 4.7. Displaying the record count of the filtered Dynaset.

```
Private Sub Form_Load()
    '
    ' create data object variables
    Dim dat As Database ' create a database object
    Dim dyn1 As dynaset ' create a dynaset object
    Dim dyn2 As dynaset ' create dynaset object
    '
    ' create standard variables
    Dim cDbName As String
    Dim cRecSource As String
    Dim nRecs As Integer
    Dim cFilter As String
    '
    ' initialize variables
    cDbName = App.Path + "\books.mdb"
    cRecSource = "Titles"
    cFilter = "[Year Published]>1990"
    '
    ' set values
    Set dat = OpenDatabase(cDbName) ' open the database
    Set dyn1 = dat.CreateDynaset(cRecSource) ' create the dynaset

    dyn1.MoveLast ' move to end of set to force count
    nRecs = dyn1.RecordCount ' get count
    MsgBox cRecSource + " :" + Str$(nRecs), 0, "Total Records in Set"
    '
    ' create subset of dynaset and count records
    dyn1.Filter = cFilter
    Set dyn2 = dyn1.CreateDynaset()
    dyn2.MoveLast ' move to end of set to force count
    nRecs = dyn2.RecordCount ' get count
    MsgBox cFilter + " :" + Str$(nRecs), 0, "Total Records in Set"
    '
    ' exit program
    End
    '
End Sub
```

Save and run the code to see the results. Notice that the first record count (the full data set) is larger than the second record count (the filtered data set). It is also important to notice that the second Dynaset object was created *from* the first Dynaset object. This a very powerful feature of Visual Basic. When you want to get a smaller data set, you don't have to reload the data from the database, you can use an existing Dynaset as the source for a new data set.

Now let's make one more series of changes to DBPORJ01.VBP that will illustrate the Clone method for Dynasets. Cloning a Dynaset makes a duplicate of the set. Add another data object (dyn3), and add the clone Dynaset program code in Listing 4.8.

Listing 4.8. Cloning a new Dynaset.

```
Private Sub Form_Load()
    '
    ' create data object variables
    Dim dat As Database ' create a database object
    Dim dyn1 As dynaset ' create a dynaset object
    Dim dyn2 As dynaset ' create dynaset object
    Dim dyn3 As dynaset ' create dynaset object
    '
    ' create standard variables
    Dim cDbName As String
    Dim cRecSource As String
    Dim nRecs As Integer
    Dim cFilter As String
    '
    ' initialize variables
    cDbName = App.Path + "\books.mdb"
    cRecSource = "Titles"
    cFilter = "[Year Published]>1990"
    '
    ' set values
    Set dat = OpenDatabase(cDbName) ' open the database
    Set dyn1 = dat.CreateDynaset(cRecSource) ' create the dynaset
    '
    dyn1.MoveLast ' move to end of set to force count
    nRecs = dyn1.RecordCount ' get count
    MsgBox cRecSource + " :" + Str$(nRecs), 0, "Total Records in Set"
    '
    ' create subset of dynaset and count records
    dyn1.Filter = cFilter
    Set dyn2 = dyn1.CreateDynaset()
    dyn2.MoveLast ' move to end of set to force count
    nRecs = dyn2.RecordCount ' get count
    MsgBox cFilter + " :" + Str$(nRecs), 0, "Total Records in Set"
    '
    ' clone a dynaset
    Set dyn3 = dyn1.Clone()
    dyn3.MoveLast ' move to end of set to force count
    nRecs = dyn3.RecordCount ' get count
    MsgBox "Cloned Dynaset :" + Str$(nRecs), 0, "Total Records in Set"
```

continues

Listing 4.8. continued

```
    '
    ' exit program
    End
    '
End Sub
```

Notice that all you have to do to Clone a Dynaset is to use the Clone method to load a new Dynaset object variable. When you run the program this time, you will see that the first Dynaset that is created contains 50 records. The second Dynaset—created by setting the Filter property of the first Dynaset—contains only 18 records. Notice also that the Dynaset created using the Clone method contains the same number of records as its parent.

*Dynaset*s Can Use Bookmarks, Filters, and Sorts

Dynasets can use the Bookmarks, Filters, and Sorts properties of a Dynaset to reorder data for display (Sort) or create a subset of the Dynaset (Filter). Using the Visual Basic Find method on a Dynaset forces Visual Basic to start at the first record in the Dynaset and read each one until a match is found. If no match is found when Visual Basic reaches the end of the Dynaset, the record pointer is simply left at the end of the Dynaset. If you want to get back to the record you started on, you'll need to remember where you started from. That's what Visual Basic Bookmarks do. They remember where you were.

When you search for a record in the data set using one of the Find methods, you should set Bookmarks before your search to remember where you started from. This is especially handy if your Find criteria result in a null record. Then, instead of leaving the user at some new (unwanted) location in the data set, you can recall the Visual Basic Bookmark and return the user to the place from which the search started.

Let's build a quick project to demonstrate the use of Bookmarks. Use the information in Table 4.1 to create a small form with a data control, two bound input controls, two label controls, and a single command button.

Table 4.1. Controls for BKMARK01.FRM.

Control	Property	Setting
Form1	Caption	Bookmark Demonstration
Command1	Caption	&Save Bookmark
Label1	Caption	Author ID
Label2	Caption	Author Name

Control	Property	Setting
Data1	DatabaseName	BOOKS.MDB
	RecordSource	Authors
	Caption	Authors
Text1	DataSource	Data1
	DataField	Au_ID
Text2	DataSource	Data1
	DataField	Author

Refer to Figure 4.2 as a guide for sizing and locating the controls on the form.

Figure 4.2.
Form layout for the
BKMARK01.VBP project.

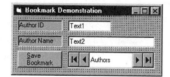

When you have completed the form layout, add the following code behind the command button. The code in Listing 4.9 is a toggle routine that saves the current place in the table by reading (and storing) the Bookmark or restores the previous place in the table by reading (and updating) the Bookmark.

Listing 4.9. Coding the `Command1_Click` event for BKMARK01.VBP.

```
Sub Command1_Click ()
    Static BkFlag
    Static cBkMark
    '
    If BkFlag = 0 Then
        '
        ' flip flag and set caption
        BkFlag = 1
        command1.Caption = "&Restore Bookmark"
        '
        ' save bookmark pointer for later
        cBkMark = data1.Recordset.Bookmark
    Else
        '
        ' flip flag and set caption
        BkFlag = 0
        command1.Caption = "&Save Bookmark"
        '
        ' restore pointer to old bookmark
        data1.Recordset.Bookmark = cBkMark
    End If
End Sub
```

> **Tip:** Listing 4.9 uses two Static variables. Static variables keep their value even after the procedure ends. Using Static variables in your program is an excellent way to keep track of flag values even after procedures or functions exit. The only other way to make sure that variables maintain their value after exit from a routine is to place them in the declaration area of the form. The problem with placing them at the form level declaration is that they now can be altered by routines in other procedures or functions on the same form. Declaring Static variables within the procedures in which they are used follows good programming practice by limiting the scope of the variable.

Save the form as BKMARK01.FRM and the project as BKMARK01.VBP, and then run the program. The program will open the BOOKS.MDB file, create a Dynaset of all the records in the Authors data table, and present the first record on the form. Note that that the command button caption says Save Bookmark. Click on the command button to create a Bookmark that points to this record of the Dynaset. The caption changes to Restore Bookmark. Now use the arrow buttons on the data control to move to another record on the form. Click on the command button. You will see that the record pointer has been returned to the first record in the Dynaset. This is because the Dynaset Bookmark property was reset to the value you stored earlier.

*Dynaset*s and ODBC

If you are accessing data from an ODBC (Open Database Connectivity) data source, the only Visual Basic data object you can use to update the underlying data table is Dynaset. You will learn more about ODBC connected databases on Day 19, "ODBC Data Access Via the ODBC API Interface."

Limitations of the *Dynaset* Data Object

Although the Dynaset is an excellent data object, it has a few drawbacks that must be considered. Chief among these is that Dynasets do not allow you to specify an existing index, and you cannot use the Visual Basic Seek method to quickly locate a single record in the Dynaset. Also, errors can occur when displaying records in a Dynaset if the records in the underlying data table have been altered or deleted by another user.

Dynaset's Access and *Seek* Limitations

Dynasets cannot make use of Index objects that exist in a database because the Index is built to control the entire data table and not just a subset of the data. Because Dynasets could be subsets of the data table, the Index is useless. Also, because you cannot specify an Index object for a Dynaset, you cannot use the Visual Basic Seek method on a Dynaset.

These are only minor limitations. If you have defined an Index in the underlying table with the Primary flag turned on, the Visual Basic data engine will use the primary key index when creating the Dynaset. This usually puts the Dynaset in optimal order. Even though you cannot use the Seek method on a Dynaset, you can use the FindFirst, FindNext, FindPrevious, and FindLast methods. Even though they are not true index searches, they are fast enough for operations on small- to medium-sized Dynasets. You will learn more about Seek, Find, and Move in Day 11, "Creating Database Programs with Visual Basic Code."

Dynamic Membership-Related Errors

If your program opens a database and creates a Dynaset from an underlying table while another user has also opened the same database and created a Dynaset based on the same underlying data table, it is possible that both users will attempt to edit the same data record. If both users edit the same record and both attempt to save the record back to the underlying table, the second person who attempts to save the record receives a Visual Basic error.

When the second person tries to save the record, Visual Basic discovers that the original record in the underlying data table has been altered. In order to maintain database integrity, Visual Basic will not allow the second person to update the table.

When to Use the *Dynaset* Data Object

The Dynaset object should be used in most database programs you write. In most cases, the Visual Basic Dynaset data object is the most effective data access object to use. It offers you a way to create a dynamic, updatable subset of data records in one or more data tables. The Dynaset object is the default object created by the bound data control and is the only updatable data object you can use to access ODBC data sources.

The Dynaset is not a good data object to use when you need to do a great deal of record-oriented processing on large data sets, such as index look-ups on large transaction files. If you have a Visual Basic program that uses Dynasets and is showing slow database performance, look for places where you can limit the size of Dynasets by narrowing your selection criteria.

The *Table* Data Object

The Visual Basic Table data object is the data object that gives you access to the physical data table, sometimes referred to as the base table. You can use the Table object to directly open the table defined by Data Manager (or some other database definition tool). The chief advantage of using the Table object is that you can specify search indexes and use the Visual Basic Seek method. Like Dynasets, Tables take a limited amount of local workstation memory.

`Table` data objects also give you instant information on the state of the data table. This is important in a multiuser environment. As soon as a user adds or deletes a record from the table, all other users who have the data table open as a Visual Basic `Table` object will also see the changes.

Visual Basic `Table` objects have their drawbacks, too. If you want to use the `Table` object, you must open the database via program code; you cannot use the data control. You cannot use a `Select` statement to initialize a `Table` object, and you cannot combine data tables to create unique views of the database when you create `Table` objects.

You cannot use bookmarks, create filters, or sort the table. Furthermore, you cannot use the `Table` data object to access ODBC data sources. Only `Dynasets` and `Snapshots` can be used with ODBC data sources.

Strengths of the *Table* Data Object

The real strength of `Table` objects is that you can specify index objects to use when searching for specific records in the table. `Table` objects also use limited workstation memory and offer instant updates whenever that data in the table changes.

Data Pointers and Instant Membership Notification

Like `Dynasets`, `Table` objects use limited workstation memory because Visual Basic caches pointers to the actual records at the workstation instead of loading all the records into workstation memory. This gives your programs the fastest access speed of all the data objects when you are searching for a single record.

Unlike `Dynasets` and `Snapshots`, `Table` objects are not subsets of the data table. They contain all the records in the table at all times. As soon as a new record is added to the data table, the record will be available to the `Table` object. Also, as soon as a user deletes a record from the table, the `Table` object will be updated to reflect the deletion.

Table Objects, Indexes, and the *Seek* Method

The Visual Basic `Table` data object enables you to specify an index to apply to the data table. You can use indexes to order the data table for displays and reports and to speed searches using the `Seek` method.

The following project (TBSEEK01.VBP) demonstrates the use of Visual Basic `Table` objects, indexes, and the `Seek` method. It opens the Titles table of the BOOKS.MDB database and gives you the ability to select one of three indexes. When the index is selected, the program loads the records from the table into a list box. When you click on the Search button, you are prompted to enter a search value to use in the `Seek` method on the table.

Use the information in Table 4.2 to build a new project that will demonstrate the use of Visual Basic `Table` objects, indexes, and the `Seek` method.

Table 4.2. Controls for the TBSEEK.VBP project.

Control	Property	Setting
Form1	Caption	Table Index and Seek Demo
Command1	Name	cmdAuthor
	Caption	&Author
Command2	Name	cmdISBN
	Caption	&ISBN
Command3	Name	cmdPublisher
	Caption	&Publisher
Command4	Name	cmdSeek
	Caption	&Seek
Command5	Name	cmdExit
	Caption	E&xit
Label1	Caption	Titles Table—Indexed by:
	Autosize	True

Refer to Figure 4.3 as a guide for placement and positioning of the controls listed in Table 4.2.

Figure 4.3.
The form layout for project TBSEEK01.VBP.

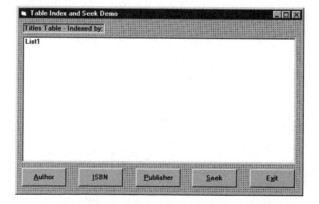

After you have placed the controls on the form and sized them, you need to place the code from Listing 4.10 in the declaration section of the form. This code declares several variables that you will use throughout the form.

Listing 4.10. Declaration code for the TBSEEK01.VBP project.

```
Option Explicit

Dim datObject As Database
Dim tblObject As Table
'
Dim cDbName As String
Dim cTblName As String
Dim cIndex As String
Dim cField As String
```

Place the code from Listing 4.11 in the Form_Load event of the form. This code opens the BOOKS.MDB database and opens the Titles table.

Listing 4.11. Coding the Form_Load routine of TBSEEK01.VBP.

```
Sub Form_Load ()
    '
    cDbName = App.Path + "\books.mdb"
    cTblName = "Titles"
    '
    ' open database and data table
    Set datObject = OpenDatabase(cDbName)
    Set TblObject = datObject.OpenTable(cTblName)
End Sub
```

Place the procedure shown in Listing 4.12 in the declaration section. This is the procedure that sets the table index and loads the list box in the proper order.

Listing 4.12. Coding the LoadList routine of TBSEEK01.VBP.

```
Private Sub LoadList()
    Dim cLine As String
    List1.Clear
    '
    tblObject.Index = cIndex
    tblObject.MoveFirst
    '
    On Error Resume Next
    '
    While Not tblObject.EOF
        cLine = tblObject.Fields("Title")
        cLine = cLine + "/" + Str(tblObject.Fields("[Year Published]"))
        cLine = cLine + "/ " + Str(tblObject.Fields("Au_ID"))
        cLine = cLine + "/" + Str(tblObject.Fields("ISBN"))
        cLine = cLine + "/" + Str(tblObject.Fields("PubID"))
        List1.AddItem cLine
        tblObject.MoveNext
    Wend
    '
```

```
    Label1.Caption = "Titles Table - Indexed by [" + cField + "]"
End Sub
```

The `LoadList` procedure is an example of a way to load a Visual Basic list box with data from a table. The routine first clears out the list box. Then the Index property of the table object is set (based on the user's input) and moves to the first record in the table.

Now the fun starts. The `While..Wend` loop reads each record in the table and creates a single line of text (`cLine`) that contains each of the fields separated by a single space. Notice that you need to use the `Str()` function to convert the numeric fields in the data table (Year Published, Au_ID, and Pub_ID) into string values before you can add them to `cLine`. After the line is built, the `cLine` is added to the list box using the `List.AddNew` method. After the line is added to the list box, the record pointer is advanced using the `Tbl0bject.MoveNext` method. This goes on until there are no more records in the table.

The following three code segments go behind the appropriate command button to set the indexes. They set values for selecting the index, setting the display, and calling the routine to load the list box.

Place this code in the `cmdAuthor_Click` event:

```
Sub cmdAuthor_Click ()
    cIndex = "Au_ID"
    cField = cIndex
    LoadList
End Sub
```

Place this code in the `cmdISBN_Click` event:

```
Sub cmdISBN_Click ()
    cIndex = "Primarykey"
    cField = "ISBN"
    LoadList
End Sub
```

Place this code in the `cmdPublisher_Click` event:

```
Sub cmdPublisher_Click ()
    cIndex = "PubID"
    cField = cIndex
    LoadList
End Sub
```

The `Seek` routine shown in Listing 4.13 calls an input box to prompt the user for a search value, performs the seek, and reports the results of the search. The routine first checks to see whether the user has filled the list box by selecting an index. If the list box contains data, the routine calls the Visual Basic `InputBox` function to get user input, and then invokes the `Seek` method of the table object. If the record is *not* found, you see a `Search Failed` message. If you entered a record that is on file, you see a `Record Found` message.

Listing 4.13. Coding the Seek routine for TBSEEK01.VBP.

```
Private Sub cmdSeek_Click()
    Dim cSearch As String
    '
    If List1.ListCount = 0 Then
        MsgBox "Select Index First", 0, "Missing Index"
    Else
        cSearch = InputBox("Enter Search Value for " + cField)
        tblObject.Seek "=", cSearch
        If tblObject.NoMatch Then
            MsgBox cSearch + " not in Table", 0, "Search Failed"
        Else
            MsgBox tblObject.Fields("Title"), 0, "Record Found"
        End If
    End If
End Sub
```

Of course, every project should have an Exit button. Enter the following line for the Exit button.

```
Sub cmdExit_Click ()
    End
End Sub
```

When you have completed the coding, save the form as TBSEEK01.FRM and the project as TBSEEK01.VBP, and then run the program. Click on the Author, ISBN, or Publisher buttons to set the index and load the list box. Note that each time you select a different button, the list is loaded in a different order. After the list is loaded, click on the Seek button to perform an indexed search on the data table. If you enter a value that is in the index, the program reports the title of the book in a message box; otherwise, you will see an error message.

Limitations of the *Table* Data Object

Even though the Visual Basic Table object provides the fastest search speed of any of the data objects, it also has certain drawbacks. You cannot sort a table; you can't use the Table object when accessing ODBC data sources; and you can't use the Visual Basic data control to access a Table object.

*Table*s Can't Use Bookmarks, Sorts, or Filters

Unlike Dynasets and Snapshots, Visual Basic Table objects cannot be sorted, filtered, or have Bookmarks set. Instead of sorting the data, you can use Index objects to establish the order of the data in the table. If you need to filter the table (usually because it is a large table), you need to create a Dynaset or Snapshot that contains a subset of the data in the table.

`Table` objects can't use Bookmarks, so you can't mark your place in a table, move around, and then return to the location using Visual Basic Bookmarks. You can, however, save the table index value instead. The table must have an index declared, and you must know the fields used in the declared index. You can get this information from the Design form of Data Manager, or you can get it at runtime by reading the `Index.Name` and `Index.Fields` properties of the `Table` object. Refer to the section on the `Database` data object for an example of how to read the `Index.Name` and `Index.Fields` properties of a data table.

ODBC Data Source Limitations

If you plan to do any work with ODBC data sources, you will have to forget using the Visual Basic `Table` object. It does not matter whether the ODBC source is an SQL Server data source or a spreadsheet on your local workstation. You will not be able to establish a `Table` object to access the data. You must use a `Dynaset` or `Snapshot` object for ODBC data requests.

The reason for this limitation is that the ODBC driver gives Visual Basic access to virtually any type of data. There is no requirement that the data source comply with the Visual Basic data engine data table format. Because the `Table` object is designed specifically to provide direct access to Visual Basic data tables, it can only be used to access a data table that exists as data table in a Microsoft Access database.

4

When to Use the *Table* Data Object

The Visual Basic `Table` object is the best choice when you need to provide speedy searches of large data tables. As long as you do not need to access ODBC data sources, and you do not need to get a set of data for processing, the `Table` object is an excellent choice.

If, however, you will need to process sets of data instead of single records, the `Table` object will not work as easily or as quickly as a `Dynaset` or `Snapshot` object.

The *Snapshot* Data Object

Visual Basic `Snapshot` objects are almost identical to `Dynaset`s in behavior and properties. However, there are two major differences between `Snapshot` objects and `Dynaset` objects. These two differences with `Dynaset`s are the two most important aspects of `Snapshot`s.

☐ `Snapshot`s are stored entirely in workstation memory
☐ `Snapshot`s are read-only and nonupdatable objects

Instead of reviewing strengths and limitations of the `Snapshot` data object, let's look at these two properties of `Snapshot`s in depth.

Snapshot Storage

You'll need to consider several things when using Snapshot data objects. For example, unlike Visual Basic Dynasets, Snapshot objects are stored entirely at the workstation. If you create a Snapshot that contains 500 data records, all 500 records are sent from the data table directly to your workstation and loaded into RAM memory. If the workstation does not have enough RAM available, the records will be stored in a temporary file on a local disk drive.

Because all the requested records are loaded on the local machine, initial requests for data can take longer with Snapshots than with Dynasets. However, when the data records are retrieved and stored locally, subsequent access to records within the Snapshot object is faster than with the Dynaset object. Also, because all records must be stored locally, you must be careful not to request too large a data set; you might quickly run out of local RAM or disk space.

Snapshots are static views of the underlying data tables. If you request a set of data records in a Snapshot object, and then someone deletes several records from the underlying data table, the Snapshot data set will *not* reflect the changes in the underlying table. The only way you can learn about the changes in the underlying data tables is to create a new Snapshot by making a new request.

*Snapshot*s are Read-Only Data Objects

Visual Basic Snapshots are read-only data objects. You cannot use Snapshots to update data tables. You can only use them to view data. This is because Snapshots are actually a copy of the data records created at your local workstation.

The project in Listing 4.14 illustrates the static aspect of Snapshot data objects compared to the dynamic aspect of Dynaset and Table data objects. There are no controls in this project. The entire source code is listed. Enter it into a single form and save it as SNAPDYNA.FRM and SNAPDYNA.VBP.

Listing 4.14. Comparing Snapshots and Dynasets.

```
Option Explicit
'
' declare form-level variables
Dim datObject As Database
Dim dynObject As Dynaset
Dim snpObject As Snapshot
Dim tblObject As Table
Dim cDbName As String
Dim cSelect As String
Dim cTblname As String
'
Dim vFields As Variant
Dim nFields As Integer
```

```
Sub CountDynaset ()
    Dim nCount As Integer
    '
    ' count records in dynaset
    dynObject.MoveFirst
    dynObject.MoveLast
    nCount = dynObject.RecordCount - 1
    Me.Print , "Total Dynaset Records:"; nCount
End Sub

Sub CountSnapshot ()
    Dim nCount As Integer
    '
    ' count records in snapshot
    snpObject.MoveFirst
    snpObject.MoveLast
    nCount = snpObject.RecordCount - 1
    Me.Print , "Total Snapshot Records:"; nCount
End Sub

Sub CountTable ()
    Dim nCount As Integer
    '
    ' count records in dynaset
    tblObject.MoveFirst
    tblObject.MoveLast
    nCount = tblObject.RecordCount
    Me.Print , "Total Table Records:"; nCount
End Sub

Sub DelDynRecord ()
    '
    ' delete first record in dynaset
    dynObject.MoveFirst
    dynObject.Delete
End Sub


Sub Form_Activate ()
    '
    ' set variables
    cDbName = App.Path + "\books.mdb"
    cSelect = "Titles"
    cTblname = "Titles"
    nFields = 5
    '
    ' put up title
    Me.Cls
    Me.Print "Comparing Dynaset, Snapshot, and Table Objects"
    Me.Print
    '
    ' open files and print counts
    OpenFiles
    Me.Print ">First Pass"
```

continues

Listing 4.14. continued

```
        CountDynaset
        CountSnapshot
        CountTable
        Me.Print
        '
        ' save a record, delete it, then count again
        SaveDynRecord
        DelDynRecord
        Me.Print ">After Dynaset Delete"
        CountDynaset
        CountSnapshot
        CountTable
        Me.Print
        '
        ' restore the record, then count aagin
        RestoreDynRecord
        Me.Print ">After Dynaset Restore"
        CountDynaset
        CountSnapshot
        CountTable
        Me.Print
End Sub

Sub OpenFiles ()
        '
        ' open database, dynaset, & snapshot, & table
        Set datObject = OpenDatabase(cDbName)
        Set dynObject = datObject.CreateDynaset(cSelect)
        Set snpObject = datObject.CreateSnapshot(cSelect)
        Set tblObject = datObject.OpenTable(cTblname)
End Sub

Sub RestoreDynRecord ()
        Dim x As Integer
        '
        ' add a new rec, write out, and save
        dynObject.AddNew
        For x = 0 To nFields - 1
            dynObject.Fields(x).Value = vFields(x)
        Next x
        dynObject.Update
End Sub

Sub SaveDynRecord ()
        Dim x As Integer
        '
        ' save record before deleting
        dynObject.MoveFirst
        For x = 0 To nFields - 1
            vFields(x) = dynObject.Fields(x).Value
        Next x
End Sub
```

When you run the SNAPDYNA.VBP program, you'll see three record count reports. The first report occurs right after the data objects are created. The second count report occurs after a record has been removed from the Dynaset object. The last count report occurs after the record has been restored to the Dynaset object. Note that both the Table and the Dynaset objects reflect the changes in the data table, but the Snapshot does not.

When to Use the *Snapshot* Data Object

Visual Basic Snapshot objects work best if you have a small set of data that you need to access frequently. For example, if you have a list of valid input values for a particular field stored in a control table, you can load these valid values into a Snapshot and refer to that data set each time you need to verify user input.

If the data set is not too large, Snapshots are very good for use in creating calculated reports or graphic displays. It is usually a good idea to create a static data set for use in calculating reports. This way, any changes in the data set that might occur in a multiuser environment from the time you start the report to the time you end it will not confuse any calculations done by the report.

Tip: It's a good idea to keep your Snapshots to less then 64K in size. You can estimate the eventual size of your Snapshots by calculating the number of bytes in an average data record and estimating the average number of records you can expect in your Snapshot. You can refer to Day 2, "Creating Databases," for information on the size of Visual Basic data types.

Special Visual Basic Data Objects

Visual Basic has two special data objects, which are both actually runtime properties of the data control. The Database object enables you to access properties of an underlying database attached to the data control with the DatabaseName property. The Recordset object enables you to access properties of an underlying data table attached to the data control with the RecordSource property.

The *Recordset* Data Object

Because the Recordset data object is actually a property of a Visual Basic data control, you can only use the Recordset as a subobject of the data control. The Recordset acts the same as a Visual Basic Dynaset. It allows you access to all the properties and methods associated with the data set object created by the data control. This data set object is always a Visual Basic Dynaset data object. The Recordset data object is only available as a property of the data control. Any operations you would normally perform on a Dynaset object can be performed on a Recordset object.

The *Database* Data Object

The Database object of a Visual Basic data control allows you access to all the properties and methods associated with the database underlying the data control. By using the related data objects TableDefs, Fields, and Indexes, you can get information about all the tables in the database, all the indexes in the database, and all the fields in each table. Also, you can get additional information about the field types and index parameters.

The Database data object is most useful when you are developing generic database routines. Because the Database object gives you access to all the field names and properties, you can use this information to write generic data table display and update routines instead of having to write routines that have hardcoded field names and data types. TableDefs objects are covered in more detail on Day 10. For now, though, let's write a short routine that lists all the tables, fields, and indexes in the BOOKS.MDB database.

Use the information in Table 4.3 to set the form property settings and place the data control on the form.

Table 4.3. The controls for project 04ABC1.MAK.

Control	Property	Setting
Form	Caption	Database Demo
	WindowState	Maximize
DataControl	DatabaseName	BIBLIO.MDB
	RecordSource	Authors

Place the data control at the very bottom of the form. It is only there to give you access to the various database properties that you will print on the form itself. Enter the program code in Listing 4.15 in the Form_Activate event.

Listing 4.15. Listing Database objects.

```
Private Sub Form_Activate()
    Dim i As Integer
    Dim j As Integer
    '
    ' open the database
```

```
      Data1.DatabaseName = App.Path + "\books.mdb" ' Set Database file.
      Data1.Refresh
      '
      ' Read and print the table info
      For i = 0 To Data1.Database.TableDefs.Count - 1
         Me.Print "Table Info"
         Print " "; Data1.Database.TableDefs(i).Name
         For j = 0 To Data1.Database.TableDefs(i).Fields.Count - 1
            Print " -"; Data1.Database.TableDefs(i).Fields(j).Name
         Next j
         MsgBox "Press OK to Continue."
         Me.Cls
      Next i
      '
      ' read and print index info
      On Error Resume Next
      '
      For i = 0 To Data1.Database.TableDefs.Count - 1
         Me.Print "Index Info"
         Print " "; Data1.Database.TableDefs(i).Name
         For j = 0 To Data1.Database.TableDefs(i).Indexes.Count - 1
             Print " -"; Data1.Database.TableDefs(i).Indexes(j).Name;
             Print " ["; Data1.Database.TableDefs(i).Indexes(j).Fields; "]"
         Next j
         MsgBox "Press OK to Continue."
         Me.Cls
      Next i
      End
      '
End Sub
```

After you enter the code, save the form as DBO.FRM and the project as DBO.VBP, and then run the program. You will see a list on the screen showing the table name, a list of all the fields in the table, and a dialog box. Click the dialog box to continue on to the next table. After clicking OK through the table listing, you will see a list of each index defined for each table, which you can also click through one at a time. Your two screens should look something like the one in Figure 4.4 for tables and the one in Figure 4.5 for indexes.

Note: As you click through the database tables, you will see several tables that start with Msys. These are system tables used by the Microsoft JET database engine and are not used for data storage or retrieval. You will also notice that each Index object consists of a unique name and one or more fields (displayed in brackets). You will not see a data table associated with the index because the Microsoft JET engine does not store that information in a manner you can easily see (it's actually in one of those Msys tables!).

Figure 4.4.

Using the Database *object to create a Table Info listing.*

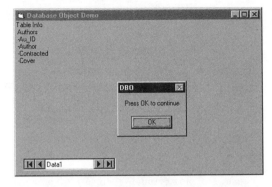

Figure 4.5.

Using the Database *object to create an index listing.*

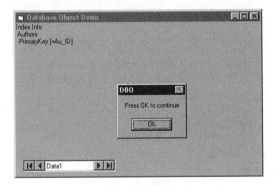

Summary

In today's lesson, you learned that there are three main types of Visual Basic data objects:

☐ Table objects: These are used when you have a large data set and need to do frequent searches to locate a single record. You can use the Visual Basic Seek method and use Visual Basic Indexes with the Table object.

☐ Dynaset objects: These are used in most cases when you need read and write access to data sets. The Dynaset uses little workstation memory and allows you to create virtual tables by combining fields from different tables in the same database. The Dynaset is the only data object that allows you to read and write to ODBC data sources.

☐ Snapshot objects: These are used when you need fast read-only access to data sets. Snapshot objects are stored in workstation memory, so they should be kept small. Snapshots are good for storing validation lists at the workstation or for small reports.

You also learned that there are two other Visual Basic data objects, both associated with the Visual Basic data control.

☐ The Recordset object is the data control equivalent of the Dynaset object. If you use the Visual Basic data control, you can access the Recordset object to read and set properties of the Dynaset created by the data control.

☐ The Database object is another subobject of the data control. You can use the Database object to get a list of tables in the database, a list of indexes associated with the tables, and a list of fields in each of the tables.

Quiz

1. Are Visual Basic Database objects data set oriented or record oriented?

2. What is the most common Visual Basic data object?

3. Do Dynasets use a relatively large amount or small amount of workstation RAM? Why?

4. What are the weaknesses of using a Dynaset object?

5. What are the main advantages of using the Table data object?

6. Do you use the Refresh method with the Table data object?

7. Can you open a Table data object by setting the properties of a data control?

8. What is the difference between a Snapshot and a Dynaset data object?

9. Which data object do you use to extract table and field names from a database definition?

Exercises

1. What data object would you use—Dynaset, Table, or Snapshot—to create an attachment to an ODBC data source that you would like to update periodically? Why?

   Write the code to open this type of data object. Assume that the database name is C:\DATA\ACCTPAY.MDB, with your desired table named Vendors.

2. Given the same data source as in Exercise 1, write the code to open a data object to be used in the generation of a report. (Assume the RAM memory is adequate on the machine running the program.)

3. Given the same data source as in Exercise 1, write the code that will open the data object so that you can access the data often in a multiuser environment to search for single records.

Creating Data Entry Forms with Bound Controls

Today's lesson is a review of all the bound data controls that are shipped with Visual Basic Professional. You'll review the special properties, events, and methods that relate to database programming, and you'll create short examples to illustrate how each of the bound controls can be used in your database programs.

You'll also review general rules for designing quality forms for Windows programs, covering alignment, font selection, control placement and spacing, and color choices.

Finally, you'll create a short project that establishes customizable color schemes for your application. This project will show you how to use the Windows Control Panel Color applet to set colors for your applications.

What Are Bound Data Controls?

Before you get into the details of listing the properties, events, and methods of Visual Basic bound data controls, let's review what a bound control is and why it's so useful.

Bound data controls are no different than any other Visual Basic control objects, except that they have been given additional properties, events, and methods that allow you to "bind" them directly to one or more data tables. This binding makes it easy to create data-aware input and display objects that you can use to perform data input and display with very little program code. Using bound controls simplifies your programming chores a great deal. Most bound controls automatically handle the various chores related to processing data entry and display for databases. The bound controls make it easy to write Visual Basic programs that handle all (or nearly all) of the following processes:

☐ Loading data from the database into a Visual Basic data object

☐ Selecting the data record(s) requested by the user

☐ Loading form controls with values in the requested record(s)

☐ Trapping simple user input errors

☐ Enforcing database integrity rules

☐ Updating the data object with modified data from the form controls

You do not need to use bound data controls in your database programs. In fact, as you will see in the lessons next week, there are times when it is better to use unbound controls in your programs. However, when you use unbound controls, you need to take responsibility for handling all the processes outlined in the preceding list. Although this is not an insurmountable task, it's a good idea to take advantage of the power of bound data controls whenever possible. Using the prebuilt and tested bound controls helps you create solid, functional database entry forms in a short period of time.

The Data Control

The Visual Basic data control is the control used to gain access to database tables. The data control allows you to establish a link to a single Dynaset data object in a database. You can have more than one data control in your program and more than one data control on a single form.

Like all Visual Basic controls, there are properties, events, and methods associated with the data control. Because the focus of this book is on databases, this lesson will focus on the properties, events, and methods that are important in dealing with database activity. In the process, you will build a small program that illustrates these database-related aspects of the Visual Basic data control.

Data Control Properties

There are five data control properties that deserve special attention. Here's a list of them:

- ☐ DatabaseName
- ☐ Exclusive
- ☐ Options
- ☐ ReadOnly
- ☐ RecordSource

There is a sixth data control property that is used only for data access: the Connect property. The Connect property is used when you are accessing non-Microsoft Access databases. You'll learn more about using the Connect property in the lesson on Day 10.

Setting DatabaseName and RecordSource Properties

The DatabaseName and RecordSource properties have been discussed on Day 4. The DatabaseName property contains the name of the database you want to access. In Microsoft Access databases, this would be the complete drive, path, and filename of the Microsoft Access database file. For example, to connect to the BOOKS.MDB Microsoft Access database, you would set the DatabaseName property to BOOKS.MDB. You can do this through the Property box at design time or through Visual Basic code at runtime.

Let's start a project to illustrate the data control properties, events, and methods. Load Visual Basic and start a new project. Drop the data control on a blank form. For this project, you'll accept the default control name of DATA1. In the examples on Day 4, you have set the

DatabaseName and RecordSource properties at design time using the Visual Basic properties window. Visual Basic will allow you to set most control properties at runtime (that is, while the program is running). The advantage of setting properties at runtime is that you can build programs that allow users to decide what database and data table they want to access. This is how the Visual Basic Data Manager works. For this project, you'll set these properties at runtime using Visual Basic code.

> **Note:** Design time refers to the time when you are designing your Visual Basic application. Runtime refers to the time when your finished application is running.

You will set these data control values in a separate procedure, called OpenDB. If you haven't done so, start Visual Basic and open a new project. To create a new procedure in Visual Basic, double-click anywhere on the form in order to bring up a Visual Basic code window. Now select Insert | Procedure from the Visual Basic main menu. You'll see a dialog box that asks you for the name of the procedure (see Figure 5.1).

Figure 5.1.

Creating a new Visual Basic procedure.

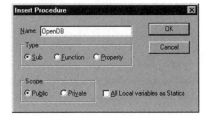

Enter OpenDB. Make sure the radio button for Sub is selected and then click OK. You now see the new Visual Basic procedure header and footer, ready for you to enter your program code.

The following procedure sets the DatabaseName property of the data control on the current form. Notice that App.Path is used as part of the database name. The Path property of the App object returns the drive and directory in which the project has been stored. This is a very good way to locate important project files. If you have stored them in the same directory as the program you are running, you can use the App.Path to find those files without having to know the exact directory name.

Place the following code in the general declarations section of your form:

```
Public Sub OpenDB()
    Dim cDBName As String     ' declare a string variable
    '
    cDBName = App.Path + "\books.mdb" ' point to database
    '
```

```
Data1.DatabaseName = cDBName ' set database property
    '
    Data1.Refresh ' update data control properties
End Sub
```

> **Tip:** When you enter Visual Basic program code, Visual Basic looks for typing errors automatically. Each time you press the Enter key, Visual Basic scans the line, capitalizes Visual Basic reserved words (if everything has been typed correctly), adds spaces between the equal signs, and so on. When you enter code, don't try to capitalize or space properly; let Visual Basic do it for you. That way, if you finish a line and press the Enter key and then notice that Visual Basic has not "edited" for you, you'll know that there is probably something on that line that Visual Basic didn't understand. Now you'll catch your typing errors as you code!

The last line in the procedure forces the data control to update all the new properties that have been set in the routine. Any time you use Visual Basic code to change data control properties, you must invoke the Refresh method to update the data control. This is just one of the data control methods. Other data control methods are discussed throughout today's lesson.

> **Tip:** Notice that in the code example you declare a variable, set the variable to a value, and then set the data control property with the variable. This could all be done in a single line of code. Here's an example:
>
> ```
> Data1.DatabaseName= App.Apth + "\BOOKS.MDB"
> ```
>
> By declaring variables and using those variables to set properties, you'll create a program that is easier to understand and modify in the future.

When you set the DatabaseName property, you are telling Visual Basic the *database* you are using. However, at this point, Visual Basic does not know what *data table* you want to use with the data control. Use the RecordSource property to indicate the data table you want to access.

Now, modify the OpenDB procedure you created earlier by adding code that sets the RecordSource property of the data control to access the Authors data table. Be sure to declare a variable, initialize it to the correct table, and then use the variable to set the data control property. When you are finished, your procedure should look like the one shown in the following code example:

```
Public Sub OpenDB()
    Dim cDBName As String    ' declare a string variable
    Dim cTblName As String   ' declare a string variable
    '
```

```
    cDBName = App.Path + "\books.mdb" ' point to database
    cTblName = "Authors" ' point to authors table
    '
    Data1.DatabaseName = cDBName ' set database property
    Data1.RecordSource = cTblName ' set recordsource property
    '
    Data1.Refresh ' update data control properties
End Sub
```

Before you get too far into the project, you should save your work. Save the form as BNDCTRL1.FRM and the project as BDNCTRL.VBP.

Setting the ReadOnly and Exclusive Properties

There are two more data control properties that you'll need to set in this example: ReadOnly and Exclusive. The ReadOnly and Exclusive properties are Boolean (True/False) properties that you can use to limit access to the database. When you set the Exclusive property to True, you are opening the database for *your* use only. In other words, no one else can open the database (or any of the tables in the database) while you have it open. This is handy when you want to perform major updates or changes to the database and do not want anyone else in the file at the same time.

For the example, you'll open the database for exclusive use. Modify the OpenDB procedure so that it sets the Exclusive property to True. Your code should look like the following code:

```
Public Sub OpenDB()
    Dim cDBName As String    ' declare a string variable
    Dim cTblName As String   ' declare a string variable
    Dim bExclusive As Boolean ' declare true/false var
    '
    cDBName = App.Path + "\books.mdb" ' point to database
    cTblName = "Authors" ' point to authors table
    bExclusive = True ' set to exclusive open
    '
    Data1.DatabaseName = cDBName ' set database property
    Data1.RecordSource = cTblName ' set recordsource property
    Data1.Exclusive = bExclusive
    '
    Data1.Refresh ' update data control properties
End Sub
```

Caution: When you open the database with Exclusive set to True, no other programs that access the database can be run without errors until you close the database. Use the Exclusive property sparingly!

The ReadOnly property opens the database with read rights only. You will not be allowed to make any changes, adds, or deletions in any table while you have the database open in read-only mode. This is handy when you are using the data for creating a report or for display purposes only. (Read-only mode is faster, too.)

> **Note:** Don't confuse the Exclusive property and the ReadyOnly property; they are not the same! The Exclusive property makes sure that *no one else* can access the database while you have it open. The ReadOnly property makes sure that *your program* cannot update the database while you have it open. The Exclusive property affects everyone who wants to access the database. The ReadOnly property affects only the person running your program.

Again, for this example, you'll open the file as read-only. Make changes to the OpenDB procedure to include variables that set the ReadOnly property to True. When you are done, your code should look something like the following code:

```
Public Sub OpenDB()
   Dim cDBName As String     ' declare a string variable
   Dim cTblName As String    ' declare a string variable
   Dim bExclusive As Boolean ' declare true/false var
   Dim bReadOnly As Boolean  ' declare true/false var
   '
   cDBName = App.Path + "\books.mdb" ' point to database
   cTblName = "Authors" ' point to authors table
   bExclusive = True ' set to exclusive open
   bReadOnly = True ' set to read only
   '
   Data1.DatabaseName = cDBName ' set database property
   Data1.RecordSource = cTblName ' set recordsource property
   Data1.Exclusive = bExclusive
   Data1.ReadOnly = bReadOnly
   '
   Data1.Refresh ' update data control properties
End Sub
```

Now, save your work before entering more Visual Basic code.

Setting the Options Property

All the properties you have set in the previous code relate to the database that Visual Basic is accessing. The Options property of the Visual Basic data control allows you to establish the properties of the *dynaset* opened in the RecordSource property of the data control. There are several options that can be set in the Options property of the data control. In today's lesson, you will learn about the three most commonly used options.

5

Here are the three Options values for the data control that is covered today:

- [ ] `dbDenyWrite`
- [ ] `dbReadOnly`
- [ ] `dbAppendOnly`

The preceding three options are actually Visual Basic constants that are predefined in the language. These constants are like Visual Basic variables, except that they have a single, set value that cannot be changed. Table 5.1 shows the three constants and their numeric values.

Table 5.1. Dynaset Option values.

Dynaset Option	Numeric Value
`dbDenyWrite`	1
`dbReadOnly`	4
`dbAppendOnly`	8

Setting the `dbDenyWrite` option prevents other users from changing the data in the dynaset while you have it open (similar to the Exclusive database property). The `dbReadOnly` option prevents you from changing the data in the dynaset (similar to the ReadOnly database property). The `dbAppendOnly` option lets you add new data to the dynaset but does not let you modify or delete existing records. Setting the `dbReadOnly` option speeds processing of the dynaset and is handy for generating displays or reports. The `dbDenyWrite` option is useful for when you want to make major changes to the dynaset and want to prevent other users from accessing the records in the dynaset until you are done making your changes. Using the `dbAppendOnly` option lets you create data entry routines that limit user rights to adding records without deleting or modifying existing ones.

Now you'll add the code that sets the Options property of the data control. You'll notice that you do not have a property for each of the three options. How do you set them individually? You do this by adding up the constants and placing the result in the Options property of the data control.

For example, if you want to open the dynaset for only appending new records, set the Options property of the data control to `dbAppendOnly`. If you want to open the dynaset to deny everyone the right to update the database and to allow read-only access for the current user, set the Options property to `dbDenyWrite + dbReadOnly`.

For now, set the data control options to `DenyWrite` and `ReadOnly`. When you are done, your procedure should look like this:

```
Public Sub OpenDB()
   Dim cDBName As String     ' declare a string variable
```

```
    Dim cTblName As String    ' declare a string variable
    Dim bExclusive As Boolean ' declare true/false var
    Dim bReadOnly As Boolean  ' declare true/false var
    '
    cDBName = App.Path + "\books.mdb" ' point to database
    cTblName = "Authors" ' point to authors table
    bExclusive = True ' set to exclusive open
    bReadOnly = True ' set to read only
    '
    Data1.DatabaseName = cDBName ' set database property
    Data1.RecordSource = cTblName ' set recordsource property
    Data1.Exclusive = bExclusive
    Data1.Options = dbDenyWrite + dbReadOnly
    Data1.ReadOnly = bReadOnly
    '
    Data1.Refresh ' update data control properties
End Sub
```

You have now completed the procedure for opening the BOOKS.MDB database and creating a dynaset from the Authors table. The database and the dynaset will be opened exclusively for read-only access. Only one thing is missing. You must first make sure the OpenDB procedure is executed! Place the following code line in the Form_Load procedure:

```
Sub Form_Load ()
    OpenDB ' open the database, set dynaset
End Sub
```

Now save the project and run the program. This program run will give you a report of any errors that might exist. If you get an error report, review the code examples and then make the necessary changes before going on to the next section, where you'll add a few more routines that illustrate how data control methods work.

Data Control Methods

Most Visual Basic controls have associated methods. Each method can be thought of as a function or process that you can tell the program to run. The Visual Basic data control has several methods, but only three are database related. Here's a list of them:

☐ Refresh

☐ UpdateControls

☐ UpdateRecord

You have used the Refresh method in today's example already. This method is used any time you change any of the properties of the data control. Using the Refresh method updates the data control and forces it to rebuild the dynaset. This refresh updates not only the behaviors and properties of the dynaset but also the records in the set. If records are added to the table by another user after your program has created its dynaset, invoking the Refresh method will make sure your dynaset contains the most recent records.

The `UpdateControls` method is used to update any bound input controls. Invoking the `UpdateControls` method is the same as reading the current record and putting the values in the fields of the data table into the input controls on a form. This happens automatically each time you press the arrow buttons on the data control. But you can force the update to occur any time during the data entry process. It's especially handy if you want to undo user changes to a data record.

Now, add a single field to the form and test the `UpdateControls` method. Add a text box control to the form and set the DataSource property to Data1. You'll set the DataField property using Visual Basic code in just a moment; leave it blank for now. Refer to Figure 5.2 for positioning and sizing of the control.

Figure 5.2.

Adding the bound text box control.

Now add the following new procedure (`BindControls`) to your form. Remember to use the Insert | Procedure item from the main menu of Visual Basic. This new procedure links the text box to the field in the dynaset using the DataField property of the text box.

```
Sub BindControls ()
    Dim cField1 As String
    '
    cField1 = "Author"
    '
    Text1.DataField = cField1
End Sub
```

Now, add the `BindControls` procedure to the `Form_Load` event to make sure it gets called when the program starts. Your `Form_Load` event should look like this:

```
Sub Form_Load ()
    OpenDB ' open the database, set dynaset
    BindControls ' link controls to data fields
End Sub
```

You need to add a command button to the form to activate the `UpdateControls` method. Place a single command button on the form and set its Name property to cmdRestore and its caption to &Restore. Also, add the following code line behind the `cmdRestore_Click` event:

```
Sub cmdRestore_Click ()
    data1.UpdateControls ' restore textbox values
End Sub
```

Your form should look like the one shown in Figure 5.3.

Figure 5.3.
Adding a Restore button to the form.

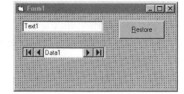

Now save and run the project. When the first record comes up, edit the field. Change the name or add additional information to the field. Before you click an arrow button, press the Restore button. You'll see that the data in the text box reverts to the value initially read into it when you first started the program.

Now, add a button that invokes the UpdateRecord method. The UpdateRecord method tells Visual Basic to save the values of the bound input controls (the text box in this project) to the dynaset. Refer to Figure 5.4 for sizing and positioning of the button.

Figure 5.4.
Adding the Update button to the form.

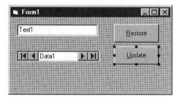

Using the UpdateRecord method updates the dynaset without moving the record pointer. Now, add a command button to the form, set its Name property to cmdUpdate and its Caption property to &Update, and then place the following code line behind the button in the cmdUpdate_Click event:

```
Sub cmdUpdate_Click ()
    data1.UpdateRecord 'write controls to dynaset
End Sub
```

Note: It is important to remember the difference between the UpdateControls method and the UpdateRecord method. The UpdateControls method reads from the data object and writes to the form controls. It updates the controls. The UpdateRecord method reads from the form controls and writes to the data object. It updates the record.

Save and run the project again. This time, after you edit the text box, click the Update button. Now, move the record pointer forward to the next record and then back to the record you edited.

What do you see? The record was not updated! Remember, you set the ReadOnly property of the database to True and turned on the ReadOnly value of the Options property. Now change the ReadOnly property to False and drop the dbReadOnly and dbDenyWrite constants from the Options property by setting the Options property to 0.

When you rerun the program, you can now edit the text box, restore the old value with the Restore button, or save the new value with the Update button. You can also save the new value by moving the record pointer.

This last behavior of the data control can cause some problems. What if you changed a field and didn't want to save the changes, but instead of clicking the Restore button, you moved to the next record? You would change the database and never know it! In the next section, you'll use one of the data control's events to help you avoid just such a situation.

Data Control Events

All Microsoft Windows programs contain events. These events occur each time the computer senses that a user clicks a button or passes the mouse over an object on the form, or when any other process occurs. When an event takes place, the Windows operating system sends a message that tells all processes currently running that something has happened. Windows programs can then "listen" for messages and act, based on their programming code, when the right message comes along.

In Visual Basic, you can create program code that will execute each time a specific event occurs. There are three data control events that relate to database functions. Here's a list of them:

- ☐ Reposition
- ☐ Validate
- ☐ Error

The Reposition event occurs each time the data control moves to a new position in the dynaset. The Validate event occurs each time a data control leaves the current record. The Error event occurs each time a database error occurs when the arrow buttons on the data control are used to move the record pointer. Visual Basic automatically creates procedure headers and footers for all the events associated with a control. When you place a data control on your form, Visual Basic creates the procedures Data1_Reposition, Data1_Validate, and Data1_Error.

Now, add some code to the project that will tell you when an event occurs. First, you need to get a message box to pop up each time you reposition the record pointer using the arrow buttons on the data control. To do this, place the following code in the Data1_Reposition event:

```
Sub Data1_Reposition ()
   MsgBox "Repositioning the pointer..."
End Sub
```

Next, to get a message box to pop up each time you leave a record using the data control's arrow buttons, place the following code in the Data1_Validate event:

```
Sub Data1_Validate (Action As Integer, Save As Integer)
    MsgBox "Validating Data..."
End Sub
```

Now save and run the project. You'll notice that the message from the Reposition event is the first thing you see after the program begins. This is because the pointer is positioned on the first record in the dynaset when the dynaset is first created. (See Figure 5.5.)

Figure 5.5.

The Reposition event at the start of the program.

After you click the OK button in the message box, you'll see the Visual Basic form with the data control. Click one of the arrow buttons. You'll see that the message from the Validate event pops up. This message is sent before Visual Basic leaves the current record. (See Figure 5.6.)

Figure 5.6.

The Validate event message.

After you click the OK button in the message box, you'll see the message from the Reposition event again. This is the event message sent when Visual Basic reads the next record.

You might have noticed that the header for the Validate event contains two parameters: Action and Save. These two parameters can be used to learn more about what action is currently being attempted on the data control and can give you control over whether the user should be allowed to save the new data to the dynaset. These parameters are set by Visual Basic while the program is running. You can read the values in these parameters at any time during the program. For now, you'll explore the Action parameter. The next set of code will add a routine to the Validate step that pops up a message box each time the arrow buttons of a data control are clicked.

Just like the Options property constants, Visual Basic also provides a set of predefined constants for all the possible Action values reported in the Validate event. Although these constants are handy, they are not very useful to users of your programs. The following code example shows you how to translate those constants into a friendly message using a string array. Add the following line to the general declarations section of the form.

```
Option Explicit

Dim VldMsg(4) As String ' declare message array
```

Now add the following procedure, which loads a set of messages into the array you declared previously. These messages are displayed each time the corresponding action occurs in the `Validate` event. Notice that you are using the predefined Visual Basic constants.

```
Public Sub MakeVldMsgArray()
    VldMsg(vbDataActionMoveFirst) = "MoveFirst"
    VldMsg(vbDataActionMovePrevious) = "MovePrevious"
    VldMsg(vbDataActionMoveNext) = "MoveNext"
    VldMsg(vbDataActionMoveLast) = "MoveLast"
End Sub
```

Update the `Form_Load` event to call the `MakeVldMsgArray` procedure. You can see that `MakeVldMsgArray` has been added at the start of the event. Here's the code:

```
Sub Form_Load ()
   MakeVldMsgArray ' create message array
   OpenDB ' open the database, set dynaset
   BindControls ' link controls to data fields
End Sub
```

Now you need to add the one bit of code that will be executed each time the `Validate` event occurs. This code displays a simple message each time you click the arrow buttons of the data control. The actual message is determined by the Action value that Visual Basic passes to the `Validate` event. The Action value is, of course, determined by the arrow button on the data control that you click while the program is running.

Notice that you have replaced the `Validating data...` message that you entered in the previous example. Here's the code:

```
Private Sub Data1_Validate(Action As Integer, Save As Integer)
    MsgBox VldMsg(Action) ' message based on user action
End Sub
```

Save and run the program to see a message box that tells you what you probably already know! There are several other actions that can occur during the `Validate` event. You'll explore these actions on Day 6, "Input Validation."

For the rest of the project, comment out the `Validate` event code and the `Reposition` event code. Now you'll concentrate on adding additional Visual Basic bound controls to the project.

The Bound Text Control and the Bound Label Control

There are no database-related methods or events associated with the bound text control or bound label control. And there are only two properties of the bound text control and the bound label control that are database related. Here's a list of them:

☐ DataSource

☐ DataField

The DataSource property is the name of the data control that maintains the link between the data table and the text or label control. The DataField property identifies the actual field in the data control dynaset to which the text box or label control is bound. You cannot set the DataSource property at runtime—it's a design time–only property. You can, however, set the DataField property at either runtime or design time.

Bound text controls give you the ability to add input fields to your data forms that automatically link to the dynaset defined in the data control. Bound label controls are handy when you want to display information without letting users update it. You've already added a bound text control to the project, so now add a bound label control, too.

You'll add the label control to display the Au_ID field of the Authors table. This will give users the chance to see the author ID but not update it. Add a label control to the form, and set its DataSource property to Data1. Also, set the BorderStyle property to Fixed Single to make it look similar to a text box control. Refer to Figure 5.7 for positioning and placement.

Figure 5.7.
Adding the bound label control.

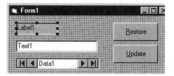

Now update the `BindControls` procedure to bind set the DataField property of the label control. Your code should look like this:

```
Sub BindControls ()
    Dim cField1 As String
    Dim cField2 As String
    '
    cField1 = "Author"
    cField2 = "Au_ID"
    '
    Text1.DataField = cField1
    Label1.DataField = cField2
End Sub
```

Now save and run the project. You'll see that the label control contains the values stored in the Au_ID field of the dynaset. As you move through the dynaset using the arrow buttons, the label control is updated just as the text control is updated.

The Bound Checkbox Control

The bound checkbox control is basically the same as the text control. It has no special database-related events or methods and has the same two database-related properties: DataSource and DataField. The difference between the text box control and the checkbox control is in how the data is displayed on the form and saved in the dynaset.

Checkboxes are linked to Boolean data type fields. You'll remember that these fields can only hold –1 or 0. Checkboxes do not display –1 or 0. They display an empty box (0) or a checked box (–1). By clicking the display of the checkbox, you can actually update the Boolean value of the bound dynaset field.

Using Figure 5.8 as a guide, add a checkbox control to the form. Set its DataSource property to Data1 and its Caption property to Under Contract.

Figure 5.8.

Adding the bound checkbox control.

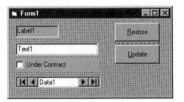

Now, update the BindControls procedure to link the checkbox control to the field Contracted in the Authors table. When you are done, your BindControls procedure should look like this:

```
Sub BindControls ()
    Dim cField1 As String
    Dim cField2 As String
    Dim cField3 As String
    '
    cField1 = "Author"
    cField2 = "Au_ID"
    cField3 = "Contracted"
    '
    Text1.DataField = cField1
    Label1.DataField = cField2
    Check1.DataField = cField3
End Sub
```

Save and run the project. You will see that some checkboxes are turned on, and some are turned off. You now have a bound checkbox control!

The Bound Image Control

Like the bound text control and the bound label control, the Visual Basic bound image control has no database-related events or methods and only two database-related properties: DataSource and DataField. Like the bound checkbox control, the image control has unique behaviors regarding displaying bound data. The image control is used to display binary pictures stored in a dynaset field in the binary data type format.

Now, add an image control to the form and bind it to a field in the Authors table. Drop an image control on the form. Set its DataSource property to Data1. Refer to Figure 5.9 for control sizing and placement.

Figure 5.9.
Adding the bound image control.

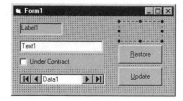

After you add the control to the form, update the `BindControls` procedure to bind the image control to the Cover field in the Authors table. When you're done, the procedure should look like this:

```
Sub BindControls ()
    Dim cField1 As String
    Dim cField2 As String
    Dim cField3 As String
    Dim cField4 As String
    '
    cField1 = "Author"
    cField2 = "Au_ID"
    cField3 = "Contracted"
    cField4 = "Cover"
    '
    Text1.DataField = cField1
    Label1.DataField = cField2
    Check1.DataField = cField3
    Image1.DataField = cField4
End Sub
```

Save and run the project. You'll now see icons displayed in the top-right corner of the form (only for the first few records). These icons are stored in the binary data type field of the database. Note that you don't have to do any fancy "loading" of the picture into the image control, because the data control binding handles all that for you!

When you run your completed project, it should look like the one shown in Figure 5.10.

Figure 5.10.
The completed project.

You have just completed a form that contains bound controls for handling text, numeric, Boolean, and binary image data stored in a database.

General Rules for Designing Quality Forms

Now that you know how to use the Visual Basic data controls, it's time to learn about form design. Microsoft encourages developers to adhere to a general set of guidelines when designing the look and feel of their programs. In this project, you'll focus on the layout and design of quality forms. I will define guidelines for the following aspects of form design:

☐ Control placement and spacing

☐ Label alignment

☐ Standards fonts

☐ Use of colors

The guidelines set here will be used throughout all the rest of the projects in this book. In the next lesson, you'll design the main input form for the CompanyMaster data table.

Note: The style guidelines used in this book adhere to the look and feel of Microsoft Windows 95. Even if you are still using Windows 3.1 or Windows for Workgroups, we encourage you to adopt the Windows 95 layout standards because many of the people using your programs may already be running Windows 95 on their PCs.

Guidelines for Win95-Style Forms

There are a few general guidelines for developing Win95-style forms. The primary things to consider are listed in Table 5.2 with comments. This table describes the standard measurements Microsoft recommends for form controls. It also contains recommended spacing for these controls. Refer to Figure 5.11 when reading this section. This figure shows an example of a data entry form that is built using the Windows 95 standards described in this section.

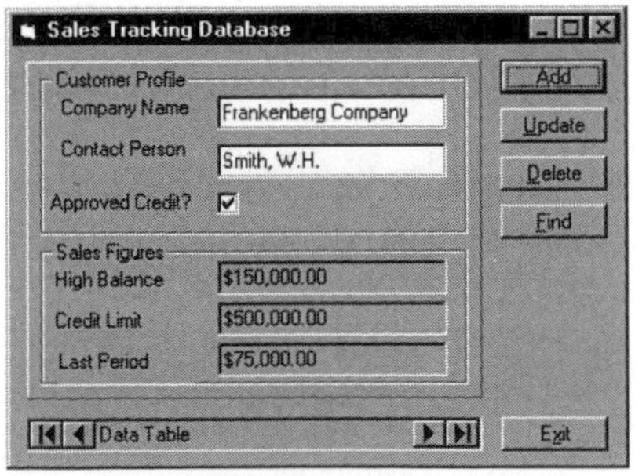

Figure 5.11.
A Win95-style input form.

The Default Form Color

When you first start your form, set its BackColor property to light gray. Set the BackStyle property for labels to Transparent so that the background color can show through. For controls that do not have a BackStyle property (such as checkbox controls and radio button controls), set the BackColor property to light gray. The gray tones are easier to read in varied light. Using gray tones also reduces the chance that a user who experiences color-blindness will have difficulty with your input screens.

Using the Panel3D Control to Lift Input Areas Off the Page

Use the Panel3D control to create a palette on which to place all display and input controls. Do not place buttons or the data control on the palette unless they act as part of the input dialog box (see Figure 5.11). Use only one palette per form. The palette is not the same as a frame around a set of controls. The palette is used to raise the set of controls up from the page. This makes it easy for the user to see that these controls are grouped together and that they deserve attention.

The Default Font

Use 8-point sans serif, regular (not bold) as the default font for all controls. If you want to use larger type in a title, for example, do so sparingly. Keep in mind that the default font is a proportionally spaced font. The space taken up by the letter W is greater than the space taken up by the letter j. This can lead to difficulty aligning numbers and columnar data. If you are doing a lot of displays and lists that include numeric amounts or other values that should line up, you should consider using a monospaced font such as Courier or FixedSys.

Input Areas and Display Areas

Use the color white to indicate areas where the user can perform input. If the field is for display purposes only, set it to gray (or to the form color if it is not gray). This means that all labels should appear in the same color as the form background (such as gray labels for gray forms). Also, make all display-only areas appear recessed on the palette. All text boxes that are active for input should appear white. This makes the action areas of your form stand out to the user. By keeping to the standard of white for input controls and gray (or form-colored) for display-only controls, users will not be so quick to attempt to edit a read-only control.

Using the Frame Controls to Group Related Information

When placing controls on a form, you should group related items together by enclosing them within a frame control. This frame control is sometimes called a *group box* because it boxes in

117

a group of related controls. The frame caption is optional, but it is recommended. Using the frame control to group related items helps the user to quickly understand the relationship among fields on the form.

Alignment of Controls on the Form

All controls should be left-justified on the form. Show a clean line from top to bottom. This makes it easy to read down a list of fields quickly. Try to avoid multicolumn labels. If you must have more than one column of labels and input controls, be sure to left-align the second column, too.

Standard Sizing and Spacing for Controls

All controls should have standard height, spacing, and width where appropriate. Microsoft publishes its Win95 spacing standards in pixels or DLU (dialog units). Because Visual Basic controls work in twips instead of pixels, you need to know that one pixel equals 15 twips. Table 5.2 shows the recommended spacing and sizing for various controls on a form. Use these as a guide when creating your forms.

Table 5.2. Control spacing and sizing.

Form Control	Size/Spacing
Control height	330 twips
Command button width	1200 twips
Vertical spacing between controls	90 twips for related items 210 twips for unrelated items
Border widths (top, bottom, and side)	120 twips

Notice that the height of all controls is the same. This makes it easy to align controls on a form regardless of their type (command buttons, text boxes, checkboxes, and so on). The recommended spacing between controls seems quite wide when you first begin designing forms with these standards. However, you'll find that once you get the hang of these numbers, you'll be able to put together very clean-looking forms in a short amount of time.

Colors

Color standards for Win95 are quite simple—use gray! Although Microsoft recommends the gray tones for all forms, the color settings are one of the most commonly customized GUI properties in Windows programs. In this section you will learn two ways you can approach adding color to your applications: system colors and custom colors.

First, put together a simple form using Table 5.3 and Figure 5.12 as a guide. Remember that you are building a Win95-style form! You won't spend time linking the input controls to a data control right now—just concentrate on building the form and adding color-switching capabilities.

Tip: Here's a few suggestions to help you build the form:

☐ Before you begin placing controls on the form, set the Grid Height and Grid Width properties in the Options | Environment menu to 60 each. This will give you a smaller grid to work with and will make it easier to place controls on the form.

☐ Place the Panel3D you will use for your palette on the form first. Then place all other controls directly on the palette. Do not place controls on the palette by double-clicking the tool in the tools window or using the Copy command. Click the control icon once and then paint the control on the palette with the mouse. This will set the control as a "child" of the palette. Now, any time you move the palette, the controls will move along with it.

☐ Place the bound command buttons on the palette one after the other without setting any properties. When you want to set the command button properties, click one of the command buttons and then hold the Shift key while you click each of the other three. Now you can use the properties window to set values for all four of the controls at once. Set the command button's FontBold, Height, and Width properties this way to save time.

☐ You can easily set border widths if you remember that the grid dots appear every 60 twips on the form. All border widths should be set at 120 twips. This Microsoft standard makes it easy to distiguish separate controls and keeps a nice border around the form and around palettes and frames. Because border widths should be set at 120 twips, make sure that you can see two grid dots between the edge of the form and the edge of any other control (panel, command button, and so on).

☐ Remember that controls should be separated from each other by at least 90 twips. The value of 90 twips is an odd value when compared to the 60 twips between items and the 120 twips between borders. This odd spacing causes the user to break up the sections of the form a bit. This makes it easy for the user to see the separation between controls. When placing controls in a vertical line, use the Top property to determine where the control appears on the form. Because each control is 330 twips in height and the controls must be 90 twips apart, add 420 twips (330 + 90) to the Top value to determine where the next control should appear underneath.

Figure 5.12.
The color-switching project.

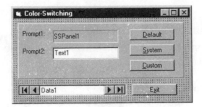

Table 5.3. Controls for the color-switching project.

Control	Property	Setting
Form	Caption	Color-Switching
	Name	frmColor
Panel3D	Caption	(set to blank)
	Name	pnlPalette
Text box	Name	txtOneLine
	FontBold	False
	Height	330
	Width	1800
Panel3D	Name	pnlDisplayOnly
	FontBold	False
	Height	330
	Width	1800
	Caption	Display-Only
	BevelInner	Sunken
	BorderWidth	1
	Alignment	Left Justify - MIDDLE
Label	Caption	Prompt1:
	FontBold	False
	BackStyle	2 - Transparent
Label	Caption	Prompt2:
	FontBold	False
	BackStyle	2 - Transparent
Data Control	Caption	Data
	FontBold	False
	Height	330
	Width	1800

Control	Property	Setting
Command Button	Name	cmdDefault
	Caption	&Default
	FontBold	False
	Height	330
	Width	1200
Command Button	Name	cmdSystem
	Caption	&System
	FontBold	False
	Heigth	330
	Width	1200
Command Button	Name	cmdCustom
	Caption	&Custom
	FontBold	False
	Height	330
	Width	1200
Command Button	Name	cmdExit
	Caption	E&xit
	FontBold	False
	Height	330
	Width	1200

Save the form as COLORS.FRM and the project as COLORS.VBP. You have built a form that has three command buttons: Default, System, and Custom. You'll add code to the project that makes each of these buttons change the color scheme of the form. First, you'll add the code that sets the colors to the Win95 default: light gray.

Standards Colors

First, create a Visual Basic constant to represent the hex value for light gray, white, and black. Here's the code:

```
Option Explicit

'
' constant for colors
Const LIGHT_GRAY = &HC0C0C0
Const WHITE = &HFFFFFF
Const BLACK = &H0
```

Next, add a new procedure, `SetColors`, which sets the colors of the form. Because you'll be using this code to set more than one color scheme, add a parameter called nSet to the procedure header. You only have one set right now, but you'll add others soon. The following code sets the BackColor property of the form and data control to light gray:

```
Sub SetColors (nSet As Integer)
    '
    ' set to default colors
    If nSet = 0 Then
        pnlDisplayOnly.BackColor = LIGHT_GRAY
        pnlPalette.BackColor = LIGHT_GRAY
        frmColor.BackColor = LIGHT_GRAY
        Data1.BackColor = LIGHT_GRAY
        '
        txtOneLine.BackColor = WHITE
        txtOneLine.ForeColor = BLACK
    End If
End Sub
```

Finally, add a single line of code to the Default command button to execute the `SetColors` procedure.

```
Sub cmdDefault_Click ()
    SetColors 0
End Sub
```

Save and run the project. You'll now see that the background for the form and the data control are set to light gray when you click the Default button. The form now meets the default color standards for Win95 forms.

Custom Colors

You may want to set your own customized colors for your form. The following code will do just that. Suppose you want the background to appear in red and the text to appear in blue.

First, add the constants for blue and red to your declaration section:

```
Option Explicit

'
' constant for colors
Const LIGHT_GRAY = &HC0C0C0
Const WHITE = &HFFFFFF
Const BLACK = &H0
Const BLUE = &H800000
Const RED = &H80
```

Next, modify the `SetColors` procedure to include your new colors. Notice that you now need to set both the ForeColor and the BackColor properties of all the controls along with the BackColor of the form itself. This time, you'll set the colors to the custom set if the parameter is set to 1. Here's the code:

```
Sub SetColors (nSet As Integer)
    '
    ' set to default colors
    If nSet = 0 Then
        pnlDisplayOnly.BackColor = LIGHT_GRAY
        pnlPalette.BackColor = LIGHT_GRAY
        frmColor.BackColor = LIGHT_GRAY
        Data1.BackColor = LIGHT_GRAY
        '
        txtOneLine.BackColor = WHITE
        txtOneLine.ForeColor = BLACK
    End If
    '
    ' set to custom colors
    If nSet = 1 Then
        pnlDisplayOnly.BackColor = RED
        pnlPalette.BackColor = RED
        frmColor.BackColor = RED
        Data1.BackColor = RED
        '
        txtOneLine.BackColor = WHITE
        txtOneLine.ForeColor = BLUE
    End If
End Sub
```

Now, add the following code to the Custom button:

```
Sub cmdCustom_Click ()
    SetColors 1
End Sub
```

Save and run the program to see the results. Not such a good color scheme, you say? Well, some may like your custom setting; some may want to keep the default setting. Now you can select the scheme you want with a click of the mouse!

System Colors

As you can see in the previous code example, some people's ideas of a color scheme can be less than perfect. Many programmers add routines to allow users to customize the color scheme to their own taste. The easiest way to do this is to let Windows set the color scheme for you. The code example that follows uses the color scheme selected via the Windows 95 Display applet. This is an excellent way to give your users the power to customize their application color without writing a lot of Visual Basic code.

There are several Windows constants for the system colors that are set by the Control Panel program. For this example, you'll use only three. The following code shows a modified declaration section with the Windows system color constants added:

```
Option Explicit

'
' constant for colors
```

```
Const LIGHT_GRAY = &HC0C0C0
Const WHITE = &HFFFFFF
Const BLACK = &H0
Const BLUE = &H800000
Const RED = &H80
'
' windows system color values
Const WINDOW_BACKGROUND = &H80000005      ' Window background.
Const WINDOW_TEXT = &H80000008            ' Text in windows.
Const APPLICATION_WORKSPACE = &H8000000C ' Background color of MDI apps
```

Next, you'll add code to the SetColors routine that sets the colors to the Windows system colors.

```
Sub SetColors (nSet As Integer)
    '
    ' set to default colors
    If nSet = 0 Then
       pnlDisplayOnly.BackColor = LIGHT_GRAY
       pnlPalette.BackColor = LIGHT_GRAY
       frmColor.BackColor = LIGHT_GRAY
       Data1.BackColor = LIGHT_GRAY
       '
       txtOneLine.BackColor = WHITE
       txtOneLine.ForeColor = BLACK
    End If
    '
    ' set to custom colors
    If nSet = 1 Then
       pnlDisplayOnly.BackColor = RED
       pnlPalette.BackColor = RED
       frmColor.BackColor = RED
       Data1.BackColor = RED
       '
       txtOneLine.BackColor = WHITE
       txtOneLine.ForeColor = BLUE
    End If
    '
    ' set to system colors
    If nSet = 2 Then
       pnlDisplayOnly.BackColor = APPLICATION_WORKSPACE
       pnlPalette.BackColor = APPLICATION_WORKSPACE
       frmColor.BackColor = APPLICATION_WORKSPACE
       Data1.BackColor = APPLICATION_WORKSPACE
       '
       txtOneLine.BackColor = WINDOW_BACKGROUND
       txtOneLine.ForeColor = WINDOW_TEXT
    End If
End Sub
```

Finally, add this line of code to the System button to activate the system color scheme:

```
Sub cmdSystem_Click ()
   SetColors 2
End Sub
```

Save and run the program. When you click the System button, you'll see the color scheme you selected in the Control Panel as the color scheme for this application. Now, while the program

is still running, start the Control Panel application and select a new color scheme for Windows. Your Visual Basic program instantly changes its own color scheme!

Summary

Today you have learned the following about creating data entry forms with Visual Basic bound data controls.

The Visual Basic data control has five database-related properties. Three refer to the *database* and two refer to the *dynaset*.

☐ The database properties of the Visual Basic data control are DatabaseName, which is used to select the database to access; Exclusive, which is used to prevent other users from opening the database; and ReadOnly, which is used to prevent your program from modifying the data in the database.

☐ The dynaset properties of the Visual Basic data control are Recordsource, which is used to select the data table within the database; and Options, which is used to set ReadOnly, DenyWrite, and AppendOnly properties to the dynaset.

The Visual Basic data control has three database-related methods:

☐ `Refresh` updates the data control after setting properties.

☐ `UpdateControls` reads values from the fields in the dynaset and writes those values to the related form controls.

☐ `UpdateRecord` reads values from the form controls and writes those values to the related fields in the dynaset.

The Visual Basic data control has three database-related events:

☐ `Reposition` occurs each time the record pointer is moved to a new record in the dynaset.

☐ `Validate` occurs each time the record pointer leaves the current record in the dynaset.

☐ `Error` occurs each time a database error occurs.

The Visual Basic bound form controls can be used to link form input and display controls to data fields in the database.

☐ The bound text box control is used for data entry on character and numeric data table fields.

☐ The bound label control is used for display-only character and numeric data table fields.

☐ The bound checkbox control is used for data entry on the Boolean data type field.

5

☐ The bound image control is used to display images stored in the binary data type field.

☐ The Three-D panel control behaves the same as the label control; the Three-D checkbox control behaves the same as a standard checkbox control.

You have also learned the following general rules for creating Visual Basic forms in the Windows 95 style:

☐ The default color is light gray for backgrounds.

☐ The Panel3D control is used to create a palette on which to place all other controls.

☐ The default font is 8-point sans serif, non-bold.

☐ Input areas should have a white background, and display areas should have a light gray background. Also, display areas should be recessed into the input palette.

☐ Frame controls are used to group related items on a form.

☐ All controls, including field prompts, should be left-justified. Field prompts should be written in mixed case and followed by a semicolon.

☐ The standard spacing and sizing of common controls should be as follows:

The control height is 330 twips.

The command button width is 1200 twips.

The vertical spacing between controls is 90 twips for related items and 210 twips for unrelated items.

The border widths (top, bottom, and side) should be 120 twips.

Finally, you learned how to write code that sets control colors to the Windows 95 default colors, how to create your own custom color scheme, and how to link your control colors to the color scheme selected with the Windows Control Panel Color applet.

Quiz

1. How do you establish a database name for a data control using Visual Basic code?

2. What property do you set to define a table in Visual Basic code?

3. What is the main difference between the UpdateControls and the UpdateRecord methods?

4. What two values can a bound checkbox produce?

5. What property do you use to bind a control to a field in a table?

6. What is the standard form color for Windows 95 applications? What is the standard color of the input areas? What is the standard color of display-only text? How are labels aligned?

Exercises

1. Write Visual Basic code to set the properties to open a database (named STUDENTS.MDB) for a data control named Data1.

2. Modify the code you wrote in the first exercise and set the properties to open a table (Addresses) in STUDENTS.MDB.

3. Modify the code you wrote in the second exercise by binding controls to the data fields in the Addresses table. Include fields for StudentID (which you should declare as cField1), Address (cField2), City (cField3), State (cField4), and Zip (cField5).

5

Input Validation

WEEK
1

Today you'll learn about one of the most important aspects of database programming—input validation. Validating user input *before* it is written to the database can improve the quality of the data stored in your tables. Good validation schemes can also make your program user friendly and, in many cases, can increase the speed at which users can enter valid data.

We'll cover several specific topics on input validation including the following:

- ☐ Field level validation versus form level validation
- ☐ How to speed data entry by filtering keyboard input
- ☐ How to use input masks to give users hints when entering data
- ☐ How to limit user choices and speed input with validation lists
- ☐ How to handle required field inputs in Windows forms
- ☐ How to handle conditional field input validation in Windows forms

After you learn how to develop input validation routines, you will build a validation library. This library will have seven valuable routines that you can use in your projects throughout the book. Because these routines are designed to be reuseable, you will be able to use them in any project you build in the future.

Also, today is the day you build the main data entry form for the CompanyMaster database you created earlier in the week. You'll use all the techniques you've learned this week, including the use of bound data controls and input validation to build a solid data entry form.

Before you get into the details of how to perform input validation, let's first talk about what input validation is and why it is so important to good database application design.

What is Input Validation?

Input validation is the process of checking the data entered by the user *before* that data is saved to the database. Input validation is a proactive process—it happens while data is being entered. Input validation is not the same thing as error trapping. Error trapping is a reactive process—it happens after the data has been entered. This is an important point. Input validation should be used to prevent errors. If you have good input validation schemes, you'll have fewer errors to trap! You'll learn more about the reactive process on Day 14, "Error Trapping."

Input validation can be used to give users guides on how to enter valid data. The best example of this kind of input validation is the use of a validation list. A validation list is a list of valid inputs for a field. If the user has only a limited number of possible valid choices for an input field, there is much less chance of a data entry error occurring. Good validation schemes give the user a list of valid input from which to choose while performing data entry.

Input validation can automatically edit data as the user enters it, instead of telling the user to fix invalid entries. For example, if the data entry for a field must be all in capital letters, the

program should automatically convert lowercase characters to uppercase instead of waiting until the user enters mixed case, and then reporting an error and forcing the user to reenter the data.

Input validation reaches beyond the individual keystroke and field. It is also important to validate data at the form level. Input validation schemes should make sure that all required fields on a form are completed properly. If you have several fields that must be filled with valid data before the record can be saved to the database, you must have a method for checking those fields before you allow the user to attempt to save the record.

Conditional input fields must be validated, too. A conditional field is slightly different from a required field. Usually conditional fields occur when a user has checked a Yes/No box and then must enter additional data to complete the process. For example, if the user indicates on a form that the customer requests all products to be shipped instead of picked up, input validation should make sure that valid data has been entered into the shipping address fields. Another example of conditional field validation is when entering a value in one field requires that the value in another field be within a certain range. For example, if the customer's credit limit is above $50,000, you must enter a valid credit-worthiness code of 5 or above. In this case, the two fields must be checked against one another and verified before the user can save the record to the database.

As you can see from the preceding examples, input validation is more than just making sure the data entered in a field is correct. Input validation should be viewed as a set of rules to ensure that quality data is entered into the system. Before you begin writing your data entry forms, you should spend time developing a comprehensive set of validation rules. Once you develop these rules, you will be ready to start creating your data entry form.

Common Input Validation Rules

Almost every field in your database will require some type of input validation. Before you design your form, put together a list of all the fields you will need on the form and answer the following questions for each input field:

- [ ] Must data be entered in the field? (Is it a required field?)
- [ ] What characters are valid/invalid for this field? (Numeric input only, capital letters only, no spaces allowed, and so on.)
- [ ] For numeric fields, is there a high/low range limit? (Must be greater than zero and less than 1000, can't be less than 100, and so on.)
- [ ] Is there a list of valid values for this field? (Can user only enter Retail, Wholesale, or Other; Name must already be in the Customer table, and so on.)
- [ ] Is this a conditional field? (If users enter Yes in field A, then they must enter something in field C.)

Even though each data entry form is unique, you can use some general guidelines when putting together input validation schemes.

☐ If possible, limit keystrokes to valid values only. For example, if the field must be numeric, don't allow the user to enter character values. If spaces are not allowed, make sure the space bar is disabled. Help the user by limiting the kinds of data that can be entered into the field.

☐ Limit input choices with lists. If there is a limited set of valid inputs for a field, give the user a pick list or set of radio buttons to choose from.

☐ Inform the user of range limits. If a field has a high or low range limit, tell the user what the limits are.

☐ Point out required fields on a form. Mark required fields with a leading asterisk (*) or some other appropriate character. Possibly change the background color of required fields.

☐ Group conditional fields together on the form. If entering Yes in one field means that several other fields must be completed, put the additional fields close to the Yes/No field to help the user. Keep conditional fields of this type disabled until the Yes/No flag has been set. This will help the user see that new fields must be entered.

Field Level Validation

The first level of validation is at the field level. This is the place where you can make sure the user is entering the right characters in the field, entering the data into the field in the proper format, and entering a valid value based on a list of possible choices.

For the rest of this section, you'll be building a sample application that illustrates the various input validation methods this chapter will cover. If you haven't done so already, start up Visual Basic 4 and create a new project. Set the caption of the form to Input Validation, save the form as INPVAL.FRM, and save the project as INPVAL.VBP.

Filtering Keyboard Input

One of the easiest ways to perform input validation is to filter keyboard input. Filtering keyboard input requires capturing the keystrokes of the user *before* they appear on the screen and filtering out the keystrokes you do not want to appear in the input controls. You can filter invalid or undesirable keystrokes by creating a beep for the user each time an invalid key is pressed (beep each time a letter is pressed in a numeric field). You can also convert the invalid key to a valid one (change lowercase to uppercase). Or you can simply ignore the keystroke completely and prevent the invalid values from ever appearing in the input control.

Tip: Keep in mind that not all your potential users may be able to hear an audible beep and could become confused at the inability to input data. Windows 95 has several useful Accessibility Options that you may want to review, including the use of message boxes for the hearing-impaired.

For the first keyboard filtering example, you will build an input control that only accepts numerals zero through nine. First, add a label control and a text box control to the form. Set the caption property of the label control to Numbers. Set the Name property of the text box control to txtNumber and set the text property to blank. Your form should resemble the one in Figure 6.1.

Figure 6.1.
Adding the Numbers input control.

Save and run the program. You can enter any type of data in the text box that you wish— numbers, letters, spaces, and so on. Now you'll add a small bit of code that will filter out all but the numerals zero through nine. You'll do this by using the text box control KeyPress event.

The KeyPress event occurs each time a user presses a key while the field has the focus. Each time a key is pressed while the cursor is in the text box control, the ASCII value of the key is sent to the KeyPress event where you can evaluate it and act accordingly.

Note: Each key on the keyboard has an ASCII (American Standard Code for Information Interchange) numeric value. Your Visual Basic 4 documentation has a list of the ASCII codes for each key on the keyboard.

In this example, you want to ignore any keystroke that is not a 0, 1, 2, 3, 4, 5, 6, 7, 8, or 9. To do this, you need to add a small bit of code (see Listing 6.1) to the KeyPress event of the txtNumbers text box.

Listing 6.1. Limiting data entry in the Keypress event.

```
Sub txtNumbers_KeyPress (KeyAscii As Integer)
   Dim cValid As String
   '
   cValid = "0123456789"
   '
   If InStr(cValid, Chr(KeyAscii)) = 0 Then
      KeyAscii = 0
   End If
End Sub
```

In Listing 6.1, you declared a string variable that holds the list of valid keys. The next line loads the string with the valid keys for this field, and the next line checks to see whether the key pressed is in the string of valid keys. It does this by converting the numeric value passed by Visual Basic 4 in the KeyAscii parameter (the ASCII value of the key pressed) into a readable character using the Visual Basic 4 Chr function and searching for the result in the list of valid keys in the cValid string. If the key pressed is not in the cValid string, the keystroke is set to zero. Setting the keystroke to zero is telling Visual Basic 4 to pretend nothing was ever typed!

Now save and run the program. No matter what keys you type, only the numerals zero through nine appear in the text box. You have filtered out all but numerals. You may also notice that keystrokes, such as the backspace and delete keys, no longer work! You've told Visual Basic 4 to ignore them. You can fix that by adding a statement that checks to see whether the keystroke is a control code. Control codes are used in Visual Basic 4 to indicate that the key the user pressed was not a printable character but a keyboard control character. Common control characters are the Escape key, the Return key, the Backspace key, and so on.

You can also add any other characters to the validity list if you like. For example, you probably want to be able to enter a minus sign, a plus sign, and a decimal point in this number field. To do this, all you need to do is add those three characters to the cValid string. Your program code should now look like Listing 6.2.

Listing 6.2. The KeyPress event with control characters.

```
Sub txtNumbers_KeyPress (KeyAscii As Integer)
   Dim cValid As String
   '
   cValid = "0123456789+-."
   '
   If KeyAscii > 26 Then ' if it's not a control code
      If InStr(cValid, Chr(KeyAscii)) = 0 Then
         KeyAscii = 0
      End If
   End If
End Sub
```

Notice that in Listing 6.2, you have first tested to see whether the key pressed was greater than 26. ASCII code 26 is the last Visual Basic 4 control code. The routine in Listing 6.2 now skips over filtering of control codes. When you save and run the program, you will be able to pass the plus, minus, and decimal point characters into the text box, too.

Now let's create validation code that only accepts uppercase characters. This will be a bit trickier. Instead of ignoring lowercase input, you'll convert it to uppercase, and then pass it through to the text box.

First add another label and text box control. Set the label caption to Uppercase. Set the Name property of the text box to txtUpper and set the text property to blank. Your form should look like the one in Figure 6.2.

Figure 6.2.
Adding the Uppercase control and conversion to the form.

The code needed for the txtUpper `KeyPress` event is in Listing 6.3. Notice that if the keystroke is not an uppercase letter, instead of setting the Visual Basic 4 KeyAscii parameter to zero (discarding it), this routine converts it to an uppercase value by subtracting 32 from the ASCII value.

Listing 6.3. The `KeyPress` event to force letters to uppercase.

```
Sub txtUpper_KeyPress (KeyAscii As Integer)
   If Chr(KeyAscii) >= "a" And Chr(KeyAscii) <= "z" Then
      KeyAscii = KeyAscii - 32
   End If
End Sub
```

When you save and run the program you'll see that any letter key you enter converts to an uppercase letter and passes through to the text box.

The two types of keyboard filters illustrated here (discard or convert) can be combined to form a powerful input validation tool. Let's create a validation example that allows only uppercase letters A through Z or numerals zero through nine—no spaces or any other characters.

First add a new label/text box control pair. Set the label caption property to Combined. Set the text box name property to txtCombined and the text property to blank. Refer to Figure 6.3 for positioning and sizing.

Figure 6.3.

Adding the Combined control to the form.

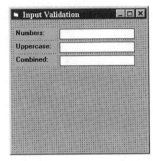

Listing 6.4 shows how to combine a check against a valid list and a conversion of keystrokes into a single input validation.

Listing 6.4. A single `KeyPress` event to check for valid entry and force uppercase.

```
Sub txtCombined_KeyPress (KeyAscii As Integer)
   Dim cValid As String
   '
   cValid = "0123456789"
   '
   If KeyAscii > 26 Then ' it's not a control code
      If InStr(cValid, Chr(KeyAscii)) = 0 Then
         If Chr(KeyAscii) >= "a" And Chr(KeyAscii) <= "z" Then
            KeyAscii = KeyAscii - 32
         Else
            KeyAscii = 0
         End If
      End If
   End If
End Sub
```

Input Masking

It is very common to have fields on your form that require special input formats. Examples of special formats would be telephone numbers, US social security numbers, hour/minute time entry, and so on. Visual Basic 4 ships with a bound data control that handles special input and display formatting—the MaskedEdit control. The MaskedEdit control works like the standard Visual Basic 4 text box control, with a few added properties that make it a powerful tool for your input validation arsenal.

Let's add a phone number input field to the form. Add a new label to the form and set its caption property to Phone. Now add a MaskedEdit control to the form. Set its Name property to mskPhone, the Mask property to (###) ###-#### and the PromptInclude property to False.

> **Tip:** It is essential that you set the PromptInclude property to False when using the MaskedEdit control as a bound control. If the PromptInclude property is set to True, you will get a database error each time you add a new record to the table or attempt to save or read a record that has a null value in the data field linked to the MaskedEdit bound control.

Your form should resemble Figure 6.4.

Figure 6.4.
Adding the MaskedEdit Phone control to the form.

The Masked Edit control button ⟶

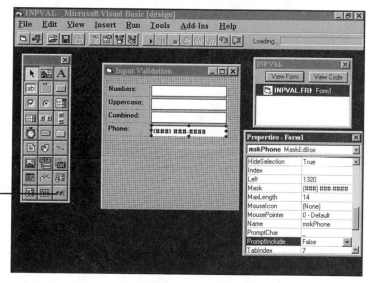

You do not need to add any additional filtering to the control because the MaskedEdit control makes sure that only digits are entered and that the input is limited to 10 digits formatted as a standard US phone number.

Save and run the program. You can see that when the control is initialized, the phone number mask is displayed. When the MaskedEdit control receives the focus, a series of underlines appear as an input guide for the user. The underlines disappear when control is given to an object other than the MaskedEdit control.

Note: The formatting characters of the MaskedEdit control are *not* saved to the database field when the PromptInclude property is set to False. This means that in the previous example, only the phone number digits would be saved to the data table, not the parentheses or the dash.

The Visual Basic 4 MaskedEdit control offers an extensive set of input masking tools. It ships with several input masks predefined, including dollar amounts, US phone numbers, and several date and time formats. To view these formats, select the MaskedEdit control, click the right (alternate) mouse button, and select Properties from the menu that appears. You will find the formats on the General tab.

You can also create custom input format masks for inventory part numbers, e-mail addresses, and so on. Although we won't cover all the possibilities here, there is one other MaskedEdit format option that you will illustrate on your form in this lesson because it is very useful when displaying dollar amounts.

The MaskedEdit control gives you the power to add a *display* mask in addition to an *input* mask. Up to this point, you have been using the input mask capabilities of the MaskedEdit control. Now let's add a control that shows the display capabilities, too.

Add another label control and another MaskedEdit control to the form. Set the label caption property to Dollars. Set the MaskedEdit control name property to mskDollars and the format property to `$#,##0.00;($#,##0.00)`.

Tip: The MaskedEdit display property actually has three parts, each separated by the semicolon (;). Part one determines how positive values will be displayed. Part two determines how negative values will be displayed. Part three determines how zero values will be displayed.

This property affects the display of the data, not the input, so you will not see any input guides when you set the format property or when you save and run the program. Your form should look like the one in Figure 6.5.

Now run the program and enter a numeric value in the Dollars text box. When you leave the text box to go to another control, you'll see the MaskedEdit control format the display of the amount you entered. Your screen should resemble Figure 6.6. Please note that two decimal places will always appear to the right of the decimal.

Figure 6.5.

Adding the Dollar control to the form.

Figure 6.6.

The display results of the MaskedEdit control.

Validation Lists

One of the most common field level input validation routines is the use of a validation list. The list contains a set of possible inputs for the field—usually displayed in a list box or a drop-down list control. Instead of having to guess at a valid value, the user can simply scan the list and click on the proper choice. Validation lists require a bit more programming to use, but the rewards far exceed the effort. Using validation lists virtually guarantees that you will not have a data entry error occur on the input field.

Before you can use a validation list for input validation, you must first have a list. It is usually a good idea to load any validation lists you need for a form at the time you load the form. This means that validation lists should be loaded in the Form_Load event. Let's add some code to your project that loads a drop-down list box with a list of possible customer types.

First add another label and a drop-down combo control to the form. Set the label caption to CustType, and set the drop-down combo box Name property to cboCustType and the Style property to 2—DropDown List. Your form should look like the one in Figure 6.7.

Note: You cannot change the height of the combo box control in Visual Basic 4. It is set at 300 twips and cannot be updated.

Figure 6.7.
*Adding the DropDown List
control to the form.*

Now add Listing 6.5 to load the list box with valid values.

Listing 6.5. The form load event to load a list box.

```
Sub Form_Load ()
    '
    ' load dropdown list box
    cboCustType.AddItem "Retail"
    cboCustType.AddItem "Wholesale"
    cboCustType.AddItem "Distributor"
    cboCustType.AddItem "Other"
End Sub
```

In Listing 6.5, you are adding values directly to the list using program code. Each `AddItem` method adds an additional valid selection to the list. You could also load the control with values from a data table. This would give you a more dynamic list of valid values. For now, stick to the direct load example here; later in this book, you will add validation lists loaded from data tables.

Now save and run the program. You can now click on the down arrow of the drop-down list box and see the list of valid values. Now the user can't help but pick a correct item for the input field.

Up to this point, you have been developing methods for handling field level validation. The next step is to add validation routines at the form level.

Form Level Validation

Form level validation is an essential part of designing a good validation scheme for your form. Although many input errors can be caught and corrected at the field level, there are several validation steps that can only be performed well at the form level.

Although field level validation is performed at the time a key is pressed or at the time a field loses focus, form level validation is performed at the time the user presses Enter, or clicks the OK or Save button. These are validations that are done after all fields have been entered by the user, but *before* any attempt is made to store the values to a data table.

Form level validation can be divided into three groups:

☐ Independent content validation
☐ Required field validation
☐ Dependent field validation

Now let's look at each type of form level validation.

Independent Content Validation: High/Low Ranges

A common form level validation routine is one that checks the upper and lower values of a numeric entry and makes sure the value is within the high/low range. This is very useful on all types of forms that have dollar amounts or unit count minimum and maximum values.

Note: Although it might seem that this kind of validation should be done at the field level, it is better to perform it at the form level. If a user enters a value that is not within the acceptable range, the field that contains the invalid data must be given focus so that the user can correct the entry. Setting the control's focus is best done outside of any other control's GotFocus or LostFocus event. Also, because a user can use the mouse to skip over any field on the form, placing independent content validation routines within the controls' events means that users may skip important validation steps in the process.

To set up the form level validation, first add a single command button to the form. Set its Name property to cmdOK and its caption property to &OK. Now add another label/text box pair to the form. Set the label caption to High/Low. Set the text box Name property to txtHighLow and the text property to blank. Refer to Figure 6.8 for sizing and placement.

Figure 6.8.
Adding the High/Low control and OK button to the form.

Next add Listing 6.6 to the `cmdOK_click` event.

Listing 6.6. The form level validation routine to check for values in a range.

```
Sub cmdOK_Click ()
    Dim nHigh As Integer
    Dim nLow As Integer
    '
    nHigh = 100
    nLow = 1
    '
    If Val(txtHighLow) < nLow Or Val(txtHighLow) > nHigh Then
        MsgBox "High/Low field must contain a value between " +
        ➥Str(nLow) + " and " + Str(nHigh)
        txtHighLow.SetFocus
    Else
        Unload Me
    End If
End Sub
```

The code in Listing 6.6 establishes the integer variables for the high and low range, sets them to 100 and 1 respectively, and then checks the value entered into the txtHighLow text control. If the value is out of the allowed range, a message is displayed, and the input cursor is moved back to the field that contains the invalid data. Notice that the message not only tells the user that the data is invalid, it also tells the user what values are acceptable. If the data entered is within range, the program exits normally.

Now save and run the program. If you skip to the OK button without entering data or enter data outside the allowed range, you'll see the validation message.

Independent Content Validation: Min/Max Field Lengths

Another common form level validation step is to make sure that character strings meet the minimum or maximum length requirements. This is done in the same way numeric values are checked for high and low ranges.

Let's add input validation to ensure that the Uppercase text box you placed on the form earlier is no longer than 10 characters, and at least 3 characters in length. You just need to add the code in Listing 6.7 to the `cmdOK_click` event that checks the txtUpper field for length.

Listing 6.7. The form level validation routine to check the length of fields and a valid range of values.

```
Sub cmdOK_Click ()
    Dim nHigh As Integer
    Dim nLow As Integer
```

```
    Dim nMinLen As Integer
    Dim nMaxLen As Integer
    Dim nOK As Integer
    '
    nHigh = 100
    nLow = 1
    nMinLen = 3
    nMaxLen = 10
    nOK = True
    '
    ' check highlow field
    If Val(txtHighLow) < nLow Or Val(txtHighLow) > nHigh Then
        MsgBox "High/Low field must contain a value between " +
        ➥ Str(nLow) + " and " + Str(nHigh)
        nOK = False
        txtHighLow.SetFocus
    End If
    '
    ' check upper field
    If Len(txtUpper) < nMinLen Or Len(txtUpper) > nMaxLen Then
        MsgBox "Upper field must be between " + Str(nMinLen) +
        ➥" and " + Str(nMaxLen) + " long."
        nOK = False
        txtUpper.SetFocus
    End If
    '
    ' see if it's all ok
    If nOK = True Then
        Unload Me
    End If
End Sub
```

In Listing 6.7, you added variables for the minimum and maximum length of the entry field and a flag variable to show that all validation steps passed. Notice that you changed the structure of the validation steps from a simple If…Then…Else to a series of If…Then routines. If the validation does not pass, a flag is set to make sure the form does not unload.

Save and run the form to test the validation rule. You'll see that now both form level validation rules must be met before the form will unload.

Note: The txtUpper field has both field level and form level validation rules applied to it. The field level routine executes when data is entered into the field. The form level validation routine executes when this data record is saved. It is perfectly acceptable, and sometimes recommended, to have both field level and form level validation for the same control.

6

Required Fields

Almost every form has at least one field that is required input. Some forms may have several. Checking for required input fields is done at the form level. Let's add code at the `cmdOK_Click` event that makes sure that users fill out the Combined field every time.

All you need to do is validate that the txtCombined field contains valid data. Listing 6.8 shows how this is done.

Listing 6.8. The form level validation routine to check for required fields.

```
Sub cmdOK_Click ()
    Dim nHigh As Integer
    Dim nLow As Integer
    Dim nMinLen As Integer
    Dim nMaxLen As Integer
    Dim nOK As Integer
    '
    nHigh = 100
    nLow = 1
    nMinLen = 3
    nMaxLen = 10
    nOK = True
    '
    ' check highlow field
    If Val(txtHighLow) < nLow Or Val(txtHighLow) > nHigh Then
        MsgBox "High/Low field must contain a value between " +
        ➥Str(nLow) + " and " + Str(nHigh)
        nOK = False
        txtHighLow.SetFocus
    End If
    '
    ' check upper field
    If Len(txtUpper) < nMinLen Or Len(txtUpper) > nMaxLen Then
        MsgBox "Upper field must be between " + Str(nMinLen) + "
        ➥and " + Str(nMaxLen) + " long."
        nOK = False
        txtUpper.SetFocus
    End If
    '
    ' check combined field
    If Len(Trim(txtCombined)) = 0 Then
        MsgBox "Combined field is a required field"
        nOK = False
        txtCombined.SetFocus
    End If
    '
    ' see if it's all ok
    If nOK = True Then
        Unload Me
    End If
End Sub
```

The only change you made is to check the length of the string in the txtCombined text box. If the result is zero, an error message is displayed. Notice the use of the Trim function to remove any trailing or leading spaces from the txtCombined string. This makes sure that users who enter blank spaces into the field will not get past the validation step.

Conditional Fields

There are times when entering a value in one field of the form means that other fields on the form must also contain valid data. Fields of this type are called conditional fields. A good example of a conditional field validation can be found in an order tracking system. For example, when a user enters Yes in the Ship to Site? field, he then must enter a valid value in the Shipping Address field. The Shipping Address field is a conditional field because its validation is based on the condition of the Ship to Site? field.

Now add a conditional validation to the project. Make the field CustType conditional to the field Upper. In other words, if the Upper field contains data, then the CustType field must contain data. See Listing 6.9 for an example of how to do this.

Listing 6.9. The form level conditional validation routine.

```
Sub cmdOK_Click ()
    Dim nHigh As Integer
    Dim nLow As Integer
    Dim nMinLen As Integer
    Dim nMaxLen As Integer
    Dim nOK As Integer
    '
    nHigh = 100
    nLow = 1
    nMinLen = 3
    nMaxLen = 10
    nOK = True
    '
    ' check highlow field
    If Val(txtHighLow) < nLow Or Val(txtHighLow) > nHigh Then
        MsgBox "High/Low field must contain a value between " +
        ➥Str(nLow) + " and " + Str(nHigh)
        nOK = False
        txtHighLow.SetFocus
    End If
    '
    ' check upper field
    If Len(txtUpper) < nMinLen Or Len(txtUpper) > nMaxLen Then
        MsgBox "Upper field must be between " + Str(nMinLen) +
        ➥" and " + Str(nMaxLen) + " long."
        nOK = False
        txtUpper.SetFocus
    End If
    '
```

continues

Listing 6.9. continued

```
' check combined field
If Len(Trim(txtCombined)) = 0 Then
  MsgBox "Combined field is a required field"
  nOK = False
  txtCombined.SetFocus
End If
'
' check conditional upper/custtype fields
If Len(Trim(txtUpper)) <> 0 And Len(Trim(cboCustType)) = 0 Then
  MsgBox "If Upper field contains data then the
  ➥CustType field must contain data"
  nOK = False
  cboCustType.SetFocus
End If
'
' see if it's all ok
If nOK = True Then
  Unload Me
End If
End Sub
```

Save and run the program. Now you must enter valid data in both fields before the form will unload. You have probably also found out that each time you click the OK button, all the form level validation steps are performed. It is good programming practice to deliver all the validation results to the user at once. It can be very frustrating to fill out a form, receive an error message, and then fix the message, only to receive another one, and another one, and so on.

Creating Generic Validation Routines

The input validation routines you have created today cover most of the situations you are likely to encounter when designing data entry forms. In fact, after you design one or two of these forms, you'll begin to see that you are writing the same validation code over and over again. Instead of repeatedly writing the same code, or even constantly performing cut, copy, and paste operations, you can modify these routines slightly and create a reusable set of validation routines that can be plugged into all your data entry programs.

Before you build the CompanyMaster data entry form, you need to build an Input Validation Library module. This module can be used for the CompanyMaster and any other data entry form you design in the future.

Creating a Global BAS Module

The first step in writing a reusable library routine is to open a Visual Basic code module—often called a BAS module (pronounced *bass*—like the fish). This module will contain procedures and

functions that can be called from any form or code module. To create a new BAS module, select Insert I Module or click on the module button of the tool bar. This opens a code window with a default name of MODULEX.BAS, where X is a number starting at one (see Figure 6.9).

Figure 6.9.
Opening a Visual Basic
BAS module.

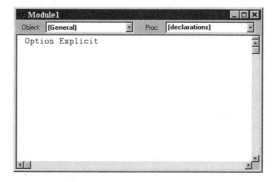

For now, save this empty module as LIBVALID.BAS. This is where you can build all your generic input validation routines.

Adding a New Function to the Library

The next step in building a library is adding a new function that can be called from any Visual Basic 4 program. Let's create a keyboard filter function that only allows numeric values to pass through to the underlying control.

The first thing you have to do is create the function header and footer. Use Insert I Procedure to create a new function called KeyNumbers (see Figure 6.10).

Figure 6.10.
Creating a new function for
the LIBVALID.BAS library.

Now, enter the code in Listing 6.10 to build the function. The code in the KeyNumbers routine is almost identical to the code you wrote earlier in this chapter for the txtNumbers field (see Listing 6.1).

A few things are different from the original validation routine in Listing 6.1. First, the function now has a passed parameter—nKeyValue. This is the ASCII value of the key the user presses. Second, the last line of code sets the function return value. The rest of the code is unchanged.

Listing 6.10. The `KeyNumbers` field level validation function.

```
Function KeyNumbers (nKeyValue As Integer) As Integer
   Dim cValid As String
      '
   cValid = "0123456789+-."
      '
   If nKeyValue > 26 Then ' if it's not a control code
      If InStr(cValid, Chr(nKeyValue)) = 0 Then
         nKeyValue = 0
      End If
   End If
   KeyNumbers = nKeyValue
End Function
```

The last thing you need to do is replace the code in the `txtNumbers_KeyPress` event with a call to the new `KeyNumbers` function.

```
Sub txtNumbers_KeyPress (KeyAscii As Integer)
   KeyAscii = KeyNumbers(KeyAscii)
End Sub
```

The preceding code excerpt gets executed each time the user presses a key in the txtNumbers text box. Each time a key is pressed, a call is made to the `KeyNumbers` function. The `KeyNumbers` function filters out all keystrokes except control codes and numeric input. Save and run the program to test the `KeyNumbers` function.

The *KeyUpper* Library Function

Now add another validation function to the library that forces all letters to uppercase. Call the function `KeyUpper`. Listing 6.11 shows how the function should look.

Listing 6.11. The `KeyUpper` field level function to force uppercase letters.

```
Function KeyUpper (nKeyValue As Integer) As Integer
      '
   If Chr(nKeyValue) >= "a" And Chr(nKeyValue) <= "z" Then
      nKeyValue = nKeyValue - 32
   End If
      '
   KeyUpper = nKeyValue ' set the return value
End Function
```

The KeyUpper function takes a single ASCII key value as an input parameter and scans the value to see if it is a lowercase letter. If it is, the routine converts the value to an uppercase letter. Finally, KeyUpper returns the key value as an output parameter.

The following lines replace the code you wrote earlier (see Listing 6.3) in the txtUpper_KeyPress event.

```
Sub txtUpper_KeyPress (KeyAscii As Integer)
   KeyAscii = KeyUpper(KeyAscii)
End Sub
```

Save and run the program to test the new KeyUpper function.

The *KeyUpperNumber* Library Function

Listing 6.12 contains the library function to handle uppercase or numeric input. Create a new function KeyUpperNumber and enter the following code.

Listing 6.12. The KeyUpperNumber function to force uppercase letters and pass control codes.

```
Function KeyUpperNumber (nKeyValue As Integer) As Integer
   '
   ' passes uppercase letters
   ' converts lowercase to uppercase
   ' passes 0123456789 and control codes
   ' rejects all else
   '
   If nKeyValue > 26 Then
      If Chr(nKeyValue) >= "a" And Chr(nKeyValue) <= "z" Then
         nKeyValue = nKeyValue - 32
      End If
      '
      If Chr(nKeyValue) >= "A" And Chr(nKeyValue) <= "Z" Then
         nKeyValue = nKeyValue
      Else
         nKeyValue = KeyNumbers(nKeyValue)
      End If
   End If
   KeyUpperNumber = nKeyValue
End Function
```

The new function, KeyUpperNumber, ignores control codes, converts lowercase letters to uppercase, and passes numeric characters. Replace the existing code (entered from Listing 6.4) in the txtCombined_KeyPress event with the following code. Save and run the program.

```
Sub txtCombined_KeyPress (KeyAscii As Integer)
   KeyAscii = KeyUpperNumber(KeyAscii)
End Sub
```

6

The *InRange* Library Function

Now let's add a function to handle range validation for numeric fields. Create a new function called InRange and enter the code in Listing 6.13.

Listing 6.13. The InRange function to handle validation of numeric ranges.

```
Function InRange (ctlName As Control, cFieldName As String, vHigh As Variant,
➡ vLow As Variant, nMsg As Integer) As Integer
    '
    ' ctlName     = name of control to check
    ' cFieldName  = name of field to display
    ' vHigh       = high end of range
    ' vLow        = low end of range
    ' nMsg        = flag to show message
    '
    If ctlName.Text < vLow Or ctlName.Text > vHigh Then
        If nMsg = True Then
            MsgBox cFieldName + " must be between " + Str(vLow) +
            ➡" and " + Str(vHigh), 0, "Validation Error"
        End If
        ctlName.SetFocus
        InRange = False
    Else
        InRange = True
    End If
End Function
```

A few things in the InRange function deserve attention. First, notice that the actual control is being passed to the function. This is done so that the function can invoke the SetFocus method. Notice also that not just the control name is passed—the form reference (Me) is passed also. This is required because the library functions have no idea what form is being used. You'll also see that all the numeric values are declared as Visual Basic 4 Variant type. This is done because you do not know whether the numeric values passed to InRange will be Integer, Single, Double, or Long. The Visual Basic 4 Variant type will handle any type it is given.

Finally, you added a parameter to control the display of an error message. Most of the time you will want to display an informative message to the user after an error is caught. However, there are times when you would rather not display an error. For example, when you want to test a single field for a combination of validations—such as when it must be within a range, *and* it is a dependent field—you may want to test for both, get the result, and display a single custom message instead of two messages.

Listing 6.14 shows how InRange is called. Place this in the cmdOK_Click event, and then save and run the project.

Listing 6.14. Calling the `InRange` function from the `cmdOK_Click` event.

```
Sub cmdOK_Click ()
    Dim nMinLen As Integer
    Dim nMaxLen As Integer
    Dim nOK As Integer
    '
    nMinLen = 3
    nMaxLen = 10
    nOK = True
    '
    ' check highlow field
    nOK = InRange(Me.txtHighLow, "HighLow", 100, 1,True)
    '
    ' check upper field
    If Len(txtUpper) < nMinLen Or Len(txtUpper) > nMaxLen Then
        MsgBox "Upper field must be between " + Str(nMinLen) + "
        ➥and " + Str(nMaxLen) + " long."
        nOK = False
        txtUpper.SetFocus
    End If
    '
    ' check combined field
    If Len(Trim(txtCombined)) = 0 Then
        MsgBox "Combined field is a required field"
        nOK = False
        txtCombined.SetFocus
    End If
    '
    ' check conditional upper/custtype fields
    If Len(Trim(txtUpper)) <> 0 And Len(Trim(cboCustType)) = 0 Then
        MsgBox "If Upper field contains data then the
        ➥CustType field must contain data"
nOK = False
        cboCustType.SetFocus
    End If
    '
    ' see if it's all ok
    If nOK = True Then
        Unload Me
    End If
End Sub
```

6

The following code was inserted into the `cmdOK_Click` event to call the `InRange` function:

```
nOK = InRange(Me.txtHighLow, "HighLow", 100, 1,True)
```

The first parameter passed, Me.txtHighLow, identifies the control to check. The Me is used in front of the control name to denote the current form. This is used, rather than the form name, to identify the currently active form in case there are multiple instances of the same form open.

The second parameter, HighLow, is the string that is passed to the error statement in case values entered into the field do not meet the specified range set by the vHigh (100) and vLow (1) parameters. Finally, the nMsg value is set to True to tell the InRange function to display a message box if an error occurs.

The *CheckSize* Library Function

The next function to add to the library is called CheckSize. This function receives the actual length of a data entry string and compares it to a minimum and maximum length. If either limit is exceeded, a message is displayed and the function returns False. If all is okay, the function simply returns True. Listing 6.15 contains the code for the CheckSize function.

Listing 6.15. The `CheckSize` function to check field length.

```
Function CheckSize (ctlName As Control, cFieldName As String, nMinLen As
➡ Integer, nMaxLen As Integer, nMsg As Integer) As Integer
   Dim nLen As Integer
   '
   ' ctlName     = name of control to check (including form)
   ' cFieldName = string name of field (for display)
   ' nMinLen     = minimum length of string
   ' nMaxLen     = maximum length of string
   ' nMsg        = flag to show message
   '
   nLen = Len(ctlName.Text)' get length for checking
   If nLen < nMinLen Or nLen > nMaxLen Then
      If nMsg = True Then
         MsgBox cFieldName + " must be between " + Str(nMinLen) + " and " +
         ➡Str(nMaxLen) + " bytes long.", 0, "Validation Error"
      End If
      ctlName.SetFocus
      CheckSize = False
   Else
      CheckSize = True
   End If
End Function
```

Listing 6.16 shows the updated cmdOK procedure that shows how CheckSize can be used.

Listing 6.16. The updated `cmdOK_Click` event that calls the `CheckSize` function.

```
Sub cmdOK_Click ()
   Dim nMinLen As Integer
   Dim nMaxLen As Integer
   Dim nOK As Integer
   '
   nMinLen = 3
   nMaxLen = 10
   nOK = True
   '
```

```
' check highlow field
nOK = InRange(Me.txtHighLow, "HighLow", 100, 1,True)
'
' check upper field
nOK = CheckSize(Me.txtUpper, "Upper", 3, 10,True)
'
' check combined field
If Len(Trim(txtCombined)) = 0 Then
   MsgBox "Combined field is a required field"
   nOK = False
   txtCombined.SetFocus
End If
'
' check conditional upper/custtype fields
If Len(Trim(txtUpper)) <> 0 And Len(Trim(cboCustType)) = 0 Then
   MsgBox "If Upper field contains data then the CustType
   ➥field must contain data"
   nOK = False
   cboCustType.SetFocus
End If
'
' see if it's all ok
If nOK = True Then
   Unload Me
End If
End Sub
```

The *IsValid* Library Function

The next function to add to the library is called IsValid. This function can be used to find required fields that have been left blank or are set to null. Listing 6.17 defines the IsValid function. Place this function in LIBVALID.BAS.

Listing 6.17. Code for the `IsValid` function to check for required fields left blank or set to null.

```
Function IsValid (ctlName As Control, cFieldName As String,
➥ nMsg As Integer) As Integer
   If Len(Trim(ctlName.Text)) = 0 Then
      If nMsg - True Then
         MsgBox cFieldName + " is a required field.", 0, "Validation Error"
      End If
      ctlName.SetFocus
      IsValid = False
   Else
      IsValid = True
   End If
End Function
```

Listing 6.18 shows how to call the IsValid function in a program.

Listing 6.18. The modified `cmdOK_Click` event to call the `IsValid` function.

```
Sub cmdOK_Click ()
   Dim nOK As Integer
   '
   nOK = True
   '
   ' check highlow field
   nOK = InRange(Me.txtHighLow, "HighLow", 100, 1, True)
   '
   ' check upper field
   nOK = CheckSize(Me.txtUpper, "Upper", 3, 10, True)
   '
   ' check combined field
   nOK = IsValid(Me.txtCombined, "Combined", True)
   '
   ' check conditional upper/custtype fields
   If Len(Trim(txtUpper)) <> 0 And Len(Trim(cboCustType)) = 0 Then
      MsgBox "If Upper field contains data then the
      ➥CustType field must contain data"
      nOK = False
      cboCustType.SetFocus
   End If
   '
   ' see if it's all ok
   If nOK = True Then
      Unload Me
   End If
End Sub
```

The *IsConditional* Library Function

The last validation function to add to the library is called IsConditional. This routine has two parameters—both Visual Basic 4 controls. The first is the control field; the second is the conditional field. If the control field is not blank, the conditional field must also not be blank. Refer to Listing 6.19 for the IsConditional function.

Listing 6.19. The `IsConditional` function to check for required entry if a conditional field is completed.

```
Function IsConditional (ctlMaster As Control, cFldMaster As String,
➥ ctlChild As Control, cFldChild As String, nMsg As Integer) As Integer
   Dim nMaster As Integer
   Dim nChild As Integer
   '
   ' ctlMaster  = master control
   ' cFldMaster = master field name
   ' ctlChild   = conditional control
```

```
      ' cFldChild  = conditional field name
      ' nMsg       = toggle to display message
      '
      nMaster = IsValid(ctlMaster, cFldMaster, False)
      nChild = IsValid(ctlChild, cFldChild, False)
      If nMaster And Not nChild Then
         If nMsg = True Then
            MsgBox "If " + cFldMaster + " is filled in then " +
            ➥cFldChild + " must be filled in."
            ctlChild.SetFocus
         End If
         IsConditional = False
      Else
         IsConditional = True
      End If
End Function
```

Notice that the IsConditional function calls the IsValid function with the messages toggled
False, and then analyzes and reports the results. Listing 6.20 is the final modification to the
cmdOK_Click procedure. This includes all the calls to the LIBVALID.BAS library file.

Listing 6.20. The modified cmdOK_Click event that calls the IsConditional function.

```
Sub cmdOK_Click ()
   Dim nOK As Integer
   '
   nOK = True
   '
   ' check highlow field
   nOK = InRange(Me.txtHighLow, "HighLow", 100, 1, True)
   '
   ' check upper field
   nOK = CheckSize(Me.txtUpper, "Upper", 3, 10, True)
   '
   ' check combined field
   nOK = IsValid(Me.txtCombined, "Combined", True)
   '
   ' check conditional upper/custtype fields
   nOK = IsConditional(Me.txtUpper, "Upper", Me.cboCustType, "CustType", True)
   '
   ' see if it's all ok
   If nOK = True Then
      Unload Me
   End If
End Sub
```

The preceding library code samples (Listing 6.10 through Listing 6.20) are meant to show how
you can build reuseable input validation routines and employ them in your data entry forms.
These routines are by no means an exhaustive list of what you might need or what is possible—

they're just a start. But these are useful basic routines that you can insert, modify, and build upon in any Visual Basic 4 project. By creating reuseable routines, you can take advantage of new concepts you learn on each project and incorporate the knowledge into future projects with very little modification.

Now that you have created an input validation library, you are finally ready to create the CompanyMaster data entry screen.

Building the CompanyMaster Input Form

Now that you've learned about data controls and form design in Day 5, "Creating Data Entry Forms with Bound Controls," and developed an input validation library in the first part of today's lesson, you are ready to design the first data entry form for the CompanyMaster data table you built on Day 3, "Using the Data Manager."

The following are four basic steps to coding data entry forms in Visual Basic 4:

- [ ] Definition of the basic form
- [ ] Placement of input controls and prompts
- [ ] Adding and coding command buttons
- [ ] Coding input validation

You can use these steps in coding any forms for Visual Basic 4. You'll follow these steps while you construct the CompanyMaster data entry form.

Definition of the Basic Form

The first step is to set the size of the data entry form, add the input palette, and add any frames needed. These are the basic components of the form. All other controls will be placed upon the palette within the frames you install in this step.

Tip: If you put the palette and frames up first, you can place all other controls as so-called children of the palette and frames. This way, when you move the frame, all controls within that frame will also move. The same thing happens when you move the large palette. Creating forms this way makes it easy to make slight adjustments later on.

At this time, you'll also add the data control and the final exit button to the form. Use the information in Table 6.1 and Figure 6.11 as a guide for sizing and placement of the basic form components. Save your form as Mast01.FRM, and save the project as Master.VBP.

Figure 6.11.

Basic form components for the CompanyMaster data entry form.

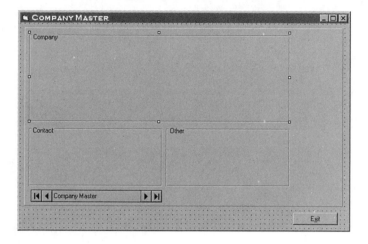

Table 6.1. CompanyMaster form components.

Object	Property	Setting
Form	Name	frmMaster
	BackColor	Light Gray
	Border Style	1—Fixed Single
	Caption	Company Master
	Height	5955
	Left	195
	Max Button	False
	Top	330
	Width	9105
	Save Filename	Mast01.FRM
SSPanel	Caption	"" (blank)
	Height	4815
	Left	120
	Top	120
	Width	8715

continues

Table 6.1. continued

Object	Property	Setting
Data Control	BackColor	Light Gray
	Caption	Company Master
	Databasename	C:\TYSDBVB\CHAP06\MASTER.MDB
	FontBold	False
	Height	330
	Left	300
	RecordSource	CompanyMaster
	Top	4500
	Width	3615
Command Button	Name	cmdExit
	Caption	E&xit
	FontBold	False
	Height	330
	Left	7500
	Top	5100
	Width	1200
SSFrame	Caption	Company
	FontBold	False
	Height	2355
	Left	120
	Top	180
	Width	7155
SSFrame	Caption	Contact
	FontBold	False
	Height	1635
	Left	120
	Top	2640
	Width	3675

Object	Property	Setting
SSFrame	Caption	Other
	FontBold	False
	Height	1635
	Left	3900
	Top	2640
	Width	3375

Placement of Input Controls and Prompts

Now you are ready to place the input controls on the form. Each input control has an associated screen prompt. All screen prompts are done using the Visual Basic 4 Label control. You'll use Text box, MaskedEdit, and Check3D controls for input fields. You will also use SSPanel3D controls for the read-only display fields.

Note: Do not double-click controls onto the form. Always single-click the control icon in the Tools window, and then use the mouse to paint the control within the proper frame control. This will make sure that the controls will be children of the frame control and will move whenever you move the frame. To play it safe, always select the panel by clicking on it prior to selecting a control to place on it.

Because you are using the Win 95 design specifications, you'll need to spend time aligning and sizing controls accordingly. All the information you need to properly size and place the controls is contained in Table 6.2 and Figure 6.12.

Table 6.2. CompanyMaster input controls and prompts.

Object	Property	Setting
Text Box	Name	txtCompanyName
	DataField	CompanyName
	DataSource	Data1
	FontBold	False

continues

Table 6.2. continued

Object	Property	Setting
	Height	330
	Left	1380
	Top	240
	Width	2100
Text Box	Name	txtAddr1
	DataField	Addr1
	DataSource	Data1
	FontBold	False
	Height	330
	Left	1380
	Top	660
	Width	2100
Text Box	Name	txtAddr2
	DataField	Addr2
	DataSource	Data1
	FontBold	False
	Height	330
	Left	1380
	Top	1080
Text Box	Name	txtCity
	DataField	City
	DataSource	Data1
	FontBold	False
	Height	330
	Left	1380
	Top	1500
	Width	2100
Text Box	Name	txtCountry
	DataField	Country
	DataSource	Data1
	FontBold	False

Object	Property	Setting
	Height	330
	Left	1380
	Top	1920
	Width	2100
SSPanel3D	Name	pnlEntryNbr
	Alignment	4—Right Just Middle
	BevelOuter	1—Inset
	BorderWidth	1
	DataField	EntryNbr
	DataSource	Data1
	FontBold	False
	Height	330
	Left	5160
	Top	240
	Width	1800
SSPanel3D	Name	pnlLastUpdated
	Alignment	4—Right Just Middle
	BevelOuter	1—Inset
	BorderWidth	1
	DataField	LastUpdated
	DataSource	Data1
	FontBold	False
	Height	330
	Left	5160
	Top	660
	Width	1800
SSCheck3D	Name	chkCustFlag
	Alignment	1—Right Justify
	Caption:	Customer Flag:
	DataField	CustFlag
	DataSource	Data1

6

continues

Table 6.2. continued

Object	Property	Setting
	FontBold	False
	Height	330
	Left	3900
	Top	1080
	Width	1455
Text Box	Name	txtStProv
	DataField	StateProv
	DataSource	Data1
	FontBold	False
	Height	330
	Left	5160
	Top	1500
	Width	1800
MaskEdBox	Name	mskPostCode
	DataField	PostalCode
	DataSource	Data1
	FontBold	False
	Height	330
	Left	5160
	Mask	#####-####
	PromptInclude	False
	Top	1920
	Width	1800
TextBox	Name	txtLastName
	DataField	LastName
	DataSource	Data1
	FontBold	False
	Height	330
	Left	1380
	Top	240
	Width	2100

Object	Property	Setting
TextBox	Name	txtFirstName
	DataField	FirstName
	DataSource	Data1
	FontBold	False
	Height	330
	Left	1380
	Top	660
	Width	2100
TextBox	Name	txtTitle
	DataField	Title
	DataSource	Data1
	FontBold	False
	Height	330
	Left	1380
	Top	1080
	Width	2100
MaskEdBox	Name	mskVoicePhone
	DataField	VoicePhone
	DataSource	Data1
	FontBold	False
	Height	330
	Left	1380
	Mask	(###) ###-####
	PromptInclude	False
	Top	240
	Width	1800
MaskEdBox	Name	mskExtension
	DataField	Extension
	DataSource	Data1
	FontBold	False
	Height	330

continues

163

Table 6.2. continued

Object	Property	Setting
	Left	1380
	Mask	####
	PromptInclude	False
	Top	660
	Width	1800
MaskEdBox	Name	mskFAXPhone
	DataField	FAXPhone
	DataSource	Data1
	FontBold	False
	Height	330
	Left	1380
	Mask	(###) ###-####
	PromptInclude	False
	Top	1080
	Width	1800
Label	Caption	Company Name:
	BackStyle	0—Transparent
	FontBold	False
	Height	330
	Left	120
	Top	240
	Width	1200
Label	Caption	Address Line1:
	BackStyle	0—Transparent
	FontBold	False
	Height	330
	Left	120
	Top	660
	Width	1200
Label	Caption	Address Line2:
	BackStyle	0—Transparent

Object	Property	Setting
	FontBold	False
	Height	330
	Left	120
	Top	1080
	Width	1200
Label	Caption	City:
	BackStyle	0—Transparent
	FontBold	False
	Height	330
	Left	120
	Top	1500
	Width	1200
Label	Caption	Country:
	BackStyle	0—Transparent
	FontBold	False
	Height	330
	Left	120
	Top	1920
	Width	1200
Label	Caption	Entry Number:
	BackStyle	0—Transparent
	FontBold	False
	Height	330
	Left	3900
	Top	240
	Width	1200
Label	Caption	Last Updated:
	BackStyle	0—Transparent
	FontBold	False
	Height	330
	Left	3900

continues

Table 6.2. continued

Object	Property	Setting
	Top	660
	Width	1200
Label	Caption	State/Prov:
	BackStyle	0—Transparent
	FontBold	False
	Height	330
	Left	3900
	Top	1500
	Width	1200
Label	Caption	Postal Code:
	BackStyle	0—Transparent
	FontBold	False
	Height	330
	Left	3900
	Top	1920
	Width	1200
Label	Caption	Last Name:
	BackStyle	0—Transparent
	FontBold	False
	Height	330
	Left	120
	Top	240
	Width	1200
Label	Caption	First Name:
	BackStyle	0—Transparent
	FontBold	False
	Height	330
	Left	120
	Top	660
	Width	1200

Object	Property	Setting
Label	Caption	Title:
	BackStyle	0—Transparent
	FontBold	False
	Height	330
	Left	120
	Top	1080
	Width	1200
Label	Caption	Voice Phone:
	BackStyle	0—Transparent
	FontBold	False
	Height	330
	Left	120
	Top	240
Label	Caption	Extension:
	BackStyle	0—Transparent
	FontBold	False
	Height	330
	Left	120
	Top	660
	Width	1200
Label	Caption	FAX Phone:
	BackStyle	0—Transparent
	FontBold	False
	Height	330
	Left	120
	Top	1080
	Width	1200

Note: Please note that we have used the USA nine-digit Zip code in this exercise. You might want to modify this mask if you live in a country that has a different Zip code format.

Figure 6.12.
Adding the input controls and prompts.

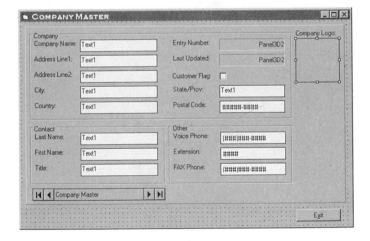

You need to add one more set of input controls to the form—the Company Logo controls. Refer to Table 6.3 and Figure 6.13 for sizing and placement of the Image control that holds the picture and the associated label control for the prompt. You will add code behind the image control in the next section.

Figure 6.13.
Adding the Company Logo controls.

Table 6.3. CompanyMaster Company Logo controls.

Object	Property	Setting
Image	BorderStyle	1—Fixed Single
	DataField	CompanyLogo
	DataSource	Data1

Object	Property	Setting
	Height	1200
	Left	7380
	Stretch	-1 True
	Top	360
	Width	1200
Label	Caption	Company Logo:
	BackStyle	0—Transparent
	FontBold	False
	Height	330
	Left	7380
	Top	120
	Width	1200

Adding and Coding Command Buttons

Next, add the command buttons. Although you already have the Visual Basic 4 data control on the form, you'll need additional buttons to allow the user to perform adds, deletes, updates, finds, and so on. You'll also add a button to pop up a small form for adding comments to the data record. Refer to Table 6.4 and Figure 6.14 for sizing and placement information.

Figure 6.14.

Adding command buttons to the Company Master form.

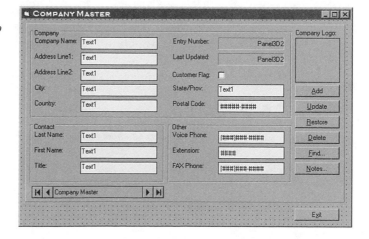

Table 6.4. CompanyMaster command buttons.

Object	Property	Setting
CommandButton	Name	cmdAdd
	Caption	&Add
	FontBold	False
	Height	330
	Left	7380
	Top	1620
	Width	1200
CommandButton	Name	cmdUpdate
	Caption	&Update
	FontBold	False
	Height	330
	Left	7380
	Top	2040
	Width	1200
CommandButton	Name	cmdRestore
	Caption	&Restore
	FontBold	False
	Height	330
	Left	7380
	Top	2880
	Width	1200
CommandButton	Name	cmdDelete
	Caption	&Delete
	FontBold	False
	Height	330
	Left	7380
	Top	3300
	Width	1200

Object	Property	Setting
CommandButton	Name	cmdFind
	Caption	&Find
	FontBold	False
	Height	330
	Left	7380
	Top	3720
	Width	1200
CommandButton	Name	cmdNotes
	Caption	&Notes
	FontBold	False
	Height	330
	Left	7380
	Top	4140
	Width	1200

The following code sections should be placed behind each button. You have placed identical code behind other examples earlier this week. Begin with Listing 6.21, which shows the code to enter behind the cmdAdd command button.

Listing 6.21. Adding data records.

```
Sub cmdAdd_Click ()
    Data1.Recordset.AddNew ' add a new record to table
End Sub
```

Now add the code in Listing 6.22 to the cmdExit button. This code will unload the form when the exit button is selected.

Listing 6.22. Unloading the CompanyMaster form.

```
Sub cmdExit_Click ()
  Unload Me ' close myself (better than END)
End Sub
```

Now enter the code in Listing 6.23 to the cmdFind_Click event. When executed, this code will query the user to enter an appropriate search string.

6

Listing 6.23. Finding data records.

```
Sub cmdFind_Click ()
   Dim nResult As Integer
   Dim cFind As String
   Dim cBookmark As String
   '
   cFind = InputBox("Enter Search String:", "CompanyMaster FIND")
   If Len(cFind) > 0 Then
      cBookmark = Data1.Recordset.Bookmark
      Data1.Recordset.FindFirst cFind
      If Data1.Recordset.NoMatch Then
         MsgBox "Can't Find [" + cFind + "]", 0, "Find Error"
         Data1.Recordset.Bookmark = cBookmark
      End If
   End If
End Sub
```

The code in Listing 6.24 should be entered into the `cmdRestore_Click` event to restore the controls to their original value when the cmdRestore command button is selected.

Listing 6.24. Restoring the data controls.

```
Sub cmdRestore_Click ()
   Data1.UpdateControls ' restore controls from table
End Sub
```

Now enter code to save the data. Use Listing 6.25 as a guide and enter this code into the `cmdUpdate_Click` event.

Listing 6.25. Writing a record.

```
Sub cmdUpdate_Click ()
   Data1.RecordSet.Update ' write reocord to table
End Sub
```

Listing 6.26 contains the code that should now be entered into the `cmdDelete_Click` event. This code will delete the displayed record after the user confirms the deletion.

Listing 6.26. Deleting a record.

```
Sub cmdDelete_Click ()
   Dim nResult As Integer
   '
   ' give user chance to reconsider
```

```
    nResult = MsgBox("Are you sure?", 1, "Delete Record")
    If nResult = 1 Then
        Data1.Recordset.Delete
    End If
End Sub
```

You need to add code behind the Image control to allow users to update the CompanyLogo field. Users should be able to locate a file on the disk, and then save it to the field. The form will then display the saved image. You can give users access to loading files by adding the Visual Basic 4 CommonDialog control to the form. Select the CommonDialog control from the Tools window and place it at the bottom of the form. It does not really matter where it is placed—the command dialog control is invisible at runtime. Once the control is on the form, add the code in Listing 6.27 to the Image1_DblClick event.

Listing 6.27. Updating the company logo.

```
Sub Image1_DblClick ()
    '
    ' set dialog properties
    CMDialog1.Filter = "Bitmap (*.bmp)¦*.bmp¦Icon (*.ico)¦*.
    ➥ico¦Metafiles (*.wmf)¦*.wmf¦"
    CMDialog1.DialogTitle = "Load Company Logo"
    '
    ' run dialog box
    CMDialog1.Action = 1
    '
    ' if they picked a file, load it up
    On Error GoTo PicErr ' in case user picks a bad file
    If Len(CMDialog1.Filename) <> 0 Then
        Image1.Picture = LoadPicture(CMDialog1.Filename)
    End If
    On Error GoTo 0 ' trun off error trapping
    '
    ' all done, go to exit
    GoTo PicExit
    '
    ' handle bad picture error
PicErr:
    MsgBox "Unable to load selected file.", 0, "Picture Error"
Resume Next
    '
    ' final exit of procedure
PicExit:
End Sub
```

6

The code in Listing 6.27 sets file type and caption properties of the common dialog box, runs the dialog and then, if a file has been selected, attempts to save it to the image control. You add a little error trapping here in case the user selects an invalid file type.

Adding Input Validation

The last step in creating Visual Basic 4 data entry forms is adding the input validation routines. The following is a list of the input rules you should use when coding the validation routines:

☐ The following fields are required for each form:

CompanyName

Addr1

City

State/Province

PostalCode

☐ The following dependent field rules apply to the form:

If the Addr2 field has data, the Addr1 field must have data.

If the FirstName field has data, the LastName field must have data.

If the Extension field has data, the VoicePhone field must have data.

☐ The StateProv field should allow only uppercase data entry.

You can perform all these validation checks in a single procedure—the `ValidateForm()` function. Listing 6.28 shows the code that fulfills the validation rules. Create a new function called `ValidateForm` and insert this code.

This code calls routines from the `IsValid` module created earlier today. Add this module to the project by right-clicking on the Project window and selecting the Add menu item.

Listing 6.28. Performing validation checks.

```
Function ValidateForm () As Integer
   Dim nOK As Integer
   Dim nValidErr As Integer
   '
   ' perform input validations
   nOK = IsValid(Me.txtCompanyName, "Company Name", True)
   If nOK = False Then
      nValidErr = True
   End If
   '
   nOK = IsValid(Me.txtAddr1, "Address Line1", True)
   If nOK = False Then
      nValidErr = True
   End If
   '
```

```
      nOK = IsValid(Me.txtCity, "City", True)
      If nOK = False Then
         nValidErr = True
      End If
      '
      nOK = IsValid(Me.txtStProv, "State/Prov", True)
      If nOK = False Then
         nValidErr = True
      End If
      '
      nOK = IsValid(Me.txtCountry, "Country", True)
      If nOK = False Then
         nValidErr = True
      End If
      '
      nOK = IsValid(Me.mskPostCode, "Postal Code", True)
      If nOK = False Then
         nValidErr = True
      End If
      '
      nOK = IsConditional(Me.txtAddr2, "Address Line2", Me.txtAddr1,
      ➡"Address Line1", True)
      If nOK = False Then
         nValidErr = True
      End If
      '
      nOK = IsConditional(Me.txtFirstName, "First Name",
      ➡Me.txtLastName, "Last Name", True)
      If nOK = False Then
         nValidErr = True
      End If
      '
      nOK = IsConditional(Me.mskExtension, "Extension",
      ➡Me.mskVoicePhone, "Voice Phone", True)
      If nOK = False Then
         nValidErr = True
      End If
      '
      ' set return value
      If nValidErr = True Then
         ValidateForm = False
      Else
         ValidateForm = True
      End If
End Function
```

6

After you enter this code, you need to add a few lines to the Data1_Validate event. The code in
Listing 6.29 calls the validation routine each time the Update button is clicked or the arrow keys
are pressed on the data control.

Listing 6.29. Calling validation routines when the Update button is pressed.

```
Sub Data1_Validate (Action As Integer, Save As Integer)
   Dim nResult As Integer
   '
   nResult = ValidateForm()
   If nResult = False Then
      Save = 0' cancel update
      MsgBox "Update Cancelled", 0, "Update Error"
   End If
End Sub
```

In Listing 6.29, if an error is returned by the ValidateForm() function, the save action is canceled and a warning message is displayed.

Summary

Today you learned how to perform input validation on data entry forms. You learned that input validation tasks can be divided into three areas:

- [ ] Key Filtering: Preventing unwanted keyboard input.
- [ ] Field Level Validation: Validating input for each field.
- [ ] Form Level Validation: Validating input across several fields.

You also learned that you should ask yourself a few basic questions when you are developing validation rules for your form.

- [ ] Is it a required field?
- [ ] What characters are valid/invalid for this field? (Numeric input only, capital letters only, no spaces allowed, and so on.)
- [ ] For numeric fields, is there a high/low range limit? (Must be greater than zero and less than 1000, can't be less than 100, and so on.)
- [ ] Is there a list of valid values for this field? (Can the user only enter Retail, Wholesale, or Other; Name must already be in the Customer table, and so on.)
- [ ] Is this a conditional field? (If users enter Yes in field A, then they must enter something in field C.)

You learned how to write keyboard filter validation functions using the Visual Basic 4 KeyPress event. You learned how to write field level validation functions that check for valid input ranges, input that is part of a list of valid data, and input that is within minimum and maximum length requirements. You also learned how to write validation functions that make sure dependent fields have been filled out properly. Finally, you learned how to create a Visual Basic 4 library module containing validation functions that can be used in any Visual Basic 4 program.

You also applied your knowledge of bound data controls, Visual Basic 4 data entry form design, and validation processing to create the data entry form for the CompanyMaster data table.

Quiz

1. What is the difference between input validation and error trapping?
2. What value must you subtract from a lowercase character to get its uppercase ASCII value?
3. What Visual Basic 4 event occurs every time a key is pressed on your keyboard?
4. Do characters in a validation list need to be entered in any particular order?
5. What does the following code mean?

   ```
   If Len(Trim(txtUpper)) <> 0 then
   ```
6. Should conditional field validation be performed at the field level or the form level?
7. When should you load validation lists?
8. What do the three sections of the format property of the MaskedEdit control represent? What character separates these sections?

Exercises

1. Write code to allow entry of only capital letters in a field. The user should be able to enter control codes, but not numbers or symbols.
2. Write the format property for a MaskedEdit control that rounds the entered number to the nearest hundredth, includes commas in all numbers, and places an en dash (–) in front of negative numbers.
3. Write a form level validation routine that requires that entry be made into a field named txtDate before a record can be saved by pressing a button named cmdOK.
4. Write the code to fill a combo box named cboEmployees with your employees' last names of Smith, Andersen, Jones, and Jackson. What property do you set in the combo box control to sort these names alphabetically?

Creating Reports
with Crystal
Reports Writer

Today you'll learn how to create reports that can be called from within your Visual Basic 4 programs. To do this, you'll use the Crystal Reports Writer, which ships with Visual Basic 4. You'll learn some basic concepts on how a report writer works, including the following:

☐ The concepts of report headers, detail lines, and footers.

☐ The three main field types: Database, Text, and Formula.

When you have an understanding of the basics, you'll take a quick tour of Crystal Reports to learn how to create list reports. Finally, you'll learn how to use the Crystal Reports Control in Visual Basic 4 programs to run reports directly from your Visual Basic 4 applications.

What Is Crystal Reports Writer?

The Crystal Reports Writer is a complete program that gives you the ability to define reports, save these report definitions to disk, and then run these reports against databases in order to create final printouts. Crystal Reports has an added feature that lets you run the final reports from within your Visual Basic 4 application using the Crystal Reports Control, which ships with Visual Basic 4.

Throughout this day, you'll use Crystal Reports to illustrate concepts and to work out practice examples. Start Crystal Reports now and follow along through the rest of the day. You can start Crystal Reports in one of two ways: from the Visual Basic 4 main menu by selecting Add Ins | Report Designer, or by selecting the Crystal Reports icon from the Visual Basic 4 program group. If you have not already done so, start Visual Basic 4 and select Report Designer from the Add Ins menu. (See Figure 7.1.)

Figure 7.1.

Starting Crystal Reports from Visual Basic 4.

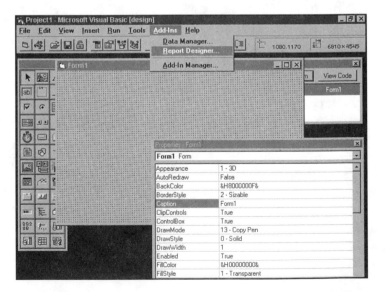

When you start Crystal Reports, you'll see the Crystal Reports greeting dialog box. Press Proceed to Crystal Reports. You'll now see the main Crystal Reports screen (see Figure 7.2). This is where you create, modify, and run your reports.

 Note: You will see the Crystal Reports Registration form the first time you load Crystal Reports. Complete this form and follow its instructions to register your software. After it is completed, you will not see this form again.

Figure 7.2.
The Crystal Reports main screen.

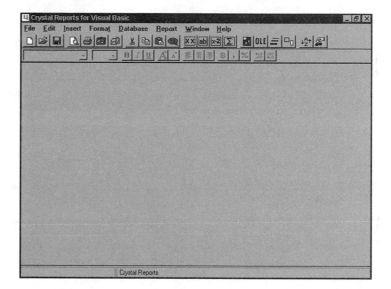

Crystal Reports Bands

Crystal Reports is a banded report writer. A *banded report writer* treats all output as "bands" of data. Each band has its own processes (such as functions it performs) and settings (properties) that you can manipulate in order to create the report layout and behaviors you need. Here are the main bands in Crystal Reports:

☐ The header and footer bands
☐ The detail band

The header and footer bands contain information that appears at the top and bottom of every page of the report. This could be report titles, page numbers, print date and time, and so on. Every report has a header and a footer band.

The detail band contains the actual print lines. The detail band is the report version of a data table record. You use the report writer to lay out a detail band the same way you use a Visual Basic 4 form to lay out a data entry screen. Detail bands can have more than one physical line. However, detail bands only describe one logical record.

Crystal Reports Fields

Within each band, you place fields to be displayed. Crystal Reports recognizes three types of fields:

☐ Database fields

☐ Text fields

☐ Formula fields

Database fields are fields taken directly from data tables in the database you open when you first start Crystal Reports. You can load any database format recognized by the Visual Basic 4 database object (for example, Microsoft Access, FoxPro, dBASE), including ODBC data sources. You add fields by selecting them from a list of available fields and placing them in the desired location on the report form.

Text fields are fields that contain explicit text you want to appear on the report form. This text is not stored in a data table. An example of a text field is Print Date. If you want this text to appear at the top of every page, you would create a text field that contains it and then you would place it in the header band.

Formula fields are fields that are calculated results of either database fields or text fields (or a combination of both). Crystal Reports requires you to declare a formula field name and then allows you to use any existing text field, database, or other formula field as part of the new formula field. Formula fields can be numeric or character-based. For example, if you want to print the values Expiration Date: followed by the database field DataTable.Expire, but do not want to have to place two field objects in the detail band, you could create a single formula field, called ExpDate, that contains the following expression:

```
"Expiration Date: "+DataTable.Expire
```

Crystal Reports has several predefined formula fields available, along with a host of functions and operators that you can use to construct complex formulas, including the use of nested If statements to test data.

In the following sections, you'll begin a report definition to illustrate how bands and fields are used in Crystal Reports.

The Detail Band

If you haven't already done so, start Crystal Reports from the Visual Basic 4 main menu bar. Select New | Report from the File menu and use the Open File dialog box to locate and load the CRYSRPT.MDB Microsoft Access database file. This file can be copied from the CD that ships with this book. It can be found in the TYSDBVB\CHAP07 directory. Your screen should look similar to the one shown in Figure 7.3.

Figure 7.3.

Loading a database with Crystal Reports.

When the database is loaded, Crystal Reports creates a blank report definition and displays the list of available tables and fields in a box in the lower-right corner of the screen. (See Figure 7.4.)

Figure 7.4.

Starting a new report with Crystal Reports.

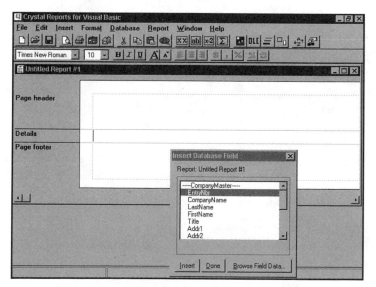

First, you'll add a database field to the detail band of the report. Double-click the EntryNbr field in the Insert Database Field box, and then move the pointer onto the report form. You'll see that a rectangle outline appears, showing you where the database field will appear. Position the rectangle at the left corner of the detail band and click the mouse button once to drop the field on the report form. Notice that the field name automatically appears as a column title in the header band above the field in the detail band. Your report form should look like the one shown in Figure 7.5.

Figure 7.5.

Placing a database field in the detail band.

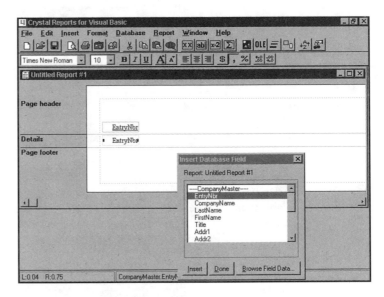

Now you'll add the company name and address to the detail band. But before you do this, expand the detail band to accept more than one line of data. Move the pointer over the solid line that separates the detail band from the footer band. When the cursor turns to a double-sided arrow, press the left mouse button and pull down the detail band line to allow for several lines of data (just a rough guess will do fine). When you are satisfied that the detail area is large enough, release the mouse button to drop the detail band line. (See Figure 7.6 for a reference.)

Now, add the following fields to the detail area:

- ☐ CompanyName
- ☐ Addr1
- ☐ Addr2
- ☐ City
- ☐ StateProv
- ☐ PostalCode

Figure 7.6.
Expanding the detail band.

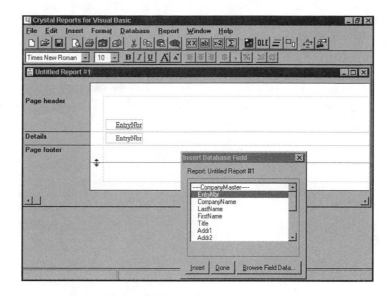

Place the CompanyName, Addr1, and Addr2 fields under each other and next to the EntryNbr field. Place the City, StateProv, and PostalCode fields together on one line. As you place each field in the detail band, you'll see the field names appear, one on top of another, in the header section. Delete all the field names except CompanyName. See Figure 7.7 for sizing and placement of the database fields.

Figure 7.7.
Placing the CompanyName and Address fields on the report.

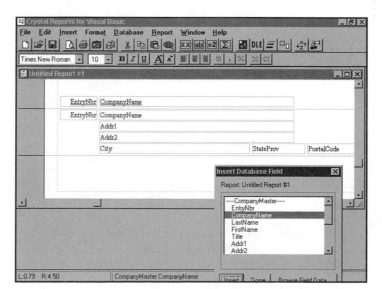

Before going any further, you should save this report definition. Select Save As from the File menu. Enter COMAST1.RPT as the report name and then click OK to save the report. (See Figure 7.8.)

Figure 7.8.

Saving the report form as COMAST1.RPT.

Now run the report to see whether everything is working. Select Print Preview from the File menu. Crystal Reports automatically opens the data table, loads the records, and sends the report to a display window. You should see something like the example shown in Figure 7.9.

Figure 7.9.

Running the first report to a window.

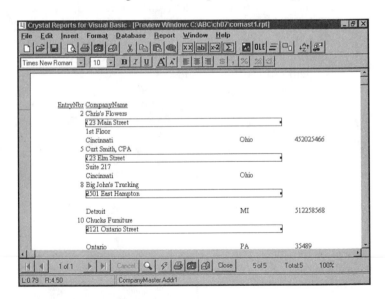

Notice that you can use this window to scroll up and down the page, to "walk" through the pages of the report, to zoom in and out with the magnifying glass, and to send the report to the default printer. These options are covered in more depth later. For now, close the report.

The Header and Footer Bands

You can add information that will appear at the top and bottom of every page by adding fields to the header and footer bands. Add a report title and date in the header band and a page number in the footer band.

You'll need to use a text field to create a report title for the header band. Select Text Field from the Insert menu and enter the text Company Master Report in the dialog box. (See Figure 7.10.)

Figure 7.10.
Creating a text field.

Click the Accept button to store the text. Move the rectangle cursor to the top center of the header band and press the left mouse button to drop the text field on the header band. Your report form should look like the one shown in Figure 7.11.

Figure 7.11.
Dropping the text field in the header band.

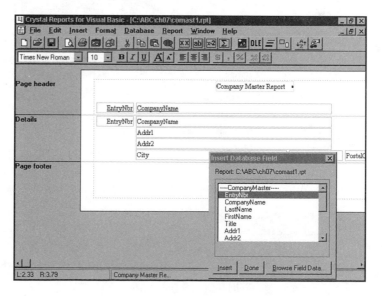

You can type text directly on the report form. This is easier than creating text fields, but it has its drawbacks. Once you type text on the form, you cannot move the text or resize it in any way.

If you want to move the field later, you'll have to erase it and re-enter the data in the new location. If you use text fields, you can simply select the field and move it or resize it as needed.

To illustrate the process of adding text directly to the report form, move the cursor to the top-left corner of the report form and type Date:. Next, select Special Field | Print Date Field from the Insert menu. Now, move your rectangle cursor to a location near Date: and press the left mouse button to drop the report date onto the form. Your report form should now look like the one shown in Figure 7.12.

Figure 7.12.

Adding direct text and a data field to the report.

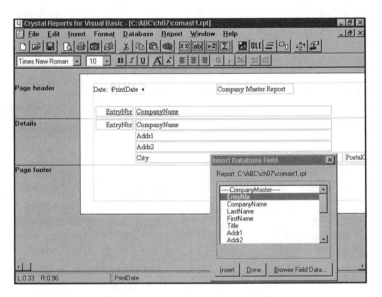

You can also add page numbers to the footer band. This time, create a text field that contains the text Page:. Place this text field at the bottom of the footer band. Select Special Field | Page Number Field from the Insert menu, and then place this field next to the text field. Refer to Figure 7.13 for placement and sizing.

Save and preview the report by selecting Print Preview from the File menu. You'll see the report title, print date, and page numbers display on each page of the report.

You need to add one more improvement to your report. Notice how the City, StateProv, and PostalCode fields print very far apart? You need to allow enough space for long city names, but you do not want to see lots of empty space on the form. What you need is a formula field that combines all three fields into a single field that has extra spaces removed.

Select Formula Field from the Insert menu. In the dialog box enter CityLine as the name for the formula field. (See Figure 7.14.)

Figure 7.13.
Adding page numbers to the report form.

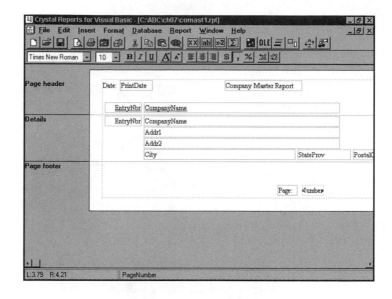

Figure 7.14.
Naming a new formula field.

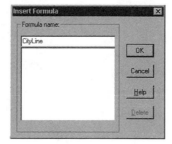

After you click OK, you'll see the formula window. This is where you put together the details of the CityLine formula. You see the following four sections in this window:

☐ Fields: This is a list of available database fields.

☐ Functions: This is a list of available Crystal Reports functions.

☐ Operators: This is a list of arithmetic and logical operators.

☐ Formula Text: This is where you build your formula.

You can type all the information into the Formula Text window, or you can use your mouse to point-and-click items from the Fields, Functions, and Operators windows through most of the formula-building process. The point-and-click method saves time and reduces typing errors.

You need to remove trailing spaces from the right of the fields, so start the formula by double-clicking the `TrimRight()` function from the Functions list. Notice that when you add a function to the Formula Text window, your cursor is positioned ready to insert the required parameters.

Because the cursor is already between the two parentheses of the `TrimRight()` function, double-click City from the Fields list. Crystal Reports will place the field name (along with the data table name) inside the `TrimRight()` function. (See Figure 7.15.)

Figure 7.15.

Adding the `TrimRight()` *function and the City field.*

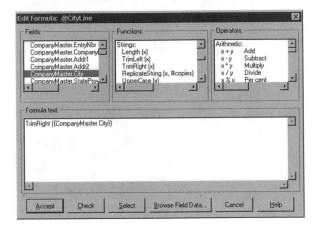

You need to add a similar function that does the same thing to the StateProv database field. First, move the cursor in the Formula text box to the end of the formula string and enter a plus sign (+). Next, add another `TrimRight()` function and insert the StateProv field into the function. Compare your screen to the one shown in Figure 7.16.

Figure 7.16.

Adding the `TrimRight()` *function and the StateProv field.*

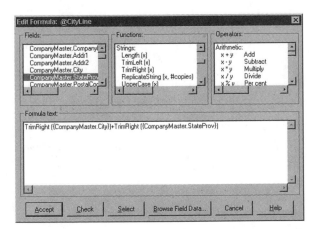

Now you need to add the PostalCode field to the formula. You don't need to trim spaces from the PostalCode field, so just add the plus sign and select the PostalCode field. Your formula should look like the one shown in Figure 7.17.

Figure 7.17.
Adding the PostalCode field to the formula.

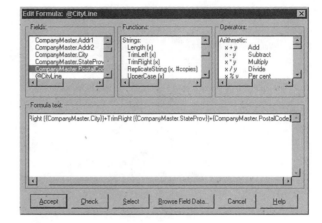

Before you save the field, you can check the syntax by using the Check button. When you click the Check button, Crystal Reports checks the formula for any errors and then reports the results in a message box. (See Figure 7.18.)

Figure 7.18.
Checking the formula.

If you have no errors, press the Accept button. Crystal Reports will return you to the report form. You are ready to place the newly constructed formula field on the form. Place the new field anywhere on the report form (wherever you have space). Next, delete the City, StateProv, and PostalCode fields from the detail band. You can do this by selecting all three fields with the mouse button and then pressing the Delete key on your keyboard. When all three fields are gone, move the CityLine formula field into place in the detail band. Your form should look like the one shown in Figure 7.19.

Save and run the report. You'll see that there are no spaces between the City, StateProv, and PostalCode fields. But you need some spaces, right? You need to edit the formula field in order to insert a comma and a space between the City and the StateProv fields and to insert two spaces between the StateProv and the PostalCode fields.

To edit an existing formula field, select the field by clicking it with the mouse. Then, select Formula from the Edit menu. Crystal Reports will present you with the formula window with the CityLine formula already loaded. Go directly to the Formula text box and make the needed changes to the formula. Your formula should now look like the one shown in Figure 7.20.

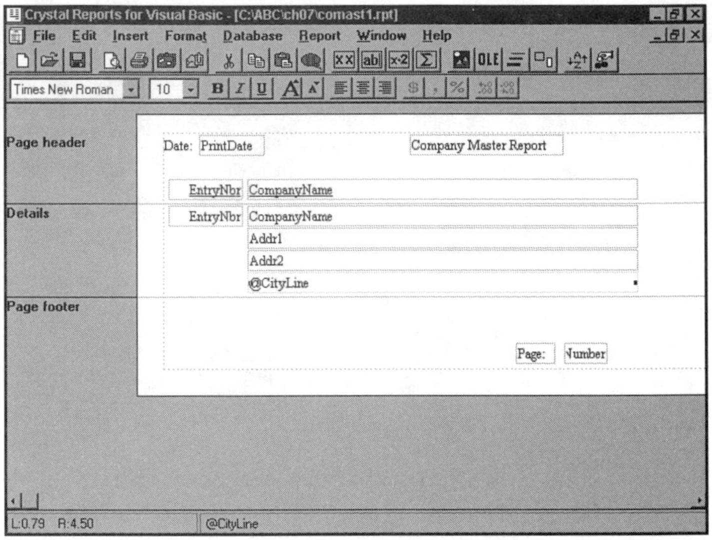

Figure 7.19.
Placing the CityLine formula field on the report form.

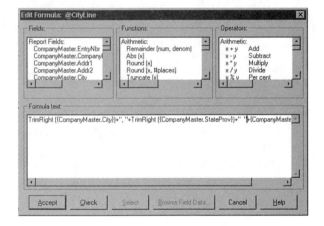

Figure 7.20.
Editing the CityLine formula.

Press the Accept button to save the formula; then save and run the report. You now see a much better looking final line on the address.

Using Crystal Reports Writer

Crystal Reports is a great tool for putting together simple list reports. It is also excellent for creating a wide variety of labels, including mailing labels, name tags, diskette labels, and others as well. What follows is a quick tour of Crystal Reports. For a more in-depth treatment of Crystal Reports, refer to the documentation that ships with Visual Basic 4.

File Menu

The items in the File menu allow you to define new reports, open existing reports, save reports, print the current report, and set program-level options such as default directories, default display formats, and default database formats. Table 7.1 contains a summary of the menu items and their uses.

Table 7.1. Crystal Reports File menu options.

Menu Option	Description
New | Report...	Use this to create a brand new report. You are first prompted to select a database (even if you already have one open). When the database is open, you can assemble a basic report by selecting fields from a list box.
New | Cross-Tab...	This selection brings up a dialog box that will help you build a cross-tab report. This type of report arranges data in rows and columns, similar to those of a spreadsheet.
New | Mailing Labels Report	Use this selection to create a label. There are many default label formats, including user-defined. You are first prompted to select a database and then select (or define) a label format.
Open...	This selection prompts you to open an existing Crystal Reports report definition (*.RPT). When the definition is open, you can edit the report and save the changes.
Save	Use this selection to save the report definition to the current report name. If no name exists, you will be prompted to supply one. The default file extension is .RPT.
Save As...	Use this option to save an existing report under a new name. It is handy if you want to use an existing report as a "template" for creating a new, slightly different report.
Close	This selection closes the current report. If you have made changes, you will be asked whether you want to save the report definition before it is closed.

continues

Table 7.1. continued

Menu Option	Description
Print Preview	This selection displays the report on-screen for your review.
Print | Printer	This selection sends the current report to the attached printer. See the Printer menu for more options.
Print | Export	This selection allows you to print to a file in numerous formats, including Lotus and Excel.
Print | Report Definition	This selection prints an abstract of the current report. Information is displayed regarding the fields, headers, database, formulas, and other items placed on the report.
Printer Setup	This selection displays a dialog box of the current printer settings.
Page Margins	This selection allows you to set the top, bottom, left, and right margins of the report.
Options…	Use this item to set program-level defaults for all reports. You can set defaults for the directory to which reports are saved and the directory from which databases are read. You can also set the default database and index formats.
	You can set the default display formats for string, numeric, currency, date, and boolean data formats. You can also set the default fonts for the header, footer, detail, group, and total bands.
	There are also several preference settings that control how Crystal Reports displays menu bars, fields on a report, and so on.
Exit	This selection exits Crystal Reports. If you have made any changes to any open report definition, you will be asked whether you want to save the changes before exiting.

Edit Menu

The Edit menu contains the usual Cut, Copy, Paste, and Clear options, plus several other options that allow you to edit formulas, text fields, and summary and group bands. See Table 7.2 for a brief summary of the Edit menu.

Table 7.2. Crystal Reports Edit menu options.

Menu Option	Description
Cut	Use this selection to cut out selected text. This only works for text that is placed directly on the report form. It does not work for any field type objects (database, text, or formula).
Copy	Use this selection to copy selected text from your report form to the Clipboard. This copies text that was placed directly onto a form and does not work for any field type objects (database, text, or formula).
Paste	Use this selection to paste text from the Clipboard directly into your report form. This does not place the selected text into database, formula, or text fields.
Paste Special	This selection allows you to use the Windows Clipboard to copy information from other applications and place the information into your Crystal Report. Objects can either be embedded or linked. If they are linked, changes in the source will flow through to your report.
Select Fields	This item allows you to use a "lasso" to draw a rectangle around and select an entire group of objects. You can accomplish the same effect by holding the Shift key as you select objects; however, this process is not as quick.
Formula...	Use this option to edit an existing formula field. First, you must select the formula field to edit; then you select this menu item to call up the formula editor.
Text Field...	Use this option to edit an existing text field. First, you must select the text field to edit; then you select this menu item to call up the Text Field edit box.
Summary Field...	Use this option to edit an existing summary operation field. First, you must select the summary field to edit; then you select this menu item to call up the Summary Operation dialog box. Summary options include Sum, Average, Min, Max, Count, Variance, and Standard Deviation.
Browse Field Data...	Use this option to view a list of all the possible values in a data field. First, you must select the data field on the report form to browse; then you select this menu item to see a list box containing all the unique values for this field. You'll also see field definition information in the upper-left corner of

continues

Table 7.2. continued

Menu Option	Description
	the list box (string type, length 30, and so on). This is handy if you want to review the data behind the form while you are constructing a report.
Show/Hide Sections...	This option displays a dialog box that allows you to hide or display different sections of your report. This option is also available by pressing the right mouse button while on a section heading.
Send Behind Others	Use this command to access fields on the report form that are stacked underneath each other. It is common practice to place more than one field in the same location on the form and allow criteria in the report to decide which of the stacked fields actually gets displayed. This menu item allows you to work down the stack in order to find the field you want to edit.
Group Section...	Use this menu item to edit an existing group section. When you select this menu item, you'll be presented with a list box showing all the existing groups. Select the group you want to edit; then you'll see a dialog box that lets you set the grouping field and the sort order (ascending or descending).
Delete Section...	Use this menu item to delete an existing group from the report.
Object	This menu item allows you to edit an OLE object that you have embedded in your report. An object must first be selected before you can choose this item. The types of objects within your report will appear at the bottom of the Edit menu. Each object type will have submenus of actions that can be performed on that type of object.
Links...	This menu item allows you to update and change links to objects embedded within your report.

Insert Menu

The Insert menu allows you to add database, text, and formula fields to your report definition. You can also add graphic images, lines, and boxes. Crystal Reports gives you shortcuts to add page numbers, record numbers, print date, and group numbers to the report definition. The

Insert menu is the menu you use to add new sections, subtotal bands, summary bands, and the report grand total band. Table 7.3 provides a short summary of the Insert menu options.

Table 7.3. Crystal Reports Insert menu options.

Menu Option	Description
Database Field…	Use this option to select a field from the attached database. You can select any field in any table. You can select the same field more than once.
Text Field…	Use this option to create a text field for your report form. After you create the text field, you can manipulate the format, font, and color the same way you can in a database field.
Formula Field…	Use this option to create a new formula field or edit an existing formula field. Select this menu item and you'll see a list box showing all the formula fields defined for this report. If you double-click one of the fields in the list, you'll see the formula editor with the selected formula loaded, ready for editing. If you type in a new formula name, you'll see the formula editor ready for you to create a new formula.
Special Field | Page Number Field	Use this option to create a page number field for your report form. This field will always report the current page number.
Special Field | Record Number Field	Use this option to create a record number for your report. This field will always report the current sequential record number in the selected records as sorted by the report. This does not report the position of the record in the physical table, it reports the position of the record in the sorted report list.
Special Field | Group Number Field	Use this option to create a group number field to place on your reports. This field can be used to report counts of group breaks within the report.
Special Field | Print Date Field	Use this option to create a Today's Date field to place on your report form. This field reports the date on which the report is printed.
Subtotal…	Use this option to create a subtotal band for your report form. First, you must select a numeric field to subtotal.

7

continues

Table 7.3. continued

Menu Option	Description
	When you create a subtotal field, a new section will automatically be created (if it does not already exist). You can select the grouping field to use for each subtotal as well as the sort order of the grouping field.
Grand Total...	Use this menu item to create a grand total band on your report form. First, you must select a field to total; then you select this menu item. You do not have to select a numeric field for the grand total band because the grand total band can report a count as well as a numeric total.
Summary...	Use this option to insert fields for counts, sums, averages, minimums, maximums, sample variances, sample standard deviations, population variances, or population standard deviations of selected fields.
Group Section...	This option allows you to set the points at which your report will break and total.
Line	Use this item to draw lines on your report. After a line has been placed on the report, you can resize it using the mouse pointer. You can set the line thickness, type, and color by double-clicking anywhere on the line to call up a dialog box.
Box	Use this item to place a box anywhere on the report form. You can use the mouse pointer to resize the box. When you double-click the selected box, you'll call up a dialog box that lets you set the border style, thickness, and color. You can also set the fill color of the box.
Graphic...	Use this item to place a bitmap graphic image on your report. When you select this item you'll be shown the Choose Graphics dialog box, which you use to locate a graphic image file. When you select a file and press OK, Crystal Reports will allow you to place and size that image anywhere on the report.
Object	This option allows you to select and insert an OLE object into your report. You can either embed or link the object.

Format Menu

The Format menu gives you options for changing the font, borders, color, and display format of existing fields. You use this menu to edit the graphic, line, and box objects on your report. You can also set formatting options for existing section bands of your report. Table 7.4 provides a short summary of the Format menu options.

Table 7.4. Crystal Reports Format menu options.

Menu Item	Description
Font...	Use this menu item to edit the font attributes of the selected fields. You must first select one or more fields; then you select this menu item.
Field...	Use this menu item to change the display format of the selected field. Different dialog boxes appear depending on the field type selected.
Border and Colors...	Use this menu option to set field colors, to set borders around fields, to set the width of the borders, to add shadows to the borders, and so on.
Graphic...	Use this item to modify the sizing, scaling, and positioning of graphic images loaded from the Insert | Graphics menu item. (See Table 7.3.)
Line	Use this menu item to modify the thickness, type, and color of existing line objects on the report form.
Box	Use this menu item to modify the attributes of a box object already on the report form.
Section...	Use this menu item to set attributes of all the sections (bands) of the report. There are several attributes that can be set from this dialog box, but not all apply to all objects. They are Hide Section, Print at Bottom of Page, New Page After, New Page Before, Reset Page Number After, Keep Section Together, Suppress Blank Lines, and Format with Multi-Columns.

Database Menu

The Database menu can be used to set and update table links, to add and remove database files, to establish table aliases to correct naming conflicts, to make sure the data set currently being used by Crystal Reports is updated, and to log on or off ODBC data sources. Table 7.5 provides a short summary of the Database menu options.

Table 7.5. Crystal Reports Database menu options.

Menu Option	Description
Links...	Use this menu option to create links between data tables. When you select this item, you will be presented with a dialog box that allows you to add, update, or delete file links. A link allows you to associate a field in one table to a field in another table, thus linking the two files. This allows you to establish one-to-one or one-to-many relationships using Crystal Reports.
Add Database to Report...	Use this menu item to add additional database files to your report definition. It is possible to have more than one Microsoft Access database as a source for your report definition.
Remove from Report...	Use this menu item to remove a database file from your report definition.
Set Location...	This option allows you to set the physical location of the databases being used in your report. This option is extremely helpful if databases are moved or if network mappings vary for the users of your reports.
Set Alias...	Use this menu item to establish helpful alias names for the tables in your report. Using meaningful alias names can make it easier to maintain your reports in the future.
Verify Database	Selecting this menu item forces Crystal Reports to refresh all data tables used in the report. This is a one-time action that makes sure you have the most up-to-date data to work with for your report.
Verify on Every Print	This menu item is a toggle on/off option. When the item is toggled on, Crystal Reports performs a refresh each time it runs the report. This is an "automated" version of the Verify Database menu option.
Log On Server	Use this menu item to attach an ODBC data source to the report definition.
Log Off Server	Use this menu item to detach an ODBC data source from the report definition.
Show SQL Query	Use this option to view the SQL query that Crystal Reports is generating and sending to your data source. You can edit the query that is displayed.

Report Menu

The Report menu contains all the options for record selection, grouping, and sorting. Also available are options for database refreshing and report defaults. Table 7.6 provides a short summary of the Report menu options.

Table 7.6. Crystal Reports Report menu options.

Menu Option	Description
Select Records	Use this menu item to create record-level selection criteria for your report. You must first select a report field that you will use as the start of your criteria. You are then prompted to select from a list of criteria, which includes >, <, =, as well as other operators.
Edit Record Selection Formula	This function is similar to the Select Records menu item. The difference is that this function allows you to work in the Crystal Reports script language in order to write your Pick criteria.
Record Sort Order	Use this menu item to establish the sort order of the report. When you select this item, you'll see a sort dialog box that lists all the possible sort fields on the left and shows the selected sort order on the right. You can use more than one report field in the sort criteria. Also, you can indicate an ascending or descending sort at the field level.
Select Groups	Use this menu item to establish selection criteria for report groups (bands). This option is similar to the Select Records option. The criteria built here is applied to the designated group field each time it is printed. In this way, you can set selection criteria for your report that are actually the result of the subtotaling of the data.
Edit Group Selection Formula	Use this menu item to develop your own group selection formula using the formula editor. This is useful if you want to build selection criteria that do not easily fit into the options available in the Select Groups menu option.
Group Sort Order	Use this item to establish the sort order of the existing report groups (bands). You'll see a dialog box similar to the one used in the Record Sort Order menu item. Use this option to control the order in which groups appear on your report.

continues

Table 7.6. continued

Menu Option	Description
Refresh Report Data	Crystal Reports automatically retrieves data only under a few circumstances while in print preview mode. Use this option to reload your data if you expect that it has changed since the last time you previewed the report.
Save Data with Closed Report	This option allows you to save the data records with the report definition. This is a handy feature if you want to archive information. It does (as you would expect) take more disk space to save a report with data records.
Report Title	Use this option to set the title bar text that appears on your report.
Set Print Date	Use this option to set the date that will appear in all date fields on your report.

Calling the Report from Within Visual Basic 4

When you have developed and saved your report definition using Crystal Reports, you are ready to modify your Visual Basic 4 program to run the report from within your Visual Basic 4 application. Throughout the rest of this day you'll be modifying the data entry form you built on Day 6, "Input Validation." If you haven't done so yet, start Visual Basic 4 and load the CompanyMaster data entry program you created on Day 6.

The Crystal Reports Control

It is very easy to run reports defined using Crystal Reports from Visual Basic 4. Crystal Reports for Visual Basic 4 ships with a special control (the Crystal Reports Control) that can be added to any Visual Basic 4 form. Once you drop the control on your form, you only need to set a few properties to get a report printout from your program. The control has several properties that you can alter when setting up or running a report.

First, place the Crystal Reports Control onto the CompanyMaster data entry form. It doesn't matter where you place the control because it's invisible at runtime. Once you have placed the control on the form, set the ReportFileName property to C:\TYSDBVB\ CHAP07\COMAST1.RPT and the WindowTitle property to Company Master Report. Leave CrystalReport1 as the default name for the control. Next, add a command button to the form. Refer to Figure 7.21 for placement and sizing.

Figure 7.21.
Adding the Print command button.

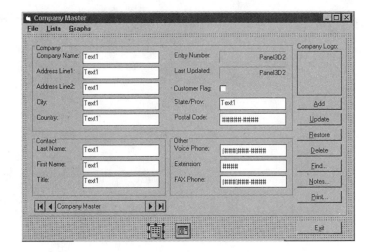

Use the information in Table 7.7 to set the properties of the command button.

Table 7.7. Property settings for the Print command button.

Control	Properties	Settings
Command Button	Name	cmdPrint
	Caption	&Print
	FontBold	False
	Height	330
	Left	7380
	Top	4140
	Width	1200

Now add the following line of code behind the cmdPrint_Click event (this code line starts Crystal Reports):

```
Sub cmdPrint_Click ()
    CrystalReport1.Action = 1 'force Crystal Reports to run report
End Sub
```

Now save and run the program. When you click the Print button, Crystal Reports creates the report and sends it to a screen window. You can preview this report in the window and, if you like, use the Print button on the report window toolbar to send the report to the printer. (See Figure 7.22.)

Figure 7.22.
Viewing the report from Visual Basic 4.

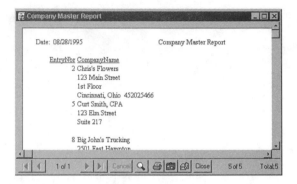

Designing the Print Report Dialog Box

There are a handful of report parameters that you can set using the Crystal Reports Control. Instead of setting them in Visual Basic 4 code, you'll create a simple report dialog box that can be used to set the most common parameters. This dialog box will be *portable*, so you'll be able to use it in any future Visual Basic 4 program.

Use Figure 7.23 and the information in Table 7.8 to construct a generic Print Report dialog box. Please note that you will be adding text boxes that have their Visible property set to False, meaning that they won't appear at runtime. These controls should simply be placed in a convenient position (such as the open space between the Printer Setup and Exit command buttons).

Figure 7.23.
Building a generic Print Report dialog box.

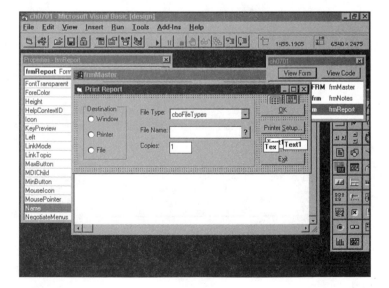

Table 7.8. Control information for the Print Report dialog box.

Control	Property	Setting
Form	Name	frmReport
	BackColor	Light Gray
	Caption	Print Report
	Height	2475
	Width	6540
	Save As	Report.frm
Command Button	Name	cmdOK
	Caption	&OK
	FontBold	False
	Height	330
	Left	5100
	Top	240
	Width	1200
Command Button	Name	cmdPrnSetup
	Caption	Printer Setup...
	FontBold	False
	Height	330
	Left	5100
	Top	720
	Width	1200
Command Button	Name	cmdExit
	Caption	E&xit
	FontBold	False
	Height	330
	Left	5100
	Top	1560
	Width	1200
SSPanel	BorderWidth	1
	Caption	(blank)

continues

Table 7.8. continued

Control	Property	Setting
	Height	1815
	Left	120
	Top	120
	Width	4815
Text Box	Name	txtReportName
	Visible	False
Text Box	Name	txtWindowTitle
	Visible	False
Text Box	Name	txtReportDBName
	Visible	False
Common Dialog	Left	5700
	Top	1
Crystal Report	Left	5200
	Top	1
SSFrame	Caption	Destination
	FontBold	False
	Height	1515
	Left	120
	Top	120
	Width	1200
SSOption	Name	opt3dDest(0)
	Caption	Window
	FontBold	False
	Height	330
	Left	120
	Top	240
	Width	1000
SSOption	Name	opt3dDest(1)
	Caption	Printer
	FontBold	False

Control	Property	Setting
	Height	330
	Left	120
	Top	660
	Width	1000
SSOption	Name	opt3dDest(2)
	Caption	File
	FontBold	False
	Height	330
	Left	120
	Top	1080
	Width	1000
Combo Box	Name	cboFileTypes
	FontBold	False
	Left	2475
	Style	2 - DropDown
	Top	240
	Width	2220
Text Box	Name	txtFileName
	FontBold	False
	Height	330
	Left	2475
	Text	(blank)
	Top	720
	Width	1995
Command Button	Name	cmdFileName
	Caption	"?"
	Height	330
	Left	4440
	Top	720
	Width	260

continues

Table 7.8. continued

Control	Property	Setting
Text Box	Name	txtCopies
	FontBold	False
	Height	330
	Left	2475
	Text	1
	Top	1140
	Width	600
Label	BackStyle	Transparent
	Caption	File Type:
	FontBold	False
	Height	330
	Left	1680
	Top	240
	Width	900
Label	BackStyle	Transparent
	Caption	File Name:
	FontBold	False
	Height	330
	Left	1680
	Top	720
	Width	900
Label	BackStyle	Transparent
	Caption	Copies:
	FontBold	False
	Height	330
	Left	1680
	Top	1140
	Width	900

Adding the Print Report Dialog Box Code

After you have constructed the form, you need to add some code behind the form. First, declare two form-level variables in the declarations section. You'll use these variables to set the properties of the Crystal Reports Control:

```
Option Explicit

Dim cFileName As String
Dim cReportName As String
```

The `LoadFileTypes` procedure loads the various report file types recognized by Crystal Reports into a drop-down combo box. Add this procedure to your project:

```
Sub LoadFileTypes ()
    '
    ' load type selections
    cboFileTypes.Clear
    cboFileTypes.AddItem "Record"
    cboFileTypes.AddItem "Tab Separated"
    cboFileTypes.AddItem "Text"
    cboFileTypes.AddItem "DIF"
    cboFileTypes.AddItem "CSV"
    cboFileTypes.AddItem "*RESERVED*"
    cboFileTypes.AddItem "Tab Separated Text"
End Sub
```

The code in the `Form_Activate` event initializes the form caption and the Crystal Reports window caption. It also checks to see that a report name and database name have been passed to the form. This is where you load the combo box, too.

```
Sub Form_Activate ()
    '
    ' fix up form caption
    If Len(Trim(Me.txtWindowTitle)) = 0 Then
        Me.txtWindowTitle = "Print Report"
    End If
    Me.Caption = Me.txtWindowTitle
    '
    ' check for passed database name
    If Len(Trim(Me.txtReportDBName)) = 0 Then
        MsgBox "Missing Database Name!"
        Unload Me
    End If
    '
    ' check for passed report name
    If Len(Trim(Me.txtReportName)) = 0 Then
        MsgBox "Missing Report Name!"
        Unload Me
    End If
    '
    ' set default copies
```

```
    txtCopies = 1
    '
    LoadFileTypes ' fill drop down list box
End Sub
```

The following code section handles the selection of the report destination. Notice that this code toggles the enabled/disabled properties of the file-related controls. The controls are kept disabled unless the user select the "file" destination option. Here's the code:

```
Sub opt3dDest_Click (Index As Integer, Value As Integer)
    Dim nFile As Integer
    '
    ' send report to window
    If opt3dDest(0) = True Then
        CrystalReport1.Destination = 0
        nFile = False
    End If
    '
    ' send report to printer
    If opt3dDest(1) = True Then
        CrystalReport1.Destination = 1
        nFile = False
    End If
    '
    ' send report to file
    If opt3dDest(2) = True Then
        CrystalReport1.Destination = 2
        nFile = True
    End If
    '
    ' enable/disable file controls
    txtFileName.Enabled = nFile
    cboFileTypes.Enabled = nFile
    cmdFileName.Enabled = nFile
End Sub
```

The next section of code calls the Visual Basic 4 common dialog box to allow the user to select a filename as the destination for the report output. Notice the use of the &H2 value in the Flags property. This forces the common dialog box to issue a warning message if the user selects a filename that already exists. Once a valid file is selected, it is loaded into a form-level variable for later use. Here's the code:

```
Sub cmdFileName_Click ()
    '
    ' set some parms
    CMDialog1.DialogTitle = "Save Report File Name"
    CMDialog1.Filter = "Text (*.txt)¦*.txt¦"
    CMDialog1.Flags = &H2
    '
    ' run the save as dialog
    CMDialog1.Action = 2
    '
    ' load the selected filename into control
    If Len(CMDialog1.Filename) > 0 Then
        cFileName = CMDialog1.Filename
```

```
    End If
    Me.txtFileName = cFileName
End Sub
```

You need a bit of code to enable the Print Setup command button. Notice that you set the Flags property to &H40. This forces the common dialog box to display the Printer Setup dialog box. Here's the code:

```
Sub cmdPrnSetup_Click ()
    CMDialog1.Flags = &H40 ' force the printers setup dialog box
    CMDialog1.Action = 5 ' run the printer setup
End Sub
```

The code for the OK command button is the most involved of the form. This routine performs input validation, sets final report properties, sets up an error trap, and then runs the Crystal Reports report. The input validation should look familiar. Note that an additional input validation had to be invented to check the combo box. After the validation pass, a few properties of the report control are set. Afterwards, the report is generated.

The report run is wrapped in an error trapping routine. Error trapping is covered in greater detail next week. For now, you should note that after the error trap is turned on, the code attempts to erase the output filename, if necessary, and then runs the report. Once the report is done, the error trapping is turned off.

The error routine is simple. It displays a Message box for any encountered error, except for the error that occurs when the user attempts to erase a file that does not exist. Here's the code:

```
Sub cmdOK_Click ()
    Dim nOK As Integer ' validation results
    Dim nVldErr As Integer ' validatoin pass/fail flag
    Dim cMsg As String ' report error string
    Dim cTitle As String ' error title
    '
    ' peform validation
    If CrystalReport1.Destination = 2 Then
        nOK = IsValid(txtFileName, "Save File Name", True)
        If nOK = False Then
            nVldErr = True
        End If
        '
        If cboFileTypes.ListIndex = -1 Then
            MsgBox "Missing Print File Type", 0, "Validation Error"
            cboFileTypes.SetFocus
            nVldErr = True
        End If
    End If
    '
    ' did we find an error?
    If nVldErr = True Then
        GoTo OKExit ' leave now!
    End If
    '
```

```
' set some final parameters
CrystalReport1.WindowTitle = txtWindowTitle ' set the window title
CrystalReport1.DataFiles(0) = txtReportDBName ' set the database location
CrystalReport1.ReportFileName = txtReportName ' set the report location
CrystalReport1.CopiesToPrinter = txtCopies ' set the copies parm
'
' if it's going to a file
If cboFileTypes.ListIndex <> -1 Then
   CrystalReport1.PrintFileType = cboFileTypes.ListIndex
   CrystalReport1.PrintFileName = txtFileName
End If
'
On Error GoTo ReportErr  ' set error trap
Kill txtFileName         ' delete file if it's there
CrystalReport1.Action = 1     ' run report
On Error GoTo 0          ' trun off error trap
GoTo OKExit              ' exit sub

' report any error you get
ReportErr:
   If Err <> 53 Then ' skip file not found msg
      '
      ' see if the error is from CRW
      If CrystalReport1.LastErrorNumber <> 0 Then
         cMsg = Str(CrystalReport1.LastErrorNumber)
         cMsg = cMsg + ":" + CrystalReport1.LastErrorString
         cTitle = "Crystal Reports Error"
      Else
         '
         ' error was from VB
         cMsg = Str(Err) + ":" + Error$(Err)
         cTitle = "Visual Basic Error"
      End If
      '
      ' show the error # and text
      MsgBox cMsg, 0, cTitle
   End If
   Resume Next

'
' end of this procedure
OKExit:
End Sub
```

Finally, you need a bit of code behind the Exit button:

```
Sub cmdExit_Click ()
   Unload Me
End Sub
```

Save the form as REPORT.FRM before you continue. You now need to make a few changes to the code behind the Print button on the CompanyMaster data entry form. You'll get rid of the Crystal Reports Control on the main form because you have one on the Print Report dialog box now. You'll also set two parameters behind the Print button before you call the Print Report dialog box.

 Tip: Notice in the following code that you load the form (without showing it), set the values of the form's controls, and then show the form modally. This is a good way to pass parameters between forms—load it, pass them, show it.

```
Sub cmdPrint_Click ()
    '
    ' load the next form
    Load frmReport
    '
    ' set values on the next form
    frmReport.txtReportDBName = "c:\tysdbvb\chap07\Crysrpt.mdb"
    frmReport.txtReportName = "c:\tysvbdb\chap07\comast1.rpt"
    frmReport.txtWindowTitle = "Company Master Report"
    '
    ' show the form modally
    frmReport.Show 1
End Sub
```

Now save and run the project. You should see the Company Master Report dialog box prompting you to set parameters for your print job. (See Figure 7.24.)

Figure 7.24.
Running the Company Master Print Report dialog box.

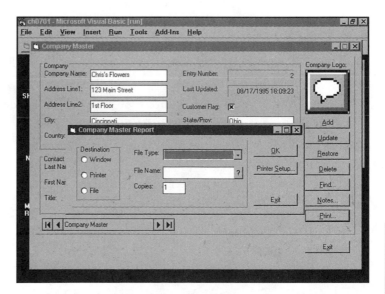

Not only have you finished a report routine for the CompanyMaster project you have been working on this week, but you also have the Print Report dialog box, which can be used in any future Visual Basic 4 project that uses the Crystal Reports report writer.

Summary

Today you have learned how to use the Crystal Reports report writer to create a simple list report using the data tables you created earlier in the week. You have also learned that Crystal Reports is a banded report writer. Here are the main bands in a report:

- ☐ The header and footer bands: These bands appear on every page.
- ☐ The detail band: This band contains the equivalent of a data table record.
- ☐ The section band: This band contains subtotals or groupings of the data.

You have also learned that Crystal Reports recognizes three types of fields on the report form:

- ☐ Database fields: These fields are from attached data tables.
- ☐ Text fields: These fields are made up of literal text created by the user.
- ☐ Formula fields: These fields are calculated fields created by the user.

You have also learned how to use the Crystal Reports Control to run a report from within your Visual Basic 4 program. Finally, you created the Print Report dialog box, which lets you control the report destination, the file type, and the number of copies printed.

Quiz

1. List and describe each of the three bands in a Crystal Report.
2. To which database types can Crystal Reports attach?
3. How do you insert text directly on a Crystal Reports design form?
4. How do you produce mailing labels in Crystal Reports?
5. In Crystal Reports, can you browse data contained in a database that you are using for a report?
6. How do you insert select criteria in a Crystal Reports report?
7. How do you join tables in Crystal Reports?

Exercises

1. Write a formula that can be used in Crystal Reports to count the number of records in a list of last names. Assume a field name of NameLast.
2. Write a formula to display a list of vendors that have not supplied their federal tax ID numbers to your accounting manager. This information is stored in a field named EmployerID.

3. Build a Crystal Reports report using the Book.mdb database that can be found in the TYSDBVB\CHAP07 directory of the CD that shippped with this book. Include the following items in your report:

    ☐ Modify the page to print in landscape mode.

    ☐ Insert the fields PubID, Publisher, and Comments from the Publisher Comments table.

    ☐ Insert the Name field from the Publishers table. Make sure that you link the PubID field in the Publisher Comments table to the PubID field in the Publishers table.

    ☐ Set a descending sort order on the Publishers.Name field.

    ☐ Insert the report title Comments on Publishers. Format this title with Arial, 14 point bold text.

    ☐ Insert a grand total record count.

    ☐ Insert a page number in the bottom right of the page footer.

    ☐ Insert the current date in the bottom left of the page footer.

Print the report and the report definition when you have finished the layout.

7

1

2

3

4

5

6

7

In the first week, you learned about the relational database model, how to use the Visual Basic database objects to access and update existing databases, and how to use the Visual Basic Data Manager program to create and maintain databases. You also learned how to design and code data entry forms, including use of the Visual Basic bound data controls, and how to create input validation routines at the keystroke, field, and form levels. Finally, you learned how to use the Visual Basic Crystal Reports report writer to design simple reports, and you learned how to use the CRYSTAL.VBX control to run those reports from within your Visual Basic programs.

Day 1, "Your First Database Program in Visual Basic"

The first day's lesson gave you a crash course in how to build a fully functional data entry form in Visual Basic with minimal programming code. On Day 1, you learned the following:

☐ How to use the data control to bind a form to a database and data table by setting the DatabaseName and RecordSource properties.

☐ How to use the Text box bound input control to bind an input box on the form to a data table and data field by setting the DataSource and DataField properties.

☐ How to combine standard command buttons and the AddNew and Delete methods to provide Add and Delete record functionality to a data entry form.

Day 2, "Creating Databases"

The lesson on Day 2 concentrated on the fundamentals of relational databases. You learned the following about relational databases:

☐ A relational database is a collection of related data.

☐ The three key building blocks of relational databases are data fields, data records, and data tables.

☐ The two types of database relationships are one-to-one (which uses qualifier fields) and one-to-many (which uses pointer fields).

☐ There are two types of key (or index) fields: primary key and foreign key.

You also learned the data field types recognized by Visual Basic 4. You constructed a data entry form that allows you to test the way Visual Basic behaves when attempting to store data entered into the various data field types.

Day 3, "Using the Data Manager"

On Day 3 you learned how to use the Data Manager that comes with Visual Basic 4 to perform the following database maintenance operations on Microsoft Access databases:

☐ Create new databases

☐ Open existing databases

☐ Create, modify, and delete data tables

☐ Perform data entry on existing tables including adding, updating, finding, and deleting records

You also learned how the Data Manager can be used to perform database operations on non-Microsoft Access databases including the following:

☐ Creating FoxPro and dBASE databases using the DOS Make Directory (md) operation to create a DOS directory

☐ Creating, modifying, and deleting tables in non-Microsoft Access databases

Day 4, "Visual Basic Database Objects"

In this day's lesson, you learned that there are three types of Visual Basic data objects:

☐ Table objects are used when you have a large data set and need to do frequent searches to locate a single record. You can use the Visual Basic Seek method and use Visual Basic indexes with the Table object.

☐ Dynaset objects are used in most cases in which you need read and write access to data sets. The Dynaset uses little workstation memory and allows you to create virtual tables by combining fields from different tables in the same database. The Dynaset is the only data object that allows you to read and write to ODBC data sources.

☐ Snapshot objects are used when you need fast read-only access to data sets. Snapshot objects are stored in workstation memory, so they should be kept small. Snapshots are good for storing validation lists at the workstation or for small reports.

You also learned that there are two other Visual Basic data objects, both associated with the Visual Basic data control.

☐ The RecordSet object is the data control equivalent of the Dynaset object. If you use the Visual Basic data control, you can access the RecordSet object to read and set properties of the Dynaset created by the data control.

☐ The Database object is another subobject of the data control. You can use the Database object to get a list of tables in the database, a list of indexes associated with the tables, and a list of fields in each of the tables.

Day 5, "Creating Data Entry Forms with Bound Controls"

On Day 5, you learned about creating data entry forms with Visual Basic bound data controls.

You learned that the Visual Basic data control has five database-related properties. Three refer to the database and two refer to the Dynaset.

The Database properties of the Visual Basic data control are

1. DatabaseName: Used to select the database to access.
2. Exclusive: Used to prevent others from opening the database.
3. ReadOnly: Used to prevent your program from modifying the data in the database.

The Dynaset properties of the Visual Basic data control are

1. RecordSource: Used to select the data table within the database.
2. Options: Used to set ReadOnly, DenyWrite, and AppendOnly properties to the Dynaset.

You learned that the Visual Basic data control has three database-related methods:

1. `Refresh`: Used to update the data control after setting properties.
2. `UpdateControls`: Used to read values from the fields in the Dynaset and write those values to the related form controls.
3. `UpdateRecord`: Used to read values from the form controls and write those values to the related fields in the Dynaset.

You learned that the Visual Basic data control has three database-related events:

1. `Reposition`: Occurs each time the record pointer is moved to a new record in the Dynaset.
2. `Validate`: Occurs each time the record pointer leaves the current record in the Dynaset.
3. `Error`: Occurs each time a database error occurs.

You learned how to use Visual Basic bound form controls to link form input and display controls to data fields in the database.

1. Bound text box control: Used for data entry on character and numeric data table fields.
2. Bound label control: Used for display-only character and numeric data table fields.
3. Bound checkbox control: Used for data entry on the BOOLEAN data type field.
4. Bound image control: Used to display images stored in the BINARY data type field.
5. The 3-D panel control behaves the same as the label control, and the 3-D checkbox control behaves the same as a standard checkbox control.

You also learned several general rules for creating Visual Basic forms in the Windows 95 style.

1. The default color is light gray for backgrounds.
2. Use the panel3D control to create a palette on which to place all other controls.
3. The default font is 8-point sans serif, regular.
4. Input areas should have a background that is white; display areas should have a background that is light gray. Display areas should be recessed into the input palette.
5. Use frame controls to group related items on a form.
6. Left-justify all controls, including field prompts. Field prompts should be written in mixed case and followed by a semicolon.
7. Standard spacing and sizing for common controls are as follows:

   ☐ Control height is 330 twips.
   ☐ Command button width is 1200 twips.
   ☐ Vertical spacing between controls is 90 twips for related items and 210 twips for unrelated items.
   ☐ Border widths (top, bottom, and side) should be 120 twips.

Lastly, you learned how to write code that sets control colors to the Windows 95 default colors, how to create your own custom color scheme, and how to link your control colors to the color scheme selected with the Windows Control Panel color applet.

Day 6, "Input Validation"

On this day, you learned how to perform input validation on data entry forms. You learned that input validation tasks can be divided into three areas:

☐ Key Filtering: Preventing unwanted keyboard input.
☐ Field-Level Validation: Validating input for each field.
☐ Form-Level Validation: Validating input across several fields.

You also learned that there are a few basic questions you can ask yourself when you are developing validation rules for your form.

☐ Is it a required field?
☐ What characters are valid or invalid for this field? (Numeric input only, capital letters only, no spaces allowed, and so forth.)
☐ For numeric fields, is there a high or low range limit? (Must be greater than zero and less than 1000, can't be less than 100, and so on.)

□ Is there a list of valid values for this field? (For example, you can only enter Retail, Wholesale, or Other; Name must already be in the customer table.)

. □ Is this a conditional field? (If users enter Yes in field A, they must enter something in field C.)

You learned how to write keyboard filter validation functions using the Visual Basic `KeyPress` event. You learned how to write field-level validation functions that check for valid input ranges, input that is part of a list of valid data, and input that is within minimum and maximum length requirements. You also learned how to write validation functions that make sure dependent fields have been filled out properly. Finally, you learned how to create a Visual Basic library module containing validation functions that can be used in any Visual Basic program.

You also applied your knowledge of bound data controls, Visual Basic data entry form design, and validation processing to create the data entry form for the CompanyMaster database.

Day 7, "Creating Reports with Crystal Reports Writer"

You wrapped up your first week of study by learning how to use Crystal Reports to create a simple list report using the data tables you created earlier in the week. You also learned that Crystal Reports is a *banded* report writer. These are the main bands in a report:

□ Header and Footer bands appear on every page.

□ Detail bands contain the equivalent of a data table record.

□ Section bands contain subtotals or groupings of the data.

You also learned that Crystal Reports recognizes three types of fields on the report form:

□ Database fields are from attached data tables.

□ Text fields are literal text created by the user.

□ Formula fields are calculated fields created by the user.

You also learned how to use the CRYSTAL.VBX to run a report from within your Visual Basic program. Finally, you created a generic print report dialog that lets you control the report destination, file type, and number of copies.

2

In this week, you will build upon the skills you developed in Week 1. Emphasis will move to developing skills you need for application development in a workgroup environment. In addition, you will create tools that you use in every Visual Basic database application.

Note: Most of the material covered this week requires the Professional Edition of Visual Basic. However, if you are working with the Standard Edition of Visual Basic, you will still be able to learn a great deal from this week's lessons.

You will learn about Visdata, a data management tool more powerful than the Data Manager. You will have lessons on the SQL data definition language, Visual Basic Data Access Objects (DAO). Other lessons cover how to use Visual Basic code to create database applications; displaying data with graphics; error trapping; and data-bound lists, combo boxes, and grids.

When you've completed this week's lessons, you will know most of the techniques needed to build solid Visual Basic database applications using Visual Basic code. You'll also have several Visual Basic code libraries that you can use in future Visual Basic projects. The following sections describe this week's lessons in more detail.

Day 8: Today, you learn how to use Visdata, which is a data management tool similar to Data Manager, but with many more features. You learn how to compile this project as well as add it to the Visual Basic Add-Ins menu. This tool assists you in building databases, defining tables, and executing SQL statements.

Day 9: You begin the first of three days devoted to one of the most important topics in database programming—Structured Query Language (SQL). After learning a definition of what SQL can do for you, you learn the basics of this powerful and simple language. You learn about SQL clauses you can use to select and sort records from your databases. You also learn SQL keywords such as SELECT, ORDER BY, WHERE, DISTINCTROW, TOP N, TOP N PERCENT, and GROUP BY. You also study SQL Aggregate functions (SUM, AVG, and so on), joins, unions, and cross tab queries.

Day 10: In this lesson, you delve into the database engine that ships with Visual Basic 4—Microsoft JET. You learn the hierarchical design and use of the Data Access Object (DAO) available to you in your development. The emphasis is on the methods, properties, and events of each object.

Day 11: In the previous week, you used the data control to attach databases. Today, you temporarily abandon use of the data control in favor of writing Visual Basic code to manage data. You learn the pluses and minuses of this practice. During the lesson, you build a library of tools that can be dropped into any Visual Basic application to assist in data management.

Day 12: You get graphical in Day 12. Users can identify trends and deviations in data much more quickly with graphics and charts than they can with raw data. You learn how to use the graph tool that ships with Visual Basic 4 to give your applications a polished, graphical appearance. During the lesson, you construct a graph library of routines that you can use in all your future Visual Basic projects.

Day 13: This day won't be unlucky because you learn about the data-bound list boxes, combo boxes, and grids that ship with Visual Basic 4. You also learn how to use subforms to display data.

Day 14: The final lesson this week focuses on error trapping. No one intends to release a product with bugs in it, but it does happen. Error trapping manages these bugs, and many other unforeseen kinds of problems. Emphasis is on different kinds of errors an application can encounter and how to handle each. You also build a reusable error trapping module that can be dropped into any Visual Basic application.

You've got a great deal of information to cover—so, let's begin Week 2!

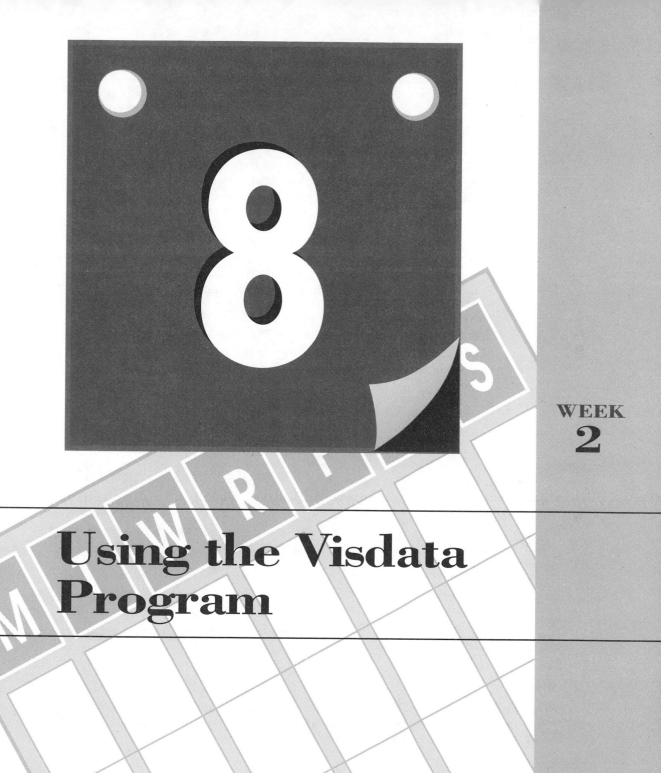

Using the Visdata Program

Today you will learn everything you need to know about using one of the most valuable sample programs that is shipped with Visual Basic 4—The Visdata sample application. You learn how to compile the Visdata sample application, and how to turn it into a Visual Basic 4 Add-In. You also learn how to use the Visdata sample application to maintain your database files, including creating and modifying database tables, performing simple data entry on existing tables, and using Visdata to make backup copies of existing databases.

On Day 2, "Creating Databases," you learned how to use the Data Manager to build and manage databases. Although Data Manager is an excellent tool, Visdata contains additional features that make it more suitable for database development in the enterprise environment. Some of the key advantages of Visdata over the Data Manager include the following:

- ☐ Visdata can open multiple tables at one time. Data Manager limits you to just one.
- ☐ Visdata allows you to create and administer JET, desktop databases such as dBASE and Paradox, and ODBC databases. Data Manager provides the ability to create JET databases, but only the ability to attach to other data sources.
- ☐ Visdata contains additional utilities to perform global data replacements and to preview list and combo boxes.
- ☐ Visdata provides the ability to print report definitions of table structures.

Note: This lesson does not cover the source code for Visdata or talk about how Visdata works. You can, however, learn a great deal by bringing the Visdata project up within Visual Basic 4 and studying the modules and forms. Studying Visdata in this manner is an excellent way to learn how to create dynamic data entry forms, handle SQL processing, and link your Visual Basic 4 programs to back-end database servers using ODBC drivers.

Using Visdata to Maintain Databases and Tables

Visdata is an excellent tool for constructing and managing databases for your Visual Basic 4 applications. You can use it to create new databases, add or modify tables and indexes, establish relationships, set user and group access rights, test and store SQL query statements, and perform data entry on existing tables.

Visdata can present dynamic data entry forms in page format or grid layout format. You can add, edit, or delete records in any table using Visdata. You can connect to Microsoft JET versions 1.1, 2.0, or 3.0 databases, as well as versions of dBASE, FoxPro, and Paradox. You can even access data from Excel spreadsheets, delimited text files and ODBC-connected databases.

Visdata is a great tool for building sample tables and entering test data for your Visual Basic 4 applications. It is also a good tool for compacting, repairing, and managing user and group access rights for Microsoft JET databases.

Visdata allows you to test SQL queries and save them in your Microsoft JET database as stored queries that you can access from your Visual Basic 4 programs. You can also use Visdata to copy records from one table to another—even copy whole data tables from one database to another. This capability gives you the power to create backups of selected information from your existing databases.

Finally, you can use Visdata to inspect the properties of Microsoft JET data objects such as fields, relationships, tables, and indexes. You can learn a great deal about how the Microsoft JET database engine operates by using Visdata to peek under the hood to see the heart of the Visual Basic 4 data access engine.

Compiling the Visdata Project

Before you can take advantage of this great Visual Basic 4 program, you must first load and compile Visdata. To do this, you need to load and run Visual Basic 4 and then select File | Open Project from the main Visual Basic 4 menu. Now locate the SAMPLES\VISDATA subdirectory. This subdirectory is located directly under the home directory in which you installed Visual Basic 4. Find the VISDATA.VBP file and load it. Your screen should look like Figure 8.1.

Figure 8.1.
Visdata loaded into Visual Basic 4.

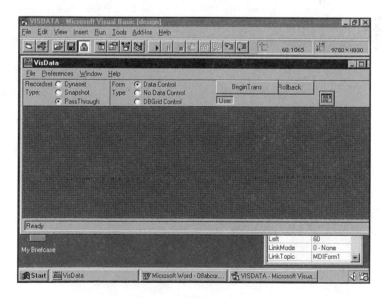

Once you load the project, select File | Make EXE File to compile the project into an executable file. Visual Basic 4 suggests a filename for you. If you are compiling using the 32-bit version of Visual Basic 4, you see the name VISDAT32.EXE. If you are compiling using the 16-bit version of Visual Basic 4, you see the name VISDAT16.EXE. It is recommended that you use the suggested filenames. Depending on your processor speed and available RAM, this might take a minute or two. Be patient because this is a large Visual Basic 4 project.

After Visual Basic 4 completes its work, you'll have a fully executable version of Visdata on your system. Add it to the Visual Basic 4 program group so that you can access Visdata easily in the future. Now click the Visdata icon to start the program. An even easier way to start Visdata exists. You can make it a Visual Basic 4 Add-In application and add it to the Add-Ins menu in Visual Basic 4. You learn how to do this in the next section.

Making Visdata a Visual Basic 4 Add-In

Visual Basic 4 has the capability to accept Add-In applications as part of its operating environment. Add-Ins are applications that are written to operate as if they are a part of the Visual Basic 4 development environment. These applications can also be designed to work independently of Visual Basic 4. The Visdata application operates in this way. Adding Visdata to the main menu of Visual Basic 4 can make it even easier to use the Visdata application to maintain your Visual Basic databases.

To make Visdata an Add-In application, you must first load and compile a small Visual Basic 4 project called VDADDIN.VBP. This short application registers Visdata as a class object and establishes it as an application that can be called by other OLE-compliant programs.

> **Note:** The theory and practice of creating OLE-compatible class objects goes beyond the scope of this book. You can refer to the documentation that ships with Visual Basic 4 for more information on how to create OLE class objects.

Use Visual Basic 4 to load the VDADDIN.VBP project. The file appears in the same directory that contains VISDATA.VBP. Select File | Make EXE File. Visual Basic 4 supplies a default filename for the executable—do not change this name. When the compiler finishes, exit Visual Basic 4 completely.

> **Caution:** You must exit Visual Basic 4 completely in order to make sure the Visdata class object gets properly registered and recognized as a valid Add-In the next time you load Visual Basic 4.

8

Load and run the *compiled* version of Visdata that you created in the previous part of this lesson. Select File | Make Visdata a VB Add-In from the Visdata main menu. You won't see anything happen on-screen, but by selecting this option, you instructed Visdata to call the vdaddin module you just created and use it to register Visdata as an OLE-compatible application. The next time you load Visual Basic 4, you can make Visdata an Add-In application.

Now reload Visual Basic 4 and register Visdata as an Add-In. To do this, you must first select Add-Ins from the main Visual Basic 4 menu. Find the Visdata Add-In Stub entry and make sure the checkbox is filled in (see Figure 8.2).

Figure 8.2.

Selecting the Visdata Add-In Stub.

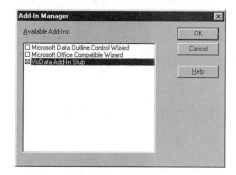

By selecting this item, you tell Visual Basic 4 to add the Visdata application to the Add-Ins menu. Now, when you select the Add-Ins menu, you see the Visdata menu item (see Figure 8.3).

Figure 8.3.

The new Visual Basic 4 Add-Ins menu.

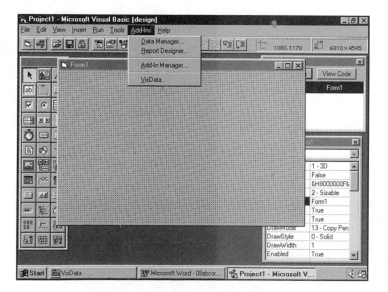

Now you can load the Visdata application by selecting it from this menu! Depending on the speed of your processor and the amount of RAM available on your machine, you may find running Visdata from the Visual Basic 4 menu a bit slow. If you want to speed up Visdata, you can load it directly from a Windows program group or from the Windows File Manager or Explorer shell.

Now let's start exploring Visdata.

The Visdata Opening Screen

If you don't already have Visdata running, start it now. You can start Visdata by selecting it from the Visual Basic 4 program group or, if you installed Visdata as an Add-In application, you can start it by selecting Add-Ins | Visdata.

> **Note:** The rest of today's lesson discusses how to use the Visdata application. Although you do not have to have Visdata up and running to learn about it, you'll probably get more out of the lesson if you run the examples given here. If you have not already loaded and compiled the Visdata program, refer to the sections "Compiling the Visdata Project" and "Making Visdata a Visual Basic 4 Add-In," earlier in this chapter.

When you first start Visdata, the main startup screen appears (see Figure 8.4).

Figure 8.4.

The Visdata main screen.

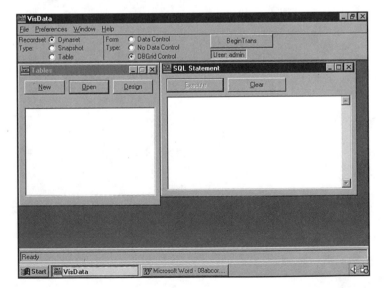

This MDI form is *data central* for the Visdata application. All database activity starts from this screen. Four major components to this screen deserve attention:

☐ The Main Menu: This menu gives you access to all the features of Visdata. This menu also expands once you open a database.

☐ The Table Window: This window shows all the major table objects present in the database you currently have open.

☐ The SQL Window: This window allows you to write and execute standard SQL statements against the database you currently have open.

☐ The Radio Buttons: You use these to determine the type of data objects you want to work with.

Now let's go through each of the four components of the Visdata main screen in a bit more depth.

The Main Menu

The Visdata Main Menu contains four items before you load a database: File, Preferences, Window, and Help. After you load a database, additional items appear between the File and Preferences items. When you load a Microsoft JET format database, you see two additional items: Jet and Utility. If you load a non-Microsoft JET format database, you see only the Utility option added to the menu.

The Visdata Main Menu gives you access to all the features and options of the program. You'll learn each menu option in depth later, but first, let's explore the File menu options just a bit.

The File | Open Database option allows you to open an existing database. This database can be any one of several formats. The most common database format you'll probably deal with is the Microsoft JET format (also known as the Microsoft Access database format). As an example, use Visdata to open an existing Microsoft JET database.

Select File | Open Database | Jet Engine MDB. The Visdata program presents you with an Open Jet Database dialog box (see Figure 8.5).

Locate and select the CH801.MDB database that can be found in the \TYSDBVB\CHAP08 directory on the CD that ships with this book. Click the Open button to load the database. Once the database is loaded, Visdata updates the Table window to show all the primary data access objects in the currently opened database. Your screen should now look something like Figure 8.6.

Figure 8.5.

*Opening a Jet Engine MDB
database.*

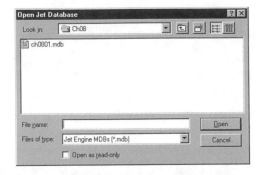

Figure 8.6.

*Visdata with an open
database.*

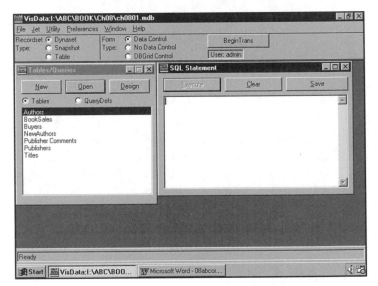

You can close the database by selecting File | Close Database from the Visdata main menu.

The Table Window

The Table window shows all the major data access objects in the currently opened database. The Table window is where you go to add new tables to the database (New button) and modify the design of one of the current tables (Design button). You can also use the Open button to add records to existing data tables. If you click the alternate mouse button within the Table window while you have a table highlighted, you see several other table management options.

Note: By using the term alternate mouse button, we're trying to avoid the left-handed/right-handed confusion. If you have your mouse set for left-handed use, choose the right button; if you have your mouse set for right-handed use, the alternate button is the left button.

Properties

The Properties option shows the various properties of the highlighted table. With the CH0810.MDB database open, highlight a table, click the alternate mouse button, and select Properties to view the data table's properties. Your screen should look like Figure 8.7.

Figure 8.7.
Viewing the table properties.

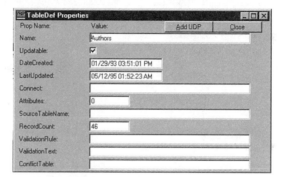

Note: Many of the properties listed on this screen are available only in the Version 3.0 Microsoft JET MDB format. Don't be alarmed if your screen has several empty fields. You learn more about the difference between the various MDB formats later.

Rename

The Rename option allows you to rename the highlighted table without deleting the data. Highlight the Authors table by clicking it once with the primary mouse button. Now click the alternate mouse button to bring up the context menu. Select Rename from the menu and enter MoreAuthors as the new name; then click the OK button. Your screen should look like Figure 8.8 as you rename the Authors table.

Figure 8.8.
Renaming a data table.

Before you continue with the project, change the MoreAuthors table back to Authors using the same technique previously described.

Copy Structure

The Copy Structure option lets you copy the highlighted table's field layout and design, with or without existing data, to a different database. Select the Authors table and click the alternate mouse button to bring up the context menu. Select Copy Structure from the menu list, and you see a dialog box like the one in Figure 8.9.

Figure 8.9.
Copying a table.

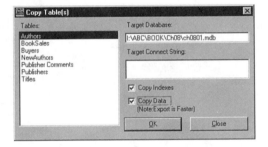

Notice that you can enter a new database name and connect string in the dialog box. This capability means you can copy the structure to an entirely different database. Leave the database name and connect string alone for now. Check the Copy Indexes and Copy Data checkboxes, and click OK. You are then prompted for a table name. Enter MoreAuthors and click OK. A message from Visdata appears, telling you that the new table has been created. When you exit the dialog by clicking Close, Visdata refreshes the Window List automatically. You should now see a new table in the list—MoreAuthors.

Delete

The Delete option lets you delete the highlighted table and all its contents. To delete a table and all its contents, select the table you want to delete and click the alternate mouse button.

Select the MoreAuthors table and click the alternate mouse button to bring up the context menu. Select Delete from the list. Click Yes at the confirmation dialog message to delete the MoreAuthors table. Your window list refreshes automatically.

Remove All Records

The Remove All Records option allows you to remove all the records from the highlighted table without deleting the table structure. To delete all records from a table, select NewAuthors from the list. Click the alternate mouse button to bring up the context menu and click Remove All Records. Visdata displays a confirmation message. Click OK to remove the records from the selected data table.

Refresh

The Refresh option updates the window to reflect changes in the data access objects that are part of the database. Usually, Visdata refreshes the Table window each time you take an action that affects the contents of the list. Some actions, however, do not automatically update the window. For example, if you use the SQL window to enter SQL statements to create a new data table in the database, Visdata does not automatically refresh the Table window.

To refresh the Table window, you must first select one of the table items by clicking it once with the primary mouse button. Then, click once with the alternate mouse button to bring up the context menu. Select Refresh from the list. Visdata then refreshes the Table window to reflect the current state of the data access objects in the opened database.

The SQL Window

The SQL window enables you to enter and execute standard SQL statements against the opened database. You can also save the SQL query for later use in your Visual Basic 4 programs.

Select the SQL window by clicking on the top border of the window one time. Now enter the following SQL query into the text window:

```
SELECT * FROM Authors
```

This statement selects all the data in the Authors table and presents it to the screen. Your screen should look like the one in Figure 8.10.

Figure 8.10.
Results of an SQL query.

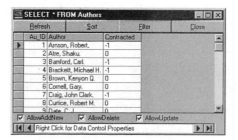

235

> **Note:** We will cover SQL SELECT Queries in depth in the lesson on Day 9, "Selecting Data with SQL." For now, just remember that you can write, test, and save your SQL queries using the Visdata SQL window.

You can save this query for later use within your Visual Basic 4 programs by clicking the Save button in the SQL window and answering No when a dialog asks whether this is an SQL PassThrough Query. Next, supply the query object name qryTest, and click OK in the dialog box that appears (see Figure 8.11).

Figure 8.11.
Saving a query.

Each time you load Visdata, the program remembers the last SQL query you entered in the SQL window. You can click the Clear button to clear out the text in the SQL window.

The Radio Buttons

Two sets of radio buttons appear near the top of the Visdata main screen. You use these buttons to establish the type of data object Visdata uses to access the data and the type of data entry form Visdata uses to present the selected data on the screen.

Selecting the Default Data Access Object

The first set of radio buttons controls the type of data access object Visdata uses to open the data table. The default data access object is the Visual Basic 4 Dynaset, the most flexible Visual Basic 4 data access object. You can use the Dynaset object to create updateable views of more than one table or open an existing table for read/write access.

You can use the Snapshot data access object to open a read-only view of one or more data tables. Snapshot objects are faster than Dynasets, but require more workstation memory.

Finally, if you only need access to the physical base table in the database, you can select the Table radio button. Tables are fast and require little workstation memory. The disadvantage of the Table data access object is that you cannot use it to combine two or more tables into a single view.

Even though most of the work you do from Visdata is with base tables, you should set this radio button to use the Dynaset data access object. Dynasets are fast enough for most all Visdata work, and they provide the most flexibility when dealing with multitable views.

Selecting the Default Data Form

The second set of radio buttons enables you to select the type of data form you see when you load your data access object. Visual Basic 4 now ships with a very nice data-bound grid tool. This grid automatically loads all the fields in the selected data access object and scrolls data records into the table as needed. This grid object may be the most useful selection of the three. Click the DBGrid radio button to make this your default data form.

The other two radio buttons select two versions of a standard data entry form. The first button, Data Control, loads the records from the data access object one at a time, using the Visual Basic 4 data control tool. The second radio button, No Data Control, presents a similar form, but without using the Visual Basic 4 data control tool. The advantage of the Data Control form is that it handles BIT and BINARY data type fields better than the No Data Control form. The No Data Control form, however, allows users to press F4 to display the entire contents of a data field whose contents overflow the control's display area. This zooming feature is handy when dealing with large text fields or memo fields.

You can switch the Form Type radio button after each table is opened and displayed, which enables you to open one or more tables using different data forms. Let's open three tables, each using a different data form.

First, select the DBGrid data form radio button. Now double-click the Authors table. This action brings up the Authors table in a grid display. Your screen should look like Figure 8.12.

Figure 8.12.

Authors table using the grid data form.

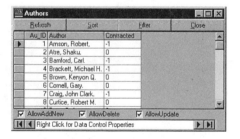

Note: Please note that the columns in this view can be resized. Simply select a column divider with your mouse and drag to the desired width.

Next, select the Data Control button and double-click the Authors table again. Now you see the same data presented in a standard data entry from. Your screen should now look like Figure 8.13.

Figure 8.13.
Authors table using the data control form.

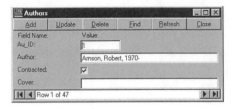

Next, select the No Data Control button and double-click the Authors table a third time. Now, you see the Authors data presented in a slightly different data entry form. Notice the differences in the way the Contracted field appears on the No Data Control (as text) form and the Data Control form (checkbox). Figure 8.14 shows a tiled view of the three data forms side by side.

Figure 8.14.
Three data forms side by side.

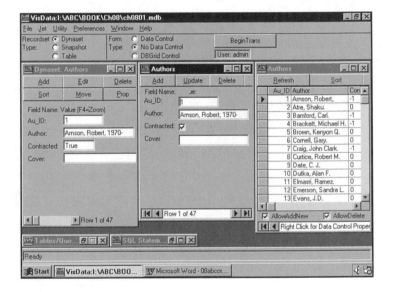

Now that you have seen the major components of the Visdata main screen, let's review each of the menu items in greater detail.

The Visdata File Menu

The Visdata File menu contains 10 items. You can open and close databases from the file menu, log into a designated workspace, learn about the properties of the database, and review any errors that have been logged since you started Visdata. You can compact or repair Microsoft JET databases from the File menu. You can run a routine that registers Visdata as an Add-In Application, and you also exit the program from the File menu.

If you have used Visdata before, you see a list of the most recently used databases in this menu. You can reload one of those databases by clicking on its name in the File menu.

Open Database and Close Database

Before you can begin working on an existing database, you must first load it using the Open Database menu option. This menu option enables you to load one of several database formats. Each format has a slightly different set of options in the menu tree. You can load Microsoft JET, dBASE, FoxPro, Excel, and text files using the 32-bit version. If you are running the 16-bit version, you can load Btreive format databases as well.

> **Note:** You can load only one database at a time into Visdata. If you need to work on tables from more than one database, you need to use the Attach menu option to attach the *foreign* data tables (the tables that are contained within a database other than the one on which you are working) to the database you currently have open. We cover the Attach option later in this lesson.

When you select Open Database, you see several other menu choices. You select one of the secondary items depending on the database format you want to access. The following sections cover each of the secondary menu choices and how you use them to open existing databases.

JET Engine MDB

When you select the Jet Engine MDB option, Visdata brings up a File Open dialog box and prompts you to select the Microsoft JET database you want to load (see Figure 8.15).

Figure 8.15.
Loading a Microsoft JET database.

Visdata is able to load Microsoft JET version 1.1 and 2.0/2.5. If you are running the 32-bit version of Visdata, you can load the Microsoft JET version 3.0 databases. You do not have to tell Visdata which database format you are loading—it figures that out. If you are running the 16-bit version of Visdata and you attempt to load a database built using Microsoft JET version 3.0, you get an error message.

Note: Microsoft documentation is a bit fuzzy on the use of Microsoft JET 2.5 and Microsoft JET 2.0 databases. The 2.5 number refers to the Microsoft JET engine version number. This version of Microsoft JET was released as an interim upgrade to Visual Basic 3.0 to allow it access to Microsoft Access version 2.0 databases. Throughout the text, the terms Microsoft JET 2.5 and Microsoft Access 2.0 are used interchangeably. Both names refer to the same physical database format.

dBASE (IV and III)

You can also use Visdata to load dBASE format databases. When you select the dBASE menu option, you see an additional menu that asks you to select version III or version IV format database.

Caution: You must tell Visdata what dBASE format you are loading so that it knows what index files and memo field formats to expect. If you load an incorrect format into Visdata, you will not see an error message right away. You may receive error messages, however, when you attempt to read or write data to the database. These errors may permanently corrupt your database. Be sure you load the FoxPro and dBASE databases using the correct menu option to avoid problems.

When you select the correct format, you see the File Open dialog box prompting you to locate and load a database. After the database is loaded you see the list of available tables. You also see a message at the bottom of the screen suggesting that you use the Attach option to access the dBASE format data tables (see Figure 8.16).

Figure 8.16.
Viewing a loaded dBASE database.

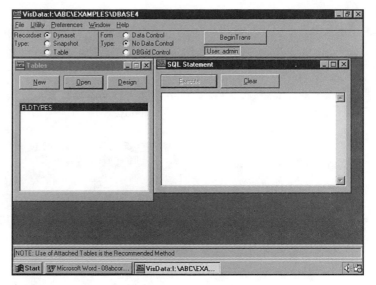

> **Tip:** When you deal with non-Microsoft JET data formats, you get better speed performance if you access them via the Attach option. We cover the Attach menu option later in today's lesson.

FoxPro (2.6, 2.5, and 2.0)

Loading the FoxPro format databases works the same as loading the dBASE format databases. When you select FoxPro from the menu, you see an additional menu list that asks you to select the proper database format. When you select the format, you see the File Open dialog prompting you to locate and load the proper database. The same warnings mentioned in the preceding dBASE section apply here. Do not attempt to load a FoxPro 2.6 format database using the FoxPro 2.5 format menu option. Even if the file loads initially without errors, you will probably get unpredictable results and may even corrupt your database.

Paradox (4.*x*, 3.*x*)

Opening Paradox files with Visdata works much like opening FoxPro or dBASE format databases. You select the database version you wish to access, and then fill out the File Open dialog box to locate and load the database. The CD that ships with this book contains a Paradox 4.*x* format database called PDSAMPLE.DB. You can locate and load this file from the \TYSDBVB\CHAP08 directory.

Excel

Visdata can also directly load Microsoft Excel spreadsheet files and enable you to manipulate their contents. When you select Excel from the Open Database menu, you see the File Open dialog box that prompts you to locate and load the Excel spreadsheet.

Visdata locates all sheets and named ranges defined in the Excel file and presents them as table objects in the Table window (see Figure 8.17).

Figure 8.17.
Using Visdata to directly load an Excel spreadsheet.

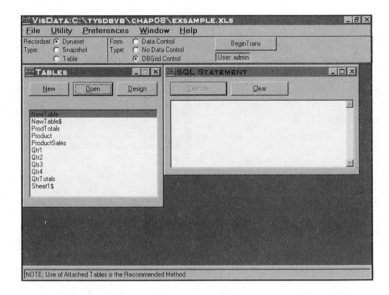

Figure 8.18 shows the sample Excel spreadsheet \TYSDBVB\CHAP08\EXSAMPLE.XLS as it appears in Excel. The range name box is opened in the illustration so that you can see how the range names in Excel compare to the table names in Visdata.

Figure 8.19 shows the same Excel file opened using Visdata. In Figure 8.19, the table object Sheet1$ has been opened as a Dynaset object.

Figure 8.18.
Viewing CH0802.XLS with Excel.

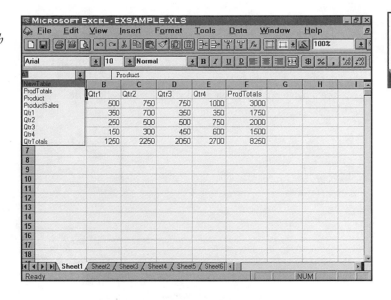

Figure 8.19.
Viewing CH0802.XLS with Visdata.

Caution: Visdata opens Excel data files for exclusive use only. If you have an Excel spreadsheet open with Visdata, no other program on your workstation, or any other program on the network, can open the same spreadsheet. If some other program has an Excel spreadsheet open, you cannot open it using Visdata until the other program closes that file.

After you open the Excel file, you can perform all data entry operations on that file including creating new tables and editing data in existing tables in the spreadsheet.

Text Files

Visdata can load various standard formats of ASCII text files for read-only access. When you select a file to load (using the File Open dialog box), you actually open the entire directory as a database. Visdata permits you to select any file with a .TXT extension from the Table window and open it as a read-only data table. Figure 8.20 shows the file \TYSDBVB\CHAP\TXSAMPLE.TXT opened as a read-only data file.

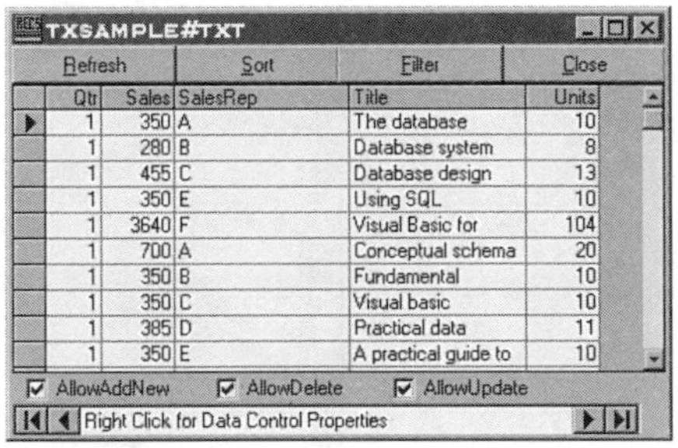

Figure 8.20.

Opening a text file from Visdata.

Visdata recognizes several types and formats of ASCII text files. The default format is comma-delimited fields with character fields surrounded by quotes. You can control this default with settings under the [Text ISAM] section of the VISDATAINI file. You can also establish more complex text file interfaces by creating a SCHEMA.INI file in your default Windows directory.

The details of creating and maintaining INI file settings for text files is beyond the scope of this book and is covered in the Visual Basic 4 Help file under the topic "SCHEMA.INI."

ODBC

The ODBC menu option is slightly different from the previously discussed Open commands. This option enables you to use Visdata to open predefined ODBC data sources. When you select the ODBC menu option, you see a screen that asks you for the data source type, data source name, user ID, and password for that data source (see Figure 8.21).

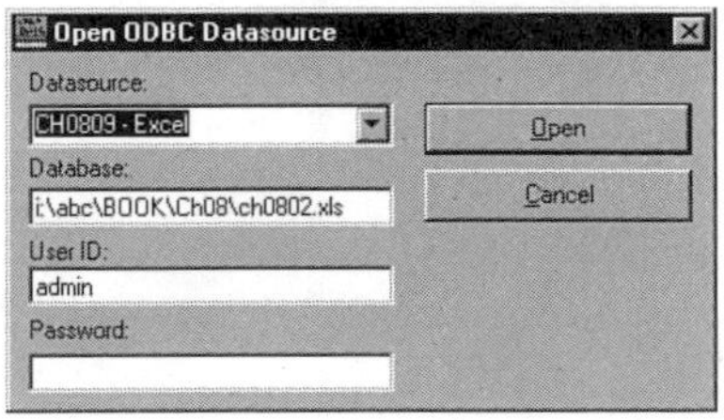

Figure 8.21.

Using Visdata to open an ODBC data source.

After you fill out the ODBC dialog box, Visdata locates and opens the data source and updates the Table window.

Before you can open an ODBC data source, you must first define that data source using the ODBC (or ODBC32) program from the Control Panel. You learn about defining and accessing ODBC data sources in depth in Week 3. If you want more information on defining ODBC data sources, you can refer to the help available when you load the ODBC or ODBC32 programs from the Control Panel.

Close Database

The Close Database menu option simply closes the open database. All tables are closed at the same time.

Errors

The Errors menu option shows the last error or set of errors reported to Visdata (see Figure 8.22).

Figure 8.22.
Viewing the Errors collection.

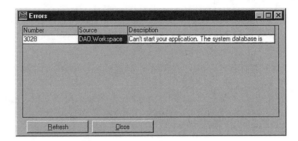

Some data sources return more than one error message per transaction (usually ODBC data sources), which is referred to as the errors collection. This menu option lets you review the errors collection in a grid listing. If no errors have been returned, this grid is empty.

Tip: Even if you have had several successful database transactions since your last error, the most recent error remains in this grid display.

Properties

The Properties menu item only appears after a database has been loaded into Visdata. This menu item has three submenu items:

- ☐ DBEngine: Returns information about the database engine currently in use.
- ☐ Workspace: Returns information about the current defined workspace.
- ☐ Database: Returns information about the database you currently have open.

DBEngine

Visual Basic 4 uses the Microsoft JET database engine for all database handling. Starting with Visual Basic 4, however, third-party vendors can design and install other database engines to work within Visual Basic. This screen allows you to view the basic properties of the current database engine. Figure 8.23 shows the dialog box that appears when you select the DBEngine menu item.

Figure 8.23.
Viewing the DBEngine properties.

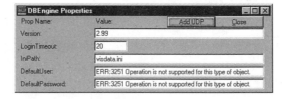

Workspace

The Workspace menu item displays properties of the currently open workspace. Workspaces are collections of databases, users, and groups. You can log into a workspace to access related databases. When you select Workspace from the menu, you see a dialog box that lists the properties of the current workspace (see Figure 8.24).

Figure 8.24.
Viewing the Workspace properties.

Workspace data objects are covered in detail on Day 10.

Database

The Database menu option shows all the properties of the currently opened database, including the database format, any connection strings that are in effect, the format version number, and several other parameters about the database. Figure 8.25 shows the Database Properties dialog box for a typical Microsoft Access database.

Figure 8.25.
Viewing the Database properties (32-bit).

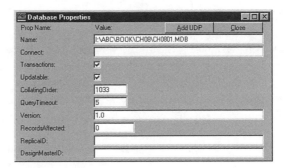

Note: The last three fields are not available in the 16-bit version.

The meaning and use of these property settings is covered on Day 10.

New

The New menu option enables you to use Visdata to create entirely new databases in several formats. This section concentrates on the Microsoft JET database format. Most of the rules for creating Microsoft JET databases apply equally to non-Microsoft JET formats. Although the Visdata application can create a non-Microsoft JET database, you should not use Visdata to create non-Microsoft JET databases very often. If you need to work in non-Microsoft JET formats, use the native database engine to create the data files. You can then use Visdata to access and manipulate the non-Microsoft JET databases.

JET (3.0, 2.0, 1.1)

When you select the JET menu item, Visdata asks you to select one of three versions of Microsoft JET data format: 1.1, 2.0, or 3.0. (Please note that the 16-bit version of Visdata does not support the 3.0 JET data format). The 1.1 format can be read by all versions of Microsoft Access and Microsoft Visual Basic versions 3.0 and later. The version 2.0 format can be read by Microsoft Access version 2.0 and by Visual Basic versions 3.0 and later. Version 3.0 format databases can only be read by 32-bit Visual Basic 4 and by the 32-bit version of Microsoft Access. The advantage of the older formats is that the data can be read by most versions of the software. The advantage of the version 3.0 format is that it allows for additional database properties that are not available in the older formats.

 **Caution:** Attempting to read a version 3.0 Microsoft JET database with Access version 2.0 or Visual Basic version 3.0 results in an error that tells you your database is invalid or corrupt. If you know that you will be working only with software that can read version 3.0 files, you should select the version 3.0 format because it provides additional features. If, however, you plan to deploy your database in an environment that contains both 16- and 32-bit versions of the software, you should stick with the version 2.0 data format.

After you select a database format from the submenu, Visdata presents you with a dialog box prompting you to enter a filename for the new database (refer to Figure 8.26).

Figure 8.26.

Creating a new Microsoft JET database.

Creating a new database does not automatically create data tables; you must use the New command button in the Table window to create a new table.

dBASE, FoxPro, and Paradox

Creating dBASE, FoxPro, and Paradox format databases is similar to creating Microsoft JET databases. When you select one of these formats, you are prompted to indicate the exact version of the database you wish to create. After you select a version, Visdata presents you with a simple dialog box prompting you to enter a name for the database. This name will not be a data file; it will be a file directory (called a folder in Windows 95). You can include any valid drive designator and directory path you wish when you create the database. See Figure 8.27 for an example of creating a FoxPro database directory.

Figure 8.27.
Creating a FoxPro database
directory.

Caution: Remember that Visdata creates directories (or folders), not data files, when you create dBASE, FoxPro, or Paradox databases. Make sure to use names that make sense as directories or folders.

Text

You can use Visdata to create text data files. These files are comma-delimited ASCII text files that you can open for read-only access from Visdata. Even though you can create the database files and tables, you cannot add any data to the tables or create indexes on the data tables. This might be useful if you want to create ASCII text data files that will be used by other applications.

When you select the text menu option, Visdata prompts you to enter a name for the database. This name will be used to create a directory (Windows 95 folder) on the designated drive. You can use any valid device designator and directory path you wish when you create the database.

Compact Database (3.0, 2.0, 1.1)

You can use Visdata to compact existing Microsoft JET databases. Compacting a database removes empty space in the data file once occupied by records that have been deleted. Running the Compact menu option also reorganizes any defined indexes stored in the database.

You can also use the Compact Database menu option to upgrade the version of Microsoft JET database formats. For example, if you have a database built in the Microsoft JET 1.1 format, you can convert it to the Microsoft JET 3.0 format using the Compact Database menu.

Note: You can only use the Microsoft JET version 3.0 format if you are running applications in 32-bit mode. The Microsoft JET version 3.0 is not available in 16-bit mode.

When you select Compact Database, you have to select a database format. If you select 3.0 from this menu, the database you selected will be compacted and stored as a Microsoft JET version 3.0 database. If you select 1.1 from this menu, the database you select will be compact and stored as a Microsoft JET version 1.1 database.

Note: You can use the Compact Database menu option to convert older database formats to newer ones, but you cannot use the Compact Database menu option to convert newer formats to older ones. For example, you cannot convert a 3.0 Microsoft JET database to a 2.0 Microsoft JET database.

When you select the target format, you see a File Open dialog box asking you to select the database you wish to compact. The database you select cannot be opened by any other program while it is being compacted. After you select the source database, you have to enter the name of the destination database file. If you select the same name as the source, your current data file is overwritten with the new format. If you select a new database filename, all information is copied from the source database to the target database.

Caution: Even though Visdata allows you to compact a database file onto itself, this practice is not recommended. If anything happens midway through the compacting process, you could lose some or all of your data. Always compact a database to a new database filename.

Before Visdata compacts your database, you will be asked if you want to encrypt the data. If you say Yes, Visdata copies all data and encrypts the file so that only those who have access to the security files can read the data. We talk more about data encryption on Day 20.

Repair Database

If you get a database corrupt error attempting to open a Microsoft JET database file, you may need to repair your database. Database files can become damaged due to power surges during read/write operations or due to physical device errors (damaged disk drive plates, and so on). You can repair an existing database by selecting Repair Database from the File menu. You then see a File Open dialog box that asks you for the database filename. Once you select the filename, Visdata loads and repairs the database to the best of its capabilities. You may receive a message saying some of the data could not be recovered.

> **Tip:** Remember to make copies of your database on a regular basis. You should not depend on the Repair routine to recover all your data. If you experience a program crash due to corrupted data, you can always restore the file from the most recent backup.
>
> You should also use the Windows 95 or DOS defragment utility on your hard drive after performing a Compact or Repair function to improve the overall performance of your application.

Make Visdata a VB Add-In

The Make Visdata a VB Add-In menu option runs a short compiled program (VDADDIN.EXE) that makes updates to the Windows registry files. These updates make it possible to run Visdata from the Visual Basic 4 Add-Ins menu option.

If you have not already done so, you can make Visdata an Add-In application by selecting this option. You must first load and compile the VDADDIN project. For more information on making Visdata an Add-In application, refer to the sections "Compiling the Visdata Project" and "Making Visdata a Visual Basic 4 Add-In" earlier in this chapter.

Exit Visdata

The Exit item does just what you expect. When you exit Visdata, your current database closes, along with all open database objects. If you have text in the SQL window, it will be saved and restored the next time you load Visdata. Visdata also remembers the windows you had open, as well as their sizes and their locations for the next time you load Visdata.

Adding Tables and Indexes to the Database

When you have created a new database, you can add new tables and indexes to the database. You can also add new tables and indexes to existing databases. To illustrate the process of managing database tables using Visdata, let's create a new Microsoft JET database, add a new table, add a new index, and then modify the table structure.

Creating the New **CH08NEW.MDB** Database

If you haven't already done so, load and start Visdata. Select File | New | JET | 2.0 from the main menu and enter CH08NEW.MDB in the Select Jet Database to Create dialog box (see Figure 8.28). Click the Save button to create the new database.

Figure 8.28.
Creating CH08NEW.MDB.

Adding a New Table to the Database

To add a new table to the database, click the New command button in the Table window to bring up the Table Definition dialog box. Your screen should look like Figure 8.29.

Figure 8.29.
Defining a new table.

Enter NewTable in the Table Name field at the top of the dialog box. Now you can add fields to the data table. Click the Add Field command button to bring up the Add Field dialog box. Your screen should look like Figure 8.30.

Figure 8.30.
Adding a new field to the table.

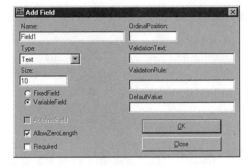

Enter the field name Field1. Set the type to Text and the length to 10. Notice that you can set default values and validation rules here, as well. We'll cover these properties on Day 10.

After you have entered the information you need to define the field, click the OK button to save the field properties to the database.

Caution: Be sure you click the OK button after each field you define. If you fill out the dialog box and then click the Close button, the information you entered on the form won't be saved to the database.

Now that you have defined Field1, let's define one more field. Enter Field2 as the name, and select Currency as the Field Type. Notice that you cannot set the field size. Only Text type fields allow you to set a field size. Now click the OK button to save this field definition; then exit the field definition dialog by clicking the Close button. The Table Structure dialog box should now show two fields defined. Refer to Figure 8.31 as a guide.

Figure 8.31.
Table Structure with two fields defined.

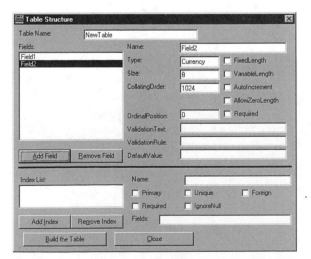

Editing an Existing Field

When you return to the Table Structure screen, you will notice that the same set of properties you saw in the Add Field dialog box appears to the right of the Fields list. You can edit any one of these values for the field by highlighting the field in the list on the left and editing the dialog values on the right. Make Field2 required by selecting the Required checkbox at the right side of the dialog box.

Building the Table

Before you leave this screen, you must first click the Build Table button to actually create the table in your database. Up to this point, Visdata has stored the data table and index definitions in memory. Clicking the Build the Table button is the step that actually creates the data table.

Caution: If you click the Close button before you click the Build Table button, you lose all your table definition information. You have to enter all the table definition data again before you can build the new table.

When you add data to an existing data table, you cannot use Visdata to modify the table structure. You must first remove all records from the data table before you can make any modification to the structure. You can, however, add new fields to a table after data has been entered.

Adding a New Index to the Database Using the Design Button

You can add indexes to existing tables using the Design command button of the Table window. This button brings up the same input form you used to add fields to the database. Now add a Primary Key index for the NewTable you just created.

Caution: Even though Visdata allows you to enter New Index information during the New Tables process, you cannot build a new table and a new index for the same table at one time. Visdata must see the data table that already exists before it can create an index for that table. Use the Design mode of the Table Structure dialog box to add indexes to existing tables.

Click the Add Index command button to bring up the Add Index dialog box. Enter `PKNewTable` as the index name. Double-click Field1 in the field list to make that field the source of the Primary Key index. Your screen should look like Figure 8.32.

Figure 8.32.
Adding a new index to the database.

Be sure to click the OK button to add the index definition to the database. When you have added the index definition, click Close to exit the dialog. Your screen should now look like Figure 8.33.

Figure 8.33.
The Table Structure dialog after adding new index.

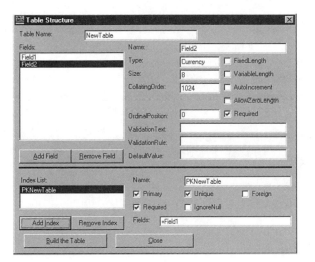

Printing the Table Structure

While you are in the Design mode of the Table Structure dialog, you can click the Print Structure button to get a hard copy printout of the selected table and index objects you have defined. Visdata sends the information directly to the default printer defined for Windows and does not prompt you for any options. Please note that the Print Structure button does not appear when creating a New table; it appears only when you select Design after the table has been created.

Tip: If you want to save the structure to a file, you can use the printer applet in the Control Panel to define a printer as a file, and then set that print device as the default printer before you click the Print Structure button in Visdata. Be sure to reset your default printer after you send your table structures to a disk file.

The Visdata JET Menu

If the currently open database is a Microsoft JET format database, you will see the JET item on the main menu. This item lets you establish attachments to external databases, define relationships between tables in your database, manage security groups and users, and set parameters for dealing with multiple users for a single database.

Attachments

Visdata allows you to attach external database files to an existing Microsoft JET format database. When you create an attachment, you actually create a link between your own Microsoft JET database and another database. You don't actually import any data from the external database into your own MDB. By creating attachments, you can access and manipulate external data files as if they are native Microsoft JET tables. Attached tables appear in the Table window as local table objects in your database, even though they are only links to external data files.

Tip: Not only is the attachment method convenient, it provides the fastest way to access external data using Visual Basic 4 programs. You can load, index, and display attached external tables faster than you can if you use ODBC or directly open the external data files in their native format.

Now create an attached table in the CH08NEW.MDB database that you created earlier today.

Note: If you skipped the section where CH08NEW.MDB was created, you can go back now and create the database. Or, if you like, you can create an attachment to any other Microsoft JET format database you already have on hand.

First, if you don't have it loaded already, select File | Open Database from the main menu to load the CH08NEW.MDB database created earlier in this lesson. Then select the Jet | Attachments menu option. You will see a grid that shows all the current attachments for this database. Because you just created this database, you should see no attachments at this time. Click the New command button to open the New Attached Table dialog box. Your screen should now look like Figure 8.34.

Figure 8.34.

Adding an attachment to a Microsoft JET database.

Table 8.1 shows the information you should enter into the Attachment dialog box.

Table 8.1. New Attached Table dialog box values.

Dialog Field	Value
Attachment Name	Test FoxPro File
Database Name	\TYSDBVB\CHAP08\
Connect String	FoxPro 2.5
Table to Attach	FLDTYPES.DBF

If you are attaching to a data source that requires a password in the connect string, you could check the AttachSavePWD checkbox to prevent a login dialog each time you open the database. If you want to create an exclusive attachment, you could check the AttachExclusive checkbox. Leave both of these fields blank for now.

Note: The FLDTYPES.DBF database is available from the \TYSDBVB\CHAP08 directory of the CD that ships with this book.

After filling out the dialog form, click Attach to commit the attachment. After you close the Attachment dialog box, you see that the grid updates to show the new attachment you just added to the database. Close this grid. You now see a new entry in your Tables/Queries window list. This shows a new table object. The right arrow (->) next to the entry shows that it is an attached table. Your screen should look something like the one in Figure 8.35.

Figure 8.35.

Viewing an attached table object.

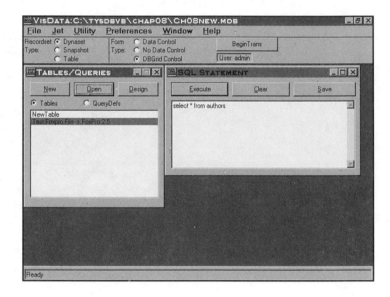

You can now access this attached table just like you would any table you created using Visdata.

Relations

The Relations menu item is where Visdata lets you define relationships between tables in your database. Data relationships are used to enforce improved data integrity in relational databases. You can use Visdata to create one-to-one and one-to-many relationships. You can enforce update and delete cascades for one-to-many relationships, too.

Note: The Relations options are only available from Microsoft JET version 3.0 database formats. If you are not using the Microsoft JET 3.0 database format, skip this section.

Note: Database relationships were first described in Day 2. We will cover creating and maintaining related objects in Day 10. For now, just remember that Visdata is a good tool for managing relationships in databases.

Let's define a relationship using Visdata. First, load the CH0801.MDB data file located in the \TYSDBVB\CHAP08\ directory on the CD that came with the book. After you load this database, select JET | Relations, which brings up the Relations dialog box. Your screen should look like Figure 8.36.

Figure 8.36.
Adding a relation object.

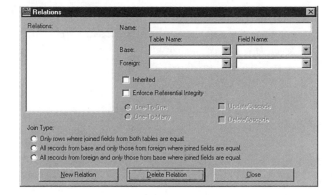

To add a new relation, click the New Relation command button, which activates the dialog form. Table 8.2 shows the values that you should enter into the fields on the Relations form.

Table 8.2. Relations form parameters.

Property	Setting
Name	Relation1
Base Table Name	Titles
Field Name	Au_ID
Foreign Table Name	Authors
Field Name	Au_ID
Join Type	Only rows where joined fields from both tables are equal

Enter these values into the form and click the Add Relation button to perform the transaction. Your screen should now look like Figure 8.37.

Figure 8.37.
*Completed relationship
added to database.*

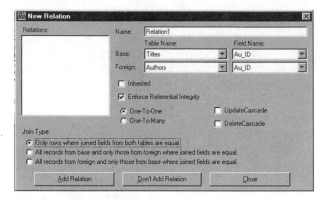

You can use the same screen to delete existing relationships. You cannot modify relationships, however. If you need to change a parameter of the relationship, you must first delete the existing relationship and then add a new one with the values you need.

Modifying data table relationships is a tricky business—especially when the tables already have data in them. It is best to establish relationships when you first create the data tables, before any data is added to them.

Caution: Changing or adding relationships after data has been added to the tables can lead to unpredictable results and possible loss of data.

Multiuser Settings

The Multiuser Settings menu option enables you to set some local values that control how Visdata behaves when accessing multiuser databases. You can edit these settings to improve the performance of Visdata and to help you diagnose read/write traffic in your database. Table 8.3 lists each of the settings and what they mean for Visdata.

Table 8.3. Multiuser settings.

Property	Setting
Retry Count	Controls the number of retries that Visdata performs when attempting locks on data tables.
Delay	Sets the number of seconds Visdata waits before attempting a Retry.

Property	Setting
Pessimistic Locks on Edit	When this radio button is active, Visdata performs a page lock whenever a record edit begins.
Optimistic Locks on Update	When this radio button is active, Visdata performs a page lock whenever a record update occurs.
Set for All Records	Clicking this button sets the current locking type for all open data objects. You should click this button each time you change parameters in the Multiuser Settings dialog box.
Add Rows Per Page Prop	Clicking this button adds a user-defined property to every Microsoft JET table object. This property shows the number of rows per locked page. You can inspect values using the Properties sheet of the table object.
Free Locks	Clicking this button forces Visdata to pause to allow the database engine to catch up to any changes that have occurred in the underlying data tables.

When you select JET | Multiuser Settings from the main menu, a small dialog box appears at the bottom of the form. Your screen should resemble Figure 8.38.

Figure 8.38.
Viewing the Multiuser Settings dialog box.

SYSTEM.MDA

Use the SYSTEM.MDA menu option to locate and load the SYSTEM.MDA security file. The SYSTEM.MDA file contains information about Microsoft JET file security, including defined users, groups, workspaces, passwords, and data object rights. You must create this file using Microsoft Access.

The JET | SYSTEM.MDA menu option presents you with a File Open dialog so that you can locate and load a SYSTEM.MDA file. Once it is loaded, Visdata will add this information to the VISDATA.INI file so that you won't have to reload it in the future.

The Visdata Utility Menu

The Visdata Utility menu contains several options to help you manage your data tables. You can create, test, and save query objects using the Query Builder; perform global replace routines on

existing data tables; import and export data in various formats, and test data bound lists and combo boxes. A menu option also exists to quickly close all the open data tables you might have on the screen.

Query Builder

The Query Builder serves as a good tool for testing queries and then saving them to the database as query objects. You can later access these objects from your Visual Basic 4 programs. The Query Builder enables you to perform complex queries without having to know all the details of SQL syntax.

> **Note:** We will cover SQL SELECT queries in detail on Day 9. For now, if you are not familiar with SQL statements, just follow along with the example. The important thing to remember is that you can use the Visdata Query Builder to create, test, and store SQL queries.

Let's build a query, test it, and save it in a database. First, make sure you have CH0801.MDB open, and then select Utility | Query Builder from the main menu. You see a data entry form ready for your input (see Figure 8.39).

Figure 8.39.
Using the Query Builder.

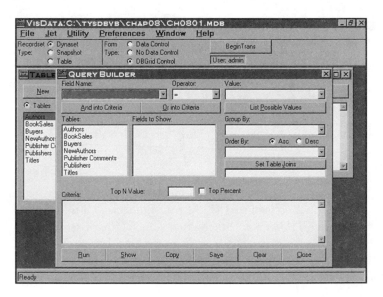

You have several options on this screen. It's easy to get confused if you are not quite sure of what to look for. Instead of going through all the possible options for a query, this example goes step-by-step through a rather simple SELECT query and views the results. Table 8.4 shows the values to select and Figure 8.40 shows the completed form. Refer to these items as you build your query.

Figure 8.40.
The completed query.

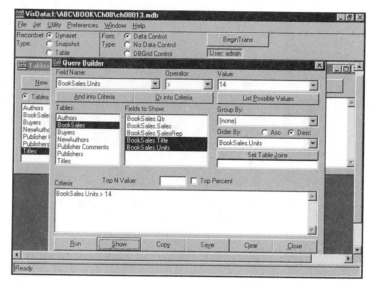

Be sure to set the values in the screen in the order they appear in Table 8.4. After you enter the Field Name, Operator, and Value settings, click the And into Criteria button to force the settings into the Criteria box at the bottom of the window.

Table 8.4. Building a query.

Property	Setting
Tables	BookSales
Field Name	BookSales.Units
Operator	>
Value	14
Fields to Show	BookSales.Title
BookSales.Units	
Order by	BookSales.Units, Desc

After you have entered all the values, click Save and enter qryTest at the dialog prompt. You have just saved the query for future use. Now try running it. Click Run to get Visdata to execute the query. Click No when Visdata asks you if this is a Passthrough Query. Visdata then executes the query and displays the results on your screen, as shown in Figure 8.41.

Figure 8.41.

Results of the executed query.

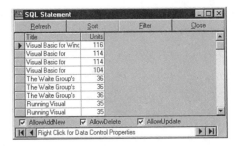

Global Replace

The Global Replace menu option enables you to perform a mass update of existing tables, which comes in handy when you need to *zero* values in test data or need to perform mass updates on a database.

For this example, set all the fields in a data table to the same value. Load the CH0801.MDB database, and then select Utility | Global Replace from the menu. You see the Global Replace dialog box as shown in Figure 8.42.

Figure 8.42.

Entering a Global Replace command.

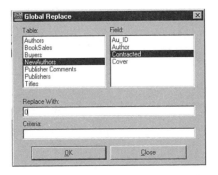

Select the NewAuthors table and the Contracted field. Set the Replace With value to zero and leave the Criteria field blank. When you click the OK button, Visdata resets all the NewAuthors.Contracted fields to zero. You can limit the number of records affected by the Global Replace command by entering an appropriate logical statement in the Criteria box. For example, if you wanted to update only the records that have an Au_ID value of 30, you could enter the following line in the Criteria box:

```
Au_ID=30
```

We cover Criteria more in depth in the lesson on Day 9, and you'll learn more about the global replace command in the lesson on Day 14, "Error Trapping."

Import/Export

You can use the Import/Export menu option to transfer data to and from external databases. You can import a data table from a non-Microsoft JET format into a Microsoft JET database. You can also export Microsoft JET data to non-Microsoft JET databases.

Let's export the Titles table to a text file formatted data table. Select Utility | Import/Export from the main menu. The Imp/Exp dialog appears. Select the Titles table, and then click the Export button. When prompted, select the text data file format. Then, when the Select Text File dialog box appears, enter NEWTITLES.TXT for the filename. Your screen should look like the one in Figure 8.43.

When the export is complete, you see a dialog box telling you the export was successful. You can use the same dialog box to import data from other databases.

DBList/DBCombo

The DBList/DBCombo menu option of Visdata enables you to experiment with the data-bound list and data-bound combo controls available in Visual Basic 4. You can use this menu option to create and test data-bound lists and combo controls, but you cannot save the list or combo settings to use in Visual Basic 4 programs later on. You can open as many DBList/DBCombo forms as you wish because the forms are not modal dialog boxes.

When you first select Utility | DBList/DBCombo from the main menu, you see the blank DBList/DBCombo form (see Figure 8.44).

Using the data tables in the CH0801.MDB data file, let's create a DBList example. First, you need to fill in the information for the List Filling Source data table. This information fills the list (or combo) control. Usually this data comes from a validation table.

For this example, enter the following values in the List Filling Source fields:

☐ RowSource: Select the Authors table.
☐ ListField: Select the Author field.
☐ BoundColumn: Select the Au_ID field.

You have just told Visdata to use the Au_ID field of the Authors table as the lookup field and to display the Author field within the list box.

Figure 8.43.

Exorting a data table.

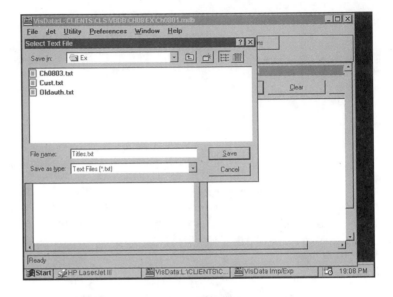

Figure 8.44.

*The blank DBList/
DBCombo form.*

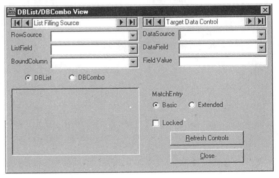

Now you need to fill in the target data control values. The target data control values define the
table object that you update using the information in the List Filling Source. For this example,
enter the following values in the Target Data Control fields:

☐ DataSource: Select the Titles table.

☐ FieldSource: Select the Au_ID field.

☐ Field Value: Visdata updates this field.

Now click the Refresh Controls command button. Visdata loads the list box with the validation
values and displays the selected field value in the Target Data Control area. Your screen should
look like Figure 8.45.

Figure 8.45.
The refreshed DBList form.

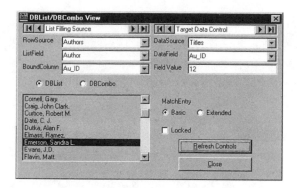

If you click on the right arrow button of the target data control, you see the values in the Field Value box change. As this value changes, you see the List Filling Source list control move to highlight the value in the Target Data Control field. This is the bound list box in action. You can perform the same operations on a combo control by clicking the DBCombo radio button.

Close Items

You can use the final three options on the Utility menu to quickly close out open forms. You can close out all RecordSet Forms, all Property Forms, or all DBList/DBCombo Forms from this menu.

The Visdata Preferences Menu

The Preferences menu option lets you customize the way Visdata shows you information. Three toggle settings control the way Visdata displays data, and two parameter settings control the way Visdata performs database logins and queries.

Open Last Database

When you toggle on the Open Last Database option, Visdata remembers the last database you had open when you last exited Visdata and automatically attempts to open that file the next time you start Visdata.

Show Performance Numbers

When you toggle on the Show Performance Numbers option, Visdata shows you on-screen timing results each time you perform a table open or query statement, which comes in handy when you want to test the relative speed of ODBC, direct external, or attached data table access options.

Include System Files

When you toggle on the Include System Files option, you see several tables maintained by Microsoft JET to keep track of table, user, group, relation, and query definitions. Users cannot access these tables, and the tables should not be altered or removed at any time.

Query Time-Out Value

You can use the Query Time-Out Value menu option to adjust the number of seconds Visdata waits before reporting a time-out error when attempting a query. If you work with slow external data files or ODBC connections, you can adjust this value upward to reduce the number of errors Visdata reports when you run queries.

Login Time-Out Value

You can use the Login Time-Out Value menu option to adjust the number of seconds Visdata waits before reporting a time-out error when attempting to log into a remote data source. Adjust this value upward if you get time-out errors when dealing with slow ODBC or external data sources.

The Visdata Windows and Help Menus

The last two items on the Visdata main menu are the Windows menu and the Help menu. These two items contain the usual options that all good Windows programs have.

The Windows Menu

This menu helps you control how all the child windows are displayed within the main MDI form. You can Cascade, Tile, or Arrange Icons from this menu. You can also force the focus to one of the three default Visdata windows: Table window, SQL window, or MDI form.

The Help Menu

The Help menu gives you access to the Visdata Help file included with your version of Visual Basic 4. You can also view the About box from this menu.

Summary

Today you learned how to use the Visdata sample application to perform all the basic database operations needed to create and maintain databases for your Visual Basic 4 applications.

You learned how to

☐ Open existing databases.

☐ Create new databases.

☐ Add tables and indexes to existing databases.

☐ Attach external data sources to existing Microsoft JET databases.

☐ Register new ODBC data sources for use through all Visual Basic 4 applications.

☐ Access data using the three data access objects: Table, Dynaset, and Snapshot.

☐ View data on-screen using the three data forms: form view with the data control; form view without the data control; and grid view using the data-bound grid.

☐ Test data-bound lists and data-bound combo boxes using the DBGrid and DBList options.

☐ Build and store SQL queries using the Query Builder.

You learned to use Visdata to perform database utility operations, including

☐ Copying tables from one database to another.

☐ Repairing corrupted Microsoft JET databases.

☐ Compacting and converting versions of Microsoft JET databases.

☐ Performing global replace operations on tables.

You learned to use Visdata to adjust various system settings that affect the way Visual Basic 4 displays data tables and processes local and external database connections and parameters that control how Visual Basic 4 locks records at update time.

Finally, you also learned how to compile the Visdata program and how to turn it into a Visual Basic 4 Add-In application using the Visual Basic 4 Add-In Manager.

Quiz

1. Where can you find a copy of Visdata?
2. How do you copy a table in Visdata?
3. When do you need to Refresh the Tables/Queries window?
4. Can you manipulate spreadsheet data with Visdata?
5. What information can be obtained by selecting Files | Properties | DbEngine?
6. Why would you compact a database?
7. Can you compact a database onto itself with the Compact MDB command?
8. Can you utilize Visdata to modify a table's structure once data has been entered?
9. Can you save queries in Visdata?

10. In what formats can you export data using the Visdata tool?

11. How would you use Visdata to convert an existing JET 1.1 database into JET 2.0 format?

Exercises

You have been asked to build a database to track entities that purchase from and sell to your organization. Complete the following tasks using Visdata as your development tool.

1. Build a new database and name it Contacts. This database should have a format that can be read by Microsoft Access 2.0.

2. Build a table of customers (tblCustomers). Include the following fields:

Field	Type	Size
IDText	10	
Name	Text	50
Address1	Text	50
Address2	Text	50
CityText	50	
StateProv	Text	25
ZipText	10	
Phone	Text	14
FaxText	14	
Contact	Text	50
Notes	Memo	NA

3. Build a primary key (PKtblCustomers) on the ID field for the tblCustomers table.

4. Print the table structure for tblCustomers.

5. Enter five sample records into the tblCustomers table.

6. Because you also need to track those whom you purchase from, copy the structure (no records) from tblCustomers to a new table, tblVendors.

7. Export the data in the tblCustomers table to a text file.

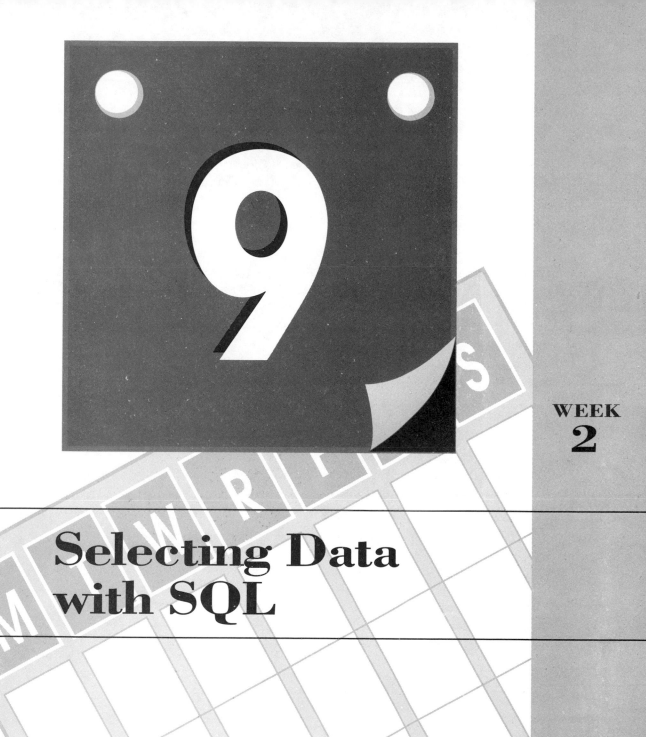

WEEK
2

Selecting Data
with SQL

Today is your first lesson in Structured Query Language (SQL). SQL is a powerful manipulation language used by Visual Basic and the Microsoft Access JET database engine as the primary method for accessing the data in your databases. SQL statements fall into two broad categories: data manipulation language statements (DML) and data definition language statements (DDL). The DDL statements enable you to define data tables, indexes, and database relationships. DML statements are used to select, sort, summarize, and calculate the information stored in the data tables.

Today, you will learn about the DML statements. When you complete this lesson, you will be able to use SQL statements to construct database queries that can be retrieved, and you will be able to reorder data in any format recognized by Visual Basic. Because SQL is used in almost all relational database systems (SQL Server, Oracle, Gupta, and so on), you will also be able to apply the knowledge you gain here in almost any other relational database environment you might encounter in the future.

In this lesson, you will learn how to use the SELECT…FROM statement to select data from one or more tables and present that information in a single table for update or review. You will also learn how to limit the data you select to only the records that meet your criteria using the WHERE clause. You'll learn how to easily reorder the data in tables using the ORDER BY clause. You will also learn how to create simple statements that automatically summarize and total the data using the GROUP BY…HAVING clause.

You will learn about typical SQL functions to manipulate numbers and strings. This lesson also covers advanced DML statements such as PARAMETERS, UNIONS, JOINS, and TRANSFORM…PIVOT.

Today, you will create actual SQL queries (and in some cases, store them for later use) using the Visual Basic Visdata program you learned about on Day 8.

What Is SQL?

Before jumping into specific SQL statements and their use, you should understand the definition of SQL and its uses and origins. SQL stands for *Structured Query Language*. It was developed in the 1970s at IBM as a way to provide computer users with a standardized method for selecting data from various database formats. The intent was to build a language that was not based on any existing programming language, but could be used within any programming language as a way to update and query information in databases.

Note: The word *SQL* should be pronounced *ess-que-ell* instead of *sequel*. The confusion about the pronunciation of the word stems from the database language's origin. The SQL language is a successor of a language called Sequel developed by IBM in the late 1960s. For this reason, many (especially those familiar with IBM's Sequel language) continued to pronounce the new database language improperly.

SQL statements are just that—statements. Each statement can perform operations on one or more database objects (tables, columns, indexes, and so on). Most SQL statements return results in the form of a set of data records, commonly referred to as a *view*. SQL is not a particularly friendly language. Many programs that use SQL statements hide these statements behind point-and-click dialogs, query-by-example grids, and other user-friendly interfaces. Make no mistake, however, that if the data you are accessing is stored in a relational database, you are using SQL statements, whether you know it or not.

ANSI Standard SQL Versus Microsoft JET SQL

SQL syntax is determined by a committee that is part of the American National Standards Institute (ANSI). The ANSI-SQL committee is made up of information system professionals who take on the job of establishing and enforcing standards on the rapidly moving computer programming industry. Although each computer programming language and database interface has its own unique versions of SQL, nearly everyone has agreed to adhere to the basic standards defined by the ANSI-SQL committee. The most widely used SQL standard is SQL-89. This standard was first promulgated in 1989. An updated set of standards (SQL-92) was developed three years later.

Within each set of SQL standards, there are three levels of compliance. A database product must meet Level I compliance in order to call itself an SQL-compatible product. Levels II and III are optional levels of compliance that products can also attain in order to increase interoperability among database systems.

The Microsoft JET database engine that is used to process all Visual Basic SQL statements is ANSI SQL-89 Level I compliant. There are very slight differences between ANSI SQL-89 and Microsoft JET SQL at Level II and Level III. We won't dwell on these differences here. Those who are interested in learning more about ANSI SQL standards and Microsoft JET compliance can find additional documentation elsewhere. The lessons in this book focus strictly on the Microsoft JET SQL syntax. Be assured that once you master the concepts covered here, you will be able to use the same skills in almost all SQL-based programming and query tools you encounter.

SQL Basics

Now it's time to start building SQL statements. If you haven't already done so, load the Visual Basic Visdata application you learned about on Day 8. Using Visdata, load the BOOKS.MDB that is included in the \TYSDBVB\CHAP09 directory of the CD that ships with this book. You will use this database for most of today's lesson.

> **Note:** This book shows reserved SQL words in uppercase letters (for example, SELECT). This is not required by Visual Basic, but it is a good programming habit.

The *SELECT...FROM* Statement

In this section, you will learn about the most commonly used SQL statement, the SELECT...FROM statement. The SELECT...FROM statement lets you pick records from one or more tables in a database. The results of a SELECT...FROM statement are returned as a *view*. This view is a subset of the source data. In Visual Basic, the view can be returned as a Recordset, Table, Dynaset, or Snapshot. Because today's lesson focuses on getting results you can display, views will be returned as Visual Basic Snapshot data objects.

In its simplest form, a SELECT...FROM statement contains two parts:

- ☐ A list of one or more table columns to select
- ☐ A list of one or more tables that contain the requested columns

>
> **Note:** Standard SQL syntax uses the word *column* to describe a field and *row* to describe a record. This book uses the terms *column* or *field* and *row* or *record* interchangeably.

A simple example of a valid SQL statement is

```
SELECT Au_ID FROM Authors
```

This SQL statement tells the Microsoft JET database engine to return a data object that contains the Au_ID from the Authors table. Enter this SQL statement into the Visdata SQL window and click the Execute button to see the returned result set. Your screen should look similar to the one in Figure 9.1.

Figure 9.1.
The result set from the first
SELECT statement.

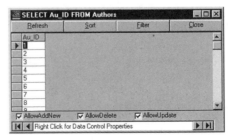

As you can see from the result set, the SELECT...FROM statement returns all the rows in the table. Whether the table contains 10 or 10,000 records, you can get a complete result set with just one SELECT...FROM statement. This is quite handy, but it can also be quite dangerous. If the result of your SELECT...FROM statement contains too many records, you can slow down the network, possibly run out of memory on your local workstation, and eventually lock up your PC. Later in this lesson, you will learn how to use the WHERE clause to limit the size of your view to only those records you need.

To return all the columns from a table, you can list each column in the SELECT statement. This works if you have only a few columns in the table. However, if you have several columns, it can become quite tedious. There is a shortcut. To automatically list all columns in the table in your result set, instead of typing column names, you can type the asterisk (*). The asterisk tells SQL to return all columns in the requested table. The SELECT statement to display all columns of the Author table would look like this:

```
SELECT * FROM Authors
```

Enter the preceding SELECT statement into the Visdata SQL window and review the results. Your screen should look like the one in Figure 9.2.

Figure 9.2.

The results of the SELECT *
query.

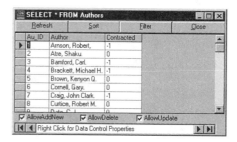

Notice that even though you listed no fields in your SELECT statement, all fields were returned in the result set. This is very useful when you want to display a data table but do not know names of all the columns. As long as you know a valid table name, you can use the SELECT...FROM statement to display the entire table.

The order in which you list columns in the SELECT...FROM statement controls the order in which they are displayed in the result set. Figure 9.3 shows the results of the following SELECT...FROM statement:

```
SELECT Authors, Au_ID FROM Authors
```

Figure 9.3.

Using the SELECT...FROM statement to change column display order.

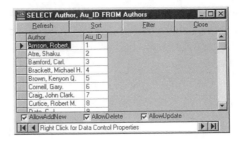

The *ORDER BY* Clause

When you use the SELECT...FROM statement, the records returned in the result set are returned in the order in which they were found in the underlying table. But what if you wanted to display the results of your SELECT...FROM statement in a specialized sorted order? You can use the ORDER BY clause to do just that.

Placing ASC or DESC after each field in the ORDER BY clause indicates the order in which you want to sort the column, ascending or descending. If no order is supplied, SQL assumes that you want the set sorted in ascending order.

The following SQL example shows how you can display the records in the Authors table in descending sorted order, by Author Name.

```
SELECT * FROM AUTHORS ORDER BY Author DESC
```

Enter this statement in the SQL window of Visdata and execute it. Compare your results to Figure 9.4.

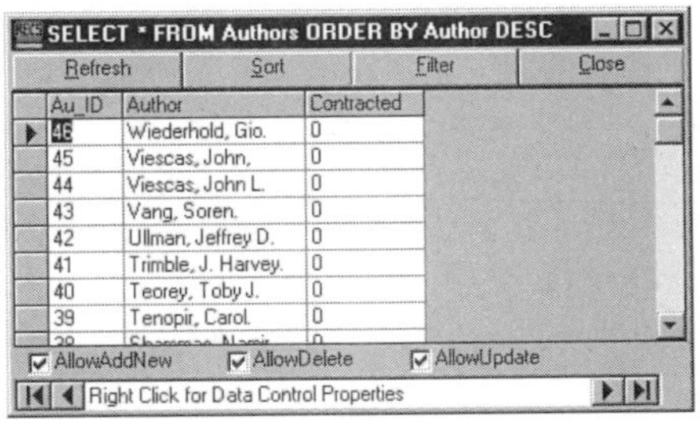

Figure 9.4.

The results of the descending ORDER BY clause.

You can enter more than one field in the ORDER BY clause. SQL will create a result set that reflects the aggregate sort of the ORDER BY clause. Using Visual Basic Visdata, enter and execute the following SELECT...FROM statement. Compare your results to those in Figure 9.5.

```
SELECT State, City FROM Publishers ORDER BY State DESC, City ASC
```

Figure 9.5.

The multiple-column ORDER
BY *clause.*

Notice in the example shown in Figure 9.5 that you have combined the ability to alter the row order of the data in the result set with the ability to alter the column order of the data in the result set. These are powerful tools. Now that you know how to use SQL to display complete, single-data tables, you can learn how to limit the result set to only those records you need.

The *WHERE* Clause

One of the most powerful aspects of the SELECT...FROM statement is its capability to control the content of the result set using the WHERE clause. There are two ways to use the WHERE clause to control the content of the result set:

☐ Use WHERE to limit the contents of a result set.

☐ Use WHERE to link two or more tables in a single result set.

Using *WHERE* to Limit the Result Set

The WHERE clause enables you to perform logical comparisons on data in any column in the data table. In its simplest form, the WHERE clause consists of the following:

```
WHERE column = value
```

In this line, *column* represents the name of the column in the requested data table, and *value* represents a literal value such as NY or Smith. It is important to know that the WHERE clause is always preceded by a SELECT...FROM statement. Use Visdata to enter and execute the following SQL statement, and compare your results to those in Figure 9.6.

```
SELECT Name, State FROM Publishers
    WHERE State = 'CA'
```

Tip: This book uses the single quote marks (') around string literals within SQL statements. Visual Basic SQL accepts both single and double quote marks within SQL. Because you will often be building SQL statements in Visual Basic code, using single quotes marks within SQL statements makes it easier to construct and maintain SQL statements as Visual Basic strings.

Figure 9.6.

The results of a simple WHERE clause SQL query.

The previous SQL statement returns a *subset* of the data in the result set. That is, the resulting view does not contain all of the rows of the Publishers table. Only those rows that have columns meeting the WHERE clause criteria will be returned in the result set.

You can link WHERE clauses using the AND and OR operators. Enter and execute the following SQL statement, and compare your results to Figure 9.7.

```
SELECT Name, State, City FROM Publishers
    WHERE State = 'CA' AND City <> 'Redwood City'
```

Figure 9.7.

The results of a complex WHERE clause.

You can use several AND and OR operators to link valid logical comparisons together to form a single WHERE clause. You can also use more than just =, <>, >, <, <=, and >= logical comparisons. Visual Basic SQL supports the use of BETWEEN...AND, IN, and LIKE comparisons. The following SQL statement illustrates the use of BETWEEN...AND in a WHERE clause. Check your results against those shown in Figure 9.8

```
SELECT PubID, Name, State, City FROM Publishers
    WHERE PubID BETWEEN 10 AND 15
```

The result set will only contain rows that have a PubID value between 10 and 15. Note that the values listed in the BETWEEN...AND clause (10 and 15) are included in the result set.

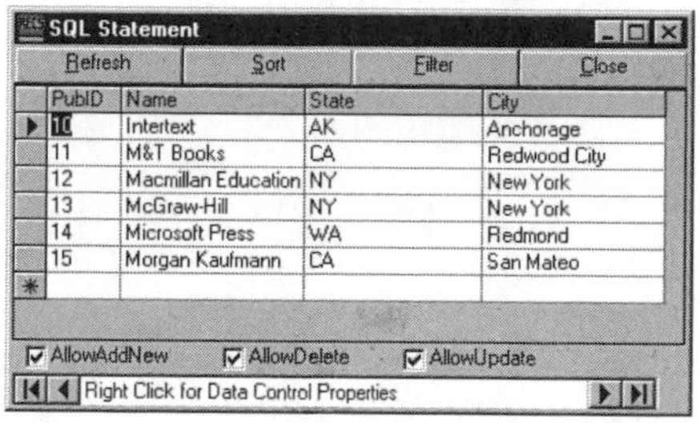

Figure 9.8.

Using BETWEEN...AND in a WHERE clause.

You can also use SQL to return a result set that contains rows that match a set of noncontiguous data. For example, if you wanted a list of all the publishers in the state of New York, California, and Alaska, you could use the IN keyword followed by the desired values, separated by commas, within parenthesis, as part of the WHERE clause. Enter and execute the following SQL statement, and check your result against those shown in Figure 9.9.

```
SELECT PubID, Name, City, State FROM Publishers
    WHERE State IN ('NY','CA','AK')
```

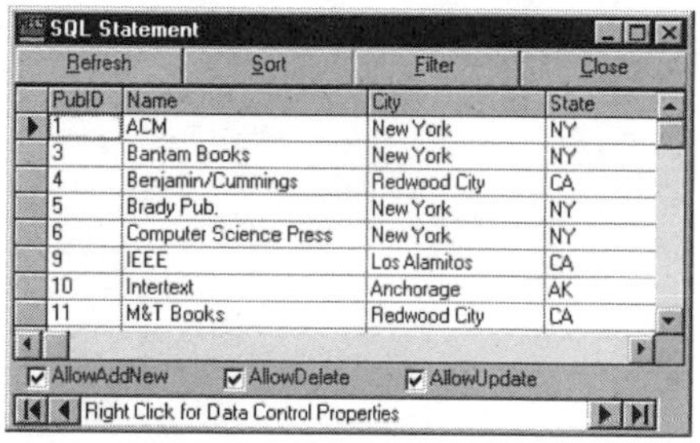

Figure 9.9.

Using the IN keyword in the WHERE clause.

You can also use the LIKE function to return all rows whose column's contents are similar to the literals passed in the function. For example, to return all rows with a State column that has the letter A in any position, you would use the following SQL SELECT...FROM statement (see Figure 9.10 for results):

```
SELECT PubID, Name, City, State FROM Publishers
    WHERE State LIKE('*A*')
```

Figure 9.10.

Using the LIKE function in a WHERE clause.

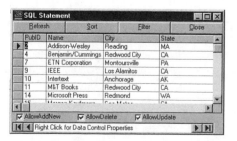

279

The LIKE function is a very powerful tool. It is covered in more depth in the next section of today's lesson, "SQL Aggregate Functions."

Using *WHERE* to Link Two or More Tables in a Result Set

You can use the WHERE clause to compare columns from different tables. In doing so, you can set up criteria that can link two or more tables in a single result set. The syntax for this form of the WHERE clause is

```
SELECT table1.columnA, table2.columnA FROM table1, table2
WHERE table1.columnA = table2.columnA
```

table1 and table2 are different data tables in the same database. columnA represents a single column in each of the tables. Use Visdata to enter and execute the following SQL statement. Compare your result set to the one in Figure 9.11.

```
SELECT Titles.Title, Publishers.Name
    FROM Publishers, Titles
    WHERE Publishers.PubID =Titles.PubID
```

Figure 9.11.

Using the WHERE clause to link two tables in a single result set.

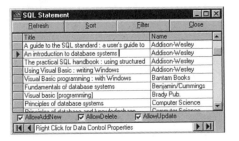

The preceding SQL statement creates a result set that displays the book title and publisher's name. This is accomplished using the WHERE clause to tell SQL to select only those rows where the PubID values in each table match up. Keep in mind that this is done without any programming code, special indexing, or sorting commands. SQL handles all those tasks for you. Also, there are a few new items in this SQL statement that bear further review.

This is the first SQL statement you have encountered today that lists columns from two different tables. When selecting columns from more than one table, it is good programming practice to precede the column name with the table name and join the two with the period (.). As long as the column name is unique among all columns in the tables from which you are selecting, SQL does not require you to use the *table.column* syntax. But it is a good habit to do so, especially when you are building SQL statements in Visual Basic code.

You should also notice that the WHERE clause comparison columns (Publishers.PubID and Titles.PubID) were not included in the SELECT portion of the statement. You do not have to

include the column in the SELECT portion of the statement to use it in the WHERE portion of the statement, as long as the column already exists in the underlying table.

Combining tables using the WHERE clause will always return a nonupdateable result set. You cannot update the columns in a view created in this manner. If you want to link tables together and also be able to update the underlying tables for that view, you need to use the JOIN clause, which is covered later today.

You can combine the link-type and limit-type versions of the WHERE clause in a single SQL SELECT...FROM statement. Execute the following statement and compare your results to those in Figure 9.12.

```
SELECT Titles.PubID,Titles.Title,Publishers.Name
   FROM Titles, Publishers
   WHERE Titles.PubID = Publishers.PubID
      AND Publishers.PubID BETWEEN 10 AND 15
```

Figure 9.12.

Combining link-type and limit-type WHERE clauses.

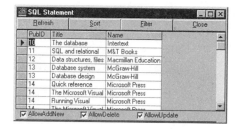

The preceding SQL statement selects only those records in which the PubID columns match *and* the PubID values are between 10 and 15.

You can use the WHERE clause to link more than two data tables. The linking column for table1 and table2 does not have to be the same column for table2 and table3. Execute the following statement and review your results against those in Figure 9.13.

```
SELECT Titles.PubID,Titles.Title,Publishers.Name,Authors.Author
   FROM Titles, Publishers,Authors
   WHERE Titles.PubID = Publishers.PubID
      AND Titles.Au_ID = Authors.Au_ID
```

Figure 9.13.

Using the WHERE clause to link three tables.

In the previous example, the Publishers table and the Titles table are linked using the PubID column. The Titles table and the Authors table are linked using the Au_ID field. When the link is done, the selected columns are displayed in the result set.

You might have noticed that SQL assigns column names to the result sets. There are times when these assigned names can be misleading or incomplete. You can use the `AS` keyword to rename the columns in the result set. The following SQL statement is one example of using the `AS` keyword in the `SELECT` statement to rename the column headers of the result set. This renaming does not affect the original column names in the underlying tables. Execute the following SQL statement and compare your results to those in Figure 9.14.

```
SELECT Titles.PubID AS PubCode,    Titles.Title AS BookTitle,
   Publishers.Name AS PubName,
   Authors.Author AS AuthorName
   FROM Titles, Publishers,Authors
   WHERE Titles.PubID = Publishers.PubID
      AND Titles.Au_ID = Authors.Au_ID
```

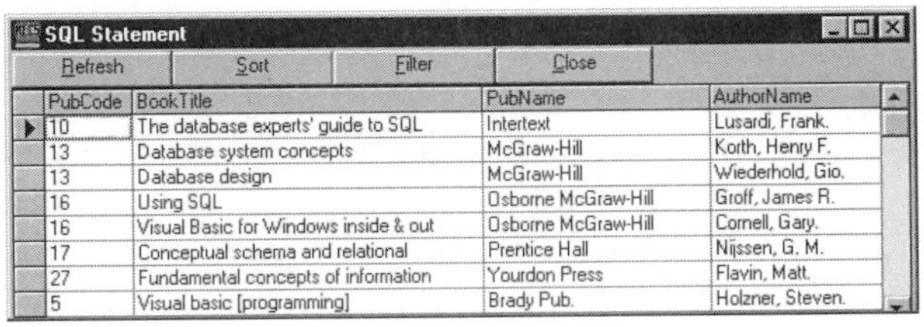

PubCode	BookTitle	PubName	AuthorName
10	The database experts' guide to SQL	Intertext	Lusardi, Frank.
13	Database system concepts	McGraw-Hill	Korth, Henry F.
13	Database design	McGraw-Hill	Wiederhold, Gio.
16	Using SQL	Osborne McGraw-Hill	Groff, James R.
16	Visual Basic for Windows inside & out	Osborne McGraw-Hill	Cornell, Gary.
17	Conceptual schema and relational	Prentice Hall	Nijssen, G. M.
27	Fundamental concepts of information	Yourdon Press	Flavin, Matt.
5	Visual basic [programming]	Brady Pub.	Holzner, Steven.

Figure 9.14.
Using the `AS` keyword to rename columns in the result set.

Now that you know how to use the `SELECT...FROM` statement to select the desired rows and columns from data tables, read about how to use SQL functions to calculate and manipulate data within your selected columns and rows.

SQL Aggregate Functions

The SQL standards define a core set of functions that are present in all SQL-compliant systems. These functions are known as *aggregate functions.* Aggregate functions are used to quickly return computed results of numeric data stored in a column. The SQL aggregate functions available through the Microsoft Access JET database engine are as follows:

- `AVG`: Returns the average value of all the values in a column.
- `COUNT`: Returns the number of columns and is usually used to determine the total rows in a view. `COUNT` is the only standard SQL aggregate function that can be applied to a non-numeric column.
- `SUM`: Returns the total of all the values in a column.
- `MAX`: Returns the highest amount of all the values in a column.

☐ MIN: Returns the lowest amount of all the values in a column.

The following SQL statement illustrates all five of the SQL aggregate functions. Enter and execute this statement, and check your results against Figure 9.15.

```
SELECT COUNT(Units) AS UnitCount,
    AVG(Units) AS UnitAvg,
    SUM(Units) AS UnitSum,
    MIN(Units) AS UnitMin,
    MAX(Units) AS UnitMax
    FROM BookSales
```

Figure 9.15.
Using SQL aggregate functions.

You can use the WHERE clause and aggregate functions in the same SELECT...FROM statement. The following statement shows how you can use the WHERE clause to limit the rows included in the aggregate calculation. Refer to Figure 9.16 for results. Compare these numbers to the ones in the view returned in the previous query (Figure 9.15).

```
SELECT COUNT(Units) AS UnitCount,
    AVG(Units) AS UnitAvg,
    SUM(Units) AS UnitSum,
    MIN(Units) AS UnitMin,
    MAX(Units) AS UnitMax
    FROM BookSales
    WHERE Qtr = 1
```

Figure 9.16.
Using the WHERE clause to limit the scope of aggregate functions.

Using Visual Basic Functions in a *SELECT* Statement

When you call the Microsoft Access JET database engine from within a Visual Basic program, you can use any valid Visual Basic functions as part of the SQL statement. For example, if you want to create a result set with a column that holds only the first three characters of a field in the underlying table, you could use the Visual Basic Left$ function as part of your column list in the SELECT...FROM statement, in the following line (see Figure 9.17).

```
SELECT Left$(Author,3), Author
    FROM Authors
```

Figure 9.17.

*Using Visual Basic functions
in an SQL statement.*

You can also use Visual Basic syntax to combine several data table columns into a single column
in the result set. Enter and execute the following example and compare your results to Figure 9.18.

```
SELECT Name, City+", "+State+"  "+Zip AS ADDRESS
    FROM Publishers
```

Figure 9.18.

*Using Visual Basic syntax to
combine columns.*

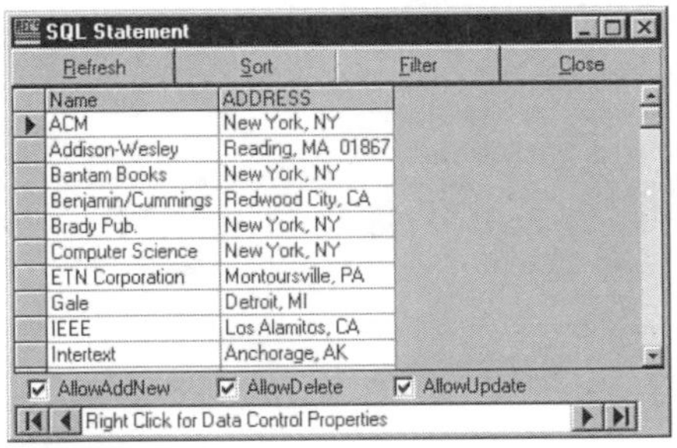

You can also use Visual Basic functions as part of the WHERE clause in an SQL statement. The
following example (see Figure 9.19) will only return rows that have the letter *a* as the second
character in the Name column.

```
SELECT Name FROM Publishers
    WHERE Mid$(Name,2,1)="a"
```

Figure 9.19.

*Using Visual Basic functions
in an SQL WHERE clause.*

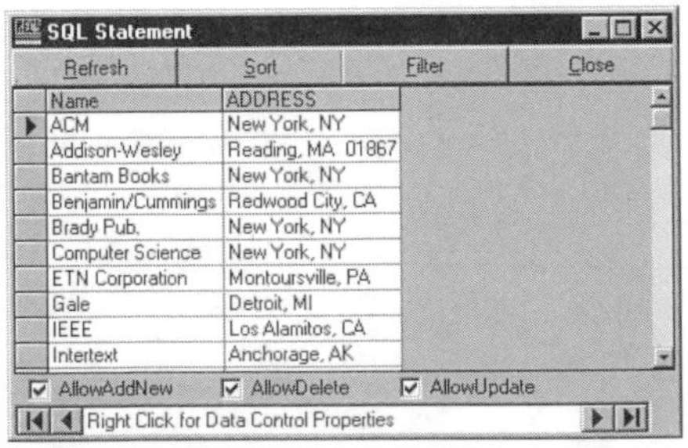

Even though using familiar Visual Basic functions and syntax is very handy, it has its drawbacks. Chief among them is the fact that after you create a SQL statement that uses VB-specific portions, your code is no longer portable. If you ever move the SQL statements to another database engine (such as SQL Server), you must remove the VB-specific portions of the SQL statements and replace them with something else that will work with the database engine you are using. This will not be an issue if you plan to stick with the Microsoft Access JET engine for all your database access.

Another possible drawback that you'll encounter if you use VB-specific syntax in your SQL statements is that of speed. Extensive use of VB-specific code within SQL statements will result in a slight performance hit. The speed difference is minor, but it should be considered.

It is better to use as few VB-specific functions in your SQL statements as possible. You will not limit the portability of your code, and you will not suffer from unduly slow processing of the SQL statements.

> **Note:** You can't use user-defined functions within your SQL statements when you use the Microsoft Access JET database engine from within Visual Basic. You can only use the built-in SQL functions and the predefined Visual Basic functions.

More SQL DML Statements

Now that you know how to create basic SQL SELECT...FROM statements and you know how to use the built-in SQL functions, return to the basic SELECT...FROM statement and add a few more enhancements to your SQL tool kit.

The *DISTINCT* and *DISTINCTROW* Clauses

There are times when you select data from a table that has more than one occurrence of the rows you are trying to collect. For example, you want to get a list of all the customers that have at least one order on file in the Orders table. The problem is that some customers have several orders in the table. You don't want to see those names appear more than once in your result set. You can use the DISTINCT keyword to make sure that you do not get duplicates of the same customer in your result set.

Enter and execute the following statement. As a test, execute the same SQL statement without the DISTINCT clause and compare the result sets. Refer to Figure 9.20 as an example.

```
SELECT DISTINCT Au_ID FROM Titles
    ORDER BY Au_ID
```

Figure 9.20.

Using the DISTINCT keyword to remove duplicates from a result set.

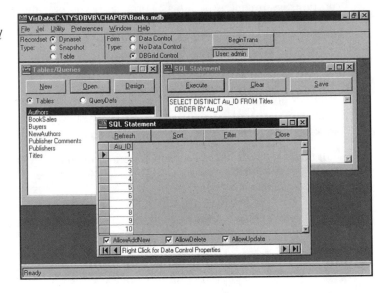

If you include more than one column in the SELECT list, all columns will be used to evaluate the uniqueness of the row. Execute and compare the result sets of the following two SQL statements. Refer to Figure 9.21 as a guide.

```
SELECT DISTINCT Title
    FROM BookSales
```

```
SELECT DISTINCT Title, Units
    FROM BookSales
```

Notice that the first SQL statement returns a single record for each Title in the data table. The second SQL statement returns more records for each Title because there are distinct Units values for each Title.

There are also times when you want to collect data on all rows that are distinct in any of the fields. Instead of using the DISTINCT keyword and listing all the fields in the table, you can use the DISTINCTROW keyword. The following SQL statement (see Figure 9.22) uses DISTINCTROW to return the same records as the SQL statement in the previous example.

```
SELECT DISTINCTROW *
    FROM BookSales
    ORDER BY Title
```

Figure 9.21.
Using DISTINCT on multiple columns.

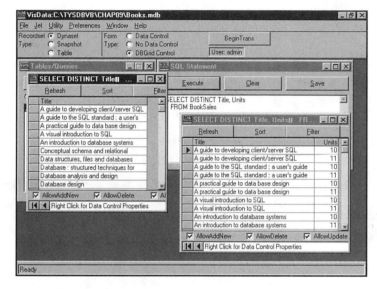

Figure 9.22.
Using DISTINCTROW in an SQL statement.

Both the DISTINCT and DISTINCTROW keywords enable you to limit the contents of the result set based on the uniqueness of one or more columns in the data table. In the next section, you'll learn how you can limit the contents of the result set to the records with the highest numeric values in selected columns.

The *TOP n* and *TOP n PERCENT* Clauses

You can use the TOP *n* or TOP *n* PERCENT SQL keywords to limit the number of records in your result set. Suppose you want to get a list of the five top-selling books in a data table. You can use the TOP *n* clause to get just that. TOP *n* returns the first *n* number of records. If you have two records of the same value, SQL will return both records. For the previous example, if the fifth and sixth records were both equal, the result set would contain six records, not just five.

When you use the `TOP` clause, you must also use the `ORDER BY` clause to make sure that your result set is sorted. If you do not use the `ORDER BY` clause, you will receive an arbitrary set of records because SQL will first execute the `ORDER BY` clause and then select the `TOP` *n* records you requested. Without the `ORDER BY` clause, it is quite likely that you will not get the results you intended. If a `WHERE` clause is present, SQL will perform the `WHERE` clause, the `ORDER BY` clause, and then the `TOP` *n* clause. As you can see, failure to use the `ORDER BY` clause will most certainly return garbage in your result set (see Figure 9.23).

```
SELECT TOP 5 * FROM BookSales
   ORDER BY Sales DESC
```

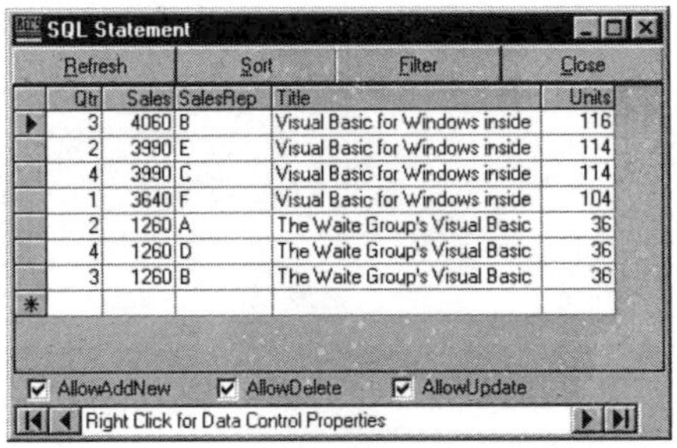

Qtr	Sales	SalesRep	Title	Units
3	4060	B	Visual Basic for Windows inside	116
2	3990	E	Visual Basic for Windows inside	114
4	3990	C	Visual Basic for Windows inside	114
1	3640	F	Visual Basic for Windows inside	104
2	1260	A	The Waite Group's Visual Basic	36
4	1260	D	The Waite Group's Visual Basic	36
3	1260	B	The Waite Group's Visual Basic	36

Figure 9.23.
Using `TOP n` *to limit the result set.*

Notice that the previous example uses the `DESC` keyword in the `ORDER BY` clause. Whether you use the `DESC` or `ASC ORDER BY` format, the result set will still contain the first *n* records in the table (based on the sort). Also note that the result set contains more than five records, because several records have the same Sales value.

The `TOP n PERCENT` version returns not the top 5 records, but the top 5 percent of the records in the underlying data table. The results of the following SQL statement (see Figure 9.24) contain several more records than the result set shown previously.

```
SELECT TOP 5 PERCENT * FROM BookSales
   ORDER BY Sales
```

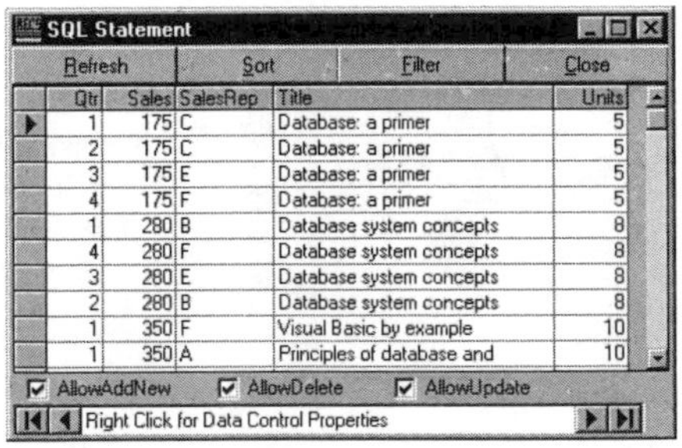

Qtr	Sales	SalesRep	Title	Units
1	175	C	Database: a primer	5
2	175	C	Database: a primer	5
3	175	E	Database: a primer	5
4	175	F	Database: a primer	5
1	280	B	Database system concepts	8
4	280	F	Database system concepts	8
3	280	E	Database system concepts	8
2	280	B	Database system concepts	8
1	350	F	Visual Basic by example	10
1	350	A	Principles of database and	10

Figure 9.24.
Using `TOP n PERCENT` *to limit the result set.*

The *GROUP BY...HAVING* Clause

One of the more powerful SQL clauses is the GROUP BY...HAVING clause. This clause lets you use the SQL aggregate functions discussed earlier today to easily create result sets that contain a list of subtotals of the underlying data table. For example, you might want to be able to create a data set that contains a list of Titles and the total Units sold, by Title. The following SQL statement (see Figure 9.25) can do that:

```
SELECT Title, SUM(Units) AS UnitsSold
    FROM BookSales
    GROUP BY Title
```

Figure 9.25.

Using GROUP BY to create subtotals.

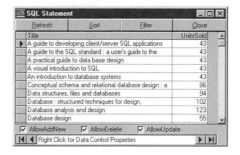

The GROUP BY clause requires that all numeric columns in the SELECT column list be a part of an SQL aggregate function (SUM, AVG, MIN, MAX, and COUNT). Also, you cannot use the * as part of the SELECT column list when you use the GROUP BY clause.

What if you wanted to get a list of all the book titles that sold more than 100 units for the year? The first thought would be to use a WHERE clause:

```
SELECT Titles, SUM(Units) AS UnitsSold
    WHERE Sum(Units) > 100
    GROUP BY Units
```

However, if you try to run this SQL statement, you discover that SQL does not allow aggregate functions within the WHERE clause. You really want to use a WHERE clause *after* the aggregate function has created a resulting column. In plain English, the query needs to perform the following steps:

☐ Add up all the units.

☐ Write the results to a temporary table.

☐ Display only those rows in the temporary table that have a unit total greater than 100.

Luckily, you don't have to actually write all this in a series of SQL statements. You can get the same results by adding the HAVING keyword to the GROUP BY clause. The HAVING clause acts the same as the WHERE clause, except that the HAVING clause acts upon the resulting columns created by the GROUP BY clause, not the underlying columns. The SQL following statement (see Figure 9.26) will return only the Titles that have sold more than 100 units in the last year:

```
SELECT Title, SUM(Units) AS UnitsSold
    FROM BookSales
    GROUP BY Title HAVING SUM(Units)>100
```

Figure 9.26.

*Using the HAVING clause
with GROUP BY.*

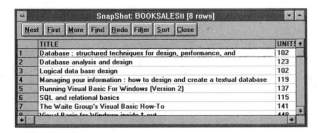

The columns used in the HAVING clause do not have to be the same columns listed in the SELECT clause. The contents of the HAVING clause follow the same rules as those for the contents of the WHERE clause. You can use logical operators AND, OR, and NOT, and you can include VB-specific functions as part of the HAVING clause. The following SQL statement (see Figure 9.27) returns sales in dollars for all titles that have more than 100 units sold and whose titles have the letter *a* as the second letter in the title:

```
SELECT Title, SUM(Sales) AS SalesAmt
    FROM BookSales
    GROUP BY Title
    HAVING SUM(Units)>100 AND Mid$(Title,2,1)="a"
```

Figure 9.27.

*Using a complex HAVING
clause.*

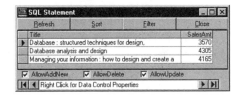

SQL *JOIN*s

The JOIN clause is a very powerful optional SQL clause. Remember when you learned how to link two tables together using the WHERE `table1.column1 = table2.column1` line? The only problem with using the WHERE clause is that the result set is not updateable. What if you need to create an updateable result set that contains columns from more than one table? You use JOIN.

There are three types of JOIN clauses in Microsoft Access JET SQL:

- ☐ INNER JOIN
- ☐ LEFT JOIN
- ☐ RIGHT JOIN

The following sections describe each form of JOIN and how each is used in your programs.

The *INNER JOIN*

The INNER JOIN can be used to create a result set that contains only those records that have an exact match in both tables. Enter and execute the following SQL statement (see Figure 9.28):

```
SELECT [Publisher Comments].Comments,
    Publishers.Name, Publishers.State
    FROM [Publisher Comments] INNER JOIN Publishers
    ON [Publisher Comments].PubID = Publishers.PubID
```

Note: The preceding SQL statement introduces the use of square brackets ([ ]). These are used to enclose a Microsoft Access data table name that contains embedded spaces. The square brackets are not part of standard SQL and are only there to handle the Microsoft Access table name. This is a good time to point out that it is a bad idea to use embedded spaces as table names!

Figure 9.28.
Using the INNER JOIN SQL clause.

Comments	Name	State
GENERAL TRADE BOOKS -	ACM	NY
Introductory to advanced-level	Addison-Wesley	MA
PROFESSIONAL BOOKS	Bantam Books	NY
DICTIONARIES,	McGraw-Hill	NY
PROFESSIONAL BOOKS	Microsoft Press	WA
Professional & reference books in	Morgan Kaufmann	CA
PAPERBACK BOOKS - TRADE	SYBEX	CA
DATABASES	Wiley	NY

The previous SQL statement returns all the records from the Publisher table that have a PubID that matches a PubID in the [Publisher Comments] table. This type of JOIN returns all the records that reside within both tables—thus, an INNER JOIN.

This is handy if you have two tables that you know are not perfectly matched against a single column and you want to create a result set that contains only those rows that match on both sides. The INNER JOIN also works well when you have a parent table (such as a CustomerTable) and a child table (such as a ShipAddressTable) with a one-to-one relationship. Using an INNER JOIN, you can quickly create a list of all CustomerTable records that have a corresponding ShipAddressTable record on file.

INNER JOINs work best when you create a JOIN on a column that is unique in both tables. If you use a table that has more than one occurrence of the JOIN column, you'll get a row for each occurrence in the result set. This might be an undesirable result. The following example illustrates the point (see Figure 9.29):

```
SELECT Titles.Title,BookSales.Units
    FROM Titles INNER JOIN BookSales
    ON Titles.Title = BookSales.Title
```

Figure 9.29.

Using an INNER JOIN on a non-unique column.

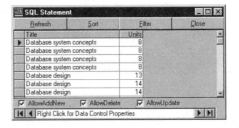

In the previous example, the table BookSales has four occurrences of Title (one for each quarter of the year), so the result of the INNER JOIN returns each Title four times.

The *LEFT JOIN*

The LEFT JOIN is one of the two outer joins in the SQL syntax. Although INNER JOIN returns only those rows that have corresponding values in both tables, the outer joins return all the records from one side of the join, whether or not there is a corresponding match on the other side of the join. The LEFT JOIN clause returns all the records from the first table on the list (the leftmost table) and any records on the right side of the table that have a matching column value. The following example (see Figure 9.30) shows the same SQL query that was shown in Figure 9.28.

```
SELECT Publishers.Name,[Publisher Comments].Comments
    FROM Publishers LEFT JOIN [Publisher Comments]
    ON Publishers.PubID = [Publisher Comments].PubID
```

Figure 9.30.

Using the LEFT JOIN clause.

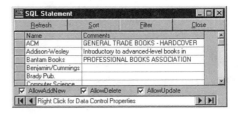

Notice that the result set has blank comments in several places. The LEFT JOIN is handy when you want a list of all the records in the master table and any records in the dependent table that are on file.

The *RIGHT JOIN*

The RIGHT JOIN works the same as the LEFT JOIN except that the result set is based on the second (right-hand) table in the JOIN statement. You can use the RIGHT JOIN in the same manner you would use the LEFT JOIN.

UNION Queries

Another powerful SQL clause is the UNION clause. This SQL keyword lets you create a union between two tables or SQL queries that contain similar, but unrelated, data. A UNION query is handy when you want to collate information from two queries into a single result set. Because UNION queries return non-updateable result sets, they are good for producing on-screen displays, reports, and base data for generating graphs and charts.

For example, if you have a customer table and a vendor table, you might want to get a list of all vendors and customers who live in the state of Ohio. You could write an SQL statement to select the rows from the Customers table. Then write an SQL statement to select the rows from the Vendors table. Combine the two SQL statements into a single SQL phrase using the UNION keyword. Now you can get a single result set that contains the results of both queries.

In the following SQL statement (see Figure 9.31), you are creating a result set that contains all Publishers and Buyers that are located in the state of New York.

```
SELECT * FROM Publishers WHERE State='NY'
   UNION
SELECT * FROM Buyers WHERE State='NY'
   ORDER BY Zip
```

Figure 9.31.
An example of a UNION query.

BuyerID	Name	Company Name	Address	City	State	Zip
1	ACM	Association for Computing	11 W. 42nd St., 3rd	New York	NY	10036
3	Bantam Books	Bantam Books Div of:	666 Fifth Ave	New York	NY	10103
26	Wiley	John Wiley & Sons Inc.	605 Third Ave	New York	NY	10158
CC01	New Age Books	NA Books, Inc.	121 First Street	New York	NY	34567-7890

Notice that in the previous example, the Publishers.PubID column is not present even though the column contents are in the result set. The contents of Publishers.PubID has been inserted into the Buyers.BuyerID column. SQL had to do a data type override to accomplish this. The

293

UNION query will use the column names of the first SQL query in the statement and will create a result set that displays the data even if data types must be altered to do so.

Each portion of the UNION query must have the same *number* of columns. If the first query results in six displayable columns, the query on the other side of the UNION statement must also result in six columns. If there is not an equal number of columns on each side of a UNION query, you will receive an SQL error message.

You can also use UNION queries on the same table. The following SQL statement (see Figure 9.32) shows how you can use SQL to return the top-selling titles and the bottom-selling titles in the same result set:

```
SELECT SUM(Sales) AS TotSales,Title FROM BookSales
    GROUP BY Title HAVING SUM(Sales)>4000
UNION
    SELECT SUM(Sales) AS TotSales,Title FROM BookSales
    GROUP BY Title HAVING SUM(Sales)<1000
ORDER BY TotSales
```

Figure 9.32.

Using UNION *on the same data table.*

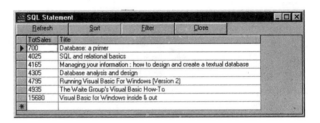

You can use Visual Basic stored queries (QueryDefs) as replacements for the complete SQL statement on either side of a UNION keyword. You can also link several SQL queries together with successive UNION keywords.

Crosstab Queries with *TRANSFORM...PIVOT*

The last SQL statement covered today is the TRANSFORM...PIVOT statement. This is a very powerful SQL tool that enables you to create result sets that contain summarized data in a form known as a *crosstab query*. Instead of trying to explain a crosstab query, let's look at a sample problem.

Suppose you have a data table that contains information on book titles and sales by quarter (sound familiar?). You have been asked to produce a view set that lists each book title down the left side and each quarter across the top with the sales figures for each quarter to the right of the book title. The only problem is that your data table has a single record for each quarter for each book. For example, if book A has sales in three quarters this year, you have three rows in your

data table. If book B has sales for four quarters, you have four rows, and so on. How can you produce a view that lists the quarters as columns instead of rows?

You can accomplish this with a complicated set of subsequent SQL statements that produces temporary views, merges them together, and so on. Thanks to the folks who invented the Microsoft Access JET database engine, however, you can use the TRANSFORM...PIVOT statement instead. You can produce the entire result set in one SQL statement using TRANSFORM...PIVOT. The following SQL statement shows how this can be done. See Figure 9.33 for a sample result set.

```
TRANSFORM SUM(BookSales.Sales)
    SELECT Title FROM BookSales
    GROUP BY Title
PIVOT BookSales.Qtr
```

Figure 9.33.

The TRANSFORM...PIVOT example.

Title	1	2	3	4
A guide to developing client/server SQL applications	350	385	385	385
A guide to the SQL standard : a user's guide to the standard relational	350	385	385	385
A practical guide to data base design	350	385	385	385
A visual introduction to SQL	350	385	385	385
An introduction to database systems	350	385	385	385
Conceptual schema and relational database design : a fact oriented	700	770	770	770

Notice the form of the TRANSFORM...PIVOT statement. It starts with the TRANSFORM keyword, not the SELECT keyword. Also notice that a single SQL aggregate function immediately follows the TRANSFORM keyword. This is required, even if no real totaling will be performed. After the TRANSFORM aggregate function clause, you have the standard SELECT...FROM clause. Notice that the previous example did not include the Booksales.Sales column in the SELECT statement because it will be produced by the TRANSFORM...PIVOT clause automatically. The GROUP BY clause is required in order to tell SQL how to treat the successive rows that will be handled for each BookSales.Title. Finally, add the PIVOT keyword, followed by the column that you want to use, as the set of headers that follow out to the right of the GROUP BY column.

TRANSFORM...PIVOT uses the data in the PIVOT column as column headers in the result set. You will have as many columns in your result set as you have unique values in your PIVOT column. This is important to understand. Using columns that contain a limited set of data (such as months of the year) will produce valuable result sets. However, using a column that contains unique data (such as the CustomerID column) will produce a result set with an unpredictable number of columns.

The nice thing about TRANSFORM...PIVOT is that it is easy to produce several different views of the same data by just changing the PIVOT column. For example, what if you wanted to see the book sales results by BookSales.SaleRep instead of by BookSales.Qtr? All you have to do is change the PIVOT field. See the following code example and Figure 9.34.

```
TRANSFORM SUM(BookSales.Sales)
   SELECT Title FROM BookSales
   GROUP BY Title
PIVOT BookSales.SalesRep
```

Figure 9.34.
Changing the PIVOT field.

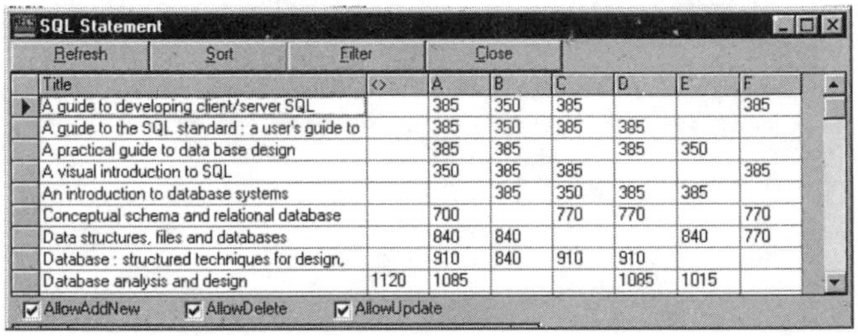

Notice, in Figure 9.34, that you can see a column with the header <>. When Microsoft Access JET ran the SQL statement, it discovered some records that had no value in the BookSales.SaleRep column. SQL automatically created a new column (<>) to hold these records and make sure they were not left out of the result set.

Even though TRANSFORM...PIVOT is a powerful SQL tool, there is one drawback to its widespread use in your programs. The TRANSFORM...PIVOT clause is not an ANSI-SQL clause. Microsoft added this clause as an extension of the ANSI-SQL command set. If you use it in your programs, you will not be able to port your SQL statements to other back-end databases that do not support the TRANSFORM...PIVOT SQL clause. Despite this drawback, you will find TRANSFORM...PIVOT a very valuable SQL tool when it comes to producing result sets for summary reports, data graphs, and charts.

Summary

Today you learned how to create basic SQL statements that select data from existing tables. You learned that the most fundamental form of the SQL statement is the SELECT...FROM clause. This clause is used to select one or more columns from a table and display the results of that statement in a result set, or view.

You also learned about the optional clauses that you can add to the SELECT...FROM clause:

☐ The WHERE clause: Used to limit the rows in the result set using logical comparisons (for example, WHERE Table.Name = "SMITH") and to link two tables in a single, nonupdateable, view (for example, WHERE Table1.Name = Table2.Name).

☐ The ORDER BY clause: Used to control the order in which the result set is displayed (for example, ORDER BY Name ASC).

☐ The GROUP BY clause: Used to create a subtotal result set based on a break column (for example, GROUP BY Name).

☐ The HAVING clause: Used only with the GROUP BY clause, the HAVING clause acts as a WHERE clause for the GROUP BY subtotal clause (for example, GROUP BY Name HAVING SUM(SalesTotal)>1000).

☐ The INNER JOIN clause: Used to join two tables together into a single, updateable result set. The INNER JOIN returns rows that have a corresponding match in both tables.

☐ The LEFT JOIN and RIGHT JOIN: Used to join two tables into a single, updateable result set. The LEFT JOIN includes all records from the first (left-hand) table and all rows from the second table that have a corresponding match. The RIGHT JOIN works in reverse.

☐ The UNION clause: Used to combine two or more complete SQL queries into a single result set (for example, SELECT * FROM Table1 UNION SELECT * FROM Table2).

☐ The TRANSFORM...PIVOT clause: Used to create a crosstab query as a result set (for example, TRANSFORM SUM(MonthlySales) FROM SalesTable GROUP BY Product PIVOT Month).

You also learned about additional SQL keywords that you can use to control the contents of the result set:

☐ BETWEEN...AND logical operators

☐ DISTINCT and DISTINCTROW

☐ AS to rename columns in the result set

☐ TOP *n* and TOP *n* PERCENT

☐ The SQL aggregate functions AVG, COUNT, MAX, MIN, and SUM

Quiz

1. What does SQL stand for? How is SQL pronounced?
2. What SQL statement enables you to select data from table fields?
3. What wildcard character do you use in a SELECT...FROM statement to include all fields of a table in your result?
4. What clause do you use in a SQL statement to sort the displayed data?
5. Identify two functions that a WHERE clause performs in a SQL statement?
6. How do you rename the column headings in a SQL statement?
7. What are SQL aggregate functions? List the SQL aggregate functions available through the Microsoft Access JET database engine.
8. What are the drawbacks of using Visual Basic functions in SQL statements?
9. What is the difference between the DISTINCT and DISTINCTROW SQL clauses?

10. What clause should you always use with the TOP *n* or TOP *n* PERCENT clause?

11. What are the three join types available in Microsoft JET SQL? Briefly explain how each is used.

12. When would you use a UNION query?

Exercises

As a corporate MIS staff member, you are given the task of assisting the Accounting Department in extracting data from its accounts payable and accounts receivable systems. As part of your analysis, you determine that these systems possess the following data tables and fields:

CustomerMaster

CustomerID
Name
Address
City
State
Zip
Phone
CustomerType

CustomerType

CustomerType
Description

OpenInvoice

InvoiceNo
CustomerID
Date
Description
Amount

Suppliers

SupplierID
Name
Address
City
State
Zip
Phone

Use this information to answer the questions that follow:

1. Write a SQL statement to list all of the customers. Include their IDs, names, addresses, phone numbers, and customer types.

2. Display all of the information in the Open Invoice table, but display CustomerID as Account.

3. Display the same information requested in Exercise 2, but sort the data by customer and then by invoice number within each customer.

4. Display all suppliers that can be found within New York City. Display their IDs, names, addresses, and phone numbers.

5. Display the Customer types, names, and address for all customers with a customer type of ABC.

6. Select and display customer IDs and names whose names begin with AME.

7. Display the CustomerID and Name of all customers who have an open invoice. Sort your information by CustomerID.

8. Select and display the five largest outstanding invoices.

9. Display a listing of names and phone numbers of all customers and vendors who reside in Ohio.

Visual Basic and the Microsoft JET Engine

Today you'll learn the details of the heart of the Visual Basic database system—Microsoft JET, the part of Visual Basic that handles all database operations. Whether you are reading a Microsoft Access format database, accessing a FoxPro file, or connecting to a back-end database server using ODBC, Microsoft JET is there. You can also use Visual Basic to create a link between an existing Microsoft JET database and data in non-Microsoft JET databases. This process of attaching external data sources provides an excellent way to gain the advantages of the Microsoft JET data access object layer without having to convert existing data to Microsoft JET format.

Today you will learn about several object collections that exist in Visual Basic Microsoft JET databases. These objects include the following:

- [ ] The DBEngine object
- [ ] The Workspace object
- [ ] The Database object
- [ ] The TableDef object
- [ ] The Field object
- [ ] The Index object
- [ ] The Relation object

Throughout this lesson, you will build a single Visual Basic project that illustrates the various data access objects you are learning about today. You can apply the Visual Basic coding techniques you learn today in future Visual Basic database projects.

What Is the Microsoft JET Database Engine?

The *JET* in *Microsoft JET* stands for Joint Engine Technology. The idea behind Microsoft JET is that you can use one single interface to access multiple types of data. Microsoft designed Microsoft JET to be able to present a consistent interface to the user regardless of the type of data the user is working with. Consequently, you can use the same Microsoft JET functions that you use to access an ASCII text file or Microsoft Excel spreadsheet to perform data operations on Microsoft Access databases.

Microsoft JET is not a single program; it is a set of routines that work together. The Microsoft JET talks to a set of translation routines. These routines convert your Microsoft JET request into a request that the target database can understand. Translation routines exist for Microsoft Access databases, and for non-Microsoft Access ISAM files such as dBASE, FoxPro, Paradox, and so on. A translation set even exists to handle ODBC data sources using the Microsoft JET interface. In theory, you could access any data file format via the Microsoft JET, as long as some set of translation routines is made available to Microsoft JET.

Note: The detailed inner workings of the Microsoft JET go beyond the scope of this book. If you want to learn more about how the Microsoft JET interface works, you can obtain copies of several white papers Microsoft has released on the topic of Microsoft JET and the data access object layer. You can get these papers through various online sources, and through the Microsoft Developers Network CDs.

Advantages of Microsoft JET over the Data Control

So far, you have learned to use the Data Control to perform database administrative tasks. The Data Access Objects (DAO) addressed in this chapter perform all of the services that the Data Control does, as well as many more. The data access objects give you complete control over database management.

If possible, use the Data Control to manage your data. It is a much easier tool to use, because many of the administrative function are handled for you. You can always add DAO in your code to work with the Data Control.

Microsoft JET Data Objects

The Microsoft JET is organized into a set of data access objects. Each of the objects has collections, properties, and methods.

- ☐ Collections: Data access objects that contain the same type of objects.
- ☐ Properties: The data contained within an object (control button, form, and so on) that defines its characteristics. You *set* an object's properties.
- ☐ Methods: The procedures that can be performed on an object. You *invoke* a method.

The Microsoft JET data access objects exist in a hierarchy, which means that a top-down relationship exists between the data access objects. You learn the various Microsoft JET data access objects in the order they reside in the hierarchy. As you push deeper into the data access object hierarchy, you move toward more specific data objects. For example, the first data object in the hierarchy is the DBEngine data access object. All other data access objects exist underneath the DBEngine data access objects.

Note: Throughout the rest of this chapter you will see the phrase data access objects and data objects. They both refer to the Data Access Object layer of the Microsoft JET.

If you do not already have Visual Basic up and running, start it now and begin a new project. Make sure that your system can reference the Data Access Object set.

> **Warning:** If you don't have a reference to the Data Access Object layer in your project, you cannot access any of the features of the Microsoft JET database engine.

If you can't tell whether your reference to the data access object is activated, select Tools | References from the Visual Basic main menu. If you are running the 32-bit version of Visual Basic 4, you should make sure the Version 3 Data Access Object checkbox is turned on. If you are running the 16-bit version of Visual Basic 4, you should make sure that the checkbox for Version 2.5 Data Access Object is turned on. Use Figure 10.1 as a reference.

Figure 10.1.
Reviewing the data access object reference.

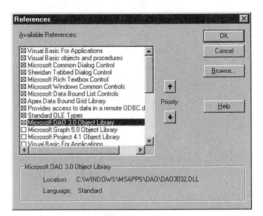

The *DBEngine* Data Object

The DBEngine data object is the default data object for all access to the database operations under Visual Basic 4. Even if you use the old Visual Basic 3 syntax to open and update database objects, you still use the DBEngine data object because it is invoked by default when Visual Basic 4 begins any database work.

> **Tip:** Even though Visual Basic 4 does not require that you explicitly use the DBEngine data object, you should use the object in all your future Visual Basic projects to ensure maximum compatibility with any future versions of Visual Basic.

The *DBEngine* Object Collections

The DBEngine object contains three different object collections. Each of these collections in turn contains other data access objects. To put it another way, the DBEngine is the top level of the DAO hierarchy, and it contains the following collections:

- ☐ Workspaces: A collection of all the defined Workspace objects. The next section of this chapter covers Workspace objects. The Workspace collection is the default collection for the DBEngine object.

- ☐ Errors: A collection of the most recent database-related errors encountered in this session. Error objects are covered later in this chapter.

- ☐ Properties: A collection of all the properties of the DBEngine object.

The *DBEngine* Object Properties

Like all Visual Basic objects, you can list the properties of the object by accessing the Properties collection. Let's write a short bit of code that will list (enumerate) all the properties of the DBEngine data access object.

First, add a single button to the bottom of the current form. Set its Name property to cmdDBEngine and its Caption property to &DBEngine. Now double-click the button to bring up the cmdDBEngine_Click event window and enter the code shown in Listing 10.1.

Listing 10.1. Coding the cmdDBEngine_Click event.

```
Private Sub cmdDBEngine_Click()
    On Error Resume Next
    '
    Dim oItem As Object
    '
    For Each oItem In DBEngine.Properties
        Me.Print oItem.Name; " | ",
        Me.Print oItem.Type; " | ",
        Me.Print oItem.VALUE; " | ",
        Me.Print oItem.Inherited; " | "
    Next
    '
End Sub
```

In Listing 10.1, you first tell Visual Basic to ignore any errors it might receive while enumerating the DBEngine properties. Then you declare a single variable as an object to represent the property you are inspecting. You then use the Visual Basic 4 For...Each loop to list each of the properties of the DBEngine object. Separate each property with the pipe character. Each property has four parameters: its name, its data type, its value, and the inheritance flag.

305

Save the form as CH1001.FRM and the project as CH1001.VBP. When you run the project, you see a single button at the bottom of the form. Click that button to force Visual Basic to enumerate the properties of the DBEngine data access object. Your screen should look like Figure 10.2.

Figure 10.2.

The enumerated DBEngine properties.

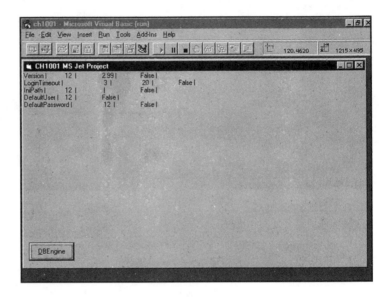

Setting the *DBEngine* Properties

You can set the properties of the DBEngine object in your program, too. For example, if you want to set the IniPath property of the DBEngine, you could add a single code line.

```
DBEngine.IniPath= App.Path + "\ch1001.ini" ' set the default ini path
```

Add this code line to the project just before the For…Each statement. Save and run the project. You should now see that the IniPath property of the DBEngine has been set. The DefaultUser and DefaultPassword properties are covered when you learn about the Workspace data access object.

The *DBEngine* Object Methods

Five Visual Basic methods are associated with the DBEngine data access object:

☐ RepairDatabase is used to fix corrupted Microsoft JET database files.

☐ CompactDatabase is used to clean up, and also convert, existing Microsoft JET databases.

☐ RegisterDatabase is used to create a link between an external data source and an existing Microsoft JET database.

□ Idle is used to force Visual Basic to pause processing while the DBEngine updates the contents of any existing data access objects.

□ CreateWorkspace is used to establish a workspace for accessing one or more databases. You'll learn about this method in the section on Workspace objects later in this chapter.

Using the *RepairDatabase* Method

You can use the RepairDatabase method to fix corrupted Microsoft JET database files. The default syntax to invoke this method is

```
DBEngine.RepairDatabase databasename
```

Add another command button to the current project. Place it at the bottom of the screen. Set its Name property to cmdRepair and its Caption property to &Repair. Add the code in Listing 10.2 in the cmdRepair_Click code window.

10

Listing 10.2. Coding the cmdRepair_Click event.

```
Private Sub cmdRepair_Click()
    '
    ' attempt to fix a currupted database
    '
    Dim cDBName As String
    '
    cDBName = InputBox("Enter Database To Repair:", "RepairDatabase Example")
    If Len(Trim(cDBName)) <> 0 Then
        DBEngine.RepairDatabase cDBName
        MsgBox cDBName + " Repaired"
    End If
End Sub
```

The code in Listing 10.2 declares a local variable for the database name and then prompts the user to enter the name of a database to repair. After checking to make sure a database name was entered, the code executes the RepairDatabase method and reports the results.

Save and run the program. When you click the Repair button, enter CH1001.MDB in the input dialog box (see Figure 10.3).

Figure 10.3.
Entering a database to repair.

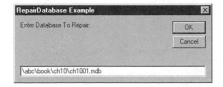

The repair method executes and the final message box appears.

> **Warning:** The RepairDatabase method overwrites the existing file with the repaired database file. You might want to make a backup copy of your database files before you execute the RepairDatabase method.

Using the *CompactDatabase* Method

The CompactDatabase method cleans out empty space in Microsoft JET databases and performs general optimization chores that improve access speed. You can also use the CompactDatabase method to convert older versions of Microsoft JET databases to newer versions.

The syntax for this method is

```
DBEngine.CompactDatabase oldDatabase, NewDatabase, locale, options
```

In this line, *oldDatabase* is the name (including path) of the database to be compacted; *NewDatabase* is the name (including path) of the new, compacted database; and *locale* is the language in which the data is written. Options can be added to encrypt or decrypt a database, as well as to change versions. Multiple options must be joined with the plus (+) sign.

Add another button to the CH1001.VBP project. Set its Name property to cmdCompact and its Caption property to &Compact. Enter the code in Listing 10.3 into the cmdCompact_Click event window. This code will compact any Microsoft JET database.

Listing 10.3. Coding the cmdCompact_Click event.

```
Private Sub cmdCompact_Click()
    Dim cOldDB As String
    Dim cNewDB As String
    Dim nEncrypt As Integer
    Dim cVersion As String
    Dim nVersion As Integer
    Dim cHeader As String
    '
    ' start of routine
cmdCompactClickStart:
    ' init vars
    cOldDB = ""
    cNewDB = ""
    cVersion = ""
    nEncrypt = False
    cHeader = "CompactDatabase Example"
    '
    ' get file to convert/compact
    cOldDB = InputBox("Enter File to Compact/Convert", cHeader)
    If Len(Trim(cOldDB)) = 0 Then
        GoTo cmdCompactClickEnd
    End If
```

```
    '
    ' get target filename
    cNewDB = InputBox("Enter Target File Name", cHeader)
    If Len(Trim(cNewDB)) = 0 Then
       GoTo cmdCompactClickStart
    End If
    '
    ' get target version
cmdCompactClickVersion:
    nVersion = 0
    cVersion = InputBox("Enter Target Version Number" + Chr(13) +
    ➥Chr(10) + "1.0, 1.1, 2.5, or 3.0", cHeader)
    Select Case Trim(cVersion)
        Case Is = ""
            GoTo cmdCompactClickStart
        Case Is = "1.0"
            nVersion = dbVersion10
        Case Is = "1.1"
            nVersion = dbVersion11
        Case Is = "2.5"
            nVersion = dbVersion20
    ' Add the next two lines only if you are working in 32-bit mode
        Case Is = "3.0"
            nVersion = dbVersion30
        Case Else
            MsgBox "Invalid Version!", vbCritical, "Input Error"
            GoTo cmdCompactClickVersion
    End Select
    '
    ' ask about encryption
    nEncrypt = MsgBox("Encrypt Database?", vbInformation + vbYesNo, cHeader)
    If nEncrypt = vbYes Then
       nEncrypt = dbEncrypt
    Else
       nEncrypt = dbDecrypt
    End If
    '
    ' now try to do it!
    DBEngine.CompactDatabase cOldDB, cNewDB, dbLangGeneral, nVersion + nEncrypt
    GoTo cmdCompactClickEnd
    '
cmdCompactClickEnd:
    '
End Sub
```

The code in Listing 10.3 declares its local variables and then prompts the user to enter the
database file to compact or convert. If no filename is entered, the routine skips to the exit. If a
filename is entered, the user is prompted to enter a target filename. If no name is entered, the
program returns to try the whole thing again. After getting the filename, the user is prompted
to supply the target MSJH version number. The value entered is checked and the user is returned
to the input box if an invalid option was entered. Finally, the user is asked whether the database
should be encrypted. After that, the CompactDatabase method is invoked.

Save your work and execute this program. You are prompted to enter the name of the database to compact. Enter the path and name for CH1001.MDB. You then must enter a database to compact to. Enter the same path, but enter the name as CH1001X.MDB. Next, enter the version. Users of 16-bit systems should enter 2.5 (3.0 is available in 32-bit mode only). Answer Yes when you are prompted with the encryption question. The new database is now compacted and saved as CH1001X.MDB.

Note: A good program would present the user with the File Open dialog box to locate the files. This example uses the InputBox to save time and simplify the code example.

Using the *RegisterDatabase* Method

The RegisterDatabase method enables you to register an ODBC data source for Microsoft JET access. The Visual Basic documentation encourages programmers to rely on the Windows Control Panel ODBC Setup utility instead of using the RegisterDatabase method. If, however, you want to perform the ODBC registration process within your Visual Basic program, you can use the RegisterDatabase method to do so.

The easiest way to provide ODBC registration capabilities in your program is to supply a limited number of parameters and force Windows to present the ODBC registration dialog for you—a fairly easy task. For this example, add a new command button to the bottom of the form. Set its Name property to cmdODBC and its Caption property to &ODBC. Add the following code in the cmdODBC_Click code window.

```
Private Sub cmdODBC_Click()
    On Error Resume Next
    '
    ' simple call to register an ODBC data source
    DBEngine.RegisterDatabase "MyODBC", "SQL Server", False, ""
End Sub
```

The preceding code first tells Visual Basic to ignore any reported errors, and then it supplies a set of parameters for creating an ODBC data source. The parameters for the RegisterDatabase method are as follows:

- SourceName: The name that will be used as the database name for the OpenDatabase method.

- DriverName: The name of an ODBC driver installed and available on your workstation.

- SilentFlag: Setting this to False forces Windows to present the ODBC registration dialog box. If it is set to True, Windows attempts to register the ODBC data source without prompting the user with the ODBC registration dialog box.

☐ AttributeList: A list of attribute settings for the ODBC source. Examples of attributes include any server device name, database name, and any other parameters required by the back-end database server.

Save and run the project. When you click the ODBC button, you see the Windows ODBC Registration dialog box appear with some of the parameters already entered. You can complete the information and click OK to register the ODBC data source on your system. Refer to Figure 10.4 as an example. For now, select Cancel and don't register.

Figure 10.4.

Registering an ODBC data source.

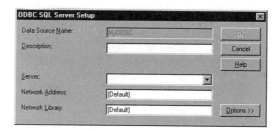

Completing an ODBC registration inserts data into the ODBC.INI file on 16-bit systems and adds information to the Windows Registry file on 32-bit systems. You can add features to the earlier cmdODBC_Click example by prompting the user to enter the SourceName and DriverName. You could also fill out all values within the program and set the SilentFlag to True. In this way, you could use the routine to install new ODBC connections for your Visual Basic applications without requiring the user to know anything at all about ODBC or Microsoft JET.

> **Warning:** Failure to register an ODBC data source properly can result in unexpected errors and possible loss of data. Be sure to test your RegisterDatabase routines completely before using them on live data.

The *Idle* Method

The Idle method forces Visual Basic to pause while the DBEngine catches up on any changes that have been made to all the open data access objects. This method becomes useful when you have a lot of database traffic or a lot of data access objects in a single program. The syntax is simple:

```
DBEngine.Idle
```

The *Workspace* Data Object

The Workspace data object identifies a database session for a user. Workspaces are created each time you open a database using the Microsoft JET. You can create Workspace objects to manage database transactions for users and to provide a level of security during a database session. Even if you do not explicitly create a Workspace object, Visual Basic 4 will create a default Workspace each time you begin database operations.

Note: Although you can create Workspace data objects, you can't save them. Workspace objects are temporary. They cease to exist as soon as your program stops running or as soon as you close your last data access object.

The Workspace object contains three collections, two properties, and eight methods. The Workspaces collection contains one property (Count) and one method (Refresh). The Workspaces collection enables you to access multiple Workspace objects. The Workspace object enables you to access the properties, collections, and methods of the named Workspace object.

The *Workspace* Object Collections

The Workspace data access object contains three object collections:

- ☐ Databases: A collection of all the Database objects opened for this Workspace object. This is the default collection.
- ☐ Groups: A collection of all the defined Group objects that have access to this Workspace.
- ☐ Users: A collection of all the defined User objects that have access to this Workspace.

Note: You can only access the Group and User objects if the Microsoft JET security is activated. You can only activate Microsoft JET security through Microsoft Access. Although Visual Basic cannot *initiate* database security, you can manage the security features using Visual Basic 4. Security features are covered on Day 20.

The *Workspace* Object Properties

Three Workspace object properties exist: the workspace name, the workspace user name, and the Isolate ODBC Trans property. The Isolate ODBC Trans property can be used to control the number of ODBC connections used during the database session.

> **Note:** ODBC connections are covered in depth in Week 3 of the book. For now, just remember that you can control the number of connections used by the session by altering the Isolate ODBC Trans property of the `Workspace` object.

When you begin a database operation, Visual Basic 4 creates a default workspace with the name `#Default Workspace #` and the user name `admin`. Let's add some code to the CH1001.VBP project to enumerate the default `Workspace` properties.

Add a new button to the form. Set its Name property to cmdWorkspace and its Caption property to &Workspace. Enter the code in Listing 10.4 into the `cmdWorkspace_Click` code window.

Listing 10.4. Coding the `cmdWorkspace_Click` event.

```
Private Sub cmdWorkspace_Click()
    On Error Resume Next
    '
    Dim oItem As Object
    Dim x As Integer
    '
    ' show properties
    Me.Cls
    For x = 0 To DBEngine.Workspaces.Count - 1
        For Each oItem In DBEngine.Workspaces(x).Properties
            Me.Print oItem.Name; " ¦ ",
            Me.Print oItem.Type; " ¦ ",
            Me.Print oItem.VALUE; " ¦ ",
            Me.Print oItem.Inherited; " ¦ "
        Next
    Next
End Sub
```

The code in Listing 10.4 should look familiar to you. It is almost identical to the code used to enumerate the `DBEngine` properties. The only change that has been made is in the `For...Each` code line. Instead of enumerating the `DBEngine` properties, this time you enumerated the properties of `DBEngine.Workspaces(x)`. You also added an additional loop that will enumerate the properties of all `Workspace` objects that might exist.

Save and run the program. When you click on the Workspace button, the program lists all the properties of the object. Your screen should look like Figure 10.5.

Figure 10.5.

Enumerating the Workspace
object properties.

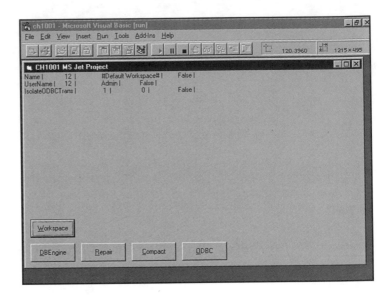

Creating a New *Workspace* Object

You can create new Workspace objects using the CreateWorkspace method of the DBEngine. Even though Visual Basic 4 will create and use a default Workspace object when you first begin database operations, you should create an explicit Workspace from within Visual Basic. When you create a unique Workspace object, you isolate all your database operations into a single session. You can then group a set of database transactions into a single session to improve database integrity and security.

Let's add a new command button to the CH1001.VBP project that will create a new Workspace object. Set the button's Name property to cmdNewWrkSp and set its Caption property to &New WS. Add the code in Listing 10.5 into the cmdNewWrkSp_Click code window.

Listing 10.5. Coding the cmdNewWrkSp_Click event.

```
Private Sub cmdNewWrkSp_Click()
    '
    Dim wsNew As Workspace
    Dim cWSName As String
    Dim cWSUser As String
    Dim cWSPassword As String
    '
    ' init vars
    cWSName = "NewWorkspace"     ' this can be any name
    cWSUser = "admin"            ' user must already exist
    cWSPassword = ""             ' password must match user
    '
    ' create workspace object
    Set wsNew = DBEngine.CreateWorkspace(cWSName, cWSUser, cWSPassword)
```

```
'
' add object to collection
DBEngine.Workspaces.Append wsNew
'
' show the entire collection now
cmdWorkspace_Click
'
End Sub
```

The code in Listing 10.5 establishes local variables and then initializes them to the correct values. Notice that you can use any unique name you like for the Workspace object, but you must use valid User and Password parameters. These values must already exist in the SYSTEM.MDA or as the default values if Microsoft Access security is not active. Because you do not use Microsoft Access security here, this example used the default admin user name and empty password.

You used the CreateWorkspace method to create a valid Workspace object. Before the system can use the object, you must add the new object to the Workspaces collection, which you do using the Append method. After adding the new object, you force Visual Basic to display the Workspaces collection to see your results.

Save and run the project. After you click the New WS button, you see two workspaces displayed on the form. Check your screen against the one in Figure 10.6.

Figure 10.6.
The results of adding a new Workspace object.

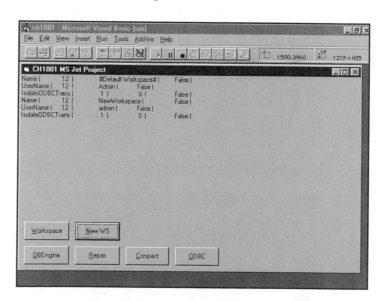

Using the *Workspace* Object Methods

Eight methods exist for the Workspace object. The Close method is used to close an existing Workspace object. Three of the methods enable you to manage transaction processing (BeginTrans,

`CommitTrans`, and `Rollback`). Transaction processing is covered on Day 18, "Multiuser Considerations." Two other methods are used to create `User` and `Group` objects. You'll learn more about those on Day 20, "Securing Your Database Applications." The remaining two methods enable you to create, open, and close `Database` objects.

Using the Database Methods

The two database-related `Workspace` methods are `CreateDatabase` and `OpenDatabase`. You use the `CreateDatabase` method to create a new database, and you use the `OpenDatabase` method to open an existing database.

Let's first add a command button to create a new database. Set the button's Name property to cmdCreateDB and its Caption property to CreateDB. Add the code in Listing 10.6 to the `cmdCreateDB_Click` code window.

Listing 10.6. Coding the `cmdCreateDB_Click` event.

```
Private Sub cmdCreateDB_Click()
    On Error Resume Next        ' ignore errors
    '
    Dim dbNew As DATABASE       ' new db object
    Dim cDBName As String       ' new db name
    Dim wsNew As Workspace      ' new workspace object
    Dim cWSName As String       ' new workspace name
    Dim cWSUser As String       ' new workspace user
    Dim cWSPassword As String   ' new workspace password
    Dim dbTemp As DATABASE      ' for enumerating dbs
    '
    ' init vars
    cDBName = App.Path + "\ch1001x.mdb"
    cWSName = "ch1001x Workspace"
    cWSUser = "admin"
    cWSPassword = ""
    '
    ' erase the new db if it's already there
    Kill cDBName
    '
    ' create workspace for session
    Set wsNew = DBEngine.CreateWorkspace(cWSName, cWSUser, cWSPassword)
    DBEngine.Workspaces.Append wsNew
    '
    ' create new JET database
    Set dbNew = DBEngine.Workspaces(cWSName).CreateDatabase(cDBName, _
    ➥dbLangGeneral, dbVersion20)
    '
    ' now show the databases for the workspace
    Me.Cls
    For Each dbTemp In Workspaces(cWSName).Databases
        Me.Print dbTemp.Name
    Next
    '
End Sub
```

The code in Listing 10.6 declares some variables, initializes them, and then goes on to create a workspace for this session. Then, it creates the new Database object, and finally shows you all the databases that are a part of the current workspace. Database objects are covered in greater detail in the next section of today's lesson. It is important to note here that you create a Workspace object before you create the database to make sure that the Database object becomes a part of the Workspace object. Now all activity on that database is a part of the Workspace. You can open more than one database in the same workspace and group the database operations together.

Save and run the project. When you click on the CreateDB button, the program creates the new database and then shows the results on the form. Your screen should look like Figure 10.7.

Figure 10.7.
Creating a new database.

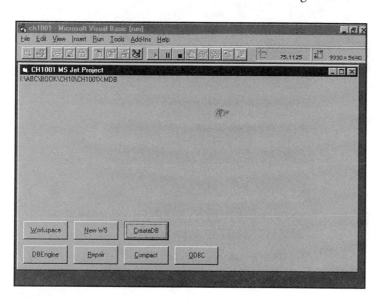

You can also open the same database in two different workspaces. Modify the project to open the newly created database under two different workspaces at the same time. Add a new command button and set its Name property to cmdOpenDB and its Caption property to &OpenDB. Add the code in Listing 10.7 to the cmdOpenDB_Click code window.

Listing 10.7. Coding the cmdOpenDB_Click event.

```
Private Sub cmdOpenDB_Click()
    On Error Resume Next       ' ignore errors
    '
    Dim wsOne As Workspace     ' for first ws
    Dim wsTwo As Workspace     ' for second ws
    Dim cWSOneName As String   ' first ws name
    Dim cWSTwoName As String   ' second ws name
    Dim cWSUser As String      ' for both ws
```

continues

Listing 10.7. continued

```
Dim cWSPassword As String    ' for both ws
Dim dbOne As DATABASE        ' first db object
Dim dbTwo As DATABASE        ' second db object
Dim cDBName As String        ' db name
Dim wsTemp As Workspace      ' for listing
Dim dbTemp As DATABASE       ' for listing
'
' init vars
cWSOneName = "WorkspaceOne"
cWSTwoName = "WorkspaceTwo"
cWSUser = "admin"
cWSPassword = ""
cDBName = App.Path + "\ch1001x.mdb"
'
' create first workspaces
Set wsOne = DBEngine.CreateWorkspace(cWSOneName, cWSUser, cWSPassword)
Set wsTwo = DBEngine.CreateWorkspace(cWSTwoName, cWSUser, cWSPassword)
DBEngine.Workspaces.Append wsOne
DBEngine.Workspaces.Append wsTwo
'
' now open database first time
Set dbOne = Workspaces(cWSOneName).OpenDatabase(cDBName)
'
' now open database second time
Set dbTwo = Workspaces(cWSTwoName).OpenDatabase(cDBName)
'
' show workspaces and databases
Me.Cls
For Each wsTemp In DBEngine.Workspaces  ' enumerate workspaces
    Me.Print wsTemp.Name; "¦",          ' workspace name
    For Each dbTemp In wsTemp.Databases ' enumerate databases
        Me.Print dbTemp.Name; "¦",      ' database name
    Next
    Me.Print "" ' complete print line
Next
'
End Sub
```

The code in Listing 10.7 declares and initializes several variables for the two Workspace and Database object pairs. Then each workspace is created and appended to the collection, and the single database is opened once under each workspace session. Finally, all the workspaces and all their databases are listed to the screen. Note that you do not have to use different user names and passwords for the two Workspace objects.

Save and run the project. When you click the OpenDB button, the program opens the database under two different workspaces and shows the results. Notice that the #Default Workspace# appears in the list. It will always exist in the Workspaces collection. Check your screen against Figure 10.8.

Figure 10.8.
The results of the
`OpenDatabase` *method in*
two workspaces.

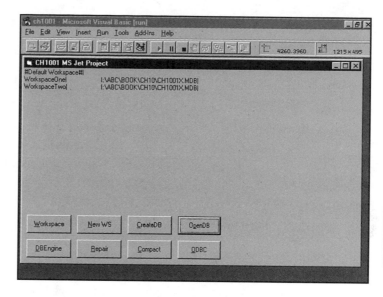

Creating and Opening Non-Microsoft JET Databases

You can only create Microsoft JET format databases using the `CreateDatabase` method. The other ISAM-type databases (dBASE, FoxPro, Paradox, and Btreive) all use a single directory or folder as the database object. To create non-Microsoft JET databases, you have to create a new directory or folder on the disk drive. You can then use the `OpenDatabase` method to open the non-Microsoft JET database. When it is opened, you can add tables and indexes using the existing Visual Basic data objects and methods. You'll learn about opening non-Microsoft JET databases in the next section.

The *Database* Data Object

The `Database` data object has five collections, eight properties, and 16 methods. The `Database` object contains all the tables, queries, and relations defined for the database. The `Database` object is also part of the Databases collection of the `Workspace` object. The `Database` object is created whenever you open a database with the `OpenDatabase` method. `Database` objects continue to exist in memory until you use the `Close` method to remove them.

Warning: Do not confuse the `Database` *object* with the database *file*. The `Database` object is a Visual Basic program construct used to access the physical database file. Throughout this section, you will hear about the `Database` object.

The Collections of the *Database* Object

The Database object has five collections:

- [ ] TableDefs is the collection of Table objects that contain the detailed definition of each data table in the database. This is the default collection.

- [ ] QueryDefs is the collection of SQL queries stored in the database.

- [ ] Relations is the collection of database integrity relationship definitions stored in the database.

- [ ] Recordsets is the collection of active Recordsets opened from this database. Recordsets include any Tables, Dynasets, or Snapshots currently open. Recordsets are temporary objects and are not stored with the database file.

- [ ] Containers is the collection of all TableDefs, QueryDefs, and Relations stored in the physical database file. You can use the Containers collection to enumerate all the persistent (stored) objects in the database.

The data access objects just described are covered in later sections of this chapter. This section focuses on the properties and methods associated with the Database data access object.

The Properties of the *Database* Object

The Database object has eight properties. To illustrate these properties, add another command button to the CH1001.VBP project. Set its Name property to cmdDBProps and its Caption property to DB&Props. Enter the code in Listing 10.8 into the cmdDBProps_Click code window.

Listing 10.8. Coding the cmdDBProps_Click event.

```
Private Sub cmdDBProps_Click()
    On Error Resume Next        ' ignore errors
    '
    Dim dbFile As DATABASE      ' data object
    Dim cDBName As String       ' db name
    Dim oItem As Object         ' to hold properties
    '
    cDBName = App.Path + "\ch1001.mdb"    ' db to open
    '
    ' open db in default workspace
    Set dbFile = OpenDatabase(cDBName)
    '
    ' enumerate the db properties
    Me.Cls
    For Each oItem In dbFile.Properties
        Me.Print oItem.Name; "|",
        Me.Print oItem.Type; "|",
        Me.Print oItem.VALUE; "|",
        Me.Print oItem.Inherited
    Next
```

```
'
    dbFile.Close      ' close the database
'
End Sub
```

In Listing 10.8, you opened an existing Microsoft JET database in the default workspace (but did not explicitly declare a session) and then enumerated the properties of the Database object. Save and run the project. Click the DBProps button and compare your screen to the one in Figure 10.9.

Figure 10.9.

The results of enumerating Database *object properties.*

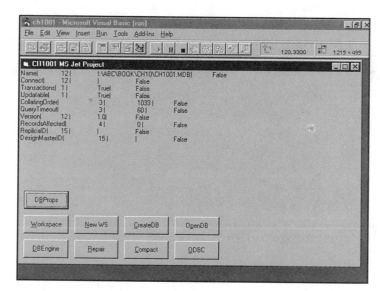

Table 10.1 lists the Database object properties and their meanings.

Table 10.1. Database object properties.

Property	Type/Value	Meaning/Use
Name	String	The name of the physical database file or the name of the ODBC data source.
Connect	String	If the data source is not a Microsoft JET database, this property contains additional information needed to connect to the data using Microsoft JET.
Transactions	True/False	If set to True, this data source supports the use of the BeginTrans, CommitTrans, and Rollback methods.

Table 10.1. continued

Property	Type/Value	Meaning/Use
Updatable	True/False	If set to True, Visual Basic can provide updates to this data source. If set to False, this is a read-only data source.
Collating Order	Numeric	This value controls the order in which Microsoft JET sorts or indexes the records. It is set via the locale parameter of the CreateDatabase method.
Query Time Out	Numeric (seconds)	This is the amount of time Microsoft JET will wait before reporting an error while waiting for the results of a query.
Version	String	Indicates the Microsoft JET version used to create the database.
Records Affected	Numeric	Shows the number of records affected by the last database operation on this file.

Let's modify the routine to open a non-Microsoft JET database in order to compare the differences in the property values between Microsoft JET and non-Microsoft JET databases. Change the code to match the following example and run the program again to review the results.

```
Private Sub cmdDBProps_Click()
    On Error Resume Next        ' ignore errors
    '
    Dim dbFile As DATABASE      ' data object
    Dim cDBName As String       ' db name
    Dim cConnect As String      ' connect parameters
    Dim oItem As Object         ' to hold properties
    '
    cDBName = App.Path    ' db to open
    cConnect = "Text;"                      ' open a text file
    '
    ' open db in default workspace
    Set dbFile = OpenDatabase(cDBName, False, False, cConnect)
..... (code continues).....
```

Only the first section of the code appears here because that section contains the modifications. Make the changes to your program, save it, and run it. When you click the DBProps button this time, you will see different property values.

The Methods of the *Database* Object

The Database object has 16 methods, but this text won't cover all of them here. Three relate to transaction management (BeginTrans, CommitTrans, and Rollback). Three relate to managing

QueryDef objects (CreateQueryDef, OpenQueryDef, and DeleteQueryDef). These methods are covered in the section titled, "The QueryDef Data Object," later in this chapter. CreateTableDef methods appear in the section on the Table data object. You will also learn about a CreateRelation method during the Relation data objects section. Finally, the Close method is used to close a Database object.

Of the remaining seven methods, three exist only for backward compatibility with older versions of Visual Basic. The new OpenRecordset method has replaced the CreateDynaset, CreateSnapshot, and OpenTable methods. The OpenRecordset, CreateProperty, Execute, and ExecuteSQL methods are covered in this section.

The *OpenRecordset* Method of the *Database* Object

You use the OpenRecordset method to access data in existing tables in the database. You can use OpenRecordset to create Dynaset, Snapshot, or Table data objects.

The format of the OpenRecordset method is as follows:

```
Set Variable = Database.OPENRECORDSET(Source, Type, options)
```

In this syntax, Database is the name of the database that will be used to create the Recordset. Type indicates whether the Recordset created will be a Table (dbOpenTable), a Dynaset (dbOpenDynaset), or a Snapshot (dbOpenSnapshot). A Table type is created if you don't specify a type. You can also add options for security and record viewing. See Visual Basic online help for a complete description of these options.

Add a new command button to the CH1001.VBP project. Set its Name property to cmdRecordset and its Caption property to R&ecordset. Add the code in Listing 10.9 in the cmdRecordset_Click code window.

Listing 10.9. Coding the cmdRecordset_Click event.

```
Private Sub cmdRecordset_Click()
    On Error Resume Next     'ignore errors
    '
    Dim wsArea As Workspace
    Dim dbFile As DATABASE
    Dim rsTable As Recordset
    Dim rsDynaset As Recordset
    Dim rsSnapshot As Recordset
    Dim cDBName As String
    Dim cTable As String
    Dim cDynaset As String
    Dim cSnapshot As String
    Dim rsTemp As Recordset
    '
    ' init vars
```

continues

Listing 10.9. continued

```
cDBName = App.Path + "\ch1001.mdb"
cTable = "Buyers"
cDynaset = "Publishers"
cSnapshot = "Authors"
'
' create workspace and open database
Set wsArea = DBEngine.CreateWorkspace("wsArea", "admin", "")
DBEngine.Workspaces.Append wsArea
Set dbFile = wsArea.OpenDatabase(cDBName)
'
' create recordset objects
Set rsTable = dbFile.OpenRecordset(cTable, dbOpenTable)
Set rsDynaset = dbFile.OpenRecordset(cDynaset, dbOpenDynaset)
Set rsSnapshot = dbFile.OpenRecordset(cSnapshot, dbOpenSnapshot)
'
' enumerate recordsets for database
Me.Cls
For Each rsTemp In dbFile.Recordsets
    Me.Print rsTemp.Name
Next
'
End Sub
```

The code in Listing 10.9 creates three Recordsets, one of each type, and then displays the list of open Recordsets on the form. Save and run the form. Compare your results with those in Figure 10.10.

Figure 10.10.

The results of the OpenRecordset method.

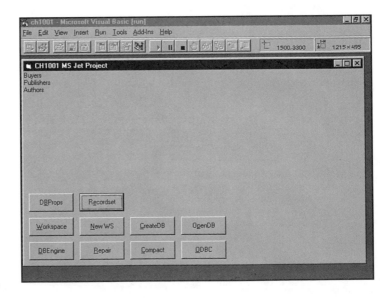

324

Using the *Execute* and *ExecuteSQL* Methods

You can use the Execute and ExecuteSQL methods on a database to perform SQL action queries. The only difference between Execute and ExecuteSQL is that the latter statement returns the number of rows affected by the SQL statement. The Execute method updates the RecordsAffected property of the Database object with the same information returned by ExecuteSQL. It is also faster and uses Microsoft JET resources more efficiently. You should use the Execute method whenever you need to perform an SQL action query on your database.

> **Note:** An action query is an SQL statement that performs an action on a database (add, edit, or delete records; create or remove data tables; and so on). Action SQL queries are covered in detail on Day 15, "Creating Databases with SQL."

10

Add a new command button to your project. Set its Name property to cmdExecute and its Caption property to E&xecute. Add the code in Listing 10.10 to the cmdExecute_Click event.

Listing 10.10. Coding the cmdExecute_Click event.

```
Private Sub cmdExecute_Click()
    ' on error resume next   ' ignore errors
    '
    Dim dbFile As DATABASE
    Dim cDBName As String
    Dim cSQL As String
    '
    ' init vars
    cDBName = App.Path + "\ch1001.mdb"
    cSQL = "DELETE FROM NewAuthors WHERE Au_ID < 10"
    '
    ' open db in default workspace
    Set dbFile = OpenDatabase(cDBName)
    '
    ' perform SQL action query
    dbFile.Execute cSQL
    '
    ' show number of records affected
    MsgBox Str(dbFile.RecordsAffected), vbInformation, "Records Affected"
    '
    dbFile.Close
    '
End Sub
```

The code in Listing 10.10 opens a database and performs an SQL action query that deletes records from a table. The routine displays the RecordsAffected property to show you how many records were deleted, and then it closes the database.

Save and run the project. Click Execute and compare your on-screen results with the screen in Figure 10.11.

Figure 10.11.
The results of the Execute *method.*

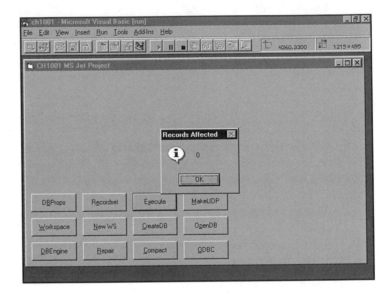

Using the *CreateProperty* Method

Visual Basic 4 lets you create user-defined properties (UDPs) for most data access objects. These UDPs get stored with the database and can be read and updated by your Visual Basic program. In this example, you use the CreateProperty method to add a UDP to a database.

 Warning: The capability to create and store UDPs is only available when you use the Microsoft JET version 3.0 database format. If you are not using Microsoft JET 3.0, you can't complete the example in this exercise.

Add a command button to CH1001.VBP. Set its Name property to cmdMakeUDP and its Caption property to &MakeUDP. Add the code in Listing 10.11 to the cmdMakeUDP_Click window.

Listing 10.11. Coding the cmdMakeUDP_Click event.

```
Private Sub cmdMakeUDP_Click()
    On Error Resume Next
    '
    Dim dbFile As DATABASE
```

```
    Dim cDBName As String
    Dim cUDPName As String
    Dim nUDPType As Integer
    Dim vUDPValue As Variant
    Dim pDBAdmin As Property
    Dim pProgrammer As Property
    Dim pTemp As Property
    '
    ' open db
    cDBName = App.Path + "\ch1003.mdb" ' open version 3.0 JET db
    Set dbFile = OpenDatabase(cDBName)
    '
    ' add first UDP
    cUDPName = "DBAdmin"
    nUDPType = dbText
    vUDPValue = "Joe DB Guru"
    dbFile.Properties.DELETE cUDPName    ' delete it if it's already here
    Set pDBAdmin = dbFile.CreateProperty(cUDPName, nUDPType, vUDPValue)
    dbFile.Properties.Append pDBAdmin
    '
    ' add second UDP
    cUDPName = "Programmer"
    nUDPType = dbText
    vUDPValue = "Fred Bitwise"
    dbFile.Properties.DELETE cUDPName    ' delete it first
    Set pProgrammer = dbFile.CreateProperty(cUDPName)
    pProgrammer.Type = nUDPType
    pProgrammer.VALUE = vUDPValue
    dbFile.Properties.Append pProgrammer
    '
    ' enumerate the db properties
    Me.Cls
    For Each pTemp In dbFile.Properties
        Me.Print pTemp.Name; "|",
        Me.Print pTemp.Type; "|",
        Me.Print pTemp.VALUE
    Next
    '
    dbFile.Close
    '
End Sub
```

The routine in Listing 10.11 adds two user-defined properties to the database. Notice that you attempted to delete the properties first. That way you can run this example several times without getting an error. Notice that you also used two different code structures to create the properties. Either one is correct.

Save and run the project. When you click the MakeUDP button, you should see a screen similar to Figure 10.12.

Figure 10.12.

The results of the CreateProperty *method.*

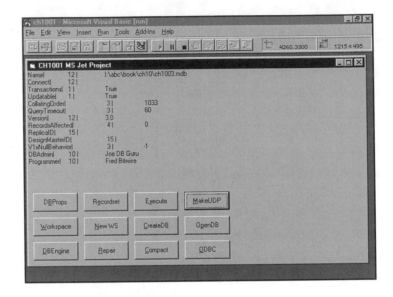

The *TableDef* Data Object

The TableDef data object contains all the information needed to define a Base table object in the Database. You can access Base table objects using the OpenRecordset method. You use TableDef objects to create and maintain Base tables. TableDef objects have three collections, five methods, and 10 properties.

The *TableDef* Collections

The TableDef object has three collections:

☐ Fields: This collection contains all the information about the database fields defined for the TableDef object. This is the default object.

☐ Indexes: This collection contains all the information about the database indexes defined for the TableDef object.

☐ Properties: This collection contains all the information about the current TableDef object.

Details of the Field and Index objects are covered later in this chapter.

The *CreateTableDef* Method and the TableDef Properties

The TableDef properties are set when the table is created. The values of the properties differ depending on whether the `TableDef` object is a native Microsoft JET object or an attached object. Listing 10.12 shows the properties of a native Microsoft JET `TableDef` object.

Add another button to the CH1001.VBP project. Set its Name property to cmdTableDef and its Caption property to &TableDef. Add the code in Listing 10.12 to the `cmdTableDef_Click` event.

Listing 10.12. Adding the TableDef button.

```
Private Sub cmdTableDef_Click()
    On Error Resume Next ' ignore errors
    '
    Dim dbFile As DATABASE
    Dim cDBName As String
    Dim tdTemp As TableDef
    Dim cTable As String
    Dim proTemp As Property
    '
    ' init vars
    cDBName = App.Path + "\ch1001.mdb"
    cTable = "BookSales"
    '
    ' open db in default ws
    Set dbFile = DBEngine.OpenDatabase(cDBName)
    '
    ' open data table
    Set tdTemp = dbFile.CreateTableDef(cTable)
    '
    ' enumerate the tabledef properties
    Me.Cls
    For Each proTemp In tdTemp.Properties
        Me.Print ">";
        Me.Print proTemp.Name,
        Me.Print proTemp.VALUE;
        Me.Print "<"
    Next
    '
    dbFile.Close
    '
End Sub
```

The code in Listing 10.12 opens a database, creates a `TableDef` object using the `CreateTableDef` method, and then lists the properties to the form. Save and run the project. Click the TableDef button and compare your screen with the one in Figure 10.13.

329

Figure 10.13.

Viewing the TableDef properties.

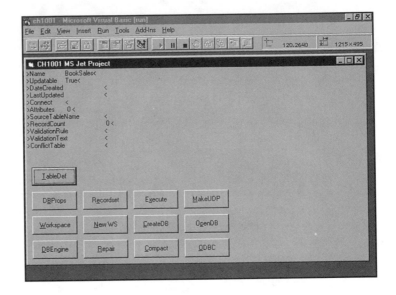

The *TableDef* Methods

Five methods exist that you can apply to the TableDef object:

☐ OpenRecordset enables you to open a Table, Dynaset, or Snapshot Recordset from the TableDef object.

☐ RefreshLink updates and refreshes any attached table links for the TableDef object.

☐ CreateProperty enables you to create and store a user-defined property. See the UDP example under the Database object elsewhere in this chapter.

☐ CreateIndex enables you to add an index to the TableDef object. This method is covered in "The Index Data Object" section later in this chapter.

☐ CreateField enables you to add a new field to an existing TableDef object. You learn more about this method in "The Field Data Object" section.

Creating a New Table in the Database

The code in Listing 10.13 enables you to create a very simple database and table. Add another command button to the form. Set its Name property to cmdCreateTable and its Caption property to &CreateTable. Add the code in Listing 10.13 to the cmdCreateTable_Click event.

Listing 10.13. Coding the `cmdCreateTable_Click` event.

```
Private Sub cmdCreateTable_Click()
    On Error Resume Next
    '
    Dim dbFile As DATABASE
    Dim cDBName As String
    Dim tdTemp As TableDef
    Dim cTable As String
    Dim fldTemp As Field
    Dim cFldName As String
    Dim nFldType As Integer
    Dim proTemp As Property
    '
    ' init values
    cDBName = App.Path + "\ch100x.mdb"
    cTable = "NewTable"
    cFldName = "NewField"
    nFldType = dbText
    '
    ' erase it if it's already there
    Kill cDBName
    '
    ' create new database
    Set dbFile = DBEngine.CreateDatabase(cDBName, dbLangGeneral, dbVersion20)
    '
    ' create tabledef
    Set tdTemp = dbFile.CreateTableDef(cTable)
    '
    ' create field
    Set fldTemp = tdTemp.CreateField(cFldName, nFldType)
    '
    ' append objects
    tdTemp.Fields.Append fldTemp
    dbFile.TableDefs.Append tdTemp
    '
    ' enumerate new table properties
    Me.Cls
    For Each proTemp In tdTemp.Properties
        Me.Print proTemp.Name,
        Me.Print proTemp.VALUE
    Next
    '
    dbFile.Close
    '
End Sub
```

The code in Listing 10.13 creates a new database (erasing any old one first), creates a new table object, creates a single field object for the table, and then appends the new objects to their respective collections. Finally, the properties of the new table are listed to the form. Save and run the project. Check your results against Figure 10.14.

Figure 10.14.
The results of adding a new table.

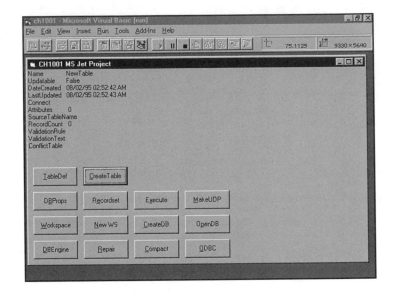

Modifying and Deleting Existing Tables

You can add new fields or delete existing fields by using the Append or Delete methods on the TableDef object. Add a command button with the Name property cmdModTable and a Caption property of M&odTable. Add the code in Listing 10.14 to the cmdModTable_Click event.

Listing 10.14. Coding the cmdModTable_Click event.

```
Private Sub cmdModTable_Click()
    On Error Resume Next
    '
    Dim dbFile As DATABASE
    Dim cDBName As String
    Dim tdTemp As TableDef
    Dim cTable As String
    Dim fldTemp As Field
    Dim cFldName As String
    Dim nFldType As Integer
    Dim fldNew As Field
    Dim proTemp As Property
    '
    ' init vars
    cDBName = App.Path + "\ch100x.mdb"
    cTable = "NewTable"
    cFldName = "NewField2"
    nFldType = dbDate
```

```
      '
      ' first create the database
      ' by calling the previous example
      cmdCreateTable_Click
      '
      ' let user see this
      MsgBox "Click OK to continue..."
      '
      ' now open that db
      Set dbFile = DBEngine.OpenDatabase(cDBName)
      '
      ' set tabledef object
      Set tdTemp = dbFile.TableDefs(cTable)
      '
      ' add a new field
      Set fldNew = tdTemp.CreateField(cFldName, nFldType)
      tdTemp.Fields.Append fldNew
      '
      ' now display field list
      Me.Cls
      Me.Print "Added Field - Table Field List:"
      For Each fldTemp In tdTemp.Fields
          Me.Print fldTemp.Name
      Next
      '
      ' delete the new field
      tdTemp.Fields.DELETE cFldName
      '
      ' display field list again
      Me.Print ""
      Me.Print "Deleted Field - Table Field List:"
      For Each fldTemp In tdTemp.Fields
          Me.Print fldTemp.Name
      Next
      '
      dbFile.Close
      '
End Sub
```

In Listing 10.14, you call the previous code section to create the table again. Then you add a new field using the Append method, and delete that field using the Delete method. Save and run the project, and check your final results against Figure 10.15.

Figure 10.15.
The results of adding and deleting fields.

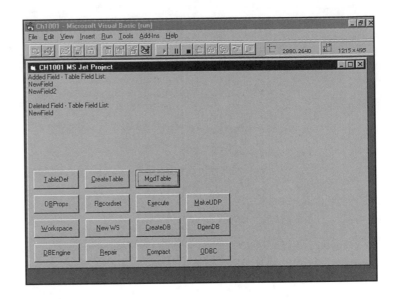

Attaching External Data

You can attach an existing external, non-Microsoft JET database table to an existing Microsoft JET format database. Attaching tables in this way gives you access to the external data using the standard Visual Basic data access object interface. It also enables you to mix Microsoft JET and non-Microsoft JET data in the same database, which is great for handling queries that combine data from both sources.

 Note: You can create and store queries on the attached external data, too. Queries are covered later in this chapter.

You cannot open a table-type Recordset on an attached table. You must use the Dynaset or Snapshot objects for accessing attached tables. Even though you must use Dynaset data objects, attached tables respond faster than external data links.

Let's illustrate attachments by adding another command button to the form. Set its Name property to cmdAttach and its Caption property to &Attach. Add the code in Listing 10. 15 to the cmdAttach_Click event.

Listing 10.15. Coding the `cmdAttach_Click` event.

```
Private Sub cmdAttach_Click()
    On Error Resume Next
    '
    Dim dbFile As DATABASE
```

```
        Dim cDBName As String
        Dim tdTemp As TableDef
        Dim cAttName As String
        Dim cAttDBType As String
        Dim cAttDBName As String
        Dim cAttSrcName As String
        '
        ' init vars
        cDBName = App.Path + "\ch1001x.mdb"
        cAttName = "FoxAttached"
        cAttDBType = "FoxPro 2.5;"
        cAttDBName = App.Path
        cAttSrcName = "fldtypes.dbf"
        '
        ' call routine to create database
        cmdCreateTable_Click
        '
        ' now open db
        Set dbFile = OpenDatabase(cDBName)
        '
        ' create a new table in the MSJet database
        Set tdTemp = dbFile.CreateTableDef(cAttName)
        '
        ' now build attachment info
        tdTemp.Connect = cAttDBType + "DATABASE=" + cAttDBName
        tdTemp.SourceTableName = cAttSrcName
        '
        ' append new attachment to the database
        dbFile.TableDefs.Append tdTemp
        '
        ' show list of tables in database
        Me.Cls
        For Each tdTemp In dbFile.TableDefs
            Me.Print tdTemp.Name
        Next
        '
        dbFile.Close
End Sub
```

The code in Listing 10.15 calls the routine that creates your test database and then opens the created database and creates a new table definition. This time, instead of creating field definitions to append to the new table definition, you create an attachment to another external database. Attachments always have two parts: the Connect string, and the SourceTableName.

The Connect string contains all information needed to connect to the external database. For desktop (ISAM-type) databases, you need to supply the driver name (dBASE III, Paradox 3.*x*, and so on) and the device/path where the data file is located. For back-end database servers, you might also need to supply additional parameters.

The SourceTableName contains the name of the data table you want to attach to the Microsoft JET database. For desktop databases, this is the database filename in the device location (names.dbf, customers.dbf, and so on). For back-end database servers, this is the data table name that already exists in the server database.

Save and run the project. When you click the Attach button, you see a few screens flash by. The final screen lists all the tables in the database. Notice that the FoxAttached table now appears. You can now manipulate this table like any native Microsoft JET data table object.

> **Note:** You also see several internal data tables in this listing. The tables that start with *mSys* are used by Microsoft JET to keep track of indexes, relationships, table definitions, and so on. Do not attempt to modify these tables. Doing so can permanently damage your database.

The *Field* Data Object

The Field object contains all the information about the data table field. In the previous section on TableDef objects, you created and deleted fields. You can also access the Field object to get information on field properties. The Field object has only one collection, the Properties collection. There are 17 properties and four methods.

The *Field* Properties

There are 17 Field properties. You can use these properties to determine the size and type of a field, and whether it is a native Microsoft JET field object or an attached field from an external database. In version 3.0 Microsoft JET formats, you can set the default value for the field, and define and enforce field-level validation rules.

Listing 10.16 shows all the properties for selected fields. Add another button to the form. Set its Name property to cmdFields and its Caption property to &Field. Add the code in Listing 10.16 to the cmdFields_Click event window.

Listing 10.16. Coding the cmdFields_Click event.

```
Private Sub cmdFields_Click()
    On Error Resume Next
    '
    Dim dbFile As DATABASE
    Dim cDBName As String
    Dim tdTemp As TableDef
    Dim fldTemp As Field
    Dim proTemp As Property
    '
    cDBName = App.Path + "\ch1001z.mdb"
    '
    ' open db
    Set dbFile = OpenDatabase(cDBName)
    '
```

The *Index* Data Object

The Index object is used to contain information on defined indexes for the associated table. Indexes can only be built for native Microsoft JET data tables (no attached tables allowed). You can use indexes for two purposes: to enforce data integrity rules, and to speed access for single-record lookups.

Indexes are always associated with an existing data table. You must create a native Microsoft JET data table before you can create an index. Listing 10.17 shows how to create an index through Visual Basic code and view its properties.

Add a command button to the form with a Name property of cmdIndex and a Caption property of &Index. Add the code in Listing 10.17 to the cmdIndex_Click event.

Listing 10.17. Coding the `cmdIndex_Click` event.

```
Private Sub cmdIndex_Click()
    ' on error resume next
    '
    '
    Dim dbFile As DATABASE
    Dim cDBName As String
    Dim tdTemp As TableDef
    Dim idxTemp As Index
    Dim idxField As Field
    Dim cIdxName As String
    Dim cIdxField As String
    Dim proTemp As Property
    '
    ' init vars
    cDBName = App.Path + "\ch1001x.mdb"
    cIdxName = "PKNewTable" ' name of index
    cIdxField = "NewField"  ' name of field
    '
    ' call routine to create database
    cmdCreateTable_Click
    '
    ' now open created db
    Set dbFile = OpenDatabase(cDBName)
    '
    ' let's make an index!
    Set idxTemp = dbFile.TableDefs("NewTable").CREATEINDEX(cIdxName)
    ' define field object for index
    Set idxField = idxTemp.CreateField(cIdxField)
    idxTemp.PRIMARY = True  ' make it primary index
    idxTemp.Required = True ' make it required
    idxTemp.Fields.Append idxField  ' add field object
    ' add whole thing to index collection
    dbFile.TableDefs("NewTable").Indexes.Append idxTemp
    '
    ' show index properties
    Me.Cls
    For Each idxTemp In dbFile.TableDefs("newTable").Indexes
```

```
    ' get table definitions
    Debug.Print String(10, "*") + "ch1001x.mdb"
    For Each tdTemp In dbFile.TableDefs
        Debug.Print String(5, "*") + tdTemp.Name
        For Each fldTemp In tdTemp.Fields
            Debug.Print String(3, "*") + fldTemp.Name
            For Each proTemp In fldTemp.Properties
                Debug.Print proTemp.Name,
                Debug.Print ">";
                Debug.Print proTemp.VALUE;
                Debug.Print "<"
            Next
        Next
    Next
    '
    ' tell user to look at debug window.
    MsgBox "Data was Written to the DEBUG Window."
    '
    dbFile.Close
End Sub
```

The code in Listing 10.16 creates the database and then loops through the collection to list the properties of every field and every table in the database. Because the Field collection is a long list, you send the output to the Debug window instead of to the form. Save and run the project. When you click the Fields button, the program sends all the data to the Debug window. Because this process takes time, you send out a message when the job finishes.

Before you exit the program, click the Pause button on the main toolbar to bring up the Debug window. You see a lengthy list of the fields and their properties. Check your screen against the one in Figure 10.16.

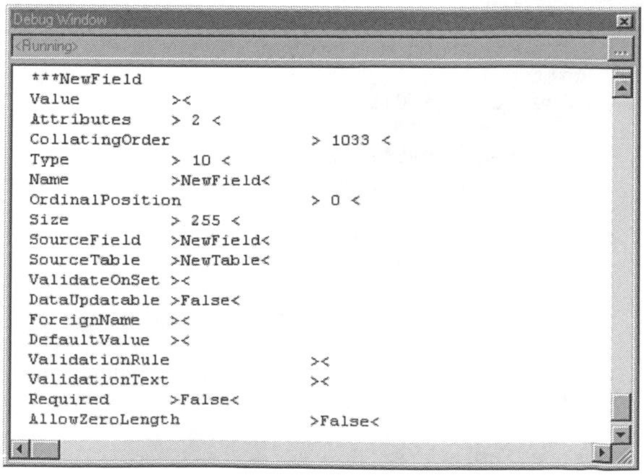

Figure 10.16.

The Field properties in the Debug window.

```
        For Each proTemp In idxTemp.Properties
            Me.Print proTemp.Name,
            Me.Print ">";
            Me.Print proTemp.VALUE;
            Me.Print "<"
        Next
    Next
    '
    dbFile.Close
End Sub
```

The code in Listing 10.17 seems pretty familiar, right? After creating a database and adding a table (handled by cmdCreateTable), you build and add the index. Notice that you first name the index, and then create a Field object for the target index. By adding the Field object and setting some other properties, you have completed the index definition. Finally, you append the index to the collection of indexes for the specific table.

Tip: Even though you append indexes to a specific table object, the index name is global for the entire database. You cannot create an Index object called Index1 for Table1 and then create another Index1 for Table2. You must have unique Index names.

Save and run the project. Click the Index button and check your results against those in Figure 10.17.

Figure 10.17.
The results of adding an index.

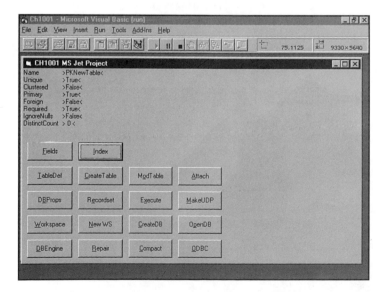

The *QueryDef* Data Object

The QueryDef object contains information about a stored SQL query. SQL queries can be used as record sources for the Visual Basic data control, or as the first parameter in the Recordset object. QueryDef objects run faster than inline SQL queries, because Visual Basic must go through a processing step before executing an SQL query. Stored queries (QueryDef objects) are stored in their processed format. Using QueryDef objects means there is one less processing step to go through before you see your data.

The example in Listing 10.18 creates a simple SELECT SQL query and stores it for later use. After creating the query, you apply it as a record source when creating a Recordset object. Finally, you enumerate the QueryDef properties. Add another button with the Name property set to cmdQuery and the Caption property set to &Query. Add the code in Listing 10.18 to the cmdQuery_Click code window.

Listing 10.18. Coding the cmdQuery_Click event.

```
Private Sub cmdQuery_Click()
    ' on error resume next
    '
    '
    Dim dbFile As DATABASE
    Dim cDBName As String
    Dim tdTemp As TableDef
    Dim rsTemp As Recordset
    Dim qryTemp As QueryDef
    Dim idxField As Field
    Dim cQryName As String
    Dim cQryText As String
    Dim proTemp As Property
    '
    ' init vars
    cDBName = App.Path + "\ch1001x.mdb"
    cQryName = "qryTestSelect" ' name of query
    cQryText = "SELECT * FROM NewTable"  ' text of query
    '
    ' call routine to create database
    cmdCreateTable_Click
    '
    ' now open created db
    Set dbFile = OpenDatabase(cDBName)
    '
    ' now add querydef to database
    Set qryTemp = dbFile.CreateQueryDef(cQryName)
    qryTemp.SQL = cQryText
    '
    ' now create a record set using query
    Set rsTemp = dbFile.OpenRecordset(cQryName, dbOpenDynaset)
    '
    ' now show us all the properties
    Me.Cls
```

```
For Each qryTemp In dbFile.QueryDefs
    For Each proTemp In qryTemp.Properties
        Me.Print proTemp.Name,
        Me.Print ">";
        Me.Print proTemp.VALUE;
        Me.Print "<"
    Next
Next
'
dbFile.Close
'
End Sub
```

Save and run the project. Check your final screen against the one in Figure 10.18.

Figure 10.18.
The results of creating a
`QueryDef` *object.*

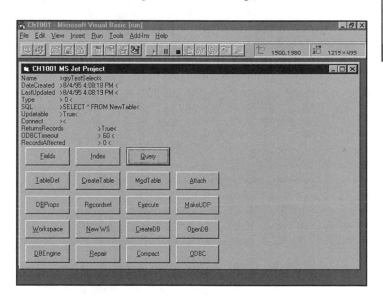

10

The *Relation* Data Object

The last data access object covered today is the `Relation` data object. This object contains information about established relationships between two tables. Relationships help enforce database referential integrity. Establishing a relationship involves selecting the two tables you want to relate, identifying the field you can use to link the tables together, and defining the type of relationship you want to establish.

Note: The details of defining relationships are covered in the chapters on Advanced SQL next week (Days 15 and 16). For now, remember that you can use the `Relation` objects to create and maintain database relationships within Visual Basic code.

The final coding example for today is to create a new database, add two tables, define fields and indexes for those two tables, and then define a relationship object for the table pair. This example calls on most of the concepts you have learned today.

Add one more button to the project. Set its Name property to cmdRelation and its Caption property to Re&lation. Add the code in Listing 10.19 to the cmdRelation_Click event window.

Listing 10.19. Coding the cmdRelation_Click event.

```
Private Sub cmdRelation_Click()
    On Error Resume Next
    '
    Dim dbFile As DATABASE
    Dim tdTemp As TableDef
    Dim idxTemp As Index
    Dim fldTemp As Field
    Dim relTemp As Relation
    Dim proTemp As Property
    '
    Dim cDBName As String
    Dim cTblLookUp As String
    Dim cTblMaster As String
    Dim cIdxLookUp As String
    Dim cIdxMaster As String
    Dim cRelName As String
    '
    cDBName = App.Path + "\ch1001q.mdb"
    cTblLookUp = "ValidUnits"
    cTblMaster = "MasterTable"
    cIdxLookUp = "PKUnits"
    cIdxMaster = "PKMaster"
    cRelName = "relUnitMaster"
    '
    ' erase datbase if it's already there
    Kill cDBName
    '
    ' create database
    Set dbFile = CreateDatabase(cDBName, dbLangGeneral, dbVersion20)
    '
    ' create list table
    ' this has the stuff to lookup
    Set tdTemp = dbFile.CreateTableDef(cTblLookUp)
    '
    ' add fields to the table
    Set fldTemp = tdTemp.CreateField("UnitID", dbText, 10)
    tdTemp.Fields.Append fldTemp
    '
    Set fldTemp = tdTemp.CreateField("UnitDesc", dbText, 30)
    tdTemp.Fields.Append fldTemp
    '
    ' add main index to ValidUnits table
    Set idxTemp = tdTemp.CREATEINDEX(cIdxLookUp)
    idxTemp.PRIMARY = True
    idxTemp.Required = True
    Set fldTemp = tdTemp.CreateField("UnitID")
    idxTemp.Fields.Append fldTemp
```

```
            tdTemp.Indexes.Append idxTemp
            '
            ' append table def to database
            dbFile.TableDefs.Append tdTemp
            '
            ' now create master table
            ' this table will need a reference to lookup
            Set tdTemp = dbFile.CreateTableDef(cTblMaster)
            '
            ' now add some fields
            Set fldTemp = tdTemp.CreateField("MasterName", dbText, 20)
            tdTemp.Fields.Append fldTemp
            '
            Set fldTemp = tdTemp.CreateField("MstrUnitID", dbText, 10)
            tdTemp.Fields.Append fldTemp
            '
            ' add main index to master table
            Set idxTemp = tdTemp.CREATEINDEX(cIdxMaster)
            idxTemp.PRIMARY = True
            idxTemp.Required = True
            Set fldTemp = tdTemp.CreateField("MasterName")
            idxTemp.Fields.Append fldTemp
            tdTemp.Indexes.Append idxTemp
            '
            ' append table to db
            dbFile.TableDefs.Append tdTemp
            '
            ' now set a relationship
            Set relTemp = dbFile.CreateRelation(cRelName)
            relTemp.TABLE = cTblLookUp ' table for lookups
            relTemp.ForeignTable = cTblMaster ' table to check
            Set fldTemp = relTemp.CreateField("UnitID") ' field to lookup
            fldTemp.ForeignName = "MstrUnitID"  ' field to check
            relTemp.Fields.Append fldTemp    ' add field object to relation object
            relTemp.Attributes = dbRelationUpdateCascade ' for cascading updates
            dbFile.Relations.Append relTemp ' book the completed relation object
            '
            ' enumerate the relation object
            Me.Cls
            For Each relTemp In dbFile.Relations
                For Each proTemp In relTemp.Properties
                    Me.Print proTemp.Name,
                    Me.Print ">";
                    Me.Print proTemp.VALUE;
                    Me.Print "<"
                Next
                '
                Me.Print "Relation Fields:"
                For Each fldTemp In relTemp.Fields
                    Me.Print "",
                    Me.Print "Name: ";
                    Me.Print fldTemp.Name,
                    Me.Print "ForeignName: ";
                    Me.Print fldTemp.ForeignName
                Next
            Next
            '
End Sub
```

10

The code in Listing 10.19 performs the basic tasks. Create a database and build two tables with two fields each. Construct primary key indexes for both tables. Then create the relationship object.

Save and run the project. When you click on the Relation command button the program will create all the data objects, and then display the resulting Relation object on the form. Compare your results to the screen in Figure 10.19.

Figure 10.19.

The results of adding a Relation object.

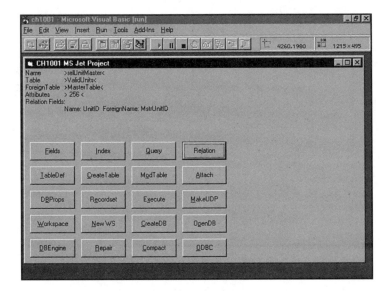

Notice that you added an attribute to make this relationship enforce cascading updates, which means that any time a value is changed in the lookup table, all the corresponding values in the foreign table will automatically be updated too. You can also set delete cascades. If the value is deleted from the lookup table, all corresponding records in the foreign table are deleted.

Summary

In today's lesson, you learned the features and functions of Visual Basic Microsoft JET data access objects. These objects are used within Visual Basic code to create and maintain workspaces, databases, tables, fields, indexes, queries, and relations. You learned the properties, methods, and collections of each object. You also learned how to use Visual Basic code to inspect the values in the properties, and how to use the methods to perform basic database operations.

Quiz

1. What does the *JET* in the Microsoft JET Database Engine stand for?
2. Describe the difference between a property and a method.
3. What is the top level data access object (DAO)?
4. What command would you issue to repair a database? Is this a method or a property?
5. What is the syntax of the `CompactDatabase` method?
6. What happens if you don't declare a `Workspace` when you open a database?
7. What data object types can be created with the `OpenRecordset` method?
8. What is the difference between the `Execute` and the `ExecuteSQL` methods?
9. Which `TableDef` method can be used to create a table in an existing database? What syntax does this method follow?
10. Which data access object would you use to determine the data type of a table column?
11. Can you use the `Index` data object to build an index for a FoxPro 2.5 database?
12. What information does the `QueryDef` object store?

Exercise

Assume that you are a systems consultant to a large multinational corporation. You have been assigned the task of building a program in Visual Basic that will create a database to handle customer information. In this database, you need to track CustomerID, Name, Address (two lines), City, State/Province, Zip, Phone, and Customer Type.

Start a new project and add a single command button to a form that will execute the code to build this database. Include the following in your code:

☐ A section that deletes the database if it already exists

☐ A table for customer information (called Customers) and a table for customer types (called CustomerTypes)

☐ Primary keys for both tables

☐ A relationship between the two tables on the Customer Type field

☐ A message that signifies that the procedure is complete

When you have completed the entry of this code, display the database in Visdata. Add information to both tables. Take note of how the referential integrity is enforced by deleting records in the CustomerTypes table that are used in the Customers table.

WEEK
2

Creating Database Programs with Visual Basic Code

Today you'll learn how to create complete database entry forms using Visual Basic code instead of the data control. You'll learn how to open a database, establish a recordset, and prepare a data entry form to allow record adds, edits, and deletes. You'll also learn how to create a generic record locate routine to use with any data entry form, as well as how to create a set of command buttons to handle all data entry functions.

You'll learn about the Visual Basic methods you can use to locate single records and about the Seek method for table objects and the Find and Move methods that you can apply to all recordsets.

All the routines you'll create today will be generic and portable. You'll write these routines in a library module that you'll be able to use in your future database projects. For the lesson today, you'll add these library routines to a new form for the CompanyMaster database project you started last week.

When you finish today's exercises, you'll be able to build a fully functional data entry form with less than 30 lines of Visual Basic code.

Why Use Code Instead of Data Controls?

Before jumping into the code routines, it's important to talk about the difference between writing your data entry programs with and without the Visual Basic data control. There are advantages and disadvantages to each method.

The advantage of using the data control is that you can quickly put together solid data entry forms without writing much Visual Basic code. This works well for small, one-time projects that need to be completed quickly. The disadvantage of using the data control is that once the project is completed, it is not always easy to modify the data entry form or to adapt the finished form for another data entry project. Also, forms built using the data control are not always easy to debug or maintain because most of the action goes on in the data control itself. If you think your project will need to be modified or maintained by other programmers in the future, the data control might not be your best choice.

The advantage of using complete Visual Basic code to produce data entry forms is that you have complete control over all aspects of the process. You decide when to open the database and recordset, and you control the record reads and writes, too. This can be a real advantage in multiuser settings where increased traffic can cause locking conflicts in programs that use the data control. Another advantage of using Visual Basic code for your data entry forms is that you can create generic code that you can reuse in all your database projects. When you have a fully debugged set of data entry routines, you can quickly create new forms without much additional coding. Because the forms rely on generic routines, they are also easy to modify and maintain in the future.

The primary drawback for using Visual Basic code to create data entry forms is that you'll have to handle all processes yourself; you can assume nothing. For example, locating and updating a single record in a data table requires that you account for all of the following processes:

☐ Opening the database

☐ Opening the recordset

☐ Locating the requested record

☐ Loading the input controls from the recordset

☐ Handling all user actions during the data entry process

☐ Writing the updated controls back to the recordset

Add the possibility of user errors and database errors, and you have a good bit of responsibility! And you haven't even seen what you'll need to do to add a new record to the table or delete an existing one. You'll also need a way for the user to browse the data. Remember that dropping the data control means your form will not automatically display the "VCR-style" navigation arrows.

Despite this added responsibility, writing your data entry forms with Visual Basic code can give you much greater control over the process and will result in a form that is easy for both programmers and users to deal with.

Searching for a Record

Before you create the generic data entry routines, you need to look at an important topic: record searching. Up until now, we have only touched on this issue. There are several methods you can use to search out a record in a recordset. Some are faster than others. Using the correct method in your Visual Basic program can make your programs seem fast and solid. Using the "wrong" search method can give your program the needless reputation of being a plodder.

The Visual Basic Data Access Object interface is a *set-oriented* interface. It is designed and tuned to quickly return a set of multiple records that meet your search criteria. However, a major part of data entry processing involves *key-oriented* searches. These are searches for a single, specific record that needs to be updated. Visual Basic offers the following three different approaches to handling key-oriented searches:

☐ The Move methods: You can use these methods to browse records one by one (commonly called "walking the data set"). The Move methods allow you to use Visual Basic code to move from one record to the next in the data set.

☐ The Find methods: You can use these methods to locate a single record in the data set that meets a set of criteria you establish. This criteria is similar to the SQL WHERE clause that you learned about in Day 9, "Selecting Data with SQL." The Find methods perform a sequential search of the data set to locate the first record that meets your criteria.

☐ The Seek method: You can use this method to perform an indexed search of the data set to find the first record that meets your criteria. This is the fastest search method provided by Visual Basic, and it can only be applied to recordsets that are opened tables. Dynasets and snapshots cannot use the Seek method.

Using *Move* to Navigate Recordsets

The Move methods offer the most basic form of record searching. There are four methods that you can apply to the recordset object:

☐ MoveFirst: This method moves the record pointer directly to the first record in the data set. This is the same as clicking the double-headed arrow on the left side of the data control.

☐ MovePrevious: This method moves the record pointer to the record just before the current record. This is the same as clicking the single-headed arrow on the left side of the data control.

☐ MoveNext: This method moves the record pointer to the record just after the current record. This is the same as clicking the single-headed arrow on the right side of the data control.

☐ MoveLast: This method moves the record pointer directly to the last record in the data set. This is the same as clicking the double-headed arrow on the right side of the data control.

To illustrate these methods, let's start a new Visual Basic project. Table 11.1 contains a list of controls to add to the form. Refer to Figure 11.1 as a guide as you layout the form.

Table 11.1. Controls for Project CH1101.VBP.

Control	Property	Setting
Form	Name	frmMove
	Caption	Chapter 11 Move Demo
Command Button	Name	cmdMoveFirst
	BorderStyle	Fixed Single
	Caption	&First
	Height	300
	Left	120
	Top	120
	Width	1200

Control	Property	Setting
Command Button	Name	cmdMovePrevious
	BorderStyle	Fixed Single
	Caption	&Previous
	Height	300
	Left	120
	Top	480
	Width	1200
Command Button	Name	cmdMoveNext
	Caption	&Next
	Height	300
	Left	120
	Top	840
	Width	1200
Command Button	Name	cmdMoveLast
	Caption	&Last
	Height	300
	Left	120
	Top	1200
	Width	1200
Label	Name	Label1
	Height	300
	Left	1500
	Top	120
	Width	1200
Label	Name	Label2
	Height	300
	Left	1500
	Top	480
	Width	2400

Figure 11.1.

Layout of the frmMove form.

```
frmMove                                           _ □ ×
Object: Form              ▼     Proc: Load              ▼
  Private Sub Form_Load()
    '
    ' open db and open recordset
    '
    cDBName = "\abc\book\ch11\ch1101.mdb"
    cRSName = "Authors"
    Set dbName = OpenDatabase(cDBName)
    Set rsName = dbName.OpenRecordset(cRSName, dbOpenDynaset)
    '
  End Sub
```

After laying out the form, you need to add the code. Enter Listing 11.1 in the general declarations section of the form (this declares all the form-level variables you'll use in the project).

Listing 11.1. Coding the form-level variables.

```
Option Explicit

'
' form-level vars
'
Dim cDBName As String    ' database name
Dim dbName As DATABASE   ' database object
Dim cRSName As String    ' record set name
Dim rsName As Recordset  ' record set object
```

Listing 11.2 opens the database and then opens a Dynaset for your use. Add this code to the Form_Load event.

Listing 11.2. Opening the database and a Dynaset.

```
Private Sub Form_Load()
    '
    ' open db and open recordset
    '
    cDBName = App.Path + "\ch1101.mdb"
    cRSName = "Authors"
    '
    Set dbName = OpenDatabase(cDBName)
    Set rsName = dbName.OpenRecordset(cRSName, dbOpenTable)
    '
End Sub
```

This routine initializes the database and recordset name variables and then creates the related data objects. Performing this step is similar to setting the DatabaseName, RecordSource, and RecordsetType properties of the data control.

You need to create a Sub procedure to handle the process of reading the current record and loading the data into the form controls. Create a Private Sub procedure called ReadRow and then add the following code to the routine:

```
Sub ReadRow()
    '
    ' reads current row into form controls
    '
    Label1 = rsName.Fields(0)
    Label2 = rsName.Fields(1)
End Sub
```

This routine simply copies the first column in the current row of the recordset to the first form control and then copies the second column of the recordset to the second form control.

You need to place code behind each of the four command buttons on the form. Each button needs to perform two tasks:

☐ Reposition the pointer as requested.

☐ Read the data from the new current row.

The following four code pieces do these tasks. Enter each of the code lines in Listing 11.3 into the Click event of each corresponding command button.

Listing 11.3. Coding the cmdMove events.

```
Private Sub cmdMoveFirst_Click()
    rsName.MoveFirst     ' position pointer
    ReadRow              ' load controls
End Sub

Private Sub cmdMoveLast_Click()
    rsName.MoveLast      ' position pointer
    ReadRow              ' load controls
End Sub

Private Sub cmdMoveNext_Click()
    rsName.MoveNext      ' position pointer
    ReadRow              ' load controls
End Sub

Private Sub cmdMovePrevious_Click()
    rsName.MovePrevious     ' position pointer
    ReadRow                 ' load controls
End Sub
```

You need to add two more routines to finish up the project. The following code forces the first record onto the screen at startup. Add this code to the Form_Activate event:

```
Private Sub Form_Activate()
    cmdMoveFirst_Click   ' force first record up
End Sub
```

The last code you'll add performs a safe close of the database at the end of the program. Add this code to the `Form_Unload` event:

```
Private Sub Form_Unload(Cancel As Integer)
    dbName.Close    '    close database
End Sub
```

Save the form as CH1101.FRM and save the project as CH1101.VBP. When you run the project, you'll be able to click the buttons in order to walk the data set. This operates the same as the data control arrow buttons.

> **Note:** If you click the First button and then immediately click the Previous button, you'll get a runtime error. This is caused by attempting to read past the beginning of the data set. Later today, you'll create a routine that prevents this from occurring in your programs.

These are good examples of how you can provide users with a way to browse the data set on a form. In the next section, you will see how to give your users the ability to search for a particular record in the data set.

Using *Seek* on Table Recordsets

The fastest way to locate a specific record is to use the `Seek` method on a table object. The `Seek` method performs an indexed search for the first occurrence of the record that matches the index criteria. This is the type of index used by ISAM-type databases. Indexed searches are easy to perform and are very fast.

Now you'll modify the CH1101.VBP project to illustrate index searching by adding another button to the form. Set its Name property to cmdSeek and its Caption property to &Seek. Next, add Listing 11.4 to the `cmdSeek_Click` event.

Listing 11.4. Coding the `cmdSeek_Click` event.

```
Private Sub cmdSeek_Click()
    '
    ' get input and peform table seek
    '
    Dim cSeek As String
    '
    cSeek = InputBox("Enter Au_ID Seek Value:", "Table Seek")
    cSeek = UCase(Trim(cSeek))
    '
    If Len(cSeek) <> 0 Then
        rsName.Seek "=", cSeek
        '
```

```
        If rsName.NoMatch = True Then
            MsgBox "Unable to Locate [" + cSeek + "]", vbCritical,
            ➥ "Failed Table Seek"
        Else
            ReadRow       ' load record
            MsgBox "Found [" + cSeek + "]", vbInformation,
            ➥"Successful Table Seek"
        End If
    End If
    '
End Sub
```

Listing 11.4 does three things. First, it prompts the user to enter a value for which to search. Second, the code confirms that the user entered a value and then performs the Seek operation. After performing the Seek, the NoMatch method is used to get the results of the Seek (this is the third operation performed in this routine). The results of the search are then posted in a message box. If the search was successful, the new record is loaded into the form controls, too.

Before this routine will work, you have to make a few changes to code in the Form_Load event. Change vbOpenDynaset to vbOpenTable and then add the following line to the end of the routine, just after the OpenRecordset… line:

```
rsName.Index = "PrimaryKey" ' set index property
```

Now save and run the project. This time, click the Seek button. When the dialog appears, enter 13 and click OK. You should see a message telling you that the search was successful. (See Figure 11.2.)

Figure 11.2.

The results of the table Seek operation.

Tip: You can use other comparison values besides = with the Seek method. You can use <, <=, =, >=, or > as a comparison value.

Although Seek is the fastest search method, it can only be applied to recordsets opened as table objects. If you want to locate a specific record in a dynaset or snapshot, you can use one of the Find methods. The Find methods are covered in the next section.

Using *Find* on Non-Table Recordsets

Because dynaset and snapshot objects do not use indexes, the Seek method cannot be used to search for specific records. The Find method is used to locate specific records in non-table objects (dynasets and snapshots). The Find method is not as fast as the indexed Seek method. The Find method is a sequential search. It starts at the beginning of the data set and looks at each record until it finds one that matches the search criteria. Although this is not as fast as Seek, it is still faster than using the Move methods to handle this within your own Visual Basic code.

The syntax for the Find methods is almost identical to the SQL WHERE clause (covered in Day 9). The search string consists of a field (or set of fields) followed by a comparison operator (=,<>, and so on) and a search value (for example, MyRS.FindFirst "Au_ID=13").

There are actually four Find methods: FindFirst, FindPrevious, FindNext, and FindLast. The FindFirst method starts its search from the beginning of the file. The FindLast method starts its search from the end of the file and works its way to the beginning. The FindPrevious and FindNext methods can be used to continue a search that can return more than one record. For example, if you are looking for all the records that have their ZipCode column set to 99999, you could use the FindFirst method to locate the first record and then use the FindNext method to continue the search forward until you reach the end of the data set. Similarly, you can use the FindLast and FindPrevious methods to perform continued searches starting at the end of the data set. Although the FindNext and FindPrevious methods are available, it is usually better to create a new recordset using the Find criteria if you expect to locate more than one record that meets the criteria.

Now you'll modify the CH1101.VBP project to illustrate the Find method by adding another button to the project. Set its Name property to cmdFind and its Caption property to F&ind. Next, add Listing 11.5 to the cmdFind_Click event.

Listing 11.5. Coding the cmdFind_Click event.

```
Private Sub cmdFind_Click()
    '
    ' get input and peform table seek
    '
    Dim cFind As String
    '
    cFind = InputBox("Enter Au_ID Find Value:", "Non-Table Find")
    cFind = UCase(Trim(cFind))
    '
    If Len(cFind) <> 0 Then
        cFind = "Au_ID=" + cFind   ' build criteria string
        rsName.FindFirst cFind
        '
        If rsName.NoMatch = True Then
            MsgBox "Unable to Locate [" + cFind + "]", vbCritical,
          ➥ "Failed Non-Table Find"
        Else
```

```
        ReadRow     ' load record
        MsgBox "Found [" + cFind + "]", vbInformation,
        ➥ "Successful Non-Table Find"
      End If
    End If
    '
End Sub
```

Listing 11.5 is almost identical to the one used in the cmdSeek_Click event. (See Listing 11.4.) Notice that you have to build the criteria string to include the name of the field you are searching. Because the Find method can be applied to any field (or fields) in the table, you must supply the field in the search criteria.

Before saving the project, comment out the line in the Form_Load event that sets the index. Also, change vbOpenTable to vbOpenSnapshot. Now save and run the project. When you click the Find button, enter 13 in the input box. You should see a message telling you that the Find operation was successful. (See Figure 11.3.)

Figure 11.3.
The results of the Find method.

Notice that if you click the Seek button, you'll eventually get an error message. You cannot apply a Seek method to a non-table object. Also, you cannot apply a Find method to a table object. Later, you'll learn how to write a single locate routine that is smart enough to figure out which search method to use for your recordset object.

Using Bookmarks Before Searching Recordsets

There is one more item to cover before you leave the topic of record searching. That item is the use of bookmarks. Visual Basic uses bookmarks to remember a specific location in a data set. Bookmarks can be used for all types of recordsets (table and non-table objects).

When you use Seek or Find, you are actually moving the record pointer. If the search is successful, the record pointer is now resting at the found record. If the search fails, the record pointer is resting at the end of the data set. (If you use the FindLast method, failed searches leave you at the beginning of the data set.) It is very annoying to users to see a Search failed message and then see their data entry form updated with a new record! Before performing a search (Seek or Find method), you should always bookmark your location. Then, if the search fails, you can restore the record pointer to the starting location.

> **Note:** First, you'll go through the process of building the code library. Then, after the library is built, you'll build a simple form to add to the CompanyMaster project. This form will use all the library functions covered here.

Preparing the Data Entry Form

The routines you have designed will make a few assumptions about how your data entry forms will be constructed. These assumptions are very general and will result in a solid, if not flashy, data entry form. After completing these routines, you might want to modify the library functions to add additional features and options that suit your particular data entry needs.

For each data entry form you design using these routines, you'll need to stay within the following guidelines:

☐ Each data entry form will correspond to a single data set. This is simple when dealing with table-type data sets. You can design a single form for each table. If you need to perform data entry on a set of columns that are the result of a multiple-table SQL JOIN operation, you can use the data set produced by the JOIN as the basis for the data entry form.

☐ Each data entry form will contain a control array of eight command buttons named cmdBtn(0) through cmdBtn(7). This is the button set expected by all the routines you'll build.

☐ Every column in the data set row that requires data entry will be represented by a single input control on the form. The control and the field will be related by placing the column name in the Tag property of the input control. This is how you'll be able to bind your input controls to your data set.

That's about it for the assumptions. Each form represents a data set, each form must have an eight-button control array defined, and each data field that will be updated will be represented by a single input control identified by placing the data set column name in the Tag property of the input control. After that, you can lay out your forms in any manner you like.

You'll build the library of record-handling functions first. Start a new Visual Basic project. Open up a BAS module by selecting Insert | Module from the main Visual Basic menu. Set the module name to modRecLibrary by placing the mouse over the open module and clicking the right (alternate) mouse button to bring up the context menu. Select Properties from this menu, and fill in the Name property on the property sheet.

Tip: Be sure to set the Option Explicit option to On for this project. This will force you to declare all variables before they are used in your program. Using the Option Explicit setting helps reduce the number of program bugs you'll create as you enter these routines.

Before you begin the heavy coding, complete the declaration section of the library routine. Enter Listing 11.7 at the top of the module.

Listing 11.7. Coding the global variables.

```
' global const for rec routines
'
Global Const recOK = 0           ' all ok value
Global Const recNotFound = -1    ' record not found
'
' button bar alignment constants
'
Global Const btnAlignTop = 0     ' algin btns on top
Global Const btnAlignBottom = 1  ' align btns on bottom
Global Const btnAlignLeft = 2    ' align btns on left
Global Const btnAlignRight = 3   ' align bnts on right
```

Not much here, really. The first two values are used throughout the routines to indicate the status of an operation. The final four values are used to control how the button set will appear on your data entry form.

After you have entered the preceding code, save the module as LIBREC.BAS. The next several sections contain the code for all the record-handling routines.

The *RSOpen* Routine

This routine handles the opening of an existing database and the creation of a recordset to hold the selected records. Enter Listing 11.8 on a blank line in the module. Be sure to include the Function declaration line. Visual Basic supplies the End Function line automatically.

Tip: It is a good idea to save your work after each coding section. This ensures that you do not lose much work if your computer suffers an unexpected crash.

Listing 11.8. Coding the RSOpen function.

```
Function RSOpen(cDBName As String, cRSName As String, nRSType As Integer,
➥ dbResult As DATABASE, rsResult As Recordset) As Integer
    '
    ' opens database, selects recordset
    '
    ' *** NOTE ******************************
    ' You must call this routine at least once
    ' before you use any other functions. The
    ' first time, you must include valid
    ' cDBName, and cRSName values. If you want
    ' to open additonal recordsets on the same
    ' database, pass an empty cDBName along with
    ' the previously created dbResult object
    ' and a new cRSName/rsResult set.
    ' ********************************************
    '
    ' inputs:
    '   cDBName       name of database to open
    '   cRSName       name of table or SQL Select
    '   nRSType       recordset type constant
    '
    ' outputs:
    '   dbResult      resulting database
    '   rsRecordset   resulting dataset
    '   RSOpen        recOK if no errors
    '
    On Error GoTo RSOpenErr
    '
    If Len(Trim(cDBName)) <> 0 Then
        Set dbResult = DBEngine.Workspaces(0).OpenDatabase(cDBName)
    End If
    Set rsResult = dbResult.OpenRecordset(cRSName, nRSType)
    '
    RSOpen = recOK   ' no errors, all ok
    GoTo RSOpenExit
    '
RSOpenErr:
    RecError Err, Error$, "RSOpen"
    RSOpen = Err ' problem!
    GoTo RSOpenExit
    '
RSOpenExit:
    '
End Function
```

The comment lines at the beginning of the module explain most of what is going on here. This routine reads the string values you send it and returns fully initialized Data Access Objects for your use. Notice that if you pass a blank cDBName value, the routine will attempt to open the recordset using the previously opened database. This makes it easy to create multiple data sets from the same database.

Another new twist here is that almost all the routines in this library are declared as Functions instead of Subs. These functions will return an integer value that indicates whether any errors occurred during the operation. This gives you a very easy way to check for errors from within Visual Basic code. Also, you have built a simple error handler for those times when things will go wrong. You'll cover error handling in depth in Day 14, "Error Trapping." For now, just remember that what you are doing here is creating a set of routines to trap and report any errors that might occur during the running of the program.

 Tip: It is a good idea to comment out the On Error… lines of your program while you are first entering the Visual Basic code. When the error trap is on, even simple typing errors will set it off. During the construction phase, you'll want the Visual Basic interpreter to halt and give you a full error message. When you are sure you have eliminated all the programming bugs, you can activate the error handlers by removing the comment mark from the On Error… program lines.

The *RecInit* Routine

This next routine clears out any stray values that might exist in the form controls that you are binding to your data table. Remember that you can bind a form control to a data set column by placing the name of the column in the Tag property of the field. This routine checks that property and, if it contains information, initializes the control to prepare it for receiving data set values. Enter the code in Listing 11.9 as a new function.

Listing 11.9. Coding the RecInit function.

```
Function RecInit(frmName As Form) As Integer
    '
    ' clears any values from bound controls
    '
    ' Inputs:
    '   frmName      name of form to initialize
    '
    ' Outputs:
    '   RecInit      recOK if no errors
    '
    On Error GoTo RecInitErr
    '
    Dim ctlTemp As Control
    Dim cTag As String
    '
    For Each ctlTemp In frmName.Controls
        cTag = UCase(Trim(ctlTemp.Tag))
        If Len(cTag) <> 0 Then
```

continues

Listing 11.9. continued

```
            ctlTemp = ""
        End If
    Next
    '
    RecInit = recOK ' all ok
    GoTo RecInitExit
    '
RecInitErr:
    RecError Err, Error$, "RecInit"
    RecInit = Err ' report error
    GoTo RecInitExit:
    '
RecInitExit:
    '
End Function
```

This routine contains a simple loop that checks all the controls on the form to see whether they are bound to a data set column. If they are, the control gets initialized.

The *RecLocate* Routine

This routine prompts the user to enter a value to use as a search criteria on the recordset. The routine is smart enough to use the Seek method for table objects and the Find method for non-table objects. Add the routine in Listing 11.10 to your module.

Listing 11.10. Coding the RecLocate function.

```
Function RecLocate(cFldName As String, rsName As Recordset,
➥cIndex As String) As Integer
    '
    ' prompt user to enter info on record to locate
    '
    ' inputs:
    '   cFldName    Name of Field to Search
    '   rsName      Name of recordset to search
    '   cIndex      Name of index to use (for table-type only)
    '
    ' outputs:
    '   RecLocate   RecOk        - if found
    '               RecNotFound  - if not found
    '
    On Error GoTo RecLocateErr
    '
    Dim cSearch As String
    Dim nIndex As Integer
    Dim cBookMark As String
    '
    If Len(Trim(cIndex)) <> 0 Then
        rsName.Index = cIndex
```

```
            nIndex = True
    Else
            nIndex = False
    End If
    '
    cSearch = InputBox("Enter Search Value:", "Searching " + cFldName)
    cSearch = Trim(cSearch)
    '
    cBookMark = rsName.Bookmark
    '
    If Len(cSearch) = 0 Then
        nResult = recNotFound ' report nomatch
    Else
        If nIndex = True Then
            rsName.Seek "=", cSearch
        Else
            If InStr(cSearch, ",") <> 0 Then
                cSearch = "'" + cSearch + "'"
            End If
            cSearch = cFldName + "=" + cSearch
            rsName.FindFirst cSearch
        End If
        '
        If rsName.NoMatch = True Then
            MsgBox "Unable to Locate [" + cSearch + "]",
            ➥ vbInformation, "Searching " + cFldName
            nResult = recNotFound     ' report nomatch
        Else
            nResult = recOK       ' report match
        End If
    End If
    '
    If nResult = recNotFound Then
        rsName.Bookmark = cBookMark
    End If
    '
    RecLocate = nResult
    GoTo RecLocateExit

RecLocateErr:
    RecError Err, Error$, "RecLocate"
    nResult = Err
    GoTo RecLocateExit
    '
RecLocateExit:
    '
End Function
```

Notice that if you pass an index name with this routine, it will be used with the Seek method instead of a sequential Find method. Also note the use of the Bookmark property to return the record pointer to its starting location if the search fails.

The *RecRead* Routine

Now you get one of the important routines! This routine takes values from the current record of the data set and loads them into controls on the form. This is done by checking all the controls on the form for a nonblank Tag property. If a control has a value in the Tag property, it is assumed that the value is a column name for the data set. The value in this column is then copied from the data set into the form control. Add this new routine (Listing 11.11) to your library.

Listing 11.11. Coding the `RecRead` function.

```
Function RecRead(frmName As Form, rsName As Recordset) As Integer
    '
    ' read a record of data and update the controls
    '
    ' Inputs:
    '    frmName      Name of form to load
    '    rsName       Name of recordset to read
    '
    ' Outputs:
    '    RecRead      recOk - if no errors
    '
    On Error GoTo RecReadErr
    '
    Dim ctlTemp As Control
    Dim cTag As String
    Dim cFldName As String
    '
    For Each ctlTemp In frmName.Controls
        cTag = UCase(Trim(ctlTemp.Tag))
        If Len(cTag) <> 0 Then
            ctlTemp = rsName.Fields(cTag)
        End If
    Next
    RecRead = recOK ' all ok
    GoTo RecReadExit
    '
RecReadErr:
    RecError Err, Error$, "RecRead"
    RecRead = Err
    GoTo RecReadExit
    '
RecReadExit:
    '
End Function
```

This routine and the next routine (`RecWrite`) are the heart of the record-handling functions. When you understand how these routines work, you'll be able to build your own customized routines for handling data set read and write operations.

The *RecWrite* Routine

This routine performs the opposite function of RecRead (see Listing 11.12). Again, it's a simple loop through all the controls on the form. If they are bound to a data column, the value in the control is copied to the data set column for storage.

Note: Before you can write to a data set, you need to invoke the Edit or AddNew methods. After the write, you must invoke the Update method to save the changes. You'll handle these operations in the button set routines later in today's lesson.

Listing 11.12. Coding the RecWrite function.

```
Function RecWrite(frmName As Form, rsName As Recordset) As Integer
    '
    ' update current record with data from controls
    '
    ' Inputs:
    '   frmName      Name of form w/ bound controls
    '   rsName       Name of recordset to update
    '
    ' Outputs:
    '   RecWrite     recOK - if no errors
    '
    On Error GoTo RecWriteErr
    '
    Dim ctlTemp As Control
    Dim cTag As String
    Dim lAttrib As Long
    '
    For Each ctlTemp In frmName.Controls
        cTag = UCase(Trim(ctlTemp.Tag))
        If Len(cTag) <> 0 Then
            lAttrib = rsName.Fields(cTag).Attributes
            If (lAttrib And dbAutoIncrField) = False Then
                rsName.Fields(cTag) = ctlTemp
            End If
        End If
    Next
    '
    RecWrite = recOK ' all ok
    GoTo RecWriteExit
    '
RecWriteErr:
    RecError Err, Error$, "RecWrite"
    RecWrite = Err
    GoTo RecWriteExit
    '
RecWriteExit:
    '
End Function
```

An added feature in this routine deserves mention. Because Visual Basic does not allow you to write to COUNTER data type fields, this routine checks the Attributes property of each bound column before attempting an update. If the field is a COUNTER data type, the routine will not attempt to write data to the column.

The *RecEnable* Routine

To simplify managing data entry routines, your form will only allow users to update form controls after they select the Edit or Add buttons on a form. This routine gives you an easy way to turn on or off the Enabled property of all the bound controls on your form. You'll call this often from your button-set routines.

Add the function in Listing 11.13 to the library.

Listing 11.13. Coding the `RecEnable` function.

```
Function RecEnable(frmName As Form, nToggle) As Integer
    '
    ' toggles input controls on/off
    '
    ' Inputs:
    '    frmName      form with bound controls
    '    nToggle      enable on/off (True/False)
    '
    ' Outputs:
    '    RecEnable    recOK if no errors
    '
    On Error GoTo RecEnableErr
    '
    Dim ctlTemp As Control
    Dim cTag As String
    '
    For Each ctlTemp In frmName.Controls
        cTag = UCase(Trim(ctlTemp.Tag))
        If Len(cTag) <> 0 Then
            ctlTemp.Enabled = nToggle
        End If
    Next
    '
    RecEnable = recOK ' all ok
    GoTo RecEnableExit
    '
RecEnableErr:
    RecError Err, Error$, "RecEnable"
    RecEnable = Err
    GoTo RecEnableExit
    '
RecEnableExit:
    '
End Function
```

The *RecDelete* Routine

This routine performs a delete operation on the selected data record. But before committing the deed, the user is given the chance to reverse the process. Add Listing 11.14 to the library.

Listing 11.14. Coding the `RecDelete` function.

```
Function RecDelete(rsName As Recordset) As Integer
    '
    ' delete the current record
    '
    ' Inputs:
    '   rsName          Recordset that holds rec to del
    '
    ' Outputs:
    '   RecDelete    recOK if no errors
    '
    On Error GoTo RecDeleteErr
    '
    nResult = MsgBox("Delete Current Record?", vbInformation +
    ➥vbYesNo, rsName.Name)
    If nResult = vbYes Then
        rsName.DELETE
    End If
    '
    RecDelete = recOK ' all ok
    GoTo RecDeleteExit
    '
RecDeleteErr:
    RecError Err, Error$, "RecDelete"
    RecDelete = Err
    GoTo RecDeleteExit
    '
RecDeleteExit:
    '
End Function
```

Other Record Routines

You need three more routines to complete the record-handling portion of the library: `RecError` handles any errors that occur; `RecBack` and `RecNext` provide a safe way to process Visual Basic `MovePrevious` and `MoveNext` operations without encountering end-of-file errors from Visual Basic. Add these three routines (in Listing 11.15) to the library.

Listing 11.15. Coding the `RecError` routine.

```
Sub RecError(nErr, cError, cOpName)
    '
```

continues

Listing 11.15. continued

```
    ' report trapped error to user
    '
    ' Inputs:
    '    nErr        Error Number
    '    cError      Error Message
    '    cOpName     Function/Sub that raised error
    '
    Dim cErrMsg As String
    '
    cErrMsg = "Error:" + Chr(9) + Str(nErr) + Chr(13)
    cErrMsg = cErrMsg + "Text:" + Chr(9) + cError + Chr(13)
    cErrMsg = cErrMsg + "Module:" + Chr(9) + cOpName
    '
    MsgBox cErrMsg, vbCritical + vbOKCancel, "RecError"
    '
End Sub

Function RecBack(rsName As Recordset) As Integer
    '
    ' move to previous record in set
    '
    ' inputs:
    '    rsName        name of recordset
    '
    ' outputs:
    '    RecBack       recOK if no errors
    '
    On Error GoTo RecBackErr
    '
    If rsName.BOF = True Then    ' past start?
        rsName.MoveFirst         ' move to first rec
    Else
        rsName.MovePrevious      ' move to prev rec
        If rsName.BOF Then       ' past start?
            rsName.MoveFirst     ' move to first rec
        End If
    End If
    '
    RecBack = recOK ' all ok
    GoTo RecBackExit
    '
RecBackErr:
    RecError Err, Error$, "RecBack"
    RecBack = Err
    GoTo RecBackExit
    '
RecBackExit:
    '
End Function

Function RecNext(rsName As Recordset) As Integer
    '
    ' move to the next record in the set
    '
```

```
'   inputs:
'      rsName        name of the recordset
'
'   outputs:
'      RecNext       recOK if no error
'
On Error GoTo RecNextErr
'
If rsName.EOF = True Then    ' past end?
    rsName.MoveLast          ' move to last rec
Else
    rsName.MoveNext          ' move to next rec
    If rsName.EOF Then       ' past end?
        rsName.MoveLast      ' move to last rec
    End If
End If
'
RecNext = recOK              ' all ok
GoTo RecNextExit             ' leave here
'
RecNextErr:
    RecError Err, Error$, "RecNext"
    RecNext = Err
    GoTo RecNextExit
'
RecNextExit:
'
End Function
```

You have just completed the record-handling portion of the library. Only three routines must still be built. These three routines provide the button set that users will see when they perform data entry operations on your form.

Creating Your Own Button Bar Routine

The next three routines handle all the operations needed to add a complete set of command buttons to your data entry form. This set can be used for any data entry form that provides the basic add, edit, delete, find, and browse operations needed for most data entry routines.

Warning: Before these routines can work with your programs you'll need to add a control array of eight command buttons. These routines assume the array is called cmdBtn(0) through cmdBtn(7). You'll cover the details of constructing a working form in the "Creating a Data Entry Form with the Library Routines" section of this lesson.

The *BtnBarInit* Routine

This routine builds the details of the command button array and places that array on your data entry form. You must first place an eight-button control array on the form called cmdBtn(0) through cmdBtn(7). This routine can place the button set on the top, bottom, left, or right side of the form. You control this feature by setting the alignment parameter using one of the constants you defined earlier.

Add this routine (in Listing 11.16) to the library module that contains the record-handling routines.

Listing 11.16. Coding the `BtnBarInit` routine.

```
Sub BtnBarInit(frmName As Form, nAlign As Integer)
    '
    ' sets up button bar where indicated
    '
    ' *** NOTE *****************************
    ' Before you can call this routine,    *
    ' you must first add a command button  *
    ' control array to frmName. This array *
    ' MUST be called cmdBtn. There MUST be *
    ' eight buttons in the array.          *
    ' *************************************
    ' Inputs:
    '   frmName      Name of form to use
    '   nAlign       location of bar
    '                0 = btnAlignTop
    '                1 = btnAlignbottom
    '                2 = btnAlignLeft
    '                3 = btnAlginRight
    '
    'On Error GoTo BtnBarInitErr
    '
    Dim nBtnWidth As Integer
    Dim nBtnTop As Integer
    Dim nBtnLeft As Integer
    Dim nBtnHeight As Integer
    Dim x As Integer
    Dim cCap(7) As String
    '
    cCap(0) = "&Add"
    cCap(1) = "&Edit"
    cCap(2) = "&Del"
    cCap(3) = "&Find"
    cCap(4) = "&Top"
    cCap(5) = "&Next"
    cCap(6) = "&Back"
    cCap(7) = "&Last"
    '
    ' calc button locations
    Select Case nAlign
        Case Is = btnAlignTop
            ' align top
            nBtnTop = 60
```

```
                nBtnWidth = (frmName.ScaleWidth - 60) / 8 ' width of each button
                If nBtnWidth < 660 Then
                    nBtnWidth = 660        ' no smaller than 660 wide
                End If
                nBtnHeight = 300           ' default height
            Case Is = btnAlignBottom
                ' align bottom
                nBtnTop = frmName.ScaleHeight - 360
                nBtnWidth = (frmName.ScaleWidth - 60) / 8 ' width of each button
                If nBtnWidth < 660 Then
                    nBtnWidth = 660        ' no smaller than 660 wide
                End If
                nBtnHeight = 300           ' default height
            Case Is = btnAlignLeft
                ' align left
                nBtnWidth = 660
                nBtnHeight = (frmName.ScaleHeight - 60) / 8
                If nBtnHeight < 300 Then
                    nBtnHeight = 300       ' no smaller than 300 high
                End If
                nBtnLeft = 60
            Case Is = btnAlignRight
                ' align right
                nBtnWidth = 660
                nBtnHeight = (frmName.ScaleHeight - 60) / 8
                If nBtnHeight < 300 Then
                    nBtnHeight = 300       ' no smaller than 300 high
                End If
                nBtnLeft = (frmName.ScaleWidth - 720)
        End Select
        '
        ' now place the buttons on form
        For x = 0 To 7
            If nAlign = btnAlignTop Or nAlign = btnAlignBottom Then
                nBtnLeft = x * nBtnWidth       ' calc left location
            End If
            If nAlign = btnAlignLeft Or nAlign = btnAlignRight Then
                nBtnTop = x * nBtnHeight + 60    ' calc top location
            End If
            '
            frmName.cmdBtn(x).Width = nBtnWidth
            frmName.cmdBtn(x).Left = nBtnLeft
            frmName.cmdBtn(x).TOP = nBtnTop
            frmName.cmdBtn(x).Height = nBtnHeight
            frmName.cmdBtn(x).Caption = cCap(x)
            frmName.cmdBtn(x).Visible = True
        Next x
        '
        GoTo BtnBarInitExit
        '
BtnBarInitErr:
        RecError Err, Error$, "BtnBarInit"
        GoTo BtnBarInitExit
        '
BtnBarInitExit:
        '
End Sub
```

Listing 11.16 uses the data form's dimensions to calculate the location and size of the command buttons in the button set. You'll create a working example of this in the section "Creating a Data Entry Form with the Library Routines."

The *BtnBarEnable* Routine

This is a short routine that allows you to toggle the Enabled property of the command buttons in the button set. This will be used to turn on or off selected buttons during edit or add operations. Add the routine in Listing 11.17 to the library.

Listing 11.17. Coding the `BtnBarEnable` routine.

```
Sub BtnBarEnable(frmName As Form, cList As String)
    '
    ' turns on(1)/off(0) cmdbuttons
    '
    ' inputs:
    '   frmName      name of form that holds controls
    '   cList        bit list for toggling
    '                    "1" = turn on
    '                    "0" = turn off
    '                    "1010" = turn 1&3 on, 2&4 off
    '
    On Error GoTo BtnBarEnableErr
    '
    Dim x As Integer
    '
    cList = Trim(cList)
    For x = 1 To Len(cList)
        If Mid(cList, x, 1) = "1" Then
            frmName.cmdBtn(x - 1).Enabled = True
        Else
            frmName.cmdBtn(x - 1).Enabled = False
        End If
    Next x
    '
    GoTo BtnBarEnableExit
    '
BtnBarEnableErr:
    RecError Err, Error$, "BtnBarEnable"
    GoTo BtnBarEnableExit
    '
BtnBarEnableExit:
    '
End Sub
```

The *BtnBarProcess* Routine

This routine handles all the button actions initiated by the user and makes many calls to the other routines in the library. It is the high-level routine of the module. This is also the most involved routine in this library. It might look intimidating at first glance. But, after you inspect the first several lines, you'll see a pattern developing. More than half of the routine is devoted to handling the browse buttons (First, Back, Next, and Last). The rest is used to handle the Add, Edit, Find, and Delete operations.

Enter Listing 11.18 into the library.

Listing 11.18. Coding the BtnBarProcess routine.

```
Sub BtnBarProcess(nCmdBtn As Integer, frmName As Form, rsName As Recordset,
➥ cSearch As String, cIndex As String)
    '
    ' handle button clicks
    '
    ' *** NOTE ******************************
    ' Before you can call this routine,      *
    ' you must first add a commandbutton     *
    ' control array to frmName. This array    *
    ' MUST be called cmdBtn. There MUST be    *
    ' eight buttons in the array.            *
    ' ****************************************
    ' inputs:
    '   nCmdBtn      button that was pressed
    '   frmName      name of form that holds controls
    '   cSearch      search field(s)
    '   cIndex       search index (table-type sets only)
    '
    On Error GoTo BtnBarProcessErr
    '
    Select Case nCmdBtn
        Case Is = 0
            ' peform add/save/cancel
            Select Case frmName.cmdBtn(nCmdBtn).Caption
                Case Is = "&Save"
                    nResult = RecWrite(frmName, rsName)
                    If nResult = recOK Then
                        rsName.UPDATE
                    End If
                    If nResult = recOK Then
                        nResult = RecInit(frmName)
                    End If
                    If nResult = recOK Then
                        nResult = RecRead(frmName, rsName)
                    End If
                    If nResult = recOK Then
                        nResult = RecEnable(frmName, False)
                    End If
```

continues

Listing 11.18. continued

```
                    If nResult = recOK Then
                        frmName.cmdBtn(0).Caption = "&Add"
                        frmName.cmdBtn(1).Caption = "&Edit"
                        BtnBarEnable frmName, "11111111"
                    End If
                Case Is = "&Add"
                    rsName.AddNew
                    nResult = RecInit(frmName)
                    If nResult = recOK Then
                        nResult = RecEnable(frmName, True)
                    End If
                    If nResult = recOK Then
                        frmName.cmdBtn(0).Caption = "&Save"
                        frmName.cmdBtn(1).Caption = "&Cancel"
                        BtnBarEnable frmName, "11000000"
                    End If
                Case Is = "&Cancel"
                    rsName.CancelUpdate
                    frmName.cmdBtn(0).Caption = "&Add"
                    frmName.cmdBtn(1).Caption = "&Edit"
                    BtnBarEnable frmName, "11111111"
                    '
                    nResult = RecInit(frmName)
                    If nResult = recOK Then
                        nResult = RecRead(frmName, rsName)
                    End If
                    If nResult = recOK Then
                        nResult = RecEnable(frmName, False)
                    End If
            End Select
        Case Is = 1
            ' perform edit/save/cancel
            Select Case frmName.cmdBtn(1).Caption
                Case Is = "&Save"
                    rsName.Edit
                    nResult = RecWrite(frmName, rsName)
                    If nResult = recOK Then
                        rsName.UPDATE
                    End If
                    If nResult = recOK Then
                        nResult = RecEnable(frmName, False)
                    End If
                    If nResult = recOK Then
                        frmName.cmdBtn(1).Caption = "&Edit"
                        frmName.cmdBtn(0).Caption = "&Add"
                        BtnBarEnable frmName, "11111111"
                    End If
                Case Is = "&Edit"
                    nResult = RecEnable(frmName, True)
                    If nResult = recOK Then
                        frmName.cmdBtn(1).Caption = "&Save"
                        frmName.cmdBtn(0).Caption = "&Cancel"
                        BtnBarEnable frmName, "11000000"
                    End If
```

```
            Case Is = "&Cancel"
                rsName.CancelUpdate
                frmName.cmdBtn(1).Caption = "&Edit"
                frmName.cmdBtn(0).Caption = "&Add"
                BtnBarEnable frmName, "11111111"
                '
                nResult = RecInit(frmName)
                If nResult = recOK Then
                    nResult = RecRead(frmName, rsName)
                End If
                If nResult = recOK Then
                    nResult = RecEnable(frmName, False)
                End If
        End Select
        '
        If nResult = recOK Then
            nResult = RecInit(frmName)
        End If
        If nResult = recOK Then
            nResult = RecRead(frmName, rsName)
        End If
    Case Is = 2
        ' perform delete
        nResult = RecDelete(rsName)
        If nResult = recOK Then
            nResult = RecEnable(frmName, False)
        End If
        If nResult = recOK Then
            nResult = RecNext(rsName)
        End If
        If nResult = recOK Then
            nResult = RecInit(frmName)
        End If
        If nResult = recOK Then
            nResult = RecRead(frmName, rsName)
        End If
        BtnBarEnable frmName, "11111111"
    Case Is = 3
        ' perform find
        nResult = RecLocate(cSearch, rsName, cIndex)
        If nResult = recOK Then
            nResult = RecInit(frmName)
        End If
        If nResult = recOK Then
            nResult = RecRead(frmName, rsName)
        End If
        BtnBarEnable frmName, "11111111"
    Case Is = 4
        ' perform move top
        rsName.MoveFirst
        nResult = RecInit(frmName)
        If nResult = recOK Then
            nResult = RecRead(frmName, rsName)
        End If
        BtnBarEnable frmName, "11111111"
```

continues

377

Listing 11.18. continued

```
        Case Is = 5
            ' perform move next
            nResult = RecNext(rsName)
            If nResult = recOK Then
                nResult = RecInit(frmName)
            End If
            If nResult = recOK Then
                nResult = RecRead(frmName, rsName)
            End If
            BtnBarEnable frmName, "11111111"
        Case Is = 6
            ' perform move back
            nResult = RecBack(rsName)
            If nResult = recOK Then
                nResult = RecInit(frmName)
            End If
            If nResult = recOK Then
                nResult = RecRead(frmName, rsName)
            End If
            BtnBarEnable frmName, "11111111"
        Case Is = 7
            ' perform move last
            rsName.MoveLast
            nResult = RecInit(frmName)
            If nResult = recOK Then
                nResult = RecRead(frmName, rsName)
            End If
            BtnBarEnable frmName, "11111111"
    End Select
    '
    GoTo BtnBarProcessExit
    '
BtnBarProcessErr:
    RecError Err, Error$, "BtnBarProcess"
    GoTo BtnBarProcessExit
    '
BtnBarProcessExit:
    '
End Sub
```

 Note: This is the last library function you'll be adding. Be sure to save the updated library file to disk before exiting Visual Basic.

There are several aspects to Listing 11.18 that need review. First, because you are using a command button array, all operations are dependent on which button was pushed. This is handled by the outer `Select Case` structure. The comment lines show what each button is labeled. However, the captions (and functions) of the first two buttons (Add and Edit) can

change during the course of the data entry process. Therefore, these two options have an additional `Select Case` to check the caption status of the selected button.

You'll also notice a great number of `If…End If` blocks in the code. These are present because you are constantly checking the results of previous actions. It clutters up the code a bit but provides very solid error checking and program flow control.

Each main section of the outer `Select Case` performs all the operations needed to complete a user action. For example, the very first set of operations in the routine is the completion of the `Save` operation for an `Add` command. If you ignore the constant checks of the `nResult` variable, you'll see that the essence of this section of the code is as follows:

☐ Write the record to the data set (`RecWrite`).

☐ Commit the changes (`rsName.Update`).

☐ Initialize the form controls (`RecInit`).

☐ Read the current record into the form (`RecRead`).

☐ Disable data entry in the fields (`RecEnable False`).

☐ Reset the command button labels and enable all the buttons.

The save operation is the most complicated process. The locate, delete, and browse operations are much easier to accomplish and require less coding. The key to remember here is that you are providing all the user-level processes of the data control in this set of Visual Basic code. Although it seems to be a large code piece, when you have it on file, you'll be able to use it in all your Visual Basic projects.

And that's what you'll do next.

Creating a Data Entry Form with the Library Routines

Now that you have a solid library set for creating data entry forms, let's build a new form for the CompanyMaster project. To do this, you'll add a new form to the CompanyMaster project. This form will be a simple validation list that can be used to validate input for other portions of the project.

If you haven't done it yet, start Visual Basic and load the MASTER.VBP project. This is a copy of the project you built last week.

The first thing you must do is add the LIBREC.BAS file to the project by selecting the File | Add File menu option. Then locate the LIBREC.BAS file you created earlier today. There is a version of this library in the Chap11 directory.

Modifying the Master Form

Before you add the new form, you need to add a short menu to the CompanyMaster main form. You'll use this menu to call the new form. Open the frmMaster form and add the menu items listed in Table 11.2. You can also refer to Figure 11.4 as a guide for building the menu.

Table 11.2. Menu items for the frmMaster form.

Caption	Menu
&File	mnuFile
E&xit	mnuFileExit
&Lists	mnuList
&State/Prov	mnuListStProv

Figure 11.4.
Building the menu for the frmMaster form.

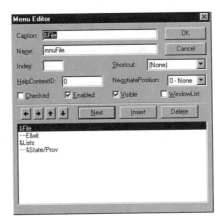

After building the menu, add the following code behind the Exit menu item.

```
Private Sub mnuFileExit_Click()
    cmdExit_Click    ' do the exit!
End Sub
```

This code simply calls the existing routine that handles the program exit.

Now you need to add the line of code that will call the new form you are going to create. Add the following code behind the State/Prov menu item.

```
Private Sub mnuListStProv_Click()
    frmStProv.Show 1
End Sub
```

This code calls the new form and forces it to display as a modal form. Because it is modal, users will not be able to change the focus within their project until they safely exit this form.

Building the State/Province List Form

Now that the housekeeping is done, you can build the new form. Use Table 11.3 and Figure 11.5 as guides as you layout the new validation form.

Table 11.3. Controls for the State/Prov list form.

Control	Property	Setting
Form	Name	frmStProv
	Caption	State/Province Validation Table
	Height	1755
	Left	1545
	Top	1110
	Width	5835
TextBox	Name	Text1
	Height	300
	Left	120
	Tag	StateProv
	Top	120
	Width	1200
TextBox	Name	Text2
	Height	300
	Left	120
	Tag	Description
	Top	540
	Width	2400

In addition to the controls listed in Table 11.3, you need to add an array of eight command buttons. To do this, add a single command button to the form (it doesn't matter where you place it on the form), and set its Name property to cmdBtn. Click on the button to give it the focus, and click the right mouse button to bring up the context menu. Select Copy from the menu. Now bring up the context menu and select Paste. You are prompted by Visual Basic to confirm that you want to create a control array. Click Yes. Do this six more times, until you have eight command buttons on your form named cmdBtn(0) through cmdBtn(7).

> ✓ **Tip:** You won't be manipulating any of the buttons in edit mode. If you like, you can place these buttons off-screen by hiding them below the edge of the display area. To do this, enlarge the form, move the buttons to the new area, and then resize the form to its original shape. Even though you can't see the buttons, Visual Basic will be able to find them at runtime.

Figure 11.5.

Laying out the State/Prov list form.

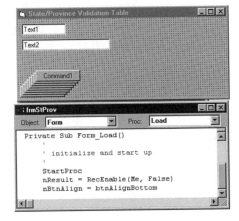

Let's add the code fragments that will make this data entry form work. You only have a few items to add because you'll be using the ModLibRec library you built earlier in this lesson. Add Listing 11.19 to the declaration section of the form.

Listing 11.19. Coding the form-level variables.

```
Option Explicit

'
' form level vars
'
Dim dbFile As DATABASE
Dim cDBName As String
Dim rsFile As Recordset
Dim cRSName As String
Dim nBtnAlign As Integer
Dim nResult As Integer
```

Create a Sub procedure to handle opening the database and creating the recordset. Add the new routine in Listing 11.20 to the form.

Listing 11.20. Coding the `StartProc` routine.

```
Sub StartProc()
    '
    ' open db and rs
    '
    ' on error goto StartProcErr
    '
    cDBName = App.Path + "\master.mdb"
    cRSName = "StateProvList"
    '
    nResult = RSOpen(cDBName, cRSName, dbOpenDynaset, dbFile, rsFile)
    If nResult = recOK Then
        nResult = RecInit(Me)
    End If
    '
    If nResult = recOK Then
        nResult = RecRead(Me, rsFile)
    End If
    '
    GoTo StartProcExit
    '
StartProcErr:
    RecError Err, Error$, "StartProc"
    GoTo StartProcExit
    '
StartProcExit:
    '
End
```

11

Listing 11.20 initializes two variables and then uses the new library routines to open the database, initialize the form, and load the first record into the controls.

Next, you need to add code to the Form_Load event that will start this whole process. Enter the code in Listing 11.21 in the Form_Load event window of the form.

Listing 11.21. Coding the `Form_Load` routine.

```
Private Sub Form_Load()
    '
    ' initialize and start up
    '
    StartProc ' open files
    nResult = RecEnable(Me, False)  ' turn off controls
    nBtnAlign = btnAlignBottom      ' set aligment var
    BtnBarInit Me, nBtnAlign        ' create button set
    BtnBarEnable Me, "11111111"     ' enable all buttons
End Sub
```

In Listing 11.21, you call the database startup routine, disable the form controls, create the button set on the bottom of the form, and then enable all buttons for the user.

Now you need to add the routine that will make the buttons call all the library routines. Add the following code to the cmdBtn_Click event of the form:

```
Private Sub cmdBtn_Click(Index As Integer)
    '
    ' this one line handles all button calls!
    '
    BtnBarProcess Index, Me, rsFile, "StateProv", ""
End Sub
```

This single line is called every time you click any of the eight buttons on the data entry form. The BtnBarProcess routine determines which button was pressed and performs the appropriate actions.

You need to add two more lines of code to this form before you are done. First, add a line of code that will allow the buttons to automatically resize each time the form is resized. Add the following code to the Form_Resize event.

```
Private Sub Form_Resize()
    BtnBarInit Me, nBtnAlign     ' repaint buttons
End Sub
```

Finally, add the following line to the Form_UnLoad event to ensure a safe close of the database when the program ends.

```
Private Sub Form_Unload(Cancel As Integer)
    dbFile.Close     ' safe close
End Sub
```

Save the new form as MAST04.FRM, and run the project. When the main form comes up, select Lists | StateProv from the menu to start the new form. Your form should look like the one in Figure 11.6.

Figure 11.6.
Running the new State/Province list form.

Notice that the button set appears on the bottom of the form. This was handled automatically by the library routines. Resize the form to see how the button bar automatically adjusts to the new form shape. Finally, click the Add button to add a new record to the StateProv table. You'll see the input controls become enabled and most of the button bar gray out (see Figure 11.7).

Figure 11.7.
Adding a new record to the StateProv table.

You can enter values in both fields and then click the Save button or the Cancel button to undo the add operation. Click Cancel for now. Test out the form by clicking the browse and find buttons. Add a record, edit it, and then delete it.

You now have a fully functional data entry form, and you added less than 30 lines of Visual Basic code to the master form!

Summary

Today you learned how to write data entry forms using Visual Basic code. These topics were covered: record search routines, the creation of a procedure library to handle all data entry processes, and creating a working data entry form for the CompanyMaster project.

You learned how to perform single-record searches using the three search methods:

☐ The Move methods for browsing the data set.

☐ The Seek method for indexed table objects.

☐ The Find methods for non-table objects (dynasets and snapshots).

You created several routines to handle adding, editing, deleting, reading, writing, and locating records in data sets. These routines were written as generic procedures that can be called from all Visual Basic programs you write in the future.

You used the new library routines to add a new form to the CompanyMaster database project. This new form reads a data set and allows the user to update and browse the table. This new data entry form was built using less than 30 lines of Visual Basic code.

Quiz

1. What are the advantages and disadvantages of using the Data Control rather than code to manage Visual Basic database applications?

2. What is the main advantage of using code to produce data entry forms?

3. Which approach to searching for a data record—the Move, Find, or Seek method—most resembles the SQL WHERE clause?

4. On what kind of recordsets can the Seek method be used to search for records?

5. What are the four Move methods that can be applied to the Recordset object?

6. Which of the Find methods starts its search from the beginning of the recordset? Which of the Find methods starts its search from the end of the recordset?

7. Which item do you utilize to remember a specific location in a data set?

8. What is the fastest search method to locate a record in a data set?

9. How do you create a control array in Visual Basic?

10. What method(s) do you need to invoke prior to using the Update method to write to a data set?

Exercise

Assume that you complete the CompanyMaster application and add the State/Prov form as discussed in this lesson. After distributing this application to your users, you quickly discover that they are having trouble obtaining Zip codes for the companies they enter. You decide to help them by adding a form to this application that lists Zip codes and their city equivalents.

Utilize code to modify the CompanyMaster application so that users can select an item from the List menu (call this item ZipCity) that displays Zip codes (field name of Zip) and city (field name of City). Use Visdata to add a data table (ZipCity) to MASTER.MDB.

Displaying Your
Data with Graphs

Today you'll learn how to add graph displays of your data to your database programs. By creating a simple graphing library that uses the graph control that ships with Visual Basic Professional, you can easily create solid visual displays of your database.

You'll also learn how to use SQL SELECT statements for creating data sets to use as the basis for your graphs. These SQL statements can be built into your code or stored as QueryDef objects in your database.

You'll also learn how to save the generated graphs to disk as bitmap files, how to share your graphs with other programs by placing them on the Windows Clipboard, and how to send the completed graphs to the printer.

And finally, when you complete this chapter, you'll have a graphing library that you can use in all your future Visual Basic projects. As an example, you'll add a set of default graphs to the CompanyMaster project you started last week.

The Advantages of Graphing Your Data

Although generating data graphs is not, strictly speaking, a database function, almost all good database programs provide graphing. Visual representations of your data are much easier for users to understand than tables or lists. Providing graphs in your database programs also gives users the chance to look at the data in more than one way. Often, users will discover important information in their data simply by looking at it from another angle.

Providing graphs also gives your programs an added polish that users appreciate. Quite often users want more than a simple data entry program with a few list reports. Many times, users will take data that was created with a Visual Basic program and export it to another Windows application in order to develop graphs and charts. Using the techniques you'll learn today, you can provide your users with all the graphing tools they will need to develop graphs and charts without using other programs!

Loading and Using Graph Control

The graph control has a multitude of properties that you can manipulate in order to customize the graph display. Not all of the options will be covered here. You can review the Visual Basic documentation for detailed information on the properties of the graph control. However, the most commonly used properties are covered. You will see how to use them to control the way graphs appear on your forms. Here is a list of the property settings covered:

☐ Setting the graph type

☐ Adding graph data using the NumPoints, NumSets, and the AutoInc, GraphData, and QuickData properties

☐ Adding titles and legends

You'll also learn how to use the DrawMode property to send the completed graph to a printer, save it as a file, or copy it to the Windows Clipboard.

Loading the Graph Control into the Visual Basic Toolbox

Note: Visual Basic ships with up to two graphing OCXs: GRAPH16.OCX and GRAPH32.OCX. Both OCXs have the same features. However, if you do not have the 32-bit version of Visual Basic, you won't have the GRAPH32.OCX. In this book, the graph control refers to either the 16-bit or the 32-bit versions of the graph control.

Before you can start using the graph control tool, you have to make sure it is loaded into the Visual Basic toolbox. To do this, load Visual Basic and select Tools | Custom Controls from the Visual Basic main menu. In the list of available controls, locate Pinnacle-BPS Graph Control (see Figure 12.1). Click the checkbox to add the control to your toolbox and then click the OK button to exit the form.

Figure 12.1.
Adding the graph control to your toolbox.

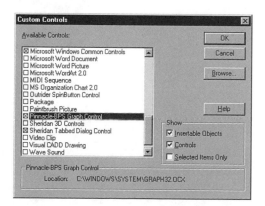

Tip: If you want to add the graph tool to all your future projects, open the AUTO16LD.VBP (or the AUTO32LD.VBP) project file and follow the steps

outlined in the preceding paragraph. After you save the Autoload project, the graph tool will automatically appear in the toolbox of all your new Visual Basic projects.

Adding the Graph Control to Your Form

It's very easy to create a good-looking graph using the graph tool. All you need to do is add the control to your form and fill it with data; the graph control will do the rest. Let's create a simple graph to illustrate this point.

Note: If you have not already loaded Visual Basic and added the graph control to the current project, review the previous section and perform the required steps.

Add the graph control to a blank form by double-clicking the graph control icon in the toolbox. You'll see that the graph control automatically displays a two-dimensional bar graph with some data. Now stretch the control so that your form looks like the one shown in Figure 12.2.

This is random data that the control automatically generates to help you get an idea of how the graph will look in your finished program. When you add your real data to the graph control, this random data will disappear.

Figure 12.2.
Adding the graph control to your form.

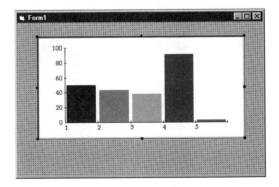

Setting the Graph Type

You determine the type of graph Visual Basic will display by setting the GraphType property. You can do this using the properties window during design time or through Visual Basic code at runtime. Because you already have the graph up on your form, move to the Properties window and locate the GraphType property. Set the property to display a three-dimensional pie chart

by clicking the property in the window and then pulling down the list box. Find and select the 3D Pie option. Your screen should look like the one shown in Figure 12.3.

Figure 12.3.
Changing the GraphType property at design time.

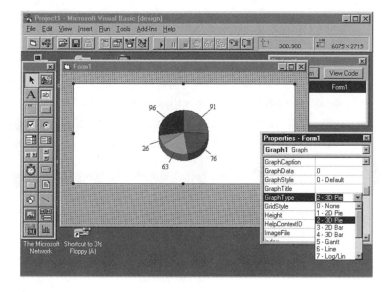

The graph control can display 11 different types of graphs including bar charts, pie charts, line and area graphs, Log/Lin graphs, Gantt charts, scatter graphs, polar graphs, and high/low/close graphs. Not all of them are covered here, but you will work with the three most commonly used formats: bar, pie, and line graphs.

How the Graph Control Organizes Your Data

Before you can display data, you have to load it into the graph control. But, before you even load it into the control, you need to know how the graph control expects to see the data. The graph control requires that you give it all the data organized in sets and points. The graph control needs to know how many points of data are in each set you want to graph. Usually, you will have a single set of data with multiple points. For example, if you want to graph company sales figures for the last 12 months, you would have a single data set (company sales figures) with 12 points (one for each month). If you want to create a graph that compares the actual monthly sales figures with the budgeted figures for the last 12 months, you would have two sets of data (actual and budget figures), each with 12 points (one for each month).

You can use the NumSets and NumPoints properties to inform the graph control how the data is to be organized. You'll now create a graph like the one just described. In design mode, use the Property box to set the NumPoints property to 12 and the NumSets property to 1. You have just told the graph control that it should prepare for one set of data containing 12 individual points.

Adding Data in Design Mode

Now add 12 data items at design time so that you can see how the graph will look. Locate the GraphData property in the Property box. It should be set to 0. Now type 1 and press the Enter key. You have just added one of the expected 12 data points for the set. Continue to add data by entering 2, 3, and so on until you have entered values up to 12.

Save the form now as GRAPHDES.FRM, and save the project as GRAPHDES.VBP. When you run the project, your graph should now look something like the one shown in Figure 12.4.

Figure 12.4.
Adding data in design mode.

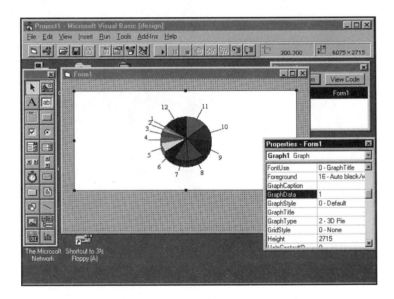

Adding Data at Runtime

You can perform the same task at runtime using Visual Basic code. Now add a command button to this form, setting its Name property to cmdSales and its Caption property to Sales. Then add the code in Listing 12.1 in the cmdSales_Click event:

Listing 12.1. Adding code to the cmdSales_Click event.

```
Private Sub cmdSales_Click()
    Dim x As Integer    ' for loop counter
    '
    Graph1.DataReset = gphAllData   'reset all properties
    Graph1.GraphType = gphBar3D     ' set to 3d bar
    '
    Graph1.NumSets = 1 ' only one set of data
```

```
    Graph1.NumPoints = 12 ' one for each month
    '
    ' now add the data items for each point
    '
    Graph1.ThisSet = 1  ' this is our only set
    For x = 1 To 12
        Graph1.ThisPoint = x    ' which point
        Graph1.GraphData = x    ' data item to load
    Next x
    '
    Graph1.DrawMode = gphDraw   ' show the completed graph
    '
End Sub
```

In Listing 12.1, you do a few things. First, you clear out any data that might already be stored in the graph control. Next, you set the GraphType property to show a three-dimensional bar graph. Also, you set the NumSets and NumPoints properties to 1 and 12, respectively, and then add the data points. Notice that the graph control must be told which set you want filled (using the ThisSet property). Next, you go through a loop—first, setting the ThisPoint property and then adding the data item. Finally, you set the DrawMode property to gphDraw to force Visual Basic to redraw the graph with the new data.

Save and run the project. When you click the Sales button, your form will look similar to the one shown in Figure 12.5.

Figure 12.5.
Creating a graph using Visual Basic code.

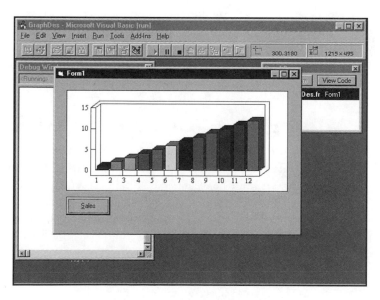

Although this method works well, there is an alternative method that is faster. By setting the AutoInc property of the graph control to 1, the graph control will automatically increment the NumPoints property. This can simplify and speed up your code. Add a new button to the form, setting its Name property to cmdAutoSales and its Caption property to &AutoSales. Then add the code in Listing 12.2 in the `cmdAutoSales_Click` event:

Listing 12.2. Adding code to the `CmdAutoSales_Click` event.

```
Private Sub cmdAutoSales_Click()
    Dim x As Integer     ' for loop counter
    '
    Graph1.DataReset = gphAllData    'reset all properties
    Graph1.GraphType = gphBar3D      ' set to 3d bar
    '
    Graph1.NumSets = 1  ' only one set of data
    Graph1.NumPoints = 12 ' one for each month
    '
    ' now add the data items for each point
    '
    For x = 1 To 12
        Graph1.GraphData = x      ' data item to load
    Next x
    '
    Graph1.DrawMode = gphDraw    ' show the completed graph
    '
End Sub
```

Save and run the project. When you press the AutoSales button, you'll see the same graph that was generated with the Sales button. Notice that, in this example, you left out the lines of code that set the ThisSet and the ThisPoint properties. These values were handled by the graph control using the AutoInc property. This might not seem like a code savings, but it really is. Single set data is relatively easy to graph. Multiple sets get pretty confusing. It's much easier to use the AutoInc property because it automatically updates the ThisSet property, too. There is yet another way to add data to a graph control: using the QuickData property.

Adding Data Using the QuickData Property

You can use the QuickData property to add graph data in a single command at runtime. The QuickData property accepts a single character string that contains all the data sets and points. Each data set must be separated by a carriage return/line feed pair. Each data point must be separated by a tab character. This is known as tab-delimited data. When you use the QuickData property to load graph data, you do not have to set any of the properties that deal with points or sets. You also do not have to force your Visual Basic code to process any For…Next loops.

Add another command button to the form, setting its Name property to cmdQuickSales and its Caption property to &QuickSales. Then add the code in Listing 12.3 in the `cmdQuickSales_Click` event window.

Listing 12.3. Adding code to the `cmdQuickSales_Click` event.

```
Private Sub cmdQuickSales_Click()
    Dim CrLf As String
    Dim cTab As String
    Dim cData As String
    '
    CrLf = Chr(13) + Chr(10) ' create CR/LF string
    cTab = Chr(9) ' create tab string
    '
    ' build three sets of data, each with four points
    '
    cData = "1" + cTab + "2" + cTab + "3" + cTab + "4" + CrLf
    cData = cData + "5" + cTab + "4" + cTab + "3" + cTab + "2" + CrLf
    cData = cData + "6" + cTab + "8" + cTab + "10" + cTab + "4" + CrLf
    '
    Graph1.GraphType = gphLine
    Graph1.DataReset = gphAllData
    Graph1.QuickData = cData
    '
    Graph1.DrawMode = gphDraw
    '
End Sub
```

You'll notice that you created a list of data that contained three sets of four points each. When you use the QuickData property, the graph control is able to determine the total number of sets and the number of points in each set without using the NumSets and NumPoints properties. Save and run this project. Your screen should look like the one shown in Figure 12.6.

Figure 12.6.
Adding graph data using the QuickData property.

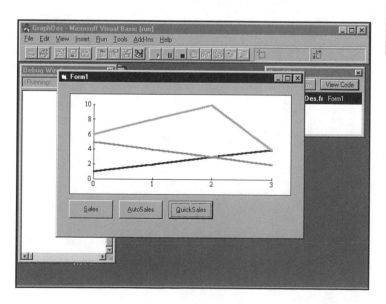

12

The real advantage of using the QuickData property is that it can accept data from most spreadsheets via Windows cut and paste operations. By placing tab-delimited data on the Windows Clipboard, you can use that data as the input for the QuickData property.

> **Note:** Because you will be working with data tables, the QuickData property will not be used to transfer data sets to the graph control. You can refer to the Visual Basic documentation for more information on using the Windows Clipboard and QuickData.

Adding Titles, Labels, and Legends

In addition to loading data and setting the graph type, you can also set graph titles, labels to the data points, and legends for the graph.

Now add another button to the project to illustrate these features of the graph control. Set its Name property to cmdTitles and its Caption property to &Titles. Add Listing 12.4 to the cmdTitles_Click event window.

Listing 12.4. Adding code to the `cmdTitles_Click` event.

```
Private Sub cmdTitles_Click()
    Dim x As Integer
    '
    ' add titles
    '
    Graph1.GraphTitle = "Graph Title"
    Graph1.BottomTitle = "Bottom Title"
    Graph1.LeftTitle = "Left Title"
    '
    ' add legends
    '
    Graph1.AutoInc = 1   ' turn on incrementing
    For x = 1 To 12
        Graph1.LegendText = "L" + Trim(Str(x))
    Next x
    '
    ' add lables
    '
    Graph1.AutoInc = 1   ' turn it on again
    For x = 1 To 12
        Graph1.LabelText = "X" + Trim(Str(x))
    Next x
    '
    Graph1.DrawMode = gphDraw ' redraw graph
    '
End Sub
```

In Listing 12.4, you initialize the three titles and then add legends and labels for the data points. Notice that you used the AutoInc property when adding the legends and labels. Notice, too, that you did not add legends and labels within the same For...Next loop. If you use the AutoInc property, you can only update one element type at a time. When you have more than one element array to update (data, legends, and labels), you must use separate loops for each element array.

Note: It is very unlikely that you would use both a legend and data point labels in the same graph. You did this here to illustrate the unique behavior of the AutoInc property.

Save and run the project. You can apply the text features of the graph control to any graph. After clicking a button to produce a graph, click the Titles button to add the text to the graph. Your screen should look like the one shown in Figure 12.7.

Figure 12.7.
Adding text features to a graph.

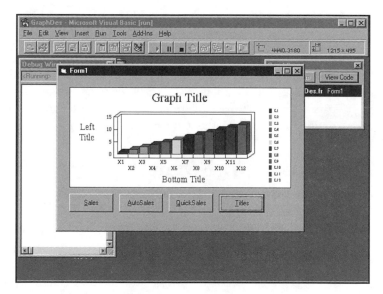

Display Options

You can also send the completed graph to a file, to the Windows Clipboard, or to your printer. All those options are covered in the next section. For now, you'll add a button that writes the completed graph to a disk file as a bitmap image.

Add one more command button to the form. Set its Name property to cmdWrite and its Caption property to &Write. Add Listing 12.5 to the cmdWrite_Click event window.

Listing 12.5. Adding code to the `cmsWrite_Click` event.

```
Private Sub cmdWrite_Click()
    '
    Graph1.ImageFile = App.Path + "\GRAPHDES.BMP" ' set file name
    Graph1.DrawMode = gphBlit   ' set for bitmap mode
    Graph1.DrawMode = gphWrite  ' force to file
    Graph1.DrawMode = gphDraw   ' redraw control
    '
End Sub
```

In Listing 12.5, you first set the name of the file that will be created. Then you set the drawing mode to bitmap. You then force the creation of the graph file and finally redraw the graph on-screen.

Save and run the project. You'll see the screen flicker when the redraw occurs. If you check your disk drive, you'll find the data file you created. You can load this file using Microsoft Paint or any other program that can read bitmap images.

Creating Your Graph Library Routines

Now that you have learned the basic techniques of using the graph control, you are ready to build your database graph routine library. This library consists of a single form that contains a graph control and a menu of graphing options. It also has a module file containing a routine that loads the form, sets the graphing values using your data set, and displays the results. You'll be able to pass any valid Visual Basic recordset object to the graph routine and display any single-set, multipoint data set without any further modification of this library.

The Graph Form

First, start a new Visual Basic project.

Note: Make sure the Pinnacle-BPS graph control is on your Visual Basic toolbox. If not, refer back to the "Loading the Graph Control into the Visual Basic Toolbox" section for instructions on how to add it to your project's toolbox.

Add the graph control to your form. Also add the CommonDialog control to the form. You'll use this control to add file and print capabilities to the graphing library. You'll also need to add a menu to the form. Refer to Figure 12.8 and Tables 12.1 and 12.2 as guides for laying out this form.

Figure 12.8.
*Laying out the graph
library form.*

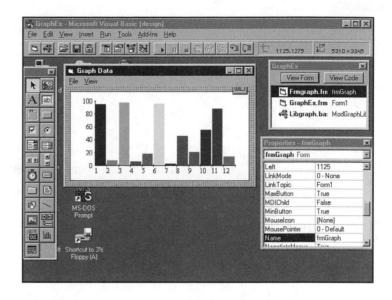

Table 12.1. The control table for the graph library form.

Control	Property	Setting
Form	Name	frmGraph
	Caption	Graph Data
	Height	3375
	Left	2145
	Top	1710
	Width	5280
Graph	Name	Graph1
	Height	2415
	Left	120
	Top	120
	Width	4935
	BorderStyle	1 - Fixed Single
CommonDialog	Name	CommonDialog1

Table 12.2. The Menu table for the graph library form.

Caption	Menu
&File	mnuFile
&Save...	mnuFileSave
&Copy	mnuFileCopy
-	mnuFileSpace0
&Print	mnuFilePrint
Print Set&Up	mnuFilePrintSetup
-	mnuFileSpace1
E&xit	mnuFileExit
&View	mnuView
&Pie Chart	mnuViewPie
&Bar Graph	mnuViewBar
&Line Chart	mnuViewLine
&Area Graph	mnuViewArea

You need to add some code to this form. But first, save this form as FRMGRAPH.FRM and use the project name GRAPHEX.VBP. Now, add Listing 12.6 to the Form_Resize event that allows users to resize the graph by resizing the form.

Listing 12.6. Adding code to the Form_Resize event.

```
Private Sub Form_Resize()
    Graph1.Left = Me.ScaleLeft + 60
    Graph1.TOP = Me.ScaleTop + 60
    Graph1.Width = Me.ScaleWidth - 120
    Graph1.Height = Me.ScaleHeight - 120
End Sub
```

Listing 12.7 goes in the mnuFileSave_Click event. This code prompts the user for a filename and saves the current graph to that filename.

Listing 12.7. Adding code to the mnuFileSave_Click event.

```
Private Sub mnuFileSave_Click()
    Dim cFile As String
    '
    ' set dialog properties
    '
    CommonDialog1.DefaultExt = ".bmp"
```

```
        CommonDialog1.DialogTitle = "Save Graph to File"
        CommonDialog1.Filter = "Bitmap (*.bmp)|*.bmp"
        CommonDialog1.ShowSave
        cFile = CommonDialog1.filename
        '
        If Len(Trim(cFile)) <> 0 Then
            Graph1.DrawMode = gphBlit    ' set to bitmap mode
            Graph1.ImageFile = cFile     ' set the file name
            Graph1.DrawMode = gphWrite   ' write the file
            Graph1.DrawMode = gphDraw    ' set to draw mode
        End If
End Sub
```

Listing 12.8 copies the current graph (as a bitmap image) to the Windows Clipboard object. You can then paste this image of the graph from the Clipboard to any other Windows program that allows image cut and paste operations (Microsoft Write, for example). Add Listing 12.8 to the mnuFileCopy_Click event.

Listing 12.8. Adding code to the `mnuFileCopy_Click` event.

```
Private Sub mnuFileCopy_Click()
    Graph1.DrawMode = gphBlit    ' set to bitmap mode
    Graph1.DrawMode = gphCopy    ' copy to clipboard
    Graph1.DrawMode = gphDraw    ' set to draw mode
End Sub
```

In order to print the graph, you'll use the PrintForm method. This method prints an exact copy of whatever is on the current form. The size of the form on-screen affects the size of the printer output. A maximized form on a 640×480 resolution screen will produce a graph that covers about half of a standard 8-1/2-inch by 11-inch sheet of paper. Add the following code to the mnuFilePrint_Click event:

```
Private Sub mnuFilePrint_Click()
    PrintForm    ' send form to default printer
End Sub
```

The next code line initiates the Printer Setup dialog box. Add this code to the mnuFilePrintSetup_Click event window:

```
Private Sub mnuFilePrintSetup_Click()
    CommonDialog1.ShowPrinter    ' run printer setup dialog
End Sub
```

The last File menu item to code is the Exit item. Add this single line to the mnuFileExit_Click event:

```
Private Sub mnuFileExit_Click()
    Unload Me    ' unload and exit
End Sub
```

401

Listings 12.9 through 12.12 allow users to change the GraphType property used to display the data. The first code snippet converts the on-screen display to a pie chart. Add this code to the mnuViewPie_Click event.

Listing 12.9. Adding code to the `mnuViewPie_Click` event

```
Private Sub mnuViewPie_Click()
    Graph1.GraphType = gphPie3D
    Graph1.DrawMode = gphDraw
End Sub
```

Listing 12.10 converts the display to a set of bars. Add this code to the mnuViewBar_Click event.

Listing 12.10. Adding code to the `mnuViewBar_Click` event.

```
Private Sub mnuViewBar_Click()
    Graph1.GraphType = gphBar3D
    Graph1.DrawMode = gphDraw
End Sub
```

The code snippet in Listing 12.11 converts the display to a set of lines. Add this code to the mnuViewLine_Click event.

Listing 12.11. Adding code to the `mnuViewLine_Click` event.

```
Private Sub mnuViewLine_Click()
    Graph1.GraphType = gphLine
    Graph1.DrawMode = gphDraw
End Sub
```

The code in Listing 12.12 converts the display into an area graph. Add this code to the mnuViewArea_Click event.

Listing 12.12. Adding code to the `mnuViewArea_Click` event.

```
Private Sub mnuViewArea_Click()
    Graph1.GraphType = gphArea
    Graph1.DrawMode = gphDraw
End Sub
```

That's all the code you need for the form. Save this form now. Next, you'll create the routine that calls this form.

The *ShowGraph* Routine

In order to display the form you just created, you need a single routine that takes a few parameters, sets all the graph control properties, and then calls the form up on-screen. That routine will be called ShowGraph. It accepts four parameters:

- ☐ nGphType: The initial graph type for the display.
- ☐ rsData: A populated Visual Basic recordset object that contains the data you want to display on the graph.
- ☐ cFldSet: The name of the column in the recordset that contains the values you'll load into the GraphData property of the graph control.
- ☐ cTitle: The title of the graph.

This is a simple graph tool that is capable of displaying a single-set, multipoint data set in the most commonly used graph types. Modifications can be made to this routine to add additional labeling, legends, and text. You could also add options in order to graph more than one set of data per graph. For now, just keep the project simple. When you complete this project, you can add your own modifications.

First, add a module to the current project (GRAPHEX.VBP) by selecting Insert | Module from the Visual Basic main menu. Set the module name to modLibRec. Add Listing 12.13 to the module.

Listing 12.13. Creating the ShowGraph function.

```
Sub ShowGraph(nGphType As Integer, rsData As Recordset,
➥cFldPoint As String, cTitle As String)
    '
    ' displays a graph form
    '
    ' inputs:
    '   nGphType    type of graph to display
    '               (see VB docs for valid types)
    '   rsData      populated recordset object
    '   cFldSet     field of recordset to use as graph set
    '   cTitle      Graph Title
    '
    '
    Dim nPoints As Integer
    Dim x As Integer
    '
    rsData.MoveLast
    nPoints = rsData.RecordCount
    '
    Load frmGraph    ' load the form w/o showing it
    frmGraph.Graph1.GraphType = nGphType
    frmGraph.Graph1.GraphTitle = cTitle
    frmGraph.Graph1.NumSets = 1
```

12

continues

Listing 12.13. continued

```
        frmGraph.Graph1.NumPoints = nPoints
        frmGraph.Graph1.AutoInc = 1
        '
        rsData.MoveFirst
        For x = 1 To nPoints
            frmGraph.Graph1.GraphData = rsData.Fields(cFldPoint)
            rsData.MoveNext
        Next x
        '
        frmGraph.Graph1.DrawMode = gphDraw
        frmGraph.Show 1
        '
End Sub
```

The first thing the code module in Listings 12.9 through 12.13 does is to get an accurate count of the total number of records in the recordset by using the MoveLast method to force the record pointer to the end of the set. Then the graph form is loaded without being shown, the initial graph control properties are set, and the data is loaded into the graph using the AutoInc property and a For...Next loop. Finally, the completed graph is updated and the form is shown on-screen. Save this module as LIBGRAPH.BAS.

That's all there is to it. You now have a reusable data graphing code library. In the next section, you'll test this library with a simple example.

Testing the Graph Library

You need to build a short program to test your new library. Suppose you have just been told that the marketing department needs a tool to display the year-to-date book sales by sales representative. The data already exists in a database, but there is no easy way to turn that data into a visual display that upper-level management can access on a regular basis. You have been asked to quickly put together a graphing front end for the sales data.

In order to complete the job, you need to open the database, create a snapshot recordset of the sales data using an SQL SELECT statement that will sum the sales by sales rep, and then pass the resultant data set to the graph library to display the graph. From there, users can select various graph styles and, if they wish, save the graph to disk, send it to the printer, or copy it to the Clipboard to paste in other documents.

Because you already have the completed graph library, you can complete your assignment with less than 15 lines of Visual Basic code.

First, if you don't have it up right now, start Visual Basic and create a new project. Add the graph control, if needed (see the "Loading the Graph Control into the Visual Basic Toolbox" section), and then add the FRMGRAPH.FRM and the LIBGRAPH.BAS files to the project using the File | Add File menu item from the Visual Basic main menu.

> **Note:** Be sure to add the Pinnacle-BPS graph control and the Microsoft common dialog control to the project before you add the FRMGRAPH.FRM file to the project. If you forget to add these two controls, Visual Basic returns an error message because it cannot find the controls in the Toolbox.

Add a single button to a blank form. Set its Name property to cmdRepSales and its Caption property to &RepSales. Add Listing 12.14 behind the button.

Listing 12.14. Adding code to the `cmdRepSales_Click` event.

```
Private Sub cmdRepSales_Click()
    Dim dbFile As DATABASE
    Dim rsFile As Recordset
    Dim cDBName As String
    Dim cRSName As String
    Dim nResult As Integer
    '
    Dim cGphField As String
    Dim cGphTitle As String
    '
    cDBName = App.Path+"\GRAPHDAT.MDB"
    cRSName = "SELECT SalesRep, SUM(Units) as UnitsSold
    ➥FROM BookSales GROUP BY SalesRep"
    cGphField = "UnitsSold"
    cGphTitle = "Units Sold by Sales Rep"
    '
    Set dbFile = OpenDatabase(cDBName)  ' open the database
    Set rsFile = dbFile.OpenRecordset(cRSName, dbOpenSnapshot) ' create dataset
    ShowGraph gphBar3D, rsFile, cGphField, cGphTitle
End Sub
```

12

This code example opens the database, populates a recordset using an SQL SELECT…GROUP BY statement, and then calls the ShowGaph routine. That's all there is to it! Save this form as GRAPHEX.FRM and run the project. After you click the single command button, you'll see the graph displayed on-screen. Your screen should look something like the one shown in Figure 12.9.

Figure 12.9.
A graph of book sales data by sales rep.

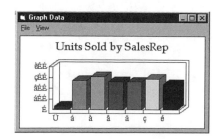

You have just completed your first database graphing project. Before you end your work on this library routine, add a few optional arguments to the ShowGraph procedure.

Adding Optional Arguments to the *ShowGraph* Routine

Visual Basic 4 allows you to declare optional arguments for your Sub and Function procedures, which means you don't have to pass all the values in the argument list each time you call the Sub or Function. You declare an argument optional by preceding it with the Optional keyword in the argument list. For example, to create a routine that has one required argument and one optional argument, you could write the following:

```
Sub MySub(cRequired as string, Optional cMaybe as variant)
```

Notice that the optional argument is at the end of the list. All optional arguments must appear at the end of the argument list. Also notice that the type declaration of the optional argument is Variant. Visual Basic requires that all optional arguments be declared as Variant type variables.

You can test to see whether an optional argument was passed to the procedure by using the IsMissing() function. The IsMissing function returns TRUE if the argument was *not* passed to the procedure. For example, to check to see whether the optional argument cMaybe was passed, you could use the following code:

```
If IsMissing(cMaybe) then
    cMaybe="Default"
End if
```

Take advantage of this new feature by adding four optional arguments to the ShowGraph routine:

☐ cFldLegend: This is the recordset column to use for setting the legends of the graph.

☐ cFldLabel: This is the recordset column to use for setting the labels of the graph.

☐ cLeftTitle: This is the string to display as the title on the left side of the graph.

☐ cBottomTitle: This is the string to display as the title at the bottom of the graph.

In order to add these new features, you need to modify the argument list at the start of the ShowGraph routine and then add the code to the routine to handle the four new arguments. The following is a listing of the modified ShowGraph routine. Add the new sections of code in Listing 12.15 to your existing routine.

Listing 12.15. Adding optional parameters to the ShowGraph function.

```
Sub ShowGraph(nGphType As Integer, rsData As Recordset, cFldPoint As String,
➥cTitle As String, Optional cFldLegend As Variant,
➥Optional cFldLabel As Variant, Optional cLeftTitle As Variant,
➥Optional cBottomTitle As Variant)
```

```
' displays a graph form
'
' inputs:
'   nGphType       type of graph to display
'                  (see VB docs for valid types)
'   rsData         populated recordset object
'   cFldPoint      field of recordset to use as graph set
'   cTitle         Graph Title
'
' optional args:
'   cFldLegend     field of recordset to use for legend set
'   cFldLabel      field of recordset to use for label set
'   cLeftTitle     title for the left of the graph
'   cBottomTitle   title for the bottom of the graph
'
'
On Error Resume Next     ' skip any error trapping
'
Dim nPoints As Integer
Dim x As Integer
'
rsData.MoveLast
nPoints = rsData.RecordCount
'
Load frmGraph    ' load the form w/o showing it
frmGraph.Graph1.GraphType = nGphType
frmGraph.Graph1.GraphTitle = cTitle
frmGraph.Graph1.NumPoints = nPoints
frmGraph.Graph1.NumSets = 1
frmGraph.Graph1.AutoInc = 1
'
' load data
'
rsData.MoveFirst
For x = 1 To nPoints
    frmGraph.Graph1.GraphData = rsData.Fields(cFldPoint)
    rsData.MoveNext
Next x
'
' load legends
'
If IsMissing(cFldLegend) = False Then
    rsData.MoveFirst
    frmGraph.Graph1.AutoInc = 1 'reset incrementing
    For x = 1 To nPoints
        frmGraph.Graph1.LegendText = rsData.Fields(cFldLegend)
        rsData.MoveNext
    Next x
End If
'
' load labels
'
If IsMissing(cFldLabel) = False Then
    rsData.MoveFirst
    frmGraph.Graph1.AutoInc = 1 'reset incrementing
```

continues

Listing 12.15. continued

```
            For x = 1 To nPoints
                frmGraph.Graph1.LabelText = rsData.Fields(cFldLabel)
                rsData.MoveNext
            Next x
        End If
        '
        ' add titles if they are passed
        If IsMissing(cLeftTitle) = False Then
            frmGraph.Graph1.LeftTitle = cLeftTitle
        End If
        '
        If IsMissing(cBottomTitle) = False Then
            frmGraph.Graph1.BottomTitle = cBottomTitle
        End If
        '
        ' draw it and display form
        '
        frmGraph.Graph1.DrawMode = gphDraw
        frmGraph.Show 1
        '
    End Sub
```

Notice that you added the new arguments to the declaration line and then added sections of code that test to see whether the parameter was passed and, if the argument exists, perform the requested task. Now, modify the cmdRepSales_Click event to pass the optional labels and the left and bottom titles to the ShowGraph routine. All you need to do is modify the line that calls ShowGraph. Replace the existing line with this:

```
ShowGraph gphBar3D, rsFile, cGphField, cGphTitle, cFldLabel:=
➥"SalesRep", cLeftTitle:=cGphField, cBottomTitle:="Sales Reps"
```

Notice that you actually told Visual Basic what optional argument you are passing (cFldLabel:="SalesRep"). This is optional as long as you are passing arguments in the same order as they are declared. In this case, because you are omitting the cFldLegend argument, you use the argument names to help Visual Basic figure out which optional parameters you want to use.

Tip: You can use *named arguments* for all your routines. When you use named arguments, you can pass parameters in any order. Refer to Visual Basic documentation for more information on the use of named and optional arguments.

Save and run the GRAPHEX.VBP project. When you click the SalesRep button, your screen should look like the one shown in Figure 12.10.

Figure 12.10.
The results of passing optional arguments to ShowGraph.

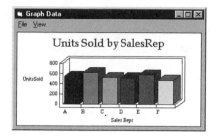

Now that you've completed your graph library routines, you can add some graphs to the CompanyMaster project you started last week.

Adding Graphs to the CompanyMaster Project

For the last project of the day, you'll add three graphs to the CompanyMaster project:

☐ A graph showing the actual year-to-date sales totals by region.

☐ A graph showing the budgeted year-to-date sales totals by region.

☐ A graph showing 10 percent of sales by customer.

First you'll have to add a new menu item to the CompanyMaster form that calls the graphs. Then you need to construct SQL statements that select the desired data and feed it to the graph library form.

Adding the Graph Menu Option

Adding the graph menu items is pretty easy. First, load the MASTER.VBP project from the CHAP12\MASTER subdirectory. Add the graph control to the project and then add the FRMGRAPH.FRM and LIBGRAPH.BAS files to the project.

Use Table 12.3 as a guide for adding the following menu items to the CompanyMaster menu.

Table 12.3. Added menu items for the CompanyMaster main menu.

Caption	Menu
&Graphs	mnuGraphs
Sales by &Region	mnuGraphsRegionSales
Sales by &Month	mnuGraphsMonthSales
Sales by &Customer	mnuGraphsCustSales

Now you need to add code to the form to make the calls to ShowGraph. For your first graph, you want to create a pie chart showing the total year's sales by region. The fields you have to work with in the SalesData table are CompanyName, Year, Month, Amount, and Region. The database contains records for each month for each customer, along with budget values for the year. These budget records are stored with a CompanyName of Budget.

To get the total customer sales by region, you would use the following SQL SELECT statement:

```
SELECT Region, SUM(Amount) AS SalesTotal
    FROM SalesData
    WHERE CompanyName<>'Budget'
    GROUP BY Region
```

This is the SQL statement you'll use to generate the snapshot object that is passed to the graph library. Place Listing 12.16 in the mnuGraphsRegionSales_Click event window.

Listing 12.16. Adding the code to the `mnuGraphRegionSales_Click` event.

```
Private Sub mnuGraphsRegionSales_Click()
    Dim rsFile As Recordset    ' rs object
    Dim dbFile As DATABASE     ' db object
    Dim cSQL As String         ' SQL statement
    Dim cField As String       ' graph data field
    Dim cTitle As String       ' graph title
    Dim cLegend As String      ' graph legend field
    Dim cLabel As String       ' graph label field
    '
    ' set the variables
    '
    cSQL = "SELECT Region, SUM(Amount) AS SalesTotal FROM
    ➥SalesData WHERE CompanyName<>'Budget' GROUP BY Region;"
    cField = "SalesTotal"         ' graph data
    cLegend = "Region"            ' graph legend
    cLabel = ""                   ' no labels
    cTitle = "Sales By Region"    ' graph title
    '
    ' set db objects
    '
    Set dbFile = OpenDatabase(App.Path + "\master.mdb")
    Set rsFile = dbFile.OpenRecordset(cSQL, dbOpenSnapshot)
    '
    ' run graph
    '
    ShowGraph gphPie3D, rsFile, cField, cTitle,
    ➥cFldLegend:=cLegend, cFldLabel:=cLabel
    '
End Sub
```

Notice that you used the SQL statement you defined earlier to create the snapshot object. The rest of the code should be familiar by now: You set several variables that are required for the database and/or the graph library. Next, you opened the database and created a snapshot data

object using the SQL statement, and then you called the graph routine. Now, save and run the project. When you select Graph | Sales by Region from the main menu, you should see a graph like the one shown in Figure 12.11.

Figure 12.11.
Displaying the Sales by Region graph.

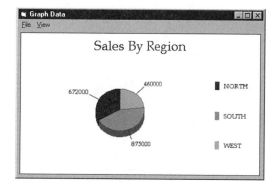

You can resize the form and the graph will resize as well. You can also use the menu on the graph to print, save, or copy the graph to the Clipboard.

> **Tip:** It is a good idea to use snapshot data objects for all your graphs and reports. Except in instances where the size of the result set is very large, snapshot objects are the fastest data object you can use for reporting and graphing.

12

Add the Sales by Month graph. This time, you need a line graph that will show the total sales by month. First, you need to construct the SQL statement. It should look like the following:

```
SELECT Month, SUM(Amount) AS SalesTotal
   FROM SalesData
   WHERE CompanyName<>'Budget'
   GROUP BY Month;
```

Now open the mnuGraphsMonthSales_Click event and add the code in Listing 12.17.

> **Tip:** Most of the code in this routine is identical to the code in the mnuGraphsRegionSales_Click event. If you are very careful, you can paste the code from the region sales routine into the month sales routine and then make minor modifications.

411

Listing 12.17. Adding the code for the `mnuGraphsMonthSales_Click` event.

```
Private Sub mnuGraphsMonthSales_Click()
    '
    Dim rsFile As Recordset
    Dim dbFile As DATABASE
    Dim cSQL As String
    Dim cField As String
    Dim cTitle As String
    Dim cLegend As String
    Dim cLabel As String
    '
    cSQL = "SELECT Month, SUM(Amount) AS SalesTotal FROM SalesData
    ➥WHERE CompanyName<>'Budget' GROUP BY Month;"
    cLegend = ""
    cLabel = "Month"
    cField = "SalesTotal"
    cTitle = "Sales By Month"
    '
    Set dbFile = OpenDatabase(App.Path + "\master.mdb")
    Set rsFile = dbFile.OpenRecordset(cSQL, dbOpenSnapshot)
    '
    ShowGraph gphLine, rsFile, cField, cTitle,
    ➥cFldLegend:=cLegend, cFldLabel:=cLabel
    '
End Sub
```

The only real difference here is the new SQL statement and the settings for the titles, labels, and legends. Save and run this code. Check your resultant graph with the one shown in Figure 12.12.

Figure 12.12.

The results of the Sales by Month graph.

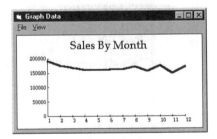

Finally, add the Sales by Company bar graph to the CompanyMaster project. Here is the SQL statement you need to produce a data set that contains the year-to-date sales figures by company:

```
SELECT CompanyName, SUM(Amount) AS SalesTotal
    FROM SalesData
    WHERE CompanyName<>'Budget'
    GROUP BY CompanyName;
```

Now add Listing 12.18 to the `mnuGraphsCustSales_Click` event.

Listing 12.18. Adding code to the `mnuGraphsCustSales_Click` event.

```
Private Sub mnuGraphsCustSales_Click()
    '
    Dim rsFile As Recordset
    Dim dbFile As DATABASE
    Dim cSQL As String
    Dim cField As String
    Dim cTitle As String
    Dim cLegend As String
    Dim cLabel As String
    '
    cSQL = "SELECT CompanyName, SUM(Amount) AS SalesTotal FROM SalesData
    ➡WHERE CompanyName<>'Budget' GROUP BY CompanyName;"
    cField = "SalesTotal"
    cLegend = "CompanyName"
    cLabel = "SalesTotal"
    cTitle = "Sales By Company"
    '
    Set dbFile = OpenDatabase(App.Path + "\master.mdb")
    Set rsFile = dbFile.OpenRecordset(cSQL, dbOpenSnapshot)
    '
    ShowGraph gphBar3D, rsFile, cField, cTitle,
    ➡cFldLegend:=cLegend, cFldLabel:=cLabel
    '
End Sub
```

Again, the only real differences are in the SQL statement and the titles, labels, and legends. Save and run the project. Your Sales by Company graph should look like the one in Figure 12.13.

Figure 12.13.
The results of the Sales by Company graph.

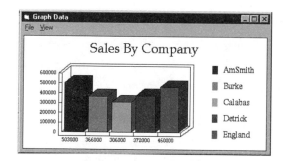

Summary

Today you have learned how to use the graph control that ships with Visual Basic in order to create visual displays of your data tables. You have learned how to add the control to your project and how to load the graph control with data points, titles, legends, and labels.

Also, you built a graph library that you can use to display virtually any data set in a variety of graph formats. This library lets you save the graph to disk, send the graph to the printer, or copy the graph to the Windows Clipboard for placement in other Windows programs via the Paste Special operation.

While building the graph library, you learned how to declare and use optional parameters for your Visual Basic Sub and Function procedures.

Finally, you used the new graph library to add three graphs to the CompanyMaster project.

Quiz

1. List the advantages of including graphics in your Visual Basic database applications.

2. Describe the purpose of the NumSets and NumPoints properties of the graph control.

3. When you are using the predefined constants for graph types, is the following code correct?

   ```
   Graph1.GraphType = graphBar3d
   ```

4. What character separates data points in a series when the QuickData property is used? What character(s) separate a set of points?

5. Is the following code correct?

   ```
   Graph1.GraphTitle = "Sales for October"
   ```

6. What do the following DrawModes constants do?

   ```
   GphBlit
   gphCopy
   gphDraw
   ```

7. What Visual Basic data type must be used for optional Sub and Function arguments?

8. What function can you use to determine whether an optional argument was passed?

9. What recordset type should you use for graphics applications?

10. Write code to get a count of records in a data set that will be used for graphing.

Exercises

Assume that you are an analyst for your regional airport. The Manager of Operations wants information on passenger activity throughout the year. He is an extremely busy individual who does not understand database applications. In order to help him perform his job better, you have decided to create some graphs for him to review.

Perform the following steps in completing this project:

1. Build a database using Visdata or Data Manager. Name this database 12ABCEX.MDB.

2. Build a table in this database and name it Activity. Include three fields: Airline (TEXT 10), Month (INTEGER), and Passengers (INTEGER).

3. Insert the following records into your table:

Airline	Month	Passengers
ABC	1	2562
ABC	2	4859
ABC	3	4235
ABC	4	4897
ABC	5	5623
ABC	6	4565
ABC	7	5466
ABC	8	2155
ABC	10	5454
ABC	11	5488
ABC	12	5456
ABC	9	5468
LMN	1	1956
LMN	2	2135
LMN	3	5221
LMN	4	2153
LMN	5	2154
LMN	6	5125
LMN	7	2135
LMN	8	5465
LMN	9	5555
LMN	10	2536
LMN	11	2153
LMN	12	2168
XYZ	1	10251
XYZ	2	12123
XYZ	3	10258
XYZ	4	12000
XYZ	5	21564
XYZ	6	21321
XYZ	7	14564
XYZ	8	12365
XYZ	9	21356
XYZ	10	21357
XYZ	11	21321
XYZ	12	12365

12

4. Start a new Visual Basic project that uses the LIBGRAPH.BAS module you have created today. Build a form and add three command buttons: cmdPie, cmdLine, and cmdBar.

5. Display the following graphs when each button is pressed:

   cmdPie: Displays a 3-D pie chart that shows comparative activity for the first month.

   cmdLine: Displays a line graph that shows total passenger activity by month. Include Passengers as the title on the vertical axis and Month as the title for the horizontal axis.

   cmdBar: Displays a 3-D bar graph for the activity of ABC Airlines for the entire year.

6. Examine the charts you have built. Notice how much easier it is to ascertain trends from these graphs than it is from the data entry table in Exercise 3.

WEEK
2

Data-Bound List Boxes, Grids, and Subforms

Today you'll learn about the use of data-bound lists, combo boxes, and grids in your Visual Basic 4 database applications. Before Visual Basic 4, this was an arduous task that required a great deal of coding and program maintenance to perform. Now, Visual Basic 4 ships with the tools you need to add lists, combo boxes, and data grids to your project with very little coding.

You'll learn how to add features to your data entry forms that provide pick lists that support and enforce the database relationships already defined in your data tables. You'll also learn the difference between data lists and combo boxes, and you'll learn where it's appropriate to use them.

We will also show you how to easily add a data grid to your form to show more than one record at a time in a table form. This grid can be used for display only, or for data entry, too. We'll show you how to decide which is the best method for your project.

After you learn how to use the data-bound list, combo box, and grid, you'll use them to create a data entry Subform that combines all three controls on a single form.

The Data-Bound List and Combo Boxes

The data-bound list and combo controls are used in conjunction with the data control to allow you to display multiple rows of data in the same control. This provides you with a pick list of values displayed in a list or combo box. You can use these types of controls on your data entry forms to speed data entry, provide tighter data entry validation and control, and give users suggested correct values for the data entry field.

Setting up data-bound lists and combo boxes are a bit trickier than standard data-bound controls. But once you get the hang of setting up data-bound list and combo boxes, you'll want to use them in every data entry screen you can.

Using the Data-Bound List Box

Although the data-bound list control looks like the standard list control, there are several differences between the two. The data-bound list control has six new properties that provide the data-binding aspects and are not found in the standard list control. The first two of these properties are the RowSource and ListField properties of the data-bound list control.

☐ RowSource: The name of the Recordset object that is providing the data set used to fill the data-bound list box.

☐ ListField: The name of the column in the RowSource data set that is used to fill the list box. This is the display field for the list.

These two properties are used to bind the list control to a data control. Once these two properties are set, Visual Basic 4 automatically populates the list control for you when you open the data entry form.

Let's start a new project and illustrate the data-bound list control. Once you start the new project, you must make sure you have added the data-bound list controls to your project. Select the Tools | Custom Controls item from the Visual Basic 4 main menu. Locate and select the Microsoft Data Bound List Controls item. Your screen should look like the one in Figure 13.1.

Figure 13.1.
Adding the data-bound list controls to your project.

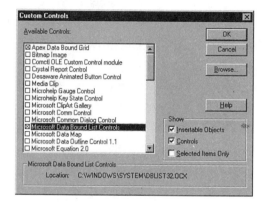

Now you need to add the data-bound list control, a standard data control, and two labels and text boxes. Use Table 13.1 and Figure 13.2 as guides as you build your first data-bound list project. Make sure to save your work periodically. Save the form as CH1301.FRM, and the project as CH1301.VBP.

 Tip: If you lay out the controls in the order in which they are listed in the table, you'll be able to use the down arrows of most of the property fields to get a selection list for the field names, and so on. This will save you some typing.

13

Table 13.1. The controls for the CH1301.VBP project.

Controls	Properties	Settings
Form	Name	frmCh1301
	Caption	Data-Bound List Controls
	Height	2670
	Left	1215

continues

419

Table 13.1. continued

Controls	Properties	Settings
	Top	1170
	Width	4995
DataControl	Name	Data1
	Caption	Data1
	DatabaseName	C:\TYSDBVB\CHAP13\CH1301.MDB
	Height	300
	Left	120
	RecordsetType	2—Snapshot
	RecordSource	ValidNames
	Top	1860
	Width	1875
DBList	Name	DBList1
	Height	1620
	Left	120
	RowSource	Data1
	ListField	NameText
	Top	120
	Width	1875
Label	Name	Label1
	Alignment	1—Right justify
	BorderStyle	1—Fixed Single
	Caption	List Field:
	Height	300
	Left	2160
	Top	120
	Width	1200
Label	Name	Label2
	Alignment	1—Right Justify
	BorderStyle	1—Fixed Single
	Caption	Text:
	Height	300
	Left	2160

Controls	Properties	Settings
	Top	540
	Width	1200
Text Box	Name	Text1
	Height	300
	Left	3540
	Top	120
	Width	1200
Text Box	Name	Text2
	Height	300
	Left	3540
	Top	540
	Width	1200
Command Button	Name	cmdGetList
	Caption	&Get List
	Height	300
	Left	2160
	Top	1860
	Width	1200

Figure 13.2.
Laying out the CH1301 form.

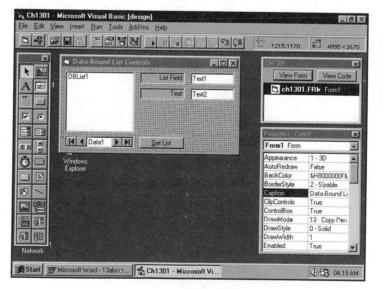

Notice that in the preceding table, we have added a single data control to open the database and create a Snapshot object of the ValidNames table. It's always a good idea to use Snapshot objects as the RowSource for data-bound lists and combo boxes. Snapshot objects are static views of the data set and, even though they take up more workstation memory than Dynaset objects, they run faster. Notice also that we set the ListField property of the data-bound list to NameText. This fills the control with the values stored in the NameText column of the data set.

Now you need to add two lines of code to the project. Open the cmdGetList_Click event and enter the following lines of code:

```
Private Sub cmdGetList_Click()
    Text1 = DBList1.ListField
    Text2 = DBList1.TEXT
End Sub
```

These two lines of code update the text box controls each time you press the GetList button on the form. That way you are able to see the current values of the ListField and Text properties of the data-bound list control.

Save the form as CH1301.FRM and the project as CH1301.VBP. Now run the project. When the form first comes up, you see the list box already filled with all the values in the NameText column of the data set (that is, the ListField used for the DBList). Select one of the items in the list box by clicking on it. Now press the GetList button. You'll see the two text controls updated with the ListField and Text values of the list control. Your screen should look like the one in Figure 13.3.

Figure 13.3.

Running the CH1301.VBP project.

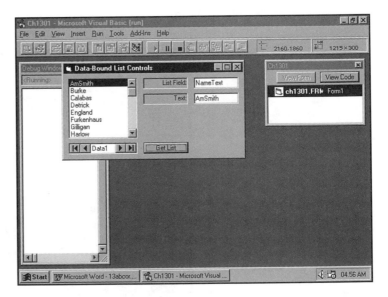

The data-bound list control has two more properties that you need to know. These are the properties that you can use to create an output value based on the item selected from the list. The two properties are

☐ BoundColumn: The name of the column in the RowSource data set that is used to provide the output of the list selection. This can be the same column designated in the ListField property, or it can be any other column in the RowSource data set.

☐ BoundText: The value of the column designated by the BoundColumn property. This is the actual output of the list selection.

Usually, data-bound lists present the user with a familiar set of names. The user can pick from these names, and then the program uses the selection to locate a more computer-like ID or code represented by the familiar name selected by the user. The table created for this example contains just such information.

Set the BoundColumn property of the data-bound list control to point to the NameID column of the ValidNames data set. Select the data-bound list control, and then press F4 to bring up the property window. Now locate the BoundColumn property and set it to NameID.

Add two more labels and text boxes to display the new properties. Do this by selecting the existing two labels and the two text controls all as a set. Then select Edit | Copy. This places the four selected controls on the Clipboard. Now select Edit | Paste from the Visual Basic 4 main menu. This places copies of the controls on your new form. Answer Yes to the prompts that ask if you want to create a control array. Set the caption properties of the two new labels to Bound Column: and Bound Text:. Use Figure 13.4 as a guide in laying out the new controls.

Figure 13.4.
Adding new controls to the CH1301.VBP project.

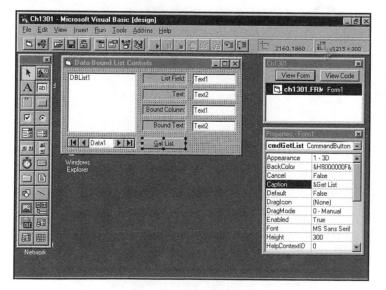

Finally, modify the code in the `cmdGetList_Click` event to match the following code. This shows you the results of the new BoundColumn and BoundText properties.

```
Private Sub cmdGetList_Click()
    Text1(0) = DBList1.ListField
    Text2(0) = DBList1.TEXT
    Text1(1) = DBList1.BoundColumn
    Text2(1) = DBList1.BoundText
End Sub
```

Notice that you added the array references to the code to account for the new control arrays. Now save and run the project. When you select an item from the list and click the GetList button, you'll see the BoundColumn and BoundText properties displayed in the appropriate text boxes, as shown in Figure 13.5.

Figure 13.5.

Displaying the new BoundColumn and BoundText properties.

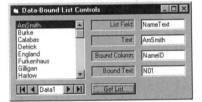

Note: You can also activate the `Get List` event by entering `cmdGetList_Click` in the `Dbl_Click` event of DBList. The user can get the same results by selecting the command button, or by double-clicking on the item in the list. This type of call provides a quick way of adding functionality to your code. You don't need to enter or maintain the code in both events.

The data that is produced by the BoundText property can be used to update another column in a separate table. The easiest way to do this is to add a second data control and link the data-bound list control to that second data control. You can do this by setting the following two properties of the data-bound list control.

☐ DataSource: The data set that is updated by the output of the data-bound list control. This is the data control used to open the destination `Recordset`.

☐ DataField: The name of the column in the `Recordset` referred to by the DataSource property.

Now let's add a second data control to the form and a bound input control that will be updated by the data-bound list. First, add a data control. Set its DatabaseName property to C:\TYSDBVB\CHAP13\CH1301.MDB and its RecordSource property to Destination. Also, set the EOFAction property of the Data2 data control to AddNew. Now add a text control to

the project. Set its DataSource property to Data2 and its DataField property to NameID. Refer to Figure 13.6 as a layout guide.

Figure 13.6.
Adding a second data control and text control.

Before you save and run the project, set the DataSource and DataField properties of the data-bound list control. Set these to Data2 and NameID, respectively. This tells the list control to automatically update the Destination.NameID field. Now, each time a user selects an item in the list, and then saves the data set of the *second* control, the designated field of the second data set is automatically updated with the value in the BoundColumn property of the data-bound list.

Save and run the project. This time, select the first item in the list by clicking on it. Now click on the GetList button to bring up the list properties in the text boxes. Force the second data control to save its contents by repositioning the record pointer by clicking the left-most arrow to force the second data set to the first record in the set. You should now see that the second data set, Destination, has been updated by the value in the BoundColumn property of the data-bound list. Your screen should look like the one in Figure 13.6.

Do this a few times to add records to the Destination table. Also notice that each time you move the record pointer of the Destination table, the data-bound control reads the value in the bound column and moves the list pointer to highlight the related NameText field. You now have a fully functional data-bound list box!

Using the Data-Bound Combo Box

The data-bound combo box works very much the same as the data-bound list control. The only difference is the way the data is displayed. The data-bound combo control can be used as a basic data entry text box with added validation. Allowing experienced users to type values they know are correct can speed up the data entry process. Also, new users are able to scan the list of valid entries until they learn them. The data-bound combo is an excellent data entry control.

Let's build a new project that shows how you can use the data-bound combo box to create friendly data entry forms. Start a new Visual Basic 4 project. Use Table 13.2 and Figure 13.7 as guides as you build your new form. Save your form as CH1302.FRM, and the project as CH1302.VBP.

Table 13.2. The controls for the CH1302.VBP project.

Controls	Properties	Settings
Form	Name	frmCh1302
	Caption	Data Bound ComboBox
	Height	2500
	Left	2750
	Top	2500
	Width	3000
DataControl	Name	dtaDestination
	Caption	Destination
	DatabaseName	C:\TYSDBVB\CHAP13\CH1301.MDB
	EOFAction	2—AddNew
	Height	300
	Left	120
	RecordsetType	1—Dynaset
	RecordSource	Destination
	Top	960
	Width	2535
DataControl	Name	dtaValidStates
	Caption	Valid States
	DatabaseName	C:\TYSDBVB\CHAP13\CH1301.MDB
	Height	300
	Left	120
	RecordsetType	2—Snapshot
	RecordSource	"ValidStates"
	Visible	0—False
	Width	2535
DataControl	Name	dtaValidNames
	Caption	Valid Names
	DatabaseName	C:\TYSDBVB\CHAP13\CH1301.MDB
	Height	300
	Left	120

Controls	Properties	Settings
	RecordsetType	2—Snapshot
	RecordSource	ValidNames
	Top	1680
	Visible	0—False
	Width	2535
DBCombo	Name	DBCombo1
	DataSource	dtaDestination
	DataField	StateCode
	Height	300
	Left	120
	RowSource	dtaValidStates
	ListField	StateName
	BoundColumn	StateCode
	Top	120
	Width	1200
DBCombo	Name	DBCombo2
	DataSource	dtaDestination
	DataField	NameID
	Height	300
	Left	120
	Top	540
	Width	1200
	RowSource	dtaValidNames
	ListField	NameText
	BoundColumn	NameID
Label	Name	Label1
	BorderStyle	1—Fixed Single
	DataSource	dtaDestination
	DataField	StateCode
	Height	300
	Left	1440

continues

13

Table 13.2. continued

Controls	Properties	Settings
	Top	120
	Width	1200
Label	Name	Label2
	BorderStyle	1—Fixed Single
	DataSource	dtaDestination
	DataField	NameID
	Height	300
	Left	1440
	Top	540
	Width	1200

Figure 13.7.
Laying out the CH1302.VBP project.

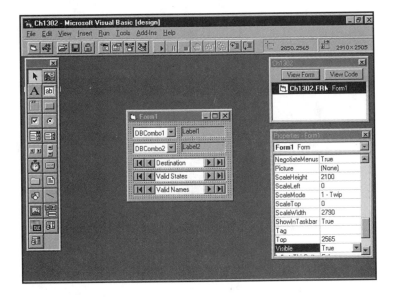

You need to add two lines of code to the project before it's complete. The following lines force Visual Basic 4 to update the form controls as soon as the user makes a selection in the combo box.

```
Private Sub DBCombo1_Click(Area As Integer)
    Label1 = DBCombo1.BoundText
End Sub
```

```
Private Sub DBCombo2_Click(Area As Integer)
    Label2 = DBCombo2.BoundText
End Sub
```

Save the form as CH1302.FRM and the project as CH1302.VBP. Now run the project and check your screen against the one in Figure 13.8.

Figure 13.8.
Running the CH1302.VBP project.

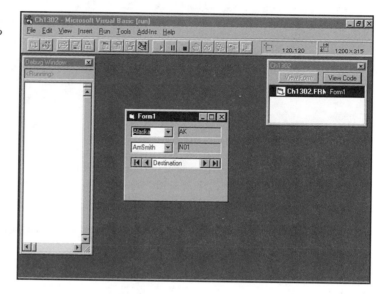

You can make selections in either of the two combo boxes and see that the label controls are updated automatically. Also, you can move through the data set using the data control arrow buttons and watch the two combo boxes automatically update as each record changes.

Deciding When to Use the List Box or Combo Box

The choice between list and combo controls depends on the type of data-entry screen you have and the amount of real estate available to your data entry form. Typically, use lists where you want to show users more than one possible entry. This encourages them to scroll through the list and locate the desired record. The data-bound list control doesn't allow users to enter their own values to the list. Therefore, you should not use the data-bound list control if you want to allow users to enter new values to the list.

The data-bound combo box is very good when you are short on form space. You can provide the functionality of a list box without using as much space. Also, combo boxes have the added benefit of allowing users to type in their selected values. This is very useful for users who are

13

performing heads-down data entry. They type the exact values right at the keyboard without using the mouse or checking a list. Also, novices can use the same form to learn about valid list values without slowing down the more experienced users.

The Data-Bound Grid

The data-bound grid control in Visual Basic 4 adds new power and flexibility to your database programs. You can now very easily provide grid access to any available database. You can provide simple display-only access for use with summary data and on-screen reports. You can also provide editing capabilities to your data grid including modify only, add rights, or delete rights.

Creating Your First Data-Bound Grid Form

It's really quite easy to create a data-bound grid form. First, start a new Visual Basic 4 project. Next, make sure you add the data-bound grid tool to your list of custom controls. To do this, select Tools | Custom Controls from the Visual Basic 4 main menu. Locate and select the Apex Data Bound Grid Control. Your screen should resemble Figure 13.9.

Figure 13.9.

Adding the data-bound grid control to your project.

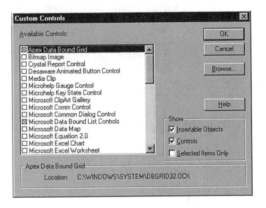

Now drop a standard data control on the form. Place it at the bottom of the form. Set the DatabaseName property to C:\TYSDBVB\CHAP13\CH1303.MDB and the RecordSource property to HeaderTable. Now place the data-bound grid tool on the form and set its DataSource property to Data1. That's all there is to it. Now save the form as CH1303.FRM and the project as CH1303.VBP and run the project. Your screen should look like the one in Figure 13.10.

You can move through the grid by clicking on the left margin of the grid control. You can also move through the grid by clicking on the navigation arrows of the data control. If you select a cell in the grid, you can edit that cell. As soon as you leave the row, that cell is updated by Visual

Basic 4. Right now, you cannot add or delete records from the grid. You'll add those features in the next example.

Figure 13.10.
Running the first data-bound grid project.

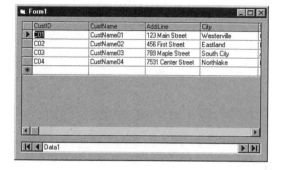

Adding and Deleting Records with the Data-Bound Grid

It's very easy to include add and delete capabilities to the data grid. Bring up the same project you just completed. Select the data grid control and press F4 to bring up the Properties window. Locate the AllowAddNew property and the AllowDelete property and set them to True. You now have add and delete power within the grid.

Before you run this project, make two other changes. Set the Visible property of the data control to False. Because you can navigate through the grid using scroll bars and the mouse, you don't need the data control arrow buttons. Second, set the Align property of the grid control to Top. This forces the grid to hug the top and sides of the form whenever it is resized.

Now save and run the project. Notice that you can resize the columns. Figure 13.11 shows the form resized with several columns adjusted.

Figure 13.11.
Resizing form and columns of a data grid control.

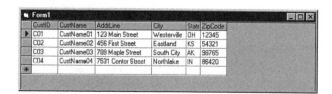

To add a record to the data grid, all you need to do is place the cursor at the first field in the empty row at the bottom of the grid and start typing. Visual Basic 4 creates a new line for you and allows you to enter data. Take note how the record pointer turns into a pencil as you type. Use Figure 13.12 as a guide. When you leave the line, Visual Basic 4 saves the record to the data set.

Figure 13.12.

Adding a record to the data grid.

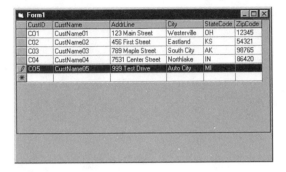

Setting Other Design-Time Properties of the Data Grid

The problem with resizing the form at runtime is that the moment you close the form, all the column settings are lost. You can prevent this by resizing the form at design time. Select the data grid control and press the right (alternate) mouse button. This brings up the context menu. Select Retrieve Fields. This loads the column names of the data set into the grid control. Select Edit from this menu. Now you can resize the columns of the control. The dimensions of these columns are stored in the control and used each time the form is loaded.

You can modify the names of the column headers at design time by using the built-in tabbed property sheet. To do this, click the alternate mouse button while the grid control is selected. When the context menu appears, select Properties from this menu. You should now see a series of tabs that allow you to set several grid-level and column-level properties. (See Figure 13.13.)

Figure 13.13.

Using the data grid tabbed properties page.

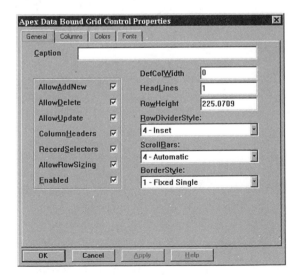

Trapping Events for the Data Grid Control

The data grid control has several unique events that you can use to monitor user actions in your graph. The following events can be used to check the contents of your data table before you allow the user to continue:

- ☐ BeforeInsert: This event occurs before a new row is inserted into the grid. Use this event to confirm that the user wants to add a new record.

- ☐ AfterInsert: This event occurs right after a new row has been inserted into the grid. Use this event to perform clean-up chores after a new record has been added.

- ☐ BeforeUpdate: This event occurs before the data grid writes the changes to the data control. Use this event to perform data validation at the record level.

- ☐ AfterUpdate: This event occurs after the changed data has been written to the data control. Use this event to perform miscellaneous chores after the grid has been updated.

- ☐ BeforeDelete: This event occurs before the selected record(s) are deleted from the grid. Use this event to perform confirmation chores before deleting data.

- ☐ AfterDelete: This event occurs after the user has already deleted the data from the grid. Use this event to perform related chores once the grid has been updated.

You can use the events listed here to perform field and record-level validation and force user confirmation on critical events, such as adding a new record or deleting an existing record. Let's add some code to the CH1303.VBP project to illustrate the use of these events.

The Add Record Events

First, add code that monitors the adding of new records to the grid. Select the grid control and open the DBGrid1_BeforeInsert event. Add the code in Listing 13.1.

Listing 13.1. Code to monitor addition of new records to a data-bound grid.

```
Private Sub DBGrid1_BeforeInsert(Cancel As Integer)
    '
    ' make user confirm add operation
    '
    Dim nResult As Integer
    '
    nResult = MsgBox("Do you want to add a new record?",
    ➥vbInformation + vbYesNo, "DBGrid.BeforeInsert")
    If nResult = vbNo Then
        Cancel = True    ' cancel add
    End If
End Sub
```

In Listing 13.1, you present a message to the user to confirm the intention to add a new record to the set. If the answer is No, the add operation is canceled.

Now let's add code that tells the user the add operation has been completed. Add the following code in the `DBGrid1_AfterInsert` event window.

```
Private Sub DBGrid1_AfterInsert()
    '
    ' tell user what you just did!
    '
    MsgBox "New record written to data set!", vbInformation,
    ➥ "DBGrid.AfterInsert"
End Sub
```

Now save and run the project. Go to the last row in the grid. Begin entering a new record. As soon as you press the first key, the confirmation message appears. (See Figure 13.14.)

Figure 13.14.
Attempting to add a record to the grid.

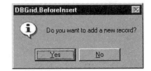

After you fill in all the columns and attempt to move to another record in the grid, you'll see the message telling you that the new record was added to the data set.

The Update Record Events

Now add some code that monitors attempts to update existing records. Add Listing 13.2 to the `DBGrid1.BeforeUpdate` event.

Listing 13.2. Code to monitor for attempted data updates.

```
Private Sub DBGrid1_BeforeUpdate(Cancel As Integer)
    '
    ' make user confirm update operation
    '
    Dim nResult As Integer
    '
    nResult = MsgBox("Write any changes to data set?",
    ➥ vbInformation + vbYesNo, "DBGrid.BeforeUpdate")
    If nResult = vbNo Then
        Cancel = True    ' ignore changes
        DBGrid1.ReBind   ' reset all values
    End If
End Sub
```

This code looks similar to the code used to monitor the add record events. The only thing different here is you that you force the ReBind method to refresh the data grid after the canceled attempt to update the record.

Now add the code to confirm the update of the record. Add the following code to the DBGrid1.AfterUpdate event.

```
Private Sub DBGrid1_AfterUpdate()
    '
    ' tell 'em!
    '
    MsgBox "The record has been updated.", vbInformation, "DBGrid.AfterUpdate"
End Sub
```

Now save and run the project. When you press a key in any column of an existing record, you'll see the message asking you to confirm the update. When you move off the record, you'll see a message telling you the record has been updated.

The Delete Record Events

Now add some events to track any attempts to delete existing records. Place Listing 13.3 in the DBGrid1.BeforeDelete event.

Listing 13.3. Code to track for record deletes.

```
Private Sub DBGrid1_BeforeDelete(Cancel As Integer)
    '
    ' force user to confirm delete operation
    '
    Dim nResult As Integer
    '
    nResult = MsgBox("Delete the current record?",
    ➥vbInformation + vbYesNo, "DBGrid.BeforeDelete")
    If nResult = vbNo Then
        Cancel = True    ' cancel delete op
    End If
End Sub
```

Again, no real news here. Simply ask the user to confirm the delete operation. If the answer is No, the operation is canceled. Now add the code to report the results of the delete. Put this code in the DBGrid1.AfterDelete event.

```
Private Sub DBGrid1_AfterDelete()
    '
    ' tell user the news!
    '
    MsgBox "Record has been deleted", vbInformation, "DBGrid.AfterDelete"
End Sub
```

13

Now save and run the project. Select an entire record by clicking on the left margin of the grid. This highlights all the columns in the row. (See Figure 13.15.) To delete the record, press the Delete key or Ctrl+X. When the message pops up asking you to confirm the delete, answer No to cancel.

Figure 13.15.
Attempting to delete a record from the grid.

Column-Level Events

Several column-level events are available for the data grid. The following are only two of them:

☐ `BeforeColUpdate`: This event occurs before the column is updated with any changes made by the user. Use this event to perform data validation before the update occurs.

☐ `AfterColUpdate`: This event occurs after the column has been updated with user changes. Use this event to perform other duties after the value of the column has been updated.

 Note: Refer to the Visual Basic 4 documentation for a list of all the events associated with the DBGrid control.

These events work just like the `BeforeUpdate` and `AfterUpdate` events seen earlier. However, instead of occurring whenever the record value is updated, the `BeforeColUpdate` and `AfterColUpdate` events occur whenever a column value is changed. This gives you the ability to perform field-level validation within the data grid.

Add some code in the `BeforeColUpdate` event to force the user to confirm the update of a column. Open the `DBGrid.BeforeColUpdate` event and enter the code in Listing 13.4.

Listing 13.4. Code to request confirmation on column updates.

```
Private Sub DBGrid1_BeforeColUpdate(ByVal ColIndex As Integer,
➥ OldValue As Variant, Cancel As Integer)
    '
    ' ask user for confirmation
    '
    Dim nResult As Integer
    '
    nResult = MsgBox("Write changes to Column", vbInformation + vbYesNo,
    ➥ "DBGrid.BeforeColUpdate")
```

```
    If nResult = vbNo Then
        Cancel = False       ' cancel change & get old value
    End If
End Sub
```

Now add the code that tells the user the column has been updated as requested. Place the following code in the DBGrid1.AfterColUpdate event.

```
Private Sub DBGrid1_AfterColUpdate(ByVal ColIndex As Integer)
    '
    ' tell user
    '
    MsgBox "Column has been updated", vbInformation, "DBGrid.AfterColUpdate"
End Sub
```

Save and run the project. Now, each time you attempt to alter a column, you are asked to confirm the column update. (See Figure 13.16.)

Figure 13.16.
Updating a grid column.

You can also see a message when you leave the column telling you that the data has been changed.

Using the Data Grid to Create a Subform

Use the data grid to create one of the most common forms of data entry screens, the Subform. Subforms are data entry forms that actually contain two forms within the same screen. Usually, Subforms are used to combine standard form layout data entry screens with view-only or view and edit lists. For example, if you want to create a form that shows the customer information (name, address, and so on) at the top of the form and the list of invoices outstanding for that customer at the bottom of the form, you have a Subform type entry screen.

Typically, Subforms are used to display data tables linked via relationship definitions. In the case just mentioned, the customer information is probably in a single master table, and the invoice data is probably in a related list table that is linked via the customer ID or some other unique field. When you have these types of relationships, Subforms make an excellent way to present data.

If you spend much time programming databases, you'll meet up with the need for a good Subform strategy. Let's go through the process of designing and coding a Subform using Visual Basic 4 data-bound controls, especially the data grid.

13

Designing the Subform

For example, you have a database that already exists, CH1303.MDB, which contains two tables. The first table is called Header. It contains all the information needed to fill out a header on an invoice or monthly statement, such as CustID, CustName, Address, City, State, and Zip. There is also a table called SalesData. This table contains a list of each invoice currently on file for the customer, and it includes the CustID, Invoice Number, Invoice Description, and the Invoice Amount. The two tables are linked via the CustID field that exists in both tables. There is a one-to-many (Header-to-SalesData) relationship defined for the two tables.

You need to design a form that allows users to browse through the master table (Header), displaying all the address information for review and update. At the same time, you need to provide the user with a view of the invoice data on the same screen. As the customer records are changed, the list of invoices must also be changed. You need a Subform.

Laying Out and Coding the Subform with Visual Basic 4

Start a new project in Visual Basic 4. Lay out the Header table information at the top of the form and the SalesTable information in a grid at the bottom of the form. You need two data controls (one for the Header table and one for the SalesTable), one grid for the sales data, and several label and input controls for the Header data. Use Table 13.3 and Figure 13.17 as guides as you lay out the Subform.

The controls table and Figure 13.17 contain almost all the information you need to design and code the Visual Basic 4 Subform. Notice that all the text box and label controls have the same name. These are part of a control array. Lay out the first label/text box pair. Then use the alternate mouse button to copy and repeatedly paste these two buttons until you have all the fields you need for your form.

Tip: Not only is it easier to build forms using data controls because you save a lot of typing, but it also saves workstation resources. To Visual Basic 4, each control is a resource that must be allotted memory for tracking. Control arrays are counted as a single resource, no matter how many members you have in the array.

Table 13.3. The controls for the Subform project.

Controls	Properties	Settings
Form	Name	frmSubForm
	Caption	Header/Sales SubForm
	Height	4545
	Left	1395
	Top	1335
	Width	6180
Data Control	Name	Data1
	Caption	Header Data Set
	DatabaseName	C:\TYSDBVB\CHAP13\CH1303.MDB
	EOFAction	2—AddNew
	Height	300
	Left	120
	RecordsetType	1—Dynaset
	RecordSource	HeaderTable
	Top	1800
	Width	5835
Data Control	Name	Data2
	Caption	Sales Data Set
	DatabaseName	C:\TYSDBVB\CHAP13\CH1303.MDB
	EOFAction	2—AddNew
	Height	300
	Left	120
	RecordsetType	1—Dynaset
	RecordSource	SalesTable
	Top	3780
	Visible	0—False
	Width	5835
Text Box	Name	Text1
	DataSource	Data1
	DataField	CustID

continues

Table 13.3. continued

Controls	Properties	Settings
	Height	300
	Left	1440
	Top	120
	Width	1200
Text Box	Name	Text1
	DataSource	Data1
	DataField	CustName
	Height	300
	Left	1440
	Top	540
	Width	2400
Text Box	Name	Text1
	DataSource	Data1
	DataField	AddrLine
	Height	300
	Left	1440
	Top	960
	Width	2400
Text Box	Name	Text1
	DataSource	Data1
	DataField	City
	Height	300
	Left	1440
	Top	1380
	Width	2400
Text Box	Name	Text1
	DataSource	Data1
	DataField	StateCode
	Height	300
	Left	4020

Controls	Properties	Settings
	Top	1380
	Width	600
Text Box	Name	Text1
	DataSource	Data1
	DataField	ZipCode
	Height	300
	Left	4740
	Top	1380
	Width	1200
Label	Name	Label1
	BorderStyle	1—Fixed Single
	Caption	CustID:
	Height	300
	Left	120
	Top	120
	Width	1200
Label	Name	Label1
	BorderStyle	1—Fixed Single
	Caption	Cust Name:
	Height	300
	Left	120
	Top	540
	Width	1200
Label	Name	Label1
	BorderStyle	1—Fixed Single
	Caption	Address Line
	Height	300
	Left	120
	Top	960
	Width	1200

continues

Table 13.3. continued

Controls	Properties	Settings
Label	Name	Label1
	Borderstyle	1—Fixed Single
	Caption	City/State/Zip
	Height	300
	Left	120
	Top	1380
	Width	1200
MSDBGrid	Name	DBGrid1
	Height	1455
	Left	120
	Top	2222
	Width	5835

Figure 13.17.

Layout design of the Subform project.

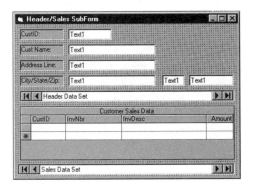

It would be nice to say that you could build a Subform without using any Visual Basic 4 code, but that's not quite true. You need just under 10 lines of code to get your data grid at the bottom of the form linked to the master table at the top of the form. Place the code in Listing 13.5 in the Data1_Reposition event of the HeaderTable data control.

Listing 13.5. Code to update the Subform with the Reposition event.

```
Private Sub Data1_Reposition()
    Dim cSQL As String
    '
    ' create select to load grid
    cSQL = "SELECT * FROM SalesTable WHERE CustID='" + Trim(Text1(0)) + "'"
    Data2.RecordSource = cSQL   ' load grid-bound data control
```

```
    Data2.Refresh    ' refresh data control
    DBGrid1.ReBind   ' refresh grid
End Sub
```

The preceding code is used to create a new SQL SELECT statement using the CustID value of the HeaderTable. This SQL statement is used to generate a new data set for the Data2 data control. This is the control that supplies the data grid. Once the new record source has been created, invoke the Refresh method to update the data control and the ReBind method to update the data grid. That's it; only seven lines of Visual Basic code, including the comments.

Now save the form as CH1304.FRM and the project as CH1304.VBP and run the program. When the form loads, you see the first record in the Header table displayed at the top of the form, and a list of all the outstanding invoices for that customer in the grid at the bottom of the form. (See Figure 13.18.)

Figure 13.18.
Running the Subform project.

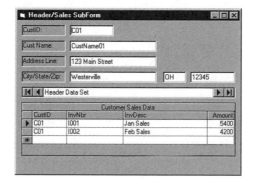

As you browse through the Header table, you'll see the data grid is updated, too. You can add records to the data grid or to the HeaderTable master. If this were a production project, you would add event trapping features like the ones mentioned in the previous section in order to maintain data integrity.

Summary

Today, you learned how to load and use three of the new data-bound controls that are shipped with Visual Basic 4.

- ☐ The data-bound list box
- ☐ The data-bound combo box
- ☐ The data-bound grid

You learned how to link these new controls to Recordsets using the Visual Basic 4 data controls, and how to use these links to update related tables.

You also learned several of the important Visual Basic 4 events associated with the data grid. These events let you create user-friendly data entry routines using just a data control and the data grid.

Finally, you drew upon your knowledge of data grids, SQL, and form layout to design and implement a data entry Subform. This form showed a master table at the top, and a related list table at the bottom of the form in a data-bound grid.

Quiz

1. What are some of the advantages of using a data-bound list or combo box?
2. What property of the data-bound list box do you set to identify the name of the Recordset object that provides the data to fill the list box?
3. What function does the BoundColumn property of the data-bound list box serve?
4. What data bound list/combo box properties do you set to identify the destination data set and field to be updated.
5. What properties of the data-bound grid control must be set to allow additions and removal of records?
6. What event of the data-bound grid control would you modify to prompt the user to confirm deletion of a record?
7. Why would you use the Column Level events of the data-bound grid control?
8. When would you use the data-bound combo box instead of the data-bound list box?
9. What data-bound grid control method do you use to refresh the grid?
10. In what scenarios would you employ a Subform using a data grid?

Exercises

Assume that you have been assigned the responsibility of maintaining the BIBLIO.MDB database application that ships with Visual Basic 4. Your organization has determined that the information contained in this database will be of value to Help Desk personnel. The Help Desk Manager has come to you and requested a Visual Basic 4 application for Help Desk use.

Build a data form that contains a data-bound list box that displays the Name field from the Publishers table. Once selection is made in this list box, text boxes should display PubID, CompanyName, Address, City, State, Zip, Telephone, and Fax of the publisher selected.

In addition, a listing of all publications of the selected publisher should appear in a data-bound grid Subform. For each entry, display the Title, Year Published, and ISBN from the Titles table.

Hint: You will need to use three data controls for this form.

Error Trapping

Today's lesson will cover a very important aspect of programming—handling runtime errors. Although you should always work to make sure your program can anticipate any problems that might occur while a user is running your software, you can't account for every possibility. That's why every good program should have a solid error handling system.

Today you will learn just what an error handler is and why error handlers are so important. You'll also learn about some of the inner workings of Visual Basic and how that affects error handling.

You'll learn about the difference between local error handling methods and global error handling methods. You'll also learn the advantages and disadvantages of each method. You'll see the various types of errors your program is likely to encounter and some guidelines on how to handle each type of error.

You'll also learn how to create error logs to keep track of errors that occur in your program. You'll learn how to create a trace log to analyze your programs. And you'll learn how you can write your programs to turn these features on or off without having to rewrite program code.

Finally, you'll build another library module today—the LIBERROR.BAS module. This module will contain all the functions and subroutines you'll need to set up error handlers in all the programs you write throughout this book and for any programs you write in the future.

Error Handling in General

Error handling is an essential part of any program. No program is complete unless it has good error handling. It is important to write your programs in a way that reduces the chances that errors will occur, but you won't be able to think of everything. Errors do happen! Well-designed programs don't necessarily have fewer errors; they just handle them better.

Writing error handlers is not difficult. In fact, you can add consistent error handling to your program by adding only a few lines of code to each module. The difficult part of writing good error handlers is knowing what to expect and how to handle the unexpected. You'll learn how to do both in today's lesson.

Adding error handling to your program will make your program seem much more polished and friendly to your users. Nothing is more annoying—or frightening—to a user than to see the screen freeze up, hear a startling beep, or watch the program (and any file your user had been working on) suddenly disappear from the screen entirely. This only needs to happen a few times before the user will vow never to use your program again.

Polite error messages, recovery routines that allow users to fix their own mistakes or correct hardware problems, and opportunities for the user to save any open files before the program halts due to errors are all essential parts of a good error handling strategy.

Error Handling in Visual Basic

Writing error handlers in Visual Basic is a bit trickier than in most PC languages. There are several reasons for this. First, Visual Basic is an *event-driven* language model, rather than *procedure-driven* like most PC languages. Second, Visual Basic uses a call stack method that isolates local variables. This means that when you exit the routine, you can lose track of the values of internal variables, which can make resuming execution after error handling difficult. Third, in Visual Basic, all errors are local. If an error occurs, it's best to handle it within the routine in which the error occurred, which means you'll have to write a short error handler for each routine in your Visual Basic program.

Note: Technically, Visual Basic does allow the use of a global error handler. However, after Visual Basic travels up the procedure stack to locate the error handler, it can't travel back down the stack to resume execution after the error has been corrected. (This is typical of most object-oriented languages.) For this reason, we highly recommend using local error handlers in your Visual Basic programs.

Creating Your Own Error Handlers

Error handlers in Visual Basic have three main parts:

- ☐ The On Error Goto statement
- ☐ The error handler code
- ☐ The exit statement

The On Error Goto statement appears at the beginning of the Sub or Function. This is the line that tells Visual Basic what to do when an error occurs, as in the following example:

```
On Error Goto ErrorHandler
```

In the preceding code line, every time an error occurs in this Sub or Function, the program immediately jumps to the ErrorHandler label in the routine and executes the error handler code.

The error handler code can be as simple or as complex as needed to handle the error. A very simple error handler would just report the error number and error message, like this:

```
ErrorHandler:
    msgbox Str(Err)+" - "+Error$
```

In the preceding code example, as soon as the error occurs, Visual Basic reports the error number (Err) and the error message (Error) in a message box.

The third, and final, part of a Visual Basic error handler is the exit statement. This is the line that tells Visual Basic where to go after the error handler is done with its work. There are four different ways to exit an error handler routine:

☐ Use the `Resume` keyword to return to the location in the program that caused the error in order to reexecute the same instruction.

☐ Use the `Resume Next` keywords to resume execution at the Visual Basic code line immediately following the line that caused the error.

☐ Use the `Resume label` keywords to resume execution at a specified location within the routine that caused the error. This location could be anywhere within the routine— before or after the line that caused the error.

☐ Use the `Exit Sub` or `Exit Function` keywords to immediately exit the routine in which the error occurred.

Which exit method you use depends on the type of error that occurred and the error handling strategy you employ throughout your program. Error types and error handling strategies are covered later in this chapter.

Now that you have the basics of error handling covered, you can write some error handling routines.

Creating a Simple Error Handler

To start, write a simple error handling routine to illustrate how Visual Basic behaves when errors occur. Start up Visual Basic and begin a new project. Add a single command button to the default form. Add the code in Listing 14.1 behind the command button.

Listing 14.1. Writing a simple error handler.

```
Sub Command1_Click ()
    On Error GoTo Command1ClickErr ' turn on error handling
    '
    Dim x As Integer          ' declare integer
    Dim cMsg as String        ' declares string
    x = 10000000              ' create overflow error
    GoTo Command1ClickExit    ' exit if no error
    '
    ' local error handler
Command1ClickErr:
    cMsg = Str(Err) + " - " + Error$ ' make message
    MsgBox cMsg, 0, "Command1Click"  ' show message
    Resume Next                      ' continue on
    '
    ' routine exit
Command1ClickExit:
    '
End Sub
```

Save the form as ERROR01.FRM, and save the project as ERROR01.VBP. Then execute the program and click on the command button. You'll see the error message displayed on the screen (see Figure 14.1).

Figure 14.1.
The results of a simple error handler.

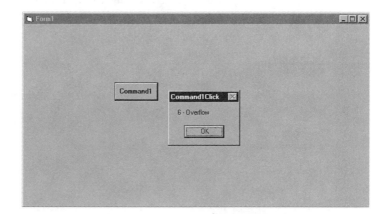

The example in Listing 14.1 has all the basic parts of a good error handler. First, the first line in the routine tells Visual Basic what to do in case of an error. Notice the naming convention used for the error handler: the name of the Sub or Function plus the letters Err. Next, you declare an integer and then purposely stuff it with an illegal value. This causes the error routine to kick in.

The error routine is very simple. It is a message that contains the error number and the associated text messages. You then display that message along with the warning symbol and the name of the routine that is reporting the error. The next line tells Visual Basic what to do after the error is handled. In this case, you tell Visual Basic to resume execution with the line of program code that immediately follows the line that caused the error (Resume at the Next line).

When Visual Basic resumes execution, the routine hits the line that tells Visual Basic to go to the exit routine (Goto Command1ClickExit). Notice again the naming convention for the exit routine. Use the name of the Sub or Function plus the word Exit.

Handling Cascading Errors

14

What happens if you get an error *within* your error routine? Although it isn't fun to think about, it can happen. When an error occurs inside the error handling routine, Visual Basic looks for the next declared error routine. This would be an error routine started in the previous calling routine using the On Error Goto *label* statement. If no error routine is available, Visual Basic halts the program with a fatal error.

As an example, let's modify the ERROR01.VBP project from Listing 14.1 to create a cascading error. First, create a new Sub procedure called NewSub. Then copy all the code from Command1_Click to NewSub. Change the names of the labels from Command1Click to NewSub. Finally, add a new error in the NewSubErr routine in order to force an error cascade in the program. Refer to the code in Listing 14.2 when creating the NewSub routine.

Listing 14.2. Creating cascading errors.

```
Sub NewSub ()
    On Error GoTo NewSubErr    ' turn on error handling
    '
    Dim x As Integer           ' declare integer
    Dim cMsg as String         ' declare string
    x = 10000000               ' create overflow error
    GoTo NewSubExit            ' exit if no error
    '
    ' local error handler
NewSubErr:
    cMsg = Str(Err) + " - " + Error$ ' make message
    MsgBox cMsg, 0, "NewSub"         ' show message
    Open "junk.txt" For Input As 1   ' create a new error
    Resume Next                      ' continue on
    '
    ' routine exit
NewSubExit:
    '
End Sub
```

Notice the new error that is introduced by attempting to open a nonexistent file from within the error handling routine of NewSub.

Before you save and run the project, you must first change the Command1_Click routine to call NewSub. Bring up Command1_Click and remove the line that declares the integer variable x and the line that sets the value of x. Your Command1_Click routine should look like the one in Listing 14.3.

Listing 14.3. Calling a subroutine to create cascading error.

```
Sub Command1_Click ()
    On Error GoTo Command1ClickErr ' turn on error handling
    '
    Dim cMsg as String         ' declare string
    NewSub                     ' call new routine
    GoTo Command1ClickExit     ' exit if no error
    '
    ' local error handler
Command1ClickErr:
    cMsg = Str(Err) + " - " + Error$ ' make message
    MsgBox cMsg, 0, "Command1Click"  ' show message
    Resume Next                      ' continue on
```

```
    '
    ' routine exit
Command1ClickExit:
    '
End Sub
```

Save the program and run it to see the results. When you first click the command button, you see the error message that announces the overflow error. Notice that the title of the message box indicates that the error is being reported by the NewSub module. (See Figure 14.2.)

Figure 14.2.
The error message
for NewSub.

When you click the OK button in the message box, you'll see another error message. This one reports an Error 53 File not Found message, which occurred when NewSub tried to open the nonexistent file (see Figure 14.3).

Figure 14.3.
The error message that
appears when a file is not
found.

Here's the important point. Notice that the second error message box tells you that the error is being reported from the Command1Click routine—even though the error occurred in the NewSub routine! The error that occurred in NewSub could not be handled locally and Visual Basic searched upward in the call stack to find the next available error handler to invoke. This action by Visual Basic can be a blessing and a curse. It's good to know that Visual Basic will use the next available error handling routine when things like this happen. But it's also likely to cause confusion for you and your users if you are not careful. For all you can tell in this example, an error occurred in Command1Click. You must keep this in mind when you are debugging Visual Basic error reports.

Using *Resume* to Exit the Error Handler

The simplest method for exiting an error handler is the Resume method. When you exit an error handler with the Resume keyword, Visual Basic returns to the line of code that caused the error and attempts to run that line again. The Resume keyword is useful when you encounter an error that the user can easily correct, such as attempting to read a disk drive when the user forgot to insert a diskette or close the drive door. You can use the Resume keyword whenever you are confident that the situation that caused the error has been remedied, and you want to retry the action that caused the error.

Let's modify the ERROR01 project to add an error handler that uses the `Resume` keyword. Add an additional button to the form. Set the caption property to Resume. Set the Name property to cmdResume. Now add the code in Listing 14.4 behind the new button.

Listing 14.4. Using the `Resume` keyword.

```
Private Sub cmdResume_Click()
    On Error GoTo cmdResumeErr
    '
    Dim x As Integer
    Dim cMsg As String
    Dim nReturn As Integer
    '
    x = InputBox("Enter an Integer Value")
    GoTo cmdResumeExit
    '
cmdResumeErr:
    cMsg = Str(Err) + " - " + Error$
    nReturn = MsgBox(cMsg, vbCritical, "cmdResume")
    Resume
    '
cmdResumeExit:
    '
End Sub
```

Your new form should look something like the one in Figure 14.4.

Figure 14.4.
Adding the Resume button to the ERROR01 project.

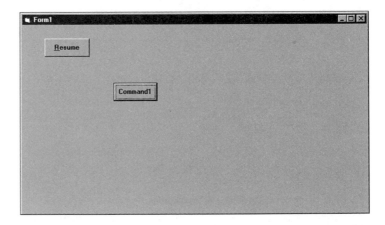

Save and run the project. When you press the Resume button, you are prompted to enter an integer value (see Figure 14.5).

Figure 14.5.
The prompt for integer input.

If you enter a value that is greater than 32,767, you invoke the error handler and receive an error message from Visual Basic (see figure 14.6).

Figure 14.6.
The error message for an invalid integer.

When you click the OK button, Visual Basic redisplays the input prompt and waits for your reply. If you enter another invalid value, you see the error message, and then you see the prompt again. This is the Resume exit method in action. You can't get beyond this screen until you enter a valid value.

If you try to press the Cancel button on the input screen, you still see an error message because selecting Cancel did not set the variable to a valid integer value. This can be very frustrating for your users. What if they don't know what value to enter here? Are they stuck in this terrible error handler forever? Whenever you use the Resume keyword, you should give your users an option to ignore the error and move on or cancel the action completely. Those options are covered next.

Using *Resume Next* to Exit the Error Handler

Using the Resume Next method to exit an error handler allows your user to get past a problem spot in the program as if no error had occurred. This is useful when you use code within the error handler to fix the problem, or when you think the program can go on even though an error has been reported.

Deciding whether to continue the program even though an error has been reported is sometimes a tough call. It is usually not a good idea to assume that your program will work fine even though an error is reported, especially if the error that occurs is one related to physical devices (missing diskette, lost communications connection, and so on) or file errors (missing, corrupted, or locked data files, and so on). The Resume Next keywords are usually used in error handlers that fix any reported error before continuing.

14

Modify your current project to contain an error handler that uses `Resume Next`. Add a new command button to the project. Set its Caption property to &Next and its Name property to cmdNext. Place the button anywhere on the form and enter the code in Listing 14.5 behind the button's cmdNext_Click event.

Listing 14.5. Using the `Resume Next` keywords.

```
Private Sub cmdNext_Click()
    On Error GoTo cmdNextErr
    '
    Dim x As Integer
    Dim cMsg as String
    Dim nReturn as Integer
    '
    x = InputBox("Enter a valid Integer")
    MsgBox "X has been set to " + Str(x)
    GoTo cmdNextExit
    '
cmdNextErr:
    If Err = 6 Then
        cMsg = "You have entered an invalid Integer Value." + Chr(13)
        cMsg = cMsg + "The program will now set X = 0 for you." + Chr(13)
        cMsg = cMsg + "Select YES to set X = 0 and continue." + Chr(13)
        cMsg = cMsg + "Select NO to return to enter a new value."
        '
        nReturn = MsgBox(cMsg, vbCritical + vbYesNo, "cmdNext")
        If nReturn = vbYes Then
            x = 0
            Resume Next
        Else
            Resume
        End If
    Else
        cMsg = Str(Err) + " - " + Error$
        MsgBox cMsg, vbCritical, "cmdNext"
        Resume
    End If
    '
cmdNextExit:
    '
End Sub
```

In Listing 14.5, you added a section of code to the error handler that tests for the anticipated overflow error. You explain the options to the user and then give the user a choice of how to proceed. This is a good general model for error handling that involves user interaction. Tell the user the problem, explain the options, and let the user decide how to go forward.

Notice, also, that you continued to include a general error trap for those cases when the error is not caused by an integer overflow. Even in cases when you think you have covered all the possible error conditions, you should always include a general error trap.

Save and run this project. When you press the Next command button and enter an invalid value (that is, any number greater than 32,767), you'll see the error message that explains your options (see Figure 14.7).

Figure 14.7.
An error message asking for user input.

Using *Resume label* to Exit an Error Handler

There are times when you need your program to return to another spot within the routine in order to fix an error that occurs. For example, if you ask the user to enter two numbers that you will use to perform a division operation, and it results in a divide by zero error, you will want to ask the user to enter both numbers again. You might not be able to simply use the Resume statement after you trap for the error.

When you need to force the program to return to a specific point in the routine, you can use the Resume *label* exit method. The Resume *label* method enables you to return to any place within the current procedure. You can't use Resume *label* to jump to another Sub or Function within the project.

Modify the ERROR01 project to include an example of Resume *label*. Add a new command button to the project. Set its Caption property to Label and its Name property to cmdLabel. Place the code in Listing 14.6 behind the cmdLabel_Click event.

Listing 14.6. Using the Resume *label* keywords.

```
Private Sub cmdLabel_Click()
    On Error GoTo cmdLabelErr
    '
    Dim x As Integer
    Dim y As Integer
    Dim z As Integer
    '
cmdLabelInput:
    x = InputBox("Enter a Divisor:", "Input Box #1")
    y = InputBox("Enter a Dividend:", "Input Box #2")
    z = x / y
    MsgBox "The Quotient is: " + Str(z), vbInformation, "Results"
    GoTo cmdLabelExit
    '
```

continues

Listing 14.6. continued

```
cmdLabelErr:
    If Err = 11 Then      ' divide by zero error
        MsgBox Str(Err) + " - " + Error$, vbCritical, "cmdLabel"
        Resume cmdLabelInput
    Else
        MsgBox Str(Err) + " -" + Error$, vbCritical, "cmdLabel"
        Resume Next
    End If
    '
cmdLabelExit:
    '
End Sub
```

Save and run the project. Enter 13 at the first input box and 0 at the second input box. This causes a Divide by zero error, and the error handler takes over from there. You'll see the error message shown in Figure 14.8 and then be returned to the line that starts the input process.

Figure 14.8.

Using the Resume label exit method.

Using the *Exit* or *End* Method to Exit an Error Handler

There are times when an error occurs and there is no good way to return to the program—for example, when you attempt to open files on a network file server and the user has forgotten to log onto the server. In this case, you need to either exit the routine and return to the calling procedure, or exit the program completely. Exiting to a calling routine can work if you have written your program to anticipate these critical errors. Usually it's difficult to do that. Most of the time, critical errors of this type mean you should end the program and let the user fix the problem before restarting the program.

Let's add one more button to ERROR01. Set its Caption property to &End and its Name property to cmdEnd. Enter the code in Listing 14.7 behind the cmdEnd_Click event.

Listing 14.7. Using the End keyword.

```
Private Sub cmdEnd_Click()
    On Error GoTo cmdEndErr
    '
    Dim cMsg as String
    Open "junk.txt" For Input As 1
    GoTo cmdEndExit
    '
```

```
cmdEndErr:
   If Err = 53 Then
       cMsg = "Unable to open JUNK.TXT" + Chr(13)
       cMsg = cMsg + "Exit the program and check your INI file" + Chr(13)
       cMsg = cMsg + "to make sure the JUNKFILE setting is correct."
       MsgBox cMsg, vbCritical, "cmdEnd"
       Unload Me
       End
   Else
       MsgBox Str(Err) + " - " + Error$, vbCritical, "cmdEnd"
       Resume Next
   End If
   '
cmdEndExit:
   '
End Sub
```

In Listing 14.7, you add a check in the error handler for the anticipated File not Found error. You give the user some helpful information and then tell him you are closing down the program. It's always a good idea to tell the user when you are about to exit the program. Notice that you did not use the Visual Basic End keyword; you used Unload Me. Remember that End stops all program execution immediately. Using Unload Me causes Visual Basic to execute any code placed in the Unload event of the form. This event should contain any file-closing routine needed to safely exit the program.

Save and run the project. When you click the End button, you see a message box explaining the problem and suggesting a solution (see Figure 14.9). When you click the OK button, Visual Basic ends the program.

Figure 14.9.
The error message that exits the program.

So far, you have seen how to build a simple error handler and the different ways to exit error handlers. Now you need to learn about the different types of errors that you will encounter in your Visual Basic programs and how to plan for them in advance.

Types of Errors

In order to make writing error handlers easier and more efficient, you can group errors into typical types. These error types can usually be handled in a similar manner. When you get an idea of the types of errors you can encounter, you can begin to write error handlers that take care of more than one error. You can write handlers that take care of error types.

There are four types of Visual Basic errors:

- ☐ General file errors: These are errors you encounter when you are attempting to open, read, or write simple files. This type of error does not include errors related to internal database operations (read/write table records).

- ☐ Database errors: These are errors that occur during database operations, usually during data read/write or data object create/delete operations.

- ☐ Physical media errors: These are errors caused by problems with physical devices— errors such as unresponsive communications ports or printers and low-level disk errors (Unable To Read Sector, and so on).

- ☐ Program code errors: These are errors that appear in your programs due to problems with your code. Errors include Divide by zero, Invalid Property, and other errors that can only be corrected by changing the Visual Basic code in your programs.

Each of these types of errors need to be handled differently within your Visual Basic programs. You'll learn general rules for handling these errors in the following sections.

General File Errors

These are errors that occur due to invalid data file information such as a bad filename, data path, or device name. Usually these errors can be fixed by the user and the program can continue from the point of failure. General file errors should be handled by an error handler that reports the problem to the user and asks for additional information to complete or retry the operation. If the retries fail, the program should allow the user to exit the program safely and give the user hints on how to fix the problem (refer to documentation, or other advice).

In Listing 14.8, the error handler is called when the program attempts to open a control file called CONTROL.TXT. The error handler then prompts the user for the proper file location and continues processing. Modify ERROR01.VBP by adding a new command button. Set its Caption property to Control and its Name property to cmdControl. Also, add a CommonDialog control to the project. Enter the code in Listing 14.8 into the cmdControl_Click event.

Listing 14.8. Adding code to the cmdControl_Click event.

```
Private Sub cmdControl_Click()
    On Error GoTo cmdControlErr
    '
    Dim cFile As String
    Dim cMsg As String
    Dim nReturn As Integer
    '
    cFile = "control.txt"
    '
    Open cFile For Input As 1
    MsgBox "Control File Opened"
    GoTo cmdControlExit
```

```
     '
cmdControlErr:
    If Err = 53 Then
        cMsg = "Unable to Open CONTROL.TXT" + Chr(13)
        cMsg = cMsg + "Select OK to locate CONTROL.TXT" + Chr(13)
        cMsg = cMsg + "Select CANCEL to exit program."
        nReturn = MsgBox(cMsg, vbCritical + vbOKCancel, "cmdControl")
        '
        If nReturn = vbOK Then
            CommonDialog1.filename = cFile
            CommonDialog1.DefaultExt = ".txt"
            CommonDialog1.ShowOpen
            Resume
        Else
            Unload Me
        End If
    Else
        MsgBox Str(Err) + " - " + Error$
        Resume Next
    End If
    '
cmdControlExit:
    '
End Sub
```

Save and run this project. When you click on the Control button, the program tries to open the CONTROL.TXT file. If it can't be found, you see the error message (see Figure 14.10).

Figure 14.10.
The File Not Found error
message.

If the user selects OK, the program calls the CommonDialog control and prompts the user to locate the CONTROL.TXT file. It can be found in the \TYSDBVB\CHAP14 directory (see Figure 14.11).

Figure 14.11.
Using the common dialog
control to locate
CONTROL.TXT.

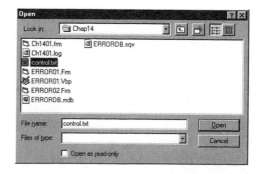

461

Notice the use of the CommonDialog control to open the file. Whenever you need to prompt users for file-related action (open, create, save), you should use the CommonDialog control. This is a familiar dialog for your users, and it handles all of the dirty work of scrolling, searching, and so on. Also, if the error here was caused by a bad value in the registry or INI file, this routine should write the corrected value back to the registry for future reference.

Table 14.1 lists errors that are similar to the File Not Found error illustrated in Listing 14.8. Errors of this type usually involve giving the user a chance to re-enter the filename or reset some value. Most of the time, you can write an error trap that anticipates these errors, prompts the user to supply the corrected information, and then retries the operation that caused the error.

Table 14.1. Common general file errors.

Error Code	Error Message
52	Bad filename or number
53	File not found
54	Bad file mode
55	File already open
58	File already exists
59	Bad record length
61	Disk full
62	Input past end of file
63	Bad record number
64	Bad filename
67	Too many files
74	Can't rename with different drive
75	Path/File access error
76	Path not found

In cases when it is not practical to prompt a user for additional information (such as during initial startup of the program), it is usually best to report the error in a message box, give the user some ideas about how to fix the problem, and then exit the program safely.

Database Errors

A very common type of error that occurs in database applications is the data-related error. These errors include those that deal with data type or field size problems, table access restrictions including read-only access, locked tables due to other users, and so on. Database errors fall into

two groups. Those caused by attempting to read or write invalid data to or from tables, including data integrity errors, make up the most common group. The second group are those errors caused by locked tables, restricted access, or multiuser conflicts.

In most cases, all you need to do is trap for the error, report it to the user, and allow the user to return to the data entry screen to fix the problem. If you use the Visual Basic data control in your data forms, you can take advantage of the automatic database error reporting built into the data control. As an example, let's put together a simple data entry form to illustrate some of the common data entry-oriented database errors.

Let's modify ERROR01.VBP to illustrate common database errors. Add a new command button to the form. Set its Caption property to Data and its Name property to cmdData. In the cmdData_Click event, add the following code:

```
Private Sub cmdData_Click()
    On Error Resume Next
    frmData.Show
End Sub
```

This code piece calls the new data entry form that you are about to create. To do that, you need to add a new form to the project and add a data control, two bound input controls, and two label controls. Use Table 14.2 as a reference for adding the controls to the form. Refer to Figure 14.12 as a guide for placing the controls. Notice that you also added a line that tells Visual Basic to ignore any error reported in this routine. This stops any cascading errors that might occur on the next form.

Table 14.2. Controls for the frmData form.

Control	Property	Setting
Form	Name	frmData
	Caption	Data Entry Form
	Height	1860
	Left	3015
	Top	2490
	Width	4170
Command Button	Name	cmdAdd
	Caption	&Add
	Height	300
	Left	2760
	Top	1020
	Width	1200

continues

Table 14.2. continued

Control	Property	Setting
Data Control	Name	Data1
	Caption	Data1
	Connect	Access
	DatabaseName	ERRORDB.MDB
	Height	300
	RecordSource	Table1
	Top	1020
	Width	2595
Text Box	Name	Text1
	DataField	Name
	DataSource	Data1
	Height	300
	Left	1440
	Top	600
	Width	2475
Text Box	Name	Text2
	DataField	KeyField
	DataSource	Data1
	Height	300
	Left	1440
	Top	120
	Width	1200
Label	Name	Label1
	Caption	Name:
	Height	300
	Left	120
	Top	600
	Width	1200

Control	Property	Setting
Label	Name	Label2
	Caption	Key Field:
	Height	300
	Left	120
	Top	120
	Width	1200

Figure 14.12.
The layout of the frmData form.

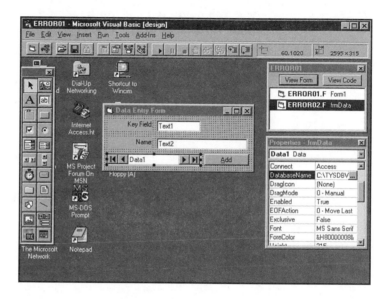

The only code you need to add to this form is a single line behind the Add button. Place the following code behind the cmdAdd_Click event.

```
Private Sub cmdAdd_Click()
   On Error Goto cmdAddClickErr
   Data1.Recordset.AddNew
   goto cmdAddClickExit
cmdAddClickErr:
   MsgBox Str(Err) + " - " + Error$
   Resume Next
cmdAddClickExit:
End Sub
```

Now save the new form as ERROR02.FRM and run the project. At the first screen, press the Data button to bring up the data entry form. To test the error trapping, edit the KeyField in the first record to create a duplicate primary key. Enter KF109 in the KeyField input box, and then press one of the arrows on the data control to force it to save the record. You should see a database error message that looks like the one in Figure 14.13.

Figure 14.13.

A sample database error message.

Are you surprised? You didn't add an error trap to the data entry form, but you still got a complete database error message! The Visual Basic data control is kind enough to provide complete database error reporting even if you have no error-coded error traps in place. In fact, it is not a good idea to attempt to override this facility with your own database errors. As long as you use the Visual Basic data control, you do not need to add database error trapping routines to your data entry forms.

If you do not use the Visual Basic data control, you need to add error handling routines to your project. For example, if you want to create a Dynaset using Visual Basic code, you need to trap for any error that might occur along the way. Let's modify the ERROR01.VBP project to create a Dynaset within the data entry form.

Add the code in Listing 14.9 to the Form_Load event of frmData. This code opens the database and creates a Dynaset to stuff into the data control that already exists on the form.

Listing 14.9. Adding code to the Form_Load event.

```
Private Sub Form_Load()
    On Error GoTo FormLoadErr
    '
    Dim db As DATABASE
    Dim ds As Dynaset
    Dim cSelect As String
    '
    Set db = OpenDatabase(App.Path + "errordb.mdb")
    cSelect = "SELECT * FROM Table2"
    Set ds = db.CreateDynaset(cSelect)
    GoTo FormLoadExit
    '
FormLoadErr:
    MsgBox Str(Err) + " - " + Error$
    Unload Me
    '
FormLoadExit:
    '
End Sub
```

The code in Listing 14.9 establishes some variables and then opens the database and creates a new Dynaset from a data table called Table2. Because there is no Table2 in ERRORDB.MDB, you get a database error. The error message is displayed and then the form is unloaded completely (see Figure 14.14).

Figure 14.14.
The database error message from the Form_Load *event.*

It is a good idea to open any data tables or files that you'll need for a data entry form during the Form_Load event. That way, if there are problems, you can catch them before data entry begins.

Physical Media Errors

Another group of common errors is caused by problems with physical media. Unresponsive printers, disk drives that do not contain diskettes, and downed communications ports are the most common examples of physical media errors. These errors might, or might not, be easily fixed by your user. Usually, you can report the error, wait for the user to fix the problem, and then continue with the process. For example, if the printer is jammed with paper, all you need to do is report the error to the user, and then wait for the OK to continue.

Let's add another button to the ERROR01.VBP project to display an example of physical media error handling. Add a new command button to the project. Set its Caption property to &Media and its Name property to cmdMedia. Enter the code in Listing 14.10 into the cmdMedia_Click event.

Listing 14.10. Trapping media errors.

```
Private Sub cmdMedia_Click()
    On Error GoTo cmdMediaErr
    Dim cMsg As String
    Dim nReturn As Integer
    '
    ' open a file on the a drive
    ' an error will occur if there
    ' is no diskette in the drive
    '
    Open "a:\junk.txt" For Input As 1
    Close #1
    GoTo cmdMediaExit
    '
```

continues

Listing 14.10. continued

```
cmdMediaErr:
    If Err = 71 Then
        cMsg = "The disk drive is not ready." + Chr(13)
        cMsg = cMsg + "Please make sure there is a diskette" + Chr(13)
        cMsg = cMsg + "in the drive and the drive door is closed."
        '
        nReturn = MsgBox(cMsg, vbCritical + vbRetryCancel, "cmdMedia")
        '
        If nReturn = vbRetry Then
            Resume
        Else
            Resume Next
        End If
    Else
        MsgBox Str(Err) + " - " + Error$
        Resume Next
    End If
    '
cmdMediaExit:
    '
End Sub
```

In Listing 14.10, you attempt to open a file on a disk drive that contains no diskette (or has an open drive door). The error handler prompts the user to correct the problem and allows the user to try the operation again. If all goes well the second time, the program continues. The user also has an option to cancel the operation.

Save and run the project. When you click on the Media button, you should get results that look like those in Figure 14.15.

Figure 14.15.
The results of a physical media error.

Program Code Errors

The final type of common errors are program code errors. These are errors that occur as part of the Visual Basic code. Errors of this type cannot be fixed by users and are usually due to unanticipated conditions within the code itself. Error messages such as Variable Not Found, Invalid Object, and so on, will be a mystery to most of your users. The best way to handle errors of this type is to tell the user to report the message to the programmer and close the program safely.

Creating Your Error Handler Library

In the previous sections, you created several error handlers, each tuned to handle a special set of problems. Although this approach works for small projects, it can be tedious and burdensome if you have to put together a large application. Also, after you've written an error handler that works well for one type of error, you can use that error handler in every other program that might have the same error. Why write it more than once?

Even though Visual Basic requires error traps to be set for each Sub or Function, you can still create a generic approach to error handling that takes advantage of code you have already written. In this section, you'll write a set of routines that you can install in all your Visual Basic programs—the Error Handling Library.

You'll create this library routine as a Visual Basic BAS file. To do this, add a module to the ERROR01.VBP project by selecting Insert | Module from the main Visual Basic menu. This opens the code window for your BAS module.

First, add some global variables that you will need for all error handling operations. Your routine will have options to simply report the errors and act as the programmer plans, or give users options to ignore or retry the operation. You need constants that reflect all those options. Add the following code to the declaration section of the module.

```
Option Explicit
'
' error handler constants
'
Global Const errExit = 0
Global Const errResume = 1
Global Const errNext = 2
Global Const errSelect = 3
```

These constants will be available to all Subs and Functions in the project. They will be used to control possible error exit options for the main error handler.

Now let's write the main error handler. You have been creating a very simple message box for all the error handling routines so far. Now you can use that basic message box as the heart of your generic error handler. This box will have option buttons on it, based on the value sent to the routine. Use the Insert | Procedure menu option to create a new Function called errHandler, which accepts three parameters and return a single integer. The declaration line should look like this:

```
errHandler(nErrNumber as integer, cErrText as string,
➥nErrOption as integer) as integer
```

Add the code in Listing 14.11 inside the new function.

Listing 14.11. Coding the errHandler function.

```
Function errHandler(nErrNumber, cErrText, nErrOption) As Integer
   Dim cMsg As String
   Dim nReturn As Integer
   '
   ' build message
   cMsg = ""
   cMsg = cMsg + "Err:" + Chr(9) + Str(nErrNumber) + Chr(13)
   cMsg = cMsg + "Text:" + Chr(9) + cErrText + Chr(13)
   '
   ' handle option
   Select Case nErrOption
      Case Is = errExit
         MsgBox cMsg, vbCritical, "Exiting Program"
         GoTo errHandlerEnd
      Case Is = errResume
         MsgBox cMsg, vbCritical, "Error"
         errHandler = errResume
      Case Is = errNext
         MsgBox cMsg, vbCritical, "Error"
         errHandler = errNext
      Case Is = errSelect
         nReturn = MsgBox(cMsg, vbCritical + vbAbortRetryIgnore, "Error")
         Select Case nReturn
            Case Is = vbAbort
               GoTo errHandlerEnd
            Case Is = vbRetry
               errHandler = errResume
            Case Is = vbIgnore
               errHandler = errNext
         End Select
   End Select
Exit Function
'
errHandlerEnd:
   MsgBox "Exiting Program"
   End
End Function
```

The Visual Basic function in Listing 14.11 first declares some local variables for internal use. Then, it builds the basic error message. This message will contain both the Visual Basic error number and the Visual Basic error message. Then the main Select…Case structure is invoked. This set of code reads the nErrOptions parameter and decides what kind of error message is displayed. If the nErrOptions parameter is set to errSelect, the message box contains command buttons that allow the user to decide what action to take at the exit of the error handler.

There is a section at the end of the error handler that exits the program if needed. You will add to this section a little later. For now, it simply ends the program.

After entering the code in Listing 14.11, save the module as LIBERROR.BAS. Because it is now part of the ERROR01.VBP project, you can use it. Modify the Command1_Click routine and the

NewSub routines to call to errHandler. To do this, call each routine up and replace the error message lines with the call to errHandler. The following code examples show how this is done in Command1_Click.

Before the change:

```
Command1ClickErr:
    cMsg = Str(Err) + " - " + Error$ ' make message
    MsgBox cMsg, 0, "Command1Click"  ' show message
    Resume Next                      ' continue on
```

After the change:

```
Command1ClickErr:
    nReturn = errHandler(Err, Error$, errNext)
    Resume Next                      ' continue on
```

Notice that you removed the two lines that created and displayed the message, and replaced them with the single line that calls errHandler. Notice also that you told errHandler that the only exit option available is Resume Next.

Make changes to the NewSub error handler so that is looks like the one in the following code section:

```
NewSubErr:
    nReturn = errHandler(Err, Error$, errNext)
    Open "junk.txt" For Input As 1   ' create a new error
    Resume Next                      ' continue on
```

Now save and run the project. When you click on the Command1 button, you'll see the new error messages (see Figure 14.16).

Figure 14.16.

An error message from errHandler.

Now let's add an option that will create an error report file whenever the error handler is activated.

Adding Error Logs to the Error Handler

When errors occur, users often do not remember details that appear in the error messages. It's much more useful to create an error log on disk whenever errors occur. This enables programmers or system administrators to review the logs and see the error messages without having to be right next to the user when the error occurs.

Listing 14.12 shows a new routine that writes the error log to the disk file. This routine creates a text file that contains the application name, error number, and error message along with a date and time the error occurred. The target directory for these error files is set with a module-level variable. This could be altered to fit your future projects. Add this routine to the library module.

Listing 14.12. Coding the `errWriteLogFile` routine.

```
Public Sub errWriteLogFile(cLogMsg)
    On Error GoTo errWriteLogFileErr
    '
    ' write error message to log file
    '
    Dim cFile As String
    Dim nFile As Integer
    '
    nFile = FreeFile() ' get first available file handle
    cFile = errDir + Format(Now, "mmddhhss") + ".err"
    '
    Open cFile For Output As nFile
    Print #nFile, "*** ERROR REPORT - [" + App.EXEName + "] ***"
    Print #nFile, ""
    Print #nFile, "DATE: " + Format(Now, "General Date")
    Print #nFile, ""
    Print #nFile, cLogMsg
    Print #nFile, ""
    Print #nFile, "*** eof ***"
    Close nFile
    GoTo errWriteLogFileExit
    '
errWriteLogFileErr:
    MsgBox Str(Err) + " - " + Error$, vbCritical, "Unable to Write Error Log"
    Exit Sub
    '
errWriteLogFileExit:
    '
End Sub
```

Notice that you create a filename that contains the month, day, hour, and second the error was created. This is a quick and simple way to create unique filenames. Notice also that you added an error handler in this routine. Because you are about to perform disk operations, you need to be ready for errors here, too!

Tip: The Visual Basic `FreeFile()` function is used to return a number that represents the first available file channel Visual Basic uses to open the data file. Using `FreeFile()` guarantees that you do not select a file channel that Visual Basic is already using for another file.

After adding the new routine to the library module, edit the errHandler function to add a line to call the errWriteLogFile routine, as shown in Listing 14.13. The only line you need to add is the errWriteLogFile cMsg line. This forces the log file to be created each time the error handler is invoked.

Listing 14.13. Adding errWriteLogFile to the errHandler function.

```
Function errHandler(nErrNumber, cErrText, nErrOption) As Integer
    Dim cMsg As String
    Dim nReturn As Integer
    '
    ' build message
    cMsg = ""
    cMsg = cMsg + "Err:" + Chr(9) + Str(nErrNumber) + Chr(13) + Chr(10)
    cMsg = cMsg + "Text:" + Chr(9) + cErrText
    '
    errWriteLogFile cMsg ' write log file
    '
    ' handle option
    Select Case nErrOption
      Case Is = errExit
         MsgBox cMsg, vbCritical, "Exiting Program"
         GoTo errHandlerEnd
      Case Is = errResume
         MsgBox cMsg, vbCritical, "Error"
         errHandler = errResume
      Case Is = errNext
         MsgBox cMsg, vbCritical, "Error"
         errHandler = errNext
      Case Is = errSelect
         nReturn = MsgBox(cMsg, vbCritical + vbAbortRetryIgnore, "Error")
         Select Case nReturn
            Case Is = vbAbort
               GoTo errHandlerEnd
            Case Is = vbRetry
               errHandler = errResume
            Case Is = vbIgnore
               errHandler = errNext
         End Select
    End Select
Exit Function
'
errHandlerEnd:
    MsgBox "Exiting Program"
    End
End Function
```

14

Now save and run the project. When you click the Command1 button, the system creates a log file for each error message displayed on the screen. You can use Notepad (or any other ASCII editor) to view the resulting log file. Look for a file with the .ERR extension. An example error report is shown in the following lines.

```
*** ERROR REPORT - [ERROR01] ***
DATE: 7/25/95 5:49:07 PM
TIME: 5:49:07 PM
Err:    6
Text:   Overflow
```

You can add a toggle variable to turn the error reporting on or off. This toggle could be set by a value in an INI file or registry entry. Listing 14.14 contains the added code for the toggle switch.

Add a global variable for the toggle switch by adding it to the declarations section of the library module.

Listing 14.14. Declaring global variables for the error handler.

```
Option Explicit
'
' error handler constants
'
Global Const errExit = 0
Global Const errResume = 1
Global Const errSelect = 2
Global Const errNext = 3
'
' module level stuff for log files
Const errDir = "\abc\examples\"
Global errLogFile As Integer
```

Now set the toggle value at the start of the project. In the first loaded form, add the following code to the Form_Load event.

```
Private Sub Form_Load()
    errLogFile = True ' set the err log file on
End Sub
```

Now alter the errHandler function to query the toggle switch before calling the log report routine.

```
If errLogFile = True Then
    errWriteLogFile cMsg ' write log file
  End If
```

All you did here is wrap the existing line that calls the error log report in an If…Then statement. Now save and run the project and check your results. Because you set the toggle to True at the start of the project, you should see two more error reports when you click the Command1 button.

Adding a Module Trace to the Error Handler

The final touch to add to your error handler library is the option to keep track of and print a module trace. A module trace keeps track of all the modules that have been called and the order in which they were invoked. This can be very valuable when you're debugging programs. Often, a routine works just fine when it is called from one module, but reports errors if called from another module. When errors occur, it's handy to have a module trace to look through to help find the source of your problems.

In order to keep track of the modules that have been called, you need a routine that maintains an array of all the modules currently running in your application. You also have to add a few lines of code to each module that update that array as your program runs.

First add some variables (in Listing 14.15) in the declaration area of LIBERROR.BAS.

Listing 14.15. Adding variables for the Module Trace option.

```
Option Explicit
'
' error handler constants
'
Global Const errExit = 0
Global Const errResume = 1
Global Const errSelect = 2
Global Const errNext = 3
'
' module level stuff for log files
Const errDir = "\abc\examples\"
Global errLogFile As Integer
'
' global stack constants
Global errStackFlag As Integer
Global Const errPush = 0
Global Const errPop = 1
Global Const errList = 2
Global Const errFile = 3
Global gblNProc As Integer   ' stack pointer
Global gblAProc() As String ' array of routines
```

You have added four constants that control how the stack routine behaves. You can add values to the stack (errPush), remove values from the stack (errPop), list the stack to the screen (errList), or send the list to a file (errFile). You also declared a pointer to the stack and an array that holds the names of all the routines called in your Visual Basic program. Finally, you added a toggle switch (errStackFlag) that lets you turn the stack operations on or off.

14

Now add the routine that handles all the stack processing—errProcStack. Create a new Sub that accepts two parameters called nStackAction and cProcName. Then enter the code in Listing 14.16.

Listing 14.16. Coding the `errProcStack` routine.

```
Sub errProcStack(nStackAction, cProcName)
   On Error GoTo errProcStackErr
   '
   Dim cMsg As String
   Dim x As Integer
   Dim nFile As Integer
   Dim cFile As String
   '
   ' skip it if toggle is off
   If errStackFlag = False Then
      GoTo errProcStackExit
   End If
   '
   ' handle stack action
   Select Case nStackAction
      Case Is = errPush
         ' add new procedure to stack
         gblNProc = gblNProc + 1
         ReDim Preserve gblAProc(gblNProc)
         gblAProc(gblNProc) = UCase$(cProcName)
      Case Is = errPop
         ' remove procedure from stack
         gblNProc = gblNProc - 1
         ReDim Preserve gblAProc(gblNProc)
      Case Is = errList
         ' list stack to screen
         cMsg = ""
         For x = gblNProc To 1 Step -1
            cMsg = cMsg + Trim(Str$(x)) + " - "
         ➥+ gblAProc(x) + Chr(13) + Chr(10)
         Next x
         MsgBox cMsg, vbInformation, "Stack Dump [" + App.EXEName + "]"
      Case Is = errFile
         ' list stack to file
         nFile = FreeFile
         cFile = Format(Now, "mmddhhss") + ".stk"
         Open cFile For Output As nFile
            Print #nFile, "*** PROCEDURE STACK DUMP [" + App.EXEName + "] ***"
            Print #nFile, "DATE: " + Format(Now, "General Date")
            Print #nFile, ""
            '
            Print #nFile, String(40, "-")
            For x = gblNProc To 1 Step -1
               Print #nFile, Chr(9) + Trim(Str(x)) + " - " + gblAProc(x)
            Next x
            Print #nFile, String(40, "-")
            Print #nFile, ""
            Print #nFile, "*** eof ***"
         Close #nFile
```

```
    End Select
    GoTo errProcStackExit
    '
errProcStackErr:
    '
    ' unexpected error
    MsgBox Str(Err) + " - " + Error$, vbCritical, "Unable to
    ➥Process Stack Request"
    Exit Sub
    '
errProcStackExit:
    '
End Sub
```

This routine handles all the operations needed to keep track of all routines running in your program. It can also send the list of routines to the screen or printer. Before this can happen, however, you have to add some code to each module. At the start of each module, you have to add code that tells the system what new routine is running. That way, if an error occurs, the system knows what routine caused it. Also, at the end of the routine, you need to add code that removes the routine's name from the active list.

Let's use the `Command1_Click` routine as an example. Modify the `Command1_Click` routine to match Listing 14.17.

Listing 14.17. Adding `errProcStack` to `Command1_Click`.

```
Private Sub Command1_Click()
    On Error GoTo Command1ClickErr ' turn on error handling
    '
    errProcStack errPush, "Command1"    ' add routine to list
    '
    NewSub                  ' call new routine
    GoTo Command1ClickExit  ' exit if no error
    '
    ' local error handler
Command1ClickErr:
    nReturn = errHandler(Err, Error$, errResume)
    Resume Next                    ' continue on
    '
    ' routine exit
Command1ClickExit:
    ProcStack errPop, "" ' remove routine from list
    '
End Sub
```

Notice that you added a line at the start of the routine and a line at the end of the routine. This is all you need to do in order to update the procedure stack for the program. But, for this to be really valuable, you have to do this for each routine that you want to track. For now, let's add the same code to the `NewSub` routine. The modified code is shown in Listing 14.18.

14

Listing 14.18. Adding `errProcStack` to `NewSub`.

```
Private Sub NewSub()
   On Error GoTo NewSubErr  ' turn on error handling
   '
   errProcStack errPush, "NewSub" ' add to stack
   Dim x As Integer          ' declare integer
   x = 10000000              ' create overflow error
   GoTo NewSubExit           ' exit if no error
   '
   ' local error handler
NewSubErr:
   nReturn = errHandler(Err, Error$, errNext)
   Open "junk.txt" For Input As 1   ' create a new error
   Resume Next                      ' continue on
   '
   ' routine exit
NewSubExit:
   errProcStack errPop, "" ' remove from stack
   '
End Sub
```

You only added the two lines that add and remove the routine from the stack. Now, add a bit of code (see Listing 14.19) to the `errHandler` routine that forces the program to display the error stack on-screen each time the error handler is activated.

Listing 14.19. Modifying `errHandler` to call `errProcStack`.

```
Function errHandler(nErrNumber, cErrText, nErrOption) As Integer
   Dim cMsg As String
   Dim nReturn As Integer
   '
   ' build message
   cMsg = ""
   cMsg = cMsg + "Err:" + Chr(9) + Str(nErrNumber) + Chr(13) + Chr(10)
   cMsg = cMsg + "Text:" + Chr(9) + cErrText
   '
   If errLogFile = True Then
      errWriteLogFile cMsg ' write log file
   End If
   '
   ' handle option
   Select Case nErrOption
      Case Is = errExit
         MsgBox cMsg, vbCritical, "Exiting Program"
         GoTo errHandlerEnd
      Case Is = errResume
         MsgBox cMsg, vbCritical, "Error"
         errHandler = errResume
      Case Is = errNext
         MsgBox cMsg, vbCritical, "Error"
         errHandler = errNext
      Case Is = errSelect
```

```
        nReturn = MsgBox(cMsg, vbCritical + vbAbortRetryIgnore, "Error")
        Select Case nReturn
            Case Is = vbAbort
                GoTo errHandlerEnd
            Case Is = vbRetry
                errHandler = errResume
            Case Is = vbIgnore
                errHandler = errNext
        End Select
    End Select
    '
    errProcStack errList, "" ' force list to screen
Exit Function
'
errHandlerEnd:
    MsgBox "Exiting Program"
    End
End Function
```

The only line you added here is the call to errProcStack with the parameter that forces the list to the screen.

Finally, add the code at the Form_Load event of the first form, which turns on the stack processor.

```
Private Sub Form_Load()
    errLogFile = True ' set the err log file on
    errStackFlag = True ' set stack flag on
End Sub
```

Now save and run the project. When you click on the Command1 button, you'll see the usual error messages and a new message box that shows the modules that are currently running. Running this routine brings out a very handy aspect of the stack routine. Look carefully at the second stack message box (see Figure 14.17).

Figure 14.17.
The second stack message box.

Notice that the second stack message tells you that two routines are active in the program. The last routine (#2) to run was the NewSub routine. That is the current routine. Remember who reported this second error? It was the Command1 routine's error handler that caught the error due to an error cascade. Now, even under cascade circumstances, the errProcStack routine gives you accurate information on the routine that really caused the error.

In a real application environment, you wouldn't want to show the procedure stack each time an error is reported. The best place for a stack dump is at exit time due to a fatal error. You should probably use the errFile option to write the stack to disk instead of displaying it to the user.

Other Error Handler Options

Now that you have the basics of error handling under your belt, you can continue to add features to the generic error handler. As you add these features, your programs take on a more professional look and feel. Also, using options, such as error report logs and procedure stack logs, makes it easier to debug and maintain your applications.

Additional features that you can add to your error handler include the following:

- [ ] Add the name of the user or workstation address to the reports.
- [ ] If you have created an error trap for common errors, such as error 53—File Not Found, add that recovery code to your generic handler. Now you can count on a consistent handling of common errors without adding code to every project.

Summary

Today's lesson covered all the basics of creating your own error handling routines for Visual Basic applications. You learned that an error handler has three basic parts:

- [ ] The On Error Goto statement
- [ ] The body of the error handler code
- [ ] The error handler exit

You learned that an error handler has four possible exits:

- [ ] Resume: Reexecutes the code that caused the error.
- [ ] Resume Next: Continues processing at the line immediately following the code line that caused the error.
- [ ] Resume *label*: Continues processing at the location identified by the *label*.
- [ ] EXIT or END: EXIT ends processing for the current routine, and END exits the program completely.

You learned about the major types of errors that you are likely to encounter in your program:

- [ ] General File Errors: These include errors such as File not Found and Invalid Path. Errors of this type can usually be fixed by the user and then re-attempted. Use Resume as an exit for these types of errors.
- [ ] Database Errors: These include errors related to data entry mistakes, integrity violations, and multiuser-related errors, such as locked records. Errors of this type are best handled by allowing the user to correct the data and attempt the operation again. If you use the Visual Basic data control, you do not have to write error handlers—the data control handles them for you. For operations that do not use the data control, you need to write your own error handling routines.

☐ Physical Media Errors: These errors relate to device problems, such as unresponsive printers, downed communications ports, and so on. Sometimes users can fix the problems and continue (such as refilling the paper tray of the printer). Other times, users cannot fix the problem without first exiting the program. It is a good idea to give users an option of exiting the program safely when errors of these types are reported.

☐ Program Code Errors: These errors occur due to problems within the Visual Basic code itself. Examples of program code errors include `Object variable not Set` and `For loop not initialized`. Usually the user cannot do anything to fix errors of this type. It is best to encourage the user to report the error to the system administrator and then exit the program safely.

You also learned that you can declare a global error handler or a local error handler. The advantage of the global error handler is that it allows you to create a single module that handles all expected errors. The disadvantage is that, due to the way Visual Basic keeps track of running routines, you are not able to resume processing at the point the error occurs once you arrive at the global error handler. The advantage of the local error handler is that you are always able to use `Resume`, `Resume Next`, or `Resume label` to continue processing at the point the error occurs. The disadvantage of the local error handler is that you need to add error handling code to every routine in your program.

Finally, you learned how you can create an error handler that combines local error trapping with global error messages and responses. This combined error handler was developed as part of the `LIBERROR.BAS` library module you built in this lesson. The `LIBERROR.BAS` library also contains modules to keep track of the procedures currently running at the time of the error, a process for printing procedure stack dumps to the screen and to a file, and a process that creates an error log on file for later review.

Quiz

1. What are the three main parts of error handlers in Visual Basic?
2. What are the four ways to exit an error handler routine?
3. When would you use `Resume` to exit an error handler?
4. When would you use `Resume Next` to exit an error handler?
5. When would you use `Resume label` to exit an error handler?
6. When would you use the `EXIT` or `END` command to exit an error handler?
7. List the four types of Visual Basic errors.
8. Should you utilize error trapping for the Visual Basic data control?
9. In what Visual Basic event should you open data tables or files in which the user enters data?
10. What are the advantages and disadvantages of global error handlers?

Exercises

1. Create a new project and add code to a command button that opens the file C:\ABC.TXT. Include an error handler that notifies the user that the file cannot be opened, and then terminates the program.

2. Modify the project started in Exercise 1 by adding a new command button. Attach code to this button that attempts to load a file named C:\ABC.TXT. Notify the user that this file cannot be opened, and give the user the option and the dialog box to search for the file. Exit the program when a selection has been made or if the user chooses not to proceed.

   Run this program and elect to find the file. Cancel out of any common dialogs that appear. After this, create the file using Notepad and run the process again. Finally, move the file to a location other than the C drive and run the program. Use the common dialog to search for and select the file.

2

Week 2 concentrated on topics that are of value to developers in the stand-alone and workgroup environments. A wide variety of topics were covered in Week 2, including the following:

- ☐ How to use Visdata to build and manage databases.
- ☐ How to use the Structured Query Language (SQL) to extract data from existing databases.
- ☐ What the Microsoft JET engine is, and how you can use Visual Basic code to create and maintain Data Access Objects.
- ☐ How to create data entry forms with Visual Basic code.
- ☐ How to use the Microsoft graph control to create graphs and charts of your data.
- ☐ How to use data-bound list boxes, data-bound combo boxes, and data-bound grids to create advanced data entry forms.
- ☐ How to make applications more solid with Error Trapping.

The following is a more detailed look at the topics covered in each lesson.

Day 8, "Using the Visdata Program"

On Day 8, you learned how to use the Visdata application to build and manage databases. You learned how to compile the Visdata project and how to add it to the Visual Basic Add-Ins menu.

Highlights of this chapter include learning how to use Visdata to perform the following tasks:

☐ Create databases, tables, fields, and indexes.

☐ Perform data entry using automatically generated Grid or Form Layout screens.

☐ Copy existing tables with or without data.

☐ Export data to other data sources, including Excel spreadsheets.

☐ Create, execute, and store SQL queries.

☐ View existing data as a Table, Dynaset, or Snapshot object.

☐ Test data-bound list and combo boxes.

☐ Copy tables from one database to the next, repair corrupted databases, convert databases from older versions of Microsoft JET, compact databases, and perform global replace operations on tables.

Day 9, "Selecting Data with SQL"

On Day 9, you learned what Structured Query Language is and what it can do. You learned how to use the SELECT clause to extract data. Several additional clauses were presented that work with the SELECT clause.

☐ The WHERE clause is used to limit the rows in a result set and can also be used to link two tables into a single, nonupdatable view.

☐ The ORDER BY clause is used to control the order in which the result set is displayed (either ascending or descending).

☐ The GROUP BY clause can be used to create a subtotal result set.

☐ The HAVING clause can be used with the GROUP BY clause to act as a WHERE clause for the GROUP BY subtotal clause.

☐ The INNER JOIN clause can be used to merge two tables together into a single, updatable result set.

☐ The LEFT JOIN and RIGHT JOIN clauses create single, updatable record sets from two tables that include everything from the side selected (LEFT or RIGHT) and only the records with a corresponding match in the second table.

☐ The UNION clause can be used to combine two or more complete SQL queries into a single result set.

☐ The TRANSFORM...PIVOT clause can be used to create a cross tab query as a result set.

Day 10, "Visual Basic and the Microsoft JET Engine"

You spent Day 10 learning about the hierarchically structured database engine that ships with Visual Basic—the Microsoft Joint Engine Technology (JET). You learned about the different objects contained within the engine, and their properties, events, and methods.

☐ The DBEngine data object is the default data object that contains all other data objects. The methods of this object include RepairDatabase, CompactDatabase, RegisterDatabase, Idle, and CreateWorkSpace.

☐ The WorkSpace data object identifies the user's database session. This object contains three collections: Databases, Groups, and Users.

☐ The Database data object contains all the tables, queries, and relations defined for the database.

☐ The TableDef data object contains all the information needed to define a base table in a database. The collections within this object are Fields, Indexes, and Properties.

☐ The Field data object contains all the information regarding a data table field.

☐ The Index data object contains all information on defined indexes for the associated table.

☐ The Relation data object contains all the information about a stored SQL query. These objects run faster than SQL queries because they actually perform preprocessing that Visual Basic would normally need to perform on an SQL statement.

Day 11, "Creating Database Programs with Visual Basic Code"

On Day 11, you learned how to abandon the data control and use Visual Basic code to manage databases. Using code to create your applications produces a product that is easier to maintain. You also gain complete control over the database administration process.

You learned the following in this chapter:

☐ The three approaches to handling key-oriented searches are Move, Find, and Seek.

☐ Seek is the fastest method to locate a record. This method can only be used on RecordSets opened as tables.

☐ Bookmarks can be utilized to remember a specific record's position in a data set.

You also created a series of library functions that you can use to create data entry forms without using the data control.

Day 12, "Displaying Your Data with Graphs"

On Day 12, you learned how to convert your data into pictures and display it for users' interpretation.

☐ You can use the NumSets and NumPoints properties of the Visual Basic graph tool to declare the number of data sets and the number of data points that will be included in the graph.

☐ You can use the QuickData property to quickly add graph data at runtime.

☐ The Graph tool has many options to set the appearance of the graph.

Also during this lesson, you created library routines that allow you to make simple calls from within your Visual Basic code to quickly create graphical displays. These graphs can be displayed in numerous formats with output directed to the screen, printer, or a file.

Day 13, "Data-Bound List Boxes, Grids, and Subforms"

In the lesson on Day 13, you learned how to use the data-bound list box, the data-bound combo box, and the data-bound grid to select and display information. You learned how to set the properties of these controls to read from and write to specified data sources. You also learned how to create subforms to display related information.

In this chapter, you learned the following:

☐ How to set the RowSource property of the data-bound list control to define the RecordSet object that will be used to fill the list box. You concentrated on using data controls as the record source in the exercises.

☐ The ListField property determines the field that will be displayed in the list box. The BoundColumn property displays the name of the field that will be saved from this control. These two properties do not have to be equivalent.

☐ The DataSource and DataField properties are set to identify the destination RecordSet and field that will be updated by the list box.

- A data-bound grid can be dropped on a form and linked to a data control by setting the DataSource property. Code can be added to the Reposition event of the data control that will filter data for the grid, which serves as a subform.

- The data-bound grid control has numerous events that can be used to monitor users' actions to the underlying data. These events include BeforeInsert, AfterInsert, BeforeUpdate, AfterUpdate, BeforeDelete, and AfterDelete.

Day 14, "Error Trapping"

No program is complete until error trapping routines are included. Problems can arise in your code, as well as in numerous other unforeseen events, which can cause erratic behavior in your programs. On Day 14, you learned about the different problems that can occur and how to guard against them.

An error handler has three basic parts:

- The On Error Goto statement
- The body of the error handler code
- The error handler exit

There are four possible exits to an error handler:

- Resume reexecutes the code that created the error.
- Resume Next continues processing at the line immediately after the line of code that caused the error.
- Resume label continues processing at the location designated by the label.
- Exit ends processing of the current routine, and END exits the program.

You also learned several types of errors and how to manage them:

- General File errors can occur when files cannot be found or opened. Use Resume as the exit for this type of error.

- Database errors occur when data has been entered incorrectly, or if records are locked. The Data Control manages these errors for you.

- Physical media errors occur when printers are turned off, communication ports are not responding, hard drives cannot be read, and so forth. You should give your users the option to correct the error or safely exit from the program if these problems are encountered.

- Program code errors are bugs in your Visual Basic code. It is best to notify the user to contact the programmer, and then shut down the process safely.

☐ Global error handlers can be used rather than local error handlers. This reduces the time it takes to write code but has a significant drawback because processing will not be able to return to the point at which the problem occurred.

3

Week 1 focused on developing skills necessary to build Visual Basic database applications in the desktop environment. Week 2 focused on the skills needed in the workgroup environment. This week focuses on skills needed for developing enterprise-level Visual Basic applications.

The following topics are covered this week:

☐ Using Advanced SQL statements to construct databases and tables, and also to add, edit, and delete data from database tables.

☐ Using database normalization techniques to improve the organization, integrity, and performance of your databases.

☐ Issues to consider when developing multiuser applications including JET locking schemes, the use of cascading updates and deletes for referential integrity, and how transaction management can improve both the speed of your programs and the quality of your data.

☐ How to use the ODBC (Open Database Connectivity) API set to build ODBC-enabled applications that run on both 16-bit and 32-bit platforms.

☐ How to add application-level security features to your program, including user login/logout, programmable access rights for critical operations, and the use of audit trails to track database updates and all secured user activity.

☐ How to use your current word processor to create document files that can be compiled into valid help files for your Visual Basic applications.

When you complete this week, you will have several reusable code modules that you can place into any Visual Basic application.

Day 15: This is the first of two days dedicated to learning Structured Query Language (SQL). In Day 9, you learned how to use SQL to SELECT data from tables. In this lesson, you learn how to use SQL Data Manipulation Language (DML) to create and modify databases, tables, relationships, and indexes. You also learn how to use SQL-VB, a tool that can read text file scripts developed in any standard text editor or word processor to create and modify databases.

Day 16: You continue your study of SQL, using Data Manipulation Language to insert records into tables, append records to tables, and update records that currently exist in data tables. You also learn how to use Make Table queries to build tables with data from other tables. Finally, you learn how to create Delete Table queries that remove multiple records from a data table.

Day 17: This lesson focuses on using data normalization to increase database integrity processing speed. The "Five Rules" of data normalization are covered, with logical examples that build upon your knowledge of SQL.

Day 18: Today's exercises center on multiuser considerations. You learn the nuances of cascading updates and cascading deletes. You spend time on transaction management using the BeginTrans, CommitTrans, and Rollback methods. By the time you finish, you will have a good understanding of database-level, table-level, and page-level locking schemes.

Day 19: Open Database Connectivity (ODBC) via the ODBC API interface is today's topic. You learn how to create data forms that use low-level API calls to access existing databases. This chapter presents topics that are essential in development of client-server Visual Basic applications that can run on both 16-bit and 32-bit operating systems. You see how to build Visual Basic applications that bypass the Microsoft JET database engine and link directly to the data source through the ODBC interface. You also learn how to build reuseable code that creates data-entry screens for applications that connect to ODBC data sources.

Day 20: Securing your Visual Basic database applications is the main focus of Day 20. All quality applications have security to protect the precious data they control. Database security, encryption, and the securing of processes are covered. You look at applying audit trails to track critical activities in your application. Throughout the day, you build security modules that you can insert into any Visual Basic project you create.

Day 21: In this final lesson, you learn how to add Windows Help to your database application. You learn how to use word processing footnotes to add titles, contents, jumps, and keywords to a help file. You also learn how to compile help files and attach them to your Visual Basic database application.

Creating Databases with SQL

Your final week will start with another chapter on SQL keywords. The previous SQL chapter (Day 9, "Selecting Data with SQL") focused on SQL's Data Manipulation Language (DML) keywords. Today's work will focus on SQL's Data Definition Language (DDL) keywords.

On Day 9, you learned how easy it is to select and order data using the SQL SELECT...FROM clause. You also learned that using SQL statements to perform data selection means that your Visual Basic programs will work with almost any back-end database server you might encounter in the future.

In today's lesson, you'll learn that you can use SQL statements to create your databases, too. Using SQL keywords to create your data tables, set relationships, and create indexes gives your programs an added level of portability. The SQL words you learn today work not only on Microsoft Access formatted databases, but also on any database format that is SQL-compliant. The skills you learn today can be applied to almost every database engine on the market.

By the time you are through with today's lesson, you will be able to use SQL keywords to perform the following tasks:

- ☐ Create and delete data tables with the CREATE TABLE and DROP TABLE keywords.
- ☐ Add and delete fields in an existing data table using the ADD COLUMN and DROP COLUMN keywords.
- ☐ Create and delete indexes using the CREATE INDEX and DROP INDEX keywords.
- ☐ Define table relationships including foreign keys using the PRIMARY KEY and FOREIGN KEY...REFERENCES keywords.

Throughout today's lesson, you use a program called SQL-VB. This is a VB program that processes SQL scripts. All the commands you learn today are in the form of SQL scripts. You can use the SQL-VB program without knowing much about how it was built. However, if you are curious about how SQL-VB works, you can refer to Appendix A. This appendix walks you through a step-by-step construction of SQL-VB. It also contains information on how to use SQL-VB with this book and with other projects you will create in the future.

Using the SQL-VB Interpreter

Before you begin today's lesson in advanced SQL commands, you will take a quick tour of the SQL-VB program. You'll learn how to use SQL-VB to create, edit, and run SQL scripts. The SQL-VB interpreter is a program that reads and executes SQL command scripts. You will use this program throughout the lesson today. You might also find that this program will be useful in the future for creating and managing SQL databases.

Loading and Running the SQL-VB Interpreter

To load the SQL-VB Interpreter, locate the TYSDBVB\SQLVB directory that was created from the installation CD (for installation information, refer to the last page of this book). Select either SQLVB.EXE (32-bit version) or SQLVB16.EXE (16-bit version) depending on your operating system. After the program loads, you should see a screen that looks similar to the one in Figure 15.1.

Figure 15.1.

The opening screen for SQL-VB Interpreter.

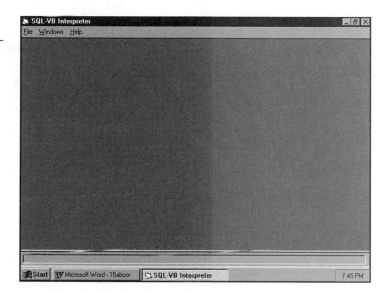

The opening screen is actually a multidocument interface. You can load and run one or more scripts from this interface. To test the system, load and run a simple test script. Using SQL-VB, select File | Run, and at the File | Open dialog, locate and select SQLVB01.SQV (refer to Figure 15.2).

When you select the script, SQL-VB begins to read and process the SQL commands in the file. This test script opens the BOOKS.MDB database and then creates six result sets and displays them on the screen. When the script is completed, you see a dialog box announcing the completion of the script along with several result sets displayed on the screen as shown in Figure 15.3.

Figure 15.2.
*Loading the
SQLVB01.SQV SQL script.*

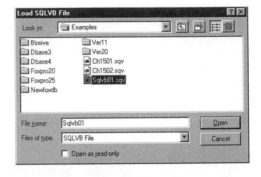

Figure 15.3.
*The completed
SQLVB01.SQV script.*

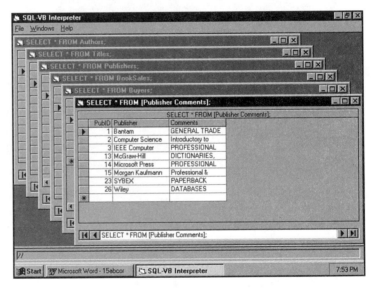

SQL-VB creates all result set forms in a cascade starting at the top left of the screen. You can change this to a tiled view by selecting Windows | Tile from the main menu (refer to Figure 15.4).

You can also use your mouse pointer to resize, minimize, or maximize any form. You can even resize individual columns and rows within a form. Figure 15.5 shows several of the ways you can alter the view of forms.

Creating and Editing SQL-VB Scripts

You can also use SQL-VB to create and edit SQL command scripts. For example, edit the SQLVB01.SQV script you tested earlier. First, load the script for editing by selecting File | Edit from the main menu. Locate and select the SQLVB01.SQV script. When you select the script, SQL-VB launches the Notepad editor and loads the selected SQL script.

Figure 15.4.
Tiling the open forms.

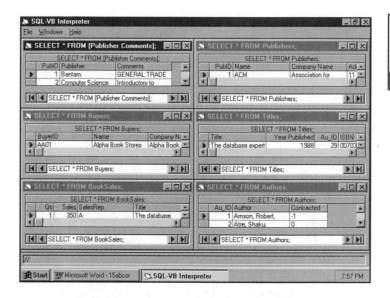

Figure 15.5.
Altering the form views within SQL-VB.

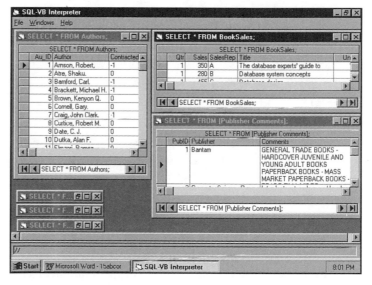

Let's change the SQL script so that the first result set includes only authors whose Au_ID is greater than 10. To do this, add the text WHERE Au_ID>10; to the first SELECT statement. Be sure to place the semicolon (;) at the end of the line. SQL-VB needs this character to indicate the end of an SQL statement. Also, let's comment out the rest of the view sets for now. You only want to see one result set in this test. To do this, add two slashes (//) to the start of all the other lines that contain SELECT statements. Be sure to place a space after the // comment sign. Your script should now resemble Listing 15.1.

Listing 15.1. Modifying an SQL-VB script.

```
//
// test sql command file for sqlvb interpreter
//

// open the database
dbOpen \tysdbvb\sqlvb\book.mdb;

// open some tables to view
SELECT * FROM Authors WHERE Au_ID>10;
SELECT * FROM Titles;
SELECT * FROM Publishers;
SELECT * FROM BookSales;
SELECT * FROM Buyers;
SELECT * FROM [Publisher Comments];


//
// eof
//
```

After you have changed the script, save it using the File | Save command of Notepad. Now select File | Run from the SQL-VB main menu to run the updated SQLVB01.SQV command script. Your results should look similar to those in Figure 15.6.

Figure 15.6.

The results of the edited SQLVB01.SQV script.

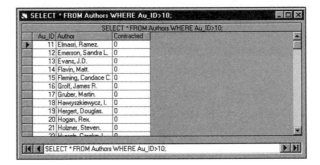

You can create new SQL-VB scripts by selecting File | New from the menu and entering any valid SQL statement into the editor. After you've created your script, save it with an .SQV file extension. Then use the File | Run menu option to execute your script.

You need to know a few SQL-VB command syntax rules before you can create your own SQL-VB scripts. This is covered in the next section.

SQL-VB Command Syntax

The command syntax for SQL-VB is very similar to standard ANSI SQL syntax. In fact, any valid SQL command is a valid SQL-VB command. However, there are a few additional commands in SQL-VB that you should know about.

Three special command words work in SQL-VB, but they are not SQL commands. These special commands are used to create, open, and close Microsoft JET databases. SQL-VB also has a comment command. The comment command indicates to SQL-VB that the information on this line is for comment only and should not be executed. Finally, each command line must end with a semicolon (;). The semicolon tells SQL-VB where the command line ends. The special command words, their meanings, and examples are included in Table 15.1.

Table 15.1. Special SQL-VB commands.

SQL-VB Command	Example	Description
//	// this is a comment	Any line that begins with // is treated as a comment line and is not processed by the SQL-VB interpreter. Comments cannot be placed at the end of SQL command lines, but must occupy their own line of text. Don't use the single quote mark for comments as in VB because the single quote is a valid SQL character. Also, you must leave at least one space after the // for SQL-VB to recognize it as a comment marker.
dbOpen	dbOpen C:\DATA.MDB;	The dbOpen command opens a Microsoft JET database. SQL-VB can only open and process Microsoft JET format databases. A dbOpen command must be executed before any SQL statements are processed.
dbMake	dbMake C:\NEWDATA.MDB;	The dbMake command creates a new, empty Microsoft JET database on the drive path indicated in the command. When a database is created using the dbMake command, you do not have to issue a dbOpen command.

continues

Table 15.1. continued

SQL-VB Command	Example	Description
dbClose	dbClose;	The dbClose command closes the Microsoft JET database that was opened using the dbOpen or dbMake command word.
;	SELECT * FROM Table1;	The semicolon is used to indicate the end of a command. Commands can stretch over several lines of text but each command must always end with a semicolon (;).

You now have enough information about SQL-VB to use it in the rest of the lesson today. As you go through the examples in today's lesson, you will learn more about SQL-VB and how you can create your own SQL scripts. If you want to know more about how SQL-VB works, refer to Appendix A.

Why Use SQL to Create and Manage Data Tables?

Before you jump into the details of SQL keywords, let's talk about the advantages of using SQL statements to create and manage your data tables.

Even though Visual Basic offers several powerful commands for performing the same functions within a Visual Basic program, you might find that using SQL keywords to perform database management gives you an advantage. By using SQL statements to create and maintain your database structures, you can easily create useful documentation on how your databases are structured. Are you trying to debug a problem at a client site and can't remember how the tables are laid out? If you used a set of SQL statements to create the tables, you can refer to that script when you are solving your client's problems.

It is also easy to generate, test, or sample data tables using SQL statements. If you are working on a database design and are still experimenting with table layouts and relationships, you can quickly put together an SQL DDL script, run it through SQL-VB, and review the results. If, after experimenting, you find you need a new field in a table, you can alter your existing script and rerun it. Or, you can write a short script that makes only the changes you need, preserving any data you have loaded into the existing tables.

You can even use SQL statements to load test data into your new tables. After you have created the tables, you can add SQL statements to your script that load test data into the columns. This

test data can exercise defined relationships, check for data table integrity, and so on. Using an SQL script to load data is an excellent way to perform repeated tests on changing data tables. As you make changes to your table structures, you can use the same data each time until you know you have the results you are looking for.

Also, you can use the same SQL statements to create your data tables within other database systems, including Microsoft's SQL Server, Oracle, and others. After you create the test files using Microsoft Access JET databases, you can then regenerate the tables for other database engines using the same SQL statements. This increases the portability of your application and eases the migration of your data from one database platform to another.

Table Management SQL Keywords

The type of SQL keywords you'll learn today are the table management keywords. These keywords enable you to create new data tables, alter the structure of existing data tables, and remove existing data tables from the database.

Designing New Tables with *CREATE TABLE*

The CREATE TABLE keyword allows you to create new tables in an existing database. In its most basic form, the CREATE TABLE statement consists of three parts: the CREATE TABLE clause; a *TableName*; and a list of column names, column types, and column sizes for each column in the new table. The following example shows a simple CREATE TABLE SQL statement.

```
CREATE TABLE NewTable (Field1 TEXT(30), Field2 INTEGER);
```

This SQL statement creates a data table called NewTable that has two columns. The column named Field1 is a TEXT column 30 bytes long. The column named Field2 is an INTEGER column. Notice that no size was designated for the INTEGER column. Microsoft Access JET SQL statements only accept size values for TEXT columns. All other columns are set to a predefined length. See Table 2.1 in Day 2, "Creating Databases" for a list of the default field lengths for Microsoft Access JET data fields.

> **Note:** If you omit the size definition for the TEXT field, Microsoft Access JET uses the default value of 255 bytes. Because this can result in rather large tables with empty space, it's a good habit to declare a size for all TEXT fields.

Test this SQL statement by creating the SQL script in Listing 15.2 and running it using the SQL-VB application. Start the application and select File | New to create a new script called SQLVB02.SQV. Enter the following script commands into Notepad.

Listing 15.2. Creating the SQLVB02.SQV script.

```
//
// SQLVB02.SQV - Testing SQL Table Management Keywords
//
// create a new database for our tests
dbMake sqlvb02.mdb;
// create a simple table
CREATE TABLE NewTable (Field1 TEXT(30), Field2 INTEGER);
// show the empty table
SELECT * FROM NewTable;
// eof (end of file)
```

This script creates a new database, creates a new table in the database, and displays the empty table in a result set. Use SQL-VB to run the script by selecting File | Run and locating and loading the SQLVB02.SQV script file. Your results should appear as shown in Figure 15.7.

Figure 15.7.

Results of the CREATE TABLE statement.

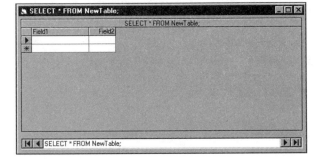

You can also use the PRIMARY KEY command when you CREATE a data table. This can be done by following the name of the primary key field with a CONSTRAINT clause. Use SQL-VB to edit the SQLVB02.SQV script so that it sets the Field1 column as a primary key. Refer to Listing 15.3 for an example.

Listing 15.3. Adding the PRIMARY KEY CONSTRAINT.

```
//
// testing SQL Table Management Keywords
//
// create a new database for our tests
dbMake sqlvb02.mdb;
// create a simple table
CREATE TABLE NewTable
    (Field1 TEXT(30) CONSTRAINT PKNewTable PRIMARY KEY,
     Field2 INTEGER);
// show the empty table
SELECT * FROM NewTable;
// eof
```

Notice that the CREATE TABLE SQL statement is spread out over more than one line of text. SQL statements can stretch over several lines, as long as each complete SQL statement ends with a semicolon. The continued lines need not be indented, but doing so makes it easier to read the SQL scripts.

You'll look at the CONSTRAINTS clause in depth a bit later. For now, remember that you can create both primary and foreign keys in a CREATE TABLE statement.

Modifying Tables with *ALTER TABLE...ADD COLUMN* and *DROP COLUMN*

There are two forms of the ALTER TABLE statement: the ADD COLUMN form and the DROP COLUMN form. The ADD COLUMN form enables you to add new columns to an existing table without losing any data in the existing columns. Edit the SQLVB02.SQV script using SQL-VB so that it matches the script in Listing 15.4.

Listing 15.4. Using the ADD COLUMN clause.

```
//
// testing SQL Table Management Keywords
//
// create a new database for our tests
dbMake sqlvb02.mdb;
// create a simple table
CREATE TABLE NewTable
    (Field1 TEXT(30) CONSTRAINT PKNewTable PRIMARY KEY,
     Field2 INTEGER);
// add a two new columns
ALTER TABLE NewTable ADD COLUMN Field3 DATE;
ALTER TABLE NewTable ADD COLUMN Field4 CURRENCY;
// show the empty table
SELECT * FROM NewTable;
// eof
```

Notice that you had to add two ALTER TABLE statements to add two columns to the same table. The ALTER TABLE statement can only deal with one column at a time. Run the SQLVB02.SQV script and inspect the results. Your screen should look similar to the one in Figure 15.8.

Note: Note that the ADD COLUMN clause always adds columns starting at the left-most column in the table. You can always control the order of the columns in a display using the SELECT...FROM clause (see Day 9). If you want to control the physical order of the fields, you must add the fields in a CREATE TABLE statement.

Figure 15.8.

Results of using ALTER
TABLE...ADD COLUMN *key-
words.*

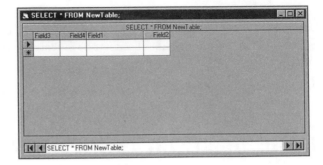

You can also use the ALTER TABLE statement to remove columns from an existing table without losing data in the unaffected columns. This is accomplished using the DROP COLUMN clause. Edit CH1501.SQV to match the example in Listing 15.5.

Listing 15.5. Using the DROP COLUMN clause.

```
//
// testing SQL Table Management Keywords
//
// create a new database for our tests
dbMake sqlvb02.mdb;
// create a simple table
CREATE TABLE NewTable
    (Field1 TEXT(30) CONSTRAINT PKNewTable PRIMARY KEY,
     Field2 INTEGER);
// add a two new columns
ALTER TABLE NewTable ADD COLUMN Field3 DATE;
ALTER TABLE NewTable ADD COLUMN Field4 CURRENCY;
// drop one of the new columns
ALTER TABLE newTable DROP COLUMN Field3;
// show the empty table
SELECT * FROM NewTable;
// eof
```

Run the SQLVB02.SQV script and check your results against the screen shown in Figure 15.9.

Figure 15.9.

Results of the ALTER
TABLE...DROP COLUMN
keywords.

Note: You can also use the ALTER TABLE statement to ADD or DROP CONSTRAINTS. We'll cover CONSTRAINTS in depth later in this chapter.

Deleting Tables with *DROP TABLE*

You can use the DROP TABLE statement to remove a table from the database. This is often used to remove temporary tables, or it can be used as part of a process that copies data from one table to another or from one database to another. Edit and save CH1501.SQV to match the code example in Listing 15.6.

Listing 15.6. Using the DROP TABLE clause.

```
//
// testing SQL Table Management Keywords
//
// create a new database for our tests
dbMake sqlvb02.mdb;
// create a simple table
CREATE TABLE NewTable
    (Field1 TEXT(30) CONSTRAINT PKNewTable PRIMARY KEY,
     Field2 INTEGER);
// add a two new columns
ALTER TABLE NewTable ADD COLUMN Field3 DATE;
ALTER TABLE NewTable ADD COLUMN Field4 CURRENCY;
// drop one of the new columns
ALTER TABLE NewTable DROP COLUMN Field3;
// remove the table from the database
DROP TABLE NewTable;
// show the empty table
SELECT * FROM NewTable;
// eof
```

Save and run the updated SQLVB02.SQV. You should see an SQL error message telling you that it could not find the table NewTable. This happened because the script executed the DROP TABLE statement just before the SELECT...FROM statement. The error message appears in Figure 15.10.

Figure 15.10.
Results of the DROP TABLE statement.

Relationship SQL Keywords

You can create and delete indexes or constraints on a data table using the SQL keywords CREATE INDEX and DROP INDEX, and the CONSTRAINT clause of CREATE TABLE and ALTER TABLE statements. SQL constraints are just indexes with another name. However, CONSTRAINT clauses are usually used with CREATE TABLE statements to establish relationships between one or more tables in the same database. INDEX statements are usually used to add or delete search indexes to existing tables.

Managing Indexes with *CREATE INDEX* and *DROP INDEX*

The CREATE INDEX statement is used to create a search index on an existing table. The most basic form of the CREATE INDEX statement is shown in the following line:

```
CREATE INDEX NewIndex ON NewTable (Field1);
```

There are several variations on the CREATE INDEX statement that allow you to add data integrity to the data table. Table 15.2 shows a list of the various CREATE INDEX options and how they are used.

Table 15.2. The CREATE INDEX options.

CREATE INDEX Statement	Meaning and Use
CREATE INDEX NewIndex ON NewTable (Field1) WITH PRIMARY	Creates a primary key index. A primary key index ensures that each row of the table has a unique value in the index field. No nulls are allowed in the index field.
CREATE UNIQUE INDEX NewIndex ON NewTable(Field1)	Creates a unique index on the designated field. In this example, no two columns could have the same value, but null values would be allowed.
CREATE INDEX NewIndex ON NewTable (Field1) WITH DISALLOW NULL	Creates an index that is not unique, but does not allow null columns.
CREATE INDEX NewIndex ON NewTable (Field1) WITH IGNORE NULL	Creates a non-unique index that allows null records in the index column.

Use SQL-VB to create a new SQL script that contains the code from Listing 15.7. After you enter the code, save the script as SQLVB03.SQV.

Listing 15.7. Testing the relationship SQL keywords.

```
//
// sqlvb03.sqv - Test Relationship SQL keywords
//
// create a database
dbMake sqlvb03.mdb;
// create a test table to work with
CREATE TABLE NewTable1
   (EmployeeID   TEXT(10),
    LastName     TEXT(30),
    FirstName    TEXT(30),
    LoginName    TEXT(15),
    JobTitle     TEXT(20),
    Department   TEXT(10));
// create primary key
CREATE INDEX PKEmployeeID
   ON NewTable1(EmployeeID) WITH PRIMARY;
// create unique key column
CREATE UNIQUE INDEX UKLoginName
   ON NewTable1(LoginName) WITH IGNORE NULL;
// create non-null column
CREATE INDEX IKJobTitle
   ON NewTable1(JobTitle) WITH DISALLOW NULL;
// create multi-column sort key
CREATE INDEX SKDeptSort
   ON NewTable1(Department,LastName,FirstName);
// show empty table
SELECT * FROM NewTable1;
// eof
```

The preceding SQL script shows several examples of the CREATE INDEX statement. You can use SQL-VB to run this script. Your screen should look similar to the one in Figure 15.11.

Figure 15.11.
Results of SQLVB03.SQV script.

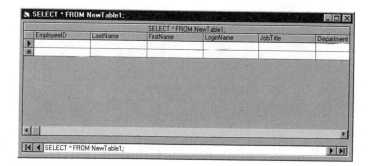

In the code example in Listing 15.7, we introduced a naming convention for indexes. This convention is widely used by SQL programmers. All primary key indexes should start with the letters PK (PKEmployeeID). All keys created for sorting purposes should begin with the letters SK (SKDeptSort). All index keys that require unique values should begin with UK (UKLoginName). All keys that define foreign key relationships should start with FK. (You'll learn more about foreign keys in the next section.) Finally, any other index keys should start with IK (IKJobTitle) to identify them as index keys.

Using the *ASC* and *DESC* Keywords in the *INDEX* Statement

You can control the index order by adding ASC (ascending) or DESC (descending) keywords to the CREATE INDEX SQL statement. For example, to create an index on the LastName column, but listing from Zilckowicz to Anderson, you would use the following CREATE INDEX statement:

```
CREATE INDEX SKLastName ON NewTable1(LastName DESC);
```

Notice that the DESC goes inside the parentheses. If you want to control the index order on a multiple column index, you can use the following CREATE INDEX statement:

```
CREATE INDEX SKDeptSort ON NewTable1(Department ASC, LastName DESC);
```

If you omit an order word from the CREATE INDEX clause, SQL uses the default ASC order.

Using Indexes to Speed Data Access

In the SQL-VB Listing 15.7, the index SKDeptSort is a special index key. This is a sort key index. Sort key indexes can be used to speed data access while performing single-record lookups (using the Visual Basic Find method), or for speeding report processing by ordering the data before running a list report. Sort key indexes are not used to enforce data integrity rules or perform data entry validation.

Although sort key indexes are very common in non-relational databases, they are not often used in relational databases. All the related indexes in a database must be updated by the database engine each time a data table is updated. If you have created several sort key indexes, you might begin to see a performance degradation when dealing with large data files or when dealing with remote (ODBC-connected) databases. For this reason, we do not recommend extensive use of sort key indexes in your database.

Using Indexes to Add Database Integrity

You have just about all the possible indexes created in the SQLVB03.SQV example. Many of the indexes serve as database integrity enforcers. In fact, only one of the indexes is meant to be

used as a tool for ordering the data (SKDeptSort). All the other indexes in SQLVB03.SQV add database integrity features to the table. This is an important point. In SQL databases, you have much more opportunity to build database editing and field-level enforcement into your database structures than you do with non-relational desktop databases. When you use the database enforcement options of SQL databases, you can greatly decrease the amount of Visual Basic code you need to write to support data entry routines. Also, by storing the database integrity enforcement in the database itself, all other programs that access and update the database have to conform to the same rules. The rules are no longer stored in your program; they're stored in the database itself!

PRIMARY KEY Enforcement

The PRIMARY KEY index (PKEmployeeID) is familiar to you by now. By defining the index as the primary key, no record is allowed to contain a NULL value in the column EmployeeID, and every record must contain a unique value in the EmployeeID column.

IGNORE NULL UNIQUE Enforcement

The index key UKLoginName allows records in the table that have this field blank (IGNORE NULL). However, if a user enters data into this column, the database checks the other records in the table to make sure that the new entry is unique (UNIQUE keyword). This shows an excellent method for enforcing uniqueness on columns that are not required to have input. For example, if you have an input form that allows users to enter their social security number, but does not require that they do so, you can ensure that the value for the field is unique by using the IGNORE NULL and UNIQUE keywords in the INDEX definition.

DISALLOW NULL Enforcement

The index key IKJobTitle is another example of using the SQL database engine to enforce data integrity rules. By defining the IKJobTitle index as DISALLOW NULL, you have set a data rule that defines this field as a required field. No record can be saved to the data table unless it has a valid value in the JobTitle column. Notice that you have not required that the value be unique. That would require every person in the database to have a unique job title. Instead, you allow duplicate job titles in this column. In real life, you would probably want to check the value entered here against a list of valid job titles. That involves creating a foreign key relationship using the CONSTRAINT keyword. Read the next section for more on CONSTRAINTS.

Managing Relationships with CONSTRAINTS

CONSTRAINTS are really the same as indexes from the standpoint of SQL statements. The CONSTRAINT keyword is used to create indexes that add data integrity to your database. You must use the CONSTRAINT keyword with the CREATE TABLE or ALTER TABLE SQL statement. There is no such thing in Microsoft Access JET SQL as CREATE CONSTRAINT.

There are three forms of the CONSTRAINT clause:

- ☐ PRIMARY KEY
- ☐ UNIQUE
- ☐ FOREIGN KEY

Microsoft Access SQL syntax does not allow you to use the IGNORE NULL or DISALLOW NULL keywords within the CONSTRAINT clause. If you want to create data integrity indexes that include the IGNORE NULL or DISALLOW NULL keywords, you have to use the CREATE INDEX keyword to define your index.

Using the *PRIMARY KEY CONSTRAINT*

The most commonly used CONSTRAINT clause is the PRIMARY KEY CONSTRAINT. This is used to define the column (or set of columns) that contains the primary key for the table. The SQL-VB script in Listing 15.8 creates a new database and a single table that contains two fields, one of which is the primary key column for the table. The other field is a MEMO field. MEMO fields can contain any type of free-form text and cannot be used in any CONSTRAINT or INDEX definition.

Listing 15.8. Testing the PRIMARY KEY CONSTRAINT.

```
//
// sqlvb04.sqv - Test CONSTRAINT SQL keyword
//
// create a database
dbMake sqlvb04.mdb;
// create jobs title table
CREATE TABLE JobsTable
    (JobTitle TEXT (20) CONSTRAINT PKJobTitle PRIMARY KEY,
     JobDesc  MEMO
     );
// show the table
SELECT * FROM JobsTable;
// eof
```

Enter this code into the SQL-Visual Basic editor, save the script as SQLVB04.SQV, and execute it. You will see a simple table that shows two fields. Refer to Figure 15.12 as an example.

The SQL script in Listing 15.9 performs the same task, except it uses the CREATE INDEX keyword to define the primary key index.

Figure 15.12.
*Defining the PRIMARY KEY
CONSTRAINT.*

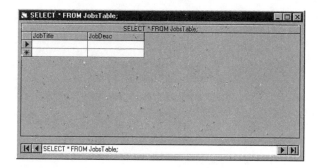

Listing 15.9. Using CREATE INDEX to define the PRIMARY KEY.

```
//
// create index using CREATE INDEX keywords
//
// create database
dbMake sqlvb04.mdb;
// create table
CREATE TABLE JobsTable
   (JobTitle TEXT(20),
    JobDesc MEMO
    );
// create index
CREATE INDEX PKJobTitle ON JobsTable(JobTitle) WITH PRIMARY;
// eof
```

Although the code examples in Listing 15.8 and Listing 15.9 both perform the same task, the second code example (15.9) is the preferred method for creating primary key indexes. Listing 15.9 documents the creation of the index at the time the table is created. This is easier to understand and easier to maintain over time. It is possible to create primary key indexes using the CREATE INDEX statement, but this can lead to problems. If you attempt to use the CREATE INDEX…PRIMARY KEY statement on a table that already has a primary key index defined, you get a database error. It is best to avoid this error by limiting the creation of primary key indexes to CREATE TABLE statements.

Using the *UNIQUE KEY CONSTRAINT*

Another common use of the CONSTRAINT clause is in the creation of UNIQUE indexes. By default, the index key created using the UNIQUE CONSTRAINT clause allows null entries in the identified columns. However, when data is entered into the column, that data must be unique or the database engine returns an error message. This is the same as using the IGNORE NULL keyword in the CREATE INDEX statement. You should also note that you cannot use the DISALLOW NULL keywords when creating a UNIQUE CONSTRAINT clause. By default, all keys created using the UNIQUE CONSTRAINT are IGNORE NULL index keys.

The SQL script in Listing 15.10 shows a new column in the JobsTable data table that was created in the last SQL-VB script. The new column, BudgetCode, is defined as an optional data column that must contain unique data. Update your version of the SQLVB04.SQV script, save it, and execute it. Your result set should resemble the one shown in Figure 15.13.

Listing 15.10. Adding a UNIQUE CONSTRAINT.

```
//
// sqlvb04.sqv - Test CONSTRAINT SQL keyword
//
// create a database
dbMake sqlvb04.mdb;
// create jobs title table
CREATE TABLE JobsTable
   (JobTitle TEXT (20) CONSTRAINT PKJobTitle PRIMARY KEY,
    BudgetCode TEXT(10) CONSTRAINT UKJobCode UNIQUE,
    JobDesc  MEMO
    );
// show table
SELECT * FROM JobsTable;
// eof
```

You can use the UNIQUE CONSTRAINT clause in a multicolumn index. This is especially handy if you have a data table containing more than one field that must be evaluated when deciding uniqueness. For example, what if the preceding data table in addition to BudgetCode, had BudgetPrefix and BudgetSuffix, too? You can make sure that the combination of the three fields is always unique by building a multicolumn CONSTRAINT clause. Use the code sample in Listing 15.11 as a guide. Update your SQLVB04.SQV script to match the example in Listing 15.11 and execute it to make sure you have written the syntax correctly.

Figure 15.13.

Defining a UNIQUE
CONSTRAINT index.

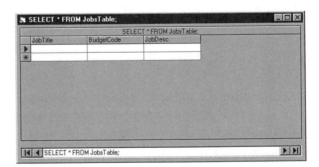

Listing 15.11. Defining a multicolumn UNIQUE CONSTRAINT.

```
//
// sqlvb04.sqv - Test CONSTRAINT SQL keyword
//
```

```
// create a database
dbMake sqlvb04.mdb;
// create jobs title table
CREATE TABLE JobsTable
    (JobTitle TEXT (20) CONSTRAINT PKJobTitle PRIMARY KEY,
     BudgetPrefix TEXT(5),
     BudgetCode   TEXT(10),
     BudgetSuffix TEXT(5),
     JobDesc MEMO,
     CONSTRAINT UKBudget UNIQUE (BudgetPrefix,BudgetCode,BudgetSuffix)
    );
// show table
SELECT * FROM JobsTable;
// eof
```

Once the script has executed, your screen should look similar to the one in Figure 15.14.

Figure 15.14.

The results of a multicolumn CONSTRAINT *clause.*

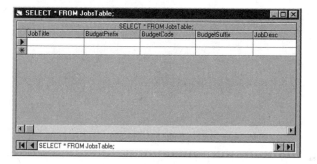

You should also be aware of an important difference between the single-column and multicolumn CONSTRAINT clause formats. Notice that when you are defining a *single-column* CONSTRAINT, you place the CONSTRAINT clause directly after the column definition *without* a comma between the column type and the CONSTRAINT keyword. In the *multicolumn* CONSTRAINT clause, you separate the CONSTRAINT clause *with* a comma and enclose the column names within parentheses. Mixing these two formats can lead to frustration when you are trying to debug an SQL script!

> **Tip:** Think of it this way. In the case of a single-column CONSTRAINT, these are additional qualifiers of the column; the constraint belongs *within* the column definition. A multicolumn CONSTRAINT, however, is a stand-alone definition that is not an extension of any one column definition. For this reason, multicolumn constraints are treated as if they are on an equal level with a column definition. They stand alone in the column list.

Using the *FOREIGN KEY...REFERENCES* Relationship

The most powerful of the CONSTRAINT formats is the FOREIGN KEY...REFERENCES format. This format is used to establish relationships between tables. Most commonly, a FOREIGN KEY relationship is established between a small table containing a list of valid column entries (usually called a *validation table*) and another table. The second table usually has a column defined with the same name as the primary key column in the validation table. By establishing a foreign key relationship between the two files, you can enforce a database rule that says the only valid entries in a given table are those values that already exist in the primary key column of the validation table. Once again, you are using the database engine to store data integrity rules. This reduces your volume of Visual Basic code and increases database integrity.

Let's use the previous script from Listing 15.11 (SQLVB04.SQV) to create a foreign key relationship. You already have a table defined—JobsTable. This is an excellent example of a validation table. It has few fields and has a single column defined as the primary key. Now let's add another table—the EmpsTable. This table holds basic information about employees, including their respective job titles. Listing 15.12 shows modifications to SQLVB04.SQV that include the definition of the EmpsTable data table.

Listing 15.12. Adding a PRIMARY KEY CONSTRAINT to the EmpsTable.

```
//
// sqlvb04.sqv - Test CONSTRAINT SQL keyword
//
// create a database
dbMake sqlvb04.mdb;
// create jobs title table
CREATE TABLE JobsTable
    (JobTitle TEXT (20) CONSTRAINT PKJobTitle PRIMARY KEY,
     BudgetPrefix TEXT(5),
     BudgetCode   TEXT(10),
     BudgetSuffix TEXT(5),
     JobDesc MEMO,
     CONSTRAINT UKBudget UNIQUE (BudgetPrefix,BudgetCode,BudgetSuffix)
     );
// create a test table to work with
CREATE TABLE EmpsTable
    (EmployeeID   TEXT(10) CONSTRAINT PKEmployeeID PRIMARY KEY,
     LastName     TEXT(30),
     FirstName    TEXT(30),
     LoginName    TEXT(15),
     JobTitle     TEXT(20),
     Department   TEXT(10)
     );
// show empty table
SELECT * FROM JobsTable;
SELECT * FROM EmpsTable;
// eof
```

The SQL-VB script in Listing 15.12 defines the EmpsTable with only one CONSTRAINT—that of the PRIMARY KEY index. Now let's define a relationship between the EmpsTable.JobTitle column and the JobsTable.JobTitle column. You do this by using the FOREIGN KEY CONSTRAINT syntax. The modified SQLVB04.SQV is shown in Listing 15.13.

Listing 15.13. Adding the FOREIGN KEY...REFERENCES CONSTRAINT.

```
//
// sqlvb04.sqv - Test CONSTRAINT SQL keyword
//
// create a database
dbMake sqlvb04.mdb;
// create jobs title table
CREATE TABLE JobsTable
   (JobTitle TEXT (20) CONSTRAINT PKJobTitle PRIMARY KEY,
    BudgetPrefix TEXT(5),
    BudgetCode   TEXT(10),
    BudgetSuffix TEXT(5),
    JobDesc MEMO,
    CONSTRAINT UKBudget UNIQUE (BudgetPrefix,BudgetCode,BudgetSuffix)
   );
// create a test table to work with
CREATE TABLE EmpsTable
  (EmployeeID  TEXT(10) CONSTRAINT PKEmployeeID PRIMARY KEY,
   LastName    TEXT(30),
   FirstName   TEXT(30),
   LoginName   TEXT(15),
   JobTitle    TEXT(20) CONSTRAINT FKJobTitle REFERENCES JobsTable(JobTitle),
   Department  TEXT(10)
   );
// show empty table
SELECT * FROM JobsTable;
SELECT * FROM EmpsTable;
// eof
```

Notice that the exact SQL syntax for single-column foreign key indexes is

```
CONSTRAINT IndexName REFERENCES Tablename(ColumnName)
```

As long as the column name you are referencing defines the PRIMARY KEY of the referenced table, you can omit the *(ColumnName)* portion of the CONSTRAINT clause. However, it is good programming practice to include the column name for clarity.

Use the SQL-VB editor window to load SQLVB04.SQV. Modify the script to match the code in Listing 15.13, save it, and run the script. Your screen should resemble Figure 15.15.

What you have defined here is a rule that tells the Microsoft JET database engine that, any time a user enters data into the EmpsTable.JobTitle column, it should refer to the JobsTable.JobTitle column to make sure that the value entered in EmpsTable.JobTitle can be found in one of the rows of JobsTable.JobTitle. If not, return an error message to the user and do not save the record to the data table. All of that is done without writing any input validation code at all!

Figure 15.15.

A foreign key constraint cascades the related tables on-screen.

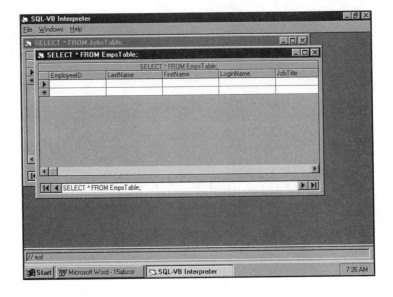

You can set up foreign key relations between any two columns in any two tables. They need not have the same column name, but they must have the same data type. For example, you can add a table to the SQLVB04.MDB database that holds information about job titles and pay grades. But in this table the column that holds the job title will be called JobName. Enter the script in Listing 15.14, save it, and execute it. Refer to Figure 15.16 as a guide.

Listing 15.14. Creating a foreign key relationship on unmatched field names.

```
//
// sqlvb04.sqv - Test CONSTRAINT SQL keyword
//
// create a database
dbMake sqlvb04.mdb;
// create jobs title table
CREATE TABLE JobsTable
   (JobTitle TEXT (20) CONSTRAINT PKJobTitle PRIMARY KEY,
    BudgetPrefix TEXT(5),
    BudgetCode   TEXT(10),
    BudgetSuffix TEXT(5),
    JobDesc MEMO,
    CONSTRAINT UKBudget UNIQUE (BudgetPrefix,BudgetCode,BudgetSuffix)
    );
// create job pay grade table
CREATE TABLE PayGrades
   (GradeID  TEXT(5)  CONSTRAINT PKGradeID PRIMARY KEY,
    JobName  TEXT(20) CONSTRAINT FKJobName REFERENCES JobsTable(JobTitle),
    PayMin   CURRENCY,
    PayMax   CURRENCY
    );
```

```
// create a test table to work with
CREATE TABLE EmpsTable
  (EmployeeID  TEXT(10) CONSTRAINT PKEmployeeID PRIMARY KEY,
   LastName    TEXT(30),
   FirstName   TEXT(30),
   LoginName   TEXT(15),
   JobTitle    TEXT(20) CONSTRAINT FKJobTitle REFERENCES JobsTable(JobTitle),
   Department  TEXT(10)
   );
// show empty table
SELECT * FROM JobsTable;
SELECT * FROM PayGrades;
SELECT * FROM EmpsTable;
// eof
```

Figure 15.16.

Results of a FOREIGN KEY
CONSTRAINT on unmatched
column names.

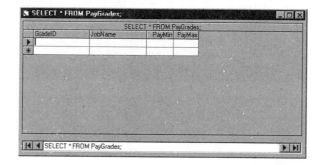

Notice that the column PayGrades.JobName does not have the same name as its referenced column (JobsTable.JobTitle). You can still define a foreign key relationship for these columns. This relationship will operate exactly the same as the one defined for EmpsTable.JobTitle and JobsTable.JobTitle.

It is also important to point out the order in which you must create tables when you are establishing foreign key constraints. You must always create the *referenced* table before you refer to it in a CONSTRAINT clause. Failure to adhere to this rule will result in a database error when you run your SQL-VB script. SQL must see that the table exists before a foreign key reference to it can be established.

It is also possible to create a multicolumn foreign key constraint. When you create multicolumn foreign key constraints, you must reference the same number of columns on each side of the relationship. For example, if you have a primary key index called PKBudgetCode that contains three columns, any foreign key constraint you define in another table that references PKBudgetCode must also contain three columns.

The example in Listing 15.15 shows an added FOREIGN KEY CONSTRAINT in the JobsTable. This constraint sets up a relationship between the Budget columns in the BudgetTrack table and JobsTable. Make the changes to the SQLVB04.SQV script and execute it to check for errors. Refer to Figure 15.17 to compare your results.

Listing 15.15. Creating a multicolumn FOREIGN KEY CONSTRAINT.

```
// create a database
dbMake sqlvb04.mdb;
// create budget tracking file
CREATE TABLE BudgetTrack
   (BudgetPrefix TEXT(5),
    BudgetCode   TEXT(10),
    BudgetSuffix TEXT(5),
    CONSTRAINT PKBudgetCode PRIMARY KEY (BudgetPrefix,BudgetCode,BudgetSuffix),
    AnnBudgetAmt CURRENCY,
    YTDActualAmt CURRENCY
   );
// create jobs title table
CREATE TABLE JobsTable
   (JobTitle TEXT (20) CONSTRAINT PKJobTitle PRIMARY KEY,
    BudgetPrefix TEXT(5),
    BudgetCode   TEXT(10),
    BudgetSuffix TEXT(5),
    JobDesc MEMO,
    CONSTRAINT FKBudget
        FOREIGN KEY (BudgetPrefix,BudgetCode,BudgetSuffix)
        REFERENCES  BudgetTrack
   );
// create job pay grade table
CREATE TABLE PayGrades
   (GradeID  TEXT(5)  CONSTRAINT PKGradeID PRIMARY KEY,
    JobName  TEXT(20) CONSTRAINT FKJobName REFERENCES JobsTable(JobTitle),
    PayMin   CURRENCY,
    PayMax   CURRENCY
   );
// create a test table to work with
CREATE TABLE EmpsTable
  (EmployeeID  TEXT(10) CONSTRAINT PKEmployeeID PRIMARY KEY,
   LastName    TEXT(30),
   FirstName   TEXT(30),
   LoginName   TEXT(15),
   JobTitle    TEXT(20) CONSTRAINT FKJobTitle REFERENCES JobsTable(JobTitle),
   Department  TEXT(10)
   );
// show empty table
SELECT * FROM JobsTable;
SELECT * FROM EmpsTable;
SELECT * FROM PayGrades;
SELECT * FROM BudgetTrack;
// eof
```

Notice that the syntax for adding multicolumn foreign key constraints differs from that used when creating single-column foreign key relationships. When creating multicolumn foreign key relationships, you have to actually use the keywords FOREIGN KEY. Also, you list the columns in parentheses in the same order in which they are listed in the referenced key for the referenced table.

Figure 15.17.

The results of adding a multicolumn FOREIGN KEY CONSTRAINT.

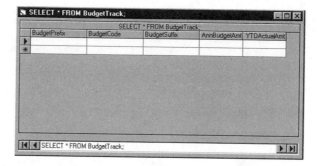

Using *ALTER TABLE* to *ADD* and *DROP* Constraints

You can also use the ALTER TABLE statement to add constraints or drop constraints from existing data tables. The code example in Listing 15.16 adds a new constraint to an existing table, and then removes it. You should be careful adding or dropping constraints outside of the CREATE TABLE statement. Although SQL allows you to do this, it can often lead to data integrity errors if data already exists within the target table. We recommend that you only establish CONSTRAINTS at the time you create the table using the CREATE TABLE statement.

Listing 15.16. Using ALTER TABLE to ADD and DROP constraints.

```
// create a database
dbMake sqlvb04.mdb;
// create budget tracking file
CREATE TABLE BudgetTrack
   (BudgetPrefix TEXT(5),
    BudgetCode   TEXT(10),
    BudgetSuffix TEXT(5),
    CONSTRAINT PKBudgetCode PRIMARY KEY (BudgetPrefix,BudgetCode,BudgetSuffix),
    AnnBudgetAmt CURRENCY,
    YTDActualAmt CURRENCY
    );
// create jobs title table
CREATE TABLE JobsTable
   (JobTitle TEXT (20) CONSTRAINT PKJobTitle PRIMARY KEY,
    BudgetPrefix TEXT(5),
    BudgetCode   TEXT(10),
    BudgetSuffix TEXT(5),
    JobDesc MEMO,
    CONSTRAINT FKBudget
       FOREIGN KEY (BudgetPrefix,BudgetCode,BudgetSuffix)
       REFERENCES  BudgetTrack
    );
// create job pay grade table
CREATE TABLE PayGrades
```

continues

Listing 15.16. continued

```
    (GradeID  TEXT(5)  CONSTRAINT PKGradeID PRIMARY KEY,
     JobName  TEXT(20) CONSTRAINT FKJobName REFERENCES JobsTable(JobTitle),
     PayMin   CURRENCY,
     PayMax   CURRENCY
     );
// create a test table to work with
CREATE TABLE EmpsTable
   (EmployeeID  TEXT(10) CONSTRAINT PKEmployeeID PRIMARY KEY,
    LastName    TEXT(30),
    FirstName   TEXT(30),
    LoginName   TEXT(15),
    JobTitle    TEXT(20) CONSTRAINT FKJobTitle REFERENCES JobsTable(JobTitle),
    Department  TEXT(10)
    );
// use alter table to add and drop a constraint
ALTER TABLE EmpsTable ADD CONSTRAINT FKMoreJobs
    FOREIGN KEY (JobTitle) REFERENCES JobsTable(JobTitle);
ALTER TABLE EmpsTable DROP CONSTRAINT FKMoreJobs;

// show empty table
SELECT * FROM JobsTable;
SELECT * FROM EmpsTable;
SELECT * FROM PayGrades;
SELECT * FROM BudgetTrack;
// eof
```

In today's lesson, you have seen SQL keywords that create and alter tables and establish table indexes and relationship constraints. Now you are ready for tomorrow's lesson in which you'll learn the SQL keywords that you can use to add data to the tables you have created. You'll also see keywords that you can use to copy tables, including the data.

Summary

In today's lesson you've learned how to create, alter, and delete database table structures using DDL (Data Definition Language) SQL keywords. You've also learned that using DDL statements to build tables, create indexes, and establish relationships is an excellent way to automatically document table layouts. You learned how to maintain database structures using the following DDL keywords:

☐ CREATE TABLE enables you to create entirely new tables in your existing database.

☐ DROP TABLE enables you to completely remove a table, including any data that is already in the table.

☐ ALTER TABLE enables you to ADD a new column or DROP an existing column from the table without losing existing data in the other columns.

☐ CREATE INDEX and DROP INDEX enable you to create indexes that can enforce data integrity or speed data access.

☐ The CONSTRAINT clause can be added to the CREATE TABLE or ALTER TABLE statement to define relationships between tables using the FOREIGN KEY clause.

Quiz

1. What are the benefits of using SQL to create and manage data tables?
2. What is the format of the CREATE TABLE statement?
3. What is the default size of a Microsoft JET TEXT field?
4. What SQL statement do you use to add a column to a table? What is its format?
5. What SQL statement do you use to remove a table from a database? What is the format of this statement?
6. What SQL statement creates an index to a data table?
7. What are the three forms of the CONSTRAINT clause?

Exercise

You have been assigned the responsibility to build a database of customers for your company. After careful review of the business processes and interviews with other users, you have determined that the following data must be maintained for the Customer database:

Table	Name	Field Type
CustomerType	CustomerType	TEXT(6)
	Description	TEXT(30)
Customers	CustomerID	TEXT(10)
	Name	TEXT(30)
	CustomerType	TEXT(6)
	Address	TEXT(30)
	City	TEXT(30)
	State	TEXT(30)
	Zip	TEXT(10)
	Phone	TEXT(14)
	FAX	TEXT(14)

Use SQL-VB to build this structure. Include a primary key for each table and an index on Zip in the Customers table. Include any foreign key relationships that you think would increase database integrity. Name your database CH15EX.MDB. (You can use any path that you like for the .MDB file.)

Updating Databases with SQL

In today's lesson, you'll learn about the SQL Data Manipulation Language (DML) keywords you can use to update and modify data in existing tables. Although most of the time you will use Visual Basic data entry forms and Visual Basic program code to perform data table updates, there are often times when it is more desirable to use SQL statements to update your data tables.

When you complete the examples in this chapter, you will be able to do the following:

- ☐ Alter the contents of existing tables using the UPDATE statement.
- ☐ Add new rows to existing tables with the INSERT INTO statement.
- ☐ Append rows from one table to another using the INSERT INTO...FROM clause.
- ☐ Copy one or more rows from an existing table to a new table using the SELECT...INTO keywords.
- ☐ Remove selected rows from a table using the DELETE...FROM clause.

Note: Throughout this chapter, you will use the SQL-VB program to create and run SQL scripts. The lesson in Day 15 contains a short tutorial on where to locate the SQL-VB program and how to use it. If you have not worked through the lesson on Day 15 yet, now is a good time to review at least the first half of the chapter.

Data Management SQL Keywords

The Data Management Language (DML) SQL keywords are used to add new data to existing tables, edit existing table data, append data from one table to another, copy data from one table to an entirely new table, and delete data rows from existing tables.

Most of the time, your Visual Basic programs will use data entry screens to perform these tasks. However, at certain other times, the DML keywords come in handy. In some back end database systems, these SQL keywords are the only way you can add, edit, or delete data from tables. At other times, these SQL keywords will give you the power to produce updates to large tables with very few lines of code and in a relatively short amount of time.

Also, many times you might need to select a small subset of data from your tables for a report or a graphic display. Instead of creating Dynaset views of existing tables, you might want to create a frozen Snapshot of the data to use for this purpose. What you need to do is copy some records from an existing table into a new table for use in reporting and displays. SQL DML keywords can help create these select tables quickly without extensive Visual Basic code.

Another example of using SQL DML keywords is when you want to append a set of records from one table to another. Instead of writing Visual Basic code routines that read a record from one

table and then write it to another, you can use SQL DML keywords to perform the table update—many times with just one line of SQL code.

Finally, SQL DML keywords allow you to quickly delete entire tables or subsets of the data in a single SQL statement. This reduces the amount of Visual Basic code you need to write and also greatly speeds the processing in most cases.

Adding Rows with the *INSERT* Statement

The INSERT statement is used to insert values into data tables. You can use the INSERT statement to populate data tables automatically—without the need for data entry screens. Also, you can perform this automatic data entry using very little Visual Basic code.

Why Use *INSERT* Statements?

Even though you will most often perform data entry using Visual Basic coded data entry screens tied to Visual Basic data controls, there are times when using the INSERT statement can prove more efficient.

An excellent example of the use of INSERT statements is the installation of a new database system. Often, several data tables need to be populated with default values before people can start using a system. You can use the INSERT statement to perform the initial data load.

Another use for the INSERT statement is in converting data from one database to another. Often, you can use INSERT statements to load existing data in one format into your newly designed relational database.

Finally, you can use INSERT statements to quickly add data to tables that would be too tedious to enter using data entry screens.

Using the *INSERT INTO* Statement

The basic form of the INSERT statement is

```
INSERT INTO TableName(field1, field2) VALUES (value1, value2);
```

Note: INSERT and INSERT INTO statements are often used interchangeably. For the most part, this book uses the latter term.

The INSERT SQL statement has three parts. The *TableName* identifies the table that you want to update. The *(field1, field2)* part of the statement identifies the columns into which you will add data. The *(value1, value2)* part of the statement identifies the exact values you will be adding to the fields you identified in the statement. You can name as few or as many fields as you like in the field portion of the statement. However, you must supply a list of values that has the same number of values and the same data type as those identified in the field portion of the statement. Also, you must list the values in the same order as the fields. The first value will be placed in the first field, the second value in the second field, and so on.

Let's use SQL-VB to create a working example of the INSERT statement. Open a new .SQV script called SQLVB05.SQV using the File | New command from the main menu. Enter the following script, save it, and execute it using the File | Run menu option. Refer to Figure 16.1 to compare your results.

Listing 16.1. Testing the INSERT INTO keyword.

```
//
// sqlvb05.sqv - Testing the INSERT INTO keyword
//
// create a new database
dbMake sqlvb05.mdb;
// create a new table
CREATE TABLE JobTitles
    (JobID TEXT(5) CONSTRAINT PKJobTitle PRIMARY KEY,
     JobName TEXT(20),
     JobDesc MEMO
     );
// insert some data
INSERT INTO JobTitles(JobID, JobName, JobDesc) VALUES
    ('J001',
     'President',
     'Presides over the company'
     );
INSERT INTO JobTitles(JobID, JobName, JobDesc) VALUES
    ('J002',
     'Vice President',
     'Does what the President tells him to do'
     );
// display results
SELECT * FROM JobTitles;
// eof
```

Notice that you must use a separate INSERT INTO statement for each row you want to add to the table. If you wanted to add 10 more job descriptions to the JobTitles table, you would need to add 10 more INSERT INTO statements to the script.

Also, because you defined the JobsTitles.JobID column as the primary key, you are required to fill that field with unique, non-null data each time you execute the INSERT INTO statement. If you provide a null value, or leave the JobsTitles.JobID field out of the INSERT INTO statement, you get a database error message.

Figure 16.1.

The results of the INSERT
INTO statement.

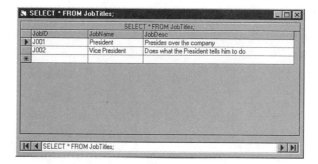

16

If you use a COUNTER data type field in your table, you can't include that in the field list of the INSERT INTO statement. Visual Basic and the SQL engine will fill the COUNTER field in with an appropriate value. Also, you do not have to add data to every column in the row. If there are fields in the data table that are not required and that can be left null, you can simply omit them from the INSERT INTO statement. The code example in Listing 16.2 illustrates these last two points. Use SQL-VB to edit the SQLVB05.SQV script to match the one in Listing 16.2. Save and execute the script. Check your results against those in Figure 16.2.

Listing 16.2. Handling COUNTER and blank fields in INSERT statements.

```
//
// sqlvb05.sqv - Testing the INSERT INTO keyword
//
// create a new database
dbMake sqlvb05/mdb;
// create a new table
CREATE TABLE JobTitles
    (JobCounter COUNTER,
     JobID TEXT(5) CONSTRAINT PKJobTitle PRIMARY KEY,
     JobName TEXT(20),
     JobPay CURRENCY,
     JobDesc MEMO
     );
// insert some data
INSERT INTO JobTitles (JobID, JobName, JobDesc, JobPay) VALUES
    ('J001',
     'President',
     'Presides over the company',
     '50000'
     );
INSERT INTO JobTitles (JobID, JobName, JobDesc, JobPay) VALUES
    ('J002',
     'Vice President',
     'Does what the President tells him to do',
     '40000'
     );
INSERT INTO JobTitles (JobID, JobPay, JobName) VALUES
    ('J003',
```

continues

Listing 16.2. continued

```
        '35000',
        'Chief Engineer'
    );
// display results
SELECT * FROM JobTitles;
// eof
```

Figure 16.2.

The results of using INSERT
INTO *with counter and
optional fields.*

Notice that the JobTitles.JobCounter column was automatically populated by Visual Basic. Also, you can see that the JobTitles.JobDesc column was left blank for the third record in the table.

Two other interesting things about the INSERT INTO statement are illustrated in the code example in Listing 16.2. Notice that the values for the JobTitles.JobPay column were surrounded by quote marks even though the data type is CURRENCY. When you use the INSERT INTO statement, all values must be surrounded by quote marks. SQL and Visual Basic will handle any type conversions needed to insert the values into the identified fields.

The second interesting thing to note in Listing 16.2 is the order in which columns are listed in the INSERT INTO statements. If you look at each of the statements, you will see that the JobTitles.JobPay column appears in different places within the field list. When you use the INSERT INTO statement, you can list the columns in any order. You only need to make sure that you list the values to be inserted in the same order in which you list the columns.

You have learned how to use the INSERT INTO statement to add individual rows to a table. This is commonly called a *single-record* insert. In the next section, you'll learn about a more powerful version of the INSERT INTO statement, commonly called an append query.

Creating Append Queries with *INSERT INTO...FROM*

The INSERT INTO...FROM version of the INSERT statement allows you to insert multiple records from one table into another table. This multirecord version of INSERT INTO is called an *append query*.

It is called an append query because it enables you to append rows from one table onto the end of another table. As long as the two tables you are working with have fields with the same name, you can use the INSERT INTO...FROM statement to append records from one table to the other.

The basic format of the INSERT INTO...FROM statement is as follows:

```
INSERT INTO TargetTable SELECT field1, field2 FROM SourceTable;
```

There are three important parts of the INSERT INTO...FROM statement. The first part is the *TargetTable*. This is the table that will be updated by the statement. The second part is the SELECT *fields* part of the statement. This is a list of the fields that will be updated in the *TargetTable*. These are also the fields that will be supplied by the third part of the statement— the *SourceTable*. As you can see, the INSERT INTO...FROM statement is really just a SELECT...FROM query with an INSERT INTO *TargetTable* in front of it.

Now, let's update the SQLVB05.SQV to provide an example of the INSERT INTO...FROM statement. First, use SQL-VB to load and edit the SQLVB05.SQV script. Make changes to the script so that it matches the one shown in the code example in Listing 16.3. Save the script and run it. Check your results against those shown in Figure 16.3.

Listing 16.3 Using the INSERT INTO...FROM statement.

```
//
// sqlvb05.sqv - Testing the INSERT INTO keyword
//
// create a new database
dbMake sqlvb05.mdb;
// create a new table
CREATE TABLE JobTitles
    (JobCounter COUNTER,
     JobID TEXT(5) CONSTRAINT PKJobTitle PRIMARY KEY,
     JobName TEXT(20),
     JobPay CURRENCY,
     JobDesc MEMO
    );
// insert some data
INSERT INTO JobTitles (JobID, JobName, JobDesc, JobPay) VALUES
    ('J001',
     'President',
     'Presides over the company',
     '50000'
    );
INSERT INTO JobTitles (JobID, JobName, JobDesc, JobPay) VALUES
    ('J002',
     'Vice President',
     'Does what the President tells him to do',
     '40000'
    );
INSERT INTO JobTitles (JobID, JobPay, JobName) VALUES
```

continues

Listing 16.3 continued

```
        ('J003',
         '35000',
         'Chief Engineer'
        );
// create a second table to hold some of the info from JobTitles
CREATE TABLE JobReport
    (JobID TEXT(5) CONSTRAINT PKJobReport PRIMARY KEY,
     JobName TEXT(20),
     JobDesc MEMO,
     DeptID  TEXT(5)
    );
// now append records from JobTitles into JobReport
INSERT INTO JobReport
    SELECT JobID, JobName, JobDesc FROM JobTitles;

// display results
SELECT * FROM JobTitles;
SELECT * FROM JobReport;
// eof
```

Figure 16.3.

The results of the INSERT INTO...FROM statement.

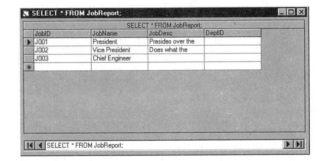

Note: You might have noticed in Listing 16.3 that you created two indexes, each on an identical column name, but you named the two indexes different names. SQL will not allow you to use the same name on two different indexes, even if they refer to a different table. Indexes appear as independent data objects in a Microsoft Access database. Each object must have a unique name.

Notice that the INSERT INTO...FROM statement lists only those fields that are present in both tables. You need to list the columns by name in this example because the JobReport table does not contain all the fields that the JobTitles table contains. If both tables were an exact match, you could use the asterisk wildcard (*) character in the SELECT clause. For example, if JobTitles and

JobReport shared all the same column names, you could use the following SQL statement to append data from one to the other:

```
INSERT INTO JobReport SELECT * FROM JobTitles;
```

You can also use the INSERT INTO statement to append rows to tables in another database. You accomplish this by adding an IN clause to the first part of the statement. For example, you can add rows from the JobTitles table in SQLVB05.MDB to a similar table in another database called SQLVB05B.MDB. The syntax for the IN clause of an INSERT INTO...FROM statement is

```
IN "DatabaseFileName" "DatabaseFormat"
```

The DatabaseFileName is the complete database filename including the drive identifier and the path name of the destination (or external) database. The DatabaseFormat is the name of the database format of the destination database, such as FoxPro, dBASE, Paradox, and so on. For example, if you want to update TableOne in the external database called EXTERNAL.MDB on drive C at the directory called DB, you would use the following IN clause for the SELECT INTO statement:

```
SELECT INTO TableOne IN "c:\db\external.mdb" "access"
```

Listing 16.4 shows how this is done using a real set of database files. Use SQL-VB to load and edit SQLVB05.SQV to match the modifications outlined in Listing 16.4. Save the script and execute it. Your results should look similar to those in Figure 16.4.

Listing 16.4. Adding the IN clause.

```
//
// sqlvb05.sqv - Testing the INSERT INTO keyword
//
// create sqlvgb05b database
dbMake sqlvb05b.mdb;
// make a table
CREATE TABLE OtherTitles
   (JobCounter COUNTER,
    JobID TEXT(5) CONSTRAINT PKJobTitle PRIMARY KEY,
    JobName TEXT(20),
    JobPay CURRENCY,
    JobDesc MEMO
    );
// insert some rows
INSERT INTO OtherTitles (JobID, JobName, JobDesc, JobPay) VALUES
   ('J004',
    'Line Foreman',
    'Supervises production line',
    '30000'
    );
INSERT INTO OtherTitles (JobID, JobName, JobDesc, JobPay) VALUES
   ('J005',
```

continues

Listing 16.4. continued

```
        'Line Worker',
        'Does what the Line Foreman tells him to do',
        '25000'
        );
// show results
SELECT * FROM OtherTitles;
// now close this database
dbClose;
// ***********************************************************
// create a new database
dbMake sqlvb05.mdb;
// create a new table
CREATE TABLE JobTitles
    (JobCounter COUNTER,
     JobID TEXT(5) CONSTRAINT PKJobTitle PRIMARY KEY,
     JobName TEXT(20),
     JobPay CURRENCY,
     JobDesc MEMO
     );
// insert some data
INSERT INTO JobTitles (JobID, JobName, JobDesc, JobPay) VALUES
    ('J001',
     'President',
     'Presides over the company',
     '50000'
     );
INSERT INTO JobTitles (JobID, JobName, JobDesc, JobPay) VALUES
    ('J002',
     'Vice President',
     'Does what the President tells him to do',
     '40000'
     );
INSERT INTO JobTitles (JobID, JobPay, JobName) VALUES
    ('J003',
     '35000',
     'Chief Engineer'
     );
// create a second table to hold some of the info from JobTitles
CREATE TABLE JobReport
    (JobID TEXT(5) CONSTRAINT PKJobReport PRIMARY KEY,
     JobName TEXT(20),
     JobDesc MEMO
     );
// now append records from JobTitles into JobReport
INSERT INTO JobReport
    SELECT JobID, JobName, JobDesc FROM JobTitles;

// display results
SELECT * FROM JobTitles;
SELECT * FROM JobReport;
// now append data from one database to another
INSERT INTO OtherTitles IN "sqlvb05.mdb" "Access"
    SELECT JobID, JobName, JobDesc, JobPay FROM JobTitles;
// close this db
dbClose;
```

```
// open other db
dbOpen sqlvb05b.mdb
// show updated table
SELECT * FROM OtherTitles;
// eof
```

Figure 16.4.

The results of the INSERT INTO...FROM statement with IN clause.

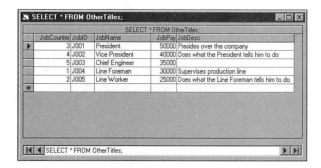

The script in Listing 16.4 first creates a database with a single table (OtherTitles) that has two records in the table. Then the script displays the table for a moment before the database is closed. Notice that the records in the table have OtherTitles.JobCounter values of 1 and 2. Then the script creates the JobTitles table in another database and populates that table with three records. Other tables are populated (this was done in previous examples), and eventually the JobTitles table is displayed. Notice that the three records have JobTitles.JobCounter values of 1, 2, and 3. Finally, the INSERT INTO...FROM...IN statement is executed to update the external data table. Then the external table is opened so that you can view the results.

Now look at the OtherTitles.JobCounter values. What has happened? When you append COUNTER data fields to another table, the new records will be renumbered. This is to ensure unique counter values in the table. If you want to retain the old numbers, you can include the COUNTER field in your INSERT INTO list. To illustrate this, add the JobCounter column name to the field list in the INSERT INTO statement that updated the external table. (See Figure 16.5.) Now execute the script again to see the results.

Figure 16.5.

The results of the INSERT INTO...FROM...IN with updated counter column.

SELECT * FROM OtherTitles;

JobCounter	JobID	JobName	JobPay	JobDesc
1	J001	President	50000	Presides over the
2	J002	Vice President	40000	Does what the
3	J003	Chief Engineer	35000	
1	J004	Line Foreman	30000	Supervises
2	J005	Line Worker	25000	Does what the Line

As you can see in Figure 16.5, you now have duplicate COUNTER values in your table. This can lead to data integrity problems if you are using the COUNTER data type as a guaranteed unique value. You should be careful when you use INSERT INTO statements that contain COUNTER data type columns.

> **Warning:** The Microsoft Visual Basic documentation for the behavior of INSERT INTO with COUNTER data types states that duplicate counter values will not be appended to the destination table. This is not correct. The only time duplicates are not included in the destination tables is when the COUNTER data type column is defined as the primary key.

We should point out here that if you attempt to append records to a table that has a duplicate primary key value, the new record will not be appended to the table—and you will not receive an error message! If you edit the SQLVB05.SQV script to renumber the OtherTitles.JobID values to J001 and J002, you will see a different set of results when you run the script. Figure 16.6 shows what you get when you attempt to update duplicate primary key rows.

Figure 16.6.

The results of attempting to append duplicate primary key rows.

JobCounter	JobID	JobName	JobPay	JobDesc
1	J001	Line Foreman	30000	Supervises
2	J002	Line Worker	25000	Does what the Line
3	J003	Chief Engineer	35000	Does what the

The fact that SQL will not append records with a duplicate key can be used as an advantage. You can easily merge two tables that contain overlapping data and get a single result set that does not contain duplicates. Anyone who has worked with mailing lists will be able to find a use for this feature of the INSERT INTO statement.

Now that you know how to insert rows into tables, it's time to learn how you can update existing rows using the UPDATE...SET statement.

Creating *UPDATE QUERIES* with the *UPDATE...SET* Statement

The UPDATE...SET statement enables you to update a large amount of data in one or more tables very quickly with very little coding. You use the UPDATE...SET statement to modify data already on file in a data table. The advantage of the UPDATE...SET statement is that you can use a single statement to modify multiple rows in the table.

For example, assume that you have a table of 500 employees. You are told by the Human Resource Department that all employees are to be given a 17.5 percent increase in their pay starting immediately (wouldn't it be nice?). You could write a Visual Basic program that opens the table, reads each record, computes the new salary, stores the updated record, and then goes back to read the next record. Your code would look something like the pseudocode sample in Listing 16.5.

Note: Listing 16.5 is not a real Visual Basic program; it is just a set of statements that read like program code. This pseudocode is often used by programmers to plan out programs without having to deal with the details of a particular programming language. Another benefit of using pseudocode to plan programs is that people do not need to know a particular programming language to be able to understand the example.

Listing 16.5. Sample code for record-oriented updates.

```
OPEN EmpDatabase
OPEN EmpTable
DO UNTIL END-OF-FILE (EmpTable)
   READ EmpTable RECORD
   EmpTable.EmpSalary = EmpTable.EmpSalary * 1.175
   WRITE EmpTable RECORD
END DO
CLOSE EmpTable
CLOSE EmpDatabase
```

This is a relatively simple process but—depending on the size of the data table and the speed of your workstation or the database server—this kind of table update could take quite a bit of time. You can use the SQL UPDATE statement to perform the same task.

```
OPEN database
UPDATE EmpTable SET EmpSalary = EmpSalary * 1.175
CLOSE database
```

The preceding example shows how you can accomplish the same task with less coding. Even better, this code will run much faster than the walk-through loop shown in Listing 16.5, and this single line of code works for any number of records in the set. Furthermore, if this statement is sent to a back-end database server connected via ODBC and not processed by the local workstation, you could see an ever greater increase in processing speed for your program.

Let's start a new program that will illustrate the UPDATE...SET statement. Use SQL-VB to create a new script file called SQLVB06.SQV and enter the commands in Listing 16.6. After you save the script, execute it and check your results against those in Figure 16.7.

Listing 16.6. Using the UPDATE...SET statement.

```
//
// sqlvb06.sqv - testing the UPDATE ... SET statement
//
// create a database
dbMake sqlvb06.mdb;
// create a table
CREATE TABLE EmpTable
   (EmpID TEXT(5) CONSTRAINT PKEmpTable PRIMARY KEY,
    EmpName TEXT(30),
    EmpSalary CURRENCY
    );
// insert some data
INSERT INTO EmpTable VALUES
   ('E001',
    'Anderson, Shannon',
    '35000'
    );
INSERT INTO EmpTable VALUES
   ('E002',
    'Billings, Jesse',
    '30000'
    );
INSERT INTO EmpTable VALUES
   ('E003',
    'Caldwell, Dana',
    '25000'
    );
// show first result set
SELECT * FROM EmpTable;
// now perform update
UPDATE empTable SET EmpSalary = EmpSalary * 1.175;
// show new results
SELECT * FROM EmpTable;
// eof
```

Figure 16.7.
The results of using the
UPDATE...SET statement.

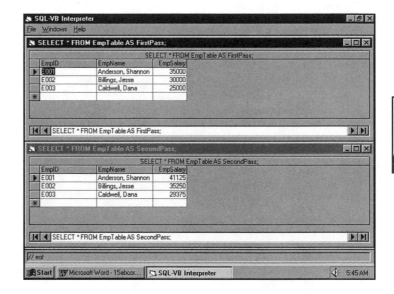

Note: Notice that you did not include the column names in the INSERT INTO statements in this example. As long as you are supplying *all* the column values for a table, in the same order that they appear in the physical layout, you can omit the column names from the statement.

As you can see in Figure 16.7, all the records in the table are updated by the UPDATE...SET statement. The SET statement works for both numeric and character fields. It can contain any number of column updates, too. For example, if you have a table that has three fields that need to be updated, you can use the following SQL statement:

```
UPDATE MyTable SET
   CustType="RETAIL",
   CustDiscount=10,
   CustDate=#01/15/96#;
```

You can also add a WHERE clause to the UPDATE statement to limit the rows that are affected by the SET portion of the statement. What if you want to give anyone whose salary is over $35,000 a 10 percent raise and anyone whose salary is $35,000 or under a 15 percent raise? You could accomplish this with two UPDATE...SET statements that each contain a WHERE clause. Use the code in Listing 16.7 as a guide to modifying the SQLVB06.SQV script. Save your changes and run the script. Check your results against Figure 16.8.

Listing 16.7. Adding the WHERE clause to the UPDATE statement.

```
//
// sqlvb06.sqv - testing the UPDATE ... SET statement
//
// create a database
dbMake sqlvb06.mdb;
// create a table
CREATE TABLE EmpTable
   (EmpID TEXT(5) CONSTRAINT PKEmpTable PRIMARY KEY,
    EmpName TEXT(30),
    EmpSalary CURRENCY
    );
// insert some data
INSERT INTO EmpTable VALUES
   ('E001',
    'Anderson, Shannon',
    '35000'
    );
INSERT INTO EmpTable VALUES
   ('E002',
    'Billings, Jesse',
    '30000'
    );
INSERT INTO EmpTable VALUES
   ('E003',
    'Caldwell, Dana',
    '25000'
    );
// show first result set
SELECT * FROM EmpTable AS FirstPass;
// now perform updates
UPDATE EmpTable SET EmpSalary = EmpSalary * 1.10
   WHERE EmpSalary > 30000;
UPDATE empTable SET EmpSalary = EmpSalary * 1.15
   WHERE EmpSalary <= 30000;
// show new results
SELECT * FROM EmpTable AS SecondPass;
// eof
```

In Listing 16.7, you use the WHERE clause to isolate the records you want to modify with the UPDATE...SET statement. The WHERE clause can be as simple or as complicated as needed to meet the criteria. In other words, any WHERE clause that is valid within the SELECT...FROM statement can be used as part of the UPDATE...SET statement.

Figure 16.8.

The results of the UPDATE QUERY with a WHERE clause.

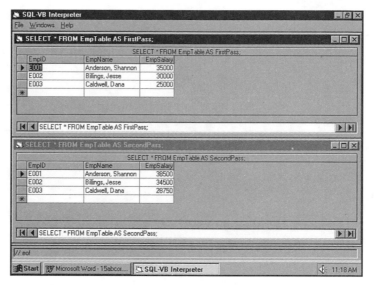

16

Creating Make Table Queries Using the *SELECT...INTO...FROM* Statement

The SELECT...INTO...FROM statement allows you to create entirely new tables, complete with data from existing tables. This is called a Make Table query because it enables you to make a new table. The difference between Make Table queries and the CREATE TABLE statement is that you use the Make Table query to copy both the table structure and the data within the table from an already existing table. Because the Make Table query is really just a form of a SELECT statement, you can use all the clauses valid for a SELECT statement when copying data tables including WHERE, ORDER BY, GROUP BY, and HAVING.

Make Table queries are excellent for making backup copies of your data tables. You can also create static read-only tables for reporting and reviewing purposes. For example, you can create a Make Table query that summarizes sales for the period and save the results in a data table that can be accessed for reports and on-screen displays. Now you can provide summary data to your users without giving them access to the underlying transaction tables. This can improve overall processing speed and help provide data security, too.

The basic form of the Make Table query is

```
SELECT field1, field2 INTO DestinationTable FROM SourceTable;
```

539

In the preceding example, the *field1, field2* list contains the list of fields in the *SourceTable* that will be copied to the *DestinationTable*. If you want to copy all the columns from the source to the destination, you can use the asterisk wildcard (*) character for the field list. Enter the SQL-VB script in Listing 16.8 as SQLVB07.SQV. Save and execute the script, and check your on-screen results against those in Figure 16.9.

Listing 16.8. Testing Make Table queries.

```
//
// sqlvb07.sqv - Testing Make Table Queries
//
// create a database
dbMake sqlvb07.mdb;
// create a base table
CREATE TABLE BaseTable
    (CustID TEXT(10) CONSTRAINT PKBaseTable PRIMARY KEY,
     CustName TEXT(30),
     CustBalance CURRENCY,
     CustType TEXT(10),
     Notes MEMO
     );
// add some data
INSERT INTO BaseTable VALUES
    ('CUST01',
     'Willingham & Associates',
     '300.65',
     'RETAIL',
     'This is a comment'
     );
INSERT INTO BaseTable VALUES
    ('CUST02',
     'Parker & Parker',
     '1000.29',
     'WHOLESALE',
     'This is another comment'
     );
INSERT INTO BaseTable VALUES
    ('CUST03',
     'Anchor, Smith, & Hocking',
     '575.25',
     'RETAIL',
     'This is the last comment'
     );
// now make a new table from the old one
SELECT * INTO CopyTable FROM BaseTable;
// show results
SELECT * FROM BaseTable;
SELECT * FROM CopyTable;
// eof
```

In Listing 16.8, you created a database with one table, populated the table with some test data, and then executed a Make Table query that copied the table structure and contents to a new table in the same database.

Figure 16.9.

The results of a simple Make Table query.

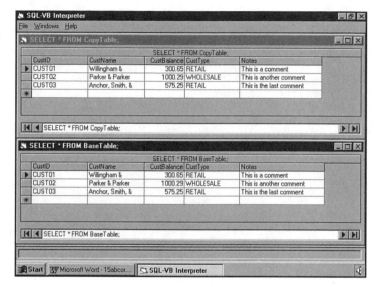

You can use the WHERE clause to limit the rows copied to the new table. Modify SQLVB07.SQV to contain the new SELECT...INTO statement and its corresponding SELECT...FROM as shown in Listing 16.9. Save the script and execute it. Your results should look similar to those in Figure 16.10.

Listing 16.9. Using the WHERE clause to limit Make Table queries.

```
//
// sqlvb07.sqv - Testing Make Table Queries
//
// create a database
dbMake sqlvb07.mdb;
// create a base table
CREATE TABLE BaseTable
   (CustID TEXT(10) CONSTRAINT PKBaseTable PRIMARY KEY,
    CustName TEXT(30),
    CustBalance CURRENCY,
    CustType TEXT(10),
    Notes MEMO
    );
// add some data
INSERT INTO BaseTable VALUES
   ('CUST01',
    'Willingham & Associates',
    '300.65',
    'RETAIL',
    'This is a comment'
    );
INSERT INTO BaseTable VALUES
   ('CUST02',
```

continues

Listing 16.9. continued

```
        'Parker & Parker',
        '1000.29',
        'WHOLESALE',
        'This is another comment'
        );
INSERT INTO BaseTable VALUES
    ('CUST03',
        'Anchor, Smith, & Hocking',
        '575.25',
        'RETAIL',
        'This is the last comment'
        );
// now make a new table from the old one
SELECT * INTO CopyTable FROM BaseTable;
// select just some of the records
SELECT * INTO RetailTable FROM BaseTable
    WHERE CustType='RETAIL';
// show results
SELECT * FROM BaseTable;
SELECT * FROM CopyTable;
SELECT * FROM RetailTable;
// eof
```

Figure 16.10.

Using the WHERE clause to limit Make Table queries.

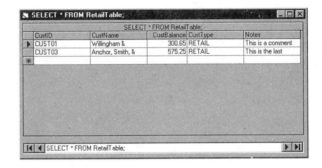

As you can see from Figure 16.10, only the rows with where CustType = 'RETAIL' are copied to the new table.

You can also use the GROUP BY and HAVING clauses to limit and summarize data before copying to a new table. Let's modify the SQLVB07.SQV script to produce only one record for each Customer Type, with each new row containing the customer type and total balance for that type. Let's also order the records in descending order by customer balance. Finally, let's rename the CustBalance field to Balance. The modifications to SQLVB07.SQV are shown in Listing 16.10. Make your changes, save and run the script, and compare your results to Figure 16.11.

Listing 16.10. Using GROUP BY and HAVING to summarize data.

```
//
// sqlvb07.sqv - Testing Make Table Queries
//
// create a database
dbMake sqlvb07.mdb;
// create a base table
CREATE TABLE BaseTable
   (CustID TEXT(10) CONSTRAINT PKBaseTable PRIMARY KEY,
    CustName TEXT(30),
    CustBalance CURRENCY,
    CustType TEXT(10),
    Notes MEMO
   );
// add some data
INSERT INTO BaseTable VALUES
   ('CUST01',
    'Willingham & Associates',
    '300.65',
    'RETAIL',
    'This is a comment'
   );
INSERT INTO BaseTable VALUES
   ('CUST02',
    'Parker & Parker',
    '1000.29',
    'WHOLESALE',
    'This is another comment'
   );
INSERT INTO BaseTable VALUES
   ('CUST03',
    'Anchor, Smith, & Hocking',
    '575.25',
    'RETAIL',
    'This is the last comment'
   );
// now make a new table from the old one
SELECT * INTO CopyTable FROM BaseTable;
// select just some of the records
SELECT * INTO RetailTable FROM BaseTable
   WHERE CustType='RETAIL';
// create a new summary table with fancy stuff added
SELECT CustType, SUM(CustBalance) AS Balance INTO SummaryTable
   FROM BaseTable
   GROUP BY CustType;
// show results
SELECT * FROM BaseTable;
SELECT * FROM CopyTable;
SELECT * FROM RetailTable;
SELECT * FROM SummaryTable;
// eof
```

Figure 16.11.

Using GROUP BY *and* HAVING *to summarize data.*

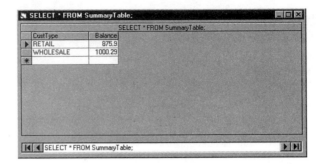

In all the examples so far, you have used the SELECT...INTO statement to copy existing tables to another table within the database. You can also use SELECT...INTO to copy an existing table to another database by adding the IN clause. You can use this feature to copy entire data tables from one database to another, or to copy portions of a database or data tables to another database for archiving or reporting purposes.

For example, if you want to copy the entire BaseTable you designed in the previous examples from SQLVB07.MDB to SQLVB07B.mdb, you could use the following SELECT...INTO statement:

```
SELECT * INTO CopyTable IN sqlvb07b.mdb FROM BaseTable;
```

You can use all the WHERE, ORDER BY, GROUP BY, HAVING and AS clauses you desire when copying tables from one database to another.

Warning: When you copy tables using the SELECT...INTO statement, none of the indexes or constraints are copied to the new table. This is an important point. If you use SELECT...INTO to create tables that you want to use for data entry, you need to reconstruct the indexes and constraints using CREATE INDEX to add indexes and ALTER TABLE to add constraints.

Creating Delete Table Queries Using *DELETE...FROM*

The final SQL statement you'll learn today is the DELETE...FROM statement, commonly called the Delete Table query. Delete Table queries are used to remove one or more records from a data table. The delete query can also be applied to a valid view created using the JOIN keyword. Although it is not always efficient to use the DELETE statement to remove a single record from a table, it can be very effective to use the DELETE statement to remove several records from a table.

In fact, when you need to remove more than one record from a table or view, the DELETE statement will outperform repeated uses of the Delete method in Visual Basic code.

In its most basic form, the DELETE statement looks like this:

```
DELETE FROM TableName;
```

In the preceding example, *TableName* represents the name of the base table from which you are deleting records. In this case, all records in the table would be removed using a single command. If you want to remove only some of the records, you could add an SQL WHERE clause to limit the scope of the DELETE action.

```
DELETE FROM TableName WHERE Field = value;
```

This example would only remove the records that meet the criteria established in the WHERE clause.

Now let's create some real DELETE statements using SQL-VB. Start a new script file called SQLVB08.SQV, and enter the script commands in Listing 16.11. Save the script and execute it. Check your results against those shown in Figure 16.12.

Listing 16.11. Using the DELETE statement.

```
//
// sqlvb08.sqv - Testing DELETE statements
//
// create a new database
dbMake sqlvb08.mdb;
// create a table to work with
CREATE TABLE Table1
    (RecID TEXT(10),
     LastName TEXT(30),
     FirstName TEXT(30),
     RecType TEXT(5),
     Amount CURRENCY,
     LastPaid DATE
    );
// add some records to work with
INSERT INTO Table1 VALUES
    ('R01',
     'Simmons',
     'Chris',
     'LOCAL',
     '3000',
     '12/15/95'
    );
INSERT INTO Table1 VALUES
    ('R02',
     'Walters',
     'Curtis',
     'INTL',
     '5000',
```

continues

545

Listing 16.11. continued

```
    '11/30/95'
    );
INSERT INTO Table1 VALUES
   ('R03',
    'Austin',
    'Moro',
    'INTL',
    '4500',
    '01/15/96'
    );
// show loaded table
SELECT * FROM Table1;
// now delete LOCAL records
DELETE FROM Table1
   WHERE RecType = 'LOCAL';
// show results
SELECT * FROM Table1;
// eof
```

Figure 16.12.

The results of a simple
DELETE statement.

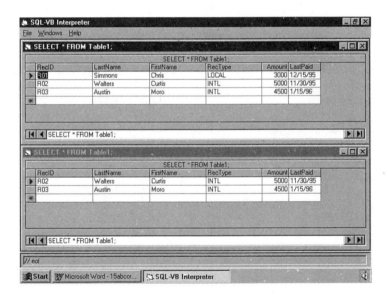

The SQLVB08.SQV script in Listing 16.11 creates a database with one table in it, populates that table with test data, and then shows the loaded table. Next, a DELETE statement is executed to remove all records that have a Table1.RecType that contains LOCAL. When this is done, the results are shown on-screen.

You can create any type of WHERE clause you need to establish the proper criteria. For example, what if you want to remove all international (INTL) records where the last payment is after

12/31/95? Edit your copy of SQLVB08.SQV. Then save and run it to check your results against Figure 16.13. Our version of the solution appears in Listing 16.12.

Listing 16.12. Using a complex WHERE clause with a DELETE statement.

```
//
// sqlvb08.sqv - Testing DELETE statements
//
// create a new database
dbMake sqlvb08.mdb;
// create a table to work with
CREATE TABLE Table1
   (RecID TEXT(10),
    LastName TEXT(30),
    FirstName TEXT(30),
    RecType TEXT(5),
    Amount CURRENCY,
    LastPaid DATE
    );
// add some records to work with
INSERT INTO Table1 VALUES
   ('R01',
    'Simmons',
    'Chris',
    'LOCAL',
    '3000',
    #12/15/95#
    );
INSERT INTO Table1 VALUES
   ('R02',
    'Walters',
    'Curtis',
    'INTL',
    '5000',
    #11/30/95#
    );
INSERT INTO Table1 VALUES
   ('R03',
    'Austin',
    'Moro',
    'INTL',
    '4500',
    #01/15/96#
    );
// show loaded table
SELECT * FROM Table1;
// now delete LOCAL records
DELETE FROM Table1
   WHERE RecType = 'INTL' AND LastPaid > #12/31/95#;
// show results
SELECT * FROM Table1;
// eof
```

Figure 16.13.

The results of the DELETE statement with a complex WHERE clause.

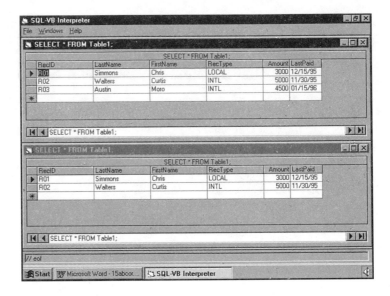

As you can see from the code in Listing 16.12, you only need to change the WHERE clause (adding the date criteria) in order to make the DELETE statement function as planned.

Note: You might have noticed that you enclose date information with the pound symbol (#). This ensures that Microsoft JET handles the data as DATE type values. Using the pound symbol works across language settings within the Windows operating system. This means that if you ship your program to Europe, where many countries use the date format *DD/MM/YY* (instead of the US standard *MM/DD/YY*), Windows will convert the date information to display and compute properly for the regional settings on the local PC.

You can also use the DELETE statement to delete records in more than one table at a time. These multitable deletes must be performed on tables that have a one-to-one relationship. The example in Listing 16.13 shows modifications to SQLVB08.SQV to illustrate the use of the JOIN clauses to create a multitable DELETE statement. Use SQL-VB to edit your copy of SQLVB08.SQV to match the one in Listing 16.13. Save and execute the script and refer to Figure 16.14 for comparison.

Listing 16.13. Using JOIN to perform a multitable DELETE.

```
//
// sqlvb08.sqv - Testing DELETE statements
```

```
//
// create a new database
dbMake sqlvb08.mdb;
// create a table to work with
CREATE TABLE Table1
    (RecID TEXT(10),
     LastName TEXT(30),
     FirstName TEXT(30),
     RecType TEXT(5),
     Amount CURRENCY,
     LastPaid DATE
     );
// add some records to work with
INSERT INTO Table1 VALUES
    ('R01',
     'Simmons',
     'Chris',
     'LOCAL',
     '3000',
     #12/15/95#
     );
INSERT INTO Table1 VALUES
    ('R02',
     'Walters',
     'Curtis',
     'INTL',
     '5000',
     #11/30/95#
     );
INSERT INTO Table1 VALUES
    ('R03',
     'Austin',
     'Moro',
     'INTL',
     '4500',
     #01/15/96#
     );
// create a second table for JOIN purposes
CREATE TABLE Table2
    (RecID TEXT(10),
     BizPhone TEXT(20),
     EMailAddr TEXT(30)
     );
// load some data
INSERT INTO Table2 VALUES
    ('R01',
     '(111)222-3333',
     'chris@link.net'
     );
INSERT INTO Table2 VALUES
    ('R03',
     '(777)888-9999',
     'moro@band.edu'
     );
INSERT INTO Table2 VALUES
```

continues

Listing 16.13. continued

```
        ('R04',
        '(222)444-6666',
        'person@mystery.uk'
        );
// show loaded table
SELECT * FROM Table1;
SELECT * FROM Table2;
// now delete records
DELETE Table1.*, Table2.* FROM
    Table1 INNER JOIN Table2 ON Table1.RecID = Table2.RecID;
// show results
SELECT * FROM Table1;
SELECT * FROM Table2;
// eof
```

Figure 16.14.

Results of a multitable
DELETE.

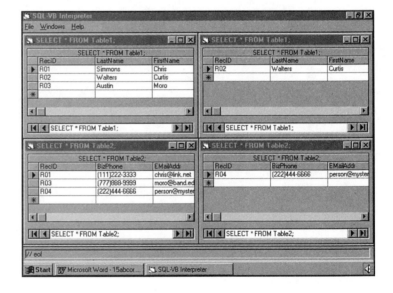

The results of this DELETE query might surprise you. Because there is no WHERE clause in the DELETE statement that could limit the scope of the SQL command, you might think that the statement will delete all records in both tables. In fact, this statement only deletes the records that have a matching RecID in both tables. The reason for this is that you used an INNER JOIN. INNER JOIN clauses operate only on records that appear in both tables. You now have an excellent way to remove records from multiple tables with one DELETE statement! It must be pointed out, however, that this technique only works with tables that have a one-to-one relationship defined. In the case of one-to-many relationships, only the first occurrence of the match on the many-side will be removed.

Here is a puzzle for you. What happens if you only list Table1 in the first part of that last DELETE statement?

```
DELETE Table1.* FROM
Table1 INNER JOIN Table2 ON Table1.RecID = Table2.RecID;
```

What records (if any) would be deleted from Table1? Edit SQLVB08.SQV, save it, and execute it to find out. Check your results against Figure 16.15.

Figure 16.15.

The results of a one-sided DELETE *using an* INNER JOIN.

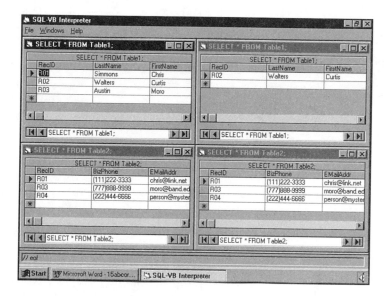

As you can see from Figure 16.15, a DELETE query that contains an INNER JOIN will only remove records from Table1 that have a match in Table2. And the records in Table2 are left intact! This is a good example of using JOIN clauses to limit the scope of a DELETE statement. This technique is very useful when you want to eliminate duplicates in related or identical tables. Note also that this INNER JOIN works just fine without the use of defined constraints or index keys.

Summary

You have learned how to add, delete, and edit data within tables using the DML (Data Manipulation Language) SQL keywords. You've learned that, by using DML statements, you can quickly create test data for tables and load default values into startup tables. You also learned that DML statements—such as Append queries, Make Table queries, and Delete queries—can outperform equivalent Visual Basic code versions of the same operations.

You learned how to manage data within the tables using the following DML keywords:

☐ The INSERT INTO statement can be used to add new rows to the table using the VALUES clause.

☐ You can create an Append query by using the INSERT INTO...FROM syntax to copy data from one table to another. You can also copy data from one database to another using the IN clause on an INSERT INTO...FROM statement.

☐ You can create new tables by copying the structure and some of the data using the SELECT...INTO statement. This statement can incorporate WHERE, ORDER BY, GROUP BY, and HAVING clauses to limit the scope of the data used to populate the new table you create.

☐ You can use the DELETE FROM clause to remove one or more records from an existing table. You can even create customized views of the database using the JOIN clause and remove only records that are the result of a JOIN statement.

Quiz

1. What SQL statement do you use to insert a single data record into a table? What is the basic form of this statement?

2. What SQL statement do you issue to insert multiple data records into a table? What is its format?

3. What SQL statement do you use to modify data that is already in a data table? What is the form of this statement?

4. What SQL statement is used to create new tables that include data from other tables? What is the format of this statement?

5. What SQL statement do you use to delete one or more records from a data table? What is the basic format of this statement?

Exercises

1. Modify the SQL-VB script you created in Exercise 1 of Day 15 to add the following records.

Data for the CustomerType table

Customer Type	Description
INDV	Individual
BUS	Business—Non-Corporate
CORP	Corporate Entity

Data for the Customers table

Field	Customer #1	Customer #2	Customer #3
CustomerID	SMITHJ	JONEST	JACKSONT
Name	John Smith	Jones Taxi	Thomas Jackson
CustomerType	INDV	BUS	INDV
Address	160 Main Street	421 Shoe St.	123 Walnut St.
City	Dublin	Milford	Oxford
State	Ohio	Rhode Island	Maine
Zip	45621	03215	05896
Phone	614-555-8975	555-555-5555	444-444-4444
Fax	614-555-5580	555-555-5555	444-444-4444

2. Create a third table that includes data from the CustomerID, City, and State fields of the Customers table. Call your table Localities.

3. Write an SQL statement that would delete the SMITHJ record from the Customers table. What SQL statement would you issue to delete the entire Customers table?

Database
Normalization

Now that you understand the Data Definition Language (DDL) portion of SQL, it's time to apply that new knowledge to a lesson on database theory. Today you'll learn about the concept of data normalization. You'll develop a working definition of data normalization and learn about the advantages of normalizing your databases. You'll also explore each of the five rules of data normalization, including reasons for applying these rules. When you have completed today's lesson, you will be able to identify ways to use data normalization to improve database integrity and performance.

Throughout today's lesson, you will be normalizing a real database using the data definition SQL statements you learned about on Day 15 and Day 16, and by using Visual Basic's Visdata application that you learned about last week (see Day 8, "Using the Visdata Program").

The topic of data normalization could easily take up an entire book—and there are several excellent books on the subject. This lesson approaches data normalization from a practical standpoint rather than a theoretical standpoint. Here you'll focus on two particular questions: What are the rules? How can these rules help me improve my Visual Basic database applications? To start out, let's develop a working definition of data normalization and talk about why it can improve your Visual Basic applications.

What Is Data Normalization?

Data normalization is a process of refining database structures to improve the speed at which data can be accessed and to increase the database integrity. This is not as easy as it might seem. Very often, optimizing a table for speed is not the same as optimizing for integrity. Putting together a database is a process of discovering the data elements you need and then creating a set of tables to hold those elements. The tables and fields you define make up the structure of the database. The database structure you decide upon will affect the performance of your database programs. Some database layouts can improve access speed. For example, placing all related information in a single table allows your programs to locate all needed data by looking in one place. On the other hand, you can lay out your database in a way that improves data integrity. For example, placing all the invoice line item data in one table and the invoice address information in another table prevents users from deleting complete addresses when they remove invoice line items from the database. Well-normalized databases strike a balance between speed and integrity.

High-speed tables have few index constraints and can have several, sometimes repetitive, fields in a single record. The few constraints make updates, insertions, and deletes faster. The repetitive fields make it easier to load large amounts of data in a single SQL statement instead of finding additional, related data in subsidiary tables linked via those slower index constraints.

Databases built for maximum integrity have many small data tables. Each of these tables can have several indexes—mostly foreign keys referencing other tables in the database. If a table is built

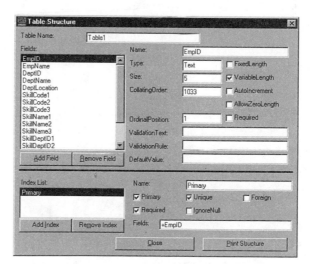

with high integrity in mind, it is difficult to add invalid data to the database without firing off database error messages. Of course, all that integrity checking eats precious ticks off the microchip clock.

Good data normalization results in data tables that make sense in a fundamental way. Well-normalized tables are easy to understand when you look at them. It is easy to see what kind of data they are storing and what types of updates need to be performed. Usually, it is rather easy to create data entry routines and simple reports directly from well-normalized tables. In fact, the rule of thumb is this: If it's hard to work with a data table, it probably needs more normalization work.

For the rest of this lesson, you will be using the Visdata application to build data tables. If you have not already compiled the Visdata application, see the lesson on Day 8 for information on how to load, compile, and save the application. Day 8 also covers how to use Visdata to maintain relational databases.

A Typical Database Before Normalization

To illustrate the process of normalization, let's start with an existing database table. The database NORMDAT1.MDB can be found in the CHAP17 directory. Load this into the Visdata application and open the Table1 data table. Your screen should look something like the one in Figure 17.1.

Figure 17.1.
Displaying Table1 before normalization.

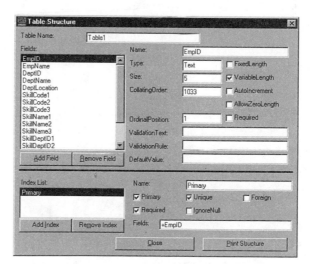

This data table holds information about employees of a small company. The table contains fields for the employee ID and employee name, and the ID, name, and location of the department to which this employee is currently assigned. It also includes fields for tracking the employee's job skills, including the skill code, the name, the department in which the skill was learned, and the ability level that the employee has attained for the designated skill. Up to three different skills can be maintained for each employee.

This table is rather typical of those you will find in existing record-oriented databases. It is designed to quickly give users all the available information on a single employee. It is also a fairly simple task to build a data entry form for this data table. The single form can contain the employee fields and the department fields at the top of the form and the three skill field sets towards the bottom of the form. Figure 17.2 shows a simple data form for this table generated by Visdata.

Figure 17.2.

The data entry form for Table1.

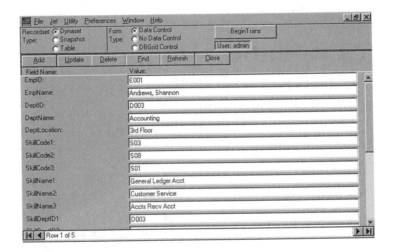

Access to the information in the table is fast and the creation of a data entry screen is easy. So this is a well-normalized table, right? Wrong. Three of the five rules of normalization that you will learn in the rest of this lesson are broken, and the other two are in jeopardy! Some of the problems are obvious, some are not. Let's go through each of the five rules of normalization and see how applying these rules can improve the data table.

Rule 1: Eliminate Repeating Groups

The first area in which Table1 needs some work is in the repeating skill fields. Why include columns in the data table called SkillCode1, SkillCode2, SkillCode3 or SkillName1, SkillName2, SkillName3, and so forth? You want to be able to store more than one set of skills for an employee, right? But what if you want to store data on more than three skills acquired by a single

employee? What if most of the employees only have one or two skills, and very few have three skills? Why waste the blank space for the third skill? Even more vexing is how easy will it be to locate all employees in the data table that have a particular skill?

Note: The first rule of data normalization states that you should make a separate table for each set of related columns and give each table a primary key. Databases that adhere to this first rule of normalization are in the First Normal Form.

The first rule of data normalization is to eliminate repeating groups of data in a data table. Repeating groups of data, such as the skill fields (SkillCodeX, SkillNameX, SkillDeptIDX, and SkillLevelX), usually indicates the need for an additional table. Creating the related table will greatly improve the readability of your tables and allow you to keep as few or as many skill sets for each employee as you need without wasting storage space.

The fields that relate to the employee skills need to be separated from the others in the table. You don't need to put all 12 skill fields in the new table, though. You only need one of each of the unique data fields. The new database now has not one, but two data tables. One, called Skills, contains only the skill fields. The other table, called Employees, contains the rest of the fields. Table 17.1 shows how the two new tables look.

Table 17.1. Eliminating repeating data.

Skills	Employees
EmpID	EmpID
SkillCode	EmpName
SkillName	DeptID
SkillDeptID	DeptName
SkillLevel	DeptLocation

Notice that the first field in both tables is the EmpID field. This field is used to relate the two tables. Each record in the Skill table contains the employee ID and all pertinent data on a single job skill (code, name, department learned, and ability level). If a single employee has several skills, there will be a single record in the Skill table for each job skill acquired by an employee. For example, if a single employee has acquired five skills, there will be five records with the same employee ID in the Skills table.

Each record in the Skills table must contain a valid value in the EmpID field or it should be rejected. In other words, each time a record is added to the Skills table, the value in the EmpID field should be checked against values in the EmpID field of the Employees table. If no match is found, the Skills record must be corrected before it is written to the database. You remember from the discussion of SQL Data Definition Language statements on Day 15 that this is a FOREIGN KEY CONSTRAINT. The field EmpID in the Skills table is a foreign key that references the field EmpID in the Employees table. Also, the EmpID field in the Employees table should be a primary field to make sure that each record in the Employee table has a unique EmpID value.

Now that you know the fields and index constraints you need, you can use SQL DDL to create two new tables. If you have not already done so, start the Visdata application and open the NORMDAT1.MDB database. Now you'll create two new tables that bring the database into compliance with the first rule of data normalization.

First, create the table that holds all the basic employee data. This table has all the fields that were in the Table1 table, minus the skill fields. Using the information in Table 17.1 as a guide, enter an SQL DDL statement in the SQL window of Visdata that creates the Employees data table. Your SQL statement should resemble Listing 17.1.

Listing 17.1. Creating the Employees table.

```
CREATE TABLE Employees
    (EmpID TEXT(5),
     EmpName TEXT(30),
     DeptID TEXT(5),
     DeptName TEXT(20),
     DeptLocation TEXT(20),
     CONSTRAINT PKEmpID PRIMARY KEY (EmpID));
```

Notice that the EmpID field has been designated as a primary key field. This guarantees that no two records in the Employees data table can have the same EmpID value. You can use the EmpID field in the next table you create (the Skills table) as the reference field that links the two tables. Because you are using the EmpID field as a link, it must be a unique value in the Employees table in order to maintain database integrity. What you are doing here is setting up a one-to-many relationship between the Employees table (the one side) and the Skills table (the many side). Any time you establish a one-to-many relationship, you must make sure that the reference field (in this case, the EmpID field) is unique on the one side of the relationship.

Now that you have built the Employees table, you can create the table that holds all the skills data. Use the information in Table 17.1 to write an SQL DDL statement that creates a table called Skills. Make sure the new table has the field EmpID and that the EmpID field is built with the correct index constraint to enforce one-to-many database integrity. Your SQL statement should look like the one in Listing 17.2.

Listing 17.2. Creating the Skills table.

```
CREATE TABLE Skills
    (EmpID TEXT(5),
     SkillCode TEXT(5),
     SkillName TEXT(20),
     SkillDeptID TEXT(5),
     SkillLevel INTEGER,
     CONSTRAINT PKSkills PRIMARY KEY (SkillCode,EmpID),
     CONSTRAINT FKEmpID FOREIGN KEY (EmpID) REFERENCES Employees(EmpID));
```

You can see in Listing 17.2 that you have used the FOREIGN KEY…REFERENCES syntax to establish and maintain the table relationship. As you remember from the SQL lessons on Day 15 and Day 16, the FOREIGN KEY…REFERENCES syntax makes sure that any entry in the Skills.EmpID field can be found in the related field Employees.EmpID. If users enter a value in the Skills.EmpID field that cannot be found in any Employees.EmpID field, Visual Basic automatically issues a database error message. This message is generated by Visual Basic, not by your program.

That's how you build tables that adhere to the first rule of data normalization. To see how these tables look when they have live data in them, use Visdata to load the CHAP17\NORMDAT2.MDB database. This database contains the Employees and Skills tables with data already loaded into them. Figure 17.3 shows how Visdata displays the two new tables that have live data.

Figure 17.3.
The new Employees and Skills tables from NORMDAT2.MDB.

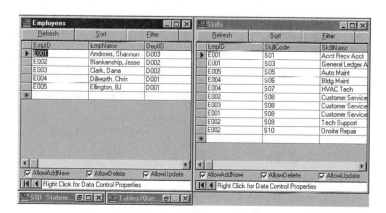

Note: Before continuing with today's lesson, load the NORMDAT2.MDB database into Visdata.

Rule 2: Eliminate Redundant Data

Another aspect to the Skills table also needs attention. Although moving the repeating skills fields into a separate table improves the database, you still have work to do. The Skills table contains *redundant data*. That is, data is stored in several places in the database. Redundant data in your database can lead to serious database integrity problems. It's best to eliminate as many occurrences of redundant data as possible.

> **Note:** The second rule of data normalization states that if a column depends only on part of a multivalued key, you remove it to a separate table. In other words, if you need to fill in two fields in order to truly identify the record (JobID and JobName), but only one of those fields is needed to perform a lookup in the table, you need a new table. Databases that conform to this rule are in the Second Normal Form.

For example, the Skills table includes a field called SkillCode. This field contains a code that identifies the specific skill (or skills) each employee has acquired. If two employees have gained the same skill, that skill appears twice in the Skills file. The same table also includes a field called SkillName. This field contains a meaningful name for the skill represented by the value in the SkillCode field. This name is much more readable and informative than the SkillCode value. In essence, these two fields contain the same data, represented slightly differently. This is the dreaded redundant data you have to eliminate!

Before you jump into fixing things, first review the details regarding redundant data and how it can adversely affect the integrity of your database.

Update Integrity Problems

When you keep copies of data elements in several rows in the same table or in several different tables (such as job names to go with the job ID codes), you'll have a lot of work ahead of you when you want to modify the copied data. If you fail to update one or more of these copies, you can ruin the integrity of your database. Redundant data can lead to what are known as *update integrity* problems.

Imagine that you have built a huge database of employee skills using the tables you built in the preceding section. All is going great when, suddenly, the Human Resources Department informs you that it has designed a new set of names for the existing skill codes. You now have to go through the entire database and update all the records in the Skills table, searching out the old skill name and updating the SkillName field with the new skill name. Because this is an update for the entire data table, you have to shut down the database until the job is complete in order to make sure no one is editing records while you're performing this update. Also, you probably have to change some Visual Basic code that you built to verify the data entry. All in all, it's a nasty job. If that isn't enough, how about a little power outage in the middle of your update run? Now you have some records that have the old names, and some have the new names. Things are really messed up now!

Delete Integrity Problems

Although the update integrity problem is annoying, you can suffer through most of those problems. In fact, almost all database programmers have had to face similar problems before. The more troublesome integrity problem resulting from redundant data comes not during updates, but during deletes. Let's assume you have properly handled the mass update required by the Human Resources Department. Now you discover that there is only one employee in the entire database that has on file the SkillCode S099 (the Advanced Customer Service course). No other employee has attained this high level of training. Now, that employee leaves the organization. When you delete the employee record from the file, you would delete the only reference to the Advanced Customer Service course! There is no record of the existence of the Advanced Customer Service course in your entire database, which is a real problem.

The Normalization Solution

The way to reduce these kinds of data integrity problems is to pull out the redundant data and place it in a separate table. You need a single table, called SkillMaster, that contains only the SkillCode and the SkillName data fields. This table is linked to the Skills table via the SkillCode field. Now, when the HR department changes the skill names, you only need to update a single record—the one in the SkillMaster table. Because the Skills table is linked to the SkillMaster table, when you delete that last employee with the certification for SkillCode S099, you won't be deleting the last reference to the skill. It's still in the SkillMaster table.

Tip: Another plus to this type of table separation is in speeding data entry. With only one field to enter, and especially a brief code, data entry operators can more quickly fill in fields on the table's form.

Also, you now have a single table that has a list of all the unique skills that can be acquired by your employees. You can now produce a Skills list for employees and managers to review. If you add fields that group the skills by department, you can even produce a report that shows all the skills by department. This would be very difficult if you were stuck with the file structure you developed in the previous section.

So now let's redefine the Skills table and the SkillMaster table to conform to the second rule of data normalization. Table 17.2 shows the fields you need for the two tables.

Table 17.2. The field list for the Skills and SkillMaster tables.

EmpSkills Table	SkillMaster Table
EmpID	SkillCode
SkillCode	SkillName
SkillDeptID	
SkillLevel	

You can see that you have renamed the Skills table to EmpSkills to better reflect its contents. You have also moved the SkillName field out of the EmpSkills table and created SkillMaster, a small table that contains a list of all the valid skills and their descriptive names. Now you have the added bonus of being able to add a FOREIGN KEY constraint to the EmpSkills table. This will improve database integrity without adding any additional programming code!

Listing 17.3 shows the two SQL DDL statements that create the EmpSkills and the SkillMaster data tables. Note the use of FOREIGN KEY constraints in the EmpSkills table.

Listing 17.3. Creating the SkillMaster and EmpSkills tables.

```
CREATE TABLE SkillMaster
   (SkillCode TEXT(5),
    SkillName TEXT(20),
    CONSTRAINT PKSkillMaster PRIMARY KEY (SkillCode))
CREATE TABLE EmpSkills
   (EmpID TEXT(5),
    SkillCode TEXT(5),
    SkillDeptID TEXT(5),
    SkillLevel INTEGER,
    CONSTRAINT PKSkills PRIMARY KEY (SkillCode,EmpID),
    CONSTRAINT FKEmpID2 FOREIGN KEY (EmpID)
      REFERENCES Employees(EmpID),
    CONSTRAINT FKSkillCode FOREIGN KEY (SkillCode)
      REFERENCES SkillMaster(SkillCode));
```

Use Visdata to add these two new tables to the NORMDAT2.MDB database. The database NORMDAT3.MDB contains a complete database with the data tables Employees, EmpSkills, and SkillMaster fully populated with data.

Figure 17.4.
The new Employees, EmpSkills, and SkillMaster tables.

Employees	
EmpID	EmpName
E001	Andrews, Shann
E002	Blankenship, Jes
E003	Clark, Dana
E004	Dillworth, Chris
E005	Ellington, BJ

EmpSkills	
EmpID	SkillCode
E001	S01
E001	S03
E005	S05
E004	S06
E004	S07
E001	S08
E002	S08
E003	S08
E002	S09
E002	S10

SkillMaster	
SkillCode	SkillName
S01	Accts Recv Acc
S02	Accts Payable A
S03	General Ledger A
S04	Fixed Assets Acc
S05	Auto Maintenanc
S06	Bldg Maintenanc
S07	HVAC Repair
S08	Customer Service
S09	Tech Support
S10	Onsite Repair

You now have a database that conforms to the first two rules of data normalization. You have eliminated repeating data and redundant data. You have one more type of data to eliminate from your tables. You'll handle that in the following section.

Note: Before continuing with the lesson, load the NORMDAT3.MDB database into Visdata.

Rule 3: Eliminate Columns Not Dependent on the Primary Key

By now, you're probably getting the idea. You are looking for hints in the table structure that lead you into traps further down the road. Will this table be easy to update? What happens if you delete records from this table? Is it easy to get a comprehensive list of all the unique records in this table? Asking questions like these can uncover problems that are not so apparent when you first build a table.

When you are building a data table, you should also be concerned about whether a field describes additional information about the key field. In other words, is the field you are about to add to this table truly related to the key field? If not, the field in question should not be added to the table. It probably needs to be in its own table. This process of removing fields that do not describe the key field is how you make your data tables conform to the third rule of data normalization—eliminate columns not dependent on keys.

17

> **Note:** The third rule of data normalization states that if a column does not fully describe the index key, that column should be moved to a separate table. In other words, if the columns in your table don't really need to be in this table, they probably need to be somewhere else. Databases that follow this rule are known to be in the Third Normal Form.

In these database examples, you have data describing the various departments in the company stored in the Employees table. Although the DeptID field is important to the Employees description (it describes the department to which the employee belongs), the *department-specific* data should not be stored with the employee data. Yes, you need another table. This table should contain only department-specific data and be linked to the Employees table via the DeptID field. Table 17.3 lists the modified Employees table and the new Departments table.

Table 17.3. The modified Employees table and the new Departments table.

Employees	Departments
EmpID	DeptID
EmpName	DeptName
DeptID	DeptLocation

Notice that the Employees table is much simpler now that you have eliminated all unrelated fields. Use Visdata to construct SQL DDL statements that create the new Departments table and then modify the Employees table and the EmpSkills table to increase database integrity (yes, more foreign keys!). First, use the SQL DDL in Listing 17.4 to create the Departments table.

Listing 17.4. Creating the Departments table.

```
CREATE TABLE Departments
  (DeptID TEXT(5),
   DeptName TEXT(20),
   DeptLocation TEXT(20),
   CONSTRAINT PKDeptID PRIMARY KEY (DeptID))
```

Now alter the Employees table. You need to do two things:

☐ Remove the DeptName column from the table.

☐ Add a FOREIGN KEY constraint to enforce referential integrity on the Employees.DeptID field.

Listing 17.5 contains the SQL DDL statements to create the modified Employees table.

Listing 17.5. Creating the new Employees table.

```
CREATE TABLE Employees
    (EmpID TEXT(5),
     EmpName TEXT(30),
     DeptID TEXT(5),
     CONSTRAINT PKEmpID PRIMARY KEY (EmpID),
     CONSTRAINT FKEmpDept FOREIGN KEY (DeptID)
        REFERENCES Departments(DeptID))
```

Now you need to modify the EmpSkills table to add the referential integrity check on the EmpSkills.SkillDeptID field. The new SQL DDL should look like Listing 17.6.

Listing 17.6. Creating the new EmpSkills table.

```
CREATE TABLE EmpSkills2
    (EmpID TEXT(5),
     SkillCode TEXT(5),
     SkillDeptID TEXT(5),
     SkillLevel INTEGER,
     CONSTRAINT PKEmpSkill2 PRIMARY KEY (SkillCode,EmpID),
     CONSTRAINT FKSkillMast FOREIGNKEY (SkillCode)
        REFERENCES SkillMaster(SkillCode),
     CONSTRAINT FKSkillDept FOREIGN KEY (SkillDeptID)
        REFERENCES Departments(DeptID));
```

Figure 17.5.

*The Departments
table added to
NORMDAT4.MDB.*

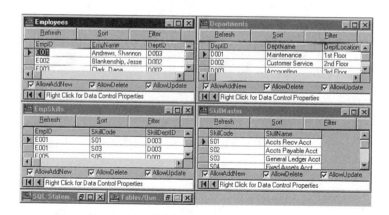

The database NORMDAT4.MDB contains a complete set of tables that conform to the third rule of data normalization. Use Visdata to load NORMDAT4.MDB and review the data tables. Attempt to add some data that does not follow the integrity rules. Try deleting records. This shows you how Visual Basic issues database error messages when you try to save a record that breaks the referential integrity rules.

The first three rules of data normalization involve the elimination of repeating, redundant, or unrelated data fields. The last two rules involve isolating multiple relationships to improve

overall database integrity. The first three rules are usually all that you need to produce well-designed databases. However, there are times when additional normalization can improve the quality of your database design. In the next two sections, you will learn rules 4 and 5 of data normalization.

Do Not Store Calculated Data in Your Tables

It is important to note here that one of the results of the third rule of data normalization is that you should not store calculated fields in a data table. Calculated fields are fields that contain derived data such as year-to-date totals, a line in the invoice table that contains the totals of several other rows in the invoice table, and so forth. Calculated fields do not describe the primary key. Calculated fields are *derived* data. It is a bad practice to store derived data in live data tables.

Derived data can easily fall out of sync with the individual rows that make up the total data. What happens if the individual rows that add up to the total are altered or deleted? How do you make sure the row that holds the total is updated each time any line item row is changed? Storing derived data might seem to be faster, but it is not easier. And dealing with derived data opens your database to possible update and delete integrity problems each time a user touches either the prime data rows or the total data rows. Calculated data should not be stored. It should always be computed using the prime data at the time it is needed.

Note: Before continuing with this lesson, load the NORMDAT4.MDB database into Visdata.

Rule 4: Isolate Independent Multiple Relationships

The fourth rule of data normalization concerns the handling of independent multiple relationships. This rule is applied whenever you have more than one one-to-many relationship on the same data table. The relationship between the Employees table and the EmpSkills table is a one-to-many relationship. There can be many EmpSkills records related to one Employee record. Let's add an additional attribute of employees to create a database that has more than a single one-to-many relationship.

Assume that the Human Resources Department has decided it needs more than just the skill names and skill levels attained for each employee. Human Resources also wants to add the level of education attained by the employee for that skill. For example, if the employee has an

accounting skill and has an associates degree in bookkeeping, Human Resources wants to store the degree, too. If an employee has been certified as an electrician and works in the Maintenance Department, the HR group wants to know that.

The first thing you might want to do is add a new column to the EmpSkills table—maybe a field called Degree, maybe even a field for YearCompleted. This makes sense because each skill might have an associated education component. It makes sense, but it is not a good idea. What about the employee who is currently working in the Customer Service Department but has an accounting degree? Just because the employee has a degree does not mean that employee has the skills to perform a particular job or is working in a position directly related to his or her degree. The degree and the job skills are independent of each other. Therefore, even though the skills data and the degree data are related, they should be isolated in separate tables and linked via a foreign key relationship.

> **Note:** The fourth rule of data normalization dictates that no table can contain two or more one-to-many or many-to-many relationships that are not directly related. In other words, if the data element is important (the college degree) but not directly related to other elements in the record (the customer service rep with an accounting degree), you need to move the college degree element to a new table. Databases that follow this rule are in the Fourth Normal Form.

Table 17.4 shows a sample Training table that can be used to hold the education information for each employee. Now the HR department can keep track of education achievements independent of acquired job skills. Note that the EmpID directly connects the two relationships. If the Training table has only one entry per employee, the two relationships are a one-to-one relationship between the Employees table and the Training table, and a one-to-many relationship between the Employees table and the EmpSkills table. Of course, if any employee has more than one degree, both relationships become one-to-many.

Table 17.4. The sample Training data table.

EmpID
Degree
YearCompleted
InstitutionName

Listing 17.7 is a sample SQL DDL statement that creates the Training data table with the proper relationship constraint. Enter this statement in the SQL window of Visdata while you have the NORMDAT4.MDB database open.

Listing 17.7. Creating the Training table.

```
CREATE TABLE Training
   (EmpID TEXT(5),
    Degree TEXT(20),
    YearCompleted INTEGER,
    InstitutionName TEXT(30),
    CONSTRAINT PKTraining PRIMARY KEY (EmpID,Degree),
    CONSTRAINT FKEmpTrn FOREIGN KEY (EmpID)
       REFERENCES Employees (EmpID))
```

Figure 17.6.

The Training table shows the degree achievements for the Employees table.

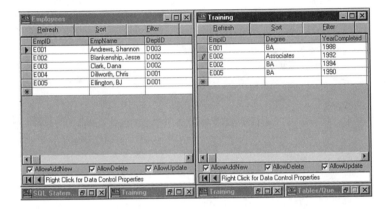

The database NORMDAT5.MDB contains a complete version of the database normalized up to the fourth rule of data normalization. Use Visdata to open the database and review the table structure.

Note: Before continuing with the lesson, load the NORMDAT5.MDB database into Visdata.

Rule 5: Isolate Related Multiple Relationships

The last remaining rule of data normalization covers the handling of related multiple relationships in a database. Unlike the fourth rule, which deals with independent, one-to-many, multiple relationships, the fifth rule is used to normalize related, many-to-many multiple relationships. Related, many-to-many multiple relationships do not occur frequently in databases. However, when they do come up, these types of data relations can cause a great deal

of confusion and hassle when you're normalizing your database. You won't invoke this rule often, but when you do it will pay off!

Imagine that the Maintenance Department decides it wants to keep track of all the large equipment used on the shop floor by various departments. It will use this data to keep track of where the equipment is located. The Maintenance Department also wants to keep a list of suppliers for the equipment in cases of repair or replacement. When you were a novice, you might have decided to design a single table that held the department ID, equipment name, and supplier name. But, as I'm sure have guessed by now, that is not the correct response. What if the Maintenance Department has more than one supplier for the same type of equipment? What if a single supplier provides more than one of the types of equipment used in the plant? What if some departments are restricted in the suppliers they can use to repair or replace their equipment?

Note: The fifth rule of data normalization dictates that you should isolate related multiple relationships within a database. In other words, if several complex relationships exist in your database, separate each of the relationships into its own table. Databases that adhere to this rule are known to be in the Fifth Normal Form.

The following list shows the relationships that have been exposed in this example:

☐ Each department can have several pieces of equipment.
☐ Each piece of equipment can have more than one supplier.
☐ Each supplier can provide a variety of pieces of equipment.
☐ Each department can have a restricted list of suppliers.

Although each of the preceding business rules are simple, putting them all together in the database design is tough. It's the last item that really complicates things. There is more than one way to solve this kind of puzzle. The one suggested here is just one of the many possibilities.

First, you need to expose all the tables that you need to contain the data. The preceding list describes two one-to-many relationships (department to equipment and department to supplier, with restrictions) and one many-to-many relationship (equipment to supplier, supplier to equipment). Each of those relationships can be expressed in simple tables. Two additional tables not mentioned, but certainly needed, are a table of all the equipment in the building (regardless of its location) and a table of all the suppliers (regardless of their department affiliation). Table 17.5 shows sample field layouts for the required tables. The Equipment and Supplier tables are shortened in this example. If you were designing these tables for a real database project, you would add several other fields.

Table 17.5. The Fifth Rule sample data tables.

Equipment Table	Supplier Table
EquipID	SupplierID
EquipName	SupplierName
DatePurchased	SupplierAddress

Listing 17.8 contains the SQL DDL statements to create these tables.

Listing 17.8. Creating the Equipment and the Supplier tables.

```
CREATE TABLE Equipment
   (EquipID TEXT (10),
    EquipName TEXT(30),
    DatePurchased DATE,
    CONSTRAINT PKEquipID PRIMARY KEY (EquipID))
CREATE TABLE Supplier
   (SupplierID TEXT (10),
    SupplierName TEXT(30),
    SupplierAddress MEMO,
    CONSTRAINT PKSupplier PRIMARY KEY (SupplierID))
```

Figure 17.7.
Supplier and Equipment tables in NORMDAT6.MDB.

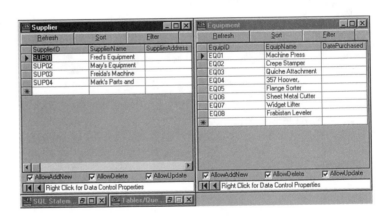

The next two data tables describe the relationships between Supplier and Equipment and between Supplier and Departments. You remember that departments can be restricted to certain suppliers when repairing or replacing equipment. By setting up a table such as the DeptSupplier table described next, you can easily maintain a list of valid suppliers for each department. Similarly, as new suppliers are discovered for equipment, they can be added to the EquipSupplier table. Refer to Table 17.6 for a sample list of fields.

Table 17.6. EquipSupplier and DeptSupplier tables.

EquipSupplier	DeptSupplier
EquipID	DeptID
SupplierID	SupplierID

These two tables are short because they are only needed to enforce expressed simple relationships between existing data tables. Creating small tables such as these is a handy way to reduce complex relationships to more straightforward ones. It is easier to create meaningful CONSTRAINT clauses when the tables are kept simple, too. The SQL DDL statements for these two tables are in Listing 17.9.

Listing 17.9. Creating the EquipSupplier and DeptSupplier tables.

```
CREATE TABLE EquipSupplier
  (EquipID TEXT(10),
   SupplierID TEXT(10),
   CONSTRAINT PKEqSpl PRIMARY KEY (EquipID,SupplierID),
   CONSTRAINT FKEqSplEquip FOREIGN KEY (EquipID)
      REFERENCES Equipment(EquipID),
   CONSTRAINT FKEqSplSupplier FOREIGN KEY (SupplierID)
      REFERENCES Supplier(SupplierID))
CREATE TABLE DeptSupplier
  (DeptID TEXT(5),
   SupplierID TEXT(10),
   CONSTRAINT PKDeptSpl PRIMARY KEY (DeptID,SupplierID),
   CONSTRAINT FKDptSplDept FOREIGN KEY (DeptID)
      REFERENCES Departments(DeptID),
   CONSTRAINT FKDptSplSupplier FOREIGN KEY (SupplierID)
      REFERENCES Supplier(SupplierID))
```

Figure 17.8.
EquipSupplier and DeptSupplier tables.

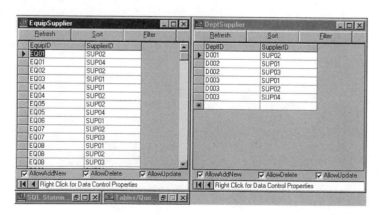

Notice that, in these two tables, the CONSTRAINT definitions are longer than the field definitions. This is common when you begin to use the power database integrity aspects of SQL databases.

Finally, you need a single table that expresses the Equipment-Supplier-Department relationship. This table will show which department has which equipment supplied by which supplier. More importantly, you can build this final table with tight constraints that will enforce all these business rules. Both the Department-Supplier relationship and the Equipment-Supplier relationship are validated before the record is saved to the database. This is a powerful data validation tool—all without writing any Visual Basic code! Table 17.7 and the SQL DDL statement in Listing 17.10 show how this table can be constructed.

Table 17.7. The Department-Equipment-Supplier data table.

DeptID

EquipID

SupplierID

Listing 17.10. Creating the DeptEqpSuplr table.

```
CREATE TABLE DeptEqpSuplr
   (DeptID TEXT(5),
    EquipID TEXT(10),
    SupplierID TEXT(10),
    CONSTRAINT PFDeptEq PRIMARY KEY (DeptID, EquipID),
    CONSTRAINT FKEqSupl FOREIGN KEY (EquipID,SupplierID)
      REFERENCES EquipSupplier(EquipID,SupplierID),
    CONSTRAINT FKDeptSupl FOREIGN KEY (DeptID,SupplierID)
      REFERENCES DeptSupplier(DeptID,SupplierID))
```

Figure 17.9.

The EquipSupplier, DeptSupplier, and DeptEqpSuplr tables.

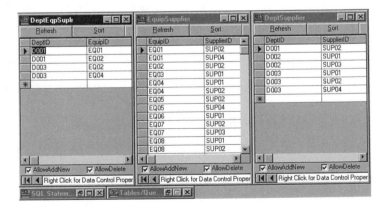

The Microsoft Access database NORMDAT6.MDB contains a set of live data for the tables described in this section. Use Visdata to open the database and review the table structure. Try adding or deleting records in ways that would break integrity rules. You'll notice that the last three tables defined (EquipSupplier, DeptSupplier, and DeptEqpSuplr) all do not allow edits on any existing record. This is because you defined the primary key as having all the fields in a record. Because you cannot edit a primary key value, you must first delete the record, and then add the modified version to the data table.

Summary

In today's lesson, you learned how to improve database integrity and access speed using the five rules of data normalization. You learned the following five rules:

☐ **Rule 1: Eliminate Repeating Groups.** If you have a set of fields that have the same name followed by a number (Skill1, Skill2, Skill3, and so forth), remove these repeating groups, create a new table for the repeating data, and relate it to the key field in the first table.

☐ **Rule 2: Eliminate Redundant Data.** Don't store the same data in two different locations. This can lead to update and delete errors. If equivalent data elements are entered in two fields, remove the second data element, create a new master table with the element and its partner as a key field, and then place the key field as a relationship in the locations that formerly held both data elements.

☐ **Rule 3: Eliminate Columns Not Dependent on Keys.** If you have data elements that are not directly related to the primary key of the table, these elements should be removed to their own data table. Only store data elements that are directly related to the primary key of the table. This particularly includes derived data or other calculations.

☐ **Rule 4: Isolate Independent Multiple Relationships.** Use this rule to improve database design when you are dealing with more than one one-to-many relationship in the database. Before you add a new field to a table, ask yourself whether this field is really dependent upon the other fields in the table. If not, create a new table with the independent data.

☐ **Rule 5: Isolate Related Multiple Relationships.** Use this rule to improve database design when you are dealing with more than one many-to-many relationship in the database. If you have database rules that require multiple references to the same field or sets of fields, isolate the fields into smaller tables and construct one or more link tables that contain the required constraints that will enforce database integrity.

Quiz

1. Is it a good idea to optimize your database strictly for speed?

2. What is meant by the term First Normal Form?

3. Explain how the second rule of data normalization differs from the first rule of normalization.

4. Should you include fields in a data table that are the calculated results of other fields in the same table?

5. When would you invoke the fourth rule of data normalization?

6. When would you invoke the fifth rule of data normalization?

Exercises

1. As a computer consultant, you have landed a contract to build a customer tracking system for your local garage. After several days of interviews with the owner, mechanics, and staff members, you have determined that the following data fields should be included in your database. Many of the customers of this garage have more than one automobile. Therefore, you are requested to leave room for tracking two cars per customer.

   Use these fields: CustomerID, CustomerName, Address, City, State, Zip, Phone, SerialNumber, License, VehicleType1, Make1, Model1, Color1, Odometer1, VehicleType2, Make2, Model2, Color2, Odometer2.

   Optimize this data into tables using the rules of data normalization discussed in today's lesson. Identify all primary and foreign keys.

2. Write the SQL statements that create the tables you designed in Exercise 1.

18

WEEK
3

Multiuser
Considerations

Today you'll learn about issues that relate to designing and coding applications that serve multiple users. Multiuser applications pose some unique challenges when it comes to database operations. These challenges are the main topics of this chapter:

☐ Database locking schemes: You'll see how the locking system is used by the Microsoft JET database engine, as well as the differences between optimistic and pessimistic locking schemes. You will also learn a scheme for performing multitable locking of data tables in highly relational databases.

☐ Cascading updates and deletes: You'll learn how to use the new features of the Microsoft JET database engine to enforce database relations using the cascading updates and deletes options.

☐ Transaction management: You'll see the process of transaction management, as well as how to add transaction management to your Visual Basic applications using the BeginTrans, CommitTrans, and Rollback methods. Transaction management using the SQL Pass-Through method with back-end databases is also covered.

By the time you complete this chapter, you'll be able to add transaction management to your Visual Basic applications and you'll know how to use cascading updates and deletes to maintain the referential integrity of your database. You will also know how to perform database-level, table-level, and page-level locking schemes in your database applications.

Database Locking Schemes

Whenever there is more than one person accessing a single database, some type of process must be used in order to prevent two users from attempting to update the same record at the same time. This process is known as a *locking scheme*. In its simplest form, a locking scheme allows only one user at a time to update information in the database.

The Microsoft JET database engine provides three levels of locking:

☐ Database locking: At this level, only one user at a time can access the database. Use this locking level when you need to perform work on multiple, related database objects (such as tables, queries, indexes, and relations) at the same time.

☐ Table locking: At this level, only one user at a time can access the locked table. Use this locking level when you need to perform work on multiple records within the same table.

☐ Page locking: At this level, only one user can access the page of records within the database table. This is the lowest locking level provided by Microsoft JET. Page locking is automatically handled by Visual Basic whenever you attempt to edit or update a record in a data set.

Database Locking

Database-level locking is the most restrictive locking scheme you can employ in your Visual Basic application. When you open the database using the Visual Basic data control, you can lock the database by setting the Exclusive property of the data control to True. When you open the database using Visual Basic code, you can lock the database by setting the second parameter of the OpenDatabase method to True. Here's an example:

```
Set db = DbEngine.OpenDatabase("c:mydb",True)
```

When the database is locked, no other users can open it. Other programs will not be able to read or write any information until you close the database. You should only use database-level locking when you must perform work that will affect multiple data objects (such as tables, indexes, relations, and queries). For example, the Visual Basic CompactDatabase operation affects all the data objects. It requires that the database be opened exclusively.

If you need to perform an operation in order to update the customer ID values in several tables and you also need to update several queries to match new search criteria, you want to use database-level locking.

Let's start a Visual Basic project to illustrate how database-level locking works. Load Visual Basic and open a new project. Add a data control to the form. Set its DataBaseName property to C:\TYSDBVB\CHAP18\MULTIUSE.MDB and its Exclusive property to True. Save the form as MULTIUS1.FRM and the project as MULTIUS1.VBP. Now create an executable version of the project by selecting File | Make EXE from the Visual Basic main menu. Use MULTIUS1.EXE as the name of the executable file.

Now run the executable file. It will load and display the data control. Run a second instance of the executable file. This is an attempt to run a copy of the same program. Because this second copy will attempt to open the same database for exclusive use, you'll see an error message when the second program starts. (See Figure 18.1.)

Figure 18.1.
Attempting to open a locked database.

You'll notice that the second program continues after the error occurs, even though the database is not opened. You can check for the error when you first load the project by adding the following code to the Error event of the data control:

```
Private Sub Data1_Error(DataErr As Integer, Response As Integer)
    If Err <> 0 Then
        MsgBox Error$(Err)+Chr(13)+"Exiting Program", vbCritical, "Data1_Error"
        Unload Me
    End If
End Sub
```

Add this code to the Data1_Error event and then recompile the program. Just as you did in the previous example, attempt to run two instances of this program. This time, when you attempt to start the second instance, you will receive a similar message, after which the program will exit safely. (See Figure 18.2.)

Figure 18.2.

Trapping the locked
database error.

Table Locking

You can use table-level locking to secure a single table while you perform sensitive operations on the table. For example, if you want to increase the sale price of all items in your inventory by five percent, you open the table for exclusive use and then perform the update. After you close the table, other users will be able to open it and see the new price list. Using table-level locking for an operation like this can help prevent users from writing sales orders that contain some records with the old price and some records with the new price.

Let's modify the MULTIUS1.VBP project to illustrate table-level locking. Reopen the project and set the Exclusive property of the data control to False. This allows other users to open the database while your program is running. Now set the RecordSource property to Master Table and set the Options property to 3. Setting the Options property to 3 opens the recordset with the DenyWrite (1) and DenyRead (2) options turned on. This prevents other programs from opening Master Table while your program is running.

Save and recompile the program. Start a copy of the executable version of the program. It will run without error. Now attempt to start a second copy of the same program. You will see an error message telling you that the table is locked. (See Figure 18.3.)

Figure 18.3.

Attempting to open a
locked table.

You can perform the same table locking by using Visual Basic code with the following code piece:

```
Sub OpenTable()
    On Error GoTo OpenTableErr
    '
    Dim db As Database
    Dim rs As Recordset
    '
    Set db = DBEngine.OpenDatabase(App.Path + "\multiuse.mdb")
    Set rs = db.OpenRecordset("Master Table", dbOpenTable,
    ➥dbDenyRead + dbDenyWrite)
    '
    GoTo OpenTableExit
    '
OpenTableErr:
    MsgBox Error$(Err) + Chr(13) + "Exiting Program", vbCritical, "OpenTable"
    GoTo OpenTableExit
    '
OpenTableExit:
    '
End Sub
```

Notice the use of the dbDenyRead and dbDenyWrite constants in the OpenRecordset method. This is the same as setting the Option property of the data control to 3. Also notice that an error trap is added to the module to replace the code in the Error event of the data control.

Page Locking

The lowest level of locking available in Visual Basic is page-level locking. *Page-level locking* is handled automatically by the Microsoft JET engine and cannot be controlled through Visual Basic code or with data-bound control properties. Each time a user attempts to edit or update a record, the Microsoft JET performs the necessary page locking to ensure data integrity.

What Is Page Locking?

A data page can contain more than one data record. Currently, the Microsoft JET data page is always 2K in size. Locking a data page will lock all records that are stored on the same data page. If you have records that are 512 bytes in size, each time Microsoft JET performs a page lock, four data records will be locked. If you have records that are 50 bytes in size, each Microsoft JET page lock can affect 40 data records.

The exact number of records that are locked on a page cannot be controlled or accurately predicted. If your data table contains several deleted records that have not been compacted out using the CompactDatabase method, you will have "holes" in your data pages. These holes will not contain valid records. Also, data pages contain records that are physically adjacent to each other—regardless of any index, filter, or sort order that has been applied to create the data set.

Even though records in a data set are listed one after another, they might not be physically stored in the same manner. Therefore, editing one of the data set records might not lock the next record in the data set list.

Pessimistic and Optimistic Locking

Even though page-level locking is performed automatically by Microsoft JET, you can use the LockEdits property of a record set to control how page-locking is handled by your application. There are two page-locking modes available: pessimistic locking (LockEdits=True) and optimistic locking (LockEdits=False). The default locking mode is pessimistic.

In pessimistic locking mode, Microsoft JET locks the data page whenever the Edit or AddNew method is invoked. The page stays locked until an Update or Cancel method is executed. When a page is locked, no other program or user can read or write any data records on the locked data page until the Update or Cancel methods have been invoked. The advantage of using the pessimistic locking mode is that it provides the highest level of data integrity possible at the page level. The disadvantage of using the pessimistic locking mode is that it can lock data pages for a long period of time. This can cause other users of the same database to encounter error messages as they attempt to read or write data in the same table.

In optimistic locking mode, Microsoft JET only locks the data page whenever the Update method is invoked. Users can invoke the Edit or AddNew methods and begin editing data without causing Microsoft JET to execute a page lock. When the user is done making changes and saves the record using the Update method, Microsoft JET will attempt to place a lock on the page. If it is successful, the record is written to the table. If Microsoft JET discovers that someone else has also edited the same record and has already saved it, the update is canceled and the user is informed with an error message saying that someone has already changed the data.

The advantage of using optimistic locking is that page locks are in place for the shortest time possible. This reduces the number of lock messages users receive as they access data in your database. The disadvantage of using optimistic locking is that it is possible for two users to edit the same record at the same time. This can lead to lock errors at update time rather than at read time.

An Example of Page-Level Locking

Let's build a new Visual Basic project to illustrate page-level locking as well as the differences between pessimistic and optimistic locking. Load Visual Basic and start a new project.

Place a command button on the form. Set its Name property to cmdEdit and its Caption property to &Edit. Add a frame control to the form and set its Caption property to Page Locking. Place two option button controls within the frame control. Set the Caption property of Option1 to Pessimistic and the Caption property of Option2 to Optimistic. Refer to Figure 18.4 as a layout guide.

Figure 18.4.
Laying out the page locking project.

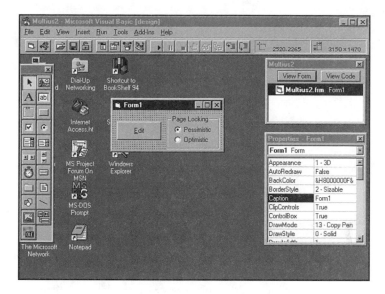

Now you need to add code to this demo. First, place the following variable declarations in the general declarations section of the form:

```
Option Explicit

Dim db As Database
Dim rs As Recordset
Dim cName As String
Dim nMax As Integer
```

Now add the following code to the Form_Load event. This code prompts you for a name for the form header. It then opens the database and data table, and it counts all the records in the table.

```
Private Sub Form_Load()
    ' get instance ID
    cName = InputBox("Enter Job Name:")
    Me.Caption = cName
    '
    ' load db and open set
    Set db = OpenDatabase(App.Path + "\multiuse.mdb")
    Set rs = db.OpenRecordset("mastertable", dbOpenTable, dbSeeChanges)
    '
    ' count total recs in set
    rs.MoveLast
    nMax = rs.RecordCount
    '
End Sub
```

Now add the following two code pieces to the Click events of the option buttons. These routines toggle the LockEdits property of the recordset between pessimistic locking (LockEdits=True) and optimistic locking (LockEdits=False).

This code snippet turns on pessimistic locking:

```
Private Sub Option1_Click()
    If Option1 = True Then
        rs.LockEdits = True
    Else
        rs.LockEdits = False
    End If
End Sub
```

This code snippet turns on optimistic locking:

```
Private Sub Option2_Click()
    If Option2 = True Then
        rs.LockEdits = False
    Else
        rs.LockEdits = True
    End If
End Sub
```

Finally, add the following code to the cmdEdit_Click event of the form. While in edit mode, this code prompts you for a record number. It then moves to that record, invokes the Edit method, makes a forced changed in a recordset field, and updates some titles and messages. When the form is in update mode, this routine attempts to update the recordset with the changed data and then resets some titles. Here's the code:

```
Private Sub cmdEdit_Click()
    On Error GoTo cmdEditClickErr    ' set trap
    '
    Dim nRec As Integer ' for rec select
    Dim X As Integer     ' for locator
    '
    ' are we trying to edit?
    If cmdEdit.Caption = "&Edit" Then
        ' get rec to edit
        nRec = InputBox("Enter Record # to Edit [1 - " +
        ➥Trim(Str(nMax)) + "]:", cName)
        ' locate rec
        If nRec > 0 Then
            rs.MoveFirst
            For X = 1 To nRec
                rs.MoveNext
            Next
            rs.Edit ' start edit mode
            ' change rec
            If Left(rs.Fields(0), 1) = "X" Then
                rs.Fields(0) = Mid(rs.Fields(0), 2, 255)
            Else
                rs.Fields(0) = "X" + rs.Fields(0)
            End If
            ' tell 'em you changed it
            MsgBox "Modified field to: [" + rs.Fields(0) + "]"
            ' prepare for update mode
            cmdEdit.Caption = "&Update"
            Me.Caption = cName + " [Rec: " + Trim(Str(X - 1)) + "]"
        End If
```

```
        Else
            rs.Update     ' attempt update
            cmdEdit.Caption = "&Edit"    ' fix caption
            Me.Caption = cName           ' fix header
            dbengine.idle dbfreelocks    ' pause VB
        End If
        '
        GoTo cmdEditClickExit
        '
cmdEditClickErr:
        ' show error message
        MsgBox Trim(Str(Err)) + ": " + Error$, vbCritical, cName + "[cmdEdit]"

cmdEditClickExit:
        '
End Sub
```

Notice that there is a new line in this routine: the DBEngine.Idle method. This method forces Visual Basic to pause for a moment to update any dynaset or snapshot objects that are opened by the program. It is a good idea to place this line in your code so that it is executed during some part of the update process. This ensures that your program has the most recent updates to the data set.

Save the form as MULTIUS2.FRM and the project as MULTIUS2.VBP. Compile the project and save it as MULTIUS2.EXE. Now you're ready to test it. Load two instances of the compiled program. When it first starts up, you will be prompted for a job name. It does not matter what you enter for the job name, but make sure that you enter different names for each instance. The name you enter will be displayed on messages and form headers so that you can tell the two programs apart. Position the two instances apart from each other on the screen. (See Figure 18.5.)

Figure 18.5.
Running two instances of the page locking project.

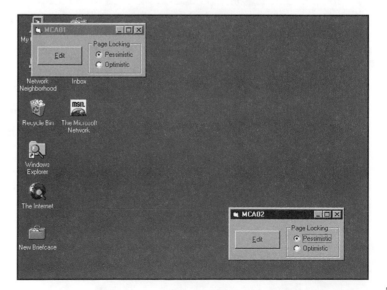

First you'll test the behavior of pessimistic page locking. Make sure the pessimistic radio button in the Page Locking frame is selected in both instances of the program. Now click the Edit button of the first instance of the program; when prompted, enter 1 as the record to edit. This program now has locked a page of data. Switch to the second instance of the program and click the Edit button. You'll see error 3260, which tells you that the data is unavailable. (See Figure 18.6.)

Figure 18.6.

A failed attempt at editing during pessimistic locking.

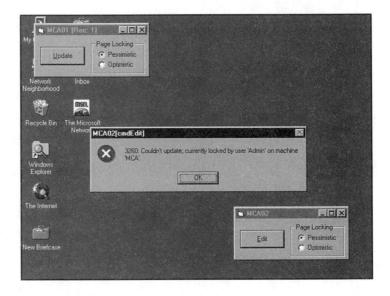

Remember that pessimistic locking locks the data page as soon as a user begins an edit operation on a record. This lock prevents anyone else from accessing any records on the data page until the first instance releases the record by using Update or UpdateCancel. Now click the error message box and then click the Update button to release the record and unlock the data page.

Now you'll test the behavior of Microsoft JET during optimistic locking. Select the Optimistic radio button on both forms. In the first form, press Edit and enter 1 when prompted. The first instance is now editing record one. Move to the second instance and press Edit. This time you will not see an error message. When prompted, enter 1 as the record to edit. Again, you'll see no error message as Microsoft JET allows you to begin editing record one of the set. Now both programs are editing record one of the set.

Press the Update button of the second instance of the program to save the new data to the data set. The second instance has now read, edited, and updated the same record opened earlier by the first instance. Now move to the first instance and press the Update button to save the changes made by this instance. You'll see error 3197, which tells you that data has been changed and the update has been canceled. (See Figure 18.7.)

Figure 18.7.
A failed attempt to update during optimistic locking.

Optimistic locking occurs at the moment the Update method is invoked. Under the optimistic scheme, a user can read and edit any record he or she chooses. When the user attempts to write the record back out to disk, the program checks to see whether the original record was updated by any other program since the user's version last read the record. If changes were saved by another program, error 3197 is reported.

When to Use Pessimistic or Optimistic Page Locking

The advantage of using pessimistic locking is that once you begin editing a record, you will be able to save your work because all other users are prevented from accessing that record. The disadvantage of using pessimistic locking is that if you have a lot of people in the database, it is possible that quite a bit of the file will be unavailable at any one time.

The advantage of using optimistic locking is that it occurs only during an update and then only when required. Optimistic locks are the shortest in duration. The disadvantage of using optimistic locking is that even though more than one user can edit a data set record at one time, only one person can *save* that data set record. This is usually the first person to complete the edit (not the person who opened the record first or the person who saves it last). This can be very frustrating for users who have filled out a lengthy data entry screen only to discover that they cannot update the data table! However, except in rare cases where there is an extreme amount of network traffic, you will probably find that optimistic locking is enough.

Tip: All ODBC data sources use optimistic locking *only*.

Using Cascading Updates and Deletes

In the lesson on Day 10 ("Visual Basic and the Microsoft JET Engine"), you learned how to identify and define cascading updates and delete relations using the relation data access object. At the time, a particular aspect of relation objects was not fully covered: the capability to define cascading updates and deletes in order to enforce referential integrity. By employing cascading updates and deletes in your database definition, you can ensure that changes made to columns

in one data table will be properly distributed to all related columns in all related tables within the database. This type of referential integrity is essential when designing and deploying database applications that will be accessed by multiple users.

Microsoft JET can only enforce update and delete cascades for native Microsoft JET format databases. Microsoft JET cannot enforce cascades that involve an attached table.

 Tip: Cascading options should be added at database design time and can be accomplished using the Visdata program (see Day 8, "Using Visdata") or through Visual Basic code (see Day 10).

Cascading occurs when users update or delete columns in one table that are referred to (via the relation object) by other columns in other tables. When this update or delete occurs, Microsoft JET automatically updates or deletes all the records that are part of the defined relation. For example, if you define a relationship between the column Valid.ListID and the column Master.ListID, any time a user updates the value of Valid.ListID, Microsoft JET will scan the Master table and update the values of all Master.ListID columns that match the updated values in the Valid.ListID column. In this way, as users change data in one table, all related tables are kept in sync through the use of cascading updates and deletes.

Building the Cascading Demo Project

Let's use Visdata to define a relation object that includes cascading updates and deletes. Start Visdata and load the C:\TYSDBVB\CHAP18\MULTIUSE.MDB database. Then select Jet | Relations from the main menu to bring up the Relations dialog box. Press the Add Relation button and enter RelCustType as the relation object name. Select ValidTypes as the base table and CustType as the base field. Select MasterTable as the foreign table and CustType as the foreign field.

 **Tip:** It might seem to you that the terms *base table* and *foreign table* are used incorrectly in the relation definition. It might help you to remember that all relation definitions are "based" on the values in the ValidTypes table. Also, it might help to remember that any data table related to the ValidTypes table is a foreign table.

Now check the Enforce Referential Integrity checkbox, select the One-To-Many radio button, and then check both the UpdateCascade and DeleteCascade checkboxes. Finally, in the Join

Type section, select the radio button "Only rows where joined fields from both tables are equal"; then press the Add Relation button to save the object to the database. Your screen should look like the one shown in Figure 18.8.

Now you'll build a project that illustrates the process of cascading updates and deletes. Use the information in Table 18.1 and Figure 18.9 to build the MULTIUS3.VBP project.

Figure 18.8.

Adding a cascading relation to the database.

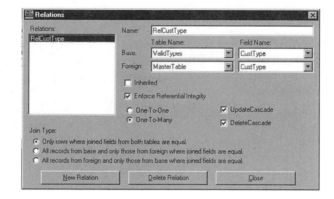

18

Table 18.1. The control table for the MULTIUS3.VBP project.

Controls	Properties	Settings
Form	Name	Ch1803
	Caption	Cascading Demo
	Left	1020
	Height	4275
	Top	1170
	Width	6480
DBGrid	Name	DBGrid1
	AllowAddNew	True
	AllowDelete	True
	Height	2715
	Left	120
	Top	120
	Width	3000
DBGrid	Name	DBGrid2
	AllowAddNew	True
	AllowDelete	True

continues

Table 18.1. continued

Controls	Properties	Settings
	Height	2715
	Left	3240
	Top	120
	Width	3000
Data Control	Name	Data1
	Caption	Master Table
	DatabaseName	C:\TYSDBVB\CHAP18\MULTIUSE.MDB
	Height	300
	Left	120
	RecordsetType	1 - Dynaset
	RecordSource	MasterTable
	Top	3000
	Width	3000
Data Control	Name	Data2
	Caption	Valid Types
	DatabaseName	C:\TYSDBVB\CHAP18\MULTIUSE.MDB
	Height	300
	Left	3240
	RecordsetType	1 - Dynaset
	RecordSource	ValidTypes
	Top	3000
	Width	3000
Command Button	Name	Command1
	Caption	Refresh
	Height	300
	Left	2580
	Top	3480
	Width	1200

Figure 18.9.

Laying out the MULTIUS3.FRM form.

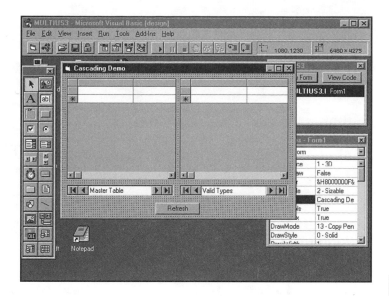

Only two lines of Visual Basic code are needed to complete the form. Add the following two lines to the Command1_Click event. These two lines update both data controls and their associated grids.

```
Private Sub Command1_Click()
    Data1.Refresh
    Data2.Refresh
End Sub
```

Save the form as MULTIUS3.FRM and the project as MULTIUS3.VBP, and then run the project. Now you're ready to test the cascading updates and deletes.

Running the Cascading Demo Project

When you run the project, you'll see the two tables displayed in each grid, side by side. First, test the update cascade by editing one of the records in the Valid Types table. Select the first record and change the CustType column value from T01 to T09. When you have finished the edit and have moved the record pointer to another record in the ValidTypes grid, press the Refresh button to update both data sets. You'll see that all records in the MasterTable that had a value of T01 in their CustType field now have a value of T09. The update of ValidTypes was "cascaded" into the MasterTable by Microsoft JET.

Now add a new record with the CustType value of T99 to the ValidTypes table (set the Description field to any text you want). Add a record to the MasterTable that uses the T99 value in its CustType field. Your screen should look something like the one shown in Figure 18.10.

Figure 18.10.
Adding new records to the
MULTIUSE.MDB
database.

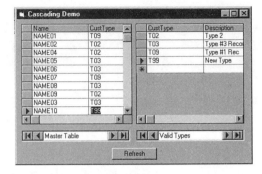

Delete the T99 record from the ValidTypes table by highlighting the entire row and pressing the Delete key. After you have deleted the record, press the Refresh button again to update both data controls. What happens to the record in the MasterTable that contains the T99 value in the CustType field? It is deleted from the MasterTable! This shows the power of the cascading delete. When cascading deletes are enforced, any time a user deletes a record from the base table, all related records in the foreign table are also deleted.

When to Use the Cascading Updates and Deletes

The capability to enforce cascading updates and deletes as part of the database definition is a powerful tool. However, with this power comes some responsibility, too. Because database cascades cannot be easily undone, you should think through your database design carefully before you add cascading features to your database. It is not always wise to add both update and delete cascades to all your relationships. There are times when you might not want to cascade all update or delete operations.

Whenever you have defined a relation object, in which the base table is a "validation" table and the foreign table is a "master" table, it is wise to define an update cascade. This will ensure that any changes made to the validation table will be cascaded to the related master table. It is not a good idea to define a delete cascade for this type of relation. Rarely will you want to delete all "master" records whenever you delete a related record from the validation table. If the user attempts to delete a record in the validation table that is used by one or more records in the master table, Microsoft JET will issue an error message telling the user that it is unable to delete the record.

Whenever you have defined a relation object in which the base table is a master table and the foreign table is a child table (that is, CustomerMaster.CustID is the base table and CustomerComments.CustID is the foreign table), you might want to define both an update and a delete cascade. It is logical to make sure that any changes to the CustomerMaster.CustID

field would be updated in the CustomerComments.CustID field. It might also make sense to delete all CustomerComments records whenever the related CustomerMaster record is deleted. However, this is not always the case. For example, if the child table is CustomerInvoice, you might not want to automatically delete all invoices on file. Instead, you might want Microsoft JET to prevent the deletion of the CustomerMaster record if a related CustomerInvoice record exists.

The key point to remember is that cascades are performed automatically by Microsoft JET, without any warning message. You cannot create an "optional" cascade or receive an automatic warning before a cascade begins. If you choose to use cascades in your database, be sure to think through the logic and the relations thoroughly, and be sure to test your relations and cascades before deploying the database in a production setting.

Transaction Management

Another important tool for maintaining the integrity of your database is the use of *transactions* to manage database updates and deletes. Visual Basic allows you to enclose all database update operations as a single transaction. Transactions involve two steps: first, mark the start of a database transaction with the BeginTrans keyword; second, mark the end of the database transaction with the CommitTrans or RollBack keyword. You can start a set of database operations (add, edit, delete records) and then, if no error occurs, you can use the CommitTrans keyword to save the updated records to the database. If, however, you encounter an error along the way, you can use the RollBack keyword to tell Microsoft JET to reverse all database operations completed up to the point where the transaction first began.

For example, suppose you need to perform a series of database updates to several tables as part of a month-end update routine for an accounting system. This month-end processing includes totaling up transactions by customer from the TransTable, writing those totals to existing columns in a CustTotals table, appending the transactions to the HistoryTable, and deleting the transactions from the TransTable. The process requires access to three different tables and involves updating existing records (appending new records to a table and deleting existing records from a table). If your program encounters an error part of the way through this process, it would be difficult to reconstruct the data as it existed before the process began. In other words, it would be difficult unless you used Visual Basic transactions as part of the update routine.

Microsoft JET Transactions and the Workspace Object

All Microsoft JET transactions are applied to the current workspace object. (See Day 10 for a discussion of the workspace object.) If you have not named a workspace object, Visual Basic will use the default workspace for your program. However, because transactions apply to an entire

workspace, it is recommended that you explicitly declare workspaces when you use transactions. This will give you the ability to isolate data sets into different workspaces and better control the creation of transactions.

Here's the exact syntax for starting a transaction:

```
Workspace(0).BeginTrans    ' starts a transaction
...
If Err=0 Then
    Workspaces(0).CommitTrans   ' completes a transaction
Else
    Workspaces(0).Rollback    ' cancels a transaction
End If
```

In this code, the default workspace for the transaction area is used. In an actual program, you should name a workspace explicitly.

Building the Microsoft JET Transaction Project

You'll now build a small project that illustrates one possible use for transactions in your Visual Basic applications. You'll create a database routine that performs the tasks listed in the previous example. You'll open a transaction table, total the records to a subsidiary table, copy the records to a history file, and then delete the records from the original table.

You'll write two main routines: one to declare the workspace and open the database, and one to perform the database transaction. First, add the following code to the general declarations section of a new form in a new project:

```
Option Explicit

Dim db As Database          ' database object
Dim wsUpdate As workspace   ' workspace object
Dim nErrFlag As Integer     ' error flag
```

These are the form-level variables you will need to perform the update.

Add the following code, which creates the workspace and opens the database. Create a new Sub called OpenDB and place the following code in the routine:

```
Sub OpenDB()
    On Error GoTo OpenDBErr
    '
    nErrFlag = 0 ' assume all is OK
    '
    Set wsUpdate = DBEngine.CreateWorkspace("wsUpdate", "admin", "")
    Set db = wsUpdate.OpenDatabase(App.Path + "\MULTIUS4.mdb", True)
    '
    GoTo OpenDBExit
```

```
      '
OpenDBErr:
    MsgBox Trim(Str(Err)) + " " + Error$(Err), vbCritical, "OpenDB"
    nErrFlag = Err
      '
OpenDBExit:
      '
End Sub
```

This routine creates a new workspace object to encompass the transaction and then opens the database for exclusive use. You don't want anyone else in the system while you perform this major update. An error trap routine has been added here in case you can't open the database exclusively.

Now you can add the code that will perform the actual month-end update. Do this by using the SQL statements you learned in the lessons on Day 15 and Day 16. Create a new Sub called ProcMonthEnd and then add the following code:

```
Sub ProcMonthEnd()
    On Error goto ProcMonthEndErr
      '
    Dim cSQL As String
    Dim nResult As Integer
      '
    wsUpdate.BeginTrans ' mark start of transaction
      '
    ' append totals to transtotals table
    cSQL = "INSERT INTO TransTotals SELECT TransTable.CustID,
    ➥SUM(TransTable.Amount) as Amount FROM TransTable
    ➥GROUP BY TransTable.CustID"
    db.Execute cSQL
      '
    ' append history records
    cSQL = "INSERT INTO TransHistory SELECT * FROM TransTable"
    db.Execute cSQL
      '
    ' delete the transaction records
    cSQL = "DELETE FROM TransTable"
    db.Execute cSQL
      '
    ' ask user to commit transaction
      '
    nResult = MsgBox("Transaction Completed. Ready to Commit?",
    ➥vbInformation + vbYesNo, "ProcMonthEnd")
    If nResult = vbYes Then
        wsUpdate.CommitTrans
        MsgBox "Transaction Committed"
    Else
        wsUpdate.Rollback
        MsgBox "Transaction Canceled"
    End If
      '
    nErrFlag = 0
    GoTo ProcMonthEndExit
```

18

```
ProcMonthEndErr:
    MsgBox Trim(Str(Err)) + " " + Error$(Err), vbCritical, "ProcMonthEnd"
    nErrFlag = Err

ProcMonthEndExit:

End Sub
```

This code executes the three SQL statements that perform the updates and deletes needed for the month-end processing. The routine is started with a BeginTrans. When the updates are complete, the user is asked to confirm the transaction. In a production program, you probably wouldn't ask for transaction confirmation; however, this will help you see how the process is working.

Finally, you need to add the code that puts everything together. Add the following code to the Form_Load event:

```
Private Sub Form_Load()
    OpenDB
    If nErrFlag = 0 Then
        ProcMonthEnd
    End If

    If nErrFlag <> 0 Then
        MsgBox "Error Reported", vbCritical, "FormLoad"
    End If
    Unload Me
End Sub
```

This routine calls the OpenDB procedure. Then, if no error is reported, it calls the ProcMonthEnd procedure. If an error has occurred during the process, a message is displayed.

Save the form as MULTIUS4.FRM and the project as MULTIUS4.VBP, and then run the project. All you'll see is a message that tells you the transaction is complete and asks for your approval. (See Figure 18.11.)

Figure 18.11.

Waiting for approval to commit the transaction.

If you choose No in this dialog box, Microsoft JET will reverse all the previously completed database operations between the Rollback and the BeginTrans statements. You can confirm this by clicking the No button, using Visdata or Data Manager to load the MULTIUS4.MDB database, and then inspecting the contents of the tables.

> **Note:** There is an SQL-Visual Basic script on the CD that ships with this book called MULTIUS4.SQV. This script can be used with the SQL-VB program (see Day 15, "Creating Databases with SQL," and Day 16, "Updating Databases with SQL") to create a "clean" MULTIUS4.MDB file. After you have run MULTIUS4.VBP once and answered Yes to commit the transaction, you might want to run the CH1804.SQV script to refresh the database.

Advantages and Limitations of Transactions

The primary advantage of using transactions in your Visual Basic programs is that they can greatly increase the integrity of your data. You should use transactions whenever you are performing database operations that span more than one table or even operations that affect many records in a single table. A secondary advantage of using transactions is that they will often increase the processing speed of Microsoft JET.

As useful as transactions are, there are still a few limitations. First, some database formats might not support transactions (for example, Paradox files do not support transactions). You can check for transaction support by checking the Transactions property of the database. If transactions are not supported, Microsoft JET will ignore the transaction statements in your code; you will not receive an error message. Some dynasets might not support transactions, depending on how they are constructed. Usually, sets that are the result of SQL JOIN and WHERE clauses or result sets that contain data from attached tables will not support transactions.

Transaction operations are kept on the local workstation in a temporary directory (the one pointed to by the TEMP environment variable). If you run out of available space on the TEMP drive, you will receive error 2004. You can trap for this error. The only solution is to make more disk space available or reduce the number of database operations between the BeginTrans and the CommitTrans statements.

Microsoft JET allows you to nest transactions up to five levels deep. However, if you are using external ODBC databases, you cannot nest transactions.

Summary

Today you have learned about the three important challenges that face every database programmer writing multiuser applications. They are

- ☐ Database locking schemes
- ☐ Using cascading updates and deletes to maintain database integrity
- ☐ Using database transactions to provide commit/rollback options for major updates to your database

You have learned that there are three levels of locking available to Visual Basic programs. These levels are as follows:

☐ The database level: You can use the Exclusive property of the data control or the second parameter of the OpenDatabase method to lock the entire database. Use this option when you need to perform work that will affect multiple database objects (such as tables, queries, indexes, relations, and so on).

☐ The table level: You can set the Options property of the data control to 3 or the third parameter of the OpenRecordset method to dbDenyRead+dbDenyWrite in order to lock the entire table for your use only. Use this option when you need to perform work that affects multiple records in a single table (for example, increasing the sales price on all items in the inventory table).

☐ The page level: Microsoft JET automatically performs page-level locking whenever you use the data control to edit and save a record, or whenever you use Visual Basic code to perform the Edit/AddNew and Update/CancelUpdate methods. You can use the LockEdits property of the recordset to set the page locking to pessimistic (to perform locking at edit time) or optimistic (to perform locking only at update time).

You have learned how to use the Visdata application to create relation objects that enforce referential integrity and automatically perform cascading updates or deletes to related records. You have learned that there are times when it is not advisable to establish cascading deletes (for example, do not use cascading deletes when the base table is a validation list and the foreign table is a master).

Finally, you have learned how to use database transactions to protect your database during extended, multitable operations. You have learned how to use the BeginTrans, CommitTrans, and Rollback methods of the workspace object. And you have learned some of the advantages and limitations of transaction processing.

Quiz

1. What are the three levels of locking provided by the Microsoft JET database engine?
2. Which form of locking would you use when compacting a database?
3. What form of locking would you use if you need to update price codes in the price table of a database?
4. What property of a recordset do you set to control whether your application's data will have optimistic or pessimistic page locking?
5. What is the difference between pessimistic and optimistic page locking?
6. Can you use pessimistic locking on an ODBC data source?
7. What happens to data when cascading deletes are used in a relationship?

8. Why would you use transaction management in your applications?

9. What are the limitations of transactions?

10. Do you need to declare a workspace when using transactions?

Exercises

1. Write Visual Basic code that will exclusively open a database (C:\DATA\ABC.MDB) during a Form Load event. Include error trapping.

2. Build on the code you wrote in the previous exercise to exclusively open the table Customers in ABC.MDB.

3. Here is a scenario. You are building a new accounts receivable system for your company. You have saved all tables and data into a single database named C:\DATA\ABC.MDB. You have discovered that all invoices created must be posted to a history file on a daily basis. Because this history file is extremely valuable (it is used for collections, reporting, and so on), you don't want your posting process to destroy any of the data that it currently contains. Therefore, you decide to use transactions in your code.

   Write the Visual Basic code that will take invoice transactions from the temporary holding table, named Transactions, and insert them into a table named History, which keeps the cumulative history information.

   The History table contains four fields: HistoryItem (counter, primary key), CustID (a unique identifier for the customer), InvoiceNo (the number of the invoice issued to the customer), and Amount.

   The Transactions table also has four fields: TransNo (counter, primary key), CustID (a unique identifier for the customer), InvoiceNo (the number of the invoice issued to the customer), and Amount.

   Complete this project by starting a new project and dropping a single command button (named Post) onto a form. Pressing this button should trigger the posting process.

   Include error trapping in your routines. Also, include messages to notify the user that the transaction posting is complete or that problems have been encountered.

18

19

ODBC Data Access Via the ODBC API Interface

Today, you'll learn how to create data entry forms that use the low-level Open Database Connectivity (ODBC) API routines to access existing databases. The ODBC API interface provides an alternative to using the Microsoft JET to access data. The ODBC interface is usually faster than Microsoft JET and uses up less workstation memory than Microsoft JET, too. The ODBC interface is capable of accessing data in client-server databases, desktop ISAM databases (such as dBASE, FoxPro, and so on), Microsoft Access format databases, and even Excel spreadsheets and text files.

Although data access via ODBC is fast, you can only work with snapshot-type data sets. All data access is done using SQL statements to pass data to and from the ODBC data source. Also, data access via the ODBC API requires more code than using data controls or Visual Basic programming code. For these reasons, the ODBC API is not a good choice for every program. After you get an idea of what it takes to write a Visual Basic program using ODBC for data access, you can decide for yourself when to use the ODBC for data access.

In today's lesson, you'll learn how to install the ODBC Administrator on your system and how to use the administrator program to define and register an ODBC data source for use with the ODBC API interface. We'll also briefly discuss the ODBC operational model and show you the minimum ODBC APIs you'll need to create your own database programs using the ODBC interface.

You will then use your knowledge of the ODBC API to construct a code library that will contain the essential API calls and a series of *wrapper* routines that you can use with all your Visual Basic programs to create data entry screens for ODBC data sources. Finally, you'll build a Visual Basic data entry form that will call the library routines and show you how to implement a simple subform using standard Visual Basic controls.

When you complete this Day's lesson, you will know how to register new data sources using the ODBC Administrator program. You will also have a code library you can use to build solid Visual Basic applications that bypass the Microsoft JET and use the ODBC API set to read and write databases.

Note: Throughout today's lesson, you will be working exclusively in the 16-bit version of Visual Basic 4. The 16-bit version has a slightly different ODBC Administrator program and uses different API calls than the 32-bit version. If you have been using the 32-bit version of Visual Basic 4 for the other chapters, switch to the 16-bit version for today. The information you learn here can easily be transported to the 32-bit version later. After you learn how to use the 16-bit version of the ODBC API, you can modify the API calls to use the ODBC32.DLL to gain access to the 32-bit ODBC drivers installed on your workstation.

What Is the ODBC Interface?

The Open Database Connectivity (ODBC) interface is a direct interface between your Visual Basic program and the target database. This interface has been developed by Microsoft as a way to provide seamless access to external data formats. The first versions of ODBC were a bit buggy and, in some cases, slow. Although the ODBC interface is now understood to be one of the fastest data interfaces available, many programmers still mistakenly think the ODBC interface is too slow for production applications. This is not the case. As you'll see in today's lesson, using the ODBC interface is usually faster than using the Microsoft JET database engine.

When you use the Microsoft JET interface to access an ODBC data source, the Microsoft JET does the talking to the ODBC interface, which then talks to the intermediate driver, which talks to the data source your Visual Basic program requested. When you use ODBC API calls, you bypass the Microsoft JET layer and your Visual Basic program talks directly to the ODBC interface. Figure 19.1 shows how this looks on paper.

Figure 19.1.

The difference between ODBC and Microsoft JET interfaces.

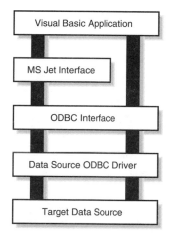

The ODBC interface doesn't really talk to databases. Instead, it links your Visual Basic program to defined data sources. These sources of data could be flat-file databases (such as dBASE and FoxPro), relational databases (such as Microsoft Access and SQL Server), or any file format for which an ODBC interface driver is available. For example, Microsoft provides an ODBC interface driver for Excel spreadsheets and even delimited text files. As long as a driver is available, you can use ODBC to access the data.

Even more importantly, when you use the ODBC interface to link to a data source, your Visual Basic program is not really talking to the data source directly. Your program talks to the ODBC front end alone. The ODBC front end uses removable drivers to translate your requests into a format understood by the target data source. The ODBC drivers exist as a middleman between the ODBC front end and the target data file. Your Visual Basic programs talk to the ODBC front end. The ODBC front end talks to the appropriate driver. The driver talks to the target data file. The advantage of this design is that you can easily replace the translator routines (the drivers) to add improved performance or functionality without having to change your Visual Basic program or the target data source. Also, because the ODBC interface rules are published information, anyone who wants to make data available to users can create a new driver, and that driver can then work with all the installed versions of the ODBC interface that already exist.

Using the ODBC API interface has its limits, however. When you use the ODBC API to select and retrieve data, you are actually dealing with Snapshot-type data objects. You collect a set of data, bring it to your machine, make additions or modifications to the data set, and send those changes back to the data source. Although this is fast, it can be a bit cumbersome. Also, when you use the ODBC API interface, you are not able to use any data-bound controls. You are responsible for reading the data, placing it into form controls, and moving the data from the form controls back to the data source when needed. This means you have more programming to do before you get a data entry form up and running. Even with these drawbacks, using the ODBC API to access your data can add increased flexibility to your Visual Basic database programs.

Installing the ODBC Interface

The most recent version of the ODBC interface is included in the Visual Basic 4 installation files. If you did not install the ODBC interface when you first installed Visual Basic 4, you need to do it now in order to continue the lesson. If you have already installed the ODBC interface, you can skip this section and move on to the section on how to define and register your own ODBC data sources.

Note: You might also have other software packages that installed the ODBC interface on your system. Look for a program called ODBCADM.EXE. If you do not find this program, refer to the Visual Basic 4 install disks or CD to install the ODBC interface.

For your lesson today, you will only use the 16-bit version of the ODBC interface. This version works on both 16-bit and 32-bit systems. If you are using Window NT or Windows 95, be sure you are using the ODBCADM.EXE administrator.

The ODBC kit that ships with Visual Basic 4 contains drivers for SQL Server and the Microsoft Code Page Translator. Installing these drivers allows your Visual Basic 4 apps to access data stored in SQL Server databases. However, there are also drivers available for accessing desktop file formats such as dBASE, FoxPro, Microsoft Access, and Excel spreadsheets.

One of the best collections of ODBC drivers for desktop databases is included in Microsoft Office. If you have Microsoft Office, you probably already have these drivers on file. If not, you can run the SETUP.EXE program in the Microsoft Office SETUP directory to install the desktop ODBC drivers (see Figure 19.2).

Figure 19.2.

Installing the desktop ODBC drivers with Microsoft Office.

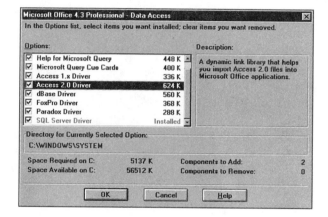

If you do not have the Microsoft Office ODBC kit, you can still install the ODBC drivers that are shipped with Visual Basic 4. Run the SETUP.EXE program in the ODBC subdirectory of the main Visual Basic 4 directory. This will allow you to install the ODBC administrator and any drivers currently available (see Figure 19.3).

Note: If you cannot find the ODBC subdirectory under the Visual Basic 4 main directory, make sure you are running the 16-bit version of Visual Basic 4. You must be running this project under the 16-bit version of Visual Basic 4 to make sure the API calls and the ODBC interface work properly.

Figure 19.3.

Installing the ODBC drivers from Visual Basic 4.

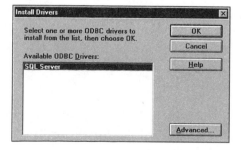

Now that you have the ODBC Administrator installed, you are ready to define an ODBC data source that you can use with your Visual Basic 4 programs.

Registering an ODBC Data Source

The ODBC interface is based on the idea that defined data sources are available for users and programs to access. Each desktop has its own list of available ODBC data sources. On 16-bit systems, this list of ODBC data sources is kept in the ODBC.INI file in the \WINDOWS\ SYSTEM directory. On 32-bit systems, the information is stored in the registry under the SOFTWARE/ODBC keys.

Warning: Even though you can call up the ODBC.INI file with a text editor or open the Windows Registry using REGEDIT.EXE, we do not recommend that you alter these entries using anything other than the ODBC Administrator program. Incorrect data in the ODBC entries in the INI file or in the registry can cause the ODBC interface to behave unpredictably or fail completely.

Each of these entries contains basic information about the defined data source, the drive used to access the data, and possibly additional information depending on the data source and driver used. It is easy to define and register a new ODBC data source. As an illustration, create an ODBC data source that you can use later in this lesson.

First, load the ODBC Administrator program. To do this, locate and execute the ODBCADM.EXE program.

Note: Throughout the lesson today, you will use the 16-bit version of the ODBC driver kit. There are slight differences between the 16-bit and 32-bit ODBC administrators. Even if you are running on a 32-bit operating system (NT or Windows 95), you will still be able to use the 16-bit ODBC administrator. After you learn how to use the 16-bit ODBC API, you can modify the API routines to use the ODBC32.DLL and access the 32-bit ODBC drivers installed on your machine.

When you first start the ODBC Administrator, you see a dialog box that lists all the data sources that are currently registered for your workstation (see Figure 19.4).

Figure 19.4.
Viewing the registered ODBC data sources.

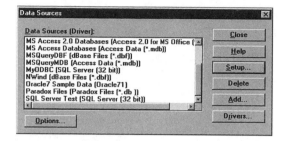

To define a new ODBC data source, click the Add button to bring up the Add Data Source dialog box. Select the Access 2.0 for Microsoft Office (*.MDB) driver and click the OK button. You then see the data entry dialog for creating a new ODBC data source (see Figure 19.5).

Figure 19.5.
Adding a new data source.

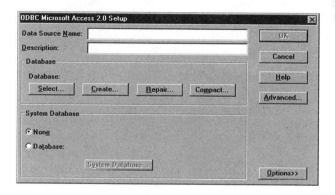

Enter TYSODBC in the Data Source Name field and Test ODBC/MDB Interface in the Description field. The Data Source name is the string you will use when you call the ODBC connection from your Visual Basic 4 program. The description is just a comment to remind you of the contents of the data source.

Now click the Select Database command button to bring up a File dialog box. Locate and select the C:\TYSDBVB\CHAP19\TYSODBC.MDB database. This is the database that your program will connect to each time it calls the ODBC data source name TYSODBC. Your screen should now resemble the one in Figure 19.6.

Click the OK button to store the new Data Source definition to the ODBC.INI file. You should now be able to see the TYSODBC data source in the list box in the first ODBC dialog form.

As a source of reference, the following code shows the entries in the ODBC.INI file that were created when you added the TYSODBC data source. Your entries might vary slightly.

19

```
[TYSODBC]
Driver=C:\WINDOWS\SYSTEM\ODBCJT16.DLL
DBQ=C:\TYSDBVB\CHAP19\TYSODBC.MDB
DefaultDir=C:\ABC\CH19
Description=Test ODBC/MDB Interface
DriverId=25
FIL=MS Access;
JetIniPath=odbcddp.ini
UID=admin
```

Figure 19.6.

The completed ODBC data source registration.

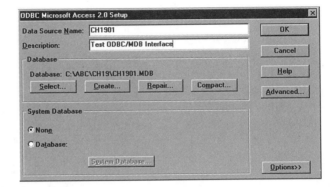

You can register as many data sources as you like. You can add various options to the data source definition depending on the target data file you are working with. For example, with Microsoft JET databases, you can add the SYSTEM security file to the data source to force users to provide valid user IDs and passwords. You can also adjust time-out values and mark the data source for exclusive use only. There are other possible entries for other data file formats, as well.

 Tip: Review the ODBC Administrator online help file for more on how to configure ODBC data sources.

Creating the ODBC API Library Routines

Now that you know how to define ODBC data sources, you are ready to put together a Visual Basic 4 program that uses the ODBC interface to read and write data. In order to build your ODBC application, you will need to declare several Windows API (Application Programming

Interface) calls. These calls, along with a handful of predefined constants are the heart of creating an ODBC-capable database program. We won't review all the ODBC API calls in this chapter—only the essential ones you'll need to get your ODBC application working.

> **Tip:** Visual Basic 4 ships with an API viewer that lets you search for a particular API call and then copy and paste the information from the viewer directly to your Visual Basic 4 application. Two other files also ship with Visual Basic 4 and contain all the ODBC API declarations and constants. Search for the files ODBC16.TXT and ODBC32.TXT. These two files contain more than you'll ever want to see on ODBC APIs.

After you declare the basic APIs, you need to create a set of Visual Basic routines that use these APIs to perform the low-level operations that are needed to execute ODBC commands from Visual Basic. After the low-level routines, you'll write a few mid-level functions that hide most of the grittier features of API programming. Finally, you'll create a few high-level routines that you can use from any Visual Basic data entry form to start off and maintain your ODBC connections.

ODBC API Crash Course

There are dozens of possible API calls for the ODBC interface. You can write calls that enable you to inspect the type of ODBC driver you are using, calls to inspect the various details of the data source (database name, format, and so on), calls to gather information about the data set (column names, data types for each field, length of each field, and so on), and calls to actually connect to the data source and move data to and from the ODBC data source. For this lesson, you will focus only on those routines that you need in order to move data back and forth through the ODBC interface.

Before you start coding the API calls and wrapper routines, you need to review the basic sequence of ODBC events that are required to connect to and share data with a registered ODBC data source. There are several preliminary steps involved before you can actually get any data from an ODBC data source. These steps involve defining an environment space for the ODBC connection, completing the actual connection, and then establishing an area of memory for passing data back and forth. Many of the API calls require or return unique values (called *handles*) to identify the memory spaces reserved for the ODBC interface. Most of the preliminary work for establishing an ODBC connection involves creating the handles you will use throughout your program. Figure 19.7 shows these operations.

Figure 19.7.

The preliminary steps to establish an ODBC data source connection.

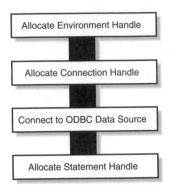

When the connection is established, you can easily share data with the target data source using standard SQL statements. You can select a set of rows using the SELECT...FROM statement. Whenever you request a data set from the ODBC source, you need to go through several steps to actually pass the rows and columns from the source to your Visual Basic program. First, you execute the SQL statement. Then, in order to receive the data set, you must determine the number of columns to receive, and then use that information to tell ODBC to queue up a row of data and send you each column in the row. You do this until you have received all the rows in the data set. Figure 19.8 illustrates the process of executing the SELECT statement and collecting the resulting data.

Figure 19.8.

Collecting results of a SELECT query from an ODBC data source.

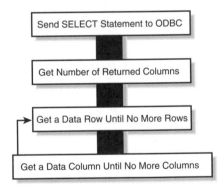

You can perform single record adds, updates, and deletes using SQL INSERT, UPDATE, and DELETE statements. You accomplish this by simply sending the SQL statement to the data source. You can even perform data table CREATE and DROP statements for most data sources.

The last set of ODBC routines that you need to call from Visual Basic are the ones that safely close down the ODBC interface before your program exits. The shutdown routine is basically the same as the startup routine in reverse. First, you need to release the statement handle; then, close the ODBC connection and release the connection handle. Finally, you release the environment handle.

Throughout the process of communicating with the ODBC interface, you need to check for any error codes returned by ODBC. Because the functions are executing outside your Visual Basic program, ODBC errors do not automatically invoke your Visual Basic error handler. Every major ODBC call returns either a success code or an error code. After you execute an ODBC API call, you need to check the return code. If it indicates that an error occurred, you can also call an ODBC routine that returns the detailed error message generated by the data source. When you build your ODBC library, you'll write a routine to perform this error checking.

The Low-Level API Calls

The first thing you need to do to build your library is to declare the necessary API calls for the ODBC interface. In your project, you'll declare only a subset of the total ODBC API calls. These are the ones that are essential for creating a basic data entry form. You also need a handful of Visual Basic constants that you'll use throughout the library.

Load the 16-bit Visual Basic 4 and start a new project. Add a BAS module to the project and set its Name property to APIODBC. Add the API calls in Listing 19.1 to the project.

> **Tip:** If you want to save yourself some typing (and possible typing errors), you can find the APIODBC.BAS file in the C:\TYSDBVB directory. You can load this file into your project using File | Add File from the main menu.

Listing 19.1. The ODBC API declarations.

```
Option Explicit

'
' 16 bit ODBC Declares
Declare Function SQLAllocEnv Lib "odbc.dll" (env As Long) As Integer
Declare Function SQLFreeEnv Lib "odbc.dll" (ByVal env As Long) As Integer
Declare Function SQLAllocConnect Lib "odbc.dll" (ByVal env As Long,
➡hdbc As Long) As Integer
Declare Function SQLConnect Lib "odbc.dll" (ByVal hdbc As Long,
➡ByVal Server As String, ByVal serverlen As Integer, ByVal uid As String,
➡ByVal uidlen As Integer, ByVal pwd As String,
➡ByVal pwdlen As Integer) As Integer
Declare Function SQLFreeConnect Lib "odbc.dll" (ByVal hdbc As Long) As Integer
Declare Function SQLDisconnect Lib "odbc.dll" (ByVal hdbc As Long) As Integer
Declare Function SQLAllocStmt Lib "odbc.dll" (ByVal hdbc As Long,
➡hstmt As Long) As Integer
Declare Function SQLFreeStmt Lib "odbc.dll" (ByVal hstmt As Long,
➡ByVal EndOption As Integer) As Integer
Declare Function SQLExecDirect Lib "odbc.dll" (ByVal hstmt As Long,
➡ByVal sqlString As String, ByVal sqlstrlen As Long) As Integer
```

continues

Listing 19.1. continued

```
Declare Function SQLNumResultCols Lib "odbc.dll" (ByVal hstmt As Long,
➥NumCols As Integer) As Integer
Declare Function SQLFetch Lib "odbc.dll" (ByVal hstmt As Long) As Integer
Declare Function SQLGetData Lib "odbc.dll" (ByVal hstmt As Long,
➥ByVal Col As Integer, ByVal wConvType As Integer, ByVal lpbBuf As String,
➥ByVal dwbuflen As Long, lpcbout As Long) As Integer
Declare Function SQLError Lib "odbc.dll" (ByVal env As Long,
➥ByVal hdbc As Long, ByVal hstmt As Long, ByVal SQLState As String,
➥NativeError As Long, ByVal Buffer As String, ByVal Buflen As Integer,
➥OutLen As Integer) As Integer
```

These are the ODBC API calls needed to implement basic connect, data transfer, and disconnect. Now add the constants in Listing 19.2 to the module.

Listing 19.2. The ODBC constant declarations.

```
' SQL/ODBC Constants
Global Const gSQLSuccess = 0
Global Const gSQLSuccessWithInfo = 1
Global Const gSQLError = -1
Global Const gSQLNoDataFound = 100
Global Const gSQLClose = 0
Global Const gSQLDrop = 1
Global Const gSQLMaxMsgLen = 512
Global Const gSQLChar = 1
```

Save the module as APIODBC.BAS, and save the project as TYSODBC.VBP. Now you are ready to build the library functions that use these API calls to perform ODBC operations.

The ODBC Library Routines

The next set of routines are separated into two groups. The first group are routines that deal primarily with the ODBC interface. These routines are just wrappers for the API calls. Wrappers are Visual Basic routines that encapsulate the API call. Using wrappers makes it easy to change the underlying API call without having to change your code. For example, if you want to use the 32-bit version of the ODBC, you only need to change the ODBC.DLL in each of the API calls to ODBC32.DLL. Because you are using Visual Basic wrappers, you won't have to make any changes to your Visual Basic programs in order to use 32-bit ODBC!

The second set of library routines deals primarily with Visual Basic. These routines take the data from the ODBC and store it in Visual Basic variables and controls for use on your data entry forms.

First, you need to add a few global variables that you'll use throughout the library. Add a new BAS module to the project and set its Name property to LIBODBC. Now add the declarations in Listing 19.3 to the file.

Listing 19.3. Adding the local variables to LIBODBC.BAS.

```
Option Explicit


' Local ODBC Vars
Global Const ODBCBuffer = 256     ' for fixed length vars
Global gblHenv As Long            ' environment handle
Global gblHdbc As Long            ' database connection
Global gblHstmt As Long           ' statement handle
Global gblNumCols As Integer      ' result set columns
Global ODBCDataSource As String   ' data source name
Global ODBCUserID As String       ' user id
Global ODBCPassword As String     ' user password
Global ODBCQuery As String        ' initial startup SQL
```

Now you're ready for the first set of Visual Basic routines.

Mid-Level Routines

These routines handle the direct calls to the ODBC API and provide simple error checking. The first of the routines allocates an environment handle. This handle is needed before you can attempt to connect to the ODBC interface.

Create a new function called `ODBCEnvironment` and add the code in Listing 19.4.

Listing 19.4. Coding the `ODBCEnvironment` function.

```
Function ODBCEnvironment(hEnv As Long)
    '
    ' establish an ODBC environment
    '
    ' inputs:
    '   hEnv      var to hold returned value
    '
    ' output:
    '   hEnv      set to unique handle value
    '
    ' returns:  gSQLSuccess if OK, oer errcode
    '
    Dim nResult As Integer
    Dim Temp As Integer
    '
    nResult = SQLAllocEnv(hEnv)
    If nResult <> gSQLSuccess Then
        MsgBox "Cannot allocate environment handle.", vbCritical,
        ➥"ODBCEnvironment"
        Screen.MousePointer = vbDefault
    End If
    ODBCEnvironment = nResult
    '
End Function
```

This routine calls the SQLAllocEnv API and checks for any errors. The SQLAllocEnv API establishes an environment for all ODBC transactions for this session. The hEnv parameter that you pass to the function is a variable of the LONG data type. This will hold a unique number that identifies all transactions that pass from your Visual Basic program to the ODBC interface.

Create a new function called ODBCConnect, as shown in Listing 19.5. This routine handles the details of completing a connection to the ODBC data source.

Listing 19.5. Coding the ODBCConnect function.

```
Function ODBCConnect(hEnv, hdbc As Long, hstmt As Long, cDataSource As String,
➡cUserID As String, cPassword As String) As Integer
    '
    ' connect to remote data source
    '
    ' inputs:
    '   hEnv        environment handle from ODBCEnvironment
    '   hdbc        database connect var (will be set)
    '   hstmt       statement var (will be set)
    '   cDataSource name of ODBC data source
    '   cUserID     ODBC user login ID
    '   cPassword   ODBC login password
    '
    ' outputs:
    '   hdbc        database connection handle
    '   hstmt       statement handle
    '
    ' returns       gSQLSuccess or error code
    '
    Dim nResult As Integer
    Dim Temp As Integer
    '
    ODBCConnect = gSQLSuccess

    ' get a connection handle
    nResult = SQLAllocConnect(hEnv, hdbc)
    If nResult <> gSQLSuccess Then
        MsgBox "Unable to allocate connection handle.", vbCritical,
        ➡"ODBCConnect.SQLAllocConnect"
        Screen.MousePointer = vbDefault
        ODBCConnect = nResult
        Exit Function
    End If

    ' now attempt to connect to database
    nResult = SQLConnect(hdbc, cDataSource, Len(cDataSource), cUserID,
    ➡Len(cUserID), cPassword, Len(cPassword))
    If nResult <> gSQLSuccess And nResult <> gSQLSuccessWithInfo Then
        MsgBox "Unable to establish DataSource connnection.", vbCritical,
        ➡"ODBCConnect.SQLConnect"
        Screen.MousePointer = vbDefault
        ODBCConnect = nResult
        Exit Function
    End If
```

```
    ' now get handle for all future statements
    nResult = SQLAllocStmt(hdbc, hstmt)
    If nResult <> gSQLSuccess Then
        MsgBox "Unable to allocate statement handle.", vbCritical,
        ➥"ODBCConnect.AllocStmt"
        Screen.MousePointer = vbDefault
        ODBCConnect = nResult
        Exit Function
    End If
    '
End Function
```

The routine in Listing 19.5 takes several parameters and uses them to perform three basic ODBC operations. The first operation is establishing a data source connection handle. The second operation is the actual attempt to connect to the data source. The cDataSource, cUserID, and cPassword parameters are used for this. You'll see how to initialize these parameters later in this chapter. The final ODBC operation is to establish an ODBC statement handle. This handle will be used as the unique identifier whenever you want to share data with the ODBC data source.

You will also need to disconnect the ODBC link when you exit the program. Create a new function called ODBCDisconnect and add the code in Listing 19.6.

Listing 19.6. Coding the ODBCDisconnect function.

```
Function ODBCDisconnect(hdbc As Long, hstmt As Long) As Integer
    '
    ' disconnect from data source
    '
    ' inputs:
    '   hdbc     database connection handle
    '   hstmt    statement handle
    '
    ' outputs:
    '   none
    '
    ' returns:  True if ok, False if error
    '
    Dim nResult As Integer
    '
    ODBCDisconnect = True
    '
    ' close statement handle
    If hstmt <> 0 Then
        nResult = SQLFreeStmt(hstmt, gSQLDrop)
        If nResult <> gSQLSuccess Then
            ODBCDisconnect = False
        End If
    End If
    '
    ' disconnect from ds
```

continues

Listing 19.6. continued

```
        If hdbc <> 0 Then
            nResult = SQLDisconnect(hdbc)
            If nResult <> gSQLSuccess Then
                ODBCDisconnect = False
            End If
        End If
        '
        ' close connection
        If hdbc <> 0 Then
            nResult = SQLFreeConnect(hdbc)
            If nResult <> gSQLSuccess Then
                ODBCDisconnect = False
            End If
        End If
        '
End Function
```

You can see that Listing 19.6 performs the same three functions as ODBCConnect, only this time in reverse. First, it releases the statement handle, and then it performs the actual disconnect of the ODBC interface. Finally, the routine releases the connection handle.

Of course, you'll need a routine to release the environment handle, too. Create the ODBCFreeHandle function and enter the code in Listing 19.7.

Listing 19.7. Coding the ODBCFreeHandle function.

```
Function ODBCFreeHandle(hEnv As Long) As Integer
    '
    ' release environment handle
    '
    ' inputs:
    '   hEnv      environment handle var
    '
    ' outputs:
    '   none
    '
    ' returns    True if OK, False if error
    '
    Dim nResult As Integer
    '
    ODBCFreeHandle = True
    '
    If hEnv <> 0 Then
        nResult = SQLFreeEnv(hEnv)
        If nResult <> gSQLSuccess Then
            ODBCFreeHandle = False
        End If
    End If
    '
End Function
```

This is a simple routine. It simply tells the ODBC interface that you are done with the session and returns any resulting codes.

The last mid-level routine you need is an ODBC error routine. This routine will gather any error information sent to your Visual Basic program from the ODBC data source. ODBC data sources are capable of sending more than one line of error information. For this reason, you'll write the routine as a loop that continues to ask for error messages until there are none to be found.

Create a new function called ODBCErrMsg and enter the code in Listing 19.8.

Listing 19.8. Coding the ODBCErrorMsg function.

```
Sub ODBCErrorMsg(hdbc As Long, hstmt As Long, cTitle As String)
    '
    ' return detailed SQL Error
    '
    ' inputs:
    '   hdbc     database connection handle
    '   hstmt    statement handle
    '   cTitle   error message title
    '
    Dim SQLState As String * 16
    Dim ErrorMsg As String * gSQLMaxMsgLen
    Dim ErrMsgSize As Integer
    '
    Dim ErrorCode As Long
    Dim ErrorCodeStr As String
    Dim nResult As Integer
    Dim Temp As Integer
    '
    SQLState = String$(16, 0)
    ErrorMsg = String$(gSQLMaxMsgLen - 1, 0)
    '
    Do
        '
        nResult = SQLError(0, hdbc, hstmt, SQLState, ErrorCode, ErrorMsg,
        ➥Len(ErrorMsg), ErrMsgSize)
        Screen.MousePointer = vbDefault
        If nResult = gSQLSuccess Or nResult = gSQLSuccessWithInfo Then
            If ErrMsgSize = 0 Then
                Temp = MsgBox("gSQLSuccess Or gSQLSuccessWithInfo Error
                ➥— No additional information available.",
                ➥vbExclamation, cTitle)
            Else
                If ErrorCode = 0 Then
                    ErrorCodeStr = ""
                Else
                    ErrorCodeStr = Trim$(Str(ErrorCode)) & "   "
                End If
```

continues

619

Listing 19.8. continued

```
                Temp = MsgBox(ErrorCodeStr & Left$(ErrorMsg, ErrMsgSize),
                ➥vbExclamation, cTitle)
            End If
        End If
    '
    Loop Until nResult <> gSQLSuccess
    '
End Sub
```

This routine checks the state of the error code and returns any messages it can find. There are times when the error code is set by ODBC, but no message is returned. The routine checks for this and creates its own message, if needed.

Save this module as LIBODBC.BAS before you continue on with the last set of ODBC library routines.

High-Level Routines

The last set of ODBC library routines deals primarily with the duties required to make Visual Basic capable of displaying, reading, and writing data via the ODBC interface. These routines take the data sets returned by ODBC and store them in Visual Basic list and grid controls. These controls are then used as holding areas by your Visual Basic program for filling and updating text boxes on your data entry form. This method of storing result sets in a Visual Basic control reduces the amount of traffic over the ODBC link and improves the response time of your program.

Note: In the examples here, you access relatively small data sets. If your ODBC interface requires the passing of very large data sets, you need to develop more sophisticated methods for storing and retrieving the resulting data sets. However, it is always a good idea to limit the size of the result set as much as possible, because passing large amounts of data over the ODBC link can adversely affect not just your Visual Basic program, but all programs that are using the same network.

The first high-level routine you'll build actually creates a data set for your Visual Basic program. This routine handles the creation of the environment handle, the completion of the ODBC connection to the data source, and the passing of the initial SQL SELECT statement that creates the data set.

Create a new function called ODBCDataSet and add the code in Listing 19.9.

Listing 19.9. Coding the `ODBCDataSet` function.

```
Function ODBCDataSet(frmName As Form) As Integer
    '
    ' get data from source
    '
    Dim nResult As Integer
    '
    ' declare an enviforment handle
    nResult = ODBCEnvironment(gblHenv)
    If nResult = gSQLSuccess Then
        ' connect to data source
        nResult = ODBCConnect(gblHenv, gblHdbc, gblHstmt, ODBCDataSource,
        ➥ODBCUserID, ODBCPassword)
        If nResult = gSQLSuccess Then
            ' build data set for list box
            nResult = ODBCLoadCtl(frmName.LstODBC, ODBCQuery, gblHstmt,
            ➥False, "*")
            ' build data set for grid control
            nResult = ODBCLoadCtl(frmName.GrdODBC, ODBCQuery, gblHstmt,
            ➥False, "*")
        End If
    End If
    '
    ODBCDataSet = nResult

End Function
```

The routine in Listing 19.9 expects you to pass it a form variable. This form must contain a list box and a grid control. These controls are filled with the records from the data set created by the SQL SELECT statement. This routine calls a new function called ODBCLoadCtl that you have not yet defined. You'll get to that a bit later in this section.

Before you look at the ODBCLoadCtl function, you need to add the function that sets the initial data source name, user ID and password, and initial SQL statement. Create a new function called ODBCStart and enter the code in Listing 19.10.

Listing 19.10. Coding the `ODBCStart` function.

```
Function ODBCStart(frmName As Form, Optional cDSN, Optional cUser,
➥Optional cPW, Optional cSQL) As Integer
    '
    ' main wrapper to launch ODBC
    '
    ' inputs:
    '   frmName name of data entry form
    '   cDSN    data source name
    '   cUser   data source user login ID
    '   cPW     data source password
    '   cSQL    initial SELECT statement
    '
```

continues

Listing 19.10. continued

```
        ' check for passed parms
        If IsMissing(cDSN) Then
            cDSN = ""

        End If
        '
        If IsMissing(cUser) Then
            cUser = ""
        End If
        '
        If IsMissing(cPW) Then
            cPW = ""
        End If
        '
        If IsMissing(cSQL) Then
            cSQL = ""
        End If

        ' check for needed inputs
        If cDSN = "" Then
            cDSN = InputBox("Enter Data Set Name to Open:", "ODBC DataSource Name")
        End If
        '
        If cUser = "" Then
            cUser = InputBox("Enter UserID:", "ODBC UserID")
        End If
        '
        If cPW = "" Then
            cPW = InputBox("Enter Password:", "ODBC Password")
        End If
        '
        If cSQL = "" Then
            cSQL = InputBox("Enter Intitial SQL Statement", "ODBC SQL Statement")
        End If

        ' now load global vars
        ODBCDataSource = cDSN
        ODBCUserID = cUser
        ODBCPassword = cPW
        ODBCQuery = cSQL

        ' now try to connect and load
        ODBCStart = ODBCDataSet(frmName)
End Function
```

As you can see, this routine has one required parameter and four optional ones. You must pass the form that contains the list and grid controls. You have the option of omitting the data source and other parameters. If you leave them out, the routine prompts the user for the necessary values. If you include them, the routine just stores these passed values for later use.

Now you can build the heart of the high-level library routines. The ODBCLoadCtl routine reads each row and column of data in the data set returned by the ODBC data source and stores that data into two Visual Basic controls. In effect, you are creating your own set of bound data controls for the ODBC interface. After these two controls are filled, you'll write another routine to move data from the list control to a predefined set of text boxes for user input.

Create a new function called ODBCLoadCtl and enter the code in Listing 19.11.

Listing 19.11. Coding the ODBCLoadCtl function.

```
Function ODBCLoadCtl(ctlName As Control, cSQL As String, hstmt As Long,
➥lFill As Boolean, cDelim As String) As Integer
    '
    ' perform query and
    ' load results into control
    '
    ' inputs:
    '   CtlName      name of control to load
    '   cSQL         SQL query to perform
    '   hstmt        statement handle for SQL calls
    '   lFill        flag to pad info
    '   cDelim       char value that separates fields
    '
    ' outputs:
    '   CtlName      loaded with data
    '
    ' returns:       gSQLSucess if OK or error code
    '
    Dim nResult As Integer   ' error var
    Dim Temp As Integer      ' local stuff
    Dim nRows As Integer     ' row counter
    Dim nCols As Integer     ' column counter
    Dim cBuffer As String * ODBCBuffer   ' receive buffer
    Dim cItem As String      ' output buffer
    Dim cData As String      ' output line
    Dim cOutLen As Long      ' local counter
    Dim nColWide As Integer  ' width of grid column
    '
    ODBCLoadCtl = gSQLSuccess
    nColWide = 1500
    '
    ' Make sure referenced control is a list box, combo box, or grid
    If TypeOf ctlName Is ListBox Then
        ElseIf TypeOf ctlName Is ComboBox Then
        ElseIf TypeOf ctlName Is Grid Then
    Else
        ODBCLoadCtl = -3
        Exit Function
    End If
```

continues

Listing 19.11. continued

```
' Do the initial query
nResult = SQLExecDirect(hstmt, cSQL, Len(cSQL))
If nResult <> gSQLSuccess Then
    Call ODBCErrorMsg(gblHdbc, gblHstmt,
    ➥"SQL Statement Error During ODBCLoadCtl")
    Temp = SQLFreeStmt(hstmt, gSQLClose)
    Screen.MousePointer = vbDefault
    ODBCLoadCtl = nResult
    Exit Function
End If

' get column count
nResult = SQLNumResultCols(hstmt, gblNumCols)
If nResult <> gSQLSuccess Then
    Temp = SQLFreeStmt(hstmt, gSQLClose)
    Screen.MousePointer = vbDefault
    ODBCLoadCtl = nResult
    Exit Function
 End If

' must not have found data!
If gblNumCols = 0 Then
    Temp = SQLFreeStmt(hstmt, gSQLClose)
    Screen.MousePointer = vbDefault
    ODBCLoadCtl = gSQLNoDataFound
    Exit Function
End If

' initialize grid
If TypeOf ctlName Is Grid Then
    ctlName.Cols = gblNumCols + 1
    ctlName.Rows = 2
End If
' clear list
If TypeOf ctlName Is ListBox Then
    ctlName.Clear
End If
' clear combo box
If TypeOf ctlName Is ComboBox Then
    ctlName.Clear
End If

' initialize receive buffer
cBuffer = String$(ODBCBuffer, 0)

'Now load get rows and put into control
nRows = 0
Do
    nResult = SQLFetch(hstmt)      ' get a row
    If nResult <> gSQLSuccess Then
        If nResult = gSQLNoDataFound Then
            Temp = SQLFreeStmt(hstmt, gSQLClose)
            Screen.MousePointer = vbDefault
            If nRows > 0 Then
```

```
                    Exit Do          ' we're all done
            Else
                ODBCLoadCtl = nResult     ' error!
                Exit Function
            End If
        Else
            Temp = SQLFreeStmt(hstmt, gSQLClose)
            Screen.MousePointer = vbDefault
            ODBCLoadCtl = nResult
            Exit Function
        End If
    End If
'
' update grid row count
nRows = nRows + 1
If TypeOf ctlName Is Grid Then
    ctlName.Row = nRows
End If
'
' now get each column
cItem = ""
cData = ""
For nCols = 1 To gblNumCols
    nResult = SQLGetData(hstmt, nCols, gSQLChar, cBuffer,
    ➥ODBCBuffer, cOutLen)
    If nResult <> gSQLSuccess Then
        Temp = SQLFreeStmt(hstmt, gSQLClose)
        Screen.MousePointer = vbDefault
        ODBCLoadCtl = nResult
        Exit Function
    End If
    '
    If TypeOf ctlName Is Grid Then
        ' load grid column
        ctlName.Col = nCols
        If cOutLen > 0 Then
            ctlName.Text = Left$(cBuffer, cOutLen)
            ctlName.ColWidth(nCols) = nColWide
        End If
    Else
        ' build single string for list/combo box
        If lFill And nCols = 1 Then
            If cOutLen > 0 Then
                cData = Left$(cBuffer, cOutLen)
            Else
                cData = ""
            End If
        Else
            If cOutLen > 0 Then
                If cItem = "" Then
                    cItem = Left$(cBuffer, cOutLen)
                Else
                    cItem = cItem & cDelim & Left$(cBuffer, cOutLen)
                End If
            Else
```

continues

Listing 19.11. continued

```
                        cItem = cItem & cDelim
                    End If
                End If
            End If
        Next nCols
        '
        ' now move string data into
        ' list/combo control.
        If cItem <> "" Then
            On Error Resume Next
            ctlName.AddItem cItem
            If Err = 0 Then
                If cData <> "" Then
                    ctlName.ItemData(ctlName.NewIndex) = Val(cData)
                End If
            Else
                MsgBox "Result Set too large to fit in control",
                ➥vbExclamation, "ODBCLoadCtl"
                Temp = SQLFreeStmt(hstmt, gSQLClose)
                Exit Do
            End If
            On Error GoTo 0
        End If
        ' increment grid row
        If TypeOf ctlName Is Grid Then
            ctlName.Rows = ctlName.Rows + 1
        End If
    Loop
    ' fix final grid row count
    If TypeOf ctlName Is Grid Then
        ctlName.Rows = ctlName.Rows - 1
    End If
    '
    ODBCLoadCtl = gSQLSuccess
    Screen.MousePointer = vbDefault
    '
End Function
```

This routine does a number of things. First, you pass it several parameters that are used to create the data set and a few to control how the Visual Basic controls are loaded. You wrote the routine to be used with more than one type of data control, so there are several lines of code that check and verify the type of control you are dealing with.

Because Listing 19.11 is a rather long routine, let's break the major sections down and inspect the operations that are taking place here. The main operations of this routine are as follows:

☐ Intialize variables for exit code and grid column width and verify that the control type passed into the routine is valid.

```
ODBCLoadCtl = gSQLSuccess
    nColWide = 1500
    '
```

```
    ' Make sure referenced control is a listbox, combobox, or grid
    If TypeOf ctlName Is ListBox Then
        ElseIf TypeOf ctlName Is ComboBox Then
        ElseIf TypeOf ctlName Is Grid Then
    Else
        ODBCLoadCtl = -3
        Exit Function
    End If
```

☐ Send the SQL statement to the ODBC data source.

```
    ' Do the initial query
    nResult = SQLExecDirect(hstmt, cSQL, Len(cSQL))
    If nResult <> gSQLSuccess Then
        Call ODBCErrorMsg(gblHdbc, gblHstmt,
        ➥"SQL Statement Error During ODBCLoadCtl")
        Temp = SQLFreeStmt(hstmt, gSQLClose)
        Screen.MousePointer = vbDefault
        ODBCLoadCtl = nResult
        Exit Function
    End If
```

☐ Find out how many columns were returned.

```
    ' get column count
    nResult = SQLNumResultCols(hstmt, gblNumCols)
    If nResult <> gSQLSuccess Then
        Temp = SQLFreeStmt(hstmt, gSQLClose)
        Screen.MousePointer = vbDefault
        ODBCLoadCtl = nResult
        Exit Function
     End If
```

☐ If you have no columns, you must not have any data to load. Exit the routine.

```
    ' must not have found data!
    If gblNumCols = 0 Then
        Temp = SQLFreeStmt(hstmt, gSQLClose)
        Screen.MousePointer = vbDefault
        ODBCLoadCtl = gSQLNoDataFound
        Exit Function
    End If
```

☐ If you have data, initialize the controls for loading into a list control. This list control acts as a receive buffer for the entire data set.

```
    ' initialize grid
    If TypeOf ctlName Is Grid Then
        ctlName.Cols = gblNumCols + 1
        ctlName.Rows = 2
    End If
    ' clear list
    If TypeOf ctlName Is ListBox Then
        ctlName.Clear
    End If
    ' clear combo box
    If TypeOf ctlName Is ComboBox Then
        ctlName.Clear
    End If
```

☐ Use a large DO...LOOP to read each data set row.

```
'Now load get rows and put into control
    nRows = 0
    Do
        nResult = SQLFetch(hstmt)      ' get a row
        If nResult <> gSQLSuccess Then
            If nResult = gSQLNoDataFound Then
                Temp = SQLFreeStmt(hstmt, gSQLClose)
                Screen.MousePointer = vbDefault
                If nRows > 0 Then
                    Exit Do            ' we're all done
                Else
                    ODBCLoadCtl = nResult    ' error!
                    Exit Function
                End If
            Else
                Temp = SQLFreeStmt(hstmt, gSQLClose)
                Screen.MousePointer = vbDefault
                ODBCLoadCtl = nResult
                Exit Function
            End If
        End If
        '
        ' update grid row count
        nRows = nRows + 1
        If TypeOf ctlName Is Grid Then
            ctlName.Row = nRows
        End If
```

☐ After reading a row, get each column of data.

```
' now get each column
    cItem = ""
    cData = ""
    For nCols = 1 To gblNumCols
        nResult = SQLGetData(hstmt, nCols, gSQLChar, cBuffer,
        ➥ODBCBuffer, cOutLen)
        If nResult <> gSQLSuccess Then
            Temp = SQLFreeStmt(hstmt, gSQLClose)
            Screen.MousePointer = vbDefault
            ODBCLoadCtl = nResult
            Exit Function
        End If
        '
```

☐ Store each column of data in a grid column or build a line for the list/combo controls.

```
If TypeOf ctlName Is Grid Then
                ' load grid column
                ctlName.Col = nCols
                If cOutLen > 0 Then
                    ctlName.Text = Left$(cBuffer, cOutLen)
                    ctlName.ColWidth(nCols) = nColWide
                End If
            Else
                ' build single string for list/combo box
                If lFill And nCols = 1 Then
                    If cOutLen > 0 Then
```

```
                        cData = Left$(cBuffer, cOutLen)
                Else
                        cData = ""
                End If
            Else
                If cOutLen > 0 Then
                    If cItem = "" Then
                        cItem = Left$(cBuffer, cOutLen)
                    Else
                        cItem = cItem & cDelim & Left$(cBuffer,
                        ➥cOutLen)
                    End If
                Else
                        cItem = cItem & cDelim
                End If
            End If
        End If
    End If
Next nCols
```

☐ Store each row of data as a string in the list control, as long as the data set is not too large to fit in the control. The Visual Basic list control can hold 64K of data.

```
' now move string data into
        ' list/combo control.
        If cItem <> "" Then
            On Error Resume Next
            ctlName.AddItem cItem
            If Err = 0 Then
                If cData <> "" Then
                    ctlName.ItemData(ctlName.NewIndex) = Val(cData)
                End If
            Else
                MsgBox "Result Set too large to fit in control",
                ➥vbExclamation, "ODBCLoadCtl"
                Temp = SQLFreeStmt(hstmt, gSQLClose)
                Exit Do
            End If
            On Error GoTo 0
        End If
        ' increment grid row
        If TypeOf ctlName Is Grid Then
            ctlName.Rows = ctlName.Rows + 1
        End If
    Loop
```

☐ If there are no more rows, exit the routine.

```
' fix final grid row count
    If TypeOf ctlName Is Grid Then
        ctlName.Rows = ctlName.Rows - 1
    End If
    '
    ODBCLoadCtl = gSQLSuccess
    Screen.MousePointer = vbDefault
```

Now that you have loaded the list and grid controls, you need a routine that moves the requested record from the list control into a set of text boxes for user input on the form. Create the new function called ODBCGetFld, and enter the code in Listing 19.12.

19

Listing 19.12. Coding the ODBCGetFld function.

```
Function ODBCGetFld(ctlName As Control, nFld As Integer, cFldDelim As String)
➥As String
    '
    ' get info from list/combo control
    ' into text control for editing
    '
    ' inputs:
    '   ctlName      control that has data set
    '   nFld number of field to retrieve
    '   cFldDelim    field delimeter
    '
    ' outputs:
    '   none
    '
    ' returns:       resulting column of data
    '
    Dim x As Integer
    Dim nPos1 As Integer
    Dim nPos2 As Integer
    Dim cSearch As String
    '
    ODBCGetFld = ""
    cSearch = cFldDelim & ctlName.List(ctlName.ListIndex) & cFldDelim
    '
    ' make sure we have the right control
    If TypeOf ctlName Is ListBox Then
    Else
        If TypeOf ctlName Is ComboBox Then
        Else
            Exit Function
        End If
    End If

    ' look for first delimiter for field nfld
    nPos1 = 0
    For x = 1 To nFld
        nPos1 = InStr(nPos1 + 1, cSearch, cFldDelim)
        If nPos1 = 0 Then
            nPos1 = -1
            Exit For
        End If
    Next x
    '
    ' get second delimeter for nFld
    If nPos1 <> -1 Then
        nPos2 = InStr(nPos1 + 1, cSearch, cFldDelim)
    End If
    '
    ' ok, we got a column of data!
    If nPos2 > nPos1 And nPos2 <> 0 Then
        ODBCGetFld = Mid$(cSearch, nPos1 + 1, nPos2 - (nPos1 + 1))
    End If
    '
End Function
```

The routine in Listing 19.12 asks for the control to read the column number and the character used to delimit the columns in the list control. It takes this information and returns a string that can be used to populate a text control (or any other control) on a data entry form. You'll see how to use this in your data entry forms in the next section.

You need only three more library functions before you have a complete ODBC database kit. You need routines that can write an updated existing record, add a new record, and delete an existing record from the data set. These three routines can be called from your data entry form and look much like the standard Add, Edit, and Delete operations used with data bound controls.

First, create the ODBCRowDel function and enter the code in Listing 19.13.

Listing 19.13. Coding the ODBCRowDel function.

```
Public Function ODBCRowDel(frmName As Form, cTable As String, cKey As String)
➥As Integer
    '
    '   inputs:
    '       frmName    form that holds the controls
    '       cTable     table name of data
    '       cKey       index key for table
    '
    ' outputs:
    '       modifies data set
    '
    ' returns:   <>0 if an error occurs
    '       ' delete a row
    '
    Dim nResult As Integer
    Dim Temp As Integer
    Dim cSQL As String
    '
    ODBCRowDel = gSQLSuccess

    ' create delete query
    cSQL = "DELETE * FROM " + cTable + " WHERE " + cKey + "='" +
    ➥Trim(frmODBC.Text1(0)) + "'"

    ' Do the delete query:
    nResult = SQLExecDirect(gblHstmt, cSQL, Len(cSQL))
    If nResult <> gSQLSuccess Then
        Call ODBCErrorMsg(gblHdbc, gblHstmt, "SQL Statement Error
        ➥During ODBCRowDel")
        Temp = SQLFreeStmt(gblHstmt, gSQLClose)
        Screen.MousePointer = vbDefault
        ODBCRowDel = nResult
        Exit Function
    End If

    ' set values and exit
    ODBCRowDel = gSQLSuccess
    Screen.MousePointer = vbDefault
    '
End Function
```

This routine is designed to delete the current record loaded into the text controls on the form, and it requires three parameters. The first is the name of the data entry form, the second is the name of the table you are updating, and the third parameter is the name of the key field. For all your ODBC data sets, you are assuming that the first field in the list is the primary key field.

> **Note:** Assuming that the primary key field is always the first physical field in the data set can be a limitation when you're dealing with secondary tables and other non-normalized data sets. For now, however, this handles most of your data entry needs. As you develop more skill with ODBC routines, you can modify these routines or add others that give you more flexibility in sharing data over ODBC connections.

The routine in Listing 19.13 builds a standard DELETE query using the parameters you supplied it, and then executes the SQL DELETE returning any error messages that might result.

Now you'll build the ODBCRowAdd function. The add routine requires the table name and the form name as parameters. The routine builds a standard APPEND query using the INSERT INTO syntax. Create the new function and add the code in Listing 19.14.

Listing 19.14. Coding the ODBCRowAdd function.

```
Public Function ODBCRowAdd(frmName As Form, cTable As String) As Integer
    '
    ' add a new row to the table
    '
    '  inputs:
    '    frnName    form that holds the controls
    '    cTable     table name for data
    '
    ' outputs:  modifies data set
    '
    ' returns:  <>0 if error occurs
    '
    Dim nResult As Integer
    Dim Temp As Integer
    Dim cSQL As String
    Dim x As Integer
    '
    ODBCRowAdd = gSQLSuccess
    '
    ' create SQL insert query
    cSQL = "INSERT INTO " + cTable + " VALUES("
    For x = 1 To gblNumCols
        cSQL = cSQL + "'" + frmName.Text1(x - 1) + "'"
        If x < gblNumCols Then
            cSQL = cSQL + ","
        End If
```

```
    Next x
    cSQL = cSQL + ")"
    '
    ' Do the insert query:
    nResult = SQLExecDirect(gblHstmt, cSQL, Len(cSQL))
    If nResult <> gSQLSuccess Then
        Call ODBCErrorMsg(gblHdbc, gblHstmt, "SQL Statement Error
        ➥During ODBCRowAdd")
        Temp = SQLFreeStmt(gblHstmt, gSQLClose)
        Screen.MousePointer = vbDefault
        ODBCRowAdd = nResult
        Exit Function
    End If
    '
    ' set values and exit
    ODBCRowAdd = gSQLSuccess
    Screen.MousePointer = vbDefault
    '
End Function
```

The last routine in your library performs an update of an existing record. The simplest way to accomplish this is to delete the existing record and replace it with the new updated version. This can be done with two SQL statements—a DELETE query followed by an INSERT INTO statement. A more sophisticated approach would be to build a series of UPDATE statements that update each field of the row, one at a time. For the example here, you'll use the DELETE/INSERT method because it takes less code and is easier to understand.

Note: In certain situations, you will not want to perform updates using the DELETE/INSERT method. If you have defined a delete cascade in a relationship between two tables, performing a DELETE/INSERT on the *one* side of the one-to-many relationship results in the deletion of all the related records on the *many* side of the relationship. In cases where you might define delete cascades, you should only use the UDPATE method.

Create the ODBCRowUdpate function and add the code in Listing 19.15.

Listing 19.15. Coding the ODBCRowUpdate function.

```
Function ODBCRowUpdate(frmName As Form, cTable As String,
➥cKey As String) As Integer
    '
    ' update row of data set
    '
    ' inputs:
    '    frmName    for that holds controls
```

continues

19

Listing 19.15. continued

```
'     cTable      name of data table
'     cKey        index key of table
'
' outputs:        modifies data set
'
'  returns        <>0 if error occurs
'     Dim nResult As Integer
Dim Temp As Integer
'
Dim cSQLInsert As String
Dim cSQLDelete As String
Dim x As Integer

ODBCRowUpdate = gSQLSuccess

' create delete query
cSQLDelete = "DELETE * FROM " + cTable + " WHERE " + cKey + "='" +
➥Trim(frmName.Text1(0)) + "'"

' create SQL update query
cSQLInsert = "INSERT INTO " + cTable + " VALUES("
For x = 1 To gblNumCols
    cSQLInsert = cSQLInsert + "'" + frmName.Text1(x - 1) + "'"
    If x < gblNumCols Then
        cSQLInsert = cSQLInsert + ","
    End If
Next x
cSQLInsert = cSQLInsert + ")"

' do delete query
nResult = SQLExecDirect(gblHstmt, cSQLDelete, Len(cSQLDelete))
If nResult <> gSQLSuccess Then
    Call ODBCErrorMsg(gblHdbc, gblHstmt, "SQL Statement Error During0
    ➥ODBCRowUpdate.Delete")
    Temp = SQLFreeStmt(gblHstmt, gSQLClose)
    Screen.MousePointer = vbDefault
    ODBCRowUpdate = nResult
    Exit Function
End If

' Do the insert query:
nResult = SQLExecDirect(gblHstmt, cSQLInsert, Len(cSQLInsert))
If nResult <> gSQLSuccess Then
    Call ODBCErrorMsg(gblHdbc, gblHstmt, "SQL Statement Error During
    ➥ODBCRowUpdate.Insert")
    Temp = SQLFreeStmt(gblHstmt, gSQLClose)
    Screen.MousePointer = vbDefault
    ODBCRowUpdate = nResult
    Exit Function
End If

' set values and exit
ODBCRowUpdate = gSQLSuccess
Screen.MousePointer = vbDefault
'
End Function
```

As you can see, this routine first executes a DELETE query, and then it executes an INSERT statement.

Save this module as LIBODBC.BAS. You have now completed the ODBC library routines. The next step is to build a simple data entry form that uses the ODBC library to open a data set and pass information to and from the data via the ODBC interface.

Using the ODBC Library to Create a Data Entry Form

Now that you have your ODBC library, you are ready to build a data entry form that uses the ODBC interface for database access. For this example, you'll build a form that is self-configuring. This form reads the number of fields in the data set and presents the correct number of text boxes for the data set. The form also displays a grid that shows the table view of the same data presented in the text boxes. Users are able to click on the grid line to bring up the data record in the text boxes. You'll also have the usual set of navigation buttons (First, Last, Next, and Back) and data table modification buttons (Add, Update, Delete, and Refresh).

You'll write the form in a way that lets you easily modify it for future Visual Basic projects. In fact, this form can be used with different data sets without any additional modification because it is able to read the data set columns and "construct itself" to create a simple data entry form.

Building the Dynamic Data Entry Form

19

Because you plan to make this form self-constructing, you have very little to do in the way of form layout. You need to add a handful of controls (some of them are control arrays), and then add some code to make sure the form can make its own decisions on how the controls should appear on the screen. You need five controls and one form for this project.

Start Visual Basic and create a new project. Set the Name and the Caption properties of the form to FRMODBC. Add a command button control to the form. Set its Name property to cmdExit and its Caption property to E&xit. Add a grid control to the form (not the data-bound grid, just the standard grid control). Set its Name property to grdODBC. Place a list control on the form and set its Name property to LSTODBC. Also set the list control's Visible property to False.

Now you need to add two control arrays to the form. First, add a single command button to the form. Set its Name and caption properties to cmdODBC. Also set its Font properties to Microsoft Sans Serif, eight-point, regular. Use the Copy and Paste operations from the Visual Basic Edit menu to add seven more cmdODBC buttons to the form. You should now have a total of eight command buttons called cmdODBC.

> **Note:** All forms and controls in this project should have their Font properties set to Microsoft Sans Serif, eight-point, regular.

The second control array that you need is a set of text boxes. Add a single text box to the form. Set its Name and Caption properties to txtODBC. Make sure the Font properties are set to Microsoft Sans Serif, eight-point, regular. Use Copy and Paste to add 11 more text boxes to the form. You should now have a total of 12 text boxes called txtODBC.

The placement of all of these controls does not matter; you'll add code to the form to make sure all controls are sized and placed properly. However, as a reference, your form should look similar to the one in Figure 19.9.

Figure 19.9.

Adding controls to the ODBC form.

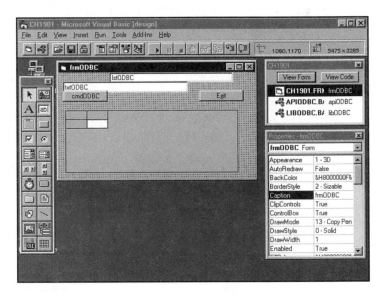

Save this form as FRMODBC.FRM and the project as CH19.VBP. Remember that this project should also contain the APIODBC.BAS and the LIBODBC.BAS modules.

Now you're ready to add the code to the form.

Coding the ODBC Data Entry Form

You need to add code to the form to make sure all the controls respond accordingly and that the form builds itself at startup time. We'll save the form-building code for the end of this section.

First, let's add some of the basic stuff. Add the form-level variables in Listing 19.16 to the declaration section of the form. You'll use these variables throughout the form.

Listing 19.16. Coding the form-level variables.

```
'
' form-level vars
'
Dim cDSN As String              ' data source
Dim cUser As String             ' userid
Dim cPW As String               ' password
Dim cRefresh As String          ' select query
Dim cTable As String            ' base table name
Dim cKeyFld As String           ' key field name
Dim cFormTitle As String        ' title for data form
```

Add the code in Listing 19.17 to the Form_Load event. This is where you set the form-level variables and then begin the process of connecting to the ODBC data source and formatting the data form.

Listing 19.17. Coding the Form_Load event.

```
Private Sub Form_Load()
    '
    Dim nResult As Integer  ' for errors
    '
    ' set form-level vars
    cDSN = "TYSODBC"            ' ODBC data source
    cUser = "Admin"            ' login ID
    cPW = " "                  ' empty password
    cTable = "Master"          ' default base table
    cKeyFld = "CustID"         ' default key field
    cRefresh = "SELECT * FROM Master ORDER BY CustID"   ' default SQL
    cFormTitle = "ODBC/Access Interface Demo"    ' form title

    ' attempt to connect
    nResult = ODBCStart(Me, cDSN, cUser, cPW, cRefresh)

    ' check results
    If nResult <> gSQLSuccess Then
        Unload Me               ' exit
        End                     ' end program
    Else
        FixForm                 ' fix up form
        lstODBC.ListIndex = 0   ' point to first rec
    End If

    ' center the form
    Me.Left = (Screen.Width - Me.Width) / 2
    Me.Top = (Screen.Height - Me.Height) / 2
End Sub
```

19

In this routine, you first initialize the variables you need for the ODBC data connection (cDSN, cUser, cPW, cRefresh), and then you initialize two more variables needed to make the ODBCRowUpdate and ODBCRowDel functions work.

> **Warning:** The values used to initialize the variables are related to the ODBC data source you defined in the "Registering an ODBC Data Source" section of this chapter. If you have not completed the first part of this chapter, you will not be able to run this program with these variables.

In the next part of Listing 19.17, you attempt the ODBC connection (ODBCStart). If an error occurs, you close the form and end the program; otherwise, you execute the routine to format the data entry form (FixForm), position the record pointer to the first record in the data set, and finally center the form on the screen.

Now let's add the code for the Form_Unload event. In Listing 19.18, you'll execute the ODBCDisconnect and ODBCFreeHandle routines.

Listing 19.18. Coding the Form_Unload event.

```
Private Sub Form_Unload(Cancel As Integer)
    '
    ' close out safely
    '
    Dim nResult As Integer
    '
    nResult = ODBCDisconnect(gblHdbc, gblHstmt)
    nResult = ODBCFreeHandle(gblHenv)
    '
End Sub
```

Now add the code in Listing 19.19 behind the cmdExit_Click event. This starts the Form_Unload routine.

Listing 19.19. Coding the cmdExit_Click event.

```
Private Sub cmdExit_Click()
    Unload Me    ' exit this form
End Sub
```

You also need code that will transfer a line of data from the list control into the array of text controls. This is your own version of moving data from a Snapshot object to a set of data-bound controls. Add the code in Listing 19.20 to the lstODBC_Click event.

Listing 19.20. Coding the `lstODBC_Click` event.

```
Private Sub lstODBC_Click()
    '
    ' load text controls from listbox
    '
    Dim x As Integer
    '
    For x = 1 To gblNumCols
        txtODBC(x - 1).Text = ODBCGetFld(lstODBC, x, "*")
    Next
End Sub
```

Here, you simulate the click of the list by moving the pointer of the list box. You want your data form to have a grid that the user can browse through and select a record from. The code line in Listing 19.21 fires off a list click each time the user clicks on a grid line. Add it to the grdODBC_RowColChange event.

Listing 19.21. Coding the `grdODBC_RowColChange` event.

```
Private Sub grdODBC_RowColChange()
    '
    ' when user clicks row, update other controls
    '
    lstODBC.ListIndex = grdODBC.Row - 1
End Sub
```

You need to add the code that handles all the user actions behind the command button array. This eight-button array handles the navigation chores (First, Last, Next, and Back) and the record modification chores (Add, Update, Delete, and Refresh). Listing 19.22 is similar to the code you wrote for the LIBRECS.BAS code library last week. This time, you keep the code a bit more basic so that you can focus on the ODBC aspects of the project. If you plan to use this ODBC code library in production applications, you might want to spruce up this code section with some error checking and other extras.

Listing 19.22. Coding the `cmdODBC_Click` event.

```
Private Sub cmdODBC_Click(Index As Integer)
    '
    ' handle user clicks
    '
    Dim nResult As Integer
    Dim x As Integer
    '
    Select Case Index
        Case Is = 0
            ' first rec
            nResult = ODBCDataSet(Me)
            lstODBC.ListIndex = 0
```

continues

19

Listing 19.22. continued

```
            Case Is = 1
                ' next rec
                If lstODBC.ListIndex < (lstODBC.ListCount - 1) Then
                    lstODBC.ListIndex = lstODBC.ListIndex + 1
                End If
            Case Is = 2
                ' previous rec
                If lstODBC.ListIndex > 0 Then
                    lstODBC.ListIndex = lstODBC.ListIndex - 1
                End If
            Case Is = 3
                ' last rec
                nResult = ODBCDataSet(Me)
                lstODBC.ListIndex = lstODBC.ListCount - 1
            Case Is = 4
                ' new rec
                If cmdODBC(Index).Caption = "&Add" Then
                    nResult = MsgBox("Add a New Record?", vbInformation +
                    ➡vbYesNo, "Add Record")
                    If nResult = vbYes Then
                        For x = 0 To gblNumCols - 1
                            txtODBC(x) = ""
                        Next x
                        cmdODBC(Index).Caption = "&Save"
                        txtODBC(0).SetFocus
                    End If
                Else
                    nResult = ODBCRowAdd(Me, cTable)
                    cmdODBC(Index).Caption = "&Add"
                    nResult = ODBCDataSet(Me)
                    lstODBC.ListIndex = 0
                End If
            Case Is = 5
                ' update rec
                nResult = ODBCRowUpdate(Me, cTable, cKeyFld)
                nResult = ODBCDataSet(Me)
                lstODBC.ListIndex = 0
            Case Is = 6
                ' delete rec
                nResult = MsgBox("Delete the Current Record?", vbInformation +
                ➡vbYesNo, "Delete Record")
                If nResult = vbYes Then
                    nResult = ODBCRowDel(Me, cTable, cKeyFld)
                    nResult = ODBCDataSet(Me)
                    lstODBC.ListIndex = 0
                End If
            Case Is = 7
                ' refresh set
                nResult = ODBCDataSet(Me)
                lstODBC.ListIndex = 0
    End Select
    '
End Sub
```

Notice that you added confirmation messages for the Add and Delete buttons. Notice also that you made the Add button play a dual role. When you're in standard mode, the button displays the Add characteristics. When the Add mode is invoked, the same button turns into the Save button. Although you did not do it here, it's a good idea to disable all the other buttons during the add process. See the code for the LIBRECS.BAS routines (on Day 11, "Creating Database Programs with Visual Basic Code") to get an example of how to implement such a feature.

Now for the last bit of code for this chapter. The FixForm routine gets information from the data set and sizes and positions all the command buttons, text boxes, grids, and the exit button. Finally, this routine makes sure the data form itself is the proper size to hold all the controls.

Create a new Sub procedure called FixForm and end the code using Listing 19.23.

Listing 19.23. Coding the FixForm routine.

```
Sub FixForm()
    '
    ' position buttons, text boxes and grid
    '
    Dim nWidth As Integer
    Dim x As Integer

    ' minimum form width
    If Me.Width < 6000 Then
        Me.Width = 6000
    End If

    Me.Caption = cFormTitle ' set form title

    ' command buttons
    nWidth = (Me.Width - 360) / 8
    cmdODBC(0).Caption = "&First"
    cmdODBC(1).Caption = "&Next"
    cmdODBC(2).Caption = "&Back"
    cmdODBC(3).Caption = "&Last"
    cmdODBC(4).Caption = "&Add"
    cmdODBC(5).Caption = "&Update"
    cmdODBC(6).Caption = "&Delete"
    cmdODBC(7).Caption = "&Refresh"
    '
    For x = 0 To 7
        cmdODBC(x).Width = nWidth
        cmdODBC(x).Left = x * nWidth + 120
        cmdODBC(x).Height = 300
        cmdODBC(x).Top = 120
    Next x

    ' text boxes
    For x = 1 To gblNumCols
        txtODBC(x - 1).Left = 120
        txtODBC(x - 1).Top = (360 * x) + 240
```

19

continues

Listing 19.23. continued

```
            txtODBC(x - 1).Width = 3600
            txtODBC(x - 1).Visible = True
    Next x
    '
    ' grid
    grdODBC.Left = 120
    grdODBC.Width = Me.Width - 360
    grdODBC.Top = (360 * x) + 360
    grdODBC.Height = 2400
    '
    ' other text boxes
    For x = gblNumCols + 1 To 12
        txtODBC(x - 1).Visible = False
    Next x

    ' adjust form length
    Me.Height = grdODBC.Top + grdODBC.Height + 960

    ' position exit button
    cmdExit.Width = 1200
    cmdExit.Height = 300
    cmdExit.Left = Me.Width - (240 + cmdExit.Width)
    cmdExit.Top = Me.Height - (480 + cmdExit.Height)
    '
End Sub
```

The routine in Listing 19.23 first sets a minimum width for the form and then sets the form title. Then the command button captions and locations are set. Next, the routine sets the number of text boxes needed to show the data from the associated ODBC data set. After the grid is sized and located, the routine makes any remaining text boxes invisible. Then, after adjusting the form height (based on the number and location of input controls), the exit button is sized and placed at the lower right corner of the form.

Save the project. You are now ready to run the ODBC data entry form.

Running the ODBC Data Entry Form

Now that both the library and the form routines have been completed, you are ready to run the program. When you first run the program, you'll see the data entry form appear (see Figure 19.10).

Notice that all the proper text boxes appear in order on the form and that the grid and Exit button are properly positioned. This is all handled by the FixForm routine.

You can now use this screen to walk through the data set by using the command buttons (First, Last, Next, and Back) or by clicking the desired row on the grid at the bottom of the form. You can also add, edit, and delete records in the data set using the appropriate buttons. The Refresh button will requery the ODBC data source to get updated information.

Figure 19.10.
Running the ODBC data entry form.

You now have a fully functional data entry screen for ODBC data sources. You can improve this form by adding field prompts to the form and by adding other additional routines that improve the error handling and increase the user friendliness of the form. You can even use this form as a basis for your own ODBC data entry forms.

Other ODBC Considerations

Now that you know how to build ODBC data entry forms, you should also keep in mind a few ODBC-related items as you build ODBC-enabled Visual Basic applications.

☐ ODBC connection usage: If you are using ODBC data sources, each connection you make counts as a user connection to the back-end data source. If your client has a 10-user SQL Server license and your Visual Basic application opens three ODBC data sets, only seven connections are left for the entire network. If you run three versions of the same program at the same time, you are using nine SQL Server connections. It is a good idea to minimize the number of open connections your Visual Basic programs require.

☐ Install files: If you are using ODBC to connect to data, you'll need to include the ODBC setup files with your Visual Basic program setup kit. See Visual Basic documentation on the Setup Wizard for more information on the required files to include for ODBC-enabled applications.

☐ .INI and registry settings: A number of ODBC-related variables can affect performance. The 16-bit ODBC interface uses ODBC.INI (the list of defined data sources), ODBCINST.INI (the list of installed ODBC drivers available), and ODBCISAM.INI and ODBCDDP.INI (which deal with the ISAM-type interfaces such as Microsoft Access, Excel, FoxPro, and so on). In 32-bit systems, this information is stored in the system registry. Although you should not edit these files directly,

19

641

you should know where these values are stored when you're debugging your ODBC applications.

☐ Tracing ODBC activity: You can turn on ODBC trace files from the ODBC Administrator program. This allows you to watch the message activity between your application and the ODBC interface, which can be very informative when you're attempting to locate bugs or performance problems. The trace log does take up a lot of disk space after a short time, though. You should only turn the trace on when you absolutely need it.

☐ Remote data control alternative: If your Visual Basic program will be operating only in a 32-bit environment and you have the Enterprise Edition of Visual Basic, you can use the Remote Data Control (RDC) and the Remote Data Objects (RDO) to connect to the ODBC data source. The RDC/RDO platform is a replacement for the ODBC API you learned today. Although it is easier to deal with the RDC/RDO platform, you must use the 32-bit version of Visual Basic and your program must run on a 32-bit operating system. If your program must run on a 16-bit OS, you can still use the ODBC API and the examples from this chapter.

Summary

Today you learned how to use the Open Database Connectivity (ODBC) API set to directly link your Visual Basic program to target data sources via the ODBC interface. The ODBC interface is generally faster than Microsoft JET when it comes to linking to ODBC defined data sources.

You also learned how to install the ODBC interface on your workstation and how to use the ODBC Administrator program to install ODBC driver sets and define data sources for ODBC connections.

You learned how to build a program library that uses a minimum set of ODBC API calls along with several Visual Basic wrapper routines. This library set provides the basic functions necessary to read and write data to and from a defined ODBC data source. You can use these routines to create fully functional data entry forms for ODBC data sources.

Finally, you used the library routines to build a data entry form that opens a link to a defined ODBC data source and allows the user to read and write data records for the ODBC data source.

Quiz

1. What do the letters ODBC stand for?

2. Why is the ODBC API interface faster than the Microsoft JET interface when connecting to defined ODBC data sources?

3. What are some of the drawbacks to using the ODBC API to link to databases?

4. What program do you use to define an ODBC data source for the workstation?

5. Can you use the ODBC interface to connect to nondatabase files, such as spreadsheets or text files?

6. When you write ODBC-enabled Visual Basic applications, can you use the same set of API declarations for the 16-bit version of Visual Basic 4 as you do for the 32-bit version of Visual Basic 4?

7. Name the four preliminary steps you must complete before you can pass an SQL SELECT statement to the newly opened ODBC data source.

Exercise

You have been given the assignment of creating a remote data entry form for reviewing and updating data in a centrally located data file. The data entry program runs on 16-bit and 32-bit workstations throughout the headquarters building. The data is currently stored in a Microsoft Access database on the central file server, but it might soon be converted to an SQL Server database in another location. You cannot always know the actual columns that exist in the data table because the layout of the table changes based on information entered each month. The form should be flexible enough to determine the columns available and present those columns to the user for data entry. The program should also be flexible enough to allow for minimum disruption of the file even when the database is converted from Microsoft Access to SQL Server database format.

Your first task is to define an ODBC data source at your workstation that has the Microsoft Access 2.0 data file C:\TYSDBVB\CHAP19\EXER19.MDB as its data source name. You want to access the Transactions table that exists in the EXER19.MDB database. The key field of the Transactions table is called OrderNbr. Then, modify the TYSODBC.VBP project to open this data source and allow users to review and update data in the spreadsheet.

19

Securing Your Database Applications

Today we'll cover topics related to securing your database and your application. Almost all software that is deployed in a multiuser environment should use some level of security. Security schemes can be used for more than just limiting user access to the database. Security schemes can also limit user access to the applications that use the database. You can also install security features in your Visual Basic database applications that will limit the function rights of users within your applications. You can even develop routines that will record user activity within your applications—including user login/logout activity—each time a user updates a database record, and even each time a user performs a critical operation such as printing a sensitive report or graph, updating key data, or running restricted routines.

Throughout today's lesson, you will build a new set of library routines. You will be able to use these routines to add varying levels of security to all your future Visual Basic database applications.

When you have completed this chapter, you will understand how Microsoft Access database security and encryption works and the advantages and disadvantages of both. You'll also know how to implement an application security scheme, including adding user login and logout history, audit trails that show when database records have been updated, and recording each time users perform critical application operations.

Database Security

The first level of security you can employ in Visual Basic database applications is at the database level. The Microsoft JET database format enables you to establish user and group security schemes using the Microsoft Access SYSTEM security file. You can also add database encryption to your Microsoft JET databases to increase the level of security within your database.

Although the Microsoft Access SYSTEM security file and Microsoft JET data encryption are powerful tools, they have some disadvantages. When adding either of these features, you should understand the limitations and pitfalls of the security features. In the following sections, you'll learn the most notable of these limitations, as well as some suggestions on how you can avoid unexpected results.

Limitations of the Microsoft Access SYSTEM Security

If you have a copy of Microsoft Access, you can install a database security scheme for your Visual Basic applications. The security scheme requires the presence of a single file (called SYSTEM.MDA). This file must be available to your Visual Basic application either in the application path, or pointed to via the application .INI file or system registry. After the SYSTEM security file is defined, all attempts to open the secured database will cause Microsoft JET to request a user name and password before opening the database.

> **Note:** Some 32-bit systems will have a Microsoft JET security file called SYSTEM.MDW (for example, Access 95). Others will continue to use the SYSTEM.MDA in both 16- and 32- bit modes (such as Visual Basic 4). The difference between these two files (SYSTEM.MDW and SYSTEM MDA) is in name only. Throughout this lesson, you will see SYSTEM, SYSTEM.MDW, and SYSTEM.MDA. They can be used interchangeably.

We won't review the details of creating and updating the SYSTEM security file here (see Day 8 for details on defining SYSTEM security). Instead, this section covers the advantages and limitations of using the SYSTEM security scheme employed by Microsoft Access and Microsoft JET.

Microsoft Access Is Required

Once you have a SYSTEM.MDA file on your workstation, you can use Microsoft Access or you can use Visdata to define the system security details. However, only Microsoft Access can create the SYSTEM.MDA file. You cannot use any Visual Basic application to create a SYSTEM file. You can only use Visual Basic to modify existing SYSTEM.MDA files.

Multiple SYSTEM Files Are Possible

You can have multiple versions of the SYSTEM.MDA security file available on your workstation or network. This way, you can create unique security schemes for each of your Microsoft JET databases. The disadvantage here is that it is possible to install the wrong SYSTEM.MDA file for an application. This could result in preventing all users from accessing any of the data. Depending on the SYSTEM.MDA file installed, it could also result in reducing security to the point of allowing all users access to critical data normally not available to them. If you are using multiple SYSTEM.MDA files, be sure to store these files in the same directory as the application files and include the specific path to this SYSTEM.MDA in all installation procedures.

Removing SYSTEM.MDA Removes the Security

Because all security features are stored in a single file, removing SYSTEM.MDA from the workstation or network can result in effectively eliminating all database security. You can limit this possibility by storing SYSTEM.MDA on a network in a directory where users do not have delete or rename rights. Setting these rights requires administrator level access to the network and knowledge of your network's file rights utilities.

Some Applications Might Not Use SYSTEM.MDA

If you are using the database in an environment where multiple applications can access the database, you might find that some applications do not use SYSTEM.MDA at all. These applications might be able to open the database without having to go through the SYSTEM.MDA security features. For example, you could easily write a Visual Basic application that opens a database without first checking for the existence of the SYSTEM.MDA file. By doing this, you can completely ignore any security features built into the SYSTEM security file.

Limitations of Microsoft JET Encryption

You can also use the encryption feature of Microsoft JET to encode sensitive data. However, you have no control over the type of encryption algorithm used to encode your data. You can only turn encryption on or off using the `dbEncrypt` or `dbDecrypt` option constants with the `CreateDatabase` and `CompactDatabase` methods.

The following list outlines other limitations to consider when using Microsoft JET encryption.

- [ ] You cannot encrypt selected tables within a database. When you turn encryption on, it affects all objects in the database. If you have only a few tables that are sensitive, you should consider moving only those tables into a separate database for encryption.

- [ ] If you are deploying your database in an environment where multiple applications will be accessing your data, it is possible that these applications might not be able to read the encrypted data.

- [ ] If you want to take advantage of the replication features of Microsoft Access 95, you will not be able to use encrypted databases.

Application Security

Application security is quite different from database security. Application security focuses on securing not only data but also processes. For example, you can use application security to limit users' ability to use selected data entry forms, produce certain graphs or reports, or run critical procedures (such as month-end closing or mass price updates).

Any good application security scheme has two main features. The first is a process that forces users to log into your application using stored passwords. This provides an additional level of security to your Visual Basic database application. As you will see later in this chapter, forcing users to log into and out of your application will also give you the opportunity to create audit logs of all user activity. These audit logs can help you locate and fix problems reported by users and give you an additional tool for keeping track of just who is using your application.

The second process that is valuable in building an application security system is an access rights scheme. You can use an access rights scheme to limit the functions that particular users can perform within your application. For example, if you only want to allow certain users to perform critical tasks, you can establish an access right for that task and check each user's rights before he or she is allowed to attempt that operation. You can establish access rights for virtually any program operation including data form entry, report generation, even special processes such as price updates, files exports, and so on.

> **Note:** Because application security only works within the selected application, it cannot affect users who are accessing the database from other applications. Therefore, you should not rely on application-level security as the only security scheme for your critical data. Still, application security can provide powerful security controls to your Visual Basic database applications.

In order to provide user login and logout and access rights checking, you will build a set of routines in a new procedure library called LIBUSER.BAS. This library will contain all the Sub and Function procedures needed to install and maintain application-level security for all your Visual Basic database applications.

Developing a User Login/Logout System

The first routines you'll need to build as part of your application security library enable application administrators to create and maintain a list of valid application users. This involves creating a simple data entry form that contains add, edit, and delete operations for a Users table. Next, you will need routines to process user logins and logouts. The login routine prompts potential users for their user ID and password and checks the values entered against the data table on file. As usual, you'll construct these routines in a way that makes it easy for you to use them in any future Visual Basic database applications.

Building the User Maintenance Form

Load Visual Basic and start a new project. The first thing you'll do is create a form to manage the list of valid application users. This form enables you to add, edit, and delete users from a table called AppUsers. This is the same table that will be used to verify user logins at the start of all your secured applications. Use Table 20.1, Table 20.2, and Figure 20.1 to build the User Maintenance form.

Before building this form, however, you need to add a number of library files, custom controls, and object references to your project. Refer to the following lists to make sure you load all the additional files needed for this project.

- ☐ Crystal Reports Control
- ☐ Microsoft Common Dialog Control
- ☐ Sheridan 3D Controls
- ☐ Microsoft DAO 2.5 Object Library

You will also need the following library modules for this project. They can be found in the C:\TYSDBVB\CHAP20 directory. Add these to your project using the File | Add Files command from the Visual Basic main menu.

```
frmRpt.frm
libError.bas
libRecs.bas
LibValid.bas
```

Caution: The library files in C:\TYSDBVB\CHAP20 contain changes that were not covered in previous chapters of this book. Be sure to use the versions stored in the C:\TYSDBVB\CHAP20 directory and not the ones you built earlier in the course.

Note: This project uses several control arrays. You can save yourself additional typing by building the first member of the control array, setting all the control properties, and then copying the additional members. You'll still have to retype some property settings, but it will be considerably less tedious than if you had to set them all manually.

Table 20.1. Controls for the User Maintenance form.

Controls	Properties	Settings
Form	Name	frmUserMaint
	Caption	User Maintenance
	Height	3495
	Left	1785
	Top	1530

Controls	Properties	Settings
	Width	5740
SSPanel	Name	SSPanel1
	Height	2235
	Left	120
	Top	120
	Width	5355
CommandButton	Name	cmdOK
	Caption	&OK
	Height	300
	Left	4080
	Top	2880
	Width	1200
CommonDialog	Name	CMDialog1
	Left	540
CommandButton	Name	cmdBtn(0–7)
(Add eight buttons)	Height	495
	Left	0
	Top	0
	Width	1215
Label	Name	Label1(0)
	BorderStyle	1—Fixed Single
	Caption	UserID:
	Height	300
	Left	120
	Top	120
	Width	1200
Label	Name	Label1(1)
	BorderStyle	1—Fixed Single
	Caption	Password:
	Height	300
	Left	120

20

continues

651

Table 20.1. continued

Controls	Properties	Settings
	Top	540
	Width	1200
Label	Name	Label1(2)
	BorderStyle	1—Fixed Single
	Caption	Name:
	Height	300
	Left	120
	Top	960
	Width	1200
Label	Name	Label1(3)
	BorderStyle	1—Fixed Single
	Caption	Last Log In:
	Height	300
	Left	120
	Top	1380
	Width	1200
Label	Name	Label1(4)
	BorderStyle	1—Fixed Single
	Caption	Last Log Out:
	Height	300
	Left	120
	Top	1800
	Width	1200
TextBox	Name	Text1(0)
	Height	300
	Left	1440
	Tag	UserID
	Top	120
	Width	1200TextBox
	Name	Text1(1)

Controls	Properties	Settings
	Height	300
	Left	1440
	PasswordChar	*
	Tag	Password
	Top	540
	Width	1200
TextBox	Name	Text1(2)
	Height	300
	Left	1440
	Tag	Name
	Top	960
	Width	2400
TextBox	Name	Text1(3)
	Height	300
	Left	1440
	Tag	LastIn
	Top	1380
	Width	1800
TextBox	Name	Text1(4)
	Height	300
	Left	1440
	Tag	LastOut
	Top	1800
	Width	1800

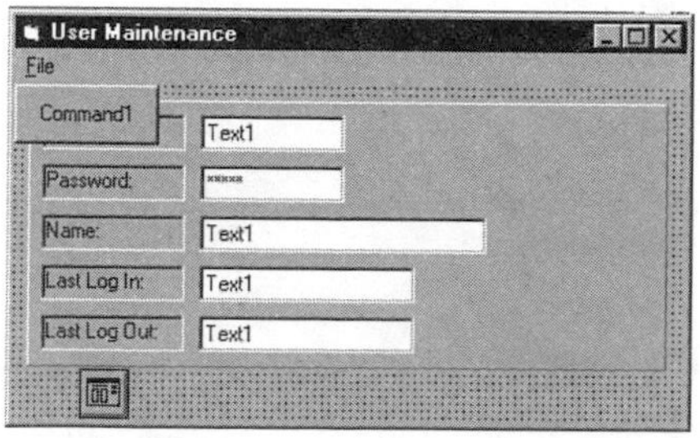

Figure 20.1.
Laying out the User Maintenance form.

Table 20.2. Menus for the User Maintenance form.

Menu Name	Menu Caption
mnuFile	&File
mnuFilePrint	&Print...
mnuFilePrintSet	Printer &Setup...
mnuFileSp01	—
mnuFileExit	E&xit

Save the form as FRMUSERM.FRM and the project as USERDEMO.VBP after you add all the controls, position them on the form, and add the menus. Now you need to add some Visual Basic code to make the form work.

Place the following initialization code in the Declaration section of the User Maintenance form.

```
Option Explicit

Dim nBtnAlign As Integer
```

Next, place the code in Listing 20.1 in the Form_Load event of the form.

Listing 20.1. Setting up the User Maintenance form.

```
Private Sub Form_Load()
    '
    ' set error trap and
    ' put name on trace stack
    '
    On Error GoTo FormLoadErr
    errProcStack errPush, Me.Name + ".FormLoad"
    '
    ' initialize the form
    ' and read the first rec
    '
    If RecInit(Me) = recOK Then
        nResult = RecRead(Me, rsUsers)
    End If
    '
    ' report error and exit
    '
    If nResult <> recOK Then
        cResult = "Unable to Open Users Table"
        nErrExit = errExit
        GoTo FormLoadErr
    End If
    '
    ' set form fields and
    ' report error if needed
    '
    If RecEnable(Me, False) <> recOK Then
```

```
            cResult = "Unable to Enable Button Bar"
            nErrExit = errExit
            GoTo FormLoadErr
        End If
        '
        usrRightsCheck ' get user rights
        '
        ' set button stuff
        nBtnAlign = btnAlignTop
        BtnBarInit Me, nBtnAlign
        BtnBarEnable Me, recEnableList
        '
        ' center form
        Me.Left = (Screen.Width - Me.Width) / 2
        Me.Top = (Screen.Height - Me.Height) / 2
        '
        GoTo FormLoadExit    ' exit
        '
FormLoadErr:
    nResult = errHandler(nResult, cResult, nErrExit)
    Unload Me
    '
FormLoadExit:
    errProcStack errPop, ""
    '
End Sub
```

Listing 20.1 performs several initialization operations. Notice that you have added the error trapping library routines to the project. You've seen most of the rest of the procedure in previous lessons.

Add the code to the cmdBtn_Click event. This code line calls the libRecs routine to handle all data entry functions.

```
Private Sub cmdBtn_Click(Index As Integer)
    '
    ' handle user clicks
    '
    BtnBarProcess Index, Me, rsUsers, "UserID", ""
End Sub
```

Next, add the code line that resizes the controls when the user resizes the form.

```
Private Sub Form_Resize()
    BtnBarInit Me, nBtnAlign    ' resize buttons
End Sub
```

You also need to add some code (see Listing 20.2) to the Text1_KeyPress event. This code prevents users from editing the Last Log In or Last Log Out fields on the form.

Listing 20.2. Disabling entry in the `Text1_KeyPress` event.

```
Private Sub Text1_KeyPress(Index As Integer, KeyAscii As Integer)
    '
    ' disable entry for lastin/lastout fields
    '
    If Index = 3 Or Index = 4 Then
        KeyAscii = 0
    End If
End Sub
```

Now, you need to add code behind the three menu items you defined earlier. First, add the code in Listing 20.3 behind the File | Print command.

Listing 20.3. Setting up the Print command.

```
Private Sub mnuFilePrint_Click()
    '
    ' set error trap and
    ' put name on stack
    '
    On Error GoTo mnuFilePrintErr
    errProcStack errPush, Me.Name + ".mnuFilePrintClick"
    '
    Load frmReport   ' load the report form
    '
    ' set report form vars
    frmReport.txtReportName = App.Path + " \UserList.rpt"
    frmReport.txtReportDBName = App.Path + " \USERDEMO.mdb"
    frmReport.txtWindowTitle = "Application User List"
    '
    ' write report run to log
    logWriteFile "RunReport", frmReport.txtReportName
    '
    frmReport.Show vbModal   ' show form to user
    '
    GoTo mnuFilePrintExit   ' all done
    '
mnuFilePrintErr:
    nResult = errHandler(Err, Error$, errResume)
    GoTo mnuFilePrintExit
    '
mnuFilePrintExit:
    errProcStack errPop, ""
    '
End Sub
```

This routine loads the library form, sets several report parameters, and then shows the report front-end form to the user. The User Application Report has already been built and is stored in the `C:\TYSDBVB\CHAP20` directory.

Now add the code in Listing 20.4 to launch the printer setup dialog behind the Printer Setup button.

Listing 20.4. Launching the Printer setup dialog.

```
Private Sub mnuFilePrintSet_Click()
    '
    ' force print setup dialog
    '
    CMDialog1.Flags = &H40
    CMDialog1.Action = 5
End Sub
```

Finally, add a line of code (see Listing 20.5) behind the File | Exit command and the OK button.

Listing 20.5. Programming the Exit and OK buttons.

```
Private Sub mnuFileExit_Click()
    Unload Me
End Sub

Private Sub cmdOK_Click()
    Unload Me
End Sub
```

Now save the project. Before you can run this project, you need to create a BAS module to handle a few general chores. Load a module into the project and set its Name property to LIBUSER.BAS. First, add some declarations to the top of the module, based on Listing 20.6.

Listing 20.6. Global declarations for the LIBUSER.BAS project.

```
Option Explicit

'
' global vars
'
Global usrAction As Integer
Global usrMaxTries As Integer
Global usrUserID As String
'
Global Const usrErr = -1
Global Const usrOK = 0
'
Global nResult As Integer
Global cResult As String
Global nErrExit As Integer
'
Global dbUsers As Database
Global rsUsers As Recordset
Global cDBName As String
Global cRSName As String
'
```

continues

Listing 20.6. continued

```
Global Const accNone = 0
Global Const accRead = 1
Global Const accModify = 2
Global Const accAdd = 3
Global Const accDelete = 4
Global Const accExtended = 5
'
Global rsAccess As Recordset
Global Const accOK = 0
Global Const accErr = -1
'
Global logWrFile As String
```

You'll use these variables for all your application security routines.

Now let's add a new routine (see Listing 20.7) that opens the user data set for you. Create a Function called usrInit and add the following code to the routine.

Listing 20.7. Opening the data set with the usrInit function.

```
Function usrInit() As Integer
    '
    ' perform basic startup for form
    '
    On Error GoTo usrInitErr
    errProcStack errPush, "LibUser.usrInit"
    '
    ' open the recordset
    nResult = RSOpen(cDBName, cRSName, dbOpenDynaset, dbUsers, rsUsers)
    If nResult <> recOK Then
        cResult = "Unable to Load Database"
        nErrExit = errExit
        GoTo usrInitErr
    End If
    '
    nResult = recOK
    GoTo usrInitExit
    '
usrInitErr:
    If Err <> 0 Then
        nResult = Err
        cResult = Error$
        nErrExit = errExit
    End If
    errHandler nResult, cResult, nErrExit
    GoTo usrInitExit
    '
usrInitExit:
    errProcStack errPop, ""
    usrInit = nResult
    '
End Function
```

Most of the code in Listing 20.7 is very familiar to you. This function opens the database and Dynaset, and reports any errors along the way.

You need one more routine that calls the User Maintenance form. Create a Sub called usrMaint and add the code in Listing 20.8.

Listing 20.8. Calling the User Maintenance form.

```
Sub usrMaint()
    '
    ' perform general maintenance on user table
    '
    On Error GoTo usrMaintErr
    errProcStack errPush, "LibUser.usrMaint"
    '
    nResult = usrInit()
    If nResult <> usrOK Then
        cResult = "Unable to continue..."
        nErrExit = errExit
        GoTo usrMaintErr
    End If
    '
    frmUserMaint.Show vbModal
    '
    GoTo usrMaintExit
    '
usrMaintErr:
    If Err <> 0 Then
        nResult = Err
        cResult = Error$
        nErrExit = errExit
    End If
    errHandler nResult, cResult, nErrExit
    GoTo usrMaintExit
    '
usrMaintExit:
    errProcStack errPop, ""
    '
End Sub
```

This routine calls the function that initializes the database files and, if all is okay, it loads and runs the maintenance form. Any errors it encounters are reported.

Finally, let's add a Main module to start the whole thing off. You'll build on this module throughout the lesson today. First, you should only call this maintenance form. Create a Sub called Main, and add the code segment that follows the Tip box.

20

> **Tip:** You'll find several advantages to using a Main() routine as the startup for your application. You can handle numerous initialization processes before you load a form, and you can even design your application to use different forms from the same Main() routine. Programs that start with a Main() routine are usually easier to maintain and modify than programs that start with a startup form.

```
Sub Main()
    '
    usrMaint    ' run main routine
    dbUsers.Close   ' close database
    End   ' exit program
    '
End Sub
```

Now save and run the project. Your screen should look similar to the one in Figure 20.2.

Figure 20.2.

Running the User Mainte-
nance form.

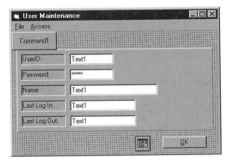

You can now add, edit, and delete user records. A few records have already been added for you. Make sure this includes a record for USERA. If one does not exist, add it. If it is already on file, edit the record and set the Password field to USERA. Notice that the Password field does not display its contents. This is because you set the PasswordChar property of the text box to show only an asterisk (*) for every character in the field. The actual characters are stored in the database table.

Building the User *LogIn* and *LogOut* Routines

Now that you have a method for managing the list of valid users, it's time to create the routines that enable users to log into and out of your applications. First you need to create a user login form. Then you need a routine to verify the login and a routine to automatically log the user out when the application is terminated.

First, build the user login form. Add a new form to the existing USERDEMO.VBP project, using Table 20.3 and Figure 20.3 as a guide in building the form.

Table 20.3. Controls for the User Login form.

Controls	Properties	Settings
Form	Name	frmUserLogIn
	Caption	User Login
	Height	2310
	Left	1995
	Top	2415
	Width	4575
SSPanel	Name	SSPanel1
	Height	1095
	Left	120
	Caption	\<blank\>
	Top	660
	Width	2835
Label	Name	lblAppTitle
	Alignment	2—Center
	BorderStyle	1—Fixed Single
	Caption	Application Title
	Font	MS Sans Serif/Bold
	FontSize	12
	Height	375
	Left	120
	Top	120
	Width	4215
Label	Name	Label1
	BorderStyle	1—Fixed Single
	Caption	UserID:
	Height	300
	Left	120

continues

Table 20.3. continued

Controls	Properties	Settings
	Top	180
	Width	1200
Label	Name	Label2
	BorderStyle	1—Fixed Single
	Caption	Password:
	Height	300
	Left	120
	Top	600
	Width	1200
TextBox	Name	txtUserID
	Height	300
	Left	1440
	Top	180
	Width	1200
TextBox	Name	txtPass
	Height	300
	Left	1440
	Top	600
	Width	1200
	PasswordChar	*
CommandButton	Name	Command1
	Caption	&OK
	Default	True
	Height	300
	Left	3120
	Top	1260
	Width	1200
CommandButton	Name	Command2
	Caption	&Cancel
	Cancel	True

Controls	Properties	Settings
	Height	300
	Left	3120
	Top	1260
	Width	1200

Figure 20.3.
Laying out the User Login form.

You only need to add a few lines of code (see Listing 20.9) to this form. First, add code to the `Form_Load` event that centers the form on the screen.

Listing 20.9. Centering a form.

```
Private Sub Form_Load()
    ' center form
    Me.Left = (Screen.Width - Me.Width) / 2
    Me.Top = (Screen.Height - Me.Height) / 2
End Sub
```

Next, add the code in Listing 20.10 to the `Form_Activate` event to initialize form values at startup.

Listing 20.10. Initializing form values.

```
Private Sub Form_Activate()
    '
    ' init input vars
    ' and set focus
    '
    txtUserID = ""
    txtPass = ""
    txtUserID.SetFocus
End Sub
```

You need to add a few lines behind the command buttons. First, add the code in Listing 20.11 for the OK button.

Listing 20.11. Code for the OK button.

```
Private Sub Command1_Click()
    '
    ' user ok exit
    '
    usrAction = usrOK    ' update global var
    Me.Hide              ' hide form (don't unload)
End Sub
```

This code sets a global variable and then hides the login form. Now add code from Listing 20.12 behind the Cancel button.

Listing 20.12. Code for the Cancel button.

```
Private Sub Command2_Click()
    '
    ' user cancel exit
    '
    usrAction = usrErr   ' usedr cancels
    Me.Hide              ' hide form (don't unload)
End Sub
```

That's it for the User Login form. Save this form as FRMUSERL.FRM.

Now you need to add code to the LIBUSER.BAS library file. You need three routines. The first routine calls the login form, the second routine validates the user's ID and password, and the third routine handles the user logout at the end of an application.

Create a new Function called usrLogin and add Listing 20.13.

Listing 20.13. Adding the `usrLogin` function to LIBUSER.BAS.

```
Function UsrLogin() As Integer
    '
    ' load form and perform login
    '
    errProcStack errPush, "LibUser.UsrLogin"
    '
    Dim nTries As Integer
    '
    ' init vars
    cDBName = App.Path + " \USERDEMO.mdb"
    cRSName = "AppUsers"
    '
    nResult = usrInit()     ' load database, etc.
    If nResult <> usrOK Then
        cResult = "Unable To Continue."
        nErrExit = errExit
        GoTo usrLoginErr
    End If
```

```
    '
    Load frmUserLogIn          ' load login form
    frmUserLogIn.lblAppTitle = "Test Login Application"
    '
    usrMaxTries = 3
    nTries = 0
    While nTries < usrMaxTries
        nTries = nTries + 1
        frmUserLogIn.Show vbModal    ' show form to user
        '
        ' check results
        If usrAction = usrOK Then
            ' user pressed OK
            nResult = usrValid(frmUserLogIn.txtUserID, frmUserLogIn.txtPass)
            ' if user is valid, exit
            If nResult = usrOK Then
                nTries = usrMaxTries
            End If
        Else
            ' user pressed cancel
            nResult = usrErr
            nTries = usrMaxTries
        End If
    Wend
    '
    GoTo usrLoginExit
    '
usrLoginErr:
    If Err <> 0 Then
        nResult = Err
        cResult = Error$
        nErrExit = errExit
    End If
    errHandler nResult, cResult, nErrExit
    GoTo usrLoginExit
    '
usrLoginExit:
    UsrLogin = nResult
    errProcStack errPop, ""
    '
End Function
```

20

The module in Listing 20.13 first sets some variables and then calls the usrInit routine to open the database and table. If that occurs without an error, the routine loads the user login form (without showing it) and then sets the application title on the form. (You can modify this for your own applications.) Next, the routine allows the user three login attempts. If the user presses the OK button on the form, the routine calls the usrValid function to check for a valid user. If the user is valid, the program exits the loop and exits the routine. If not, the loop returns to give the user another chance to log in or click Cancel. Note that the program unloads the form before leaving this routine.

Now let's code the usrValid routine. This is the module that looks up the user ID and (if it locates it) compares the password on the form to the one in the data table. Create a new Function called usrValid and enter the code in Listing 20.14.

Listing 20.14. Coding the usrValid routine.

```
Function usrValid(cUserID, cPass) As Integer
    '
    ' attempt to validate the user login
    '
    ' inputs:
    '   cUserID     user login
    '   cPassword   user login password
    '
    ' returns       usrOK if user is valid
    '               usrErr if error
    '
    ' on error goto usrValidErr
    errProcStack errPush, "LibUser.usrValid"
    '
    rsUsers.FindFirst "UserId='" + cUserID + "'"
    If rsUsers.NoMatch = False Then
        If UCase(rsUsers.Fields("password")) = UCase(cPass) Then
            nResult = usrOK
        Else
            nResult = usrErr
            cResult = "User Login Failed" + Chr(13)
            cResult = cResult + "Invalid Password"
            nErrExit = errResume
            GoTo usrValidErr
        End If
    Else
        nResult = usrErr
        cResult = "User Login Failed" + Chr(13)
        cResult = cResult + "Invalid UserID"
        nErrExit = errResume
        GoTo usrValidErr
    End If
    '
    ' all ok, so upate database
    '
    rsUsers.Edit
    rsUsers.Fields("lastin") = Now
    rsUsers.Fields("lastout") = Empty
    rsUsers.Update
    '
    nResult = usrOK
    GoTo usrValidExit
    '
usrValidErr:
    If Err <> 0 Then
        nResult = Err
        cResult = Error$
        nErrExit = errExit
    End If
```

```
        errHandler nResult, cResult, nErrExit
        GoTo usrValidExit
        '
usrValidExit:
        usrValid = nResult
        errProcStack errPop, ""
        '
End Function
```

This routine first searches the data set for the User ID. If the User ID is found, the routine then compares passwords. If all is okay, the routine updates the LastIn and LastOut fields of the data set and exits. If either entry is invalid, the user is shown an error message, and the routine exits for another attempt. After three attempts, the program exits.

You need only one more routine—the LogOut routine. This procedure needs simply to locate the requested user record and update the LastOut field. Create a new Function called usrLogOut and add Listing 20.15.

Listing 20.15. Adding the LogOut routine.

```
Function usrLogOut(cUserID As String) As Integer
    '
    ' log user out of application
    '
    ' inputs:
    '   cUserID      userid to log out of app
    '
    ' returns:       usrOK if all ok, else error
    '
    On Error GoTo usrLogOutErr
    errProcStack errPush, "LibUser.usrLogOut"
    '
    rsUsers.FindFirst "UserID='" + cUserID + "'"
    If rsUsers.NoMatch = False Then
        rsUsers.Edit
        rsUsers.Fields("lastout") = Now
        rsUsers.Update
        nResult = usrOK
    Else
        cResult = "UserLogout Failed" + Chr(13)
        cResult = cResult + "Unable to Locate UserID [" + cUserID + "]"
        nResult = usrErr
        nErrExit = errResume
        GoTo usrLogOutErr
    End If
    '
    GoTo usrLogOutExit
    '
usrLogOutErr:
    If Err <> 0 Then
        nResult = Err
```

continues

Listing 20.15. continued

```
            cResult = Error$
            nErrExit = errExit
        End If
        errHandler nResult, cResult, nErrExit
        GoTo usrLogOutExit
    '
usrLogOutExit:
    usrLogOut = nResult
    errProcStack errPop, ""
    '
End Function
```

Before continuing, save this project as USERDEMO.VBP.

You need to modify the `Main` procedure you created earlier to add the new User Login form. Modify the `Main` routine to match the lines of code in Listing 20.16.

Listing 20.16. Modifying the `Main` routine to add the new User Login form.

```
Sub Main()
    Dim nlog As Integer
    '
    nlog = UsrLogin()    ' attempt login
    If nlog <> 0 Then
        MsgBox "Login Failed!"   ' invalid user
    Else
        usrUserID = frmUserLogIn.txtUserID   ' update variable
        usrMaint   ' call main form routine
        nResult = usrLogOut(usrUserID)   ' log out user
    End If
    dbUsers.Close   ' close database
    End    ' end program
End Sub
```

Instead of just calling the usrMaint routine right away, you first make the user log in with a valid ID and password. If the user successfully logs in, the program saves the user ID and runs the usrMaint routine. When the user returns from the User Maintenance form, usrMaint executes the usrLogOut before ending the program.

Save and run this project. Your screen should look similar to the one in Figure 20.4.

When you see the login form, enter USERA as the User ID and USERA as the password (remember, you added this in the previous example). Next, you see the User Maintenance form. When you exit this form, the routine will automatically update your logout time stamp.

You now have a complete and portable user login and logout system for your Visual Basic applications. Now let's add an additional application security feature—User Access Rights.

Figure 20.4.
Running the User Login form.

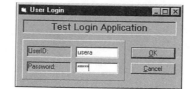

Developing a User Access Rights System

You can add an increased level of application security to your Visual Basic programs by establishing a User Access Rights scheme. An Access Rights scheme enables you to define a set of secured operations within your program and then define access rights for each of the operations on a user-by-user basis. For example, you might want to restrict the ability to print certain reports to specifically qualified users. You might also want to limit the number of users who can access data entry forms. You might even want to allow some users to modify data, but not create new records or delete existing records. Any of these arrangements can be handled by defining and implementing a User Access Rights security scheme.

Defining the User Access Rights Scheme

Before you can code the new features, you need to consider how the scheme will be implemented in your Visual Basic applications. This exercise uses a typical rights scheme that involves a scale of access rights from a level with no rights at all through a level with all possible rights. Table 20.4 shows the proposed set of access rights.

Table 20.4. The set of Access Rights levels.

Rights Level	Access Rights
Level 0	No Rights
Level 1	Read-Only Rights
Level 2	Read and Modify Rights
Level 3	Read, Modify, and Add Rights
Level 4	Read, Modify, Add, and Delete
Level 5	All, plus Extended Rights

In Table 20.4, each rights level adds additional privileges. The final level (Level 5) includes all previously defined rights plus a special extended right. You can use this level to define any special powers depending on the object or system (supervisor control, for example).

You'll set up a data table that contains three columns, User ID, Object, and Level. The User ID should match one in the AppUser table you have already defined. The Level column contains values 0 through 5, and the Object column contains the name of a secured program object. This object could be a report, a data entry form, or even a menu item or command button.

There is a single record in the data set for each secured program object. This default set will be used to establish the base security profile for the system. If an object is in the default set, it is a secured object, and any users who attempt access to the program object must have their own access record defined for the requested object. If no object is present for a particular user, the user cannot access the program object.

You need to add two primary routines to the LIBUSER library file in order to implement an access rights scheme. First, you need a routine that calls a data entry form, which allows administrators to manage user access records. Next, you need a routine to verify user access information when requested. You need a few support routines along the way, but you'll get to those later.

Building the User Access Rights Maintenance Form

The first order of business is to create the data entry form needed to create and edit user access rights. This form will be launched from the User Maintenance form. Use Table 20.5 and Figure 20.5 as guides in laying out the Access Rights Maintenance form. Save this form as FRMACCM.FRM.

Figure 20.5.

Laying out the Access Rights Maintenance form.

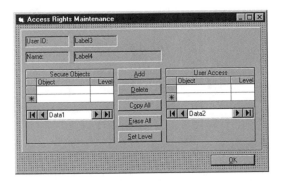

Note: This form contains a control button array. Be sure to add the first button (cmdAccess), set its properties, and then copy and paste the button on the form.

Table 20.5. Controls for the Access Rights Maintenance form.

Controls	Properties	Settings
Form	Name	FrmAccM
	Caption	Access Rights Maintenance
	Height	4365
	Left	1335
	MaxButton	False
	MinButton	False
	Top	1650
	Width	6915
SSPanel	Name	SSPanel1
	Height	3315
	Left	120
	Top	120
	Width	6555
CommandButton	Name	cmdOK
	Caption	&OK
	Default	True
	Height	300
	Left	5280
	Top	3540
	Width	6915
CommandButton	Name	cmdAccess(0)
	Caption	&Add
	Height	300
	Left	2640
	Top	1080
	Width	1200
CommandButton	Name	cmdAccess(1)
	Caption	&Delete
	Height	300
	Left	2640

20

continues

Table 20.5. continued

Controls	Properties	Settings
	Top	1500
	Width	1200
CommandButton	Name	cmdAccess(2)
	Caption	C&opy All
	Height	300
	Left	2640
	Top	1920
	Width	1200
CommandButton	Name	cmdAccess(3)
	Caption	&Erase All
	Height	300
	Left	2640
	Top	2360
CommandButton	Name	cmdAccess(4)
	Caption	&Set Level
	Height	300
	Left	2640
	Top	2760
	Width	1200
DBGrid	Name	dbgDefault
	AllowUpdates	False
	Caption	Secure Objects
	DataSource	dtaDefault
	Height	1995
	Left	120
	Top	1080
	Width	2400
DBGrid	Name	dbgUserID
	AllowUpdates	False
	Caption	Secure Objects
	DataSource	dtaUserID

Controls	Properties	Settings
	Height	1995
	Left	3960
	Top	1080
	Width	2400
DataControl	Name	dtaDefault
	Caption	Data1
	DatabaseName	USERDEMO.mdb
	Height	300
	Left	120
	RecordSource	AppAccess
	Top	2160
	Visible	False
	Width	2400
DataControl	Name	dtaUserID
	Caption	Data2
	DatabaseName	USERDEMO.mdb
	Height	300
	Left	3960
	RecordSource	AppAccess
	Top	2160
	Visible	False
	Width	2400
Label	Name	label1
	BorderStyle	1—Fixed Single
	Caption	UserID:
	Height	300
	Left	120
	Top	180
	Width	1200
Label	Name	Label2
	BorderStyle	1—Fixed single

continues

20

Table 20.5. continued

Controls	Properties	Settings
	Height	300
	Left	120
	Top	600
	Width	1200
Label	Name	lblUserID
	BorderStyle	1—Fixed Single
	Height	300
	Left	1440
	Top	180
	Width	1200
Label	Name	lblName
	BorderStyle	1—fixed Single
	Height	300
	Left	1440
	Top	600
	Width	2415

After you add the data-bound grid objects to the form, you need to set some of their properties using the pop-up menu. Select the `dbgDefault` grid and click the alternate (right) mouse button. Then select Retrieve Fields to load the fields. Now click the alternate button again and select Properties and click the Columns tab. Make the User ID column invisible. Perform the same steps for the `dbgUserID` data grid. Save the project before you add the code.

The first step in setting up the User Access Rights system is to add three form-level variables.

```
Option Explicit

Dim cSQLDefault As String
Dim cSQLUserID As String
Dim cAccDB As String
```

Next, add the code in Listing 20.17 to the `Form_Load` event to center the form on the page.

Listing 20.17. Centering the User Access Rights form.

```
Private Sub Form_Load()
    ' center the form on screen
    Me.Left = (Screen.Width - Me.Width) / 2
    Me.Top = (Screen.Height - Me.Height) / 2
End Sub
```

Then add code to the `Form_Activate` event. This line calls a routine that populates the data-bound grids. You'll add the grid code a bit later.

```
Private Sub Form_Activate()
    accLoadLists ' refresh the grids
End Sub
```

Now add a bit of code behind the `cmdOK` button.

```
Private Sub cmdOK_Click()
    Me.Hide
End Sub
```

Notice that you're just hiding the form, not unloading it. You'll need some of the information that is stored on this form a bit later on, so you need to keep it in memory for now.

Add the code from Listing 20.18 behind the cmdAccess button array. This control array handles all the routines that add and delete rights objects and set the access level for the rights object.

Listing 20.18. Setting up access levels and command buttons.

```
Private Sub cmdAccess_Click(Index As Integer)
    '
    ' handle command buttons
    '
    Select Case Index
        Case Is = 0
            ' handle single add
            accAddObject
        Case Is = 1
            ' handle single delete
            If dtaUserID.Recordset.RecordCount > 0 Then
                accDelObject
            Else
                MsgBox "No Objects to Delete", vbInformation, "Delete Object"
            End If
        Case Is = 2
            ' handle full add
            accAddAll
```

continues

Listing 20.18. continued

```
            Case Is = 3
                ' handle full delete
                If dtaUserID.Recordset.RecordCount > 0 Then
                    accDelAll
                Else
                    MsgBox "No Objects to Delete", vbInformation, "Delete All Objects"
marla               End If
            Case Is = 4
                ' handle access level
                If dtaUserID.Recordset.RecordCount > 0 Then
                    accSetLevel
                Else
                    MsgBox "No Objects on File", vbInformation, "Set Access Level"
                End If
        End Select
End Sub
```

This module calls a set of routines. Each of them handles the real dirty work. You also add some error checking here to make the program a bit more friendly, too.

Now for the tough stuff. First, you add the routine that populates the two data-bound grids. Create a Sub called accLoadLists and add the code in Listing 20.19.

Listing 20.19. Populating the two data-bound grids with accLoadLists.

```
Sub accLoadLists()
    '
    ' load data controls for DBLists
    '
    cSQLDefault = "SELECT * FROM AppAccess WHERE
    ➥UserID='Default' ORDER BY Object"
    cSQLUserID = "SELECT * FROM AppAccess WHERE UserID='" +
    ➥Trim(frmUserMaint.Text1(0)) + "' ORDER BY Object"
    cAccDB = App.Path + " \USERDEMO.mdb"
    '
    dtaDefault.DatabaseName = cAccDB
    dtaDefault.RecordSource = cSQLDefault
    dtaDefault.Refresh
    dbgDefault.ReBind
    '
    dtaUserID.DatabaseName = cAccDB
    dtaUserID.RecordSource = cSQLUserID
    dtaUserID.Refresh
    dbgUserID.ReBind
End Sub
```

This procedure initializes the two data controls and then refreshes them and rebinds the data grids.

Next, add the code that adds an object from the Default Set to the current User's Set. Create a new Sub called accAddObject and place the code in Listing 20.20 in the routine.

Listing 20.20. Creating the `accAddObject` routine.

```
Function UsrLogin() As Integer
    '
    ' load form and perform login
    '
    errProcStack errPush, "LibUser.UsrLogin"
    '
    Dim nTries As Integer
    '
    ' init vars
    cDBName = App.Path + " \USERDEMO.mdb"
    cRSName = "AppUsers"
    '
    nResult = usrInit()      ' load database, etc.
    If nResult <> usrOK Then
        cResult = "Unable to continue"
        nErrExit = errExit
        GoTo usrLoginErr
    End If
    '
    Load frmUserLogIn         ' load login form
    frmUserLogIn.lblAppTitle = "Test Login Application"
    '
    usrMaxTries = 3
    nTries = 0
    While nTries < usrMaxTries
        nTries = nTries + 1
        frmUserLogIn.Show vbModal    ' show form to user
        '
        ' check results
        If usrAction = usrOK Then
            ' user pressed OK
            nResult = usrValid(frmUserLogIn.txtUserID, frmUserLogIn.txtPass)
            ' if user is valid, exit
            If nResult = usrOK Then
                nTries = usrMaxTries
            End If
        Else
            ' user pressed cancel
            nResult = usrErr
            nTries = usrMaxTries
        End If
    Wend
    '
    GoTo usrLoginExit
    '
usrLoginErr:
    If Err <> 0 Then
        nResult = Err
```

continues

677

Listing 20.20. continued

```
        cResult = Error$
        nErrExit = errExit
    End If
    errHandler nResult, cResult, nErrExit
    GoTo usrLoginExit
    '
usrLoginExit:
    UsrLogin = nResult
    errProcStack errPop, ""
    '
End Function
```

This routine gets some variables from the form and then checks to see whether you are trying to add an object to the Default user. If so, you are prompted for the new object name, and if a valid one is entered, that object is added to the Default list. If you are attempting to add a new object to a real user, the routine checks to make sure the object does not already exist for that user before adding it to your list.

The next routine to add (see Listing 20.21) deletes an object from the User List. Create a new Sub called accDelObject and add the code in Listing 20.21.

Listing 20.21. Deleting an object with `accDelObject`.

```
Sub accDelObject()
    '
    ' attempt to remove an object
    '
    Dim cObject As String
    Dim nResult As Integer
    '
    ' get confirmation
    cObject = dtaUserID.Recordset.Fields("Object")
    nResult = MsgBox("Delete [" + cObject + "] from User Access?",
    ➥vbInformation + vbYesNo, "Delete Object")
    If nResult = vbYes Then
        dtaUserID.Recordset.Delete   ' drop it
        accLoadLists                 ' refresh lists
    End If
    '
End Sub
```

The routine first asks for confirmation before deleting the object from the list.

Now you'll tackle a tougher one. The Sub called accDelAll removes all the existing rights objects for the current user. Add the code in Listing 20.22.

Listing 20.22. Deleting all existing rights objects with `accDelAll`.

```
Sub accDelAll()
    '
    ' remove all objects for this user
    '
    Dim cUserID As String
    Dim nResult As Integer
    Dim cSQL As String
    Dim cDBLocal As String
    Dim dbLocal As Database
    '
    ' init vars
    cUserID = Trim(frmAccM.lblUserID)
    cSQL = "DELETE * FROM AppAccess WHERE UserID='" + cUserID + "'"
    cDBLocal = dtaUserID.DatabaseName
    '
    ' get confirmation
    nResult = MsgBox("Delete All Object for UserID [" + cUserID + "]?",
    ➥vbInformation + vbYesNo, "Delete All Objects")
    If nResult = vbYes Then
        Set dbLocal = DBEngine.OpenDatabase(cDBLocal)
        '
        On Error Resume Next
        Workspaces(0).BeginTrans     ' start trans
        dbLocal.Execute cSQL         ' delete SQL
        If Err = 0 Then
            Workspaces(0).CommitTrans     ' ok
        Else
            Workspaces(0).Rollback        ' oops!
            MsgBox "Unable to Complete Transaction - Request Denied",
            ➥vbInformation, "Delete All Objects"
        End If
        On Error GoTo 0
        '
        dbLocal.Close     ' close local db
        accLoadLists      ' refresh lists
    End If
    '
End Sub
```

20

Notice that you use an SQL statement to perform this task. Because you are using the Execute method, you need to open another copy of the database (dbLocal). Also, because the single SQL statement might be deleting multiple records in the same table, you encapsulate the delete process in a BeginTrans…CommitTrans loop.

Now for the hardest one of the bunch, the accAddAll routine. Because some records might already be on file, you first must delete any existing items. The routine in Listing 20.23 contains several SQL statements and, of course, they are covered by Visual Basic transactions, too.

Listing 20.23. The `accAddAll` routine.

```
Sub accAddAll()
    '
    ' add all objects for this user
    '
    Dim cUserID As String
    Dim cSQLDel As String
    Dim cSQLTmp As String
    Dim cSQLUpd As String
    Dim cSQlDrp As String
    Dim cSQLAdd As String
    Dim nResult As Integer
    Dim cDBLocal As String
    Dim dbLocal As Database
    '
    ' set error trap and put routine on trace stack
    On Error GoTo accAddAllErr
    errProcStack errPush, Me.Name + ".accAddAll"
    '
    ' init vars for this routine
    cUserID = Trim(frmAccM.lblUserID)
    cDBLocal = dtaUserID.DatabaseName
    cSQLDel = "DELETE * FROM AppAccess WHERE UserID='" + cUserID + "'"
    cSQLTmp = "SELECT * INTO AppTemp FROM AppAccess
    ➥WHERE AppAccess.UserID='Default'"
    cSQLUpd = "UPDATE AppTemp SET UserID='" + cUserID + "'"
    cSQLAdd = "INSERT INTO AppAccess SELECT * FROM AppTemp"
    cSQlDrp = "DROP Table AppTemp"
    '
    ' main event here
    nResult = MsgBox("Replace all Current Objects for UserID [" + cUserID +
    ➥"] with Default Set?", vbInformation + vbYesNo, "Copy All Objects")
    If nResult = vbYes Then
        ' open the db
        Set dbLocal = DBEngine.OpenDatabase(cDBLocal)
        '
        On Error Resume Next
        Workspaces(0).BeginTrans      ' start the trans
        dbLocal.Execute cSQLDel ' delete old recs
        dbLocal.Execute cSQLTmp ' pull out defaults
        dbLocal.Execute cSQLUpd ' rename defaults
        dbLocal.Execute cSQLAdd ' add back to access
        dbLocal.Execute cSQlDrp ' drop temp table
        If Err = 0 Then
            Workspaces(0).CommitTrans     ' all ok
        Else
            Workspaces(0).Rollback        ' oops!
            MsgBox "Unable to Complete Transaction - Request Denied",
            ➥vbInformation, "Copy All Objects"
        End If
        On Error GoTo accAddAllErr
        '
        dbLocal.Close    ' close db
        accLoadLists     ' re-load the grids
    End If
```

```
            '
            GoTo accAddAllExit  ' exit
            '
            ' local error stuff
        accAddAllErr:
            If Err <> 0 Then
                nResult = Err
                cResult = Error$
                nErrExit = errResume
            End If
            nResult = errHandler(nResult, cResult, nErrExit)
            GoTo accAddAllExit
            '
        accAddAllExit:
            errProcStack errPop, "" ' remove name from stack
            '
    End Sub
```

The last routine you need to add is the one for the Set Level button. This routine calls another
small form that you'll build next. The second form is where you can set the access level for the
selected rights object. Create a new Sub called accSetLevel and add the code in Listing 20.24.

Listing 20.24. The `accSetLevel` routine.

```
    Sub accSetLevel()
        '
        ' set vars and call access level form
        '
        Dim cTitle As String
        '
        ' init vars
        cTitle = Trim(frmAccM.lblUserID) +  "["
        cTitle = cTitle + Trim(dtaUserID.Recordset.Fields("Object")) + "]"
        frmAccR.fraRights = cTitle
        frmAccR.lblLevel = dtaUserID.Recordset.Fields("Level")
        frmAccR.Caption = "User Access Rights"
        '
        frmAccR.Show vbModal     ' show rights form
        '
        ' update object w/ new rights value
        dtaUserID.Recordset.Edit
        dtaUserID.Recordset.Fields("Level") = Val(frmAccR.lblLevel)
        dtaUserID.Recordset.Update
        '
        accLoadLists     ' refresh list
        '
    End Sub
```

This routine loads some controls on the new form and then shows the form for input. When
the form is closed, this routine transfers some of the information back into the data control and
refreshes the on-screen lists.

Now you need to build the last data form. Add a new form to the project. Use Table 20.6 and Figure 20.6 as guides in laying out the Rights List.

Figure 20.6.

Laying out the Rights List form.

Table 20.6. Controls for the Rights List form.

Controls	Properties	Settings
Form	Name	frmAccR
	Caption	Rights List
	Height	3900
	Left	2520
	MaxButton	False
	MinButton	False
	Top	1485
	Width	3435
CommandButton	Name	cmdOK
	Caption	&OK
	Height	300
	Left	1800
	Top	3060
	Width	1200
SSPanel	Name	SSPanel1
	Caption	<blank>
	Height	2835
	Left	120
	Top	120
	Width	3075

Controls	Properties	Settings
Frame	Name	fraRights
	Height	2475
	Left	180
	Top	180
	Width	2715
OptionButton	Name	Option1
	Caption	No Access
	Height	300
	Left	180
	Top	240
	Width	2400
OptionButton	Name	Option2
	Caption	Read Only
	Height	300
	Left	180
	Top	600
	Width	2400
OptionButton	Name	Option3
	Caption	Read/Modify
	Height	300
	Left	180
	Top	960
	Width	2400
OptionButton	Name	Option4
	Caption	Read/Modify/Add
	Height	300
	Left	180
	Top	1320
	Width	2400

continues

20

Table 20.6. continued

Controls	Properties	Settings
OptionButton	Name	Option5
	Caption	Read/Modify/Add/Delete
	Height	300
	Left	180
	Top	1680
	Width	2400
OptionButton	Name	Option6
	Caption	Read/Mod/Add/Del/Xtended
	Height	300
	Left	180
	Top	2040
	Width	2400
Label	Name	lblLevel
	Visible	False

There is very little code to add to this form. First, add the centering routine in Listing 20.25 to the `Form_Load` event.

Listing 20.25. Centering the new form.

```
Private Sub Form_Load()
    ' center form on screen
    Me.Left = (Screen.Width - Me.Width) / 2
    Me.Top = (Screen.Height - Me.Height) / 2
End Sub
```

Next, add some code to the `Form_Activate` event. The code in Listing 20.26 initializes the set of radio buttons based on the value in the `lblLevel` control.

Listing 20.26. Initializing radio buttons with the `lblLevel` control.

```
Private Sub Form_Activate()
    '
    ' set radio button based on label value
    '
    Select Case lblLevel
        Case Is = 0
            ' no access
            Option1 = True
```

```
            Case Is = 1
                ' read only
                Option2 = True
            Case Is = 2
                ' read/modify
                Option3 = True
            Case Is = 3
                ' read/mod/add
                Option4 = True
            Case Is = 4
                ' read/mod/add/del
                Option5 = True
            Case Is = 5
                ' read/mod/add/del/extended
                Option6 = True
        End Select
        '
    End Sub
```

Now you need to add a single line of code (see Listing 20.27) in the Click events of each of the radio buttons. This sets the new rights level each time a radio button is clicked.

Listing 20.27. Coding the radio buttons in the Click events.

```
Private Sub Option1_Click()
    ' set for no access
    lblLevel = 0
End Sub

Private Sub Option2_Click()
    ' set for read only
    lblLevel = 1
End Sub

Private Sub Option3_Click()
    ' set for read/modify
    lblLevel = 2
End Sub

Private Sub Option4_Click()
    ' set for read/mod/add
    lblLevel = 3
End Sub

Private Sub Option5_Click()
    ' set for read/mod/add/del
    lblLevel = 4
End Sub

Private Sub Option6_Click()
    ' set for read/mod/add/del/extended
    lblLevel = 5
End Sub
```

20

Finally, add a line of code behind the `CmdOK_Click` event to exit the form. Notice that you are leaving the form up in memory because you'll need some information from some of its controls.

```
Private Sub cmdOK_Click()
    Me.Hide
End Sub
```

Now save this form as FRMACCR.FRM. Before the project is complete, you need to add two more menu items to the User Maintenance form. Call up the FRMUSERM form and open the menu editor by selecting Tools | Menu Editor from the Visual Basic main menu. Add two menu items at the bottom of the list. Set the first caption to &Access and the name to mnuAccess. Set the second item, indented under the first, with a caption of &Set User Access and a name of mnuAccessSetUser.

Now add the code in Listing 20.28 in the `mnuAccessSetUser_Click` event.

Listing 20.28. The `mnuAccessSetUser_Click` event.

```
Private Sub mnuAccessSetUser_Click()
    '
    ' set some vars and load access maint
    '
    frmAccM.lblUserID = Text1(0)
    frmAccM.lblName = Text1(2)
    frmAccM.Show vbModal
End Sub
```

Save the modified FRMUSERM form. In the next section, you'll walk through a session of setting user rights and adding new secured objects to the database.

Running the Access Rights Maintenance Forms

After building the Access Rights forms, you are ready to run the project. When you start the program, you'll be prompted to enter a password. As before, enter USERA for both the User ID and the Password. This will bring up the User Maintenance form. First, add a new user, TEMPUSER. Be sure to include a password and a name. After saving the new user record, use the Find button to locate the TEMPUSER record and then select Access | Set User Access from the main menu. Your form should look similar to the one in Figure 20.7.

You can see a set of default access objects on the left of Figure 20.7, and you can see that the new user does not have any defined security levels for the objects in the box on the right. First, add one of the default objects to the user's list by clicking on a row selector in the Secure Objects list (the Default List) and clicking the Add button. You'll see that the selected object has been copied to the User Access list with the default access rights setting (see Figure 20.8).

Figure 20.7.
*Editing the access rights for
a user.*

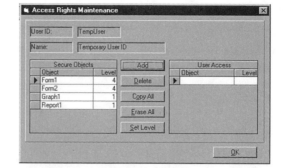

Figure 20.8.
*Adding an object to the User
Access list.*

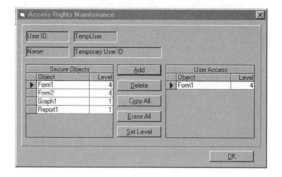

You can change the access level for the new object by pressing the Set Level button. This brings
up a window that shows all the possible access levels (see Figure 20.9).

Figure 20.9.
Changing the Access Level.

Tip: If you want to make things a little easier for your users when they move from
the numbering system for the various access levels to the text definitions in this
dialog box, you can simply add the level number to the caption shown in Table
20.6 when you create the form.

Select the Read/Modify radio button and click the OK button. When you return to the previous form, you'll see that the access level for that user has been updated.

You can practice adding, deleting, and modifying secured objects for any user you add to the database. You can define new secured objects by opening the Default user profile and selecting Access | Set User Access from the main menu. Any entirely new objects must first be added to the Default user.

Caution: Although it is possible to delete all the objects from the Default user profile, it is not recommended. Doing so will make it impossible to add or edit existing access rights of other new users.

Implementing Access Rights Security in Your Application

Now that you have the tools to create and manage user access rights, you need to build a routine to check those user rights and then add rights-checking to a working Visual Basic application.

First, you'll add two procedures to the LIBUSER.BAS library file. The first procedure creates a Snapshot set that contains all the defined rights for the requested user. The second procedure will be used to verify that the user has rights to perform a requested task.

Create a new Function in LIBUSER.BAS called accGetSet, and enter the following code. The routine in Listing 20.29 creates a Snapshot data object that contains all the defined access rights for the user that is logged into the application.

Listing 20.29. Adding the accGetSet function to LIBUSER.BAS.

```
Function accGetSet(cUserID As String, dbUsers As Database,
➥rsAccess As Recordset) As Integer
    '
    ' load the recordset with a
    ' snapshot of the users' rights
    '
    ' inputs:
    '   cUserID     user to get rights for
    '   dbUsers     init'ed db containing table
    '   rsAccess    access rights returned
    '
    ' returns:      accOK if all ok
    '               accErr if error
    '
    On Error GoTo accGetSetErr
```

```
    errProcStack errPush, LibUser.accGetSet
    '
    Dim cSQL As String
    '
    cSQL = "SELECT * FROM AppAccess WHERE USerID='" + cUserID + "'"
    Set rsAccess = dbUsers.OpenRecordset(cSQL, dbOpenSnapshot)
    '
    nResult = accOK
    GoTo accGetSetExit
    '
accGetSetErr:
    nResult = errHandler(Err, Error$, errExit)
    nResult = Err
    GoTo accGetSetErr
    '
accGetSetExit:
    accGetSet = nResult
    errProcStack errPop, ""
    '
End Function
```

Now add the routine to check the access rights for a particular secured object. Create a Function called accRights and enter the segment of code in Listing 20.30.

Listing 20.30. Checking access rights for a secured object with accRights.

```
Function accRights(cObject As String, rsSet As Recordset) As Integer
    '
    ' check for requested rights acccess
    '
    ' inputs:
    '   cObject        app object user wants
    '   rsSet          snapshot of all user's rights
    '
    ' returns:        user's rights level
    '
    Dim nTemp As Integer
    '
    rsSet.FindFirst "object='" + cObject + "'"
    If rsSet.NoMatch = False Then
        accRights = rsSet.Fields("level")
    Else
        accRights = accNone
    End If
End Function
```

This function accepts two parameters (the object and the Snapshot set), and it returns the rights level on file. If no rights level is on file, it returns zero (no access).

20

Save the LIBUSER.BAS file. Next, you will add code to the User Maintenance form that uses the access rights to limit user access to the system.

For this example, you employ security on a report and an entire data entry form, and you also set security levels for modify, add, and delete privileges on a data form. To keep this example brief, you establish all this security from the User Maintenance form.

To set all of these security rights, you need a single routine that is invoked at the form level each time the form is loaded. Load the FRMUSERM.FRM file, create a new Sub procedure called usrRightsCheck, and add the code in Listing 20.31.

Listing 20.31. The `usrRightsCheck` Sub procedure.

```
Sub usrRightsCheck()
    '
    ' check user's rights to do stuff
    '
    ' check on access to rights form
    If accRights("frmAccM", rsAccess) >= accRead Then
        mnuAccess.Enabled = True
    Else
        mnuAccess.Enabled = False
    End If
    '
    ' check on access to report
    If accRights("rptUserList", rsAccess) >= accRead Then
        mnuFilePrint.Enabled = True
    Else
        mnuFilePrint.Enabled = False
    End If
    '
    ' check on form function buttons
    Select Case accRights("frmUserM", rsAccess)
        Case Is = accModify
            recEnableList = "01011111"
        Case Is = accAdd
            recEnableList = "11011111"
        Case Is = accDelete
            recEnableList = "11111111"
    End Select
End Sub
```

In Listing 20.31, you are checking user security for three different program objects. The first is the Access Rights Form (frmAccM). Notice that you compare the results of AccRights to the accRead constant. If the user has at least read only rights, you can load the form. If not, you disable the menu option to prevent the user from attempting the operation.

You do a similar rights check on the Application User list report. In this case, as long as the user has rights to read the report, you allow her to call it up and print it. If you wanted to, you could add additional security at the report form level to prevent users from actually printing the report unless they have additional rights. This way users could view the reports, but not create hard copies.

Finally, you check the user's rights levels for access to the User Maintenance form itself. As you check the user's rights, you adjust the string used to enable the command buttons on the form.

After adding this routine to the data entry form, you need to modify an existing line of code in the User Maintenance form. Bring up the Form_Load procedure and find and replace the line that first enables the button bar.

Before modification:

```
BtnBarEnable Me, "11111111"
```

After modification:

```
BtnBarEnable Me, recEnableList
```

You also need to make a modification to the Main procedure of the LIBUSER.BAS module. This added code loads the Rights Snapshot before running the User Maintenance form. The next two excerpts (see Listing 20.32 and Listing 20.33) show a copy of the code before modification and a version after modification.

Listing 20.32. Before the change in the Main procedure.

```
    Else
        cUserID = frmUserLogIn.txtUserID
        usrMaint
        nResult = usrLogOut(cUserID)
    End If
```

Listing 20.33. After modifying the Main procedure.

```
    Else
        cUserID = frmUserLogIn.txtUserID
        If accGetSet(cUserID, dbUsers, rsAccess) = accOK Then
            usrMaint
        End If
        nResult = usrLogOut(cUserID)
    End If
```

That's it! Now save and run the project. This time, log into the application using MCA as the user and the password. This user has restricted rights for all the sections you installed in the preceding modifications. When the User Maintenance form comes up, you'll see grayed out buttons and grayed out menu items showing where the logged in user (MCA) has limited access (see Figure 20.10).

Figure 20.10.

Running the User Mainte-
nance form with restricted
access.

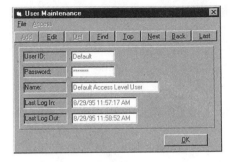

With this tool, you can create and manage any type of secured program object you like. You can create security levels that restrict user access to entire programs or individual forms or reports, disable menu items or command buttons, and even disable or hide individual fields within a form. It is also very easy to add these security features to all your Visual Basic programs.

Auditing User Actions

Now that you have a way to force users to log in and out of your application and a method of establishing and restricting user access to program objects, you can allow users to create an *audit trail* for all the secured activity. Audit trails are very valuable tools for tracking application use. With good audit trails you can tell when users log in and out of your application and what kinds of program operations they have performed. Audit trails can also provide vital information you can use to debug your applications. Often users will not be able to remember just what it was they were doing when they received an error message. Good audit trails can tell you the exact date and time the user experienced the error.

Developing a User Audit System

Adding a User Audit system to your applications is really very easy. You need only a few additional routines in your LIBUSER.BAS library. First, you need a method of writing information to an audit log file. Second, you need a method of triggering the creation of audit records. You can write audit information any time. Typically, you'll want to keep track of each time a user logs into and out of an application. You might also want to log each time a user performs any critical operation, such as printing a sensitive report or running a mass update routine. One of the most common uses for audit logs is to track any modifications made to database records. Let's look at how you can create detailed audit logs that show all the fields that were modified, including the old value and the new value for each field.

The Audit Log Library Routines

You only need to add three routines to the library in order to provide detailed audit trails for your Visual Basic applications. First, you need a routine to establish the name and location of the audit trail file. Next, you need a routine that writes the audit information to the audit file. Last, you add a routine that loops through all the controls on a data entry form and creates audit records for each field that has been updated.

Before you add code routines, you need to define a new global variable for the audit trail file. Add the following line to the `declaration` section of the LIBUSER.BAS file.

```
Global logWrFile As String
```

The first routine you need establishes the name of the audit trail file. This short routine simply initializes a global variable. If an empty string is passed, the routine creates its own name for the audit file (based on the application name). You'll make the audit trail file an ASCII text file in the comma-delimited format. This is easy to read without special programs or utilities and can also be quickly converted into a Microsoft Access format database if needed.

Create a new `Sub` called `logInitFile` in the LIBUSER.BAS module and enter the code in Listing 20.34.

Listing 20.34. Adding the `logInitFile` routine to LIBUSER.BAS.

```
Sub logInitFile(cLogFile)
    '
    ' sets up logfile name for system
    '
    If Len(cLogFile) = 0 Then
        logWrFile = App.EXEName + ".log"
    Else
        logWrFile = cLogFile
    End If
End Sub
```

Add the routine that writes the audit trail information to the log file. This routine accepts one required parameter and several optional ones. The notes in the code explain most of how this routine works. When you add the routine to check for changed fields, this will make more sense, too.

Create a new `Sub` called `logWriteFile` and add the code in Listing 20.35.

20

Listing 20.35. Recording the audit trail with the `logWriteFile` routine.

```
Sub logWriteFile(cLogType, Optional cRecordSet, Optional cKey,
➥Optional cField, Optional cOld, Optional cNew)
    '
    ' write action out to log file
    '
    ' inputs:
    '   cLogType    type of log record
    '   cRecordSet  database or program object
    '   cKey        table key field or other ID
    '   cField      record field
    '   cOld        old value
    '   cNew        new value
    '
    Dim nCh As Integer
    Dim Qt As String
    '
    On Error GoTo logWriteFileErr
    errProcStack errPush, LibUser.logWriteFile
    '
    Qt = Chr(34)
    '
    If Len(logWrFile) = 0 Then
        logInitFile ""
    End If
    '
    If Len(usrUserID) = 0 Then
        usrUserID = "SYSTEM"
    End If
    '
    nCh = FreeFile
    Open logWrFile For Append As nCh
    '
    ' write date/time, user, and action
    '
    Print #nCh, Qt + Format(Now, "General Date") + Qt + ",";
    Print #nCh, Qt + usrUserID + Qt + ",";
    Print #nCh, Qt + cLogType + Qt;
    '
    ' write recordset if we have it
    '
    If IsMissing(cRecordSet) = False Then
        Print #nCh, "," + Qt;
        Print #nCh, cRecordSet;
        Print #nCh, Qt;
    End If
    '
    ' write record key info, if we have it
    '
    If IsMissing(cKey) = False Then
        Print #nCh, "," + Qt;
        Print #nCh, cKey;
        Print #nCh, Qt;
    End If
    '
    ' write record field, if we have it
```

```
          '
          If IsMissing(cField) = False Then
              Print #nCh, "," + Qt;
              Print #nCh, cField;
              Print #nCh, Qt;
          End If
          '
          ' write old data, if we have it
          '
          If IsMissing(cOld) = False Then
              Print #nCh, "," + Qt;
              Print #nCh, cOld;
              Print #nCh, Qt;
          End If
          '
          ' write updated data, if we have it
          '
          If IsMissing(cNew) = False Then
              Print #nCh, "," + Qt;
              Print #nCh, cNew;
              Print #nCh, Qt;
          End If
          '
          ' end line and close file
          '
          Print #nCh, ""
          Close nCh
          '
          GoTo logWriteFileExit
          '
logWriteFileErr:
          nResult = errHandler(Err, Error$, errResume)
          On Error Resume Next
          Close nCh
          GoTo logWriteFileExit
          '
logWriteFileExit:
          errProcStack errPop, ""
          '
End Sub
```

In Listing 20.35, you first check to make sure that a valid audit file and user are declared. Then you open the audit file and begin adding a new line. Only one parameter is required for the routine, but it can have several optional ones. The program tests for the existence of each parameter and, if it's there, writes it to the audit line.

> **Tip:** Notice that you are enclosing all items in quotation marks. This will make it easier for you to convert this file into a database in the future (if you want to) because most conversion tools expect strings in quotations.

Now add the final routine. This one is designed to work with the LIBREC library. This new routine loops through all the controls on a data entry form and creates entries in the audit log for each field that has been changed. Create a new Sub called logChanged to the LIBUSER library file and add the code in Listing 20.36.

Listing 20.36. Tracking changes in each field with the `logChanged` routine.

```
Function logChanged(frmName As Form, rsName As Recordset) As Integer
    '
    ' checks for controls that have changed
    '
    On Error GoTo logChangedErr
    errProcStack errPush, "LibUser.logChanged"
    '
    Dim cTag As String      ' field tag
    Dim cKey As String      ' record key field
    Dim cOld As String      ' old column value
    Dim cNew As String      ' new column value
    Dim ctlTemp As Control  ' for collection
    '
    For Each ctlTemp In frmName.Controls
        cTag = UCase(Trim(ctlTemp.Tag)) ' get field name
        cKey = rsName.Fields(0).Name + "=" +
        ➥rsName.Fields(0) ' get key field info
        If Len(cTag) <> 0 Then
            If ctlTemp <> rsName.Fields(cTag) Then
                ' write out log record
                logWriteFile "RecUpdate", rsName.Name, cKey, cTag,
                ➥rsName.Fields(cTag), ctlTemp
            End If
        End If
    Next
    '
    GoTo logChangedExit
    '
logChangedErr:
    nResult = errHandler(Err, Error$, errResume)
    GoTo logChangedExit
    '
logChangedExit:
    errProcStack errPop, ""
    '
End Function
```

The routine in Listing 20.36 loops through all the controls on the form. If it finds one that has its Tag property set, the routine builds a log record to send to the audit file.

Now save the project. You have created all the routines you need in order to add detailed audit trails to any Visual Basic project. In the next section, you'll add code to the data entry forms and the Main procedure that will actually make the audit entries.

Recording User Activity in an Audit File

The next step is to add code to the current project that logs each time a user logs in or out of the application. You also add code that logs all changes to the AppUsers table. Finally, you add code that creates a log entry each time a user runs the User List report.

To add login and logout auditing to this application, you need to add two lines to the Main routine in LIBUSER. Listing 20.37 shows the modified Main routine with the new lines marked with multiple asterisk comments. Make the indicated changes to your version of Main.

Listing 20.37. The modified Main routine for login/logout auditing.

```
Sub Main()
    Dim nlog As Integer
    Dim cUserID As String
    '
    nlog = UsrLogin()
    If nlog <> 0 Then
        MsgBox "Login Failed!"
    Else
        usrUserID = frmUserLogIn.txtUserID
        logWriteFile "UserLogIn"    ' **** added audit line
        '
        If accGetSet(usrUserID, dbUsers, rsAccess) = accOK Then
            usrMaint
        End If
        '
        logWriteFile "UserLogOut"   '**** added audit line
        nResult = usrLogOut(usrUserID)
    End If
    dbUsers.Close
    End
End Sub
```

It's time to add auditing to the User Maintenance form. Actually, you'll add a single line to the RecWrite routine of the LIBREC.BAS file. Open the LIBREC.BAS file and insert the following line right after the last DIM statement and before the first FOR EACH statement.

```
logChanged frmName, rsName  ' *** added auditing
```

That's all you need to do. Of course, all applications that use the LIBREC.BAS library can now provide audit trail logs.

Finally, let's add a line to the frmUserM form to log each time a user runs the User List report. Open the frmUserM form and select the File | Print command to bring up the mnuFilePrint_Click event. Add the following line of code just before the frmReport.Show vbModal line.

```
logWriteFile "RunReport", frmReport.txtReportName
```

This line creates a log entry that shows the date and time the user ran the named report.

Save and run the project. Log into the application with default as the User ID and Password. Edit a record, run the User List report, and then exit the application. You have just created an audit file called USERDEMO.LOG in the Visual Basic default directory. Open the file using Notepad and review its contents. You'll see the login record, the list of changed fields from the time you modified a record, the record of the report run, and the final user logout. The results of a similar run are included in the following lines:

```
"08/30/95 02:36:28 PM","default","UserLogIn"
"08/30/95 02:36:56 PM","default","RecUpdate","AppUsers","UserID=Default       ",
➥"PASSWORD","default","DEFAULT"
"08/30/95 02:37:17 PM","default","RunReport",App.Path + " \UserList.rpt"
"08/30/95 02:37:23 PM","default","UserLogOut"
```

Summary

In today's lesson, you learned several methods you can use to increase the level of security for your Visual Basic database applications. You learned about the limitations of using the Microsoft Access SYSTEM security file and database encryption.

This lesson also showed you how you can add application level security to your Visual Basic programs by adding user login/logout routines and creating a user access rights scheme for your applications. In this lesson, you designed and implemented a login screen that you can use for all your Visual Basic applications, and you created several screens for maintaining user lists and managing access rights for each user.

You also learned how to add an audit trail option to your programs. You added routines to existing libraries that will log all critical user activity to an audit trail file including user logins, database modifications, and all critical program operations, such as running reports or processing mass database updates.

Best of all, the routines you built here can be used in all your future Visual Basic applications.

Quiz

1. What are the disadvantages and limitations of using the Microsoft Access SYSTEM.MDA file to secure a database?
2. What are the disadvantages of using data encryption to secure a database?
3. What is the difference between Application Security and Database Security?
4. What are the two main features of a good application security scheme?

5. Can application security schemes prevent unauthorized access of data by tools such as Visdata and Data Manager?

6. Why would you use an access rights security scheme in your application?

7. Why add audit trails to an application?

Exercise

Assume that you are a system developer for a large corporation. Your company has had a problem keeping track of the fixed assets (desks, chairs, computers) in one of its divisions. Your manager has asked you to develop a system to help manage the tracking of these fixed assets.

These assets are a large portion of the net worth of this organization. Therefore, management wants to keep track of any changes made to the items in this database. You decide that the best way to assist them in their efforts is to place an audit log in your application.

Use the skills you developed in this chapter to modify project 20ABC01.VBP to construct a fixed asset tracking system. Follow these guidelines in the construction of this project:

☐ Use Data Manager to create a new database for fixed assets. Name this database CH20EX.MDB, and add the table Assets. Include the following fields in this table:

Field	Type	Length
AssetID	TEXT	12
Description	TEXT	40
Cost	CURRENCY	
DateAcq	DATE/TIME	
SerialNo	TEXT	20
Department	TEXT	10

☐ Build a form to enter and edit the data records for this table. Use a data control to manage the records. Use the default (Text1, Text2, and so on) for text field's Name property. Set the Name property of the form to frmFixedAssets. Make this the first form displayed after the login process.

☐ Make your system write to an audit log any time a record is changed. Include Ch20ex.mdb.Assets as the name of the changed object, the user who made the change, and the AssetID of the changed record in the log. Use the same log as used by the login and logout routine. (Hint: Research the Data Changed event.)

20

Preparing Online Help for Your Database Application

Today you will learn how to build help applications for your Visual Basic database application. You will create help files in a standard word processor and attach them to your application. You will then see an application that can facilitate much of the work encountered in the creation of a help file.

To perform the exercises in this chapter, you need a word processor that can save your data files in rich text format (RTF). You also need the help compiler HC.EXE. This file installs with Visual Basic 4 and can be found in the VB4 HC subdirectory. This file can also be downloaded from the Microsoft FTP site or from Microsoft forums on CompuServe or America Online.

An Overview of Developing a Help System for Your Application

Including online help with your Visual Basic database application is important for several reasons. First, online help makes your application look "finished." The user will gain greater confidence in your application if there is an online resource that he or she can turn to for assistance.

Second, online help makes a system easier to use. Users don't have to search for printed manuals for answers to their questions. Researching information online is faster and easier than leafing through printed manuals. Users don't have to leaf through a table of contents or an index to get the appropriate answer. Instead, users can use the search feature of the online help.

Third, online help can be customized. For instance, users can enter their own comments using the Annotation function. This helps to inform others of policy decisions and system uses. It also helps in the use of the system across different functional areas.

You should also understand the drawbacks of using online help. Many users have not accepted the paradigm of searching for information online. Some users like to take manuals home with them on the weekend. Others like to write important notes in the margins of their manuals. Others find it a strain on their eyes to read long descriptions of information on-screen. Also, if the online help is poorly designed, users can get trapped in endless loops and not find the information they expect.

Overall, the benefits of attaching an online help file to your application far outweigh the drawbacks. Help of any sort, even if it is the name and phone number of the program developer, should be included with any application you develop.

Steps in Creating a Help File

You should follow these steps in order to build a help file for your application. (This lesson will focus on each step in detail.)

1. Write a topic file. This is the word processing document that contains the text and codes of the help file.
2. Save the topic file in rich text format.
3. Create a project file to tell the help compiler how to build the help file.
4. Compile your project using HC.EXE.
5. Attach help to your Visual Basic application.
6. Test and revise as needed.

Creating Topic Files

The first step in creating your online documentation is to create a topic file. The topic file contains the text that the user sees when he or she presses F1 in your application. This file also contains codes in the form of footnotes that the WinHelp program uses to determine how the system is to function.

Word 6.0 is used in this lesson's examples to create the topic file. If you are not using Word, make sure your word processor supports the following:

☐ The capability to save text in rich text format

☐ The capability to add custom footnote markings

☐ The capability to work with hidden text

Before starting, make sure that your default system options are set so that you can view hidden text. In Word, select Options from the Tools menu. Next, select the View tab. Then, under Non-Printing Characters, check the Hidden Text checkbox.

You might also want to select the Print Tab and then check the Hidden Text checkbox in the Include with Document section. This will allow you to print any hidden text codes entered into your document.

As with good programming, it is important that you design your help file before you build it. The following exercises will cover the design of the help file at the end. You will be much better at designing the help file after you have learned how it is built. Now let's build the topic file.

Writing the Text

To start the project today, begin by building a text file that contains the information the user will read when help is requested. You will build a file to attach to the Company Master application you started in Day 6.

Let's keep the text file short and enter only information for the three sections of the application: Company Information, Contact Information, and Other Information. Although you will enter a small amount of information, it will provide you with the skills you need to build help files of any size.

You should now enter into your word processor the text shown in Figure 21.1. You can find this text in the TOPICS.DOC file found in the \TYSDBVB\CHAP21 directory on the CD that ships with this book. You could also import the TOPICS.RTF file if you are using a word processor other than Word.

Figure 21.1.

The text for your sample help file.

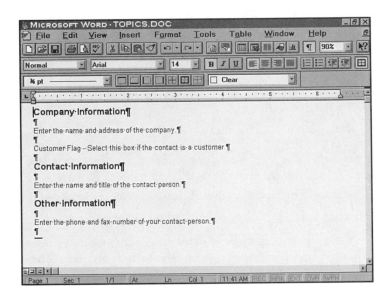

Separate Topics with Hard Page Breaks

Each topic in your text file must be separated with a hard page break. In Word, you enter hard page breaks by pressing Ctrl+Enter. Now do this between each topic. Your file should look like the one shown in Figure 21.2.

Now that the text entry is complete, you can start entering the format codes. These codes will inform the help compiler what to do with this text.

Figure 21.2.
The text file with page breaks between the topics.

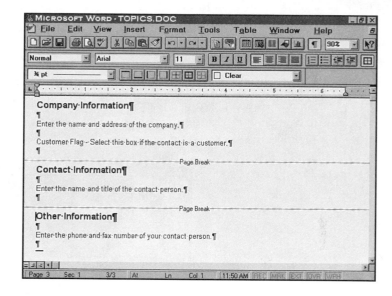

Entering the Context String

The context string is the unique identifier for a topic and serves as the unique key for the help system. Users will not see this code; it is only used by the WinHelp program for ordering the topics.

You need to insert a footnote to designate a context string for a topic. The footnote is marked with a pound sign (#). To insert a footnote, follow these steps:

1. Move the cursor in front of the title for the topic but after the page break for the previous topic. For the first topic in the exercise, place the cursor to the left of the C in the first topic heading, Company Information.

2. Select Footnote from the Insert menu. The Footnote and Endnote dialog box will appear. (See Figure 21.3.)

Figure 21.3.
The Footnote and Endnote dialog box, used for entering a custom footnote mark for a context string.

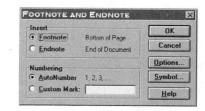

21

3. Select the Footnote checkbox (if not already checked) in the dialog that appears.

4. In the Numbering section of the Footnote dialog box, click the Custom Mark button and enter #.

5. Select OK.

The footnote section of Word now appears. Type the context string `CompanyInformation`. Make sure to have no more than one space between the # and the context string. Your screen should now look like the one shown in Figure 21.4.

Figure 21.4.

Entering the context string.

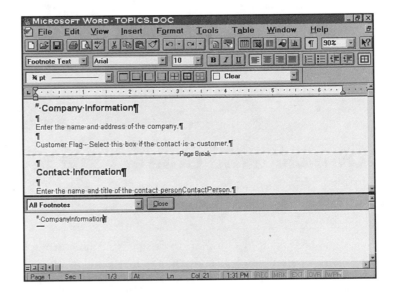

When building the context string, it is important not to leave any spaces in your text. Entering `Company Information` (with a space) results in a compile error. It is also good practice to match the context string as closely as possible to the heading you place on each topic. This will prevent confusion when dealing with a large number of context strings.

The context string is the only required footnote for each topic. The following sections discuss optional help file footnotes that you should also include with each topic.

Entering the Title

Now that you have entered the context string for the first topic, it is time to enter the title footnote. The title is displayed as the topic in the Help Topics Find tabbed dialog box of the help system. (See Figure 21.5.) It's a good practice to use the topic heading from the topics file as the title of the text for this footnote.

Figure 21.5.

The Windows 95 Help Topics Find tabbed dialog box.

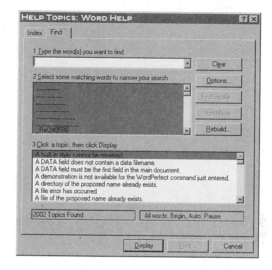

Entering the title is similar to entering the context string. However, the title footnote can include spaces between the words and is designated by the dollar sign ($) custom footnote mark rather than the pound sign (#).

Follow these steps in order to insert a title for the Company Information topic:

1. Move your cursor to the left of the letter *C* in Company Information. Footnotes can appear in any order, just as long as they are located before the topic heading and after the page break for the previous topic.

2. Select Insert | Footnote.

3. Click the Footnote button.

4. Click the Custom Mark button and then enter the dollar sign ($) as the custom mark. Click OK.

5. Type the title Company Information.

You can find help topics in the Help Topics dialog box by typing a keyword for a topic and then clicking the Display button. Determining which keywords apply to a specific topic is the focus of the next lesson.

Entering Keywords

Keywords are used in the WinHelp Help Topics Find tab to find topics. You use the same techniques for entering keyword footnotes as you did for entering context strings and titles. However, there are two differences: You can have multiple keywords for each topic (each keyword separated by a semicolons), and you use the uppercase letter *K* as the custom footnote mark for the topic.

Follow these steps in order to define a keyword for the first topic:

1. Insert the cursor before the letter *C* in Company Information and after the $ title footnote marker.

2. Select Footnote from the Insert menu

3. Select the Footnote option.

4. Select Custom Mark and enter an uppercase *K*.

5. Select OK and then enter the keyword Company in the footnote.

Note: It is possible to enter keywords for a topic and not a title. This will result in an >>Untitled Topic<< message appearing in the Topics section of the Help Topics Find tab. To avoid this, always include a title if you use a keyword.

Entering the Browse Sequence

The last code to enter is the browse sequence. The *browse sequence* defines the order in which you can move through help screens by pressing the forward (>>) and reverse (<<) buttons at the top of your help screen. This footnote is defined by the plus sign (+), and it uses the following syntax:

```
group name:sequence
```

In this line, the group name is followed by a colon and then by the order in which the topic appears in the group. The group allows you to connect all related topics in the help file so that users can move forward and backward in order to review any related information. The sequence is the position of the topic within the group.

For this exercise, let's add a browse sequence for Company Information.

1. Insert the cursor before the C in Company Information and after the K footnote mark.

2. Select Footnote from the Insert menu.

3. Check the Footnote option.

4. Select the Custom Mark option and enter a plus sign (+). Press OK.

5. Enter Company:1 as the footnote. Make sure to leave no more than one space between the footnote mark and the C.

You have entered all the necessary footnotes for the first topic. Your screen should now look like the one shown in Figure 21.6.

Figure 21.6.

All the footnotes for the Company Information topic.

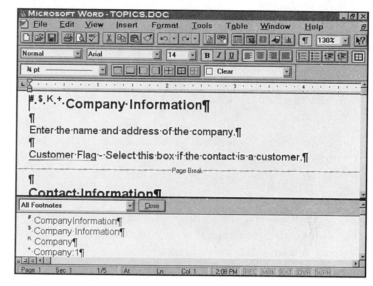

Continue this exercise by entering the footnotes for the other two topics in your file. Use Table 21.1 as a guide.

Table 21.1. Footnote information for the Contact Information and Other Information topics.

Topic	Footnote Type	Code	Footnote Text
Contact Information	Context string	#	ContactInformation
	Title	$	Contact Information
	Keyword	K	Contact
	Browse sequence	+	Company:2
Other Information	Context string	#	OtherInformation
	Title	$	Other Information
	Keyword	K	Other
	Browse Sequence	+	Other:1

Saving the File

You should now save all of the information that you have entered into your topic file. First, save the information as a Word 6 document. To do this, simply select Save from the File menu. Save your information as TOPICS.DOC.

Now save the file as an RTF file. Do this by selecting Save As from the File menu. Open the Save File As Type combo box and select Rich Text Format. Enter TOPICS.RTF in the File Name box. Then, execute the save by selecting OK.

Tracking the Topic Files

When creating large help files, keeping track of the different footnotes can become quite cumbersome. For instance, all the context strings must be unique and the browse sequence must follow an order within each group. For just three topics, this is not a hard task. But for 50, 100, or 1000 topics, this task becomes much more difficult.

Therefore, it's recommended that you keep track of all the footnotes you enter for each topic in a spreadsheet. This will help you in establishing the browse sequence and will ensure that each context string is unique. For each topic, keep the heading from the topics file as well as details on each footnote that you enter.

A sample tracking file is shipped with Visual Basic. The file is in Word 6.0 format and is named ..\VB4\HC\TRACK.DOC. (Refer to Figure 21.7.)

Figure 21.7.
TRACK.DOC, a sample help tracking tool.

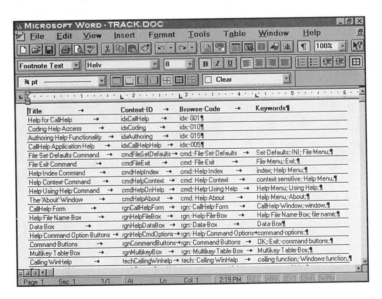

A tracking file will also help you build the project file, which is the subject of the next section.

Creating the Project File

When you have entered your help text in a document, inserted the appropriate footnotes, and saved the document as an RTF file, you are ready to build the project file. The *project file* tells the help compiler how to create a help file (HLP) from the topic file (the RTF).

The project file is very similar to an INI file. Enter information in sections, which each have a heading enclosed in square brackets ([ ]). These files can be created in a text editor and must be saved as unformatted ASCII text. Now open the Notepad accessory in Windows to create the project file.

Enter the following text to create the project file. Save your file into the same directory as your TOPICS.RTF file and name it 21ABC.HPJ.

```
; Project file for the Company Master Help
;
[Options]
Title=My Help File  ;Title to Appear on the Help Title Bar
ErrorLog = Error.TXT  ;File to store compile errors
[Files]
Topics.RTF  ;Name of the file containing the topics
[Config]
BrowseButtons()  ;Macro to place browse buttons on the help screens
[Map]; section to define context string parameters
CompanyInformation                          1
ContactInformation                          2
OtherInformation                            3
```

Components of the Project File

The first section of the project file is the [Options] section. This section, if used, should always be the first section of the topic file. Although it is not required that you use this section, it is highly recommended. This is where you identify the title that appears on your help title bar as well as the name of the file that will be used to collect compilation errors.

Here is the syntax to follow when entering an [Options] section:

```
[Options]
Title=My Help File  ;Title to Appear on the Help Title Bar
ErrorLog = Error.TXT  ;File to store compile errors
```

The second section is the Titles section. This section is required in all project files. It contains the name of the topic file (the TOPICS.RTF file in this exercise) from which the help file will be created. You entered only one line in this section:

```
[Files]
Topics.RTF  ;Name of the file containing the topics
```

The third section is the [Config] section. This section lets you declare macros to be executed when your finished help file is compiled. In the [Config] section you have entered a macro name that will place browse buttons at the top of the help screen to aid you in moving through the defined browse sequences. For this section, enter the following:

```
[Config]
BrowseButtons()  ;Macro to place browse buttons on the help screens
```

The final section in the exercise is the [Map] section. In this section, you enter numeric references to the context strings that you entered into the RTF file. Be very careful when building this section. Your context strings must be identical to the context strings entered in the RTF file. Enter the following:

```
[Map]; section to define context string parameters
CompanyInformation                      1
ContactInformation                      2
OtherInformation                        3
```

There are several other sections you can place in your project file. The [Buildtags] section, for instance, allows you to designate the topics in the RTF file that are to be compiled. There is also a [Windows] section where you can set parameters for the sizing, background colors, and locations of your help file.

You can also place an [Alias] section in your project file. Aliases allow you to assign multiple context strings to the same topic. This is useful when you delete topics in your RTF file. See the VB 4 Books Online, *The Microsoft Help Compiler Guide*, for a complete discussion on each of these sections.

Now that you have created your project file, it is time to compile your help application.

Compiling Your Help Project

Compiling your help file can't be done from within the Windows environment. Shell out to the DOS prompt or close Windows and return to DOS to begin this lesson. Go to the directory in which you saved the files TOPICS.RTF and 21ABC.HPJ. You should copy the help compiler, HC.EXE, to this directory. A copy of this file can be obtained from CompuServe or the Microsoft FTP if you do not have it.

At the DOS prompt, type the following command line to compile your help file:

```
HCP 21ABC.HPJ.
```

The program will compile and create a file with the same name as your project file, with an .HLP extension.

You will be prompted for any compilation errors that are written to the error file ERROR.LOG. Review any error messages you receive and then edit the project and topic file as needed. Then you can recompile your project.

Linking Help to Your Visual Basic Database Application

When the 21ABC.HLP file is created, it is ready to be attached to your Visual Basic database application. Before attaching it, however, let's first review the file. To do this, select Help from any Windows application by pressing F1. From the File menu, select Open, and then select the file 21ABC.HLP. The first topic, Company Information, should now appear.

You will now attach the help file to the Company Master application. First, you attach help information by setting properties. After that, you use code to assign help definitions. When you have completed that, you add menu applications to the application that automatically bring up the Contents, Search, Help on Help, and About Help information.

Using Properties to Attach Help Information

Follow these steps to attach a help file to your project:

1. Select Project from the Visual Basic 4 Tools menu. Then select the Project tab.
2. Select Help File and then enter the name of the help file (21ABC.HLP), including its path. You can also click on the ... box at the right of the field to Search for the file.
3. Select OK.

This assigns the help file to the project. You now need to assign the help context ID to the controls on the Company Master form. Follow these steps to make the attachments:

1. Open the Company Master project.
2. Select and open the Company Master form.
3. Select the txtCompanyName control.
4. Press F4 and move to the HelpContextID property.
5. Enter 1.

The entry in the HelpContextID property refers to the value you set in the project file (21ABC.HPJ) for the context string.

Save your form and run the project. Click in the Company Name field and press F1. You should now see the help you wrote for the Company Information topic.

Now exit help and return back to form design mode. Assign the remaining input fields within the Company Information frame to HelpContextID 1. Assign 2 to the HelpContextID property for all the fields in the Contact Information frame, and assign 3 to all the input fields in the Other Information frame.

Run the project and select any field on the form. Press F1 to bring up help. Select the Search box and then the Find tab. Notice that the keywords appear in the middle box and the titles appear in the lower box.

You can use the >> button in the Company Information topic to move to the Contact Information topic. This happens as a result of setting the browse sequence for both topics to the same group. Notice that Company Information comes first within this browse sequence. This is due to the browse sequence of Company:1 for the Company Information topic and Company:2 for the Contact Information topic.

While in help, select the Contents button. Company information should now be displayed. The Contents button will display the first topic in your help file if you do not declare a contents topic in your project file. Declaring this topic and building a contents page is the subject of the next lesson.

Building the Contents Page, Adding Jumps, and Modifying the Project File

To build the contents page, you will need to build a topic, assign footnotes, create jumps to the underlying topics, and modify the project file. When you have done this, you will then need to recompile the project.

Reopen your topics file (21ABC.DOC) and enter the following information for the contents page. Make sure that you insert a page break between the Other Information topic and your new topic.

```
Table of Contents
This is the page we will use for our Table of Contents.
➥Select the topic you would like to view.
Company Information
Contact Information
Other Information
```

You will now add a jump to each of the three sections in the contents page. To do this, follow these steps:

1. Use your mouse to select Company Information in the Table of Contents topic.

2. Double underline this text. In Word, this can be done by selecting Format | Font and then selecting Double from the Underline combo box.

3. Add the context string of the topic to which you would like to jump immediately after the double-underlined text (the context string itself should not be double underlined). For example, your first jump should appear as this:

```
Company InformationCompanyInformation
```

4. Assign the hidden text attribute to the context string you just added. This can be done by selecting CompanyInformation. Next, select Format | Fonts, and then check the Hidden Effect checkbox.

5. Now double underline the other two jumps, and insert the context strings of the desired topics. For Contact Information, the context string is ContactInformation. For Other Information, the context string is OtherInformation. Make sure these context strings have the hidden text effect.

Use the following list to insert the footnotes for the Table of Contents topic:

Footnote Type	Code	Footnote Text
Context string	#	TableofContents
Title	$	Table of Contents
Keyword	K	Contents;Table of Contents

Adding Pop-Ups

Let's add one more feature to your topic file—a pop-up. A *pop-up* is a box of text that displays on top of the active help topic. It is commonly used to provide term definitions without requiring the user to select a jump to a different topic. A jump should therefore be used to elaborate on the current topic, not to serve as a topic itself. See Figure 21.8 for an example.

Figure 21.8.
A pop-up.

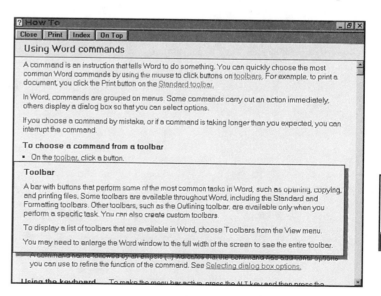

Preparing Online Help for Your Database Application

Adding a pop-up to your help topic is the same as adding a jump, except that you use a single underline for the pop-up text rather than the double underline used for the jump text. Follow these steps to add a jump:

1. Create a new topic for your pop-up text. In this exercise, you will enter the definition of Contact Person in the Contact Information topic. Enter the following text and footnotes for this topic:

```
Contact Person
The person to whom we send monthly statements.
```

Footnote Type	Code	Footnote Text
Context string	#	ContactPerson
Title	$	Contact Person
Keyword	K	Contact

2. Single underline Contact Person in the Contact Information topic.

3. Insert the context string ContactPerson immediately after the single-underlined text Contact Person.

```
Contact PersonContactPerson
```

4. Assign the hidden text effect to the ContactPerson context string added in the previous step. The text added to call the pop-up should be similar to the text displayed in Figure 21.9.

Figure 21.9.

Adding a pop-up.

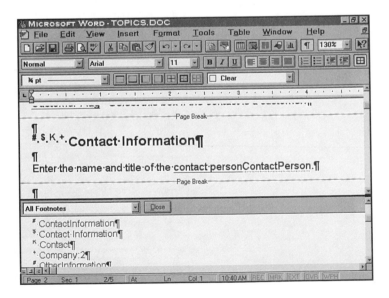

You have now completed the revisions to the topic document. Save this document in RTF format. Also, save the document a second time in your word processor's normal format.

Changing the Project File

You now need to make some changes to the project file. Remember that you created this file earlier in the Notepad application and gave it the name 21ABC.HPJ. Bring up Notepad and open this file. This file should look like the one shown in Figure 21.10.

Figure 21.10.

21ABC.HPJ, the Project file.

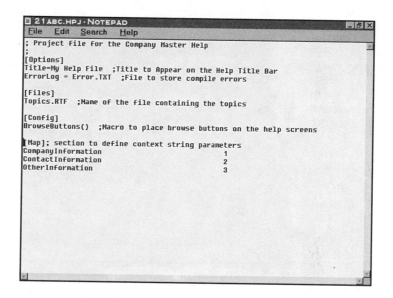

You first need to edit the [Options] section to identify the topic you want to use as your contents topic. Modify this section so that it looks like this:

```
[Options]
Title=My Help File   ;Title to Appear on the Help Title Bar
ErrorLog = Error.TXT   ;File to store compile errors
Contents = TableofContents
```

TableofContents is the context string you assigned in the earlier exercise.

You also need to modify the [Map] section for the new topics you added. Change this section of 21ABC.HPJ so that it looks like the following:

```
[Map]; section to define context string parameters
CompanyInformation            1
ContactInformation            2
OtherInformation              3
TableofContents               4
ContactPerson                 5
```

21

717

You will not add a context string for the pop-up because you will not reference it from a Visual Basic control.

Save your changes to this file, exit to the DOS prompt, and then compile your help file (command line of HC 21ABC.HPJ).

When the file is successfully compiled, return to Visual Basic and run the Company Master application. Select a control in the Contact Information frame and press F1. Select the underlined phrase Contact Person. Your definition now appears (see Figure 21.11).

Figure 21.11.
A pop-up definition.

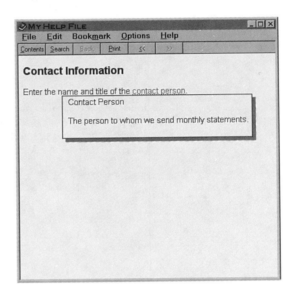

Next, select the Contents button to display the Table of Contents topic. Select any of the underlined items to jump to their topic. When you're in the topic, select the Back, History, or Contents button and return to the original screen.

Using Code to Set the Help File Project Option and the HelpContextID Property

In the previous exercise, you attached the help file name by entering it in the Project Options section and setting the HelpContextID in each control's properties. You can also set these values at runtime. Just enter the following code in the Form_Load procedure to open the help file and set help context IDs:

```
Sub Form_Load ()

   App.HelpFile = "C:\TYSDBVB\CHAP21\21ABC.HLP"
   txtName.HelpContextID = 1

End
```

You need to set a HelpContextID for each control to which you want to add help. This can be a very time-consuming chore if you have a large number of controls or a large number of forms in your Visual Basic database application.

Adding Help Functions to Menus

You will see Contents, Search, Help on Help, and About menu items on the Help menu of most Windows applications. The purpose of this exercise is to show you how to add these items to your Visual Basic database application.

Start by opening a new project and building the following menu by choosing Menu Designer from Visual Basic's Windows menu:

Menu Item	Name
&File	mnuFile
E&xit	mnuExit
&Help	mnuHelp
&Contents	mnuContents
&Search	mnuSearch
Help&onHelp	mnuHelponHelp
—	mnuSep1
&About	mnuAbout

Save this form as HELPMENU.FRM and the project as HELPMENU.VBP.

Note: The code in this example can either be entered manually or taken from the CD that ships with this book.

Now enter the following code in the Form_Load procedure of your HELPMENU.FRM file:

```
Sub Form_Load ()
   App.HelpFile = "C:\TYSDBVB\CHAP21\21ABC.HLP" 'Define the Help File to Use
End Sub
```

The line App.HelpFile = "C:\TYSDBVB\CHAP21\21abc.hlp defines the help file for the project.

Next, create a new module by selecting Module from the Insert menu, name it PRCHELP.BAS, and insert the following code inside the general declaration section:

```
Option Explicit

#If Win16 Then
    Declare Function WinHelp Lib "User" (ByVal hwnd As Integer,
    ➥ ByVal lpHelpFile As String, ByVal wCommand As Integer,
    ➥ ByVal dwData As Any) As Integer
    Declare Sub ShellAbout Lib "shell.dll" (ByVal hWindOwner As Integer,
    ➥ ByVal lpszAppName As String, ByVal lpszMoreInfo As String,
    ➥ ByVal hIcon As Integer)

#Else
    Declare Function WinHelp Lib "user32" Alias "WinHelpA" (ByVal hwnd As Long,
    ➥ By Val lpHelpFile As String, ByVal wCommand As Long,
    ➥ ByVal dwData As Any) As Long
    Declare Function ShellAbout Lib "shell32.dll" Alias "ShellAboutA"
    ➥ (ByVal hwnd As Long,
    ➥ ByVal szApp As String, ByVal szOtherStuff As String,
    ➥ ByVal hIcon As Long) As Long

#End If

Global Const HELP_QUIT = 2
Global Const HELP_INDEX = 3
Global Const HELP_HELPONHELP = 4
Global Const HELP_PARTIALKEY = &H105
```

Insert a new procedure by selecting Procedure from the Insert menu, name it HelpFile, and insert the following code:

```
Sub HelpFile (frmForm As Form, nHelpCmd As Integer)
    Dim i As Integer
    Dim nFlag As Integer
    Dim aData As Variant
    '
'Test for the naming of a help file
    If Len(LTrim(RTrim(App.HelpFile))) = 0 Then
        MsgBox "No Help File Available"
        GoTo HelpFile_Exit
    End If
'Set a text flag
    Select Case nHelpCmd
        Case Is = HELP_QUIT
            nFlag = True
        Case Is = HELP_INDEX
            nFlag = True
        Case Is = HELP_HELPONHELP
            nFlag = True
        Case Is = HELP_PARTIALKEY
            nFlag = True
        Case Else
            nFlag = False 'invalid command!
```

```
      End Select
'Pass parameters to the DLL call
   If nFlag = True Then
      If nHelpCmd = HELP_PARTIALKEY Then
         i = WinHelp(frmForm.hWnd, App.HelpFile, nHelpCmd, "")
      Else
         i = WinHelp(frmForm.hWnd, App.HelpFile, nHelpCmd, 0&)
      End If
   Else
      MsgBox "Invalid Help Command Value"
   End If
   '
HelpFile_Exit:
End Sub
```

Adding the About Box to Your Application

Create a new procedure by selecting Insert | Procedure and entering the following code:

```
Sub WinAboutPage (frm As Form)
   Dim MoreInfo$
   '
   MoreInfo$ = "Copyright " + Chr$(169) + " 1994 Software Company, Inc."
   MoreInfo$ = MoreInfo$ + Chr$(13) + "Technical Support: 800-555-7777"
   '
   Call ShellAbout(frm.hWnd, app.Title, MoreInfo$, frm.Icon)
End Sub
```

Entering Code in the Menu Events

First, enter the following code in the mnuContents_Click event:

```
Sub mnuContents_Click ()
   Helpfile Me, Help_index
End Sub
```

Second, enter the following code in the mnuSearch_Click event:

```
Sub mnuSearch_Click ()
   HelpFile Me, Help_PartialKey
End Sub
```

Third, enter the following code in the mnuHelponHelp_Click event:

```
Sub mnuHelponHelp_Click ()
HelpFile Me, Help_HelponHelp
End Sub
```

Fourth, enter the following code in the mnuAbout_Click event:

```
Sub mnuAbout_Click ()
   WinAboutPage Me
End Sub
```

21

Fifth, enter the following code inside the `mnuExit_Click` event:

```
Sub mnuExit_Click()
    Unload Me
End Sub
```

And finally, enter the following code inside the `Unload` event for your form:

```
Sub Form_Unload (Cancel As Integer)
    HelpFile Me, Help_Quit
End Sub
```

Save your form and your project. Run the project and select each of the menu items. Notice that Help | Contents displays the Contents page of the help file you created earlier today and declared in the `Form_Load` event. Selecting Help | Search displays a listing of topics from the same help file. The menu selection Help | Help on Help displays a screen similar to Figure 21.12, which shows the Win 95 help topics. Selecting Help | About displays a dialog similar to Figure 21.13, which contains information about your program. Finally, selecting Exit from the File menu stops the execution of the program.

Figure 21.12.
Help on Help.

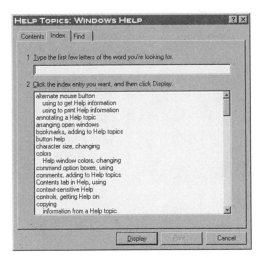

Figure 21.13.
The About box.

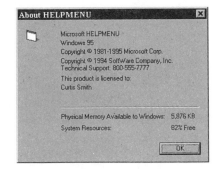

How This Program Works

You first began this project by entering code in the general declaration section for two API calls. The first call was made to the Windows help system to display the Help on Help, Search, and Contents information. The second call is solely for the About box:

```
#If Win16 Then
    Declare Function WinHelp Lib "User" (ByVal hwnd As Integer,
    ➥ ByVal lpHelpFile As String, ByVal wCommand As Integer,
    ➥ ByVal dwData As Any) As Integer
    Declare Sub ShellAbout Lib "shell.dll" (ByVal hWindOwner As Integer,
    ➥ ByVal lpszAppName As String, ByVal lpszMoreInfo As String,
    ➥ ByVal hIcon As Integer)

#Else
    Declare Function WinHelp Lib "user32" Alias "WinHelpA" (ByVal hwnd As Long,
    ➥ ByVal lpHelpFile As String, ByVal wCommand As Long,
    ➥ ByVal dwData As Any) As Long
    Declare Function ShellAbout Lib "shell32.dll"
    ➥ Alias "ShellAboutA" (ByVal hwnd As Long,
    ➥ ByVal szApp As String, ByVal szOtherStuff As String,
    ➥ ByVal hIcon As Long) As Long

#End If
```

Notice that you used the compilation directive (#if) to insert the code so that this application will run under the 16-bit version of Visual Basic 4. You then used the #Else directive to insert the 32-bit version. By doing this, the application will run under either version of Visual Basic 4 (16- or 32-bit).

The final entries into the general declaration section are to define the constants that will be called by the Help menu items:

```
Global Const HELP_QUIT = 2
Global Const HELP_INDEX = 3
Global Const HELP_HELPONHELP = 4
Global Const HELP_PARTIALKEY = &H105
```

The HelpFile procedure performs the following tasks:

☐ It declares variables:

```
Sub HelpFile (frmForm As Form, nHelpCmd As Integer)
    Dim i As Integer
    Dim nFlag As Integer
    Dim aData As Variant
```

21

☐ It tests for the declaration of a help file and returns a message if none is declared:

```
If Len(LTrim(RTrim(App.HelpFile))) = 0 Then
    MsgBox "No Help File Available"
    GoTo HelpFile_Exit
End If
```

☐ It flips a switch depending upon which value has been selected. This switch is set to true if a valid case is passed:

```
Select Case nHelpCmd
    Case Is = HELP_QUIT
        nFlag = True
    Case Is = HELP_INDEX
        nFlag = True
    Case Is = HELP_HELPONHELP
        nFlag = True
    Case Is = HELP_PARTIALKEY
        nFlag = True
    Case Else
        nFlag = False 'invalid command!
End Select
```

☐ It makes the API call depending upon the value passed:

```
If nFlag = True Then
    If nHelpCmd = HELP_PARTIALKEY Then
        i = WinHelp(frmForm.hWnd, App.HelpFile, nHelpCmd, "")
    Else
        i = WinHelp(frmForm.hWnd, App.HelpFile, nHelpCmd, 0&)
    End If
Else
    MsgBox "Invalid Help Command Value"
End If
HelpFile_Exit:
End Sub
```

The `WinAboutPage` procedure makes an API call to display an About box. Parameters are passed for a company name and a technical support number:

```
Sub WinAboutPage (frm As Form)
    Dim MoreInfo$
    '
    MoreInfo$ = "Copyright " + Chr$(169) + " 1994 Software Company, Inc."
    MoreInfo$ = MoreInfo$ + Chr$(13) + "Technical Support: 800-555-7777"
    '
    Call ShellAbout(frm.hWnd, app.Title, MoreInfo$, frm.Icon)
End Sub
```

The `Click` events for the menu items are defined to call the `HelpFile` procedure and pass the appropriate parameters:

```
Sub mnuContents_Click ()
    Helpfile Me, Help_index
End Sub

Sub mnuSearch_Click ()
    HelpFile Me, Help_PartialKey
End Sub

Sub mnuHelponHelp_Click ()
HelpFile Me, Help_HelponHelp
End Sub
```

```
Sub mnuAbout_Click ()
    WinAboutPage Me
End Sub

Sub mnuExit.Click()
    Unload Me
End Sub
```

Finally, when the form unloads, housekeeping should be performed and any help screens that have been left open should be closed. This is the role of the Form_Unload event.

```
Sub Form_Unload (Cancel As Integer)
    HelpFile Me, Help_Quit
End Sub
```

Please note that Unload Me was used in the Exit menu item rather than End. Using the End command would stop execution of the program without triggering the Unload event.

Using Help Authoring Tools to Create Your Help File

There are commercial products available that will greatly reduce the time required for developing a help file. These products automate the process by which footnotes are entered, context strings are mapped, project files are built, and the help file is compiled. In addition, these programs can "strip" footnotes from your topic file so that you can use it for your printed documentation.

There is a tradeoff that you should be aware of when using an authoring tool. Any tool will undoubtedly make you more efficient in the creation of topic files; but if it takes you more time to install and learn the product than you save by using it, you are better off producing the file manually.

The ultimate determinant in whether or not to purchase a help authoring tool will be based upon the size of your projects. Simple one- or two-screen applications are probably best documented manually. More complex, multiscreen applications will best be documented with the assistance of a help authoring tool.

There are numerous authoring tools available. They range in price from approximately $100 to $500. Many of these products must be purchased directly from their authors. It is hard for us to recommend one specific help authoring tool over another because your own personal working habits dictate which tool is best for you and your project. Please consult the advertising found in the back of trade publications to obtain the distributors, pricing, and titles of the latest authoring tools.

21

In order to learn how these tools operate, you might preview an intriguing authoring tool available free of charge from Microsoft. It is called WHAT6.EXE. This file can be obtained from the Microsoft FTP, CompuServe, and America Online services. This tool is actually a Word 6.0 document template that contains a series of macros that assist in the building of topic files. It is unsupported by Microsoft, which means you have no one to turn to if you have a problem or a question. Weigh this factor very carefully before you decide to utilize this tool on a live project.

Designing Your Help System

Let's turn to the design of your help application. As demonstrated in the exercises for this lesson, your help topic file will contain the information that users will depend upon to operate your application. An effective help system must be designed properly to meet the users' needs.

Make sure you understand who will be using your system. For instance, you would design and write one type of help topic file for highly sophisticated users and another for novice users. Different levels of users have different technical needs and viewpoints concerning the use of computers as productivity tools. Meet the expectations of your users, both technically and emotionally.

Always plan what you will include in your help system. Don't begin writing until you have given consideration to the detail you want to provide and the browse sequences you want the user to see. Plan your topics to be no more than a few pages long. The topics should also be more than a sentence or two in length. You will find it better to use one topic that is two pages long in order to describe every field on a report, rather than writing many short topics in order to explain each control.

Keep the design of your help system simple. Also, be sure to use jumps judiciously: You don't want your users jumping through page after page of information. It is better to duplicate help information rather than have the user continually jumping from screen to screen in order to find the answer to a simple question.

Don't try to model your users' business practices when building the topic file. Your system should be designed to be versatile, allowing for changing environments. Your help system should follow the same thought processes. Don't dictate how the system should be used optimally, but rather show the users how to do what they need to do. You will be surprised by the clever ways in which a well-designed system can be used.

Don't burden the users of your system with the obvious. For example, don't tell the users to enter a phone number in a field with a label Phone Number and an input mask of (###) ###-####. Everyone knows that this means to enter a phone number. Not everyone will know, however,

where this number is used throughout the system or on what reports it appears. Be informative and follow through to the end. Don't stop your explanation when only 75 percent of the process has been defined.

It is best to write your online documentation as you build your system. Help files should be read and reviewed for suitability as part of the testing cycle. Writing the topic file as you code will keep you from forgetting key features of your design. Functionality is best documented when it is fresh in your mind.

Remember to budget time in your system design plan to write your online documentation. Writing is hard work and requires patience, perseverance, and attention to detail. Allow time for numerous rewrites and edits. Many experienced technical writers estimate that it takes approximately one hour to type a page of text. Make estimates based upon this rate and then adjust it according to the speed at which you work. Double the result that you get to allow sufficient time if you run into any problems.

Do not release a programming project that has not been properly documented. It is a mistake to think that you can provide quality documentation at a future date if you can't provide it at the ship date. A help system will be needed most when users are new to the system and just beginning to learn it. Everyday work demands can distract you from the "less important" and routine responsibilities of your job. Always remember that creating a new project is exciting, but writing about a new project is often quite tedious. Discipline on your part will be required in order to get the job done.

If you are managing a team of developers, allow them the time needed in order to develop documentation. There are no shortcuts in system development or documentation. Items that are not finished when they should have been always come back to haunt you to an even greater extent some time in the future.

Know your writing abilities and seek assistance when needed. Many system programmers find it difficult to write. Their expertise lies with system design and coding, not with writing. This is not a bad thing in itself, as long as you are honest with yourself and are not ashamed to seek out technical writers for assistance.

Determine whether you will have both written and online documentation. You should provide both forms of documentation. It is easier to write the online documentation first and then use it as the starting point for your printed documentation. The online documentation will follow the natural flow of the system.

Remember that users depend on your documentation to enable them to understand how to operate the systems that help them perform their jobs. You have a great responsibility to properly document your system and to make it easy to use and quick to learn.

Summary

Every application should have a help file attached. A help file ensures that the system is used as it was intended. It also gives the application a more "finished" look and feel.

The following key points were covered in this lesson:

1. You need to create a topic file and a project file in order to build a help file.

2. The topic file you create includes all the text and footnotes for the help system. It is written in rich text format (RTF).

3. You insert footnotes to define each topic. Insert a # footnote to declare a context string, a $ footnote to denote a title, an uppercase K to denote a keyword, and a plus sign (+) to denote the browse sequence.

4. The project file contains the codes that inform the compiler how to build the help file from the topics file. It is saved as ASCII text and must have an .HPJ extension.

5. You declare your project's help file by setting its path and name in the Project Options section. You declare your topic for a control by setting its HelpContextID property.

6. Jumps can be added to your help file by double underlining your jump text and immediately inserting the context string of the topic to which the user will jump. This context string is then formatted as hidden text.

7. You can create a pop-up window the same way you create a jump; but you use single-underlined text rather than double-underlined text.

8. You can add help menu items to your application by making an API call to WinHelp.

9. There are several programs, known as authoring tools, that are available commercially. These programs can assist you in creating help files. The size of your application will dictate whether an authoring tool is worth the time and financial investment.

10. Plan your help file before writing it. Remember to write your online help first. Also, prepare your documentation as you develop your application rather than after the project is completely coded. Always keep your system simple, while making sure that all the information the user expects to find in your documentation is indeed there.

Quiz

1. What custom footnote mark do you insert for a context string? Can you put spaces in the text of this footnote?

2. What custom footnote mark do you insert for a title? Can you use spaces in this footnote?

3. Where will keywords be used in your help application? What separator do you use if you want to insert multiple keywords for a topic?

4. In what format(s) should you save your topic file? In what format(s) should you save your project file?

5. How do you declare a contents page in your help file?

6. What control property do you set in order to identify the help topic to display when the control has focus and F1 is pressed? Where does this value come from?

7. How much time should you budget to produce one typed page of documentation?

Exercises

1. Build a browse sequence that makes a topic the third topic to appear in a group called Processing.

2. Build a jump for the text Creating a New Project that opens a topic titled Creating a New Project with the context string NewProject.

3. Build a pop-up rather than a jump for the topic discussed in Exercise 2.

4. Add a topic to the help file created in this lesson to describe the Company Master form. Recompile your project and attach help to the form. (Hint: Make sure to modify the [Map] section of your project file for the context string.)

21

The third and final week of this book covered several very important topics. This week's work was focused on database issues you'll encounter when you develop database applications for multiple users or multiple sites. You learned advanced SQL language for defining databases (DDL) and manipulating records within existing databases (DML). You also learned the five rules of data normalization and how applying those rules can improve the speed, accuracy, and integrity of your databases.

You learned about Visual Basic database locking schemes for the database, table, and page level. You also learned the advantages and limitations of adding cascading updates and deletes to your database relationship definitions. You learned how to use Visual Basic keywords `BeginTrans`, `CommitTrans`, and `Rollback` to improve database integrity and processing speed during mass updates.

You learned how to write data entry forms that use the ODBC API calls to link directly with the ODBC interface to access data in registered ODBC data sources. You also learned how to install the ODBC Administrator and how to create new ODBC data sources for your ODBC-enabled Visual Basic programs.

You learned how to create application-level security schemes such as user login and logout, program-level access rights, and audit trails to keep track of critical application operations.

Finally, you learned how to design and build online help systems for your Visual Basic applications, including the 10-point checklist for creating quality help systems. You also learned how to link help files directly to fields on a Visual Basic data form.

Day 15, "Creating Databases with SQL"

You started the week by learning how to create, alter, and delete database table structures using DDL (Data Definition Language) SQL keywords. You learned that using DDL statements to build tables, create indexes, and establish relationships is an excellent way to automatically document table layouts.

You learned how to maintain database structures using the following DDL keywords:

- ☐ CREATE TABLE enables you to create entirely new tables in your existing database.
- ☐ DROP TABLE enables you to completely remove a table, including any data that is already in the table.
- ☐ ALTER TABLE enables you to add a new column or drop an existing column from the table without losing existing data in the other columns.
- ☐ CREATE INDEX and DROP INDEX enable you to create indexes that can enforce data integrity and speed data access.
- ☐ The CONSTRAINT clause can be added to the CREATE TABLE or ALTER TABLE statement to define relationships between tables using the FOREIGN KEY clause.

Day 16, "Updating Databases with SQL"

You continued your SQL studies on Day 16 with Data Manipulation Language (DML) keywords. These SQL keywords enable you to add, delete, and edit data within tables. You also learned how to use DML statements to quickly create test data for tables and load default values into startup tables. Plus, you learned that DML statements such as Append queries, Make Table queries, and Delete queries can outperform equivalent Visual Basic code versions of the same operations.

You learned how to manage data within the tables using the following DML keywords:

- ☐ The INSERT INTO statement can be used to add new rows to the table using the VALUES clause.

☐ You can create an Append query by using the INSERT INTO…FROM syntax to copy data from one table to another. You can also copy data from one database to another using the IN clause on an INSERT INTO…FROM statement.

☐ You can create new tables by copying the structure and some of the data using the SELECT…INTO statement. This statement can incorporate WHERE, ORDER BY, GROUP BY, and HAVING clauses to limit the scope of the data used to populate the new table you create.

☐ You can use the DELETE FROM clause to remove one or more records from an existing table. You can even create customized views of the database using the JOIN clause and remove only records that are the result of a JOIN statement.

Day 17, "Database Normalization"

On Day 17, you learned how to improve database integrity and access speed using the five rules of data normalization. You learned the following five rules:

☐ **Rule 1: Eliminate Repeating Groups.** If you have a set of fields that have the same name, followed by a number (such as skill1, skill2, skill3), remove these repeating groups and create a new table for them.

☐ **Rule 2: Eliminate Redundant Data.** Don't store the same data in two different locations. This can lead to update and delete errors. If the same data element is stored in two places, remove the second data element, create a new table with the element and a key field, and then place the key field in the locations that used to hold the data element.

☐ **Rule 3: Eliminate Columns not Dependent on Keys.** If you have data elements that are not directly related to the primary key of the table, these elements should be removed to their own data table. Only store data elements that are directly related to the primary key of the table.

☐ **Rule 4: Isolate Independent Multiple Relationships.** Use this rule to improve database design when you are dealing with more than one one-to-many relationship in the database. Before you add a new field to a table, ask yourself whether this field is really dependent upon the other fields in the table. If not, you should create a new table with the independent data.

☐ **Rule 5: Isolate Related Multiple Relationships.** Use this rule to improve database design when you are dealing with more than one many-to-many relationship in the database. If you have database rules that require multiple references to the same field or sets of fields, isolate the fields into smaller tables and construct one or more link tables that contain the required constraints to enforce database integrity.

Day 18, "Multiuser Considerations"

On Day 18, you learned about the following three important challenges that face every database programmer writing multiuser applications.

- ☐ Database locking schemes
- ☐ Using cascading updates and deletes to maintain database integrity
- ☐ Using database transactions to provide commit/rollback options for major updates to your database

You also learned the following three levels of locking that are available to Visual Basic programs.

- ☐ Database Level: You can use the Exclusive property of the data control or the second parameter of the OpenDatabase method to lock the entire database. Use this option when you need to perform work that will affect multiple database objects (such as tables, queries, indexes, and relations).
- ☐ Table Level: You can set the Options property of the data control (set to 3) or the third parameter of the OpenRecordset method (use dbDenyRead+dbDenyWrite) to lock the entire table for your use only. Use this option when you need to perform work that affects multiple records in a single table (for example, increasing the sales price on all items in the inventory table).
- ☐ Page Level: Microsoft JET automatically performs page-level locking whenever you use the data control to edit and save a record or whenever you use Visual Basic code to perform the Edit/AddNew and Update/CancelUpdate methods. You can use the LockEdits property of the Recordset to set the page locking to pessimistic (perform locking at edit time) or optimistic (perform locking only at update time).

You learned how to use the Visdata application to create relation objects that enforce referential integrity and automatically perform cascading updates or deletes to related records. You learned that there are times when it is not advisable to establish cascading deletes (for example, do not use cascading deletes when the base table is a validation list and the foreign table is a master).

You also learned how to use database transactions to protect your database during extended, multitable operations. You learned how to use the BeginTrans, CommitTrans, and Rollback methods of the Workspace object. You also learned some of the advantages and limitations of transaction processing.

Day 19, "ODBC Data Access Via the ODBC API Interface"

On Day 19, you learned how to use the Open Database Connectivity (ODBC) API set to directly link your Visual Basic program to target data sources via the ODBC interface. The ODBC interface is generally faster than Microsoft JET when it comes to linking to ODBC defined data sources.

You also learned how to install the ODBC interface on your workstation and how to use the ODBC Administrator program to install ODBC driver sets and define data sources for ODBC connections.

You learned how to build a program library that uses a minimum set of ODBC API calls along with several Visual Basic wrapper routines. This library set provides the basic functions needed to read and write data to and from a defined ODBC data source. You can use these routines to create fully functional data entry forms for ODBC data sources.

Finally, you used the library routines to build a data entry form that opens a link to a defined ODBC data source and allows the user to read and write data records for the ODBC data source.

Day 20, "Securing Your Database Applications"

Today's lesson covered several methods you can use to increase the level of security for your Visual Basic database applications. You learned the merits of using the Microsoft Access SYSTEM security file and the advantages and disadvantages of encrypting your database.

You also learned how to add application level security to your Visual Basic programs by adding user login/logout routines and creating a user access rights scheme for your applications. In this lesson, you designed and implemented a login screen you can use for all your Visual Basic applications, and you created several screens for maintaining user lists and managing access rights for each user.

You also learned how to add an audit trail option to your programs. You added routines to existing libraries that will log all critical user activity to an audit trail file, including user logins, database modifications, and all critical program operations, such as running reports or processing mass database updates.

Day 21, "Preparing Online Help for Your Database Application"

On Day 21, you learned how to design and build online help files for your Visual Basic applications. You learned the 10 key points to developing good online systems:

1. You need to have a Topic file and a Project file to build a help file.

2. The Topic file you create includes all the text and footnotes for the help system. It is written in Rich Text Format (RTF).

3. You insert footnotes to define each topic. Insert a pound sign (#) footnote to declare a context string, a dollar sign ($) footnote to denote a Title, a capital к to denote a keyword, and a plus sign (+) to denote the Browse sequence.

4. The Project file has the codes to inform the compiler how to build the help file from the Topic file. It is saved as ASCII text and must have the extension .HPJ.

5. You declare your project's help file by setting its path and name in Project Options. You declare your topic for a control by setting its HelpContextID property.

6. Jumps can be added to your help file by double underlining your jump text and immediately inserting the context string of the topic to which the user will jump. This context string is formatted as hidden text.

7. You can create a pop-up window in the same way you created a jump, by single underlining the text rather than double underlining the text.

8. You can add help menu items to your application by making an API call to WINHELP.

9. There are several commercially available programs that can assist you in creating help files.

10. Plan your help file in advance of writing it. Remember to write your online help first. Also, prepare your documentation as you develop your application rather than after the project is completely coded.

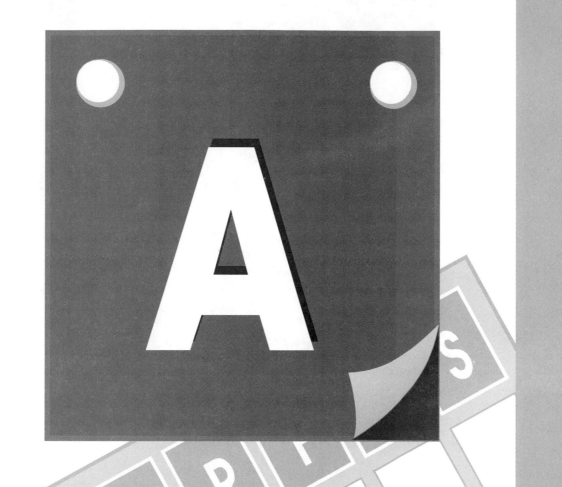

The SQL-VB Project

The SQL-VB Project

This appendix contains a step-by-step explanation of the creation of the SQL-VB Interpreter project. This program is already on the CD-ROM included with your copy of the book. The SQL-VB program in this lesson allows you to use an ASCII editor to create SQL scripts that SQL-VB can read and process. SQL-VB can handle fully commented, multiline SQL scripts. You'll find that SQL-VB will become a very handy data management tool.

Note: You do not need to construct this project from scratch. It is already shipped on the CD. However, you may want to go through this chapter as an added guide to constructing SQL-enabled applications in Visual Basic.

The Benefits of SQL-VB

You may often need to quickly generate sample database layouts for a programming project. You may even need to build some test data to run through data editing or reporting routines. The SQL-VB program enables you to do all that. The SQL-VB program is able to read SQL scripts you create with the Windows Notepad application (or any other ASCII editor). Listing A.1 is a sample SQL script that can be processed by SQL-VB.

Listing A.1. A sample SQL script.

```
//
// load and read data tables
//


// open a database
dbOpen C:\TYSDBVB\SQLVB\BOOKS.MDB

// open some tables to view
SELECT * FROM Authors;
SELECT * FROM Titles;
SELECT * FROM Publishers;
SELECT * FROM BookSales;
SELECT * FROM Buyers;
SELECT * FROM [Publisher Comments];

//
// eof
//
```

Listing A.1 opens a database and then displays several data tables on the screen. This same script could perform any valid SQL statement and show the results on the screen for the user to review or edit.

The advantage of generating database layouts using SQL-VB is that you have some documentation on the database structure that you can refer to in the future. You can also use SQL-VB to generate test SELECT queries and other SQL statements before you put them into your Visual Basic programs. Finally, SQL-VB is an excellent tool for exploring SQL and your databases.

Designing SQL-VB

Before you jump into code mode, lay out some general design parameters for the SQL-VB project. SQL-VB should be able to do the following:

- ☐ Open an ASCII file that contains valid SQL script statements.
- ☐ Process the open file sequentially and perform all SQL statements in the file, including all SQL DDL and SQL DML keywords.
- ☐ Display any result sets created by the SQL statements (SELECT...FROM) in data grids that can be reviewed by the user. To keep the project relatively simple, only allow users to view the results of queries, not update them.
- ☐ Provide an MDI interface so that more than one result set can be viewed at a time.
- ☐ Provide a simple About Box to display program information.
- ☐ Provide direct access to editing SQL script files without having to exit the SQL-VB program.
- ☐ Allow users to add comment lines in the SQL-VB script for documentation purposes.
- ☐ Provide reasonable error trapping and reporting to aid in debugging SQL scripts.
- ☐ Allow users to OPEN, CREATE, and CLOSE Microsoft Access format databases.

That last item may be a surprise to some. Remember that Microsoft Access SQL has no keyword for opening, closing, or creating a database! You'll add your own script keywords to handle this.

To accomplish all this you need three forms and one code module:

- ☐ SQLVBMain: An MDI form to enclose all activity.
- ☐ SQLVBChild: A child form that displays the result sets.
- ☐ SQLVBAbout: A simple form that displays the About Box.
- ☐ SQLVBMod: Visual Basic code module that has all the magic.

The SQLVBMain form needs some menu items and a CommonDialog control to handle the Open File dialog that runs the SQL scripts. The SQLVBChild form needs a Data control and a DBGrid control to handle the result sets. The SQLVBAbout needs a couple of Label controls and a single OK command button.

The SQLVBMod code module needs three main routines and a host of supporting routines. The three main routines are

☐ SQLFileOpen: To open the ASCII file selected by the user.

☐ SQLFileProcess: To process the SQL commands in the file.

☐ SQLFileClose: To safely close the ASCII file upon completion.

The SQLVBMod needs an error routine; some special routines to handle the database OPEN, CLOSE, and CREATE commands; a routine to handle the SQL DML commands (SELECT...FROM); and a routine to handle the SQL DDL commands (CREATE TABLE, for example). You can add these as you go along.

You'll need one other set of tools to meet the design criteria—the ability to edit scripts from within SQL-VB. Instead of trying to create your own editor, we'll show you how you can include the Windows program Notepad as part of your Visual Basic project. This can be done with minimal effort, and it is a great way to take advantage of the software already available on users' desktops. This is perfectly legal as long as you do not provide users with a copy of the NOTEPAD.EXE program. Because all Windows systems have this program already, you're all set.

Creating the SQL-VB Forms

Note: If you haven't already done so, start up Visual Basic and prepare it for a new project.

The first thing you'll do is define the MDI form for the project. This form provides the interface to the Notepad editor for managing script files. It also enables users to run existing scripts to see the results. Because it is a multidocument interface, you need to add some menu options to enable users to arrange the forms within the workspace. Finally, you add access to an About Box via the menu.

Creating the SQLVBMain Form

Add an MDI form to your project by selecting Insert | MDIForm from the Visual Basic main menu. This form contains a few controls that allow the user to open an ASCII file to edit or run, arrange the various child forms open within the SQLVBMain MDI form, and show the About Box upon request. Use Table A.1 and Figure A.1 as a guide as you build the form.

Figure A.1.
*Creating the SQLVBMain
MDI form.*

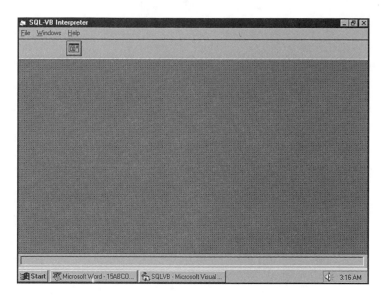

Note: In Table A.1, two controls are listed with an extra space preceding them. These controls are child controls. They must be placed directly on the controls that precede them in the table listing. For example, the CommonDialog control must be placed *on* the Picture1 control. The Label controls must be placed *on* the Picture2 control. Visual Basic does not allow standard controls to be placed directly on an MDI form. You can, however, place Picture controls on an MDI form, and then place your standard controls on the Picture controls.

Table A.1. Visual Basic controls for the SQLVBMain MDI form.

Control	Property	Setting
MDIForm	Name	SQLVBMain
	Caption	SQL-VB Interpreter
	WindowState	2—Maximized
PictureBox	Name	Picture1
	Align	1—Align Top
	Height	450
	Visible	0—False
CommonDialog	Name	CommonDialog1

continues

Table A.1. continued

Control	Property	Setting
PictureBox	Name	Picture2
	Align	2—Align Bottom
	Height	420
Label	Name	lblProgress
	BorderStyle	1—Fixed Single
	Left	60
	Height	300
	Width	9375

Now that you have created the form, you need to add the menu. Table A.2 shows the hierarchy tree of the menu items you need for the SQLVBMain form.

Table A.2. Menu tree for the SQLVBMain MDI form.

Caption	Name
&File	mnuFile
&New...	mnuFileNew
&Edit...	mnuFileEdit
—	mnuFileSp01
&Run...	mnuFileRun
—	mnuFileSp02
E&xit	mnuFileExit
&Windows	mnuWindows
&Cascade	mnuWindowsCascade
&Tile	mnuWindowsTile
&Arrange	mnuWindowsArrange
&Help	mnuHelp
A&bout	mnuHelpAbout

As you build the menu, you need to set two additional properties of the &Windows menu item. Set the Index property to zero and set the WindowList property to True. This forces Visual Basic to create a dynamic list of all the child forms open under the SQLVBMain MDI form window.

The final step in completing the SQLVBMain form is adding the Visual Basic code that activates the various menu options selected by the user. Because most of that code calls other routines you have not yet written, skip the Visual Basic code for now, and you'll get back to it at the end of the project.

Before continuing with the lesson, save this form as SQLVBMAI.FRM and save the project as SQLVB.VBP.

Creating the SQLVBChild Child Form

The SQLVBChild child form displays any result set created by SQL statements in the script being processed. You need two controls on this form—a data control and a data bound grid control. Add a new form to your project by selecting Insert | Form from the Visual Basic main menu. Use Table A.3 and Figure A.2 as a guideline for creating SQLVBChild.

Figure A.2.
Creating the SQLVBChild child form.

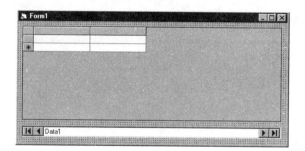

Table A.3. Visual Basic controls for the SQLVBChild child form.

Control	Property	Setting
Form	Name	SQLVBChild
	Height	3690
	Width	7485
	MDIChild	−1—True
Data	Name	Data1
	Height	300
	Left	120
	Top	2820
	Width	7095
DBGrid	Name	DBGrid1
	Height	2535

continues

743

Table A.3. continued

Control	Property	Setting
	Left	120
	DataSource	Data1
	Top	120
	Width	7095

You need to add code in three locations within the SQLVBChild form: in the Form_Load event, in the Form_Unload event, and in the Form_Resize event.

> **Tip:** To add code to one of the Form events, double-click on any empty location of the form to bring up the Visual Basic code window for SQLVBChild. The first event you should see is the Form_Load event. You can use the drop-down list box on the right to locate other events for the form object.

Open the Visual Basic code window for the Form_Load event and add the Visual Basic program code in Listing A.2.

Listing A.2. Adding code to the Form_Load event.

```
Private Sub Form_Load()
    Me.Caption = Trim(cSQLLine)
    Data1.DatabaseName = Trim(cGlobaldbName)
    Data1.RecordSource = Trim(cSQLLine)
    Data1.Caption = Trim(cSQLLine)
    DBGrid1.Caption = Trim(cSQLLine)
End Sub
```

Listing A.2 first sets the form's Caption property. Then, the code sets the Data1.DatabaseName, Data1.RecordSource, and Data1.Caption properties. Finally, it sets the DBGrid.Caption property. The variables used to set these properties (cSQLLine and cGlobaldbName) are global variables that are initialized prior to loading this form (see Listing A.4).

The `Form_Unload` event contains a single line of code. This code line decrements the count of all open child forms. This allows the MDI form (SQLVBMain) to keep track of all the result sets that are currently open. Enter the following code in the `Form_Unload` event.

```
Private Sub Form_Unload(Cancel As Integer)
    nForms = nForms - 1
End Sub
```

The last code piece needed for the SQLVBChild form is the code behind the `Form_Resize` event (see Listing A.3.). This code automatically resizes the DBGrid and Data controls whenever the user resizes the form. Note the `if` test that occurs at the start of the routine. Whenever a form is minimized, the `Form_Resize` event occurs. Attempts to resize a minimized form will result in Visual Basic errors, so you check to be sure the form is *not* minimized before you continue with the routine.

Listing A.3. Adding code to the `Form_Resize` event.

```
Private Sub Form_Resize()
    '
    ' if the form was re-sized by user
    ' and was not minimized, then
    ' re-size controls, too
    '
    If Me.WindowState <> 1 Then
        Data1.Width = Me.Width - 240
        Data1.Left = 60
        Data1.Height = 300
        Data1.TOP = Me.Height - 480 - Data1.Height
        '
        DBGrid1.Width = Me.Width - 240
        DBGrid1.Left = 60
        DBGrid1.TOP = 60
        DBGrid1.Height = Me.Height - 720 - Data1.Height
    End If
    '
End Sub
```

After you have entered these code pieces, save the form as SQLVBCHI.FRM. It's a good idea to save the project at this time, too.

Creating the SQLVBAbout Form

The last form you need for this project is the SQLVBAbout form. This is a simple form that lists the name and version of the program and its authors. Use Table A.4 and Figure A.3 as guides as you create this form for your project.

Figure A.3.
Creating the SQLVBAbout form.

Table A.4. Visual Basic controls for the SQLVBAbout form.

Control	Property	Setting
Form	Name	SQLVBAbout
	Caption	About SQL-VB
	Height	2040
	Left	2520
	MaxButton	0—False
	MinButton	0—False
	Top	2490
	Width	4380
CommandButton	Name	Command1
	Caption	&OK
	Height	300
	Left	1500
	Top	1200
	Width	1200
Label	Name	Label1
	Alignment	2—Center
	BorderStyle	1—Fixed Single
	Caption	SQL-VB Interpreter
	Font—Name	Microsoft Sans Serif
	Font—Size	15
	Height	495
	Left	120
	Top	120
	Width	3975

Control	Property	Setting
Label	Name	Label2
	Alignment	2—Center
	BorderStyle	1—Fixed single
	Caption	Copyright 1995—MCA/CLS
	Height	300
	Left	120
	Top	720
	Width	3975

You need a single Visual Basic code line behind the Command1_Click event. Double-click on the OK button to bring up the code window and insert the following line of code.

```
Private Sub Command1_Click()
    Unload Me
End Sub
```

This code line exits and unloads the form from memory when the user hits the command button. Save this form as SQLVBABO.FRM. Save the project at this time, too.

Adding the SQLVBMain Code

Now that you have created all three forms, you can go back to SQLVBMain and add the code behind the menu options. This is also the time when you add code that calls the Windows Notepad program from within SQLVB.

First, add code behind the Help menu option that shows off the SQLVBAbout form. To open the code window for the About menu option, select Help | About. When the code window pops up, insert the following line.

```
Private Sub mnuHelpAbout_Click()
    SQLVBAbout.Show vbModal
End Sub
```

Now add code that gives the user the ability to control the multiple child forms within the SQLVBMain MDI form. Select Windows | Cascade and insert the following code.

```
Private Sub mnuWindowsCascade_Click()
    SQLVBMain.Arrange vbCascade
End Sub
```

The Arrange method requires a single parameter. The vbCascade parameter tells Visual Basic to cascade all open child windows starting from the top left of the MDI form. The vbTileHorizontal parameter tells Visual Basic to tile the child forms. Select Windows | Tile from the menu and insert the following code.

The SQL-VB Project

```
Private Sub mnuWindowsTile_Click()
    SQLVBMain.Arrange vbTileHorizontal
End Sub
```

The vbArrangeIcons parameter tells Visual Basic to arrange all minimized forms in an orderly fashion at the bottom of the MDI parent form. Select Windows | Arrange to open the code window and add the following code piece.

```
Private Sub mnuWindowsArrange_Click()
    SQLVBMain.Arrange vbArrangeIcons
End Sub
```

Now add the code behind the File | Exit menu option. This code safely closes down all open child windows before exiting to the operating system.

```
Private Sub mnuFileExit_Click()
    Unload Me
End Sub
```

Select File | Run and add the following code line. Notice that the code line starts with the comment character. This tells VB to treat this line as a comment, not executable code. You have it "commented out" right now because you haven't created the SQLMain routine yet. You'll do that in the next section when you create the SQL-VB Main code module.

```
Private Sub mnuFileRun_Click()
    ' SQLMain
End Sub
```

The following two segments of code should be added behind the File | New and File | Edit menu options. The code calls a routine you will build in the SQL-VB Main module so you have commented out the calls for now to prevent Visual Basic from reporting an error at compile time.

```
Private Sub mnuFileNew_Click()
    ' LoadNotePadFile "Create New SQLVB File"
End Sub
```

```
Private Sub mnuFileEdit_Click()
    ' LoadNotePadFile "Edit an Existing SQLVB File"
End Sub
```

You need to add one more code routine to the form. As an added feature of the software, you want to be able to add a script file as a parameter when you run the program. This script would be loaded and executed automatically. You can use this feature to create associations in Windows that will automatically load and run the program when you click on the script file from the File Manager shell program.

To add command line processing to this application, you only need to add three lines of code to the Form_Activate event.

```
Private Sub MDIForm_Activate()
    If Command$ <> "" Then
      ' SQLMain Trim(Command$) ' call main job w/ parm
    End If
End Sub
```

The preceding code piece checks the Visual Basic system variable Command to see if it contains a value. If it does, you assume it is a valid script file, and then call the main processing routine just as if someone had used the File | Run menu option to select a file. Note that you have commented out the line that calls SQLMain because you have not yet created that routine.

Now that all the code is added, save this form and save the project. As a test, you can run the project. You can't do much except view the About Box and exit, but you can check for compile errors.

Creating the SQL-VB Main Module

The SQLVBMod code module contains the major portion of the system. It's here that you add the routines that can read and execute the SQL statements found in the ASCII file. You'll also add routines to handle any errors that occur along the way. Even though this module does a lot, you have only slightly more than 10 routines to define before you complete the project.

Declaring Global Variables

First, you need to declare a set of variables to be used throughout all the project. These variables contain information about the script being processed, any forms that are open, and so forth. Add a module to the project by selecting Insert | Module from the Visual Basic main menu. Set its name property to SQLVBMod and enter the lines in Listing A.4 into the declarations section. The meaning and use of these variables will become clearer as you build the various routines within the module.

Listing A.4. Adding the global variables.

```
'
' general declarations
'
Global cSQLFile As String
Global nGlobalErr As Integer
Global nSQLFlag As Integer
Global ndbFlag As Integer
Global nSQlFileHandle As Integer
Global cSQLLine As String
Global nLine As Integer
Global cLine As String
Global cGlobalSelect As String
Global cGlobaldbName As String
Global db As DATABASE
Global nForms As Integer
Global TblForms() As Form
```

Creating *SQLMain*

The topmost routine in this module is the SQLMain routine. This routine has only three tasks: open the script file, process the script commands, and close the script file. So let's write a module that does just that. To add a new procedure to the module, select Insert | Procedure from the Visual Basic main menu. Enter SQLMain(cRunFile) as the name, select the Sub radio button, and select the Public radio button. Now enter the code in Listing A.5.

Listing A.5. Coding the SQLMain routine.

```
Sub SQLMain(cRunFile)
    '
    ' main loop for interpreting SQL ASCII file
    '
    InitApp              ' clean up environment
    SQLFileOpen cRunFile ' open the script
    SQLFileProcess       ' process the script
    SQLFileClose         ' close the script
    '
    cRunFile = ""        ' clear passed parm
    MsgBox "Script Completed", vbInformation
End Sub
```

The routine in Listing A.5 does all the things mentioned earlier and adds two more actions. You perform some application initialization. You set an error condition during the SQLFileOpen routine in case something goes wrong when you open the file. Then you can check that error condition before you try to run the SQLFileProcess routine. Also, once the script processing is completed, you show the user a friendly little message box.

Creating *SQLFileOpen*

Now let's start building the next level of routines. The first is the SQLFileOpen routine. Use the CommonDialog control to get the filename from the user. If a filename was selected, open that file for processing, and then return to SQLMain. Notice that you have built in an error trap to catch any problems that may occur during file selection and opening.

Select Insert | Procedure from the Visual Basic main menu and set the name to SQLFileOpen(cSQLFile). Make this a Public Sub procedure. Now enter the code in Listing A.6 in the procedure window.

Listing A.6. Coding the SQLFileOpen routine.

```
Sub SQLFileOpen(cSQLFile)
    On Error GoTo SQLFileOpenErr
    '
    If Len(Trim(cSQLFile)) = 0 Then
```

```
         SQLVBMain.CommonDialog1.DialogTitle = "Load SQLVB File"
         SQLVBMain.CommonDialog1.DefaultExt = "SQV"
         SQLVBMain.CommonDialog1.Filter = "SQLVB File¦*.SQV"
         SQLVBMain.CommonDialog1.ShowOpen
         cSQLFile = SQLVBMain.CommonDialog1.filename
      End If
      '
      If Len(cSQLFile) = 0 Then
         nGlobalErr = True
         nSQLFlag = False
         GoTo SQLFileOpenExit
      End If
      '
      nSQlFileHandle = FreeFile(0)
      Open cSQLFile For Input As nSQlFileHandle
      nGlobalErr = False
      nSQLFlag = True
      GoTo SQLFileOpenExit
      '
SQLFileOpenErr:
      ErrMsg Err, Error$, nLine, cLine, "SQLFileOpen"
      InitApp
      '
SQLFileOpenExit:
End Sub
```

Creating *SQLFileClose*

Let's skip over the SQLProcess routine and write the SQLFileClose routine next. The only task this routine has to complete is to safely close the script file upon completion. Create a Public Sub procedure called SQLFileClose and enter the code in Listing A.7.

Listing A.7. Coding the SQLFileClose routine.

```
Sub SQLFileClose()
   On Error GoTo SQLFileCloseErr
   '
   If nGlobalErr = False Then
      If nSQlFileHandle <> 0 Then
         Close (nSQlFileHandle)
      End If
      nSQLFlag = False
   End If
   GoTo SQLFileCloseExit
   '
SQLFileCloseErr:
   ErrMsg Err, Error$, nLine, cLine, "SQLFileClose"
   InitApp
   '
SQLFileCloseExit:
   '
End Sub
```

Creating *SQLFileProcess*

Now you get to the heart of the program—SQLFileProcess. This routine reads each line of the script file and performs whatever processing is necessary to build and execute the SQL statements in the script. You also add a few lines that show the user the script lines as they are processed. Also, you'll remember that the script file has regular SQL statements, special database OPEN, CREATE, and CLOSE words, and comments. This processing routine has to handle each of these differently. Of course, you need an error handler, too.

Create a Public Sub procedure called SQLFileProcess and enter the code in Listing A.8. Don't be discouraged by the length of this code piece. Although it's about 50 lines long, it won't take you long to enter it into the project.

Listing A.8. Coding the SQLFileProcess routine.

```
Sub SQLFileProcess()
    '
    ' main loop for processing ASCII file lines
    '
    On Error GoTo SQLFileProcessErr
    '
    Dim cToken As String
    '
    If nSQLFlag = False Then
        GoTo SQLFileProcessExit
    End If
    '
    cSQLLine = ""
    While Not EOF(nSqlFileHandle)
        If nGlobalErr = True Then
            GoTo SQLFileProcessExit
        End If
        '
        Line Input #nSqlFileHandle, cLine
        nLine = nLine + 1
        cLine = Trim(cLine) + " "
        If Len(cLine) <> 0 Then
            cToken = GetToken(cLine)
            If Right(cToken, 1) = ";" Then
                cToken = Left(cToken, Len(cToken) - 1)
            End If
            '
            SQLVBMain.lblProgress.Caption = cLine
            DoEvents
            Select Case UCase(cToken)
                Case Is = "//"
                    ' no action - comment line
                Case Is = "DBOPEN"
                    SQLdbOpen
                Case Is = "DBMAKE"
                    SQLdbMake
                Case Is = "DBCLOSE"
```

```
            SQLdbClose
        Case Else
            cSQLLine = cSQLLine + cLine
            If Right(cLine, 2) = "; " Then
                SQLDoCommand
                cSQLLine = ""
            End If
        End Select
    End If
Wend
GoTo SQLFileProcessExit
    '
SQLFileProcessErr:
    ErrMsg Err, Error$, nLine, cLine, "SQLFileProcess"
    InitApp
    '
SQLFileProcessExit:
    '
End Sub
```

Despite containing less than 50 lines of code, several things are happening in Listing A.8. Let's review the routine more closely. After setting up the error trap and initializing variables, the main `While...Wend` loop starts. This loop reads a line from the script file opened by `SQLFileOpen`, updates a line counter, removes any trailing or leading spaces from the line, and then adds a single space at the end of the line. This single space is added to help the `GetToken` function do its work.

The SQL-VB program processes each line of script word by word. The first word in each command line is used to determine how SQL-VB will process the line. The `GetToken` function returns the first word in the line (you'll learn more about `GetToken` a bit later). Next, you show the current script line to the user by updating `SQLVBMain.lblProgress`. Notice that you added the `DoEvents` command right after updating the label. This forces your program to pause a moment, and that will allow Windows time to send the message that ultimately updates the SQLVBMain form.

Once the main form is updated, the program must handle the word it pulled from the script line. Usually, the word is an SQL keyword and SQL-VB can add it to the `cSQLLine` variable for eventual processing. However, there are four words that require special handling. These four words are listed in Table A.5 along with comments about how they are handled.

Table A.5. Script words that require special handling.

Script Word	Handling Comments
`//`	This is the comment word. If a line begins with this keyword, ignore the rest of the line and get the next line in the script. You must leave at least one space between the `//` and the comment. For example, `//comment` would be rejected by SQL-VB, but `//  comment` is just fine.

continues

Table A.5. continued

Script Word	Handling Comments
DBOPEN	This is the `OpenDatabase` word. If a line starts with this keyword, call a special routine (`SQLdbOpen`) that executes a Visual Basic `OpenDatabase` operation.
DBMAKE	This is the `CreateDatabase` word. If a line starts with this keyword, call a special routine (`SQLdbMake`) that executes a Visual Basic `CreateDatabase` operation.
DBCLOSE	This is the `CloseDatabase` word. If a line begins with this keyword, call a special routine (`SQLdbClose`) that executes a Visual Basic `Close` operation on a database object.

If the word found at the start of the line is not one of the four in Table A.5, the program assumes that it is a valid SQL word and adds the entire line to the variable `cSQLLine`. After doing this, the routine checks to see if the current line ends with a semicolon (;). If so, the program attempts to execute the SQL statement using the `SQLDoCommand` routine. After executing this routine, the `cSQLLine` variable is cleared in preparation for the next SQL statement.

This process is repeated until the program reaches the end of the script file. At that time, the routine exits `SQLFileProcess` and returns to the `SQLMain` routine.

Now would be a good time to save the `SQLVBMod` code module and save the project. You can't run the program at this point because you added references to several routines that do not yet exist. You'll add those final routines in the next section.

Creating the Support Routines

Now that you have entered all the main routines, you need to add several support routines. Almost all these support routines are called directly from `SQLFileProcess`. You'll concentrate on those first and add others as needed.

The first routine called from `SQLFileProcess` is `GetToken`. This routine takes a line of script and returns the first word in the list. You'll use this word (often referred to as a *token*) as a way to determine how `SQLFileProcess` handles each line of script. Because `GetToken` returns a value, it is a *function*. To create a Visual Basic function, select Insert | Procedure. Enter the function name as `GetToken(cString As String) As String` and select the Function radio button. Now enter the code in Listing A.9 in the code window.

Listing A.9. Coding the GetToken routine.

```
Function GetToken(cString As String) As String
    Dim nTemp As Integer        ' holds string location
    '
    nTemp = InStr(cString, " ")  ' search for first space
    If nTemp > 0 Then            ' if you found one,
        GetToken = Left(cString, nTemp - 1)   ' get the first 'word'
    Else
        GetToken = ""                         ' else return empty string
    End If
End Function
```

The comments in the code explain things pretty well. You use the Visual Basic InStr function to locate the first occurrence of a space within the script line, and then use that position to grab a copy of the first word in the line. If you can't find a word, you return an empty string.

The next three routines you add handle the DBOPEN, DBMAKE, and DBCLOSE script words. These are all non-SQL commands that you need in order to open, create, and close Microsoft Access JET databases. The first one you add is the routine that handles opening a Microsoft Access JET database. Use the Visual Basic menu to create a Public Sub routine named SQLdbOpen and enter the code in Listing A.10.

Listing A.10. Coding the SQLdbOpen routine.

```
Sub SQLdbOpen()
    On Error GoTo SQldbOpenErr
    '
    Dim cOpen As String
    Dim nTemp As Integer
    '
    cLine = Trim(cLine)  ' drop any spaces
    nTemp = InStr(cLine, " ") ' locate first embedded space
    cOpen = Mid(cLine, nTemp + 1, 255) ' get rest of line
    '
    ' if line ends w/ ";", dump it!
    If Right(cOpen, 1) = ";" Then
        cOpen = Left(cOpen, Len(cOpen) - 1)
    End If
    '
    ' now try to open database
    Set db = OpenDatabase(cOpen)
    ndbFlag = True
    GoTo SQldbOpenExit
    '
SQldbOpenErr:
    ErrMsg Err, Error$, nLine, cLine, "SQldbOpen"
    InitApp
    '
SQldbOpenExit:
    '
End Sub
```

Listing A.10 performs three tasks. First, it strips the DBOPEN keyword off the script line. Second, if a semicolon (;) appears at the end of the line, the routine drops it off the line. What's left is the valid database filename in the variable cOpen. The routine then attempts to open this file as a Microsoft Access JET database. Once that's done, the routine returns to SQLFileProcess.

The next routine to add handles the DBCLOSE command. This is a simple routine. Its only job is to close the Microsoft Access JET database. This routine also classes out any open child forms and clears flag variables. Create a Public Sub called SQLdbClose and add the code in Listing A.11.

Listing A.11. Coding the SQLdbClose routine.

```
Sub SQLdbClose()
    On Error Resume Next ' ignore errors here
    '
    db.Close
    '
    For x = 0 To nForms
        Unload TblForms(x)
    Next x
    '
    nForms = 0
    ndbFlag = False
End Sub
```

The final routine to handle special commands is the routine that processes the DBMAKE keyword to create new Microsoft Access JET databases. This one works much like the DBOPEN routine except that there are a few additional chores when creating a new file. Create a Public Sub called SQLdbMake and enter the code in Listing A.12.

Listing A.12. Coding the SQLdbMake routine.

```
Sub SQLdbMake()
    On Error GoTo SQLdbMakeErr
    '
    Dim cMake As String
    Dim nTemp As Integer
    '
    cLine = Trim(cLine)  ' drop any spaces
    nTemp = InStr(cLine, " ") ' locate first embedded space
    cMake = Mid(cLine, nTemp + 1, 255) ' get rest of line
    '
    ' if line ends w/ ";", dump it!
    If Right(cMake, 1) = ";" Then
        cMake = Left(cMake, Len(cMake) - 1)
    End If
    '
    ' try to open it (to see if it already exists)
    nSQLMakeHandle = FreeFile(0)
    Open cMake For Input As nSQLMakeHandle
    Close nSQLMakeHandle
    '
```

      nResult = MsgBox("ERASE [" + cMake + "]", vbYesNo + vbQuestion,
   ➥"Database Already Exists!")
      If nResult = vbYes Then
         Kill cMake
      Else
         ErrMsg 0, "Script Cancel - Database Already Exists",
         ➥nLine, cLine, "SQLdbMake"
         InitApp
      End If
   '
   ' now try to make a new database
SQLdbMake2:
      Set db = CreateDatabase(cMake, dbLangGeneral, dbVersion25)
      ndbFlag = True
      GoTo SQLdbMakeExit
   '
SQLdbMakeErr:
      If Err = 53 Then
         Resume SQLdbMake2
      Else
         ErrMsg Err, Error$, nLine, cLine, "SQLdbMake"
         InitApp
      End If
   '
SQLdbMakeExit:
   '
End Sub
```

A few things in this routine deserve attention. First, the routine drops the first word from the script line (the DBMAKE word). Then it strips the semicolon off the end of the line, if necessary. Then, instead of performing the create operation, the routine first tries to open the file. This is done to see if it already exists. If it does, you can issue a warning before you clobber that multimegabyte database that the user has been nursing for the last few months. If no error occurs when you try to open the file, the routine sends out a message warning the user and asking if it's okay to erase the existing file. If the answer is Yes, the file is erased. If the answer is No, a message is displayed, and the script processing is halted.

Now, if an error occurs during the attempt to open the file, you know that the file does not exist. The local error handler is invoked and the first thing checked by the local error handler is to see if the error was caused by an attempt to open a nonexistent file. If so, the error handler sends the routine to the file creation point without comment. If it's another error, the global error handler is called and the program is halted.

Finally, after all the file creation stuff is sorted out, the routine executes the Visual Basic CreateDatabase operation and returns to the SQLFileProcess routine. Notice that you declared two parameters during the CreateDatabase operation. The first parameter (vbLangGeneral) tells Visual Basic to use the general rules for sorting and collating data. The second parameter (vbVersion25) tells Visual Basic to create a version 2.5 Microsoft JET database. This data format can be read by Visual Basic 3.0, Visual Basic 4.0, and Microsoft Access 2.0.
```

The last routine called from `SQLFileProcess` handles the execution of SQL statements. Create a `Public Sub` called `SQLDoCommand` and enter the code in Listing A.13.

Listing A.13. Coding the `SQLDoCommand` routine.

```
Sub SQLDoCommand()
    On Error GoTo SQLDoCommandErr      ' set error trap
    '
    Dim cTemp As String               ' holds token
    '
    ' skip errors if you're deleting objects
    cTemp = GetToken(Trim(cSQLLine))  ' get first word
    Select Case UCase(cTemp)
       Case Is = "DELETE"             ' don't report error
          On Error Resume Next
       Case Is = "DROP"               ' don't report error
          On Error Resume Next
       Case Is = "ALTER"              ' don't report error
          On Error Resume Next
    End Select
    '
    ' check for queries that return a view
    Select Case cTemp
       Case Is = "TRANSFORM"
          ShowTable cSQLLine          ' show view form
       Case Is = "SELECT"
          If InStr(cSQLLine, " INTO ") <> 0 Then
             db.Execute cSQLLine      ' execute make-table SQL
          Else
             ShowTable cSQLLine       ' show view form
          End If
       Case Else
          db.Execute cSQLLine         ' execute SQL
    End Select
    GoTo SQlDoCommandExit             ' exit routine
    '
    ' local error handler
SQLDoCommandErr:
    ErrMsg Err, Error$, nLine, cLine, "SQLDoCommand"
    InitApp
    '
    ' routine exit
SQlDoCommandExit:
    '
End Sub
```

Even though it looks as though several things take place in this routine, only three tasks are being handled by `SQLDoCommand`. First, you get the first word in the script line, and then you have to make a couple of decisions on how to properly execute the SQL statement.

If the first word is `DELETE`, `DROP`, or `ALTER`, you turn off the local error handler. This is done for convenience. You want to be able to create scripts that can use the SQL words `DELETE`, `DROP`, and

ALTER to remove table objects from the database. Because the objects may not exist, you could get errors that can halt the script processing. To make life simple, SQL-VB ignores these errors. Once you write a few SQL-VB scripts, you'll appreciate this feature.

Next, you have to check for the SQL keywords that can return result sets. These are TRANSFORM and SELECT. These keywords should be handled differently from SQL statements that do not return result sets. If you see TRANSFORM, you call the ShowTable routine to load and display the SQLVBChild child form on the screen. If you see SELECT, you make one additional check. If the line contains the INTO keyword, you have an SQL statement that will create a new table. Using the INTO keyword means that the SELECT statement will not return a result set. If there is no INTO in the SQL statement, you hand the statement off to the ShowTable routine. If the line starts with any other SQL keyword, you simply execute the command using the Visual Basic Execute method on the database.

The SQLDoCommand routine calls the ShowTable routine, so you need to add that routine to the project. This is a simple routine that updates some variables, creates a new instance of the SQLVBChild child form, and shows the new form. Create a Public Sub called ShowTable and enter the code in Listing A.14.

Listing A.14. Coding the ShowTable routine.

```
Sub ShowTable(cSQL As String)
    '
    cGlobalSelect = cSQLLine
    cGlobaldbName = db.Name
    '
    nForms = nForms + 1
    ReDim Preserve TblForms(nForms) As Form
    Set TblForms(nForms) = New SQLVBChild
    TblForms(nForms).Show
End Sub
```

The only real fancy stuff in this module is the creation of new Form objects. Remember that you created a global array called TblForms in the declaration section of the module? This routine increases the size of the array by one each time it is invoked. Also, this routine uses the Visual Basic SET command to create a new *instance* of the SQLVBChild child form. This new instance is a *copy* of SQLVBChild that will have its one "life," once it is loaded and displayed with the Visual Basic SHOW method. You may also remember that you added code in the SQLVBChild.Form_Unload event that destroys the current instance of the form and decrements the array counter to keep everything in order.

You need to add another support routine. This one handles the loading of the scripts into the Windows Notepad for editing. This is called from the SQLVBMain MDI form. Create a Public Sub called LoadNotePadFile(cLoadMsg As String) and enter the code in Listing A.15.

Listing A.15. Coding the `LoadNotePadFile` routine.

```
Sub LoadNotePadFile(cLoadMsg As String)
    On Error GoTo LoadNotePadFileErr:
    '
    Dim cEditFile As String
    Dim nAppID As Long
    '
    SQLVBMain.CommonDialog1.DialogTitle = cLoadMsg
    SQLVBMain.CommonDialog1.DefaultExt = "SQV"
    SQLVBMain.CommonDialog1.Filter = "SQLVB File¦*.SQV"
    SQLVBMain.CommonDialog1.ShowOpen
    cEditFile = SQLVBMain.CommonDialog1.filename
    '
    If Len(cEditFile) <> 0 Then
        nAppID = Shell("NotePad " + cEditFile, 1)
        AppActivate (nAppID)
    End If
    GoTo LoadNotePadFileExit
    '
LoadNotePadFileErr:
    ErrMsg Err, Error$, 0, cEditFile, "LoadNotePadFile"
    InitApp
    '
LoadNotePadFileExit:
    '
End Sub
```

Most of this code should look familiar. The first part of the routine in Listing A.15 sets up and activates the `CommonDialog` object to allow the user to select an existing file or create a new file. Once this is done, the routine forces Windows to load a new instance of the Notepad application, and then gives that application the focus. Now the user sees the Notepad application (with the selected file loaded, too!). The SQL-VB application resumes processing once it gains the focus again.

The next routine you need to add to `SQLVBMod` is the global error handler. This routine (see Listing A.16) simply displays the error messages and waits for the user to click the OK button before it returns to the calling routine. Create a `Public Sub` called `ErrMsg` and enter the code in Listing A.16.

Listing A.16. Coding the `ErrMsg` routine.

```
Sub ErrMsg(nErr As Integer, cError As String, nLine As Integer,
➥cLine As String, cModule As String)
    Dim cMsg As String
    '
    cMsg = "ErrNo:" + Chr(9) + Str(nErr) + Chr(13)
    cMsg = cMsg + "ErrMsg: " + Chr(9) + cError + Chr(13)
    cMsg = cMsg + "LineNo:" + Chr(9) + Str(nLine) + Chr(13)
    cMsg = cMsg + "Text: " + Chr(9) + cLine
    '
    MsgBox cMsg, vbCritical, cModule
End Sub
```

No real magic in this routine. Listing A.15 is passed the Visual Basic error number and error message, the script line number and script line text, and the name of the SQL-VB routine that experienced the error. All this is formatted into a readable (if not entirely welcome) message that is displayed to the user. Notice that you used the tabs (Chr(9)) and carriage returns (Chr(13)) to make the information easier to read.

You need to add one more routine to SQLVBMod. The routine in Listing A.17 handles all the initialization chores for the start of a script. It is also called whenever an error is reported and when the program is exited. Create a Public Sub procedure called InitApp and enter the code in Listing A.17.

Listing A.17. Coding the InitApp routine.

```
Sub InitApp()
    On Error Resume Next ' ignore any errors here
    '
    ' close all child forms
    For x = 0 To nForms
        Unload TblForms(x)
    Next x
    '
    ' close open database
    If ndbFlag = True Then
        db.Close
    End If
    '
    ' close open script file
    If nSQLFlag = True Then
        Close (nSQlFileHandle)
    End If
    '
    ' reset flags & stuff
    nSQLFile = ""
    nSQLFlag = False
    ndbFlag = False
    nGlobalErr = False
    nLine = 0
    '
End Sub
```

That's the last routine in the SQLVBMod code module. Save this module and save the project before you continue. Before you run the program, you need to go back and remove comment marks from three locations in the SQLVBMain MDI form. Remove the comment mark from the following routines: mnuFileNew_Click, mnuFileRun_Click, and mnuFileEdit_Click. Also remove the comment mark from the Form_Activate event in SQLVBMain. Then save the project again. Now you are ready to compile and test the SQL-VB project.

Compiling and Testing SQL-VB

All you need to do now is compile the program as an executable and you're done. But first, let's run a test script through the system to make sure all is working properly. You'll run this test by starting SQL-VB from within Visual Basic. If all goes well, you'll create a final compiled version that will run faster.

Begin the testing by selecting Run | Start with Full Compile. This starts the SQL-VB project with a clean compilation. Once SQL-VB is up and running, you load two SQL-VB scripts and give them a test run.

The test script is called SQLVB01.SQV. This script contains a set of lines that open a database and then create several result sets to display. Before you run the first script, you should load it for edit and make sure the drive letter and path are correct for your desktop setup. To load the SQL script file, select File | Edit. This brings up the Open File dialog. Locate the SQLVB01.SQV script file in the TYSDBVB\SQLVB directory on your machine (see Figure A.4).

Figure A.4.
Loading an SQL-VB script
for testing.

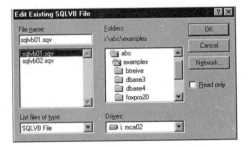

When the file is loaded into Notepad, inspect the script line that opens the database file. Make sure the path and drive letters match your desktop setup (see Figure A.5).

Figure A.5.
Editing an SQL-VB script
in Notepad.

```
//
// test sql command file for sqlvb interpreter
//

// open the database
dbOpen c:\tysdbvb\book.mdb;

// open some tables to view
SELECT * FROM Authors;
SELECT * FROM Titles;
SELECT * FROM Publishers;
SELECT * FROM BookSales;
SELECT * FROM Buyers;
SELECT * FROM [Publisher Comments];

//
```

Make any changes needed and exit Notepad. Be sure you save the script if you made any updates. Now you are ready to run the script.

To run the script, select File | Run and use the File Open dialog box to locate the SQLVB01.SQV script file. Once you select the file, the program will automatically begin processing the script. The line at the bottom of the screen shows the script lines as they are processed. The SQLVB01.SQV script opens a database and creates six result set forms before it issues a "Script Completed" message. Your screen should look like the one in Figure A.6.

Figure A.6.
Result sets created by
SQLVB01.SQV script.

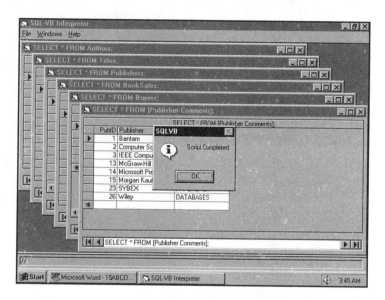

If you had problems with the script, review the SQLVB01.SQV file for errors. You may also have to review the Visual Basic code to check for program errors. If the script ran without errors, you can check out other aspects of the program, including the Windows menu and resizing the grid forms.

When you are sure that the program is working properly, you should compile it into an .EXE file. To do this, select File | Make EXE File. When prompted for the filename, enter SQLVB if you are running the 32-bit version of Visual Basic. If you are running the 16-bit version of Visual Basic, enter SQLVB16. Once the compiler has completed its work, test the file by running the .EXE version using the same SQL-VB script you used earlier.

Modifying SQL-VB

You now have a very valuable tool to add to your database programming tool kit. You can use SQL-VB to generate database layouts for all your projects in the future. You can also use

SQL-VB to test data integrity options, load test data into existing tables, and even create simple data backup and replication scripts.

You could even add more options to the project. Some additional features that you might want to consider are the following:

- ☐ Add the ability to open non-Microsoft JET database files such as dBASE, FoxPro, Paradox, and other formats via ODBC connections. This involves adding parameters to the dbOpen script line that identify the database type and any connection parameters needed. Then add code to the SQLdbOpen routine to handle the new parameters.

- ☐ Add the ability to create non-Microsoft JET database files such as dBASE, FoxPro, and Paradox. To do this, you need to add additional parameters to the dbMake script line along with corresponding code in the SQLdbMake routine to handle the added information.

- ☐ Add the ability to edit data within the grids that appear in the main form. You need to review the DBGrid control and set some additional parameters before you launch the SQLVBChild form.

- ☐ Make SQL-VB an Add-In application. This involves adding a class module to the project and declaring an SQL-VB class with at least one method that loads and processes a script. Check the Visual Basic documentation on creating OLE-enabled applications for more information on how to create a Visual Basic Add-In.

B

Answers to Quizzes and Exercises

Answers to Day 1 Quiz

1. The two properties you must set when you are linking a form to a database are the DatabaseName property and the RecordSource property.

2. Set the Caption property of the data control to display a meaningful name between the record pointer arrows.

3. You must set the DataSource property of the input control to the data table and the DataField property of the input control to the field name in the data table.

4. You only need one line of Visual Basic code (not including the Sub…End Sub statements) to add delete functionality to a data entry form when using the Visual Basic data control.

5. Set the Save Project Before Run option from the Options | Environment Menu to Yes in order to save the project before you run the program.

Answers to Day 1 Exercises

1. While in design mode, select the form by clicking anywhere on the form that doesn't have a control. Press F4 and select the Caption property. Type The Titles Program and press Enter. Note that the title appears on the title bar of the form as you type.

2. Complete the following steps to build an Exit button:

   Double-click the Command Button control on the Visual Basic toolbox to add a new button to the form.

   Set the following properties for the new button:

   Name: cmdExit

   Drag the new button to align it with the Add and Delete buttons.

   Caption: E&xit

   Enter the following code in the cmdExit_Click procedure:

   ```
   Sub cmdExit_Click()
       End
   End Sub
   ```

   Save your changes and execute your program.

   Click on the Exit button to stop the program.

3. Enter the following code in the cmdAdd_Click procedure:

   ```
   Sub Command1_Click()
       datTitles.Recordset.AddNew  ' Add a new record to the table
       Text1.SetFocus  ' Set the focus to the Text1 control (added chp3 exercise
       ➥#3
   End Sub
   ```

Answers to Day 2 Quiz

1. The three main building blocks of relational databases are data fields, data records, and data tables.

2. The smallest building block in a relational database is the data field.

3. A data record is a collection of related data fields.

4. The main role of a primary key in a data table is to maintain the internal integrity of a data table.

5. A data table can have any number of foreign keys defined. It can have only one primary key defined.

6. There are only two values that can be stored in a BOOLEAN data field: –1 (True) and 0 (False).

7. The highest value that can be stored in a BYTE field is 255. Visual Basic will allow users to enter up to 32767 without reporting an error, but any value higher than 255 will be truncated to a single-byte value.

8. Any attempt to edit and update a counter field will result in a Visual Basic error.

9. The CURRENCY data type can store up to four places to the right of the decimal. Any data beyond the fourth place will be truncated by Visual Basic without reporting an error.

10. You can use the International applet from the Windows Control Panel to determine the display format of DATE data fields.

Answers to Day 2 Exercises

1. There are three records in the table.

2. The SSN (Social Security Number) would make an excellent primary key for this table because it would be unique for all records entered.

3. The answer to part C is shown in the following table:

Field	Data Type	VISUAL BASIC Type
SSNo	Text	String
Last	Text	String
First	Text	String
Age	Byte	Integer
City	Text	String
St	Text	String
Comments	Memo	String

4. Perform the following steps to add the checkbox: First, double-click on the checkbox control. Second, position the checkbox in an aesthetically pleasing position. Third, set these properties:

Property	Setting
DataSource	datFieldTypes
DataField	BOOLEAN
Name	chkBoolean

Run your program and check the BOOLEAN box. Notice that nothing happens to the BOOLEAN text field. Now move to the subsequent record, and then return. You should see -1 displayed in the BOOLEAN text field.

This example shows how to use a checkbox to enter values into fields. Your program can now reference this field and get the value as –1 (yes) or 0 (no), which are the only two values that can be in a BOOLEAN type data field.

Answers to Day 3 Quiz

1. The advantages of using the Data Manager to create databases include the following:

   ☐ You can build the databases directly from Visual Basic 4.

   ☐ You can enter data quickly to test forms and routines that you have created to manipulate data.

   ☐ You can Compact databases.

   ☐ You can repair corrupted databases.

   ☐ You can test your SQL statements.

   ☐ You can encrypt databases to increase security.

2. The major disadvantage of the Data Manager is that it is not a complete database administration tool. You cannot print table structures or index definitions.

3. Only Microsoft Access databases (*.MDB) can be compacted with the Data Manager.

4. You can only have one Primary Key in an Access table. Remember that Access databases have multiple tables, each having at most only one primary key.

5. You can use the Data Manager to remove indexes from a table. You cannot, however, use the Data Manager to remove the field on which your index was created until the index itself is removed.

6. The statement means to display all names and phone numbers found in the CompanyMaster database.

Answers to Day 3 Exercise

Complete the following steps to build your data table and enter data:

1. Start Visual Basic 4.

2. Select Data Manager from the Add/Ins menu.

3. From the Data Manager menu bar, select File | New Database.

4. Enter an appropriate name and location in the New Database dialog box.

5. Select the New button from the Tables/QueryDefs form. Provide an appropriate name, such as Address.

6. Add fields such as SSN (a unique identifier of the individual), LastName, FirstName, Address1, Address2, StateProv, Country, and Zip.

7. Enter a Primary Key index with a descriptive name, such as PKCompanyMaster. Add the Social Security Number field, and press Add (ASC). Finally, check the Primary Index box to designate this as the primary key.

   It is recommended that you not depend on the combination of the LastName and the FirstName fields as the unique identifier for the record. It is quite possible to have two people with the same first and last name. Also, complex multifield primary keys make query design much more difficult.

   If you have followed the exercises in this chapter closely, you may remember that we did build a key for a table using the last name, first name field combination. This was for illustrative purposes only and was meant only to show how to combine fields in a key. This practice is not recommended for combinations of fields that could have multiple occurrences (how many John Smiths are there in the world?), and is definitely taboo for primary keys. In fact, a good rule of thumb to remember is that the need for a multifield primary key is indicative of a database that needs to be redesigned.

8. Close the Table Design dialog.

9. Select the Open button from the Tables dialog.

10. Select Add to enter your first record. Create information to be entered. Select Update to commit your entries. Move through entry fields by pressing the Tab key. Move backward by pressing the Shift and Tab keys simultaneously.

11. Enter several records in this fashion. Click the arrow buttons on the data control at the bottom of the screen to move through the data records after you have entered them.

Answers to Day 4 Quiz

1. Visual Basic database objects are data set oriented. You will work with a set of records at one time, not one record at a time as you would with a record-oriented database.

2. The `Dynaset` is the most common Visual Basic data object. It is the object that is created when you open a form with a data control.

3. `Dynasets` use minimal RAM resources. Visual Basic stores only the pointers to the records in the underlying table, not the actual data.

4. Weaknesses of using `Dynasets` include the following:

   ☐ You can't specify an index with a `Dynaset`. `Dynasets` are only a portion of the underlying table, whereas indexes are for the entire table.

   ☐ You can't use the `Seek` method with `Dynasets`.

   ☐ Errors can occur if records in the underlying table have been altered or deleted between the time that the `Dynaset` is created and the time that a record is updated.

5. Table data objects allow you to utilize indexes and the `Seek` method.

6. You do not use the `Refresh` method with the `Table` data object because this object is the underlying data.

7. You must use code to open a `Table` object in Visual Basic.

8. A `Snapshot` stores all the data in the workstation's memory, whereas the `Dynaset` stores only pointers to the data. The `Snapshot` is also read-only and can't be updated. A `Dynaset` can be updated.

9. You use the `Database` data object to extract field and table names from a database.

Answers to Day 4 Exercises

1. You would use the `Dynaset` data object because it is the only data object that can update an ODBC data source. Your code could look similar to the following:

```
Sub Form_Load()

'Create a database and dynaset object
Dim Dat as Database
Dim dyn1 as Dynaset

'Declare standard variables
Dim cDBN ame as String
Dim cTable as String

'Initialize variables
cDBName = "c:\DATAS\ACCTPAY.MDB"
cTable = "Vendors"
```

```
'Set values
set Dat = OpenDatabase(cDBName)
Set dyn1 = Dat.CreateDynaset(cTable)

End Sub
```

2. The Snapshot data object should be used for this purpose because it will not change after it is created. This will prevent the data used in your report from being updated while your report is generating.

Your code could look as follows:

```
Sub Form_Load()

'Create a database and snapshot object
Dim Dat as Database
Dim snpObject as Snapshot

'Declare standard variables
Dim cDBName as String
Dim cTable as String

'Initialize variables
cDBName = "c:\DATAS\ACCTPAY.MDB"
cTable = "Vendors"

'Set values
set Dat = OpenDatabase(cDBName)
Set snpObject = Dat.CreateSnapshot(cTable)

End Sub
```

3. You would use the Table data object because it will give you instant information when records are changed. Your code could look like the following:

```
Sub Form_Load()

'Create a database and table object
Dim Dat as Database
Dim tblObject as Table

'Declare standard variables
Dim cDBName as String
Dim cTable as String

'Initialize variables
cDBName = "c:\DATAS\ACCTPAY.MDB"
cTable = "Vendors"

'Set values
set Dat = OpenDatabase(cDBName)
Set tblObject = Dat.OpenTable(cTable)

End Sub
```

Answers to Day 5 Quiz

1. You can establish a database for a data control by setting the DatabaseName property of the data control to the name of the database (including the path), or to a defined variable that points to the database. For example, to attach the data control Data1 to a Microsoft Access database C:\DATAPATH\XYZ.MDB, you can enter the following:

```
Data1.DatabaseName = "C:\DATAPATH\XYZ.MDB"
```

2. You use the RecordSource property to establish the name of a table for a data control in Visual Basic. For example, to set the data control Data1 to a table of vendors in an accounts payable application, you can type the following:

```
Data1.RecordSource = "Vendors"
```

It is better form, however, to assign the RecordSource to a variable that has been defined and points to the data table. Here's an example:

```
Dim cTable as String' Declare the variable
cTable = "Vendors" ' Establish the name of the table
Data1.RecordSource = cTable ' Set the data control
Data1.Refresh ' Update the data control
```

3. The UpdateControls method takes information from the underlying database table and places it in the form controls; whereas the UpdateRecord method takes information entered into the form controls and updates the attached table.

4. Checkboxes should only be bound to Boolean fields and can only produce values of 0 (No or False) and –1 (Yes or True).

5. You use the DataField property to bind a control to a table field.

6. The standard color for a Windows 95 form is light gray. Input areas are white. Display-only controls are light gray. Labels are left-aligned.

Answers to Day 5 Exercises

1. You should enter the following code as a new procedure in the general declarations section:

```
Sub OpenDB()
'Declare the variable for the name of the database
Dim cDBName as String

'Assign the variable to a database, including the path
cdbName = App.Path + " \Students.MDB"

'Set the name of the database used by the data control
Data1.DatabaseName = cDBName

'Refresh and update the data control
Data1.Refresh

End Sub
```

2. Your code should look like this:

```
Sub OpenDB()

    'Declare the variable for the name of the database
    Dim cDBName as String
    'Declare the variable for the table
    Dim cTable as String

    'Assign the variable to a database, including the path
    cdbName = App.Path + "\Students.MDB"
    'Assign the variable to the appropriate table
    cTable = "Addresses"

    'Set the name of the database used by the data control
    Data1.DatabaseName = cDBName
    'Set the name of the table used by the data control
    Data1.RecordSource = cTable

    'Refresh and update the data control
    Data1.Refresh

End Sub
```

3. Your code should look like this:

```
Sub OpenDB()

Dim cDBName as String
Dim cTable as String
Dim cField1 as String
Dim cField2 as String
Dim cField3 as String
Dim cField4 as String
Dim cField5 as String

'Assign variables
cdbName = App.Path + "\Students.MDB"
cTable = "Addresses"
cField1 = "StudentID
cField2 = "Address"
cField3 = "City"
cField4 = "State"
cField5 = "Zip"

'Set the data control properties
Data1.DatabaseName = cDBName
Data1.RecordSource = cTable

'Bind the text fields
txtStudentID.DataField = cField1
txtAddress.DataField = cField2
txtCity.DataField = cField3
txtState.DataField = cField4
txtZip.DataField = cField5

'Refresh and update the data control
Data1.Refresh
End Sub
```

Answers to Day 6 Quiz

1. Input validation occurs as the data is entered, whereas error trapping occurs after the data is entered. Input validation is used to guarantee uniformity in the data that is saved.

2. Subtracting 32 from the lowercase value will return the uppercase value.

3. The KeyPress event occurs whenever a key is pressed.

4. No, a validation list can be entered in any order.

5. The field txtUpper is being trimmed of spaces and then is being tested to see whether the length is anything other than zero. This code is used to test whether any values are entered into a field. The Trim command is used to remove any spaces entered into the field either intentionally or inadvertently.

6. Conditional field validation should be performed at the form level. Users may skip around on the form using the mouse, thus making field level validation impractical.

7. Validation lists should be loaded by the Form_Load procedure.

8. The first section is the format of a positive number. The second section is the format of a negative number. The third section is the format of zero. Each section is separated by a semicolon (;).

Answers to Day 6 Exercises

1. Enter the following code inside your field's KeyPress event:

```
Sub FieldName_KeyPress(KeyAscii as Integer)
    If KeyAscii >26 then 'If anything other than a control code
        If Chr(KeyAscii) >= "a" and Chr(KeyAscii) <= "z" Then
            KeyAscii = KeyAscii - 32 ' Capitalize small letters
        Else
            KeyAscii = 0 ' No input from keyboard
        End if
    End if
End Sub
```

2. #,##0.00;-#,##0.00

3. Enter the following code into the cmdOK_Click event:

```
Sub cmdOK_Click ()

    Dim nOK as Integer ' Declare a test variable

    nOK = True

    If Len(Trim(txtDate)) = 0 then ' Check for entry (exclusive of spaces)
        MsgBox "Input is required in the txtDate field before this record
        ➥can be saved" ' Issue a message if no data is entered
```

```
        nOK = False 'Set test variable to False
        txtDate.SetFocus ' Place cursor in txtDate
    End if

    If nOK = True then
        Unload Me ' Exit form if data is entered
    End if
End sub
```

4. Enter the following code in the Form_Load event:

```
Sub Form_Load()

    'Load the combo box
    cboEmployees.AddItem "Smith"
    cboEmployees.AddItem "Andersen"
    cboEmployees.AddItem "Jones"
    cboEmployees.AddItem "Jackson"

End sub
```

You set the Sorted property of the combo box to True to alphabetically sort the information displayed in the combo box. This property can only be set at design time.

Answers to Day 7 Quiz

1. The three bands are the header, footer, and detail bands. The header is used to insert information that displays on the top of each page of the report. The footer band inserts information on the bottom of each page of the report. The detail band displays the actual information.

2. Crystal Reports can attach to any database type recognized by Visual Basic 4. This includes Microsoft Access, dBASE, FoxPro, Btrieve, Paradox, and any ODBC data source.

3. You can type text directly on a form in Crystal Reports, but remember that it cannot be moved or resized (you can, however, change the font size and appearance). The more versatile way to enter text is with the Text Field option from the Insert menu.

4. You can produce mailing labels in Crystal Reports by selecting New Mailing Labels Report from the File menu.

5. You can browse data in a database by choosing a field on the report during design time and selecting Browse Field Data from the Edit Menu.

6. Yes, you can add select criteria to your Crystal Reports report by choosing Select Records from the Report menu and then entering your criteria.

7. You can join tables in Crystal Reports by selecting Links from the Database menu option.

Answers to Day 7 Exercises

1. Here is the formula:

   `Count({NameLast})`

2. `IsNull({EmployerID})`

3. Perform the following steps to build the report:

   - [ ] Start Crystal Reports and select New | Report from the File menu. Select the Book.mdb. database.

   - [ ] Choose Printer Setup from the File menu and then select the Landscape option.

   - [ ] Double-click the PubID field in the Publisher Comments table and drop the field on the form.

   - [ ] Select Link from the Database menu. Create the link between the Publisher Comments and the Publishers tables on the PubID field.

   - [ ] Add the Publisher and Comments fields from the Publisher Comments table.

   - [ ] Select Record Sort Order from the Report menu. Double-click the Name field and set the sort direction to descending.

   - [ ] Select Text Field from the Insert menu. Enter `Comments on Publishers` as the title text and then select Accept. Drop the field in the middle of the header.

   - [ ] Select Font from the Format menu. Select Arial, 14 point bold and press OK.

   - [ ] To insert the count of the records, select the PubID field and then choose Grand Total from the Insert menu. Select Count from the combo box that appears and then press OK.

   - [ ] Select Special Field | Print Date Field from the Insert menu. Drop the field on the bottom left of the form.

   - [ ] Select Special Field | Page Number Field from the Insert menu. Drop the field on the bottom right of the form.

   - [ ] Print the report by selecting Print | Printer from the File menu.

   - [ ] Print the report definition by selecting Print | Report Definition from the File menu.

Answers to Day 8 Quiz

1. The Visdata project can be found in the Samples\Visdata subdirectory of Visual Basic 4.

2. To copy a table, simply select the table from the Table | Queries window, press the alternate mouse button, and select Copy Structure.

3. You need to Refresh the Tables | Queries window each time you enter an SQL statement to create a new table.

4. You can open and edit Excel spreadsheets in Visdata.

5. The Files | Properties | DbEngine menu option shows the version of the database engine in use, the login time-out, the .INI path, the default user, and the default password for the current database.

6. You compact databases to remove empty spaces where deleted records used to reside and to reorganize any defined indexes that are stored in the database.

7. You can compact a database onto itself with the Compact MDB command. This action is not advisable, however, as problems can occur during the compacting process.

8. You cannot modify a table's structure once data has been entered. You must delete all records before you can modify the structure.

9. You can save queries in Visdata for future use. You do this by building a query with the Query Builder and saving the results, or by entering an SQL statement and saving its result set.

10. Visdata can export data in the following formats:

    ☐ JET (Microsoft Access)
    ☐ dBASE IV, III
    ☐ FoxPro 2.6, 2.5, 2.0
    ☐ Paradox 4, 3
    ☐ Excel 5, 4, 3
    ☐ Text
    ☐ ODBC

11. You can use the Files | Compact Database to convert existing JET 1.1 or JET 2.0 databases to newer versions by selecting the new data format at the Compact Database submenu.

Answers to Day 8 Exercises

1. To create the new database select these menu items:

   File | New | JET Engine MDB | Version 2.0 MDB

   Next, enter the path and the name of the database and save.

2. Select New from the Table | Queries window to build the new table. Insert the name tblCustomers in the Table Name field. Next, select Add to insert the fields. Enter the

name, type, and size for each field, clicking OK after each is completed. When all fields are entered, select Close. When you return to the Table Structure form, select Build Table.

3. To build the primary key, first make sure that tblCustomers is highlighted in the Tables\Queries window, and select Design. Select Add Index button from the Table Structure window. Enter the name of the primary key (PKtblCustomers), and double-click the ID field in the Available Fields list box. Make sure that the Primary and Unique checkboxes have been checked. Finally, click OK to build the primary key index.

4. Select the tblCustomers table from the Tables | Queries window and click Design. Next, select Print Structure in the bottom right corner of the Table Structure window.

5. To enter records, first make sure that tblCustomers is highlighted. Then, select Open from the Tables | Queries window. You will be able to enter data in any Form type you would like to use. You will, however, only be able to enter Notes data in the Grid form.

6. To copy a table structure, highlight the table, click the alternate mouse button, and select Copy Structure. Leave the Target Connect String empty and make sure that neither the Copy Indexes, nor the Copy Data checkboxes are checked. Enter the table name tblVendors when prompted for the name of the new table. Select the OK button to create the table.

   Once the table is copied, you should then go into the table design and add a primary key. Build this index the same way you built the primary key for the tblCustomers table.

7. To export, select Utility | Import/Export. Select the tblCustomers table and then press Export Table(s). Next choose the text format as the data source, and click OK. You are then prompted to enter a path and a name. Select Save, and the file is created.

   Review the file. Notice that empty fields in a record are denoted by the use of two commas (,,).

Answers to Day 9 Quiz

1. SQL stands for Structured Query Language. You pronounce SQL by saying the three individual letters. It is not pronounced *sequel*.

2. Use the SELECT…FROM statement to select information from table fields.

3. Use the asterisk (*) in a SELECT…FROM statement to select all the fields in a data table. For example, to select all fields in a table of customers, you can enter the following SQL statement:

```
SELECT * FROM Customers
```

4. Use the ORDER BY clause to sort the data you display. For example, to sort the data from quiz answer 3 by a field contained within the table, CustomerID, you would enter the following:

```
SELECT * FROM Customers ORDER BY CustomerID
```

5. A WHERE clause can be used to limit the records that are selected by the SQL statement, as well as to link two or more tables in a result set.

6. Use the AS clause to rename a field heading. For example, issue the following SQL statement to rename the field CustomerID in the Customers table to Customer.

```
SELECT CustomerID AS Customer FROM Customers
```

7. SQL aggregate functions are a core set of functions available in all SQL-compliant systems used to return computed results on numeric data fields. The functions available through JET include AVG, COUNT, SUM, MAX, and MIN.

8. Chief among the drawbacks of using Visual Basic functions in your SQL statement is the loss of portability to other database engines. There is also a slight performance reduction when Visual Basic functions are used in your SQL statement.

9. Both the DISTINCT and DISTINCTROW clauses extract unique records. The DISTINCTROW command looks at the entire record, whereas DISTINCT looks at the fields you associate with it.

10. You should always use the ORDER BY clause when you use the TOP n or TOP n PERCENT clauses. The ORDER BY clause ensures that your data is sorted appropriately to allow the TOP n clauses to select the appropriate data.

11. The three types of joins found in Microsoft Access JET SQL are INNER, LEFT, and RIGHT. An INNER join is used to create updateable result sets whose records have an exact match in both tables. The LEFT join is used to return an updateable result set that returns all records in the first table in your SQL statement, and any records in the second table that have matching column values. The RIGHT join is just the opposite of the LEFT join; it returns all records in the second table of your SQL statement and any records in the first table that have matching column values.

12. UNION queries are used to join tables that contain similar information but are not linked through a foreign key. An example of a UNION query would be listing all of your company's customers and suppliers located in the state of Iowa. There won't be any foreign key relationships between a data table of supplier's information and a table of customer's information. Both tables will, however, contain fields for names, addresses, and phone numbers. This information can be joined through a UNION query and displayed as one result.

Answers to Day 9 Exercises

1. `SELECT * FROM CustomerMaster`

2. `SELECT InvoiceNo, CustomerID AS Account, Description, Amount FROM OpenInvoice`

3. `SELECT InvoiceNo, CustomerID AS Account, Description, Amount FROM OpenInvoice ORDER BY CustomerID, InvoiceNo`

4. `SELECT * FROM Suppliers WHERE City LIKE ("New York *") and State = "NY"`

5. `SELECT CustomerMaster.CustomerType, CustomerMaster.Name, CustomerMaster.Address, CustomerMaster.City, CustomerMaster.State, CustomerMaster.Zip FROM CustomerMaster WHERE CustomerMaster.CustomerType = "ABC"`

6. `SELECT CustomerID, Name FROM CustomerMaster WHERE Left(Name,3) = "AME"`

7. `SELECT DISTINCT OpenInvoice.CustomerID, CustomerMaster.Name FROM OpenInvoice INNER JOIN CustomerMaster ON  OpenInvoice.CustomerID = CustomerMaster.CustomerID ORDER BY OpenInvoice.CustomerID`

8. `SELECT TOP 5 * FROM OpenInvoice ORDER BY Amount Desc`

9. `SELECT Name, Phone FROM CustomerMaster WHERE State = "OHIO" UNION SELECT Name, Phone FROM Suppliers WHERE State = "Ohio"`

Answers to Day 10 Quiz

1. *JET* is short for Joint Engine Technology.

2. A property is data within an object that describes its characteristics, whereas a method is a procedure that can be performed upon an object. You set a property, and invoke a method.

3. The top level DAO is the `DBEngine`.

4. You use the `RepairDatabase` method to repair a database. This command uses the following syntax:

   `DBEngine.RepairDatabase DatabaseName`

5. The syntax for the `CompactDatabase` method is

   `DBEngine.CompactDatabase oldDatabase, newDatabase, locale, options`

   Please note that `oldDatabase` and `newDatabase` require the database name and path.

6. Visual Basic creates a default `Workspace` if you fail to identify one when you open a database.

7. The `OpenRecordset` method can open data from a data source as a Table, Dynaset, or Snapshot.

8. The only difference between the `Execute` and the `ExecuteSQL` methods is that the `ExecuteSQL` method returns the number of rows affected by the SQL statement.

9. The `CreateTableDef` method builds a table in a database. The syntax of this statement is

   `Database.CreateTableDef(table name)`

10. Use the Type property of the `Field` object to display the data type of a table column.

11. The `Index` data object can be used to contain information on Microsoft JET databases only.

12. The `QueryDef` object stores Structure Query Language (SQL) statements. A `QueryDef` is faster than an actual SQL statement because Visual Basic has to perform an additional preprocessing step for an SQL statement, which it does not need to perform for the `QueryDef`.

Answer to Day 10 Exercise

Drop a command button onto a form, name it cmdCreate, and then enter the following code:

```
Private Sub cmdCreate_Click()

    On Error Resume Next

    'Define Variables
    Dim dbFile As DATABASE
    Dim cDBName As String
    Dim tdTemp As TableDef
    Dim fldTemp As Field
    Dim idxTemp As Index
    Dim relTemp As Relation
    Dim ctblCustomers As String
    Dim ctblCustomerTypes As String
    Dim cidxCustomers As String
    Dim cidxCustomerTypes As String
    Dim crelName As String

    'Set variables
    cDBName = App.Path + "\10ABCEX.MDB"
    ctblCustomers = "Customers"
    ctblCustomerTypes = "CustomerTypes"
    cidxCustomers = "PKCustomers"
    cidxCustomerTypes = "PKCustomerTypes"
    crelName = "relCustomerType"

    'Delete the database if it already exists
    Kill cDBName

    'Create the database
    Set dbFile = CreateDatabase(cDBName, dbLangGeneral, dbVersion20)
```

```
'Create the Customers table
Set tdTemp = dbFile.CreateTableDef(ctblCustomers)

'Insert fields into the Customers table
Set fldTemp = tdTemp.CreateField("CustomerID", dbText, 10)
tdTemp.Fields.Append fldTemp
Set fldTemp = tdTemp.CreateField("Name", dbText, 50)
tdTemp.Fields.Append fldTemp
Set fldTemp = tdTemp.CreateField("Address1", dbText, 50)
tdTemp.Fields.Append fldTemp
Set fldTemp = tdTemp.CreateField("Address2", dbText, 50)
tdTemp.Fields.Append fldTemp
Set fldTemp = tdTemp.CreateField("City", dbText, 25)
tdTemp.Fields.Append fldTemp
Set fldTemp = tdTemp.CreateField("StateProv", dbText, 25)
tdTemp.Fields.Append fldTemp
Set fldTemp = tdTemp.CreateField("Zip", dbText, 10)
tdTemp.Fields.Append fldTemp
Set fldTemp = tdTemp.CreateField("Phone", dbText, 14)
tdTemp.Fields.Append fldTemp
Set fldTemp = tdTemp.CreateField("CustomerType", dbText, 10)
tdTemp.Fields.Append fldTemp

'Build the Primary Key index to the Customers table
Set idxTemp = tdTemp.CREATEINDEX(cidxCustomers)
idxTemp.PRIMARY = True
idxTemp.Required = True
Set fldTemp = tdTemp.CreateField("CustomerID")
idxTemp.Fields.Append fldTemp
tdTemp.Indexes.Append idxTemp

'Add the Customers table to the databases
dbFile.TableDefs.Append tdTemp

'Create the Customer Types table
Set tdTemp = dbFile.CreateTableDef(ctblCustomerTypes)

'Insert fields into the Customer Types table
Set fldTemp = tdTemp.CreateField("CustomerType", dbText, 10)
tdTemp.Fields.Append fldTemp
Set fldTemp = tdTemp.CreateField("Description", dbText, 10)
tdTemp.Fields.Append fldTemp

'Build the Primary Key index for the Customer Types table
Set idxTemp = tdTemp.CREATEINDEX(cidxCustomerTypes)
idxTemp.PRIMARY = True
idxTemp.Required = True
Set fldTemp = tdTemp.CreateField("CustomerType")
idxTemp.Fields.Append fldTemp
tdTemp.Indexes.Append idxTemp

'Add the CustomerTypes table to the database
dbFile.TableDefs.Append tdTemp
```

```
'Create the relationship
Set relTemp = dbFile.CreateRelation(crelName)
relTemp.TABLE = ctblCustomerTypes
➥' The tabl that contains the validation information
relTemp.ForeignTable = ctblCustomers
➥' The table that utilizes the validation table
Set fldTemp = relTemp.CreateField("CustomerType")
fldTemp.ForeignName = "CustomerType"
relTemp.Fields.Append fldTemp
dbFile.Relations.Append relTemp

'Issue a message when the procedure is completed
MsgBox "Database build is complete"

End Sub
```

Answers to Day 11 Quiz

1. The chief advantage of using the Data Control is that you can quickly build a Visual Basic database application without the use of much code. The disadvantages of using the Data Control include the following:

   ☐ The project will be more difficult to maintain.

   ☐ Data entry forms will not be as easily utilized in other database applications.

2. The chief advantage of using code to build Visual Basic data entry forms is that you have complete control of the process. Code can also be used in other Visual Basic projects to quickly build forms.

3. The Find method most resembles the SQL WHERE clause.

4. The Seek method can be utilized only on recordsets opened as tables. Seek cannot be utilized on Dynasets or Snapshots.

5. The four Move methods that can be applied to the recordset object are MoveFirst, MovePrevious, MoveNext, and MoveLast.

6. The FindFirst method starts its search from the beginning of the recordset. The FindLast method starts its search from the end of the recordset.

7. You use the Bookmark to remember a specific location in a data set.

8. The Seek method is the fastest way to locate a record in a data set.

9. You create a control array in Visual Basic by copying and pasting a control on a form and answering Yes when prompted to create a control array by Visual Basic.

10. You must invoke the Edit or AddNew method prior to writing to a data set with the Update method.

Answers to Day 11 Exercise

Perform the following steps to complete the addition of the ZipCity form:

1. Open Visdata and create the new table ZipCity. Add a field for Zip code (Zip) and for city (City).

2. Modify the menu on the Company master form by adding mnuListZip with a caption of &Zip/City.

3. Add the following code to the `mnuListZip_Click` event:

```
Private Sub mnuListZip_Click()

    'Open the ZipCity form
    frmZipCity.Show 1

End Sub
```

4. Create a new form (frmZipCity) and add a field for Zip and a field for City. Set the Tag property of these two text boxes to Zip and City, respectively.

5. Add a control array to this form. Do this by adding a command button, naming it cmdBtn, and then copying and pasting it seven times.

6. Make the following variable declarations in the General Declaration of your form:

```
Option Explicit

Dim dbFile As DATABASE
Dim cDBName As String
Dim rsFile As Recordset
Dim cRSName As String
Dim nBtnAlign As Integer
Dim nResult As Integer
```

7. Add the following procedure to your form:

```
Sub StartProc()
    '
    ' open db and rs
    '
    ' on error goto StartProcErr
    '
    cDBName = App.Path + "\master.mdb"
    cRSName = "ZipCity"
    '
    nResult = RSOpen(cDBName, cRSName, dbOpenDynaset, dbFile, rsFile)
    If nResult = recOK Then
        nResult = RecInit(Me)
    End If
    '
    If nResult = recOK Then
        nResult = RecRead(Me, rsFile)
    End If
    '
    GoTo StartProcExit
    '
```

```
StartProcErr:
    RecError Err, Error$, "StartProc"
    GoTo StartProcExit
    '
StartProcExit:
    '
End Sub
```

8. Add the following to the frmZipCity Form_Load event:

```
Private Sub Form_Load()

    ' initialize and start up
    '
    StartProc ' open files
    nResult = RecEnable(Me, False)    ' turn off controls
    nBtnAlign = btnAlignBottom        ' set aligment var
    BtnBarInit Me, nBtnAlign          ' create button set
    BtnBarEnable Me, "11111111"       ' enable all buttons

End Sub
```

9. Add the following to the Form_Resize event:

```
Private Sub Form_Resize()
    BtnBarInit Me, nBtnAlign      ' repaint buttons
End Sub
```

10. Add the following to the Form_Unload event:

```
Private Sub Form_Unload(Cancel As Integer)
    dbFile.Close      ' safe close
End Sub
```

From this point, save your work and run the project. Please note that most of this code can be copied directly from the StateProv example.

Answers to Day 12 Quiz

1. The use of graphics in your Visual Basic database applications offers the following advantages:

    ☐ Visual representation of data is easier to understand than tables or lists.

    ☐ Graphics offer a different view of the data.

    ☐ Graphics give your application a polished appearance.

2. The NumSets property determines how many groups of data will be plotted. The NumPoints property shows how many points will be plotted in the group.

3. No, graphBar3D should be gphBar3D.

4. The Tab character, Chr(9), separates data points in a series. The carriage return/line feed combination—Chr(13) + Chr(10)—separates data sets for QuickData.

5. Yes, GraphTitle is a valid property.

6. `gphBlit` sets the graph control to bitmap mode.

   `gphCopy` copies the graph to the Windows Clipboard.

   `gphDraw` draws the graph on-screen.

7. The Variant data type must be used for all optional arguments.

8. The `IsMissing()` function can be used to determine whether an optional argument has been passed. This function returns TRUE if the optional argument is *not* passed.

9. You should use the snapshot data type for graphics applications if possible. Snapshots might not be useable if large quantities of data are being graphed and workstation resources are limited.

10. The following code moves the data pointer to the end of a data set and counts the total number of records in the set:

```
Dim nPoints as Integer
Dim rsData as Recordset

rsData.Movelast
nPoints = rsData.RecordCount
```

Answers to Day 12 Exercises

You can complete this project by performing the following steps:

1. Create the database in Visdata. Build the table, add the fields, and enter the data.

2. Start Visual Basic and begin a new project. Insert LIBGRAPH.BAS and FRMGRAPH.FRM into your project.

3. Build the new form by adding the command buttons. Insert the following code behind each button:

```
Private Sub cmdPie_Click()

    Dim rsFile As Recordset
    Dim dbFile As DATABASE
    Dim cSQL As String
    Dim cField As String
    Dim cTitle As String
    Dim cLegend As String
    Dim cLabel As String
    Dim dbName As String

    cSQL = "Select * from Activity WHERE month =1"
    cField = "Passengers"
    cLegend = ""
    cLabel = "Airline"
    cTitle = "Market Share for January"
    dbName = "c:\abc\ch12\12abcex.mdb"

    Set dbFile = DBEngine.OpenDatabase(dbName)
    Set rsFile = dbFile.OpenRecordset(cSQL, dbOpenSnapshot)

    ShowGraph gphPie3D, rsFile, cField, cTitle,
```

```
    ➥cFldLegend:=cLegend, cFldLabel:=cLabel

End Sub

Private Sub cmdLine_Click()

    Dim rsFile As Recordset
    Dim dbFile As DATABASE
    Dim cSQL As String
    Dim cField As String
    Dim cTitle As String
    Dim cLegend As String
    Dim cLabel As String
    Dim dbName As String

    cSQL = "Select Month, Sum(Passengers) as TotPassengers from
    ➥Activity Group by Month;"
    cField = "TotPassengers"
    cLegend = ""
    cLabel = "Month"
    cTitle = "Total Activity"
    dbName = "c:\abc\ch12\12abcex.mdb"

    Set dbFile = DBEngine.OpenDatabase(dbName)
    Set rsFile = dbFile.OpenRecordset(cSQL, dbOpenSnapshot)

    ShowGraph gphLine, rsFile, cField, cTitle,
    ➥cFldLegend:=cLegend, cFldLabel:=cLabel,
    ➥cLeftTitle:="Passengers", cBottomTitle:="Month"

End Sub

Private Sub cmdBar_Click()
    Dim rsFile As Recordset
    Dim dbFile As DATABASE
    Dim cSQL As String
    Dim cField As String
    Dim cTitle As String
    Dim cLegend As String
    Dim cLabel As String
    Dim dbName As String

    cSQL = "Select * from Activity WHERE Airline='ABC';"
    cField = "Passengers"
    cLegend = ""
    cLabel = "Month"
    cTitle = "ABC Airlines Annual Activity"
    dbName = "c:\abc\ch12\12abcex.mdb"

    Set dbFile = DBEngine.OpenDatabase(dbName)
    Set rsFile = dbFile.OpenRecordset(cSQL, dbOpenSnapshot)

    ShowGraph gphBar3D, rsFile, cField, cTitle,
    ➥cFldLegend:=cLegend, cFldLabel:=cLabel,
    ➥cLeftTitle:="Passengers", cBottomTitle:="Month"

End Sub
```

B

Answers to Day 13 Quiz

1. Using a data-bound list or combo box increases the speed of data entry, gives you added control over data validation, and provides suggested values to use for entry.

2. You set the RowSource property to identify the data source for the list box.

3. The BoundColumn property sets the column that is saved in the new data record. Put another way, it's the field that is extracted from the source and placed in the destination. Remember that the bound column does not have to equal the ListField property of the control.

4. You set the DataSource property to set the name of the data set that should be updated by the contents of the data-bound list/combo box. You set the DataField property to identify the field in the data set determined by the DataSource property that will be updated.

5. You must set the AllowAddNew property to True to permit users to add records. You must set the `AllowDelete` method to True to permit removal of records.

6. Use the `BeforeDelete` event to confirm deletion of records.

7. The Column-Level events of the Data-Bound Grid control provide field level validation functionality.

8. You would use the data-bound combo box, rather than the data-bound list box, when you want to allow the user to type the entry or when space on the data entry form is limited.

9. You use the `ReBind` method to refresh a data-bound grid.

10. Subforms are typically used to display data from two different data tables that are linked through a common key. For example, Subforms can display invoice detail of a customer linked by customer ID, or work orders that have been performed on a fixed asset linked by asset ID.

Answers to Day 13 Exercises

Complete the following steps to build this form:

1. Add a data control (Data1) and a data-bound list box to a new form.

2. Set the following properties of Data1:

DatabaseName	C:\VB4\BIBLIO.MDB (include appropriate path)
RecordSource	Publishers

3. Set the DataSource property to Data1 and the ListField property to Name for the data-bound list.

4. Add a second data control (Data2) and set its Database property to BIBLIO.MDB and its RecordSource property to Publishers.

5. Add text fields in an array to the form. Set their DataSource properties to Data2 and their DataField properties to their respective fields.

6. Add a third data control to the form. Set its DatabaseName to BIBLIO.MDB (include path) and its RecordSource property to Titles.

7. Set the Visible property of all three data controls to False.

8. Add a data-bound grid to the form. Set its DataSource property to Data3.

9. Load the data set column names into the grid by selecting Retrieve Fields from the context menu of the DBGrid. Then select Properties from the context menu of the DBGrid and click on the Columns tab. Make sure that the Visible checkbox is selected only for the Title, Year Published, and ISBN columns.

10. Use the context menu again on the DBGrid and select Edit. Resize the columns as needed.

11. Set the BoundColumn property of the data-bound list control to PubID. Blank out the DataField and DataSource properties.

12. Enter the following code in the DBList1_click event:

```
Private Sub DBList1_Click()

    Dim cFind As String

    cFind = "PubID=" + Trim(DBList1.BoundText)
    Data2.Recordset.FindFirst cFind

End Sub
```

13. Enter the following code in the Data2_Reposition event:

```
Private Sub Data2_Reposition()

    Dim cSQL As String

    cSQL = "Select * from Titles WHERE PubID=" + Trim(Text1(0))

    Data3.RecordSource = cSQL ' filter the data set
    Data3.Refresh ' refresh the data control
    DBGrid1.ReBind ' refresh the data grid

End Sub
```

14. Save and execute your program.

Answers to Day 14 Quiz

1. These are the three main parts of error handlers in Visual Basic:
   - ☐ The On Error Goto statement
   - ☐ The error handler code
   - ☐ The Exit statement

2. The four ways to exit an error handler routine are as follows:
   - ☐ Resume: Returns to execute the code that caused the error.
   - ☐ Resume Next: Resumes execution of the Visual Basic code at the line immediately following the line that created the error.
   - ☐ Resume label: Resumes execution at a specified location in the program that caused the error.
   - ☐ EXIT SUB or EXIT function: Exits the routine in which the error occurred. You could also use END to exit the program completely.

3. You use Resume to exit an error handler when the user has done something that he or she can easily correct. For example, the user may have forgotten to insert a disk in drive A or close the drive door.

4. You would use Resume Next to exit an error handler when the program runs properly even though an error has been reported, or if code within the program corrects the problem.

5. You use Resume label to exit an error handler when you want the program to return to a portion of code that allows for correction of the invalid entry. For example, if the user inputs numeric data that yields improper results (division by zero, for example) you may want the code to redisplay the input screen so that entry can be corrected.

6. You would use the EXIT or END command to terminate the program when there is no good way to return to the program once the error has occurred. This may occur if the user forgot to log onto a network or if there is insufficient memory to run the program.

7. The following are the four types of Visual Basic errors:
   - ☐ GENERAL FILE ERRORS: Errors that occur when you try to open, read, or write file information.
   - ☐ DATABASE ERRORS: Errors that occur during database operations such as reads, writes, or data object creation or deletions.
   - ☐ PHYSICAL MEDIA ERRORS: Errors that are caused by physical devices, such as printers and disk drives.
   - ☐ PROGRAM CODE ERRORS: Errors that result from improper coding.

8. You should not use error trapping for the Visual Basic data control because it provides its own error trapping.

9. It is a good idea to open a data table with the FORM LOAD event. This allows you to capture most database related errors prior to any data entry.

10. The advantage of a global error handler is that it enables you to create a single module that handles all expected errors. The major disadvantage of a global error handler is that you are not able to resume processing at the point at which the error occurs. To be able to resume processing at the point of an error, you need to use Resume, Resume Next, or Resume label in a local error handler.

Answers to Day 14 Exercises

1. Insert a command button on a new form, and then double-click on that button and enter the following code:

```
Private Sub Command1_Click()
    On Error GoTo Command1Clickerr
    Dim cMsg As String ' Declare string
    Open "C:\ABC.TXT" For Input As 1 'Open file
    GoTo Command1ClickExit
'Error handler
Command1Clickerr:
    If Err = 53 Then
        cMsg = "Unable to open ABC.TXT" + Chr(13)
        MsgBox cMsg, vbCritical, "Command1Click"
        Unload Me
        End
    Else
        MsgBox Str(Err) + " - " + Error$, vbCritical, "Command1Click"
        Resume Next
    End If
'Routine exit
Command1ClickExit:
End Sub
```

2. You first need to place a common dialog on your form. Then place a command button and add the following code to it:

```
Private Sub Command2_Click()
    On Error GoTo Command2ClickErr
    'Declare variables
    Dim cFile As String
    Dim cMsg As String
    Dim nReturn As Integer
    'Define the file to open
    cFile = "C:\ABC.TXT"
    'Open the file
    Open cFile For Input As 1
    MsgBox "ABC.TXT has been opened."
    GoTo Command2ClickExit
'Error handler
```

```
Command2ClickErr:
    If Err = 53 Then
        cMsg = "Unable to open ABC.TXT!" + Chr(13)
        cMsg = cMsg + "Select OK to locate this file. "
        cMsg = cMsg + "Select CANCEL to exit this program." + Chr(13)
        nReturn = MsgBox(cMsg, vbCritical + vbOKCancel, "Command2Click")
        If nReturn = vbOK Then
            CommonDialog1.filename = cFile
            CommonDialog1.DefaultExt = ".txt"
            CommonDialog1.ShowOpen
            Resume
        Else
            Unload Me
        End If
    Else
        MsgBox Str(Err) + " - " + Error$
        Resume Next
    End If
'Routine exit
Command2ClickExit:
End Sub
```

Answers to Day 15 Quiz

1. These are the benefits of using SQL to create and manage data tables:

   ☐ SQL statements can serve as documentation for your table layouts.

   ☐ It's easy to produce test or sample data tables with SQL statements.

   ☐ You can easily load test data into new tables with SQL statements.

   ☐ You can utilize SQL for multiple data platforms.

2. The syntax is

   ```
   CREATE TABLE TableName (Field1 TYPE(SIZE), Field2 TYPE(SIZE), …);
   ```

   You first enter CREATE TABLE, followed by the name of the table, and then the fields in parentheses. The field types and sizes (sizes apply to TEXT columns only) are entered after each field.

3. The default size of an MS JET TEXT field is 255 bytes.

4. You use the ALTER TABLE...ADD COLUMN statement to add a column to a table. The ALTER TABLE...ADD COLUMN statement uses the following format:

   ```
   ALTER TABLE <Name of Table> ADD COLUMN <Name of column> <Type> <Size>;
   ```

5. You use the DROP TABLE statement to remove a table from a database. The DROP TABLE statement uses the following format:

   ```
   DROP TABLE <Table Name>;
   ```

6. You create indexes to data tables with the CREATE INDEX SQL statement.

7. The following are the three forms of the CONSTRAINT clause:

☐ PRIMARY KEY

☐ UNIQUE

☐ FOREIGN KEY

Answer to Day 15 Exercise

Enter the following code to build the CustomerType and Customers tables. Please note that the CustomerType table must be built before the Customers table, due to the foreign key constraint on CustomerType in the Customers table.

```
// Create the database
dbmake C:\CUSTOMER\CH15EX.MDB;
// Build the Customer Types Table
CREATE TABLE CustomerType(
    CustomerType TEXT(6) CONSTRAINT PKCustomerType PRIMARY KEY,
    Description TEXT(30));
// Build the Customers table
CREATE TABLE Customers(
    CustomerID TEXT(10) Constraint PKCustomerID PRIMARY KEY,
    Name TEXT(30),
    CustomerType TEXT(6) CONSTRAINT FKCustomerType
    ➡REFERENCES CustomerType(CustomerType),
    Address TEXT(30),
    City TEXT(30),
    State TEXT(30),
    Zip TEXT(10),
    Phone TEXT(14),
    Fax TEXT(14));
// Build the index on Zip
CREATE INDEX SKZip on Customers(Zip);
//Display the results
SELECT * FROM CustomerType;
SELECT * FROM Customers;
```

Answers to Day 16 Quiz

1. You use the INSERT statement to insert data into tables. The basic form of this statement is

```
INSERT INTO TableName(field1, field2,...) VALUES(value1, value2,...);
```

2. You use the INSERT INTO...FROM statement to insert multiple records into a data table. The format of this statement is

```
INSERT INTO TargetTable SELECT field1, field2 FROM SourceTable;
```

3. You use the UPDATE...SET statement to modify existing data. This statement uses the following form:

```
UPDATE <table name> SET <field to update> = <New Value>;
```

4. You use the SELECT...INTO...FROM SQL statement to create new tables and insert existing data from other tables. The format of this statement is

```
SELECT field1, field2 INTO DestinationTable FROM SourceTable;
```

In this statement, `field1` and `field2` represent the field names in the source table.

5. You use the DELETE...FROM statement to remove records from a data table. The form of this statement is

```
DELETE FROM TableName WHERE field = value;
```

Answers to Day 16 Exercises

1. Enter the following INSERT...INTO statements after your CREATE INDEX statement to insert the data.

```
INSERT INTO CustomerType VALUES('INDV', 'Individual');
INSERT INTO CustomerType VALUES('BUS', 'Business - Non-corporate');
INSERT INTO CustomerType VALUES('CORP', 'Corporate Entity');
INSERT INTO Customers VALUES('SMITHJ', 'John Smith', 'INDV',
    '160 Main Street', 'Dublin', 'Ohio', '45621',
    '614-569-8975', '614-569-5580');
INSERT INTO Customers VALUES('JONEST', 'Jones Taxi', 'BUS',
    '421 Shoe St.', 'Milford', 'Rhode Island', '03215',
    '401-737-4528', '401-667-8900');
INSERT INTO Customers VALUES('JACKSONT', 'Thomas Jackson', 'INDV',
    '123 Walnut Street', 'Oxford', 'Maine', '05896',
    '546-897-8596', '546-897-8500');
```

2. Your script should now look like this:

```
// Create the database
dbmake C:\CUSTOMER\CH15EX.MDB;
// Build the Customer Types Table
CREATE TABLE CustomerType(
    CustomerType TEXT(6) CONSTRAINT PKCustomerType PRIMARY KEY,
    Description TEXT(30));
// Build the Customers table
CREATE TABLE Customers(
    CustomerID TEXT(10) Constraint PKCustomerID PRIMARY KEY,
    Name TEXT(30),
    CustomerType TEXT(6) CONSTRAINT FKCustomerType REFERENCES
    ➡CustomerType(CustomerType),
    Address TEXT(30),
    City TEXT(30),
    State TEXT(30),
    Zip TEXT(10),
    Phone TEXT(14),
    Fax TEXT(14));
// Build the index on Zip
CREATE INDEX SKZip on Customers(Zip);
```

```
// Insert Data
INSERT INTO CustomerType VALUES('INDV', 'Individual');
INSERT INTO CustomerType VALUES('BUS', 'Business - Non-corporate');
INSERT INTO CustomerType VALUES('CORP', 'Corporate Entity');
INSERT INTO Customers Values('SMITHJ', 'John Smith', 'INDV',
    '160 Main Street', 'Dublin', 'Ohio', '45621',
    '614-569-8975', '614-569-5580');
INSERT INTO Customers Values('JONEST', 'Jones Taxi', 'BUS',
    '421 Shoe St.', 'Milford', 'Rhode Island', '03215',
    '401-737-4528', '401-667-8900');
INSERT INTO Customers Values('JACKSONT', 'Thomas Jackson', 'INDV',
    '123 Walnut Street', 'Oxford', 'Maine', '05896',
    '546-897-8596', '546-897-8500');
// Copy data into the localities table
SELECT CustomerID, City, State INTO Localities FROM Customers;
// Display the results
SELECT * FROM CustomerType;
SELECT * FROM Customers;
SELECT * FROM Localities;
```

3. You would issue the following SQL statement to delete the SMITHJ record from the Customers table:

```
DELETE FROM Customers WHERE CustomerID = 'SMITHJ';
```

You would use the DROP TABLE command to delete an entire table. To delete the Customers table, you would issue the following statement:

```
DROP TABLE Customers;
```

Answers to Day 17 Quiz

1. It is not necessarily a good idea to look at database optimization strictly from the point of view of processing performance. Other factors such as data integrity are also important. The role of data normalization is to strike a balance between speed and integrity.

2. If the term First Normal Form is applied to a database, it means that the first rule of data normalization—eliminate repeating groups—has been achieved.

3. The first rule of data normalization is to delete repeating groups, whereas the second rule of normalization requires the deletion of redundant data. Rule one requires the separation of fields that contain multiple occurrences of similar data into separate tables. Rule two requires that fields that must maintain constant relationship to other fields (for example, the name of a customer as associated with the customer ID) should be placed in a separate table.

4. Do not include calculated fields in a data table. Not only does the calculated data take up disk space, but problems can arise if one of the fields used in the calculation is deleted or changed. Calculations are best saved for forms and reports. Placing a calculated field in your data table violates the third rule of data normalization—eliminate columns not dependent on keys.

5. You would invoke the fourth rule of data normalization if you have multiple independent one-to-many relationships within the same table. You need to utilize this rule when you unwittingly create relationships that do not necessarily exist. For example, if you included educational degree in the Employee skills table in the examples used in this lesson, you mistakenly aligned skills with degrees that do not necessarily match.

6. You would invoke the fifth rule of data normalization if you have multiple dependent many-to-many relationships. To resolve any potential conflict under this rule, you might need to break the different components of the relationships into separate tables and link them through another table.

Answers to Day 17 Exercises

1. To achieve the first normal form, you must delete repeating groups. In this exercise, this includes the fields for the multiple automobiles (VehicleType1, Make1, Model1, Color1, Odometer1, VehicleType2, Make2, Model2, Color2, Odometer2). This requires that you create two tables. The first would track the customers (Customers), and the second would track their vehicles (Vehicles).

Customers Table	Vehicles Table
CustomerID (Primary Key)	SerialNumber (Primary Key)
CustomerName	CustomerID (Foreign Key)
License	VehicleType
Address	Make
City	Model
State	Color
Zip	Odometer
Phone	

Please note that by separating the VehicleTypes into a separate table, you can have any number of vehicles for a customer. Also note that SerialNumber makes a better primary key than License because the serial number of an automobile will not change, whereas a license plate can change on an annual basis.

Next, you need to reach the second normal form. This requires you to take the Customer and Vehicle tables and remove any redundant data. There is no redundant data in the Customers table. The Vehicles table, on the other hand, has redundant data describing the VehicleType. You should move the type information into a separate table to yield the following structure:

Customers	Vehicles	VehicleTypes
CustomerID (Primary Key)	SerialNumber (Primary Key)	VehicleType (Primary Key)
CustomerName	CustomerID (Foreign Key)	Make
Address	License	Model
City	VehicleType (Foreign Key)	
State	Color	
Zip	Odometer	
Phone		

To reach the third normal form, you must delete any fields that do not describe the primary key. A review of all fields shows that you have already eliminated any fields that do not describe the entire primary key.

To achieve the fourth normal form, you need to separate any independent one-to-many relationships that can potentially produce unusual answers when you query the data. The Vehicles table does have several one-to-many relationships with the CustomerID and the VehicleType fields. The combination of these two fields in the same table would not, however, lead to misleading results further down the line. Therefore, you do not need to make any changes to reach the fourth normal form.

Similarly, no changes need to be made to reach the fifth normal form because you have no dependent many-to-many relationships in your tables. Most data structures will not require you to use the fourth and fifth rules of normalization to optimize your structure.

As a final point, you might want to add a Comments field to each table. This allows users to store any miscellaneous data they choose to track. Adding a memo field to track comments is a good idea in almost every table, because memo fields do not take up room when empty, and they provide great flexibility to your system.

2. The following SQL code builds these tables.

Note: Please note that you need to create the VehicleTypes table before the Vehicles table. This is required because the Vehicles table has a foreign constraint to the VehicleTypes table. In such situations, the foreign key must be defined prior to its use in another table, or an error will occur.

```
Create Table Customers
   (CustomerID TEXT (10),
      CustomerName TEXT (40),
      Address TEXT (40),
      City TEXT (40),
      State TEXT (20),
      Zip TEXT (10),
      Phone TEXT (14),
      Comments MEMO,
      CONSTRAINT PKCustomers Primary Key (CustomerID));
Create Table VehicleTypes
   (VehicleType TEXT (10),
      Make TEXT (25),
      Model TEXT (25),
      Comments MEMO,
      CONSTRAINT PKVehicleTypes Primary Key (VehicleType));
Create Table Vehicles
   (SerialNumber INTEGER,
      CustomerID TEXT (10),
      License TEXT (10),
      VehicleType TEXT (10),
      Color TEXT (15),
      Odometer INTEGER,
      Comments MEMO,
      CONSTRAINT PKVehicles Primary Key (SerialNumber),
      CONSTRAINT FKCustomer Foreign Key (CustomerID)
      ➥REFERENCES  Customers(CustomerID),
      CONSTRAINT FKType Foreign Key (VehicleType)
      ➥REFERENCES VehicleTypes(VehicleType));
```

Answers to Day 18 Quiz

1. The Microsoft JET database engine provides three levels of locking: database locking, which locks the entire database for exclusive use; table locking, which locks a table for exclusive use; and page locking, which locks data pages 2K in size.

2. You would want to use database locking when compacting a database because compacting affects all the objects in a database.

3. You would want to use table locking when doing a mass update of a single table. You want exclusive use of the data to be changed, but you do not necessarily have to have exclusive use of the entire database when performing field update functions.

4. You use the LockEdits property of a recordset to control how page locking is handled by your application. Setting this property to True means you will have pessimistic locking. Setting this property to False means you will have optimistic locking.

5. Pessimistic locking prohibits two users from opening a data page at the same time (that is, when the Edit or AddNew method is invoked). Optimistic locking permits two users to open the same page but only allows updates to be saved by the first user to make the changes.

6. You *cannot* use pessimistic locks on an ODBC data source. ODBC data sources use optimistic locking only.

7. When cascading deletes are used in a relationship, each time a base table element is deleted, all foreign table records that contain that element will be deleted.

8. You use transaction management in your applications to provide an opportunity to reverse a series of database updates if your program fails to complete all requested data changes. This is particularly useful if you have processes that affect multiple tables within the database. Failure to fully complete such a transaction could lead to a database that has lost or inaccurate data. This can also result in a database that is difficult or impossible to repair.

9. The limitations of transactions include the following:

☐ Some database formats do not support transactions.

☐ Data sets that are the result of some SQL JOIN or WHERE clauses, and data sets that contain data from attached tables will not support transactions.

☐ Transaction operations are kept on the local workstations, which could lead to errors if the process runs out of space in the TEMP directory.

10. Declaring a unique workspace object is not required; however, it is highly recommended that you do so because transactions apply to an *entire* workspace.

Answers to Day 18 Exercises

1. Enter the following code to load a database exclusively when you bring up a form:

```
Private Sub Form_Load()

    Dim DB As Database
    Dim dbName As String

    On Error GoTo FormLoadErr

    dbName = App.Path + \abc.mdb"
    Set DB = DBEngine.OpenDatabase(dbName, True) ' Open database exclusive
    MsgBox "Database opened successfully"
    GoTo FormLoadExit

FormLoadErr:
    MsgBox "Unable to load database ABC.MDB"
    GoTo FormLoadExit

FormLoadExit:
    Unload Me

End Sub
```

2. Enter the following code in the Form_Load event to load a table exclusively:

```
Private Sub Form_Load()

    Dim db As Database
    Dim rs As Recordset
    Dim dbName As String
    Dim tabName As String

    dbName = App.Path + "\abc.mdb"
    tabName = "Customers"

    On Error GoTo FormLoadErr

    Set db = DBEngine.OpenDatabase(dbName)
    Set rs = db.OpenRecordset(tabName, dbOpenTable,
    ➥dbDenyRead + dbDenyWrite) ' table opened exclusively
    MsgBox "Table opened exclusively"
    GoTo FormLoadExit

FormLoadErr:
    MsgBox "Unable to load table exclusively"
    GoTo FormLoadExit

FormLoadExit:
    Unload Me

End Sub
```

3. To start the project, insert the following code into the general declarations section:

```
Option Explicit

'Declaration of global variables
Dim DB As Database
Dim wsUpdate As Workspace
Dim nErrFlag As Integer
```

Next, start a new procedure and insert the following code. This code creates a workspace and opens the database.

```
Public Sub OpenDB()

    On Error GoTo OpenDBErr

    Dim dbName As String

    nErrFlag = 0 'Reset the error flag
    dbName = App.Path + "\abc.mdb"

    'Open the workspace and database
    Set wsUpdate = DBEngine.CreateWorkspace("WSUpdate", "admin", "")
    Set DB = wsUpdate.OpenDatabase(dbName, True)
    GoTo OpenDBExit

OpenDBErr:
    MsgBox Trim(Str(Err)) + " " + Error$(Err), vbCritical, "OpenDB"
    nErrFlag = Err
```

```
OpenDBExit:

End Sub
```

Now build the following procedure to perform the posting:

```
Public Sub Post()

    On Error GoTo PostErr

    Dim cSQL As String

    wsUpdate.BeginTrans

    'Create the SQL statement to insert the records.
    ➥'Note that we do not use the TransNo field
    ➥'as it is a counter field necessary only
    ➥'for the Transactions table
    cSQL = "INSERT INTO History Select CustID, InvoiceNo,
    ➥Amount FROM Transactions"
    DB.Execute cSQL

    'Delete the temporary transactions data
    cSQL = "DELETE FROM Transactions"
    DB.Execute cSQL

    'Commit the transactions
    wsUpdate.CommitTrans
    MsgBox "Transactions have been committed"

    'Set the error flag and exit the program
    nErrFlag = 0
    GoTo PostExit

PostErr:
    'Display the error and rollback the transactions
    MsgBox Trim(Str(Err)) + " " + Error$(Err), vbCritical, "Post"
    wsUpdate.Rollback
    MsgBox "Post routine has been aborted"

PostExit:

End Sub
```

Finally, insert the following code into the cmdPost_Click event:

```
Private Sub cmdPost_Click()

    OpenDB
    If nErrFlag = 0 Then
        Post
    End If

    If nErrFlag <> 0 Then
        MsgBox "Error Reported", vbCritical, "cmdPost"
    End If

    Unload Me

End Sub
```

You can test this program by building the database in Visdata or Data Manager and then inserting some sample records into the Transactions table.

Answers to Day 19 Quiz

1. The letters ODBC stand for Open Database Connectivity.

2. When you use the Microsoft JET interface to connect to an ODBC data source, your Visual Basic program must first communicate with Microsoft JET, which communicates to the ODBC front end. When you use the ODBC API calls, your Visual Basic program communicates directly with the ODBC front end, skipping the Microsoft JET layer entirely.

3. When you use the ODBC API to link to your data, you are actually creating a static, Snapshot-type, data set. You must collect a set of data and bring it back to your workstation. You might also be limited by the amount of memory available on the workstation.

4. You use the ODBC Administrator to define or modify ODBC data sources. This program is part of the Windows Control Panel.

5. You can use the ODBC interface to connect to Excel spreadsheets and even text files, as long as an ODBC driver is installed on your system to handle the data format. There is no restriction to the type of data that you can access from an ODBC data source (as long as a driver exists for the format).

6. You cannot use the same set of API declarations for the 32-bit Visual Basic 4 as you do for the 16-bit Visual Basic 4. Today's exercises work with the 16-bit version only. If you want to access the ODBC interface through 32-bit API calls, you need a new set of declarations for the 32-bit ODBC API. These can be found in the file ODBC32.TXT. This file was added when you installed Visual Basic 4.

7. Before you can pass an SQL SELECT statement to a new ODBC data source, you must complete the following four preliminary steps:

   ☐ Allocate an Environment Handle (SQLAllocEnv) to create a unique identifier for this ODBC session.

   ☐ Allocate a Connection Handle (SQLAllocConnect) to create a unique identifier for this ODBC connection.

   ☐ Connect to the ODBC data source (SQLConnect) using the data source name, user login, and password.

   ☐ Allocate a Statement Handle (SQLAllocStmt) to create a unique identifier for passing data and SQL statements back and forth.

Answers to Day 19 Exercise

To complete this assignment, you must first register a new ODBC data source on your workstation. To do this, complete the following steps:

1. Call up the 16-bit ODBC Administrator and, at the Data Sources dialog box, click the Add button to add a new data source.

2. At the Add Data Source dialog box, select Access 2.0 for Microsoft Office (*.MDB) driver.

3. At the ODBC Microsoft Access 2.0 Setup dialog box, enter Ch1902 as the data source name and Chapter 19 Exercise as the description. Click the Select button to locate and select the C:\TYSDBVB\CHAP19\EXER19.MDB data file. Click OK to save this data source.

4. At the Data Sources dialog box, click OK to exit.

Now you need to call up the 16-bit version of Visual Basic and create the data entry form project by completing the following steps:

1. Load 16-bit Visual Basic 4.

2. Load the existing project called TYSODBC.VBP.

3. Select File | Save File As and save the form as EXER19.FRM.

4. Select File | Save Project As and save the project as EXER19.VBP.

5. Modify the following lines in the Form_Load event of the EXER19.FRM form:

```
cDSN = "EXER19"            ' ODBC data source
    cUser = "Admin"            ' login ID
    cPW = " "                  ' empty password
    cTable = "Transactions"    ' default base table
    cKeyFld = "OrderNbr"       ' default key field
    cRefresh = "SELECT * FROM Transactions ORDER BY OrderNbr"
    ➥' default SQL
    cFormTitle = "Chapter 19 Exercise"   ' form title
```

6. Save and run the project.

Answers to Day 20 Quiz

1. The disadvantages and limitations of using the Microsoft Access SYSTEM.MDA file to secure a database include the following points:

   ☐ You must own Microsoft Access to create a SYSTEM.MDA file. You can't use a Visual Basic utility to create a SYSTEM.MDA.

   ☐ It is possible to have multiple SYSTEM.MDA files, which could lead to problems if the wrong file is used.

☐ System security can be removed simply by deleting the SYSTEM.MDA file.

☐ Some applications do not recognize the SYSTEM.MDA file. It is possible for these applications to skirt security implemented with this file.

2. The disadvantages of using data encryption to secure a database include the following points:

☐ Encryption affects an entire database and cannot be applied only to critical tables.

☐ Encrypted databases can't be read by other programs. This makes dissemination of information more difficult.

☐ Encrypted databases cannot be replicated.

3. Application security focuses on processes, not just the underlying data. Application security focuses on granting access to forms, reports, and procedures. Database security, on the other hand, focuses strictly on the data and the database.

4. These are the two main features of any good application security scheme:

☐ It must have a process that allows users to log in to the application using stored passwords.

☐ It must have an access rights scheme that limits the functions that users can perform within the system.

5. Application security schemes can't prevent unauthorized use of your data by tools such as Visdata and Data Manager. Application security only works *within* an application. Therefore, you should not rely on it as the only means of securing your application.

6. Access rights security schemes build an added level of security into your application. This type of security allows you to define a set of secured operations within your application and then define access rights for each of the operations on a user-by-user basis.

7. You add audit trails for these reasons:

☐ To track when users log into and out of the applications.

☐ To provide detail as to the status of the application when a system error occurs. This will help with on-going system maintenance.

☐ To keep a record of major user activities, such as data table updates and the running of key reports or processes.

Answers to Day 20 Exercise

Perform the following steps to complete this process:

1. Start Visual Basic and load 20ABC01.VBP.
2. Load Data Manager from the Add/Ins menu.
3. Create the new database CH20EX.MDB.
4. Build the Assets table. Add some sample records.
5. Return to Visual Basic and build form `frmFixedAssets` by dropping a data control on a new form and adding text fields and labels for each field of your data table.
6. Modify the `Main` procedure of the LIBUSER.BAS module to call the form you created in the previous step. You simply substitute the new form for the name of the `usrMaint` form used in the example. Use the following code as a guide to make the change.

```
If accGetSet(usrUserID, dbUsers, rsAccess) = accOK Then
        frmFixedAssets.Show vbModal
        'usrMaint
    End If
```

7. Enter the following code in the `Validate` event of the data control on your `frmFixedAssets`.

```
Private Sub Data1_Validate(Action As Integer, Save As Integer)

    On Error GoTo Data1Err
    errProcStack errPush, "LibUser.logChanged"

    'Declare variables
    Dim cField As String
    Dim lFlag As Boolean

    'Reset the flag for changing of data
    lFlag = False

    'Set flag if data changes
    If Text1.DataChanged Then lFlag = True
    If Text2.DataChanged Then lFlag = True
    If Text3.DataChanged Then lFlag = True
    If Text4.DataChanged Then lFlag = True
    If Text5.DataChanged Then lFlag = True
    If Text6.DataChanged Then lFlag = True

    'Write log if record changes
    If lFlag = True Then
        logWriteFile "RecUpdate", cRecordSet:="CH20EX.MDB.Assets",
        ➥ cKey:="AssetID=" + Trim(Text1.Text)
    End If
    GoTo Data1Exit

Data1Err:
    nResult = errHandler(Err, Error$, errResume)
    GoTo Data1Exit
```

805

```
Data1Exit:
    errProcStack errPop, ""
```

```
End Sub
```

This code checks to see whether any data has been changed in the current record. If so, an entry record is made in the audit log.

8. Run the project and log in as USERA with a password of USERA. Enter some records and then edit them. Read the log file, which can be found in the Visual Basic default directory.

Answers to Day 21 Quiz

1. You use the pound sign (#) for a context string. You cannot put spaces in the context string footnote.

2. You insert the dollar sign ($) as the custom mark for a title footnote. These footnotes can include spaces.

3. Keywords will be used in the Search box of your help application. You use the semicolon (;) to separate multiple keywords in a topic.

4. You should save your topic file in a rich text format *and* in your word processor's normal file format (in case you need to make subsequent revisions). Your project file should be saved in ASCII text and given an .HPJ extension.

5. The contents page of your help file is declared in the [Options] section of the project file by making the following entry:

```
Contents = ContextString
```

In this entry, the context string is the topic you want displayed as the contents page. The first topic of your help file will default as the contents page if none is declared.

6. You set the HelpContextID property to identify the help file that displays when the control has focus and F1 is pressed. The numeric value for this field is determined in the [Map] section of the project file.

7. Allow approximately one hour for each typed page of documentation. Adjust this figure for your personal writing style.

Answers to Day 21 Exercises

1. + Processing:3

2. Creating a New ProjectNewProject

   Note that the jump text is double underlined. Also note that the context string, NewProject, should be formatted as hidden text.

3. Just change the double-underlined text to single-underlined text and the jump becomes a pop-up.

4. You will perform the following steps in order to complete this exercise:

    1. Open your topic file.

    2. Enter text for a new topic. Give the topic a descriptive heading such as The Company Master Form.

    3. Insert footnotes for the context string, title, and keywords.

    4. Save the file in RTF format.

    5. Add the context string to the [Map] section of the project file.

    6. Compile your project.

    7. Set the HelpContextID of the form to the number you have assigned the context string in the project file.

    8. Execute your program and press F1.

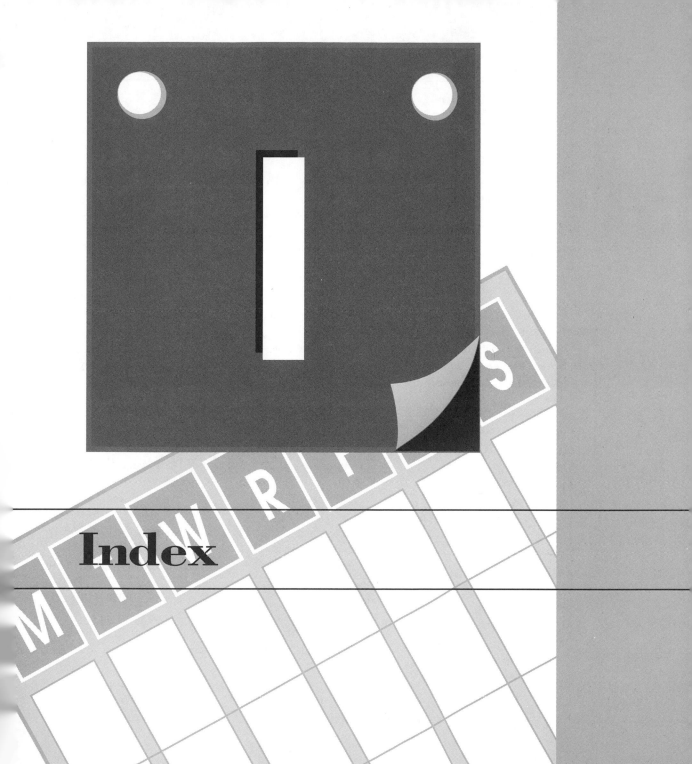

Index

Database menu commands

listings

listings

listings

Sams
Learning
Center

SAMS
PUBLISHING

listings

Q

PLUG YOURSELF INTO...

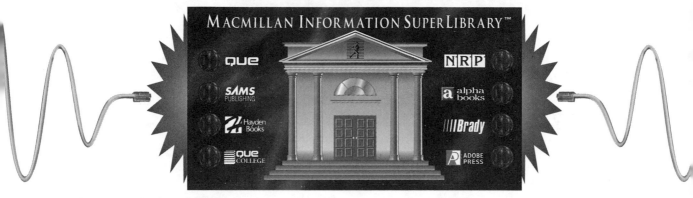

THE MACMILLAN INFORMATION SUPERLIBRARY™

Free information and vast computer resources from the world's leading computer book publisher—online!

FIND THE BOOKS THAT ARE RIGHT FOR YOU!

A complete online catalog, plus sample chapters and tables of contents give you an in-depth look at *all* of our books, including hard-to-find titles. It's the best way to find the books you need!

- **STAY INFORMED** with the latest computer industry news through our online newsletter, press releases, and customized Information SuperLibrary Reports.

- **GET FAST ANSWERS** to your questions about MCP books and software.

- **VISIT** our online bookstore for the latest information and editions!

- **COMMUNICATE** with our expert authors through e-mail and conferences.

- **DOWNLOAD SOFTWARE** from the immense MCP library:
    - Source code and files from MCP books
    - The best shareware, freeware, and demos

- **DISCOVER HOT SPOTS** on other parts of the Internet.

- **WIN BOOKS** in ongoing contests and giveaways!

TO PLUG INTO MCP: →   WORLD WIDE WEB: **http://www.mcp.com**

GOPHER: gopher.mcp.com

FTP: ftp.mcp.com

GET CONNECTED
to the ultimate source of computer information!

The MCP Forum on CompuServe

Go online with the world's leading computer book publisher! Macmillan Computer Publishing offers everything you need for computer success!

Find the books that are right for you!
A complete online catalog, plus sample chapters and tables of contents give you an in-depth look at all our books. The best way to shop or browse!

➤ Get fast answers and technical support for MCP books and software

➤ Join discussion groups on major computer subjects

➤ Interact with our expert authors via e-mail and conferences

➤ Download software from our immense library:

   ▷ Source code from books
   ▷ Demos of hot software
   ▷ The best shareware and freeware
   ▷ Graphics files

Join now and get a free CompuServe Starter Kit!

To receive your free CompuServe Introductory Membership, call **1-800-848-8199** and ask for representative #597.

The Starter Kit includes:
➤ Personal ID number and password
➤ $15 credit on the system
➤ Subscription to *CompuServe Magazine*

Once on the CompuServe System, type:

GO MACMILLAN

for the most computer information anywhere!

MACMILLAN
COMPUTER
PUBLISHING

🌐 **CompuServe**

Add to Your Sams Library Today with the Best Books for Programming, Operating Systems, and New Technologies

The easiest way to order is to pick up the phone and call

1-800-428-5331

between 9:00 a.m. and 5:00 p.m. EST.
For faster service please have your credit card available.

ISBN	Quantity	Description of Item	Unit Cost	Total Cost
0-672-30602-6		Programming Windows 95 Unleashed (Book/CD)	$49.99	
0-672-30474-0		Windows 95 Unleashed (Book/CD)	$35.00	
0-672-30855-X		Teach Yourself SQL in 14 Days	$29.99	
0-672-30462-7		Teach Yourself MFC in 21 Days	$29.99	
0-672-30619-0		Real-World Programming with Visual Basic	$45.00	
0-672-30594-1		Programming WinSock (Book/Disk)	$35.00	
0-672-30596-8		Develop a Professional Visual Basic Application in 14 Days (Book/CD)	$35.00	
0-672-30593-3		Develop a Professional Visual C++ Application in 21 Days (Book/CD)	$35.00	
0-672-30453-8		Access 2 Developers Guide, 2nd Ed (Book/Disk)	$44.95	
0-672-30-5		Visual Basic Unleashed	$45.00	
0-672-30765-0		Database Developer's Guide with Visual Basic (book/disk)	$39.99	
❑ 3 ½" Disk		Shipping and Handling: See information below.		
❑ 5 ¼" Disk		TOTAL		

Shipping and Handling: $4.00 for the first book, and $1.75 for each additional book. Floppy disk: add $1.75 for shipping and handling. If you need to have it NOW, we can ship product to you in 24 hours for an additional charge of approximately $18.00, and you will receive your item overnight or in two days. Overseas shipping and handling adds $2.00 per book and $8.00 for up to three disks. Prices subject to change. Call for availability and pricing information on latest editions.

201 W. 103rd Street, Indianapolis, Indiana 46290

1-800-428-5331 — Orders   1-800-835-3202 — FAX   1-800-858-7674 — Customer Service

Book ISBN 0-672-30832-0